OPERATION DRUMBEAT

The Dramatic True Story of
Germany's First U-Boat
Attacks Along
the American Coast
in World War II

MICHAEL GANNON

1817

HARPER & ROW PUBLISHERS, New York
Grand Rapids, Philadelphia, St. Louis, San Francisco
London, Singapore, Sydney, Tokyo, Toronto

FIRST EDITION

Designer: Cassandra J. Pappas

Cartographer: Paul Pugliese

Library of Congress Cataloging-in-Publication Data

Gannon, Michael, 1927–
    Operation Drumbeat : the dramatic true story of Germany's
first U-boat attacks along the American coast in World War II /
Michael Gannon.—1st ed.
    p. cm.
    Includes bibliographical references.
    Includes index.
    ISBN 0-06-016155-8
    1. World War, 1939–1945—Naval operations—Submarine. 2. World
War, 1939–1945—Naval operations, German. 3. World War, 1939–1945—
Campaigns—North Atlantic Ocean. 4. Merchant marine—United
States—History—20th century. 5. Atlantic Coast (North America)—
History—20th century. I. Title.
D781.G36 1990
940.54'51—dc20   89-46090

---

90 91 92 93 94 AT/RRD 10 9 8 7 6 5 4 3 2 1

To Gigi

Our U-boats are operating close inshore along the coast of the United States of America, so that bathers and sometimes entire coastal cities are witnesses to the drama of war, whose visual climaxes are constituted by the red glorioles of blazing tankers.

—ADMIRAL KARL DÖNITZ

For six or seven months the U-boats ravaged American waters almost uncontrolled, and in fact almost brought us to the disaster of an indefinite prolongation of the war.

—WINSTON S. CHURCHILL
The Hinge of Fate

The losses by submarines off our Atlantic seaboard and in the Caribbean now threaten our entire war effort.

—GENERAL GEORGE C. MARSHALL
June 1942

CONTENTS

Acknowledgments

I am indebted to many people for assistance in uncovering the documents, maps, decrypted wireless signals, and other research materials that made this book possible, principal among them Reinhard Hardegen, whose sharp and thorough recollections of events brought U-*123* to life during extensive interviews conducted at his home in Bremen, Germany, in May 1985 and December 1986. No historian is insensible of the good fortune that comes to one who can relive a major historical event through one of its principal protagonists. To him and to Frau Hardegen I express my sincere gratitude for their hospitality and numerous courtesies. Special thanks is owed as well to those other surviving members of the U-*123* complement of officers and crew who recounted their experiences in interviews conducted at a reunion in Bad König/Odenwald, Germany in November 1985: Richard Amstein, Heinz Barth, Karl Fröbel, Max Hufnagl, Walter Kaeding, Karl Latislaus, Rudolf Meisinger, Fritz Rafalski, Horst von Schroeter, and Hans Seigel. Their recollections add a different perspective and human interest to the present narrative. I was privileged to conduct a more extended interview with radio operator Fritz Rafalski at his home in Bonn, Germany, in December 1986. Also valuable, particularly for Reinhard Hardegen's expressed feelings in the year of Paukenschlag, is a propaganda document that, on the orders of superiors, he dictated to stenographers at the conclusion of his two American patrols. Published in the following year as *"Auf Gefechtssta-*

tionen!" (*Battle Stations!*) for morale and recruiting purposes, this account is useful for life data, personal thoughts, housekeeping details, and verbatim language.[1] It is not reliable for operational data, as Hardegen himself cautions, since he was required to disguise U-boat identifications, nautical positions, and most target names; to describe certain events out of sequence; and to keep attack details to a minimum. The document must be checked against the more exact and thorough record of events maintained in Hardegen's contemporaneous U-*123* war diaries, for copies of which I am indebted to Archivdirektor Hansjoseph Maierhöfer, of the Bundesarchiv/Militärchiv (Federal/Military Archive) in Freiburg, Germany, who not only provided access to the original diaries but also made available to me map tracings from Hardegen's navigator. The war diary (*Kriegstagebuch*) for each of Hardegen's patrols is abbreviated in the present text as KTB.

The staff of the Militärgeschichtliches Forschungsamt (Military History Research Office), also in Freiburg, was helpful in searching out maps used by the Kriegsmarine and Luftwaffe (Air Force). Research in the Freiburg holdings was greatly facilitated by the writer's friend Hugo Ott, o.Professor der Wirtschafts- und Sozialgeschichte (Professor [Ordinarius] of Economic and Social History) at the University of Freiburg in Breisgau. At the Bibliothek für Zeitgeschichte (Library of Contemporary History) in Stuttgart the distinguished naval historian Jürgen Rohwer provided me with numerous important documents, including the *Schussmeldungen* (shooting reports) for the torpedo or gun actions of U-*123* and the other Paukenschlag boats. A rich deposit of U-boat materials is preserved at the Traditionsarchiv Unterseeboote at Westerland on the North Sea island of Sylt, where founder and director Horst Bredow generously made available many of the photographs that accompany this book. Especially helpful, and over a long period of time, have been Timothy P. Mulligan, of the Modern Military Headquarters Branch, Military Archives Division, of the National Archives and Records Service, Washington, D.C., and Michael Walker, of the Operational Archives Branch, Naval Historical Center, Washington Navy Yard. Without their archival resources and personal assistance this history could not have been written.

Important aid in locating U-boat veterans was provided by Jochem Ahme, of the Verband Deutscher U-Bootfahrer e.V. (Association of German U-Boat Mariners), in Hamburg, Germany, who died in

May 1989, and by Robert M. Coppock, of the Naval Historical Library, Ministry of Defence, Fulham, London, England. Two skilled translators, Herbert and Kathryn Bubenik, of Unterhaching, Germany, gave particularly valuable assistance to the writer on numerous occasions: indeed, they became so engaged in the U-*123* story, and have contributed so substantially to its completion, they may truly be said to have shared in its reconstruction. Mrs. Elsa Fox kindly translated Norwegian materials. I respectfully and gratefully acknowledge the memory of Patrick Beesly, deputy chief of the Submarine Tracking Room, Operational Intelligence Centre, of the British Admiralty during the war years, who graciously afforded me an interview at his home in Lymington, England, in July 1986. Mr. Beesly died unexpectedly the following month. Similar appreciation for his valuable information goes to Captain Kenneth A. Knowles, U.S. Navy (Ret.), who established a U.S. Submarine Tracking Room on the British model in May–June, 1942. Thanks is due also to René Estienne, archivist of the Port of Lorient, France, who not only made available the resources of the Marine Nationale Service Historique but arranged for me to inspect the U-boat pens at Pointe de Keroman. Michael L. Hadley, chairman of the Department of Germanic Studies, University of Victoria, Canada, kindly shared Canadian documents on the sinking of SS *Cyclops*. Additional materials on *Cyclops* were provided me by the Directorate of History, National Defence Headquarters, Ottawa, Canada.

Special courtesies were extended by historian Gerhard L. Weinberg and by archivists John E. Taylor and Bernard F. Cavalcante. Captain Warren Kiernan, U.S. Navy (Ret.), a former submarine commander, who received the torpedo shooting award in each of the years he held command in the Atlantic Submarine Force, kindly reviewed the manuscript for technical accuracy in the torpedo attack sequences. Harry Cooper and James Frye made possible an extended study of the interior of U-*505*, a Type IXC boat preserved at the Museum of Science and Industry in Chicago. Grateful recognition is owed to staff members who assisted me in my research at the Public Record Office in Kew, England; the American Merchant Marine Museum, Kings Point, New York; the Franklin D. Roosevelt Library at Hyde Park, New York; the George C. Marshall Research Library in Lexington, Virginia; and the Library of Congress in Washington, D.C. Certainly none of this investigation would have held together without the invariable help and courtesy of various staffs, particularly that of the Interlibrary Loan Office, of the University Libraries, University of

Florida. Charles F. Sidman, historian and dean at Florida, was a supporter throughout, as were the writer's colleagues and friends Marvin Harris, David M. Chalmers, Eugene Lyon, David A. Cofrin, Helen Armstrong, Raymond Gay-Crosier, Leonidas Roberts, William Goza, and Alexander Stephan. The words of the text were decrypted and processed admirably by Myrna Sulsona, Marian Johnston, and Rebecca Haines. Special thanks for his advice and counsel is owed to my literary agent, Murray Curtin. No writer could have had on board a more discriminating navigator than executive editor at Harper & Row, Buz Wyeth.

To my wife Genevieve Haugen, without whom there would be no book, I pay a thanks that transcends words for her understanding, support, and good humor.

Various persons cited above have kindly read individual chapters of the manuscript while it was in progress but, of course, I alone bear full responsibility for the final work, for the accuracy of my facts, for the authenticity of my reconstruction of events and dialogue, and for the soundness of my interpretations.

Prologue

It was night when the message from *B-Dienst*, the radio intelligence service of the German Navy, reached Adolf Hitler's underground bunker at the Wolfsschanze (Wolf's Lair) field headquarters near Rastenburg, deep in the Görlitz forest of East Prussia. When he read it the Führer was stunned: JAPAN BEGAN HOSTILITIES AGAINST THE UNITED STATES ON 7 DECEMBER. AT 1930 HOURS CENTRAL EUROPEAN TIME STRONG AIR FORMATIONS ATTACKED PEARL HARBOR (HONOLULU).[1] A declaration of war might have been expected, but a carrier strike across 3,200 miles of open sea against the American main battle fleet? If at that moment Hitler recalled the maxim of Frederick the Great, whom he claimed to emulate— "It is pardonable to be defeated but never to be surprised"—he knew that the muse of history was not likely to absolve him. The master of Europe was caught completely by surprise.[2]

   The same message but with additional details of U.S. warship and aircraft losses flashed on the Siemens Geheimschreiber T-52 teleprinter in a handsome château requisitioned from a French sardine merchant at Kernével, a point of land bordering the mouth of the inner harbor of the German-occupied Atlantic port of Lorient. There it was read with equal amazement by Admiral Karl Dönitz, Befehlshaber der Unterseeboote (BdU) (commander in chief, U-boats). Dönitz went directly to his Situation Room and moved his dividers across the three-foot-diameter world globe that he used for rapid-distance calculations. From the principal U-boat base at Lorient he tracked the Great Circle distance to New York City on the east coast of the United States—distance: 3,000 nautical miles. Only the large Unterseeboot (submarine) Types IXB and IXC would be able to make that distance, he calculated, and still have fuel to maneuver. Quickly he made additional measurements and computations. After reaching an operations area off New York in twenty-two days the 1,050-ton Type IXB would have 60 cubic meters of diesel fuel oil for attack maneuvers against merchant ships with war cargoes; the 1,120-ton IXC with its larger fuel bunkers would need about the same number of days to cross and have 110 cubic meters available for maneuvers. That would give the IXB six or seven days in the area and the IXC about fifteen days, plenty of time for both to do great damage. Looking at other ports for comparison, Dönitz found that an IXB reaching and returning from Galveston, Texas, would have zero cubic meters for operations while an IXC would have barely 40. For Aruba, the rich oil depot in the Dutch West Indies, the figures were 25 and 65, respectively. The "SC" slow eastbound convoys, averaging six and one-half knots, with war matériel bound for England routinely assembled at Sydney, on Nova Scotia's Cape Breton Island, and the figures there were a promising 90 and 140.[3]

It was the East Coast of the United States, however, that interested Dönitz most. A strike there would have much the same effect as the Japanese had had at Hawaii, revealing American vulnerability to a determined military foe. It would intimidate U.S. defenses and humiliate the civilian population. Most important, if followed by additional and unremitting strikes during the period when U.S. naval and air forces could still be expected to be weak and inexperienced, the operation could result in damage to the U.S. and Allied war effort far exceeding the damage wreaked at Pearl Harbor. Lost in the anchorage at Hawaii, it appeared from the news flash, were aged, slow warships, obsolescent by the standards of the new capital ships of the German Fleet; lost on the United States' Atlantic doorstep, which contained the busiest sea-lanes in the world, would be a significant part of the merchant lifeblood that was keeping England in the war, not to mention fueling the United States' own nascent war industries. The prospects of going after single, unescorted vessels in American waters were all the more exciting to the admiral since, in his view, it was in the Atlantic battle against commerce that the war with England would be won or lost, and at the present moment, on orders from the Führer, all his U-boats had been withdrawn from the Atlantic in order to support operations in the Mediterranean and off Gibraltar.[4] War with the United States would get the U-boats back in the Atlantic where they belonged. The commander in chief knew that all his commanders would be of one mind with him: The Americans must be made to pay for their false neutrality; for their arrogance in declaring four-fifths of the Atlantic to be part of the Western Hemisphere; for their sighting reports on U-boats to British destroyers; and for their hitherto-untouchable convoys of war matériel and food to enemy England.

Since October, Dönitz had sent boats to intercept Britain-bound convoys as far west as the banks of Newfoundland, but now, with mounting expectancy, he jumped his gaze southward, past the St. Lawrence River and the Nova Scotia coast, to the seaports of New England; then along the south shore of Long Island to New York Harbor, where in 1941 one could count fifty arrivals and departures every twenty-four hours; from there down the shipping lanes that fed into Delaware and Chesapeake bays; past the dangerous currents off Cape Hatteras; and, finally, through the heavily trafficked Straits of Florida that funneled shipping to and from the Gulf of Mexico and the Windward Passage. Now it was the U.S. coastal waters themselves that must be attacked—from New York to Cape Hatteras to Florida. If Dönitz could persuade Oberkommando der Kriegsmarine (OKM), Naval High Command at Berlin, to release Type IX boats from west of Gibraltar, U-Boat Command (BdU) might be able to put together enough boats for a "combined surprise attack."[5] When the Führer declared war on the United States, as he soon must, Dönitz would be poised to strike a blow against the United States as sudden and as jarring as a beat on a kettledrum. And that, he decided, was what he would call it: Operation Paukenschlag ("Operation Drumbeat").

This book began as a single footnote to a history of larger scope in which I have been engaged for a number of years. It has long been known in a general way that German U-boats operated against merchant shipping along the United States East Coast during the first period of formal U.S.–German warfare in January–July 1942. But was it possible, I wondered, to identify the individual U-boat that sank the oil tanker *Gulfamerica* in a blazing display off Jacksonville Beach, Florida, on the night of 10 April 1942—and identify as well the U-boat's commander? The more the footnote fascinated, the more detective work it provoked, with the result that the footnote grew into a paragraph, a chapter, a book. It became a book because the research disclosed that there was a much larger story attached to that particular U-boat, which bore the designation U-*123*, and to its commander, twenty-eight-year-old Kapitänleutnant (lieutenant commander) Reinhard Hardegen, than the single sinking of *Gulfamerica*. It was a story that took me far from Florida waters to the approaches to New York Harbor, where on 14 January 1942, the same Reinhard Hardegen inaugurated a series of U-boat attacks on the United States so severe and extensive, and so appallingly undefended, that, taken together, they constituted an "Atlantic Pearl Harbor." In Hardegen's case the targets were not warships but freighters and tankers and their cargoes—the "sinews" of war.

It can, and will be, argued in this book that the U-boat assault on merchant shipping in United States home waters and the Caribbean during 1942 constituted a greater strategic setback for the Allied war effort than did the defeat at Pearl Harbor—particularly in that the loss of naval vessels destroyed or damaged at Hawaii had little or no bearing on the decisive carrier battles that developed soon after with the Japanese at Coral Sea and Midway; whereas the loss of nearly 400 hulls and cargoes strewn across the sands of the U.S. Navy's Eastern, Gulf, and Caribbean Sea frontiers threatened both to sever Great Britain's lifeline and to cripple American war industries. As Army Chief of Staff General George C. Marshall agonized on 19 June 1942: "The losses by submarines off our Atlantic seaboard and in the Caribbean now threaten our entire war effort."[6] If the leaching of lives and matériel had continued unchecked, one can speculate what would have been the effects on any future Allied invasion of German-occupied Europe and on Germany's ability to concentrate all her forces in the war against Russia.

German naval historian Michael Salewski has suggested that in order to understand the complex sixty-nine-month-long Battle of the Atlantic, the battle on which, more than any other, turned the outcome of World War II, one might profitably study a single heavily engaged U-boat, which "mirrored at once both the greater strategy of war and its everyday horror."[7] U-*123* was such a boat. Essentially, then, this book is the story of Kptlt. Reinhard Hardegen and of U-*123*, as recorded in on-board documents and as remembered by Hardegen and his crew. It is the story of an officer who, owing to injuries sustained in a plane crash, was not supposed to be at sea in U-boats in the first place. It is the story of an officer who was one of the most determined, daring, even reckless commanders in the Ubootwaffe, the submarine fleet. It is the story as well of U-boat warfare in general, of daily life and routine aboard the Type IXB boat that Hardegen commanded, of the woefully deficient U.S. defenses against U-boats in the opening months of U.S.–German hostilities, of U-*123*'s bold, determined destruction of enemy vessels, yet also of a commander's sometimes humanitarian concern for the enemy crews he set adrift. It is also a story of fear—the panicky fear of merchant seamen scrambling for lifeboats and the claustrophobic fear of a U-boat crew trapped under the dread pounding of depth charges. It is a story told also through the eyes of the U.S. Navy Command, so far as that story can be pieced together from the extant record (most of the principals being deceased). On the German side it is a story of lost opportunities for the Kriegsmarine (German Navy), which might well have defeated England (and thus denied the United States that island base from which to mount a joint American-British invasion of German-occupied Europe) if Adolf Hitler had permitted the timely diversion of resources from tanks for land war to U-boats for the decisive Battle of the Atlantic. On the American side it is a story of naval unpreparedness and inexperience, of negligence and dereliction of duty, of command inflexibility and unseemly arrogance—and yet of final triumph.

Though it goes without saying, Winston Churchill said it best: "Crimes were committed by the Germans under the Hitlerite domination to which they allowed themselves to be subjected, which find no equal in scale and wickedness with any that have darkened the human record."[8] This book does not attempt to portray the Kriegsmarine as anything other than an armed force in service to objective evil. At the same time it does not paint a swath of guilt across the name of every German who went to sea, for to do so would be more than indiscriminate: It would be to miss the truth that most officers and ratings went to sea for Navy, not for Nazi, reasons. The Kriegsmarine was the least politicized of the German armed forces.[9] U-boatmen fought for one another or for duty's sake. Some few, more politically sophisticated, fought to avenge the Fatherland's defeat in World War I and to redress the humiliating Versailles *Diktat*. Officers fought for the U-boat arm itself: Calling themselves *Freikorps Dönitz*, they were a "navy within the Navy." U-boat commanders recorded successes with what appears to have been a politically detached, professional pride.[10] Moreover, though they and their crews waged total war against merchant seamen of other nations, the historian of balanced perspective can find their like among U.S. Eighth Air Force and RAF Bomber Command crewmen who waged total war against civilians in German cities. Nor should it be forgotten that unrestricted U-boat warfare in the Atlantic had its exact copy in U.S. submarine warfare against Japanese merchant shipping throughout the Pacific. While Hardegen and the Drumbeat boats were consigning hundreds of Allied merchant seamen to watery graves, U.S. Navy Fleet-type submarines were sending hundreds of Japanese merchant seamen to the same dark fate. It should also be observed that members of the U.S. Merchant Marine had combatant status, and that those who died were casualties instead of victims, although that was not recognized until 1977 when the U.S. Congress granted veteran standing, including discharge certificates and benefits, to all surviving merchant sailors who served on an oceangoing ship between 7 December 1941 and 15 August 1945. The mariners suffered a casualty rate matched only by the Marines among the U.S. military branches of the Second World War. Objections to the survivors' status as veterans raised by the Department of Defense were overruled by the courts in July 1987 (again in January 1988) and the first discharge papers were mailed to those mariners still living who applied for them by the U.S. Coast Guard in March of 1988.[11]

As for the oft-alleged machine-gunning of survivors in the water by U-boat crews, there exists only one documented case of that behavior in the war (though, of course, there may have been others), when U-852, commanded by Kptlt. Heinz Eck, machine-gunned both survivors and debris in an attempt to leave no trace of its sinking of the Greek SS Peleus in the Indian Ocean on 13 March 1944. A British court-martial ordered Eck and his officers shot on 30 November 1945. Certainly there were instances when a U-boat shooting with deck guns against a merchant ship's waterline or radio house or antennae hit crewmen in the process of lowering lifeboats. This could happen inadvertently even in those cases when the U-boat commander—and Reinhard Hardegen was a consistent example—conscientiously refrained from opening gunfire until he thought the crews were safely in boats. And it could happen perforce when, short or out of torpedoes, a U-boat attempted to sink a ship by gunfire alone. Generally speaking, U-boatmen looked on survivors as seamen like themselves: After the destruction of an enemy vessel the larger bond that existed between men of the sea, irrespective of nationality, tended to preclude acts of violence upon the helpless. The ramming of lifeboats filled with survivors by U-boats apparently never happened, except in the imagination of Hollywood screenwriters (for example, in *Action in the North Atlantic*, Warner Brothers, 1943), who for wartime propaganda purposes depicted U-boat crews as evil, cunning, and ruthless outlaws of the ocean. Quite apart from the Geneva Convention and humanitarian considerations, the Kriegsmarine had very pragmatic reasons for eschewing such behavior. As the German Naval Staff expressed its position on 16 December 1942: "The killing of survivors in lifeboats is inadmissible, not just on humanitarian grounds but also because the morale of our own men would suffer should they consider the same fate as likely for themselves."[12] The historian of the U.S. submarine war against Japan provides an instructive example of this kind of "inadmissible" behavior exhibited by U.S. submariners in the Pacific.[13]

In the case of Reinhard Hardegen one concedes nothing to the odiousness of the cause for which he fought by stating that as a professional naval officer he fulfilled his assigned duties, achieved exceptional successes, and brought distinction to his service. In five war patrols as a commander he sank twenty-five ships (including two that were later refloated), for a total of 136,661 tons, a figure that compares favorably with the best record (twenty-four ships, 93,824 tons) posted by a U.S. Navy submarine skipper in the war—Richard H. O'Kane, in five patrols on USS *Tang*. He should also be credited with four ships totaling 33,247 tons damaged by his torpedoes and artillery. We can recognize Hardegen's achievements, and those of his men, even as we condemn Hitler and the Nazis who sent them to war. Their story is told in these pages with neither favor nor censure. Finally, it deserves remembering that, of 863 U-boats that sailed on operational patrols, 754 did not return to their bases; of 39,000 men who put to sea in U-boats during World War II, 27,491 rest in iron coffins, and 5,000 others were taken prisoner. That hecatomb is almost without parallel. Though relatively few in numbers, the Ubootwaffe suffered one of the greatest mortal losses of any single arm of any of the belligerent nations. Toward the end of the war, when Allied technology had overwhelmed that of the Germans and it was near suicidal for a U-boat even to stand out to sea, crew after crew did so nonetheless, without hesitation or complaint. On that other side of the Battle of the Atlantic men were no less human, no less brave.

This book represents an attempt to investigate, understand, and depict how German and American naval personnel conducted combat operations in one of the most critical, yet least-known, military chapters of World War II. I have kept strictly to what the documentary research and interviews disclose. The intention has been to tell all and to palliate nothing. On-board commands and other technical expressions for which Hardegen, his officers, and crew are quoted are based primarily on the U-*123* war diaries and shooting reports, on Hardegen's wartime writings, and on U-boat language that was common to officers and ratings. Other direct quotations are based on interviews with Hardegen and crew members; and with Patrick Beesly. No characters or events have been invented, and previous fictions devised by those who knew some little bit of the Hardegen story have been flatly discarded.[14] With sufficient drama in the facts there is no need to invent the impossible. Every incident at sea has been carefully documented. Whenever I have reconstructed an event or dialogue in order to bring U-*123* to life, that fact is acknowledged in the notes at the end of the volume. A straight academic narrative would have been one choice; recreating the U-boat environment was another.

1

U-Boats Westward

Second Flotilla U-Boat Base, Lorient, France, on the Bay of Biscay, the evening of 19 December 1941, twelve days after Pearl Harbor. Kapitänleutnant Reinhard Hardegen paced impatiently along the starboard catwalk in bay B6 of the newly commissioned Keroman I bunkers. Laid out before him in the still black water of the protective pen was the long gray hulk of his beloved U-*123*. Bright lamps high along the corrugated iron ceiling formed deep shadows beneath the movements of blue-overalled German and French workmen who swarmed over the U-boat ministering to the last of her injured parts. Twenty days had passed since Hardegen had brought *Eins Zwei Drei—One Two Three—*through steel-armored shutters into this prodigious bombproof vault, and for most of that period without stop, day or night, engine mechanics, electrical technicians, welders, armorers, and other refit specialists had reconditioned the engines, adjusted the port shaft bearings, cleaned the screws, ground in the sea valves, and hammered home corrections to flanges that lined the openings in the pressure hull to outboard cables and connecting rods. When the essential hull repairs had been completed, and the interior was fully cleaned and fumigated, Hardegen had taken *123* out to sea for test dives. At Point Laube in the bay, a navigational fix at the fifty-meter line, where the continental shelf, after deepening gradually, dropped off sharply, Hardegen conducted trial dives and trimming exercises to see, as he put it, if the parts were equal to the whole. Finding that they were and that U-*123* was ready to swim again, he had brought the boat back to Keroman with anxious urging that the maintenance crews complete their work as quickly as possible. Now from the catwalk he watched the final touches to the exterior of the hull. Highlighted by aureoles of blue light from acetylene torches employed by welders to repair depth-charge damage along the scarred surface of the deck plates and conning tower, other workers scraped away running sores of rust, applied anticorrosives, and painted the U-boat's skin afresh. Hardegen's anxiety came from the fact that he and four other U-boat commanders were assigned to an emergency mission. With two others he had received his sailing orders directly from Admiral Dönitz that very afternoon, the nineteenth. And one of the five boats committed to the mission, U-*125* of Ulrich Folkers, had already sortied the day before. Hardegen did not want to be the last to go.[1]

At 0930 on 20 December the telephone rang in Hardegen's residence in the old French Naval Prefecture. U-*123* was ready for ammunition loading. Torpedo loading could be scheduled for the following day. At once Hardegen sent his number two (IIWO), second watch officer, Leutnant zur See Horst von Schroeter to supervise the acceptance and storage on board of ammunition rounds for the two deck artillery pieces, starting with the heavier shells, each in individual packing, for the 10.5-centimeters Bootskanone on the fore casing and followed by smaller rounds for the 3.7-centimeters gun on the after casing. Then came ammo belts and magazines for the 2-centimeters C/30 antiaircraft (AA) machine gun on the rear bridge flak platform and for two small shoulder-fired machine guns kept below decks. The loading occupied von Schroeter and ratings brought in hurriedly from recreational centers at nearby Quiberon and Carnac most of the day. While von Schroeter was busy with ammunition Hardegen sent his number one (IWO), first watch officer, Oberleutnant zur See Rudolf Hoffmann to round up the rest of the crew from the back streets of Lorient, especially the torpedo mates, who would be needed for the more arduous exercise of transferring torpedoes into their six tubes and various storage cradles.

The next morning, under the lights of bay B6, torpedo loading commenced. Thirteen G7e electric and two G7a steam-driven "eels" were brought over by rail cars from the torpedo magazines northwest of the bunkers. Complex in their technology, the torpedoes had to be managed with great care. The specially designed cars transporting them moved as though they were handling eggs, since the torpedoes' delicate interior guidance systems and propellent mechanisms could easily be jarred out of tolerance. Engineers at Torpedoerpro-bungskommando (TEK), Torpedo Trials Command, had already test-launched each "eel" over a measured course, noted every deviation from the norm, and attached a service certificate to accompany the weapon on board. Once placed in the launch tubes, the G7e electrics required constant attention if they were to be available for sudden use. On a schedule of every three to five days thereafter, each one, thickly coated with grease, would have to be coaxed out of its tube onto hoist rings where a team of torpedo mates called mixers would check its battery charge, contact pistol, bearings and axles, rudder and hydro-plane controls, lubrication points, and guidance system.

The cigar-shaped G7es were seven meters long, had a diameter of 53.3 centimeters, weighed sixteen hundred kilograms (3,528 pounds), and carried an explosive charge of five hundred kilos of torpex, a high-explosive mixture consisting of Cyclonite, TNT, and aluminum flakes. Once launched by a blast of compressed air from one of *123*'s tubes—four bow, two stern—the torpedoes would become independent, self-propelled, dirigible submarines with motors, pro-pellers, rudders, and hydroplanes, that could travel at thirty knots at a specified depth over a distance of 5,000 meters (although Hardegen, like most commanders, liked to launch at 550 to 600 meters from target). Their electric motors, made possible by the development of very light lead storage batteries, left no visible wake, unlike the G7as' compressed air-steam propulsion system. The impact of the tor-pedoes' nose-contact pistols on the underwater side of a ship would detonate the torpex and tear holes in the vessel's steel hull, causing it to sink.

On this day the deck and conning tower of *123* were greatly transformed in appearance by a large winch tower, chain hoists, braces, trolleys, and other devices for lifting fifteen torpedoes into slanted position so that they could be let down the fore and aft torpedo hatches. Six of those fifteen would be stored in launch tubes, four forward and two aft, and the rest in reserve under and over floor plates or in place of the lower bunks. Once they finished manhandling the reserve torpedoes into their assigned spaces, the weary ratings se-cured the deck, took down the winch and other gear, and, with Hoffmann's permission, collapsed in place.

On 22 December von Schroeter took charge again, supervising the loading of food and fresh drinking water. This operation would closely involve the crewman who would make most direct use of the provisions, Johannes Vonderschen, the *Smutje*, or cook. To "Hannes" it would have been hard to prove that the torpedo loading was more critical to the boat's mission than the provisioning: After all, if Hannes could not get the commander and crew to the target area with life and energy intact, what good were their torpedoes? He arranged for the foodstuffs certain to be eaten last on the *Feindfahrt* (operational patrol) to be loaded first, through both the fore deck and tower hatches. Willing crew hands below received his consignments and stowed the provisions where Hannes said he could best retrieve them. Last to be eaten, as they would also be the majority of what was eaten during the mission, were canned foodstuffs.

Von Schroeter counted off the boxes in his ledger as Hannes sent down the hatches several hundred large cans of meat, vegetables, potatoes, butter, eggs, fruit, ready-cooked meals, even bread. Belowdecks, according to the cook's instructions shouted down the hatch, crewmen stacked cans on or in every available floor plate, hole, or recess of the narrow steel tube that formed the U-boat's interior. What was already an exceedingly cramped work and living space now became all the more confined as standing columns of cans crowded every compartment and passageway. Even the starboard aft head (toilet), one of only two on board for a complement of fifty-two officers and men, was requisitioned to serve as a fully stocked pantry.

Still to come were fresh foodstuffs, some of which would have to be consumed during the first weeks of travel before spoilage set in. Much of the fresh stowage would hang in overhead nets and hammocks that reduced headroom by half. Down the hatch now came fresh bread, potatoes, and hams, as well as salami, sausages, and smoked bacon, together with long-refrigerated crates of apples from Nantes and grapes from Bordeaux. They were the best rations provided to men in any of the German services.

The newly baked black bread and fruits in particular gave off a delightful aroma that wafted throughout the just-cleaned boat, but Hannes and his fellow crew members knew that it was not to last. A week into the voyage a very different fragrance would replace it: an odor compounded of stale, humid air, diesel oil, sweat, urine, semen, soiled and fusty clothing, battery gas, bilges, cooking odors, and Colibri, the eau de cologne used by the bridge watch to remove salt spray from their faces. By two weeks the U-boat's interior would deserve to be described as a sewer pipe with valves, and the reeking, putrescent atmosphere would be having its expected effect on any fresh food that remained. After three weeks the loaves of black bread, a German sailor's staple food, would be covered with a white fluffy mold; the crew would call them rabbits and eat only the centers. The sausages that hung everywhere from overhead pipes would wear their own white mildews, and the lemons that everyone on a U-boat sucked to prevent scurvy similarly would grow white coats amid the damp and the stench.

For the moment, however, Hannes and his comrades could put out of mind the hard sea days ahead. This was a time for luxuriating in the scents of dry land and for taking deserved pride in the efficiency with which they had packed their stores. Von Schroeter for his part informed IWO Hoffmann that *123* had 166 tons of diesel fuel on board, was fully stocked with ammunition, torpedoes, and provisions, and could be reported *frontreif*—ready for war front operations. She was prepared to depart Keroman at any hour for the ship *Isère* a short distance away on the Scorff River. *Isère*, an old refloated wooden prison ship that had once transported French convicts to Devil's Island and the other penal islands of French Guiana, served as a departure and arrival U-boat pontoon. Hoffmann, saluting, formally advised Hardegen of the status.

"Herr Kaleu," he reported, using the accepted diminutive form of Hardegen's rank, "*Eins Zwei Drei* is fully loaded in all categories. I have signed the release form from the yard. The maneuvering room and engine crews are on board."

"Very well, Number One," acknowledged Hardegen. "Let's take her out."

Late that day, 22 December, the tall armored gates of bay B6 pulled open with a yawning roar and in the huge silence that followed the lethally loaded U-*123*, driven by quiet electric motors, backed slowly out into the greasy harbor water. After pivoting to a forward position Hardegen and the skeleton crew fired up the starboard nine-cylinder MAN diesel and nudged *123* the short distance up the Scorff to *Isère* on the right bank where he twisted 180 degrees so that the boat faced downriver toward the harbor mouth. In her new coat of camouflage-haze gray *123* presented a striking contrast to the mottled old prison ship to which she now tied up for departure. She would look even better on the morrow, Hardegen anticipated, with her crew in fresh sea uniforms standing shoulder to shoulder on deck and her tower decorated with commissioning pennant, naval ensign, and Christmas trees.

0930 hours German War Time, 23 December 1941. Reinhard Hardegen, uniformed in formal blue, hastened down the outside ladder from the bridge of *123* in time to greet Korvettenkapitän Viktor Schütze as the flotilla commander made his way across the gangway from *Isère*. Schütze stopped when he reached deck level to salute the boat: "*Heil, Eins Zwei Drei!*" Hardegen saluted in return: "*Heil*, Herr Korvettenkapitän!" Schütze came aboard, shook Hardegen's hand, and asked the usual questions. Was his boat delivered back from refit in satisfactory condition? Was he fully loaded in all categories? Was his crew intact, in good health, and ready to board? Hardegen was able to respond to all of these in the affirmative.

Schütze then handed Hardegen his Operation Order in a large, sealed blue envelope. "You already know your initial course heading from the admiral," he said. "Notice that the cover instructions specify that you open your orders only after reaching twenty degrees longitude. Go over them carefully with your officers and, if you wish, inform your crew of their general contents. Although the plan for your cruise has been worked out in careful detail, you will notice that we did not have quite all the appropriate supporting materials to provide you. I am confident that your resourcefulness will supply the difference. You may sortie when ready. Your escort is cleared for departure. Good luck and good hunting."

The two shook hands and saluted again. Hardegen looked down at his envelope, more than ordinarily curious to know what it contained. Schütze paused on the gangway as he left, turned and said: "One thing more, Hardegen. Be alert on your way out. Two Spitfires were over Brest yesterday between 1720 and 1750. Then forty bombers hit Brest beginning about 1900. Some 175 high-explosive and 200 incendiary bombs were dropped on the harbor and the base. A few casualties. No vessels hit. The British are getting serious. Be on guard."[2]

"Yes, Herr Korvettenkapitän," Hardegen answered, then mounted the bridge ladder and went down the conning tower hatch to place the envelope in his safe.

On *Isère* a large and lively crowd was now forming. Many were crewmen, the seamen and technicians, saying goodbye to friends from the base and girls from the town. Their fresh-scrubbed appearance and clean blue-gray utility coveralls differed sharply from the unshaven, disheveled, and ragtag sight they had presented when *123* last tied up to *Isère* on 22 November following their return from the Strait of Belle Isle and Greenland. When Hardegen returned to the bridge, he was delighted to see also assembling on *Isère* a large number of Wehrmacht men in field gray, including the marching band, from a nearby infantry battalion that had befriended his crew and assumed the informal role of *Patenbataillon* (sponsoring battalion) of the boat. Following Hardegen's first patrol in *123*, the battalion had invited his crew to enjoy the open air and green fields at their base outside Lorient. There the ratings enjoyed picnics and sports, and some of the more daring among them exercised the battalion's horses. Hardegen had laughed to see his blue-clad seamen galloping awkwardly across the fields, and he had returned the favors shown his crew by inviting some of the infantrymen to have an underwater experience while he trial-dived *123* during the recent refit. That the battalion chose to sponsor the boat had pleased Hardegen greatly, and now he noticed that the soldiers gathered on *Isère* had brought with them a number of Christmas trees to join the ones he personally had already erected on the bridge and stashed belowdecks along with—unknown to the crew—presents for everyone from home. The battalion commander came on board with some of his officers and men to present the trees. He had trimmed them himself, he said, beaming, and he wondered if there were enough for every compartment to have its own. Hardegen assured him that there were. Then the commander signaled for his battalion cooks to come across the gangway with ten large cakes that they had prepared for the crew's Christmas meal at sea. Hardegen thanked them warmly. Handshakes, good wishes, and salutes followed. As the commander and his delegation walked back up to *Isère*'s venerable planking, the Patenbataillon band struck up the Christmas carol "Adeste Fideles." It was turning out to be exactly the kind of send-off that Hardegen had hoped for. Good feeling abounded and for a brief while at least even the *furor Germanicus* seemed at rest somewhere in the distance.[3]

With the propulsion systems checked and his tanks, pipes, and valves in good order for clearing port the Leitender Ingenieur (LI), chief engineering officer, Oberleutnant zur See Heinz Schulz had the temporary duty of briefing a new member of the crew, Maat Alwin Tölle.

Ordinarily an officer of Schulz's rank would not be detailed to spend time with a new crewman, much less with one who had never been on a U-boat before, but Tölle was no seaman. He wore the uniform but his armband read *Propaganda-Kompanie*. Tölle was a photographer assigned to *123* by the Ministry of Propaganda. Arriving at almost the last hour before departure he presented himself to Schulz, as ordered, saluted after a fashion, and set down his leather case and duffel bag.

Schulz asked him what was in the leather case.

Cameras, film, and notebooks, answered Tölle.

What was in the duffel bag?

Clothes and personal effects.

Schulz managed to keep his sense of humor. He told Tölle to take out two changes of underwear and socks, one for outbound, one for inbound, a sweater, and his toothbrush (not that he would have much chance to use it), hand the duffel bag with the rest of its contents to one of the dock hands and ask him to stow it at Flotilla until the boat got back. The first lesson Tölle needed to learn, Schulz told him, was that there was no room on a U-boat for more than his body, and that *123* might have trouble fitting in even that.

When Tölle returned on board, Schulz walked him to the far end of the sloping stern casing and turned his eyes back toward the bow. This, he explained, was an Unterseeboot, or U-boat for short. The term suggested that the U-boat traveled perpetually under the sea. That was what most civilians seemed to think. Was that what Tölle thought? Yes, Schulz figured as much. Now, the boat *could* go underwater, but it very rarely did so. It would dive now and then in order to evade attacking ships and planes, to escape rough seas, to seek enemy targets with underwater listening gear when visibility was poor, or very occasionally to make a submerged attack when conditions favored that kind of approach. Furthermore, it would make numerous test dives to make sure it could submerge in an emergency. For the most part, however, it cruised on the surface and fought on the surface, like a torpedo boat. The term *U-boat*, or *submarine*, tended, therefore, to give a false impression. A better term for the U-boat would be *submersible* or *diving boat*.

Speed and range were the controlling factors that led to surface travel. With diesel engine power *123* could make a maximum speed of 18¼ knots on the surface, faster than merchantmen and some escort vessels. At an economy speed of 12 knots she could cruise over a range of 8,700 nautical miles without refueling. At 10 knots the radius of action would extend to 12,000 miles. Submerged, however, she could make only 7.3 knots maximum. Even at an economy speed of 4 knots the storage batteries that ran her *E-Maschinen*, electric motors, underwater would give out of power after only 64 miles. And to fully recharge the batteries required a U-boat to run its diesels on the surface for seven hours.

Eins Zwei Drei, Schulz told Tölle, was a Type IXB Atlantikboot, an improved version of the Type IXA, which had itself evolved from the U-*81* design of the last war. Because of its large size and wide, flat deck, U-boat men called the type *See-Kuh* (sea cow), after aquatic herbivorous mammals like the manatee. Though produced in far fewer numbers than the Type VII and though unable to dive quite as fast as the smaller VII—35 seconds as compared to 28—many in the fleet thought that it was the superior boat because of its excellent seakeeping qualities. Type IXB like its more numerous sister type IXC also had a longer range than the VII because of its larger fuel bunkers, carried a third more torpedoes, and provided one additional stern launch tube. In essence it was a long-distance high-seas boat designed for extended missions. Now, if one looked at the boat from the deck, as Tölle was doing, it appeared not very different from other boats and ships with which Tölle might be familiar. It had a knife-edged stem at the bow, a rounded hull, a deck, and a stern. Most of what Tölle saw, however, was not the U-boat. What he was seeing was the outer steel skin that encapsulated the U-boat.

The boat itself was a long narrow cylindrical tube with a pressure hull made of welded high-tensile steel plates 20.5 millimeters thick and capable of withstanding some fifteen atmospheres of water pressure when submerged. This was probably the strongest hull in the whole of marine architecture. Within the pressure hull were all the engines and motors, controls, torpedoes, and, of course, the crew. The inner hull also contained trim tanks at each end and at the middle that held seawater pumped in or out to control the boat's weight and hold it at a specific angle and depth while underwater. Outside the pressure hull were other tanks whose bulging forms could be seen at the waterline. Those were the ballast, or diving, tanks, which were flooded with water when the boat dived, and the fuel bunkers, or tanks, which contained diesel fuel needed for the engines. Schulz said that he would explain both of these tank systems to Tölle later. For now it was enough to point out that the ballast and fuel tanks were enclosed by a thin outer casing that, while not pressure resistant, provided an outer hull more suitable for surface travel than did the inner cylinder or hull. The outer hull, in fact, gave a U-boat the form more or less of an ordinary ship, including the flat deck on which he and Tölle stood. The thin outer skin was kept from being crushed by maintaining the pressure in the ballast and fuel tanks equal to the surrounding sea pressures. That was accomplished by vents and piping from sea to the tanks. Slots, or limber holes, in the deck structure allowed drainage when the boat was running on the surface and taking seas over the deck. They also drained the deck when diving to prevent air bubbles from hanging up the boat.

This boat's number, by the way, *123*, did not designate her place in the sequence of U-boat construction or commissioning. U-*116, 117*, and *118*, which were also IXB boats, all came down the ways a year after *123*. The numbering system was meant to confuse the enemy— make him think there were more U-boats than actually existed. Whether it did so or not no one seemed to know. Schulz was unsure how much of this Tölle was absorbing, but he went on to cite some figures that, for an engineer, came readily to mind. The boat was 76.5 meters (251 feet) long, 6.8 meters (22¼ feet) across the beam, and 4.7 meters (15½ feet) in surfaced keel depth. Displacement surfaced was 1,051 tons, submerged 1,178 tons. Did that mean anything to Tölle? Apparently not. Schulz noticed that the correspondent's eyes were beginning to wander. Better give him something a little more human, he thought. The bridge atop the conning tower and the tower itself, with their instruments and controls, could wait for another time— someday, he mused, when Tölle was over the shock of what he would find later that same day belowdecks.

He led Tölle forward along the gray surface pointing out as he went the aft bollards, stern navigation light, diesel engine exhaust port, aft ladder, radio antenna line, 3.7-cm gun, and watertight 2-cm ammunition container. He told Tölle that he would skip for now the flak platform with its black, bristling antiaircraft gun on the after part of the bridge—though he indicated the platform's open sweeping rails and said that it was commonly called the *Wintergarten*, the only place on board where Tölle would be permitted to smoke, if he were so inclined—and that he would leave the bridge and interior of the conning tower for later; but that here, on both sides of the upper forward structure of the conning tower, was something that might interest Tölle. These, he said, were painted representations of the badge given to soldiers who had been wounded three times in battle: crossed swords against a helmet surrounded by laurel wreaths. This, Schulz said, was the insignia, or escutcheon, of the boat. Why the wounded badge? Because when *123* was under the previous command of Karl-Heinz Möhle, the boat was "wounded" three times: once when the crew accidentally shot into their own jumping wire, or net shield; another time when the boat was rammed by a steamer; and, finally, when bombs from a British aircraft damaged the outer hull. It was Möhle who chose the device. Reinhard Hardegen, when he took command, kept the device out of respect for the crew. And speaking of Möhle, Schulz continued, while the boat was under his command, it was chosen by the UFA motion picture studios for all the outboard action shots of a popular film called *U-Boote westwärts* (*U-Boats Westward*). Hardegen had seen the picture. So had most of the crew. And Schulz's guess, he expressed with a laugh, was that the admiral had seen it, too. The title was a good omen, he said. *Eins Zwei Drei* might not be going to Gibraltar after all. And why was that worth mentioning? Because that was where most of the Type IXs had been stationed recently, and it was not good water for this size boat.

One last thing, he said. When Tölle went below after departure he should ask someone right away for instructions on the operation of the head. And he should commit to memory what he heard. The valve sequence in the head was more complicated than all of Tölle's Leica lens systems and light meters. Tölle should potty-train before he did anything else. There was no one on board to clean up after him. Now Schulz had to get back to his station. He advised Tölle to stand by the tower until he saw the rest of the crew go below and then follow them through the forward hatch. Someone would show him where to stow his gear—probably on his lap.[4]

1045 hours. Hardegen wanted to be underway by 1100. He now set the maneuvering watch—mechanics in the engine room, electricians in the maneuvering room, helmsman, navigator, and deck force—and ordered the engine room to light up the twin diesels and report when they were warm. At once the deck and tower began to shake from the first uneven combustions and a harsh rumbling noise filled the air. Atop the bridge Hardegen in his white-covered commander's cap looked across at the crowd aboard *Isère*, now swelled by *Blitzmädel*, female naval telegraphers from the base, in their bright uniforms, who waved flowers at the rest of the crew now taking their positions on deck.

Hardegen ordered Hoffmann: "Number One, muster boat's company."

"*Jawohl*, Herr Kaleu!"

Under Hoffmann's orders shouted down from the bridge the petty officers lined up their men in ranks along the decks fore and aft and detailed the deck force with their heavy gloves to handle the lines and the brow. Each element reported all hands present and accounted for (some more hung over than others). Hoffmann counted fifty-two officers and men including Tölle who watched excitedly as the petty officers ordered the ratings: "Eyes front! Parade rest!" The men took a spread-ankle position facing the pontoon with hands clasped behind their backs. On *Isère* the drum major struck the air with his mace and the jackbooted battalion band, heavy on horns, broke into the traditional "Siegfried-Line." The watching crowd began to cheer.

Hoffmann reported to Hardegen: "Ready for getting under way, Herr Kaleu."

"Very well, Number One, prepare to cast off."

The diesels had now warmed from a rough, vibrating rumble to a steady roar. Hoffmann lifted a megaphone to address the deck force, most of whom stood by the four bollards bow to stern. "Stand by all lines!" he shouted. "Single up all lines!"

To others on the force who stood by the gangway he gave the order, "Take in the brow!" In peacetime departures the gangway would have been stowed on board but in wartime it was removed to the dock or pontoon, so the deck force assisted the wharf crew in snaking the brow across to *Isère*.

It was time to release the lines that held *123* fast to her base. "Take in four!"—the farthest aft. "Take in three!"

Now to draw the bow into the pontoon and get the stern angled out, "Shorten up on one!" The forward bollard crew pulled hard on their line. The boat positioned for sternway. Hoffmann put his mouth to the bridge voice pipe: "Both back one-third." The engine telegraph rang. Driveshafts engaged with a sharp report, and twin bronze screws boiled the water aft as Hoffmann followed quickly with, "Take in one!"

All that remained was the after spring as the boat moved sternway into her prop wash. "Take in two!" provided the final release.

The deck force stowed the hawsers as *123* backed smartly out from alongside *Isère*. The other crewmen on deck stood shoulder to shoulder with obvious pride. Above the bridge cowling Hardegen grinned broadly and waved. The commissioning pennant and naval ensign caught the breeze. The send-off crowd shouted hurrah three times.

"Right twenty degrees rudder." When Hoffmann had the boat in the channel he twisted to face the inlet. "Port screw ahead." And when the desired position was established, he killed sternway. "Both ahead one-third. Rudder amidships."

For a moment *123* throbbed in place until the screws bit in and she gained headway. Unleashed as though by a coiled spring *123* put to sea on her seventh Feindfahrt—Hardegen's third as her commander— trailing clouds of diesel smoke and the basso profundo of engines that almost overcame the clash and thump of "Englandlied" that drifted over the water from the battalion band. Ahead was the Bay of Biscay and, beyond it, the Atlantic.

Hoffmann reported to Hardegen: "*Eins Zwei Drei* is under way, Herr Kaleu. We rendezvous ahead with our escort through the mine field." The escort seen at station ahead, outside the harbor entrance, was a splinter-camouflaged *Räumboot* (R-boat) motor minesweeper.

"Very well," Hardegen acknowledged. "Both engines one-third to the second buoy. Fall out the crew once we pass Kernével." Hardegen knew that the Admiral would have his 7 × 50 binoculars on *123* as she passed U-boat headquarters to starboard and the old French battlements of Port-Louis to port. If this was going to be his last mission, he wanted it to look good from the start.

After the boat passed Larmor-Plage and began to leave behind the oily, brackish water of La Rade de Lorient, Hardegen yielded the conn to Hoffmann and stepped aft to the *Wintergarten*, where he could lean against the rails and watch the receding harbor structures. At the second buoy Hoffmann ordered all the boat's company except the deck force below. The petty officers and ratings passed quickly and easily down the hatches; awkwardly Tölle followed last down the forward ladder. The deck force checked all hatches and ammo containers; pushed home the watertight tampions that sealed the muzzles of the heavily greased deck guns; stowed the Christmas trees, ensign, and pennant; and cleared the AA gun. To Hoffmann they reported:

"Upper deck readied for diving, Herr Oberleutnant!"

"Very well," Hoffmann acknowledged. Calling rudder changes to the helmsman in the tower below he maneuvered *123* alongside the waiting R-boat and came to her course 250. At the same time four seaman lookouts in gray-green leather coveralls came up the tower ladder to join Hoffmann on the bridge watch. Four lookouts with the best pairs of eyes on board would attempt to get *123* safely through the first hours of the hazardous patch known as *Totenallee* — "death row" — the Bay of Biscay, a passage that normally took forty-eight hours before a U-boat reached the open Atlantic. From this point on there would be no more uniforms, no more standing in file, no more saluting, and the commander would be known by officers and ratings alike as the Old Man.

Hoffmann turned toward the Old Man in the *Wintergarten* and shouted loudly over the diesels: "First Watch Officer reporting watch set and boat ready for action, Herr Kaleu!"

"Very well, Number One. Maintain speed even with the R-boat."

Before long the navigator assistant Bootsmann Walter Kaeding ascended to the bridge to take departure sightings on the French coast. From these diopter numbers he would begin his dead-reckoning (DR) chart for the voyage. The construction cranes over Keroman provided one mark, a church steeple slightly to starboard another, and Belle Île just visible to the south a third. Kaeding called the range and bearing numbers down the tower hatch, then lingered on the *Wintergarten* with the Old Man through the next hour as the last thin streaks of land faded in the gathering sea mist and *123* cut loose from the main. He wondered how many French men and women, having sighted *123* from the shoreline, would pass word of the boat's departure through Resistance channels to London. No matter. The chambermaids would have known already. And the dockworkers. And the whores. The only secret that had remained intact was the boat's destination. Kaeding could draw the chart lines that showed where *123* had been and where she was now. Only the Old Man could draw more. Or could he? Kaeding looked across at Hardegen whose face betrayed nothing.

At 1330 from port side the R-boat escort notified *123* that she had passed safely through the swept channel of the coastal minefield and was on her own. HAPPY CHRISTMAS, concluded the semaphore, GOOD HUNTING. By voice pipe Hoffmann ordered the helmsman: "Steady on new course two-seven-five. Ring up engines both ahead two-thirds." As the R-boat turned back toward shore, her exhaust describing a tight arc and her crewmen anticipating warm baths, clean sheets, and occasional soft company, *123*'s crew, with a very different set of expectations, braced themselves for a long, hard vigil on the winter sea. Things were not bad yet: wind west, sea force 2, a slight swell, temperature 5.5 degrees Celsius. But meteorologists had been heard to say that this might be the worst Atlantic winter in fifty years. And every man on board—except Alwin Tölle—knew that nature could be a more miserable enemy than Tommies or Yankees.

> Where lies the land to which the ship would go?
> Far, far ahead, is all her seamen know.
> And where the land she travels from? Away,
> Far, far behind, is all that they can say.[5]

2

Down to the Seas

Fritz Rafalski: Sometimes he took too many risks.

Heinz Barth: Too many risks.

Richard Amstein: Yes, yes, he was full of risk.

Barth: We often thought, how can he approach so close to a tanker? After being hit by torpedoes it explodes, and then *we're* in danger. That's what we thought. I don't know if anyone ever *said* that to him. We didn't say it out loud.

Amstein: Yes, who would have told him such a thing?

Barth: Well, the LI or the first watch officer could have said, "Herr Kaleu, you shouldn't do that. Keep your distance." Or something like that. But our trips were very risky.

Karl Latislaus: And Hardegen would always be the first to attack. And then, of course, the first to sail back home. That's why we had the whole defense on our tails. But our first commander, Möhle, was more cautious.

Barth: Yes, he wasn't scared, but he considered things well before acting. But Hardegen was more or less a daredevil.

Amstein: Yes, with Möhle his first priority was the boat and the crew. We can't say that about Hardegen.

Latislaus: Yes, we were truly very lucky.

Barth: Very lucky.

Karl Fröbel: But don't forget, as young men we were inspired by his courage and his daring. We always trusted him.

Amstein: That we did.

Fröbel: Often we'd ask each other, "What's he pulling this time?" And when he stayed on the surface until the very last second, and we could already see the enemy aircraft bearing down on us, and he gave the signal to dive at the very last second, we'd say, "Well, he pulled it off again today." The older men, of course, thought differently because they had wives and children. But the young crewmembers supported their commander. We always said, "He did it again."

Kaeding: Of course, there was never a crew that was one hundred percent satisfied with their commander. The worst thing, the worst that could happen to a commander was failure. A commander who missed his targets—that would demoralize an entire crew. But you can't say that about Hardegen.

Fröbel: No. We went from success to success.

Bad König/Odenwald, Germany
8–9 November 1985

Fiercely independent men came out of Bremen, on the Weser River thirty-six miles inland from the North Sea. For twelve centuries the city-state produced mariners, merchants, and artisans who set their own peculiar style on trade routes and markets around the world and yielded to no one in their pride of place. As late as Reinhard Hardegen's birth there on 18 March 1913, one heard on the streets the special Plattdeutsch dialect that combined elements of Dutch, Danish and English, and learned from the oldest citizens how generations of burghers had resisted the reputed authority of dukes, counts, barons, and archbishops to claim sway over them. Hardegen's father was a teacher of history, geography, and French at a local *Gymnasium* (high school) and had written a number of books, including biographies of King Henry II of England and H. H. Meyer, founder of the North German Lloyd [steamship] Line. It was the sea above all that prevailed in Bremen. Through the Weser opening to the world's oceans the city offered its "virtuous Bremer youth" a frontier for exercising their inbred passion for independent life. And it was the smell of the sea and the sight of great-hulled vessels splashing to their moorings, and the inventory of cargoes from romantic ports that piled up on the docks— coffees, teas, spices, wines, and textiles—and the swagger of seamen through the market square that planted in Reinhard Hardegen's mind the resolution that when he grew up he, too, would go to sea. Not every boy his age was of the same mind: Some had heard of the sea's hard ways, of the boredom and of the fear, and they aimed for a career on land. But young Hardegen was plainly seastruck. In his games every puddle, every washbasin, became an ocean. Twigs became his frigates and matchboxes his tankers. Later it was warships that dominated his fantasies, from pirate vessels that flew the Jolly Roger to subma- rines—the latter fantasy assisted by a windup toy unterseeboot that performed heroic deeds both on and below the bathtub water.

With age the would-be seafarer took to rowboats and canoes, in which he made the Weser and its tributaries unsafe for Germany's enemies. Later he caught his first whiff of blue water at the Hanseatic Yacht School in Neustadt, Holstein, from which he made extended voyages to Copenhagen, Skagen, and Göteborg. The admiral of the yachting set was an indifferent student in Gymnasium, however. It was clear that the boating life took first place to Latin vocabulary, and eventually the priorities appeared in his deportment, as discovered during World War II when British bombers hit his old school building and a student found among the scattered papers deportment records of "our famous citizen," which he proudly forwarded to the hero: "Hardegen constantly ill-mannered"; "Hardegen interrupts the class"; "Hardegen eats breakfast during the lesson." Finally the truth was borne home on this mischievous youth that unless his academic grades and behavior improved, the chances of his admission to naval officers' training were minimal at best. Hard remedial work, com- bined with firm counsel from a longtime family friend, Paul König, retired captain in the North German Lloyd merchant fleet, turned his school life around and he successfully passed his remaining courses and the *Abitur* (final) exam while improving his deportment. On Ka- pitän König's persuasive recommendation the Kriegsmarine accepted Hardegen's application for midshipman candidacy in 1932.

Now the Kriegsmarine would find out whether or not there was any substance to this Bremer youth, and do so within three days' time, thanks to a battery of tests designed and supervised by naval psychologists of the Göttingen school. The tests, conducted at the Kiel-Wik naval barracks outside Kiel, with one psychologist assigned to observe each group of eight boys, sought to disclose a candidate's physical prowess, tenacity, courage, leadership, and ability to think and act in an emergency. The physical tests took the form of gymnastic exercises, sprinting, and chinning on a horizontal bar: A boy who struggled to chin a seventh time was rated higher than a boy who chinned himself easily eleven times and balked at a twelfth. Tenacity was measured by the *Mutprobe* ("test of courage"). Hardegen, like the other boys in his group, was placed alone in a room with one-way mirrors and told to lift a heavy metal bar. As he did so, the bar was charged with increasing currents of electricity. Those candidates who defied the shock and pain the longest received the highest grades. Hardegen held on.

In other phases of the testing Hardegen demonstrated his proficiency in carrying out complicated instructions given only once ("Carry this piece of paper over that obstacle, cross the ditch, turn left, run until you come to a tall tree, turn right, walk until you come to a man in a green coat, and say to him, 'I have been ordered to deliver this paper to you'"); wrote a short autobiography to be graded for style, grammar, and handwriting; wrote two compositions, one on a concrete and one on an abstract subject; conducted a conversation with the team psychologist before hidden cameras that recorded (it was thought) significant facial expressions and gestures; participated in a final group oral discussion on a theme such as "German Forests" or "Bismarck as a Leader" so as to reveal who was the natural leader of the conversation; and delivered an impromptu lecture before ten enlisted men whose reactions to the candidate (did he hold their attention? win their respect?) were carefully recorded. To these measurable data the examiners added their general impressions of the candidate's appearance and bearing, breeding and table manners. When the final psychological reports were presented to the Naval Board of Review (prior to expansion of the Kriegsmarine in 1935) not more than one candidate in twenty was found to meet the exacting standards. Reinhard Hardegen was one in twenty.[1]

Next after the psychological ordeal came basic training at Stralsund with many months of hard life before the mast on a square-rigger. In 1933 Hardegen's cadet class became the first to board the spanking-new tall-sail ship *Gorch Fock* (named after a poet-sailor who went down with his ship during the Battle of Jutland in May 1916) and were ferried out by the white-hulled beauty to the light cruiser *Karlsruhe* in the North Sea, on which they then embarked on a round-the-world cadet cruise. A fierce storm near the Orkney Islands north of Scotland gave the cadets their first taste of hazards on the deep, at the same time that it gave Hardegen a preview of the waters where years later he would experience his first success as a U-boat commander. After rounding the British Isles, *Karlsruhe* sailed south to the Iberian coast, entered the Mediterranean, and passed through the Suez to India, Sumatra, Java, and Australia. The final and most enjoyable stop in the Pacific sector of their voyage was Honolulu in the Hawaiian Islands.

The U.S. Navy fleet anchorage at Pearl Harbor deeply impressed Hardegen, who, with another midshipman, made friends with the local commanding officer's daughter and with that entrée gained access to the harbor, ships at anchor, and aircraft landing strips. He was particularly struck by the confined interior space of a U.S. fleet submarine that he and his friend were permitted to visit. The living quarters were incredibly small. And he wondered how anyone could make sense out of the spaghetti-like tangle of pipes and valves, hand wheels, levers, and other controls that would become so familiar an environment later in his career. What he remembered most when he was in submarines himself was that the American living quarters he had seen were actually spacious and luxurious compared with those provided in German U-boats. The Americans had a wardroom, a large kitchen, recreational space, several heads (toilets), and, it seemed, a sleeping bunk for every man. In U-boats there were no separate dining or recreational spaces for the crew, there was only one operating head for fifty officers and men, and there were so few bunks they had to be rotated constantly day and night — "hot bunks," the crew called them, because they were always warm. U-boats were spare, functional fighting machines. The Germans placed the greatest amount of fighting equipment and armament in the smallest possible space. Comfort, therefore, had to take second place. At the time of the Japanese attack on Pearl Harbor, 7 December 1941, by which date Hardegen was a U-boat veteran, he would wonder if the fact that the Americans were caught napping was due to their predilection for luxury and comfort. And he would wonder if they might not get caught napping again.

The final ports on the world cruise were New York and Boston. Like many other tourists to New York at the time, Hardegen rode the elevator to the observation floor of the Empire State Building and looked out over the city at night. What impressed him most in Manhattan, apart from the skyscrapers, was the huge sea of lights in the night-blackened city. In a matter of weeks Hardegen and his cadet class were back in Germany and enrolled in university-level classes at the Flensburg-Mürwik Naval Academy. For a year their world became physics, engineering, navigation, gunnery, strategy and tactics, and naval history and traditions. Finally, with the officers' examination successfully behind him, Hardegen moved on to short advanced coursework, including torpedo school and a fourteen-day program at the U-boat defense school at Kiel, where for the first time he experienced underwater travel on board a small three-hundred-ton Type IIA training U-boat of the kind that Germany used in the early 1930s to resurrect her 1914–18 Ubootwaffe and to produce a new generation of undersea officers and crews. The rearmament program excited his interest since he had chosen the military life, though, like his father before him, he took little interest in politics; and, in any event, all forms of party affiliation and activity were now closed off to him by oath and law in his new standing as a commissioned officer. In April 1936 he was promoted from Fähnrich zur See (midshipman) to Oberfähnrich zur See (ensign), and in October 1936 to Leutnant zur See (lieutenant junior grade). His subsequent promotions in grade would come in April 1938 (Oberleutnant zur See—Lieutenant senior grade), December 1940 (Kapitänleutnant—lieutenant commander), and March 1944 (Korvettenkapitän—commander).

When Hardegen and a number of friends from his commissioning class received their first service orders, which were handed to them in great secrecy and with instructions not to discuss them with anyone, not even among themselves, they were perplexed to find that the orders detailed them to the naval air force, which technically did not exist. Like many other young officers Hardegen had heard rumors that, in repudiation of the Versailles Treaty that had concluded the 1914–18 war and had imposed tight constraints on the German military, the Third Reich of Chancellor Adolf Hitler was building a new Luftwaffe (air force). Periodically Hardegen would see officers on the street in blue-gray uniforms that bespoke the new service. Now he learned in quick succession that he and his friends were expected to form a naval air arm (Luftkreis IV, later renamed Luftwaffenkommando See) and that they would have to go back to school. So, while most of the others in his class went out to envied sea billets on cruisers and destroyers, a disappointed Hardegen and his comrades went back to the books, this time to learn aeronautical theory and practical aircraft mechanics, all of it, it seemed at the time, a long way from the sea to which he had devoted his life interest. Only when he began flight training over the North Sea and could delight in his independence of action as a pilot as compared with the lot of his shipbound former comrades on tiny vessels far below him did he begin to find satisfaction in aviation.

With the satisfaction, however, came danger, as he learned the hard way when a Junkers W-34 aircraft in which he was a passenger crashed on takeoff and broke apart. When he regained consciousness, he beheld a broken leg hung suspended over a hospital bed and white bandages across contusions on what seemed every other part of his body. Internal injuries took the longest to recuperate from, six months altogether. The accident would leave him with a shortened right leg and a bleeding stomach, both of which threatened to end his active-duty career. For the present, though, he overcame his disabilities and completed the flight course, something that only a fraction of pilot candidates succeeded in doing, with the rest posted back to ships. By 1935, Hardegen was one of a select group of naval airmen on whom the Kriegsmarine was counting to man three hundred aircraft in twenty-five squadrons. With his own squadron he exhilarated in the experience of flying far out to sea, where he practiced both attacks on enemy submarines and maneuvers in support of Germany's own U-boats. Everything he learned about aircraft would stand him in good stead later, when as watch officer and commander on U-boats he had to contend with enemy planes, or "bees," as U-boat men called them, and he could count himself fortunate to know intimately the capabilities and the limits of airborne weaponry, the most dangerous threat to U-boats.

In 1939, after he had spent four years in naval aviation, Germany invaded Poland and, in November of that year, Hardegen together with the other navy pilots in his same date of rank were suddenly and without warning assigned to the Ubootwaffe. Luftwaffe Commander in Chief Hermann Göring had declared, "Everything that flies belongs to me." Naval aviation was no more. And Hardegen had to begin yet another career from the water up. It was a keen disappointment that he expressed in four-letter words fueled by alcohol. But, orders in hand, he soon found himself on board a seaplane to U-boat school at Flensburg. As the plane took off and made a last sentimental circle over the air base bordering "his" Kamper See, he could see below the attractive fishing village and then his own house in the pine forest where his wife Barbara, holding their first child, five-month-old Klaus-Reinhard, stood on the terrace waving.

Course followed course at U-boat school, and soon Hardegen was crammed with knowledge about the complicated diving boats. The confusion of valves and dials and handwheels that had made such an impression on him at Pearl Harbor began to clear, and eventually he and the other former aviators were actually on or under Lübeck Bay in a type IIA training boat, learning how to dive and how to keep a U-boat in trim. Their training base now was at Neustadt, Holstein, and the commander of their training boat, U-5, was Kapitänleutnant Heinrich Lehmann-Willenbrock, who would go on to become one of Germany's leading aces and a recipient of the coveted *Eichenlaub zum Ritterkreuz des Eisernen Kreuzes* (Knight's Cross of the Iron Cross, with Oak Leaves).[2] When this phase of the training was completed, Hardegen had the good fortune to spend three months assigned to the Torpedo Trials Command (Torpedoerprobungskommando) at Kiel and Eckernförde, where he developed exact skills in computing range and angle-on-bow of target vessels against which torpedoes with dummy warheads were launched. Afterward, because of his age and years in service, he was sent directly to U-boat Commanders School. It was at Commanders School on the Baltic that one day he saw two U-boats together that were both to have a major place in his future career. They came in one evening from torpedo-launching trials. One, with an edelweiss blossom painted on its tower, would be known in the fleet as the *Edelweissboot*. The other, colorfully camouflaged from bow to stern, had been used for all the outboard shots of a popular motion picture called *U-Boote westwärts* (*U-Boats Westward*). Both were Type IXB boats, the largest and most modern boats in the service. As fate would have it he would soon serve as watch officer on the first boat, U-124, and as commander on the second, U-123.

One morning while Hardegen was working in the cellar of his new house in Kiel, constructing shelves from old packing cases, a messenger arrived with orders to report in two hours' time to Holtenau airport for transport to a new assignment. He had been called up by the *System Greif*, literally "grasp system," that identified officers needed quickly for specific duties. While his wife, Barbara, made a box lunch, he hurriedly threw together his uniform and gear. A friend drove him to the airport, which he reached in good time. When the plane that was to pick him up landed and taxied to a stop, he was surprised to see a Konteradmiral flag hoisted atop the cabin.[3] As he approached the plane none other than Rear Admiral Karl Dönitz disembarked, took his salute, and reached out to shake his hand. Hardegen was instantly impressed by the clear eyes and firm handshake of this man whom the Ubootwaffe called *Der Löwe*—"the Lion." Dönitz suggested that while the plane was being refueled the two of them go into the canteen nearby and have a drink. Hardegen was still a young officer, untried and unknown to Dönitz, yet the admiral treated him with courtesy and showed genuine interest in his replies to questions.

When the admiral's aircraft was finally refueled and airborne, Hardegen thought that they might be headed to one of the new French bases. German land forces had just captured the Bay of Biscay harbors on the Brittany coast, and Dönitz was establishing U-boat bases at Lorient, Brest, St.-Nazaire, La Pallice, La Rochelle, and Bordeaux that would give U-boats direct access to the Atlantic, 450 miles west of their previous bases, without having to transit the Strait of Dover or travel north around Scotland as before. Instead, the plane landed at Wilhelmshaven on the North Sea where he learned that he was to be a replacement there for a second watch officer who had broken his hand. On reaching the pier he saw that the boat was U-*124*—the *Edelweissboot.*

When war began, fleet numbers were removed from U-boat conning towers because of their intelligence value to the enemy. Many boats chose an emblem to replace the painted numerals. Thus one boat sported a jumping dolphin, another three fish, or red devils, or golden horseshoes, and so forth. U-*124* was commanded by Kptlt. Wilhelm Schulz. He had lost a previous boat, U-*64*, when it was bombed by British aircraft near the Norwegian coast on 13 April 1940, during the Battle of Narvik. Schulz and his men were rescued by German Alpine troops on shore who came after them in rowboats. The insignia of the Alpine troops was the mountain flower edelweiss. As a gesture of gratitude Schulz emblazoned the device on the tower of his next boat, U-*124*, and had the flower design sewn onto his blue wool forage cap. Knowing this story, it was with a certain excitement that Hardegen presented himself to the commander on the deck: "Oberleutnant zur See Hardegen reporting as watch officer, Herr Kaleu!" Schulz returned his salute, shook his hand, and almost immediately called out,

"Aft line free!" Hardegen looked up at another WO on the bridge and asked him what was going on. "We're going to meet the enemy," he said. "It's the boat's first Atlantic cruise. We were just waiting for you."

So, at last, he was going against England! The boy's dream became the man's reality. He stowed his gear below while mine sweepers came alongside to begin escorting the boat out of the harbor. Soon after departure the IXB ran into heavy weather, and at midnight he drew watch on the narrow bridge atop the conning tower for the first time. Not knowing quite what to expect, despite all his training, he went up to bridge duty without changing his clothes. Soon afterward he was soaked to the skin. Violent stern seas slapped the tower. Breakers sprayed over the bridge continuously. Often he and the other members of the bridge watch were standing in water up to their hips. In those circumstances it was difficult to keep the mine sweepers' shadows in sight, as was their duty. By the time he crept into his designated bunk at 0400 hours, thoroughly chilled, soaked, and tired, he had learned a lesson about U-boats that did not come from school-books, or even from training. Then at breakfast the next morning he learned something else. Suddenly there was a loud double *Click*-CLANG! *Click*-CLANG! He thought a couple of hatch covers had sprung shut or something of the sort, until he saw a watch officer fall into the control room and watched his soup tilt to one side of the bowl. They were diving! No alarm bell had sounded, but they were diving. Everyone was watching the manometer, or depth gauge. Then another, louder *Click*-CLANG! Someone told him that a British bomber was dropping charges. Here he was, fewer than twenty-four hours since the messenger had come to his home, and he was being bombed!

The aircraft finally went away and the boat surfaced, but the wind came up and reached force eight just in time for the start of Hardegen's next watch. This time, he was dressed appropriately in a leather suit, oilskin coat, a *Südwester* (sou'wester) on his head, and heavy rubber boots. The waves were higher than before. It was daytime and he watched them with awe. He also looked about to familiarize himself with the U-shaped Type-IXB bridge. It was a tightly confined space made all the more so by the large periscope housing that ran half the length down the center line. The housing contained the retracted standards of two periscopes, one forward for underwater sky observation, the other aft for submerged torpedo attacks. Facing forward on the bridge Hardegen could see arrayed close together, where the bridge met the wind, the Siemens gyrocompass repeater, surface conning voice pipe, slot for the retracted direction finder (DF) loop, engine room telegraph, and, underfoot, the tower hatch. Off center to port and slightly astern stood the target-aiming post used for surface attacks. Farther astern on the cowling were, portside, the commander's flagpole; screened ventilator shafts, port and starboard; and portside, the hole for the long-range extendable antenna. Two other holes in the periscope housing permitted extension of short-range antennae. Altogether there was very little room for five men to collect, much less to move about, and where they stood Hardegen and the four lookouts were only five meters above the water. As the waves rose around them the men ducked their heads and braced themselves against the periscope housing. The tower hatch was closed. They were alone against the sea. And here it came! As they flinched and turned their heads crests of the huge waves slugged the back of their necks like closed fists. Slowly the boat would level out and the foaming water would run off. Then a quick glance around the horizon with their binoculars, and the seas would hit them again. After four hours of that Hardegen's neck was so tired he decided to take the water full in the face. Then the watch was over and he worked his way down the ladder into the security of the boat. Cold and wet all over, his beard and eyebrows covered with salt and his eyes stinging from the lash of the sea, he wondered if he could do that again.

By evening the waves abated, the sky cleared, and the star-strewn heaven arched over *124.* Moonlight played on the white chops and the dark frame of the U-boat appeared to be ebony dipped in liquid silver. Foam from the bow and stern wakes showed plainly. One of the ratings on night watch mistook a darting dolphin for a—"torpedo track on port side!" But better to make that kind of mistake than one of omission. In a few days they passed the Shetland Islands and made for the open Atlantic where the *Edelweissboot* and Hardegen had their first experience attacking a convoy. The date was 25 August 1940, at dusk. Close to the English coast in the Western Approaches, where their primary mission was weather reporting, the bridge watch sighted distant smoke trails in the binoculars and shouted down the voice pipe, "Commander to the bridge!" Schulz headed up the ladder with Hardegen right behind him and, after adjusting his Zeiss lens, confirmed smoke and mastheads outlined against the sinking sun. (It was Eastbound Convoy HX 65A, in six columns, position some twenty-three nautical miles north of the Hebrides.) Schulz asked for both diesels full ahead as he maneuvered the boat into torpedo launching position. Several times he had to back off as destroyer escorts moved in their direction, but the guard vessels failed to sight *124*'s low-surface silhouette in the gathering darkness. Finally, Schulz had the long parallel lines of ships in perfect attack alignment. Range, speed, and angle on the bow were computed. Now, in quick order, four torpedoes sped from the bow tubes, each meant for a separate target. Excitedly Hardegen watched the ship shadows to see what would happen. There! A bright red flame appeared on the side of a freighter, and the sound of the explosion reached him quickly afterward. Then a detonation column appeared on a second freighter. And then on a third, which sank almost immediately, its stern standing steep out of the water. The fourth torpedo missed its intended mark, but to every-one's surprise it ranged to the rear of the convoy and found its own target, yet another freighter, which ripped apart from a boiler explosion and sank in three minutes' time. It was a proud beginning for *124*, whose crew rejoiced at the hits.[4] (For its part the convoy counted the casualties, all British freighters: *Harpalyce*, 5,169 Gross Register Tons [GRT], sunk; *Firecrest*, 5,394 tons, sunk; *Stakesby*, 3,900 tons, damaged. The fourth hit claimed by Schulz has never been identified.[5])

The *Edelweissboot*'s celebration was short-lived. Destroyers steamed down the direction from which the attack had obviously come. Searchlights played back and forth across the water, star shells and signal flares began turning night into day. *"Alarm!"* Schulz yelled into the voice pipe and the bridge watch leaped down the ladder into the control room, dogging the tower hatch cover behind them. The chief engineer, whom the crew called the LI, had already begun flooding the boat, which went down on a steep forward incline, changing as it did from diesel to quiet electric power from batteries. Almost at once Hardegen could hear through the hull the onrushing *swish-swish-swish* of a destroyer's screws. And soon after the boat rocked violently. *Click*-CLANG! *Click*-CLANG! Depth charges exploded directly above them—canisters of high explosive cordite that created pressure waves to split open a U-boat's hull. Inside the boat steel frames rang with reverberations and shattered glass from bulbs and instruments flew in all directions. Then three more charges bounced them rudely about: *Click*-CLANG! *Click*-CLANG! *Click*-CLANG! And no sooner were those steel hammershocks concluded than, WHAM!, the boat was jolted by a completely different force. The bow rose sharply. The LI worked desperately to recover trim and maintain depth. What had happened? One look at the navigator's plot told

Schulz that they had slammed into the English coast in the form of an underwater cliff. Schulz killed power and hugged the cliff. The collision was a lucky accident, as it turned out, because after an hour their British pursuers, usually persistent in holding contact with a submerged U-boat, decided that they had lost their target and gave up the hunt. Hardegen's second experience of depth-charging was over. Overall he had mixed emotions of elation and relief, and he spent some time musing how small each man was in contrast to the enormous battle in which they were engaged.

As a result of their encounter with the English coast, the bow tubes no longer functioned and Dönitz reassigned 124 to weather reporting at 20 degrees West; eventually, orders came directing her to proceed to the newly opened U-boat base at Lorient for repairs. Minesweepers met the boat as Schulz and his crew approached the Brittany coast and a second boat returning from action joined them on the final surface run to harbor. Its commander sent a flag signal to 124: K. AN K. HOW DID YOU BEND YOUR SNOUT OUT OF SHAPE?[6] Schulz knew that his bow was damaged but hardly thought that the problem was that visible. When he sent Hardegen and a number of ratings forward to have a look they were astonished to find that below the upper casing the bow was torn wide open. The entire outer steel plating was in shreds, and the jagged edges had rusted. It was clear that as she completed what would come to be called the *grosse Kurve* (big bend)—the voyage from Germany to the Atlantic to Brittany—the *Edelweissboot* would remain in port for quite a while.

Lorient was not then the modern, fortified U-boat base it would become by the time of Germany's declaration of war on the United States a year and a half later. The city and naval base had been captured without a shot by the Wehrmacht on 21 June 1940. Two days later Dönitz arrived by plane to investigate its potential for a main U-boat operations base and dockyard. He found it ideal for both purposes and requisitioned a sardine merchant's château at Kernével near Larmor-Plage at the mouth of the harbor to serve as his personal headquarters. He would move into the building the following October. At the end of June advance parties from the Krupp Germania yards at Kiel and from Organisation Todt, the German construction conglomerate run by Reichsminister Dr. Fritz Todt, were on site to begin restructuring the port. By the next month facilities were adequate to receive U-boat Flotilla II from Wilhelmshaven. The first boat to arrive, on 7 July, was U-30, commanded by Kptlt. Fritz-Julius Lemp. By the date of U-*124*'s arrival on 16 September there still were no usable wharves or docks, so as a temporary expedient the hulls of old wooden prison boats, including that of *Isère*, were raised to serve as pontoons where U-boats could tie up. That was where Schulz docked, alongside *Isère*, on the right bank of the Scorff Estuary, and handed *124* over to the dockyard workmen.

The old French navy base on the Scorff, like Lorient itself, presented a picture of neglect and dilapidation. On one side were rusting old battleships that had been used by the French for housing. On another side were wrecked wharves, broken cranes, and burned-out oil tanks. Original plans called for the crew to take up lodgings in the Arsenal Maritime but they had to go instead to a small hotel, the Pigeon Blanc, because the naval quarters were found to be uninhabitable. French African troops who last occupied the barracks building before its capture had left it in such foul disorder that not until German workmen cleaned the floor did anyone know it was stone. The Second Flotilla staff that had come in from Wilhelmshaven discovered a bounty of supplies left behind by British troops—uniforms, shoes, tropical kits, arms, ammunition, food, and other items the enemy had not had time to remove or destroy, so rapid was the Wehrmacht capture of the Biscay ports. U-boat officers and men were given permission to wear the captured British army battle dress with their own insignia and collar bands, and many did so because—as Hardegen hated to admit—it was more comfortable than their own uniform cloth. Many would wear the British uniforms on board when their boats next sortied. The sight of German officers and crew standing at attention on deck in British battle dress was a shock to some newly arrived German naval officers and reporters from the Propaganda Ministry who came by to watch departures. The *Edelweissboot*'s crew watched numerous such departures during the weeks required to make their own boat seaworthy again. The crew had the opportunity to spend some of that time at a new rest hostel in Quiberon, where they could walk on the beach, go swimming if the water was not too cold, ride horseback, or just relax. Many of the men frequented the local cafés and courted the pretty Breton girls. Hardegen thought they deserved all the recreation they could get. In a very short while they would be bound away again in the cramped, dark, dangerous space of a U-boat at sea.

At first Schulz and his officers were put up in the old French Naval Préfecture, where the French admiral, his family, and staff had resided. Later they moved to a beach house at Larmor-Plage, a seaside area near the city where they could swim or walk in a park with flower gardens or just do nothing. From their windows they could catch the tangy scents from the foreshore and watch the Breton fishermen in their blue boats with red sails passing back and forth in front of the old stone island Fort St.-Louis, which guarded the entrance to the harbor. It was idyllic—except, that is, when the base nearby was bombed by British aircraft, which happened eleven days after their arrival in port. The bombers came in at high speed from the northeast at three hundred meters' altitude, directly over their heads, and released to hit the U-boats at their moorings. They failed in that, but their bombs did kill a number of U-boat crewmen and shore station personnel.

One day the officers were summoned to the base for a ceremony. Admiral Dönitz flew in from Germany to present awards. Kptlt. Fritz Frauenheim of U-*101* received the Knight's Cross, and Schulz received the Iron Cross Second and First Class. Some of *124*'s crew members also received the Iron Cross. Soon after that a number of other Knight's Cross winners put into Lorient. Hardegen met and listened with fascination to Günther Prien, the "Bull of Scapa," who had sunk the British battleship *Royal Oak* in Scapa Flow at the start of the war; Otto Kretschmer, the "tonnage king"; Joachim Schepke and Engelbert Endrass, who each accounted for 100,000 tons sunk. Lorient was becoming known as the "port of the aces." While still awaiting completion of repairs, Hardegen had a chance to go to Paris with a driver taking courier mail. For several days he took in the usual sights and, with understandable pride, watched the daily noontime Wehrmacht Guards Regiment parade from the Arc de Triomphe down the Champs-Elysées to the brass strains of "Preussens Gloria"— "Prussia's Glory." With other U-boat officers he met in his hotel he strolled at night through Montmartre, poking his head into cabarets and bars, and lingering to hear "J'attendrai" sung by Lucienne Boyer and "La Vie en rose" by the "little sparrow," Edith Piaf. He and his friends ended up at the nightclub Schéhérazade, which with its wandering violinists, soulful Russian music, and champagne for six marks, would quickly become the favorite Parisian hangout of U-boat officers from every base in France.[7]

Eventually the repairs to the bow and general refitting on the *Edelweissboot* were completed. Hardegen had asked for and received permission to stay on as WO and *Kommandantenschüler* (commander in training) with the same commander. A second war patrol and he would qualify for the U-boat badge. On 5 October he and his comrades sortied from Lorient into the Bay of Biscay on *124*'s second Feindfahrt. Once in the Atlantic they encountered heavy seas and the bridge watches were pure torment. When Hardegen was finally semidry after one watch, he experienced the dread of donning still-damp, clammy leathers for the next. Over his gray-green jacket and trousers he wore a heavy raincoat with a towel around the neck. A sou'wester and high sea boots completed his protection. Even then he was soaked through. With a following sea the bridge was constantly awash—the reason why U-boat men called it the "bathtub." And when the water was accompanied by a strong wind it could be a dangerous place to stand. On one occasion, before they could get their steel-reinforced leather harnesses attached to the bridge railings, he, Schulz, and the first mate were almost swept overboard. They had heard of men lost like that on other boats.

During the first stages of this second cruise Schulz put the crew through numerous practice emergency dives, since some of the original crew had been transferred to Petty Officer School and their replacements were greener than Hardegen. They had real emergencies, too, as time and again *124* had to dive to avoid British aircraft. Before long, however, they sighted their first steamer in the Western Approaches south of Ireland. She came out of a rainsquall in the early morning hours of 16 October. Schulz lost her briefly in the haze, but at 0345 Central European Time (CET) he sank her with a single torpedo from nine hundred meters out. Funkmaat (Radio Operator) Fritz Rafalski called out to Schulz: "It's *Trevisa*—signaling s-s-s for submarine—now signaling s-i-n-k-i-n-g." Schulz told Hardegen to look her up in the merchant registry and book of ship silhouettes that every boat kept on board. He reported back: "*Trevisa* is a British steamer, 1,813 tons." The crew celebrated their kill with a festive dinner, made the more enjoyable by a break in the weather. As the boat rode more smoothly Rafalski played radio music through the loud-speaker system while the cook served up food from their still-fresh stores: pork, sauerkraut, peas, and fruit. Some of the crew, who had trained as bakers and had found proper baking pans in France, produced their culinary specialties for dessert. Had Schulz and his men known what they had started with the sinking of *Trevisa*, there would have been even greater cause for celebration, for *Trevisa*, part of convoy SC 7, was the first of thirty-seven ships from that formation and from convoy HX 79, which blundered by, to be torpedoed within the space of four successive nights in the Western Approaches off Rockall Bank near Ireland. Participating in the sharklike feeding frenzy were Knight's Cross aces Prien (U-47), Kretschmer (U-99), Schepke (U-100), Endrass (U-46), Frauenheim (U-101), and Heinrich Liebe (U-38); also present were Heinrich Bleichrodt (U-48) who fourteen months later in U-109 would sail with Hardegen to North America on Operation Paukenschlag; and Karl-Heinz Möhle, who commanded the boat (U-123) that Reinhard Hardegen would soon make famous. The merchant ship massacre became known in the fleet as *die Nacht der Langen Messer* ("The Night of the Long Knives"), a phrase that originated as a description of Hitler's bloody purge of Ernst Röhm and his SA ("storm troopers") in 1934.[8]

Schulz's post-*Trevisa* party was premature, however. Three hours after his success *124* was spotted by three British destroyers, which kept the hastily submerged boat under attack. Pattern after pattern of *Wasserbomben*, or depth charges, which U-boat men called *Wabos* for short, fell loudly and dangerously around Hardegen and his mates. Each time the deadly canisters dropped from the destroyers' fantails, the *Click!* of their firing pistols preceding the CLANG! of their explosions, the boat heaved, lights flickered, glass cracked, and men held on tightly to any available support, including each other. With the silent-running E motors and the ballast tanks filling with seawater Schulz took *124* deeper into the protective water, as far as eight meters below factory-certified depth, in order to escape the mauling. There, hung as it were on a string, and well below the priming depth of the Wabos, they waited out the savage battering. As the hours passed *124*'s interior air became oppressively stale and foul, and carbon dioxide built up to dangerous levels. Schulz issued potassium cartridges for the men to breathe through, since potash neutralized the CO_2. Crewmen who did not have emergency duties were sent to their bunks as a means of conserving oxygen. The historian of U-*124* has written about Hardegen in this crisis: "The cold-blooded courage that would later make Hardegen a great U-boat commander was already obvious as he roamed through the boat, checking the damage and supervising repairs. His blue eyes were calm and unafraid, and men who might have panicked were strengthened by the young officer who controlled his own fear so completely, talking and joking with the men as they worked."[9]

With both oxygen and battery power running low Schulz resorted to a stratagem. He had his LI discharge some fuel oil with a couple of gloves and a shoe thrown in. The ruse worked as the destroyers, apparently convinced by the oil smear and debris on the surface that they had slaughtered their prey, moved off the target. Rafalski in the sound room confirmed by underwater sound detection (hydrophone effect, or H.E.) that the *swish-swish-swish* of the destroyers' screws was receding. Schulz decided to risk a slow ascent, and some thirty minutes later his periscope broke through the surface. A quick turn with the lens showed a clear sea. The boat surfaced, and Schulz cautiously spun the wheel-and-spider hatch open lest the built-up air pressure blow him out of the boat. Once safely on the bridge, followed by the lookouts, he swept the horizon again with his glasses. The destroyers were nowhere to be seen. His pulse rate slowed. U-*124* was alone and safe.

On 20 October U-*124* sank the Norwegian *Cubano*, 5,810 GRT, and the British *Sulaco*, 5,389 GRT. On the thirty-first she sank the British *Rutland*, 1,437 GRT, hardly bigger than herself (though Schulz claimed it as 6,000 tons—a not-uncommon phenomenon among commanders). Following one last sinking, British *Empire Bison*, 5,612 GRT, on 1 November *124* made for Lorient.[10] Except for a brief entanglement with a mine cable on the approaches to her home base, the *Edelweissboot* concluded her return cruise without incident and tied up at *Isère* with five victory pennants flying from her periscope. Hardegen, in charge of the deck force, had hardly finished docking when the flotilla commander told him that he was to fly to Kiel at once. The time had come. He was to command his own boat—a new one, just launched.

The Number 8 line of the streetcar system in Kiel was jammed with workers speaking every known European language when Hardegen rode out to the shipyard to see his new U-boat for the first time. No doubt he looked as strange to everyone else as they looked to him, since he still sported the full red beard that he had grown on the last patrol—no one shaved on a U-boat in order to conserve fresh water—and before boarding the military flight from Lorient he had had it stylishly groomed by a French barber. The beard made a great plaything for his son, but he knew that once he officially reported to his new assignment he would have to shave it off. At the end of the line he reached the Deutsche Werke yards and found waiting for him there his LI, who had been on the scene for many weeks monitoring the construction. Hardegen knew that he should have been flattered to be entrusted with a boat that had just come off the ways, but in truth he was disappointed, since his first command was U-*147*, a type IID small coastal training vessel of just over three hundred tons, the boat everyone called an *Einbaum* (dugout canoe). It had a surface speed of 12.7 knots and submerged of 7.4 knots. It carried only five torpedoes. He had wanted to go back to the Atlantic. Instead, he was to be a Lehmann-Willenbrock in the Baltic Sea to a fresh class of U-boat recruits who, up to first petty officer, had never set foot on a U-boat before. The next day he had his first chance to meet them: a Friesian fisherman's son, a locksmith from the Sudetenland, bakers, toolmakers, and merchant apprentices from every corner of Germany. They had been through training school. Now, in their bright blue uniforms, they stood ready to test themselves at sea. Hardegen admired their high-spirited natures and instantly formed a bond with them.

Not that experience was entirely lacking on the little IID. His lone WO, Oberleutnant zur See Eberhard Wetjen, was a veteran of the merchant marine and had navigational experience that would serve their boat well in the adventures ahead. He was a native of Bremen, like Hardegen, who enjoyed listening hours on end to the older man's sea stories. Ernst Hamisch, the LI, was another extremely capable officer. "*Heil*, Herr Kaleu!" he had shouted out formally when first meeting Hardegen at the shipyard, but directly after the formality he smiled and never stopped smiling thereafter. Everyone loved him for his happy nature and sense of humor.

On 11 December 1940, Hardegen and his men gathered in full uniform on deck for the *Indienststellung*, or formal commissioning, of their boat as U-*147*. The local flotilla commander officially put the boat into the service of the state. Hardegen then gave a short speech to the crew urging them to recognize that their training missions were just as important to the homeland as the battles to come. Finally he hoisted the national flag and his commander's pennant, saying, "To our Führer and commander in chief of the Armed Forces—*Sieg Heil!*" The rest of the day they spent eating and celebrating. The hard work would begin the next morning.

For weeks the commander put his crew through drill after drill, practicing underwater trims, torpedo launches, artillery fire, and bridge watches. In particular they practiced emergency dives, always seeking to improve the reading on the stopwatch, since their survival would time and again depend on their ability to clear the bridge, dog the hatch, and submerge the boat in rapid order. A gun crew might be on deck, and the drill leader would yell, *Einsteigen! Alarm!*—the emergency order to dive—and the men would pour down the tower ladder like monkeys, particularly after they learned that the slower men's fingers would be stepped on by the shoes of those who followed! By Christmas Day, Hardegen thought that the crew was in a state of near readiness—and none too soon, as it happened.

Several days after Christmas the flotilla commander asked him if he thought that the crew, whose training was not yet complete, was in condition to undertake an actual war cruise. Hardegen was surprised, since their boat was not designed for the open Atlantic, but he enthusiastically answered yes and quickly made ready to sortie. One of his last acts before departure was to choose a symbol for the boat. As a representation of his two naval careers he chose the flying fish, and the crew painted one prominently on each side of the tower. Once torpedoes, provisions, and other necessities were properly stowed on board, they put out from the Tirpitz breakwater to the hurrahs of their comrades in the flotilla and slowly followed an ice cutter through the Kaiser Wilhelm Canal that bisected the Schleswig-Holstein peninsula and connected the Baltic with the Elbe and gave it access to the North Sea. Passing a girls' school, the cutter sounded its horn and many young girls appeared waving their aprons and colorful scarves. Hardegen's crew shouted three hurrahs to them, and they responded in kind with a hearty *Zicke-Zacke*.

Despite the help given by their ice cutter, the thick ice fields in the canal and the Lower Elbe dented *147*'s outer hull and they had to put in briefly at Cuxhaven at the mouth of the Elbe for repairs. Fit for sea again, they set a course for Helgoland in the North Sea, where, following an old U-boat custom, they paused for a crew party at the canteen Tante Lotte. When Hardegen signed the canteen guest book at the end of their going-away celebration he could read there the names of all the great commanders in U-boat history, since every one of them had stopped at Tante Lotte's either before or after enemy missions to fortify himself with a Helgoland grog. Their stay on the island was prolonged unexpectedly for several days, first by dense fog and then a blinding snowstorm. Finally they were able to put out for Norway where, while awaiting operational orders, Hardegen planned to conduct practice attacks in an ice-free fjord at Bergen. They successfully entered the fjord they wanted and began practice drills. The German base at the site made available a guard vessel to serve as their target ship, and they made repeated runs on it, both submerged and on the surface. The small German detachment stationed at the remote fjord base was pleased to have them as visitors, and the seamen joined the soldiers in many an evening party.

Finally, one Friday, their Operation Order came through by radio (variously called "wireless," "W/T," and "F.T." in this narrative) from BdU. Since it was considered bad luck for a sailor to go to the front on a Friday, Hardegen delayed until 0030 hours on Saturday before making their sortie. The heading taken on departure would carry them around the Shetland and Orkney Islands off the north coast of Scotland. The sea state worsened as they traveled. Temperatures on the bridge fell below freezing. Even inside the boat, where the temperatures were six to eight degrees Celsius, the men wore bulky fur caps and coats. Between watches they tried their best to warm up, ate, and grabbed a little sleep until, four hours later, each of them had to mount the tower for another watch. On a small boat like *147* officers and ratings lived together in one single space. Gemütlichkeit was standard operating procedure. And so, on they sailed toward their designated attack area, rounding the British Isles to the convoy routes north of the Hebrides. Often the men on watch stood in freezing water up to their armpits while snow and hail whipped their faces. Thick ice encrusted the tower casing and hung from the antenna wire.

One day Wetjen fell into the control room dripping with seawater. "Herr Kaleu!" he shouted. "A Zeppelin just came out of the clouds!" Hardegen ordered an immediate dive. When they reached periscope depth the LI· trimmed the boat, and Hardegen looked through the sky scope for the gaseous intruder. It turned out to be a harmless British barrage balloon that had slipped its moorings and flown out to sea. At dawn one Sunday, though, they had a genuine war experience. They were on the surface. One of the watch shouted down the pipe, "Off the bow—a shadow!" Hardegen raced up the ladder to the bridge and saw a huge vessel coming at them at high speed. There was no time to dive. Despite the brightening sky they had to attack on the surface. And so, in that exposed position, Hardegen launched his first torpedo as a commander. No sooner was the eel released from its tube than the steamer spotted them, turned away hard, and its armed guard opened fire. At close range *147* had to dive. One shell puncture in the pressure hull would have rendered them helpless. For some reason their torpedo failed to hit, or if it did, it failed to detonate. Something like ten thousand tons GRT had slipped through their fingers. *Die ganze Sonntagsstimmung war zum Teufel!* Their whole Sunday was shot to hell! Or so it seemed.

Later that same day near dusk the lookouts sighted what appeared to be two freighters on a heading toward England, one to port, one to starboard. When they drew close—again they were on the surface—they saw a gun flash on the ship to port. Hardegen and Wetjen looked closer. *Verdammt*—it was a destroyer! Her shell created a yellow-green detonation column in their wake, fifty meters astern.

ALARM!

The U-boat dived, but she went down too fast. A hatch seal broke. Water poured into the stern and soon stood deep as the bunks. They were listing badly. The bilges could not handle the great volume of water. The crew bailed from stern to bow but it did not help. Hardegen and Hamisch could not control the boat. There was but one expedient left. They had to surface.

"Anblasen!" ("Blow tanks!")

Air pressure in the diving tanks pushed out the water that had been let into the tanks to enable them to dive. They leveled out and the LI sang out in succession:

"Boot steht!" ("Boat constant.")

"Boot steigt langsam." ("Boat rising slowly.")

"Turmluk ist frei, Boot ist raus." ("Tower hatch is free, boat is on the surface.")

Hardegen ran up the ladder, opened the tower hatch, and looked quickly around. Not more than one hundred meters to starboard lay the destroyer. Alongside, near dead in the water, was the other ship, a freighter. Overhead was a British plane. And they had to make repairs *there?* But they did. The gathering darkness helped. The crew worked feverishly. Soon the hatch seal held tight and the bilge pumps voided the leaked water. Just a few minutes more, everyone prayed. But the destroyer suddenly moved in their direction. They dived and the seals held. Men grabbed hold as they awaited the Wabos. But nothing happened! The enemy must not have seen them. Or had he no depth charges left? When the sound man reported that the destroyer had passed over them and beyond, Hardegen went to periscope depth and saw that the enemy warship had taken a position ahead of the freighter and that both were under way. He tried a torpedo approach under water but could not catch up. Eventually he surfaced. Then, as though they had not had enough bad Sunday luck, their starboard diesel would not start, and problems developed with the portside engine.

The LI concluded that the water leak had contaminated the lubricating oil. So they submerged to lick their wounds.

Late at night, though the diesels that drove the boat on the surface were still not fixed, Hardegen surfaced in order to free the antenna for any wireless signals that might be meant for them. He was barely on the bridge when he sighted a large shadow in the pale moonlight ahead. It was a freighter, heavily laden, coming right at them! And here they sat with both diesels down! He ordered full ahead on the *E-Maschinen*, the less-powerful electric motors that were for underwater use, and blew the tanks with their last remaining air.

"Auf Gefechtsstationen!" ("Battle stations!")

Wetjen scampered up with the target-aiming binoculars used for surface attacks and affixed them to the target-bearing transmitter post. In surface attacks it was the first watch officer, number one, who aimed and launched the torpedoes, while the commander analyzed the attack situation on all horizons. Meanwhile, below, the crew opened the bow caps to the two forward torpedo tubes. Hardegen had no need of his binoculars. The steamer loomed large in the moonlight and was moving exceptionally fast, so that its frothy white bow wake glistened. Wetjen cranked in the firing data—range, speed, angle on the bow—with a large aim-off allowance because of the target's speed. Now the shadow had become a giant black wall, directly in front of them. Wetjen pressed the launching button, and just a matter of seconds afterward a loud explosion blew out one fragment of that wall, a tall flame shooting up from the ship's forward cargo hatch. Their little U-boat reeled from the shock waves. The bridge party ducked their heads as large and small chunks of hot metal fell hissing in the water alongside or rattled on the bow and stern casings. Hurrahs from the happy crew sounded from below. Hardegen watched, fascinated, as the mortally wounded freighter went down forward, and because of its high speed literally drove itself beneath the water like a U-boat. Soon only the stern stuck up above the waves. Survivors clung to floating wreckage. He called out to some of them, "What ship are you?" They replied that they were the Norwegian *Augvald*, 4,811 GRT, with a full belly, bound for England.[11] He wished them well, and that was all that he could do since U-boats, because of their small size and already overcrowded interiors, were forbidden to attempt the rescue of survivors. Wondering if the Norwegians could possibly make the 150 nautical miles to land, or would be picked up by a passing vessel—which seemed more likely though still a very remote chance—

he went below to give the men a description of their kill over the loudspeaker. They were elated. Taking a turn through the boat he looked at their oil-smeared, dirty bodies, their hair plastered down on their faces by sweat, and saw, too, their toothy grins and shining eyes. This victory was theirs as much as it was his. "Herr Kaleu," one of them said, "just a few more hours and the 'sewing machines' will be running again." He meant the diesels. It was turning out to be a fairly prosperous cruise. Their Sunday had not been shot *zum Teufel*, after all.

The boat did have two great disappointments a few nights later. They spotted a freighter and a large two-funnel troop ship. On both targets they were able to close range to a point where they could not possibly miss. But they did. Or else, their torpedoes failed to detonate. Then, before they could enter a Norwegian harbor to reload, they received a wireless signal: IF FUEL SUPPLY ADEQUATE SAIL TO KIEL. Their fuel was adequate. So, with Wetjen's able navigational help, they made their way back to Helgoland, where Hardegen permitted another celebration at Tante Lotte's. After all, they were only a coastal training vessel, never intended for combat as such, but the youngsters had brought home 4,811 GRT. Not bad, he thought, for a type boat that was known throughout the fleet as a "canoe." Therefore, many a mug of grog was lifted that night to toasts of *"Ja, ja, die kleinen Boote!"* ("Yes, yes, the little boats!").

Sunshine and good seas accompanied *147* home to Kiel, where to Hardegen's great surprise he was relieved as commander. He could not believe that he would lose his boat so soon. Was he to be put on ice? Had his plane-crash injury report caught up with him at last? (Yes.) The only consolation was that Wetjen would succeed him as commander. Wetjen and the crew presented Hardegen with his commander's pennant and with the original flag at date of commissioning. Within months those were the only objects left from the boat. Under Wetjen the boat made two war cruises and sank three ships. Then on 2 June 1941, in the North Atlantic, she was depth-charged by the British destroyer *Wanderer* and the corvette *Periwinkle* with the loss of all hands. Gone were Wetjen, the LI Hamisch, and all those other fine young German men he had come to admire and love.

Hardegen was sent for medical tests and rest in the sunshine and snow of the naval recreational center at Spindelmühle in the Riesengebirge Mountains east of Dresden. When he returned to Kiel, orders awaited him to report to Admiral Dönitz's second in command, Admiral Hans-Georg von Friedeburg, at the Blücher Brücke. When he entered the admiral's office, saluted, and reported according to regulations, the admiral asked him, "Are you fit to return to sea?" To which Hardegen replied, "Yes, Herr Admiral." Von Friedeburg then spoke the magic words: "Hardegen, you are to go to France this evening to take over command of U-*123*." It was the boat that he had chanced to see while at Commander's School. He could not have been more thrilled. *Eins Zwei Drei* was a large IXB, with an experienced frontline crew. Under Kptlt. Karl-Heinz Möhle she had already sunk enough ships to earn him the Knight's Cross. Now Möhle was to command a flotilla. The next day, in a Junkers transport from the familiar Holtenau airport, but on the wings of high anticipation as well, Hardegen flew off to France, arriving five and a half hours later in Brittany where, in contrast to Kiel's raw winter weather, he found the greenery, blossoming fruit trees, and clear blue skies of that year's spring.

Much had changed at Lorient in the six months he had been absent. The Arsenal Maritime and dock areas had been cleaned up, and at Pointe de Keroman near the harbor entrance Organisation Todt, which had built the *Autobahnen,* Germany's network of superhighways, was furiously building bombproof shelters for repair and refitting of the IXB and IXC U-boats of Second Flotilla (Tenth Flotilla after January 1942). Hardegen marveled at the colossal size of the two gray structures, Keroman I and II, that were rising side by side from the bank of the Ter River where it met the Scorff. The protective bunkers were each to be 138 by 128 meters, with 18.5-meter elevations. Already he could make out the size of the individual bays, in which U-boats, two abreast, could be reconditioned and provisioned for operations. Towering cranes lifted tons of cement mixed with slag, coarse aggregates, and sand into caissons and wooden forms to create steel-reinforced walls three meters thick, and an even stouter carapace, seven meters thick, that was expected to withstand the most powerful bomb in the British arsenal. Why the RAF did not attack these U-boat lairs while they were still under construction and vulnerable no one could explain. Similar works were under way, Hardegen was told, at other Biscay bases—Brest, St.-Nazaire, and La Pallice. Fifteen thousand workmen—German, French, Czechs, Poles, Dutch, Belgians, Portuguese, Algerians, and Indochinese, most under forced labor conditions—toiled on the vast surfaces under the direction of German engineers and architects. Those not engaged in shaping the walls and roofs were operating locomotives, trucks, cement mixers, wheelbarrows, and other equipment. Huge storage buildings behind the project served as sleeping quarters for the laborers. Guards in field gray with dogs patrolled everywhere, their task to prevent both escapes and sabotage.

In other respects Lorient presented the same relaxed, familiar face, all the more engaging because of the spring air and flowers. Hardegen had time to enjoy it all because his new boat was in dry dock, where, with its dimensions exposed to view, U-*123* made the small boat he had just left look like a toy. In company with Oberleutnant zur See Herbert Schneider, his new number one, he inspected the interior, which was being entirely rebuilt. With so many panels, controls, and pipes removed they could see into the very bowels of the boat's machinery. How it would all be put back together they left to the imagination of the workmen, and Hardegen took advantage of the interval to make trial runs out of harbor with other IXB boats in order to refamiliarize himself with the large boat's characteristics. He had to appear competent to his new crew when they sortied for action. With the training boat he had just left the crew were at first all new and untried. They had no way of knowing what to expect from their commander. In the case of his new boat the crew were all experienced Atlantic fighters whose commander, Möhle, had won the Knight's Cross. Hardegen was two years younger than he, had transferred into U-boats from the Luftwaffe, and his only command experience had been in a "dugout canoe." He had a lot to prove. Nothing so built a crew's confidence, trust, and general morale as success in sinking ships. He was certain that that success would come to him, and to them. In the meantime, he got to know his men in casual settings, going out with them, for example, in the evenings to a Breton night spot that occupied an old mill and stood picturesquely on a stream. The menu featured the locally famous Brittany oysters and lobsters, which were served by girls in traditional Celtic folk costume. Through these means and others he and his crew became acquainted.

Finally, one Sunday evening, 8 June, with sealed orders from the flotilla commander in hand, he cleared harbor on his first war patrol in the new boat. After passing a navigational point specified on the sealed cover of his orders he opened them and announced their content to the crew over the loudspeaker: They were bound for Africa! They would attack British shipping on the west coast off Freetown, Sierra Leone. Hurrahs rang out from the compartments. Everyone seemed to like the idea of sinking English commerce at night under the Southern Cross. It was to be a new experience for them all. A number of commanders at Lorient had speculated that, with the lengthening of days in spring, nighttime operations in the North Atlantic would diminish and some of them might be sent south to intercept shipping that came from South America and from the Middle East and Far East around the Cape of Good Hope. At Freetown the slower merchantmen assembled to form convoys directly north to England. Faster vessels steamed independently on courses that swung farther out into the Atlantic. What *123* did not know at the time, because of the secrecy of orders, was that in the preceding month seven boats had already sailed against that southern commerce and had had exceptional successes. One boat, U-*107*, commanded by Admiral Dönitz's son-in-law, Kptlt. Günter Hessler, had sunk thirteen ships, for which he was awarded the Knight's Cross.[12]

Mechanical trouble prevented *123* from reaching her assigned patrol area on time, however. Both 7.5-meter-long periscopes, the hand-trained high-angle (ninety-degree) lens with superior light transmission that was used for general observation of sea and sky, and the foot-trained high-magnification attack scope fitted with reticle, or cross hairs, were not hoisting properly from their wells. Two days out of port Hardegen and his crew had to return to base for repairs. After four days in port they were outward bound again, on 16 June. Off the coast of Spain they sighted their first merchantman. It was daylight, so they submerged. Through the periscope Hardegen saw that the vessel was a neutral Spanish-flag steamer; rules of engagement called for it to be left to pass. The Spanish crew had no idea that someone under-water was watching them perform their daily tasks—the seamen washing down the decks, the helmsman watching his compass on the bridge, the cook coming out of the galley and stretching his arms in the warm sunlight. On 20 June, past the Strait of Gibraltar and near the coast of Morocco, Hardegen found a vessel he identified as a legitimate British target. It was daylight again, and he had to make his approach by periscope. In submerged attacks it was the commander who made the target observation, calculated the attack bearing and track, and ordered the torpedo launch. Hardegen now took his seated position at the *Standzielsehrohr*, the monocular attack-periscope sight in the conning tower just below the hatch and above the control room. By foot pedals he trained the fixed height-of-eye scope, while ordering the E motor telegraph to maintain boat speed below the five knots when vibration in the scope standard rendered vision unsatisfactory for attack. In that small space two other men had to work: the helmsman (*Rudergänger*) who directed the boat's course by pushing rudder buttons, left and right, and Schneider, the torpedo officer, who cranked Hardegen's target data into the *Vorhaltrechner*, an electromechanical calculator that fed the attack heading into the gyrocompass steering mechanism of the torpedoes in their tubes and continually adjusted that information as the U-boat moved and turned. Given these data in the gyro system a torpedo, when launched, would come onto the correct heading regardless of the direction in which the boat itself was headed. With his left hand Hardegen turned the periscope laterally, while with his right hand he focused the eyepiece in its foam-rubber housing. Now in the graduated lens he could clearly make out the target. It was a freighter, around 4,300 GRT, he estimated, drawing about seven meters draft. He called out the range, course, speed, angle on the bow, and depth setting for the torpedoes. At the same time he shouted descriptive information about the target down the voice pipe so the crew below would be aware what was going on. Those experienced frontline men were wondering, he knew, whether the "new man on board" would make it or not.

When the range closed to 600 meters he gave the order: *"Rohr los!"* ("Launch!") The boat gave a small lurch as a burst of compressed air pushed one of their "eels" out of its tube. The excess air vented inboard to prevent exterior surface bubbles; the crew felt the increase of pressure on their eardrums. Below in the control room the LI quickly adjusted the boat's trim to account for the loss of the torpedo's weight on board, while Schneider counted the seconds on his stopwatch. The sound man reported the torpedo run as hot, straight, and normal. Itself a small submarine with an electric motor and guidance system, the torpedo was speeding on its mission at a depth of 2.5 meters with a cargo of high explosives. Just at the elapsed time predicted for a hit—nothing! *Verdammt!* What had happened? Apparently the eel had passed astern of the target. Schneider checked the calculator readings and suggested that the calculator had been out of adjustment by nine degrees. Hardegen thought to himself, What a sorry beginning for a commander! They had to attack again, but their underwater speed was so slow that it took until after dusk to catch up with the target vessel and acquire an angle from which to launch again from a submerged position. This time he bypassed the calculator and "went to zero." Like a duck hunter with his shotgun, he aimed the whole boat at the point where their target would be in so many seconds. Then he launched another eel from a bow tube and started counting. WHACK! A hit! Hardegen sighted the detonation column through the scope. He had led the moving target correctly. Underwater he and the crew could easily hear the screeching of broken metal and the bursting of bulkheads in the victim's entrails.

As the minutes ticked by, however, he saw no sign that the steamer was sinking. The eel had hit exactly where he had aimed, in the engine room, and the steamer was listing to port and taking water, but still she lay stubbornly afloat. He decided to put another zero-angle torpedo shot into her side, and after he did so he watched as the freighter's crew went into lifeboats, which were heavily loaded because the two eels had crushed one boat and caused another to foul. As soon as the ship was safely abandoned he surfaced. The watch climbed to the bridge and swept all quadrants of the horizon with binoculars while Hardegen and Schneider studied their wounded prey. Still floating on her port side despite two hits, she refused to go down. Not wanting any English rescue tug to come out and haul the wreck to shore for repair and refitting, Hardegen ordered the gun crew to battle stations: They would have to put some exploding shells into her waterline. Leutnant zur See Horst von Schroeter, the number two and gunnery officer, quickly took his position commanding the 10.5-centimeter gun crew on the foredeck. Artillery shells were passed up from below. Hardegen gave the order:

"*Feuererlaubnis!*" ("Permission to fire!")

CRACK!

For a few seconds everyone on top was blinded by the bright orange flash of the ignition. When their eyes adjusted to the twilight again they could see a gaping black hole in the hull of the stopped target. Von Schroeter put several more shells into the hole, and the freighter started going down flat. Soon oil and gasoline were spilling onto the water's surface and turning the waves red with fire. With a great gurgle the mortally damaged hull at last sank from view, followed by the masts and funnel, while empty oil cans and timber came to the surface, suggesting why the vessel had floated so long. Surface fires continued to blaze and their crimson light played across the faces on the U-boat bridge as, with engines reversed, *123* backed off slowly into the gathering darkness. It was Hardegen's first submerged attack as a commander, and his first gun action. He thought that the crew felt better about their "new man on board."[13]

It was on this surface cruise southward that, one day, while Hardegen rested on his bunk, the radio operator woke him to report: "Herr Kaleu, we're at war with Russia!" Hardegen could not believe it, but the operator insisted. So he turned on the radiotelephone receiver and listened himself to the news reports from home. The announcement, it turned out, was true. Hardegen was gratified to hear of the successes of the Eastern armies, but the Russian campaign was so far away from his latitudes it bore a certain air of unreality, particularly when later he stood on the bridge at night and reflected on his very different world, one not of tanks on land but of boats gently rising and falling on warm waters that swept quietly and peacefully below Orion, the red-hued Aldebaran, blue-green Sirius, famous Arcturus, and the many other lights in the starry canopy that led seamen from point to point upon the deep. "Where are we?" he would ask his number two, von Schroeter, after the navigator had finished taking a star fix with his sextant. Such and such a latitude and longitude, von Schroeter would reply, and add something like: "Course two-oh-five, Herr Kaleu, portside diesel at slow ahead, clutched to E motors so both screws are on drive. Starboard diesel currently being examined. A water-pump bearing was worn to excess clearance. Should be cleared in two hours. Indicated surface speed seven knots."

Soon they came within sight of Pico de Teide, the highest mountain of Tenerife in the Canary Islands, and in the dark early morning hours of 25 June they reached the neutral friendly Spanish port of Las Palmas in Gran Canaria. There, on the outer extremities of the harbor, they tied up alongside a German supply tanker, *Corrientes*, from which they topped off fuel tanks and drew fresh stores. The fueling and restocking operation, which bore the code name *Culebra*, would enable Hardegen to continue operations until 23 August.[14] At 0640 the same morning, *123* stood out to sea again. Farther down the coast of Africa dolphins played around the bow of the boat and temperatures turned tropical. When the heat inside the boat reached thirty-five degrees Celsius (ninety-eight degrees Fahrenheit) Hardegen let groups of crewmen go topside to catch the breeze created by the forward motion of the boat. Some of the men rigged a saltwater shower, which further helped them cool off.

Passage to their assigned operational area off Freetown in Sierra Leone continued without incident until 27 June, in late morning, when the routine was broken by a call on the voice pipe: "Commander to the bridge! Smoke clouds!" Hardegen raced up the ladder and directed his binoculars in the direction indicated. Many times what appeared to be ships' smoke to a bridge watch turned out to be scraps of cloud, and what were thought to be attacking airplanes changed into sea gulls. This time the watch was right. Those were indeed thin columns of smoke on the southern horizon—a convoy, northbound, range closing. But that wasn't all. Overhead was a British Short Sunderland flying boat. They knew the type: *müde Bienen*—"tired bees"— they called them because of the aircraft type's slow and awkward flight characteristics. The plane carried depth charges. And it was headed straight toward them! ALARM! They submerged. They surfaced. They dived again. The circling Sunderland was keeping them underwater, even though they did not know if it had sighted them. Every so often Hardegen came to periscope depth and made an observation with the sky scope. It would take time to shake the aircraft and get into position for attack. The cat and mouse game continued for hours until, finally, darkness came. *Eins Zwei Drei* surfaced again, this time under a bright moon. Hardegen followed convoy sighting procedures and by *Funk-Telegraphie*, or F.T., their wireless transmitter (an abbreviation also used to denote a wireless message) advised BdU of the convoy's size, course, and speed: twenty-three ships in four columns, course 315 degrees, speed seven knots. As the convoy approached, the lookouts made out several destroyers and corvettes on its perimeter. Getting inside their protective screen would be difficult, especially with a moon. But as a nervous bridge watched, Hardegen did it. Closing from windward to reduce the visibility of his bow wake, he soon found himself standing on the surface inside the columns of the convoy itself. It was Kretschmer's technique—daring and dangerous. Large, pompous shadows, tankers and freighters, pushed past on the right and left at point-blank range.

Now they had to hustle before lookouts spotted *123*'s silhouette. Schneider brought up his *Uboot-Zieloptik*, or UZO, the target-aiming binoculars, and affixed it to the UZO post with its rotating base and bearing indicator ring. The UZO connected mechanically to the *Vorhaltrechner*, which computed the target data and fed them into the "brains" of the torpedoes. Schneider now took bearings on three targets in a column of ships to port and gave the orders: "Tubes one, two, and four stand by. Bow caps open." The eels would go out at one-minute intervals. Hardegen nodded to Schneider when he gave the ready sign. Three times Schneider pressed the launch button and shouted down the voice pipe his confirmations: *Los! . . . Los! . . . Los!*

The boat flinched each time in recoil. The electric eels left no wake, so the bridge had no visible way of knowing if they were running true, but the sound room called up the voice pipe that they were hot, straight, and normal. Hardegen and Schneider watched the second hands on their chronometers. Right on time—WHACK!—an eel exploded against the hull of the first ship they had taken aim at, sending a giant geyser of water skyward. Almost simultaneously another thunderous din came over the water and they watched, fascinated, as a pillar of red-and-yellow flame shot up forward of the bridge on their second target, which was closer to them, and in the fiery illumination they saw the steamer break apart in the middle and settle in the sea. Now, where was the third eel? By this time it, too, should have hit. Hardegen waited an interval, then ordered "hard-a-port" to be in position for a second salvo. Just as he began the turn he saw a high black detonation column in the convoy's last row, and a second later heard the explosion. He had been lucky. The third torpedo had missed its intended target and, instead, in a diagonal line, had wandered on to hit another ship. It was a hit of pure chance, such as he had seen once before as WO on U-*124*. (The ships sunk in this convoy, SL 76, on 27 June were British freighter *P.L.M. 22*, 5,646 GRT, which Hardegen claimed to BdU as a 10,000-ton tanker, and Dutch freighter *Oberon*, 1,996 GRT, which Hardegen claimed as 2,626 GRT. The third hit damaged a freighter, not identified.[15])

Now the whole convoy sprang to life. Ships sailed erratically on evasive courses. The first target, lying mortally wounded just barely above the water's surface, shot up illuminating flares. Tiny lights on life jackets danced on the waves, identifying the locations of survivors. So far the destroyers and corvettes had missed *123*, and Hardegen decided to seek cover alongside a lone steamer at the rear of the convoy. That turned out to be a mistake because the steamer's deck suddenly erupted in light flashes. Artillery! They were being shelled! The steamer had gun crews and she spewed ammunition from deck guns fore and aft. Her aim was bad, however, and, with their much faster surface speed, Hardegen and his crew made off safely. The gun flashes and noise alerted other ships including the escorts and soon star shells and flares were turning night into day, and searchlights were combing the water's surface. "*ALARM!*" Hardegen yelled into the voice pipe, and *123* sought the safety of the deep. There would be no more torpedoes just yet.

As they dived the sound room operator on the hydrophone

called to Hardegen in the control room: "Herr Kaleu! Destroyer—closing fast!" Hardegen ordered all hands to the bow compartments so that their weight would sharpen the boat's angle of dive. Now the destroyer was upon them with her Wabos. The first canisters exploded below the "swirl" left by their submerging, and the next pattern fell across the course the destroyer thought they had taken underwater. This Tommy captain was pretty good, Hardegen thought: He guessed well and some of his first explosions were close enough to shatter instrument glass, spray sparks, and punch the pits of a few stomachs. Now the hunter began trying to box them in, using his underwater sound-ranging device, called ASDIC.[16] That apparatus, housed in a dome on the underside of the destroyer's hull, sent out sound waves in pulses that, when they struck an underwater object such as a U-boat, returned a signal that gave the object's range and bearing. When the pulses bounced off a U-boat's hull they emitted within the boat a loud, piercing, and (for U-boatmen) ominous *PING-ping!* And that was exactly what the crew heard now as the hunter above stalked his game. Hardegen dived deeper to 150 meters, then to 200 (654 feet). Every man in the boat knew that the series of *PING-ping*s would shortly be followed by Wabos, so as the pinging increased in intensity they reached for whatever they could hold on to to steady them against the shocks. *Click-CLANG! Click-CLANG!* Each Wabo buckled the knees and jarred teeth and gums. And the bombing went on for hours. No man on board escaped the concussions that came from the explosions all around. Several times the lights shorted out, and the beams of hand-held flashlights reminded the men that they were still alive. No one broke. Discipline held. Absolute quiet prevailed within the boat. Men moved with mincing steps, and only the most necessary orders were given in whispers. While they knew that ASDIC listened to its own sound waves that echoed back from the U-boat's hull, they were likewise aware that British destroyers were equipped with an excellent hydrophone (*Horchgerät*) that "homed in" on audible sounds; though it is unlikely that a hydrophone picked up voices or footsteps inside a U-boat's thick hull. With the E motors, Hardegen tried various evasive maneuvers at great depth: "Starboard easy." "Starboard easy," the helmsman whispered down the pipe. Still, for the longest while they were not able to shake their foe. Schneider kept the count: fifty-three Wabos. It was a punishing ordeal and a sobering experience for everyone on board. In practicing their difficult three-dimensional art, the British had miscalculated *123*'s depth, with the result that their charges exploded harmlessly overhead. (For a depth charge to damage a U-boat fatally, it had to explode within seven meters [twenty-three feet] of the pressure hull. Not until 27 August when the British captured the Type VIIC U-*570* south of Iceland and subjected it to tests that demonstrated the thick hull's diving depth to 200 meters or more—the type was shipyard-certified to 250—did British war vessels adjust the priming on their charges for significantly deeper detonations.) After nearly twelve hours, the destroyer broke off the hunt. If it had remained on station for thirty-six to forty-eight hours, when *123*'s oxygen supply would have run out, the boat would have had to surface and become an easy victim. But the stalker abandoned his prey. After a prudent interval, Hardegen went to periscope depth. A quick search with the observation lens revealed an empty sea save for smoke columns far to the north. *Eins Zwei Drei* surfaced on the morning of 28 June to recharge batteries, even though it was daylight, and Hardegen ordered the helmsman to follow a northerly course to pursue the convoy. At the same time he radioed an update to BdU.

> *Hans Seigel:* It wasn't at all like what people saw in Buchheim's movie, *Das Boot.*

> *Walter Lorenz:* No, not at all. In the movie when the depth charges hit you see men falling all about. It was just not like that. Sure, your nerves got jangled, but falling about on each other? No, no.

> *Seigel:* When you heard the ASDIC, and when you heard the depth charges, you knew that you were still alive. But it's true, when the destroyer's propeller noises grew louder and closer, and when the pinging reverberated throughout the boat, and you heard the click of the explosives reaching their depth, sure it rattled your nerves. But there were never any screams or shouts like in the film. It just didn't happen. It couldn't happen—they'd locate you immediately. If just one man had shouted—

> *Richard Amstein:* I don't think there was one man on board who wasn't scared.

> *Walter Kaeding:* The man who says he wasn't scared, he's a liar. The difference was that in a U-boat you couldn't show your fear. So we didn't. But in Buchheim's film *Das Boot,*

where the men are so scared they go in their pants, not one of us had that happen, not one.

Karl Latislaus: Do you know that Buchheim also wrote a book? He is truly crazy. He made only one trip in a U-boat, as a photojournalist. How could he presume to write about U-boatmen? Some things are factual, but most are not. Before a mission we didn't drink that much or go around without our shirts—

Kaeding: We always knew where we stood. We understood from the beginning that we could be hit out there. But discussing that was taboo. Not in the family, not in the homeland, nowhere did we discuss it. We didn't even discuss it with our shipmates.

Seigel: Every boat was different. The commander of every boat was different. And I believe that if we had had a commander who was very tense, we wouldn't have been so calm either. But with Hardegen we had confidence that we would make it. And we were a well-experienced crew. You could trust your life to every single man.[17]

When darkness fell again, *123* with her superior surface speed was able to come up fast on the heels of the same convoy. Overnight, in fact, Hardegen got ahead of the convoy and waited for its lead elements in a bow attack position, but a Sunderland sighted them in the morning and sent them underwater with a brace of bombs, and *123* spent much of the daytime of 29 June submerged. Then, around dusk, there loomed into periscope view the same armed merchantman whose artillery had given them such grief two nights before. In the attack scope Hardegen easily read her name: *Río Azúl*, 4,088 GRT. What looked like a white Royal Navy war ensign on the bowstaff suggested that she was a *Hilfskreuzer*—an armed merchant cruiser (AMC). He could not think of a more satisfying target. As she steamed into his cross hairs, he made ready a single launch from tube four. Alerted to *123*'s presence by the Sunderland's attack, *Río Azúl* was zigzagging on her base course. Just when Hardegen began to worry that he might not get a clean shot at her, she zagged when she should have zigged and hove before his lens at optimum range and angle. *Eins Zwei Drei* was right on top of her at 325 meters and twenty-one seconds torpedo running time. *Los!* The torpedo went straight into her belly and the resulting blast literally blew the British ship apart. The forward gun crew could not reach their station before the bow section sank. Quickly afterward the stern section stood upright in the water and then it, too, descended below the water in loud groaning noises, with its propellers churning in the air, its Union Jack flapping, and its men sliding into the sea. Only two and a half minutes had elapsed between explosion and oil slick. To BdU Hardegen sent an F.T. announcing their triumph.[18]

    Eins Zwei Drei got one more ship on her long African patrol, an independently steaming British freighter that she hit on the port side one night about a week after their convoy adventures. The victim was *Auditor,* a British freighter, 5,444 GRT, sunk on 4 July. Schneider got the prize with a single, well-placed torpedo on a UZO aim-off and they watched the crew hastily abandon ship as the vessel went down by the stern. Faster than they could have expected only the bow stood steeply above the water. Then it heaved up in one last gasp of life and sank like a stone. It was an impressive sight. Two weeks later Hardegen would learn that two of the steamer's lifeboats, with twenty-four men aboard, successfully made Cape Verde on the African coast—a stretch of some six hundred nautical miles in an open boat, the distance, Hardegen figured, from Lake Constance to Königsberg (roughly the equivalent distance from Washington, D.C. to Chicago). He credited the survivors with excellent seamanship. *Auditor* was the U-boat's last sinking because all the rest of the shipping they saw going in or out of Freetown in Sierra Leone was American, "neutral" shipping that U-boat commanders were not allowed to attack. From the bridge Hardegen frequently sighted smoke clouds and mast tops on the horizon but when the boat closed he saw that they belonged to ships with prominently painted U.S. flags on their hulls. Everyone on board knew that the U.S. ships were delivering contraband to the enemy. Yet the rules of engagement forbade contact. To Hardegen it was infuriating and frustrating (although he could have reflected with profit on the fact that at the same time Germany was marching troops across neutral Sweden and was refueling U-boats in neutral Spanish ports).[19] Having reported to BdU that they had run out of prospects, they were ordered north, on 2 August, to waters off Gibraltar, where they patrolled, again without success and much to their grief because on two occasions, 13–14 August, British destroyers took them under depth-charging, the second time for four hours straight, and they ended up with both diesels temporarily disabled and a serious leak of lubricating oil. Schneider counted 126 toothshakers in all, 39 of which were close enough to hurt, with the result that the crew were more than a little relieved when BdU ordered *123* home for repairs. By the time (0910 on 23 August) they tied up alongside old *Isère*, the crew had been at sea for sixty-eight days. After the deck force completed their hawsers, the men raced off to the base canteen for a bottle of Beck's. Hardegen went off for a bath and shave and a long sleep between clean sheets.

At Kernével, Admiral Dönitz studied Hardegen's *Kriegstagebuch* (KTB), or war diary, in close detail and on 25 August commented on his new Type IXB commander in the BdU diary: "He first attacked a convoy and sank an auxiliary cruiser and three ships. Later he sank an independently sailing ship and observed heavy neutral traffic off Freetown. The commander behaved very skillfully throughout the operation and used his opportunities for attack to the utmost."[20] It was praise not lightly given by the Lion. Pointedly, Dönitz had left out mention of Hardegen's first sinking. There was a downside to *123*'s KTB that could only be explained to Hardegen personally. Like every other frontline commander at the conclusion of a patrol, Hardegen presented himself on the day assigned at Dönitz's headquarters château for a line-by-line analysis of his KTB by the Lion. This proved to be a daunting experience for some commanders who had little to show for their efforts or whose KTBs exhibited poor judgment, lack of aggressiveness, or incompetence. It was not unknown for commanders to be beached for flagrant or repeated failures; in one extreme instance Kptlt. Heinz Hirsacker (U-*572*) would be condemned to death by a court-martial in 1943 for "cowardice in the face of the enemy." None of these faults appeared in Hardegen's record, and Dönitz was generally complimentary, but the Lion did point out with some concern that the first ship Hardegen had sunk on the patrol—the 20 June target that required two torpedo hits and then artillery shelling to go down—was not, as Hardegen had identified her, a British vessel. She was a neutral Portuguese freighter named *Ganda*. And the diplomatic uproar caused by the incident had been somewhat allayed in Germany's favor by the fact that the Portuguese decided to blame the loss on a British submarine known to have been in the vicinity. Dönitz thereupon bound Hardegen to absolute silence about the affair and directed him to alter his KTB both to expunge all mention of the sinking and to show no action of any kind on 20 June.

This would be one of two known instances in the entire Battle of the Atlantic when Dönitz would order a U-boat commander to falsify his war diary. The other instance came in the opening days of the war with Britain, when the submerged U-*30* (Kptlt. Fritz-Julius Lemp) torpedoed and sank the British passenger liner *Athenia* 250 miles northwest of Ireland with the loss of 112 passengers, including 22 U.S. citizens. The sinking violated both international law governing warfare at sea and BdU's own strict orders. The shock and outrage that followed in every part of the world caused Dönitz to order Lemp, on his return to base, to remove all reference to *Athenia* from his KTB entry for 3 September 1939. Subsequently Hitler's Propaganda Ministry brazenly put out the story that *Athenia* had been sunk by a British submarine as a deliberate attempt to incite anti-German feelings akin to those that followed Germany's sinking of the British liner *Lusitania* in 1915, an action that helped bring the United States into the First World War.

Hardegen complied with Dönitz's second order to fake a KTB, though his effort at deception was transparent to any discriminating eye. In order to remove what must have been an elaborate account of *Ganda*'s sinking Hardegen retyped four entire pages. Instead of the tight single-spaced narrative found elsewhere in the diary, he double-spaced routine navigational data across the gap. Where the gloss failed again was in the use of a different typewriter and ribbon, four new diary-entry pages with modern typeface headings instead of Gothic as in the rest of the diary, and hand-drawn page numerals instead of typed numerals as found elsewhere. Five copies of the doctored KTB were then distributed to appropriate offices in Lorient and Germany as well as one to Hardegen's own file in U-*123*. Where the subterfuge particularly collapsed was in the *Schussmeldungen*, the shooting reports, on the *Ganda* sinking that no one thought to change. In them Hardegen provided all the technical data of the torpedo launches and gun action of his attack. Inadvertently those documents went without change to Torpedokommando (Torpedo Command) in Germany, where, if anyone was curious, the data they contained could be matched exactly with what was known of *Ganda*'s sinking. Notwithstanding the other talents of Dönitz the Lion and Hardegen the warrior, it cannot be concluded that they were adept at dissembling.[21] (At the Nürnberg War Crimes Tribunal in 1945, Dönitz testified under oath that Lemp's U-*30* KTB after *Athenia* was the only case of counterfeiting a war diary that had occurred during the war.[22])

. . .

When *123* finally came out of the yard in mid-October, her Wabo-twisted skin and innards made new and her crew rested to the point of boredom, Hardegen put out to sea again. It was the boat's sixth war cruise, his second as her commander. After passing 20 degrees longitude, he broke his sealed Operation Order and learned that *123* was to join a patrol line, or "rake," of U-boats interdicting the convoy lanes between Newfoundland and Greenland. Gone were those warm currents the crew had enjoyed under the Southern Cross, where their steel shell rose and fell in gentle waters. Now they were back bucketing through the northern high seas with cold green water in their faces. For five days they followed a generally westward course until, on 20 October, in the longitudes of Iceland, they received an F.T. from BdU alerting them to the presence of a fast-moving military convoy, probably troop transports, south of their position on an east-northeast course to England. Hardegen decrypted the report, which had originated with a contact U-boat, plotted it on the chart, and saw that *123* was already past the convoy's base course. Too bad. The more he played with the data, though, the more he thought that if he reversed course at full speed he could still intercept the convoy. Some other boats at sea that received the same message might be closer and thus better able to attack, but, he wondered, suppose there were none? Suppose *123* was the only boat in the area with a chance to attack, should he not give it a try? Against that option were the strict orders that he had received from BdU on departure to make his assigned station at fuel-saving cruising speed. Could he justify disregarding those orders and expending valuable fuel on reverse track to seek out a convoy there was no certainty of reaching? His instincts said yes. Hesitation did not win wars, he told himself. It was sometimes better to make lightning decisions based on animallike instincts than to think a problem to death. Admiral Dönitz held his U-boat men to the motto: *Angreifen! Ran! Versenken!*—Attack! Advance! Sink! Hardegen was sure that in these circumstances the Lion would agree with his decision. He turned away from the plotting board to tell Schneider: "Now, new course one zero zero, both ahead full."

It was near midnight Central European Time (CET) when they made their turn on the surface and fixed the boat on reverse heading. The diesels charged like knights' steeds going to battle. The boat pitched and plunged as it breasted the swells and the spray it created filled the bridge with foam. The crew were in a high state of excitement. No one could sleep. Schneider ran ignition tests on the torpedoes. Every man looked to his assignment and readied himself for combat. Two more wireless signals about the convoy came in from BdU. The second reported that the contact U-boat had lost sight of the convoy, it was traveling so fast. Again Hardegen studied the chart. According to his calculations *123* would reach the convoy in fewer than four hours—or not at all. And there was no point in aborting now when he had already bled the fuel bunkers this far. Then, shockingly, he received a fresh signal from BdU: Any boats west of the convoy were to break off the chase and head to their originally assigned stations at fuel-saving speeds. What to do now? A commander should not lightly disobey orders from above, not if he wanted to remain a commander. Yet neither should he disavow gut feelings that had stood him well in the past. Furthermore, if he stopped now he would have used his fuel in vain. He ordered Schneider: "Continue, both ahead full, same course, until 0400 hours." It was the most difficult order he had ever given for it constituted flat refusal to obey a legitimate command from the highest authority. He looked again at the BdU signal in his hand:

CONVOY OPERATIONS TO BE HALTED IMMEDIATELY. CONTINUE NAVIGATION WITH LOW FUEL CONSUMPTION. MORE LATER.[23]

It would be an easy order to follow. All he had to do was go hard-a-port, establish an opposite heading of 275, and ring up one engine slow ahead. That would save him from the scolding that would certainly come if he missed finding the convoy. But Hardegen had a hunch that if the admiral were in his place he would follow the same bold course. It was both a hunch and a *hope*. He bent over the chart and worried himself through the computations again. Midnight (CET) passed. Then, shortly before 0400 hours the voice pipe from the bridge barked: "Commander to the bridge! Shadows—starboard on the beam!" Hardegen went up like a shot and looked through the glasses. There they were! He counted four large two-funnel steamers and a screen of what looked like three destroyers. "*Auf Gefechtsstationen!*" ("Battle stations!")

Hardegen's sense of relief was matched only by the adrenaline that now pumped through his system. He had to move fast. Such was the convoy's speed—he estimated fourteen to fifteen knots—he had no chance to hit the first two steamers in line. He went for the third. It was a huge shadow, perhaps 14,000 GRT, zigzagging. Somehow *123* made it inside the escorts' protective envelope without anyone sighting their distinctive white-foaming bow and long stern casing. One destroyer sweeping perpendicularly to the convoy's course stood on their starboard side as they closed. Any moment it should see them. Hell was going to break loose. The watch on that quadrant yelled: "Destroyer on starboard lies course zero degrees right at us!" No more stalking—they had to launch now! Hardegen leaned forward to Schneider's ear: *Feuererlaubnis!*

Schneider pressed the launch button—*Los!, Los!, Los!*—letting loose a simultaneous spread of three eels, two of which he hoped would strike the target, since they were shooting at a distance, 1,500 meters, far greater than Hardegen would have preferred. Normally, like Kretschmer, Hardegen held to the doctrine, "one ship, one torpedo," but this was a must-sink situation and the *Fächerschuss*, or fan shot, seemed justified. Schneider had calculated target speed at fifteen knots, angle on the bow eighty degrees, time to target eighty-one seconds.[24] While the eels ran Hardegen headed away from the destroyer at top speed and it was not possible to get off a launch from a stern tube at the fourth steamer in line as he had planned. He could only seek the darkness abeam for cover and wait for some sign from the eels. Schneider counted the seconds . . . fifteen . . . ten . . . five. . . .

Officer of the Watch Lieutenant John Binfield, RNR, paced the bridge of the two-funnel, four steam turbine, twin screw HMS *Aurania*. Formerly a passenger vessel of Cunard White Star, Ltd., launched in 1924, the ship was now outfitted as an armed merchant cruiser (AMC) of the Royal Navy. En route home to the Clyde in Scotland from Halifax she had joined up with convoy SL 89 as one of five AMC escorts in the screen of the twenty-ship formation that steamed in columns five cables apart. Binfield had the ship on zigzag pattern 10, mean course 062 degrees, speed 13.5 knots. He had just paused in his pacing to check time and position—0227 Greenwich Mean Time, 50–45.5N, 18–41W—and to order the heading altered to 040 for the port leg of zigzag when a dull explosion on the port side by Number 3 Hold rocked him off his feet. Pulling himself upright he pressed the alarm rattlers for action stations, stopped the engines, put the wheel hard-a-port toward the U-boat according to standing instructions, sounded six short blasts, and switched on a red light at the yardarm to signal "torpedoed." Ship's Captain Ivan Walter Whitehorn, RN, reached the bridge thirty seconds later and found that the ship had taken a twenty-five-degrees list to port. He ordered off the red light, put the engines to Slow Ahead and the wheel hard-a-starboard to get distance from the U-boat. As a precaution he ordered ship's company to "Turn Out All Boats." Shortly afterward, finding that the ship had righted to fifteen degrees, he put on revolutions for eight knots and resumed zigzag. In the meantime someone who was not an officer passed the orders, "Clear Everybody from Down Below" and "Abandon Ship." The result of this confusion was that Gunner Charles Stewart ordered P.2 lifeboat lowered. With him in the boat were Leading Seamen Bertie E. Shaw and George R. Brown and Able Seamen Cornelius O'Keefe, Abed Graves, and Victor A. Pancott. Someone slipped the gripes, the boat swung out owing to *Aurania*'s list, and Brown went overboard. When the boat hit the water at ship's speed of five knots or better, it began to capsize and Stewart, O'Keefe, Graves, and Pancott were thrown overboard. Shaw was last seen still in the boat as it was carried astern nearly full of water. Destroyer HMS *Croome* rescued Stewart, O'Keefe, and Graves. Brown, Shaw, and Pancott were not seen again.[25]

From *123* Hardegen and the bridge watch surveyed the scene. Dull red flames glowed against the wounded hull, which listed to port and appeared to go down by the bow. Through their glasses they could see the crew lowering lifeboats. From the steamer's bridge red lights flashed Morse signals to a destroyer aft, and it hove to alongside to assist. The remainder of the convoy, alerted by the attack, changed course from 062 to 100 degrees, and though Hardegen tried to run beside them and reloaded, their speed and head start made it impossible to catch up. After an hour and a half's chase, it was daybreak and *123* was getting easy to spot. It was time to break off. When an escort turned back toward his position, Hardegen withdrew and sent a convoy position report to BdU. Perhaps another boat farther north would have a shot. Now he returned to the scene of attack to give his victim a *Fangschuss*—a coup de grace—if that was necessary. All he found there was a large oil slick, miscellaneous flotsam, and a half-foundered lifeboat. But inside the lifeboat was a survivor. As *123* approached, the sailor, on his knees in the boat, raised his hands in supplication. The crew took him on board and on interrogation he told them that his name was Bertie Shaw, that the ship they sank was HMS *Aurania*, 13,984 GRT, an armed merchant cruiser, that she had taken one hit in the forecastle and another just in front of the engine room, that the destroyer that stopped to assist had rescued most of the 250-man crew, and that some three-quarters of an hour after being torpedoed the ship blew apart from an internal explosion and sank from view bow first with her propellers in the air. *Eins Zwei Drei*'s bridge at some distance had seen a tall flame lick the sky at the attack site, and Hardegen wondered if another U-boat nearby had delivered a coup de grace. He signaled news of the sinking to BdU, and Dönitz replied with a "Bravo!" On board the principal emotion was that of vindication.

It was time to get on with their original mission. Hardegen put the boat back on a 280 heading and turned his interest to the horizon where the bridge sighted a Sunderland. They alternately dived and surfaced over most of that afternoon as Sunderlands came and went. *Eins Zwei Drei* was not far distant from the coast of England, which was one reason for the presence of the "tired bees." After a brief submergence around dusk that evening, they discovered another reason. Surfacing on a medium sea with a hazy horizon, they found themselves running alongside (but in the opposite direction) a convoy on the identical course as the one they had just attacked. Perhaps, Hardegen thought, this was a trailing element of the same convoy. In any event, it was a stunning sight. With the naked eye he could count twenty large steamers and three destroyers. Ten minutes more, and he would have surfaced directly in the middle of their columns! Now to do his duty—stay above and report. In Dönitz's system the first boat to sight a convoy did not attack but signaled position, course, and speed to BdU and continued to report while other boats, vectored to the position, undertook the attack. Proceeding ahead at full surface speed, Hardegen sent off the F.T. and awaited confirmation of the signal's receipt. A destroyer worried him. It came right at the boat. He headed away knowing that the destroyer would have to return to the convoy. But now a Sunderland came out of the haze. Where was confirmation from BdU? The Sunderland would be on them in seconds. The plane was at 3,000-meters' range and low to the water. Finally the voice pipe from the radio room below sang out: "F.T. acknowledged!" "ALARM!" Hardegen yelled. And down they went just as the Sunderland, having spotted them easily, banked in for the kill. They were just under the surface when the bombs came, one over the foredeck, one over the bridge. They shook the boat badly and did some damage, but none of it was serious. The crew got a laugh out of the experience when, as the bombs exploded, their English prisoner moaned, "No good, no good." He need not have worried. Their airborne tormentors finally went away and, several hours later when they surfaced, they found an empty sea and sky. They had lost the convoy but in the darkness astern had heard two detonations. That meant that someone had received their report through BdU and had done something about it. (U-*82* commanded by Kptlt. Siegfried Rollmann sank two ships from that convoy, SL 89, British freighters *Serbino*, 4,099 GRT, and *Treverbyn*, 5,218 GRT, at 2203 and 2231 hours respectively, on 21 October, southwest of Ireland.[26])

Their prisoner was Bertie Edward Shaw, forty-eight years old, home address 60 Wyndham Road, Kingston-on-Thames, England. His rank was Leading Seaman, pensioner rating, Naval Reserve. Once the crew got him into dry clothes and gave him some cognac he told them more about his ship and about himself, although his accent and use of slang made it very difficult to understand him. *Aurania* had been well armed, he said, with six 15.2-centimeter guns and two Lewis anti-aircraft weapons on the stern. The captain was named Whitehorn. Shaw did not know his first name. The crew were mostly naval reservists. Shaw was the oldest petty officer on board. He had joined the Navy as a young man to avoid a prison term resulting from a fight. Shortly before the war he was discharged and spent a number of peaceful years with his family working as a postman. When war came he was drafted back into the Navy and served all his time on *Aurania*. This was to have been his last voyage: He was due to be relieved of sea duty and assigned to a nice soft job with the Coastal Forces. Unfortunately for him, while he was asleep in his bunk, this U-boat interrupted his service record. When the torpedoes hit, Shaw himself sounded the signal to abandon ship. As he helped lower P.2 lifeboat, it became stuck and he went down by ladder to undo the ropes. While he stood in the boat it slipped the ropes and fell into the sea, where it nearly capsized because *Aurania* was still making about five knots. Carried astern, his boat half full of water, Shaw shouted for help but no one heard him. The wind and swells quickly separated him from his ship. Several times the rescue destroyer passed close by his boat but failed to hear his cries. After three-quarters of an hour, he said, he observed a mighty internal explosion on *Aurania*—which was already very low in the water—and after that the steamer passed from view. There was no question about the sinking.[27]

After a long voyage westward, *123* took up her assigned station as part of a patrol line called *Gruppe Schlagetot* (Group Hacker) south of Greenland. Shortly after reaching the rest of the pack, she received an FT from BdU detaching her from the rake and posting her independently to intercept ships emerging from the Strait of Belle Isle between Newfoundland and Labrador. But the boat found no hunting at all in the thick fog of the strait, leaving Hardegen frustrated and provoked, although he took some satisfaction in hearing battle sounds from other, luckier boats through the vaporous whiteout to the east.[28] Later he was reassigned to the southern coast of Greenland off Cape Farewell. The Greenland coast was a spectacular sight for the crewmen, especially for those who had never seen an alpine mountain range. Even the engine room detail was invited up to see it. Romantic and beautiful, the tall snow-covered mountains and glaciers fell sharply to the sea. Now and then the bridge sighted massive blue-white icebergs floating south with the current. It was sufficiently cold that the boat began to take on its own coat of ice, and when it got so thick that it threatened emergency readiness, or when, as happened once, the weight of the ice broke one of the antennas, Hardegen had to submerge the boat in order to melt off the crust.

Twice, south of Greenland, *123* encountered other U-boats and exchanged light-signal greetings with them—cheery and all-too-brief moments that lifted the boat's loneliness far from home. Once they were badly depth-charged by the British and had to dive so deep to avoid the Wabos that they feared the surrounding water pressure would crush them like an eggshell. But the fierce detonations finally ceased and just before their batteries were exhausted they made it to the surface safely. The most relieved man on board was their prisoner, to whom the underwater bombardment was a new and fearsome naval experience. On signal from BdU they then began the long return home, surfaced all the way, with no further incidents, which was a disappointment, for they had hoped to chance upon a convoy or a straggler. Plenty of eels were left. Though they crossed all the known steamer lanes, they failed to see a mast top. It was as though all the merchant ships had been vacuumed from the sea. For U-boatmen it was "sour-pickle time." They did find some pleasure in observing their prisoner, to whom the crew had become quite attached although they could hardly understand a word he said. "Bernhard" they called him. He gladly performed seamen's work on board and, to the delight of the cooks, freely undertook the jobs of dishwasher and potato peeler. Hardegen speculated that on future missions the cooks would look back longingly to "Bernhard" and to the free time he afforded them. The Tommy missed his cigarettes and chewing tobacco. Since the boat's tiny canteen carried some of the former, from time to time Hardegen let him go on top to smoke. "Bernhard" found the German brands just barely tolerable. The Englishman was not exactly notable for his habits of personal hygiene. When one of the crew offered him a toothbrush he refused it, saying that he had only two teeth in his mouth. By the time *123* reached her Atlantic base, "Bernhard" had a full white beard. He seemed to have thought that when they reached the English Channel his captors would free him, but as *123* moved up the Scorff Estuary toward the pontoon *Isère*, he recognized an old French warship at anchor and knew then that he would not see England again during the war. Hardegen thought he saw resignation on his face, as though "Bernhard" was reciting to himself the old German soldier's maxim: *Besser ein paar Jahre gefangen als das ganze Leben tot* — "Better a prisoner for a few years than to spend one's whole life dead." It was a moving moment when he took his leave of the crew members. Each of them wondered if he would see Bertie Shaw again.

Only one success pennant flew from the extended *Spargel* (asparagus), as U-boatmen called the periscope. During this last long patrol, *123* had sunk only one ship. But it was a warship, and thus the pennant was red. One red pennant was worth four or five whites: Hardegen was content.

Envoi

It would have come as a great shock to Hardegen had he been present at a board of inquiry held three weeks later, on 10–11 November in the wardroom of HMS *Cyclops*, docked in the Clyde Estuary near Glasgow, Scotland, and seen through the portholes HMS *Aurania* moored smartly alongside. The board, which had been convoked to investigate the torpedo hit on *Aurania* and the loss of three ratings, listened to Captain Whitehorn's explanation of how he had stabilized the ship on an even keel about fifteen feet down by the bows, held her at that with pumps, and in calm weather, escorted by HMS *Totlund*, proceeded without further incident to the Clyde, where *Aurania* safely made port on the afternoon of 23 October.

"Bernhard" had proved his mettle in the cook's gallery; as an observer and reporter his credentials were less impressive.

That *Aurania*, at nearly 14,000 GRT the largest of the twenty-nine ships that Reinhard Hardegen would torpedo as a U-boat commander, did not in fact sink he would not learn until January 1987, when he was shown the minutes of the board of inquiry conducted on *Cyclops*.

After repair to her damaged hull, *Aurania* sailed again as an escort of convoy until war's end, when she was decommissioned and scrapped.[29]

In 1962, at his father's request, Hardegen's eldest son Klaus-Reinhard visited Bertie Shaw's home in Kingston-on-Thames, outside London, to pay his father's respects. Mrs. Shaw stated that Bertie was dead and said that she would not speak further with Klaus-Reinhard "because Bertie [had] had a very hard time in POW camp."

Although Hardegen would never see the warship HMS *Cyclops*, he would very soon encounter a British freighter of the same name. It would be the same SS *Cyclops* that Admiral Dönitz thought he personally had sunk as a U-boat commander in 1918 and for which he received the Knight's Cross of the order of the House of Hohenzollern.

In early December, Hardegen and his wife, Barbara, went on leave to Italy. As he rode the Milan–Turin train over the sun-drenched Po Plain it was difficult for him to realize that just weeks before he and his crew had been dodging icebergs in the grim cold of a near arctic world. Now he was caught up in the surrealistic experience of a land-bound train clacking rhythmically along iron lanes without roll, pitch, yaw, or navigational error, from one warm city to another. Soon the mulberry and rice fields were behind him, and the steam locomotive wheezed and braked into the Turin station. Here, as in Milan, he was expected by BdU to give an inspirational lecture on the U-boat war to German locals. His was a working leave, though the speaking chores were really not so much work as fun. Hardegen enjoyed the notice and he enjoyed the talking. A welcoming delegation from the German population of Turin rushed forward as he and his wife stepped down to the platform, he with his tall, thin, erect frame; angular, even gaunt, face and penetrating blue eyes; smartly dressed in his blue naval uniform with U-boat and Air Force badges on the left breast and the gold sleeve rings of lieutenant commander rank on his jacket sleeves.

"Well, what do you think of it?" one of the delegation asked him excitedly. Hardegen answered, "Italy is wonderful." "No," his welcomers explained. "We mean the speech—Japan—Hawaii—the

Führer—Roosevelt—." Hardegen had heard nothing. As he listened he was able to put together the disjointed pieces: Japan had attacked Pearl Harbor, and the Führer had declared war on the United States! Finally the frustrations of U-boat commanders unable to shoot at U.S. targets had been removed. And what an opportunity, he thought, especially for someone like himself who commanded a long-distance boat, an IXB. With luck he could be among the first to voyage to the United States. If only he had a map, a globe, anything! He could hardly wait to measure the distance from Lorient to New York, Cape Hatteras, and Florida. He had visited New York City several years before when in training aboard the cruiser *Karlsruhe*. Unbelievable! At the newsstand in the station he purchased Italian newspapers, and his German hosts translated for him the accounts of the attack on Pearl Harbor, of the Japanese sinking of the British battleship *Prince of Wales* and battlecruiser *Repulse*, and of Hitler's declaration-of-war speech to the Reichstag. As he walked out of the station to a waiting car, now very keen about the talk he would give that night, Hardegen took his wife Barbara by the arm, smiled, and said, *"Du, auf der nächsten Fahrt besuche ich Roosevelt!"* —"You know, dear, on my next patrol I'll visit Roosevelt!"[30]

3

"We Are at War"

19 December 1941. Three U-boat commanders in dark blue caps, overcoats, and gray gloves stood in a tight circle outside the entrance to Second U-Boat Flotilla Headquarters on the River Scorff at Lorient. Reinhard Hardegen was explaining to his colleagues that he had just returned prematurely from leave in Italy when a Horch sedan sent by Admiral Dönitz's headquarters at nearby Kernével pulled up in front. The officers climbed in, Hardegen sitting alongside the naval driver for the winding three-kilometer ride through Lorient's *centre de ville.*

"Why did you say you came back early?" one of the officers in the rear asked Hardegen as the driver got under way. "Because of the Führer's declaration of war against America?"

"Exactly," Hardegen answered, turning to the officer. "I have a lot of anger toward the Americans.[1] Don't forget, two patrols ago I was off the coast of Africa, and the Americans with their hypocritical claims of neutrality made a fool of me. Time and time again I would sight smoke clouds and mast tops on the horizon only to close with them and see that they belonged to ships with large painted American flags on their hulls. So many times that happened. I knew—everyone of us on board knew—that those US ships were delivering contraband to the enemy. Yet we couldn't touch them. But we can touch those guys now."

From the back seat came sounds of approval, though one of the commanders cautioned, "Don't be so sure we're going to America. The Lion may be sending us to Gibraltar." Hardegen mused to himself, yes, the Lion could send them to Gibraltar, but more than likely he would not. All three officers commanded either Type IXB or IXC oceangoing boats designed for long-distance missions. The Lion's call for the three of them to receive orders from him in person, and at the same time, had to mean something special, something different from a Gibraltar station, where their type of boats had already operated—and for too long, in Hardegen's opinion. He guessed that the call meant an extended Feindfahrt to the coastal shipping lanes of the United States. At worst, their orders would send them to form a rake across convoy lanes south of Greenland, from which he had just returned in November. That would at least get U-boats back into the North Atlantic. But the odds favored an American patrol.

The sedan passed over the Ter River bridge onto Larmor-Plage south of the city and shortly afterward turned east on the rue du Kernével, following it to its end at the water's edge where, looking south across the roadstead, the officers could see the battlements of the eighteenth-century stone Citadelle de Port-Louis that once guarded the harbor's entrance. Their driver stopped to present passes at a guardhouse painted in red and white chevrons, then drove onto a gravel driveway and stopped again before the eight sweeping stone steps of a handsome château. Flag Lieutenant Hans Fuhrmann came rapidly down the steps to greet Hardegen and his companions as they alighted from the staff car.

"Come up to the situation room," he said, "Kapitän zur See Godt will greet you shortly. The mate has made coffee. The admiral left word he wants you to look around. There's no action right now. Be sure to see the 'museum,' as we call it—the room with our graphs and tables and tonnage tallies. Familiarize yourselves. Kapitän Godt will see you as soon as he is free."

Hardegen and his companions entered the foyer, hung up their coats and caps, and followed the flag lieutenant through the grand salon into the situation room on the ground floor. With a wave of the hand Fuhrmann left them alone with the large wall nautical charts, the operations chart with its myriad of pins with red and blue flags atop a large green baize-covered table, and the admiral's famed three-foot-diameter world globe. It did not take the commanders long to figure out that the blue flags stood for U-boats and the red for convoys. What was startling was that there were very few blue flags in the

Atlantic sea-lanes between North America and Britain. Most were bunched up in the Mediterranean and off Gibraltar. "You see?" said one of the officers, "I bet that's where we're going—Gibraltar." Hardegen shook his head. He walked over to the enlarged wall chart *Nr. 1870G Nordatlantischer Ozean.*

"Here," he said, pointing, "is where we're going—Boston, New York, Cape Hatteras, Key West. Count on it."

The others laughed. "You're awfully sure," said one. Hardegen seized on the lightened mood. "See this strait, Strait of Belle Isle?" He pointed to the body of water between Newfoundland and Labrador. "That's where I was on my last patrol in November. Now look here." He moved his finger to the right across the Atlantic to a small island south of Lorient. "That's Belle Île, which we passed when we stood out to sea. I told my officers when we reached the strait that our boat had just gone from Beautiful Island to Beautiful Island!" Again Hardegen's companions chuckled at his effervescent good humor.

"What did you find in your Beautiful Island strait when you got there?" asked one.

"Nothing," Hardegen answered. "Absolutely nothing, except fog. I spent six days looking at nothing but a milky white wall. And there was no hunting at all. I was really angry at being given such a poor station."[2]

His companions smiled indulgently. It was hard for them to imagine this man with the big smile being angry.

Richard Zapp (U-*66*), short, thickset, with deeply etched features, had a success record of five ships, 26,130 tons, sunk off Africa in the preceding June, July, and September. Redheaded Ernst Kals (U-*130*), slender as a ship's colors, had just returned to Lorient from sinking three ships, 14,971 tons, in the North Atlantic—his first kills as a commander. They knew Hardegen as spontaneous, audacious, and irrepressibly good-humored. They also knew from word passed by his officers and crew that it was a real scare to ride in his boat. He took chances that few other commanders would dream of taking. But audacity had won him seven ships claimed, nearly forty thousand tons. It was hard for some to reconcile Hardegen's aggressiveness with his delicate features and physical impairments, including a shortened right leg—result of the plane crash in 1936—that he managed successfully to camouflage. It was an open secret that the same crash had left him with a continuously bleeding stomach and a diarrhetic condition, and that on board his boat the cook regularly fed him a special bland diet. Two things could be said for certain about Hardegen, however: No officer or crewman asked to be transferred off U-123 to another boat as naval regulations freely permitted. And, in a service where the only respected commanders were those who sank ships, Hardegen was greatly respected.

However, neither his leg nor his stomach was on the mind of U-123's commander as he paced Dönitz's situation room and paused to gaze out the broad east window at Keroman I and II, the huge nearly finished U-boat bunkers that squatted directly opposite on the Ter. Thousands of workmen continued to swarm over the gray, windowless monoliths in an attempt to bring the project to completion by the end of December. Already the refit facilities at the waterline were in operation. From his vantage point Hardegen could easily make out the cavelike bays, including bay B6 where his own boat was nearing the end of refit. This was the first time his boat had been readied for combat under the newly opened shelter. In a matter of hours, he hoped, she would be ready for loading and provisioning. But first he needed Admiral Dönitz's orders. He wondered how long he would have to wait.

The admiral was doing what he always did at this time in the afternoon. He was walking his Alsatian, Wolf, across the brown countryside near Quiberon in company with his A-4 (communications officer), Korvettenkapitän Hans Meckel. It was an idyllic hour in the twenty-four, despite the December chill. Dönitz's days were precisely ordered. He awoke each morning at seven and appeared in the situation room promptly at nine where his six-man staff under Kapitän zur See Eberhard Godt, chief of operations (BdU-Ops), briefed him on the overnight situation. The dapper, sad-eyed Godt was every inch Dönitz's alter ego, and, more than anyone outside of headquarters realized at the time, the master manager of the convoy battles. From Godt's deputy, designated A-1, first operations officer, Dönitz learned the current disposition of all U-boats and of all convoys. A-1 would also describe actions taken during the night. If a major convoy battle had occurred, Dönitz would already have known about it in detail since he and Godt would have directed the strategy throughout from the green baize table. The A-1 report would close with an account of U-boats going to and returning from patrol, boats in various state of refit at all the Atlantic U-boat bases of Brest (First and Ninth Flotillas), Lorient (Second), Saint-Nazaire (Sixth and Seventh), La Pallice/La Rochelle

(Third), and Bordeaux (Twelfth), and the construction progress of new boats on stream from the major German shipyards of Kiel, Hamburg, and Bremen.

The officer designated A-2 would then report on the escort of U-boats by R-boats (motor minesweepers) as they sortied or returned through the complicated mine fields on the approaches to the various bases. The A-3, intelligence officer, presented a graphic display of convoy routes based on B-Dienst intercepts and decrypts of convoy radio traffic. The B-Dienst accomplishments in cracking British naval ciphers and codes had been persistently brilliant. While the Royal Navy tactical ciphers remained for the most part impenetrable the convoy traffic had long ago been compromised and its data on composition, course, and speed of convoys proved of inestimable value— except when, as now, Dönitz had almost none of his boats in the sea lanes that counted. A-3 also reported on other intelligence data received overnight from agents in neutral countries, Luftwaffe reconnaissance flights, and sea-level sightings of warships and merchantmen. A-4, Meckel, reviewed nighttime radio shortwave communications with surfaced U-boats at sea which were transmitted and received by his staff in the large white former residency building next to the château. From Kernével his operators keyed directly by land lines the powerful transmitters and receivers southeast of Paris that had formed the Compagnie Radio-France, which until its seizure by the Germans had been used by the French government for communications with France's far-flung colonies; the transmitters were at Sainte-Assise and the receivers at Villecresnes. Similarly, Meckel reported on longwave messages transmitted to boats in all areas, which could receive them underwater to a depth of twenty-five meters via Goliath, the enormous antenna array at Calbe, forty-three kilometers south of Magdeburg in the heart of Germany, which was also connected to Kernével by cable.[3]

A-5 and A-6 presented miscellaneous data dealing with personnel and logistics. It was A-5's unhappy duty, when a U-boat was reported lost or missing, to place a star beside the commander's name on the first receipt of a casualty report and a second star if no positive response came from the boat after several days of radio transmissions. After that the commander's name was "put on file." Among the names "on file" by this December were Prien, Kretschmer (captured though presumed dead at Kernével), Schepke, Lemp, and Endrass. Finally, Dönitz and staff prepared a "U-Boat Disposition Chart," based on the decrypted British Western Approaches daily bulletin on "U-Boat Dispositions"—as Britain believed them to be—as well as on what staff thought the enemy might have deduced about U-boat intentions from known torpedo actions, high-frequency direction-finding technology, and sightings. Dönitz and staff then asked themselves how, in the enemy's place, they would react to these data. U-boat rakes could then be deployed to ambush convoys that London thought it had safely steered from harm's way. Following the morning's work and a light lunch, Dönitz would sleep for an hour in order to build a reserve of alertness that he might have to call on during the night ahead. Upon awakening he and Wolf, with a staffer (on this particular day, Meckel), would climb into his gray Mercedes command car and, escorted front and back by naval motorcycle guards, drive the short distance from Kernével into the countryside.

On this 19 December afternoon Dönitz walked the rolling Breton landscape with more than his usual pace and energy. The shadow war with America was over. He could now think about hostilities with the United States in the clear light of day. In the 1920s, as a young officer engaged in the theoretical naval studies known as *Winterarbeiten*, he had studied the detailed contingency plan that had been prepared by the German Admiralty Staff in 1899 for a joint Navy-Army invasion of the United States. The plan called for a direct assault on New York Harbor including the initial landing of two to three battalions of infantry and one battalion of engineers on Long Island. From New York the combined naval and land forces would spread north to Boston and south to Norfolk. The plan presumed 33.3 percent naval superiority. It also presumed complete surprise. On the latter point the plan foundered, since few navy staffers thought that a large Atlantic invasion fleet could escape detection over three thousand miles of crossing. An alternate plan calling for a preliminary seizure of Puerto Rico was considered for a time, but gave way in 1900 to a *Marschplan* (plan of advance) that called for a German armada out of Wilhelmshaven to descend on either New York or Boston through Provincetown as a *Stützpunkt* (base of operations). The revised plan envisioned a landing force of one hundred thousand men that would have to be transported to the Cape Cod peninsula. The magnitude of the operation gave pause to many in the Admiralty and Prussian General Staff, particularly since even the large force assigned to the capture of coastal forts and cities would not be sufficient to operate in the interior of the United States. Though the *Marschplan* against

America would never come up as an action item on either the Kaiser's or the Führer's agenda, it continued to fascinate naval officers of strategic mind like Dönitz.[4]

Somewhat less speculative, the commander in chief U-boats was aware, were current plans for a Luftwaffe bomber offensive against American coastal cities. The plans had been under serious consideration by Hitler since at least 22 May 1941 when as Naval Staff minutes of a Hitler conference recorded in italics: *"Führer seeks the occupation of* [the Azores] *in order to deploy long-range bombers against the United States."*[5] Major planning for a war with the United States had begun in 1937 and as early as 20 October 1940 Hitler had proposed occupying the Azores "with an eye to the future war with America."[6] In Hitler's mind Azores-based bombers should attack U.S. military installations and industrial centers and thus force the United States to invest millions of dollars in antiaircraft systems that might otherwise be shipped to Britain. Unfortunately for the Führer's plan, the aircraft being designed for the purpose, the four-engine Messerschmitt Me-264, popularly called the America-Bomber, with a range of nine thousand miles and a four-thousand-pound bomb load, did not fly until a year after Pearl Harbor, and only one was ever built.[7]

An early U-boat assault against the United States had also been proposed well before Pearl Harbor when it became clear to German strategists that the United States was an armed belligerent in everything but name. In February 1941, Hitler directed the Naval Staff to study the feasibility of a surprise U-boat assault on major U.S. navy bases and anchorages on the East Coast: Boston, New London, Newport, New York, and Hampton Roads. Such a pre–Pearl Harbor strike would have constituted a clear act of war, from which Dönitz did not shrink, angry as he was at Washington's near-total involvement with Britain's war effort, and knowing as he did that Hitler intended from the beginning to make war on the United States once he had disposed of Russia and Britain. In the event, Naval Staff concluded that such an attack was not feasible owing to the known or presumed presence of antisubmarine nets and shore batteries, and to the requirement that a U-boat attacking fleet proceed submerged at a great distance from land in order to avoid detection, which would have put an unacceptable strain on batteries.[8] Dönitz and Godt thought that the conclusion was pusillanimous. They did not share the same high regard for U.S. defenses. Dönitz in particular thought that the U.S. Navy home installations were in such a poor state of readiness that a U-boat could steam directly into the throat of New York Harbor, on the surface, at night, without being challenged. As for nets and shore batteries, he doubted their effectiveness, if they even existed. But the decision had been made and now, after Pearl Harbor, it was U.S. coastal merchant shipping that he was given permission to strike. Hitler had formally approved of the seaborne blitzkrieg on 12 December. And that was going to have to be enough.

Fifty-year-old Karl Dönitz had been a naval officer for twenty-nine years, nine of them in U-boats. Born near Berlin to a Prussian family that imbued him with the overarching values of patriotism, duty, and obedience, he entered the Navy as a sea cadet in 1910 and finished thirty-ninth in his class at the Naval Academy at Flensburg-Mürwik. His first posting was to the new cruiser *Breslau*. When World War I broke out in 1914, *Breslau* was in near-continuous operations against superior Russian forces in the Black Sea and the Mediterranean. In 1915, Dönitz both learned to fly and won the hand of Sister Ingeborg Weber, a military nurse, daughter of a German general. In 1916, married, he underwent training back in Germany for service in U-boats, and subsequently became IWO on U-*39* under Kptlt. Walter Forstmann, already an established ace. Returning to southern waters off Gibraltar and in the Adriatic, Dönitz learned from Forstmann how to sink fourteen vessels by eye and mind alone, without the aid of a *Vorhaltrechner* (electromechanical calculator)—part of the equipment of U-boats a quarter century later. He also learned from Forstmann how to be "hard in war": When U-*39* sank an Italian troop ship with the loss of all one thousand infantrymen on board, Forstmann stated, "Every soft-hearted act of mercy to the enemy would be foul treason to our own striving people."[9] In a similar statement about enemy losses in an earlier sinking, Forstmann wrote, "One must energetically put aside all sympathy, all pity and every other feeling of the kind, for there is no doubt that their influence tends to weakness. The object of war is to annihilate the armed forces of the enemy whether it be on the battlefield or in a fight at sea."[10] To judge from Dönitz's actions and commands to U-boats twenty-five years later, he was an adept pupil of Forstmann's "hard war" school. The U-boat, because of its small size and vulnerable skin, was in a naval class by itself: Unlike most surface ships, it could not pick up survivors. In 1940 Dönitz would give U-boat commanders the order: "Do not rescue any men, do not take them along, and do not take care of any boats from the ship.

Weather conditions and the proximity of land are of no consequence. Concern yourself only with the safety of your own boat and with the efforts to achieve additional successes as soon as possible. We must be hard in this war."[11] U.S. Fleet Admiral Chester W. Nimitz would testify at Dönitz's Nürnberg trial in 1945 that U.S. submarines in the Pacific also practiced unrestricted warfare and that after Pearl Harbor their procedures regarding survivors were generally the same as Dönitz's. British submarines followed the same policy in the Skagerrak (an arm of the North Sea between Denmark and Norway) from May 1940 on. In the Atlantic, U.S. policy toward crewmen survivors of sunken U-boats would be expressed as follows: "The question of a small ship picking up a large number of survivors presents itself. The Commanding Officer should be able to judge for himself. At no time should he sacrifice his ship to get survivors. . . . A life raft or small boat with food may be provided for them and their recovery effected at a later date."[12]

Dönitz received command, successively, of two boats, UC-25 and UB-68. With the first he sank a 5,000-GRT Italian collier and with the second a 3,883-GRT British steamer. While pursuing a convoy east of Malta on 4 October 1918, he experienced a diving accident that left four of his crew dead and the rest, including Dönitz, prisoners on board HMS *Snapdragon*. Taken to England, he was placed in a POW camp for officers at Redmires, near Sheffield, where to gain his release he feigned insanity—with such success that he was removed for a time (though this was not his plan) to the Manchester Lunatic Asylum. Eventually, in July 1919, he was repatriated to Germany, where he joined the new postwar Navy. In the Reichsmarine, as it was then called, he rose in rank by 1921 to Kapitänleutnant and by 1928 to Korvettenkapitän. In the latter year he commanded the Fourth Torpedo Boat Half Flotilla. Two years later he visited Ceylon and other countries in the Far East, after which he put in four years as a high Naval Staff officer at Wilhelmshaven. In June 1934, as a newly minted Fregattenkapitän eager for return to sea duty, he took command of the light cruiser *Emden* and, accompanied by his adjutant, Kptlt. Eberhard Godt, he steamed with great enthusiasm around the Cape of East Africa and on to Ceylon, thence through the Red Sea and Suez Canal to the Mediterranean, where orders awaited him to return home. Germany was secretly rebuilding its U-boat fleet, starting with Type-IIA and IIB "canoes," and the capital-ship admirals who wanted to refight the Battle of Jutland (31 May–1 June 1916) had agreed, reluctantly, that there should be an auxiliary Ubootwaffe. Would Dönitz like to be considered for Führer der Uboote (FdU)? It meant giving up a new cruise on *Emden* to Borneo, Japan, China, and Australia, but Dönitz said yes. On 28 September 1935, he took over a training fleet of thirteen boats, all that then existed—Flotilla Weddigen, named after a World War I ace. A year later, as FdU, with the first Type VIIs and Type IXs on stream, Dönitz began the creation of the U-boat force that in only three years would begin slashing at Britain's economic and military sea communications.

The year 1939 was much too early for Dönitz to go to war for a second time. He lacked both the boats and the crews. Repeatedly he insisted that three hundred was the minimum number of boats required to wage successful operations against trade in the Atlantic, and thus to sever Britain's essential lifelines. But he was forced by events and had to do the best he could with what he had. In fact, those crews he did possess had been exquisitely trained to watch-movement precision by Dönitz himself. Every commander had to have completed sixty-six surface and sixty-six submerged simulated attacks before being allowed to launch a live torpedo, while Dönitz personally watched and coached either from within the boat or from his command vessel *Saar*. The U-boatmen were his men in every sense of the word. After one of them, Günther Prien (U-47), sank the battleship HMS *Royal Oak* at Scapa Flow in the Orkneys on 14 October 1939, the then Rear Admiral Dönitz was promoted from Führer to Befehlshaber (commander in chief) Unterseeboote (BdU).

A visibly commanding figure, Dönitz stood only slightly above average height, though his extraordinarily slender frame and upright bearing lent the appearance of added stature. His countenance at fifty years was serious, even stern, but it could wrinkle quickly into a smile or even give way to a loud guffaw when something struck him as incongruous. Perhaps the best clues to his personality and attributes are those found in commendations and annual fitness reports written by superior officers from 1913 on: "Charming, dashing, plucky . . . especially good professional ability . . . strength of judgment . . . very good military appearance, socially very deft . . . popular comrade, tactful messmate . . . magnificent dash and great circumspection . . . tough and brisk officer . . . absolutely reliable . . . always in good spirits . . . taut, stern . . . quick power of perception and blameless character . . . iron willpower, goal-oriented certainty and unwearying toughness."[13] This, then, was the man who had determined to vault the Atlantic moat and test his will against the U.S. Navy's.

Since Pearl Harbor and the lifting of all restrictions on U.S. targets on 9 December Dönitz and Godt had drawn up a meticulously detailed plan for twelve Type IXB and IXC boats to strike simultaneously against offshore North America from Halifax in the north to Cape Hatteras, North Carolina, in the south. The targets were to be independently routed freighters and tankers with war cargoes vital to both U.S. and British industries and defenses. Off the United States there would as yet be no convoys in place, the naval device used since medieval times to defeat a *guerre de course,* a war on commerce. Nor, Dönitz reasoned, would there be for some months to come anything resembling an effective antisubmarine defense. Twelve boats were hardly enough to do the damage, and to create the shock, intended. One hundred boats would more exactly match the operational ideal. But the Ubootwaffe was continually short of its strategic needs. Despite the fact that he had made the German U-boats the dread of the oceans, they were still available only in absurdly small numbers.

At fault, first, was Hitler himself, the land animal, who never wanted or expected a U-boat war, failed to understand the necessity of rupturing Allied sea communications in the Atlantic, and instead poured the majority of Germany's industrial resources into tanks for warfare across his obsession: the Eurasian landmass. Just days before, Hitler had sacked his army commander, taken command of the Army himself, and rejected a Kriegsmarine plan to concentrate all available naval forces on an effort to isolate Britain and take her out of the war before America could use her as "aircraft carrier England" from which to bomb and eventually invade the continent. Hitler's eyes looked only to the east. Next to blame was OKM, Supreme Naval Command, and Grossadmiral Erich Raeder, commander in chief Navy, in particular, who failed to see before 1939 that the capital ship of the next Atlantic war would not be the dreadnought, or battleship, but, as World War I had already demonstrated (excepting the stalemate Battle of Jutland in late spring of 1916), the U-boat allied with the minelayer. Dönitz had pleaded for a fleet of three hundred U-boats that would be barely adequate for a war against British trade. With one-third of the boats in repair, another third en route to or returning from patrol stations, at any one time he would have one hundred boats on combat operations. Instead, Raeder and Hitler, influenced by a Naval Staff dominated by surface gunnery officers in the Jutland tradition, opted for a mainly surface fleet: a home fleet of four superbattleships, like *Bismarck* and *Tirpitz*, two heavy cruisers, and flotillas of destroyers; a raiding force for attacking commerce composed of three pocket battleships, five armored cruisers, five light cruisers, and 190 U-boats; and two attack forces, each of which would consist of an aircraft carrier, three fast battleships, two cruisers, and destroyers. The projected construction/completion date of this Z Plan, as it was called, was 1948![14]

When war with England broke out in September 1939, Dönitz had to go to sea with fifty-seven U-boats, only forty-six of which were operational. So small was the total fleet that Dönitz could not place more than an average of thirteen attackers on station during 1939–40, the rest being in transit to or from station, or in the repair yard. At the same time he could count on only two deliveries of new boats per month since Hitler, biased toward quick victory on the Continent, had brought U-boat construction almost to a halt. By the time full-scale construction resumed, Germany's chances of dominating the Atlantic were seriously at question. Still, with one-sixth the force he had estimated as required for a war on British trade, Dönitz scored a series of staggering successes off Britain's coast in what became known as the "happy time"—a million tons sunk from July to the end of October 1940. He easily imagined the crippling blow he could have delivered with a three-hundred-boat fleet in that first year before British defenses stiffened. The war with England could have been over.

Deliveries of new boats increased to fifteen a month by June 1941 and to twenty early the next year. Meanwhile the surface, or bluewater, fleet construction envisioned in Z Plan slowed to a near halt.[15] Ironically, the surface vessels on operational status by December 1941 had been reduced to in-port "flypaper status," their function now being to tie down the British Home Fleet that might otherwise be directed at German cities, ports, and commerce, or at targets in the Mediterranean, while the lone German capital ship, the U-boat, ranged far across the compass rose seeking prey to devour. Dönitz was proud of his boats and his crews, and of what they had been able to accomplish against enemy odds. Yet other forces continued to conspire against his plans for decisive victory at sea, including the drain on his resources to support operations in the Mediterranean and off Gibraltar and the diversion of boats to weather reporting. Also frus-

trating was the practice, defended by Raeder, of drawing off maintenance workers from U-boats to repair work on surface vessels at Kiel,
Hamburg, and Bremen; at one point eight hundred dockyard workers
were reassigned from U-boat maintenance to repair fuel tanks on the
heavy cruiser *Admiral Hipper*. Revealingly, one of Dönitz's memoranda
to Naval Staff on this subject came back with the inadvertent marginal comment, "We don't want to become a navy of U-boats."[16] Dönitz
received no satisfaction on this matter, as he lamented in his December war diary alongside bitter tallies of boats lost transiting the Strait
of Gibraltar.[17] By December his force consisted of ninety-one operational boats, of which twenty-three were in the Mediterranean, three
more under orders from Naval Staff to proceed there, six deployed
west of Gibraltar, and four stationed on a line from Reykjavik to North
Cape along the Arctic Circle. Of the remaining fifty-five, thirty-three
were in shipyards undergoing repair, eleven en route to or from operational areas, six more in various states of refit, and five on North
Atlantic patrol, including one boat, U-*653*, that Dönitz had placed west
of the Faeroe Islands as a radio decoy to simulate the presence of many
more boats than actually existed.[18]

   The cruelest blow of all came that same December when, on the
tenth, the day after restrictions were lifted on American shipping,
Dönitz asked for twelve long-distance Type IX boats to be released for
attacks against the U.S. coastal sea-lanes, and Naval Staff allowed him
only six.[19] Two were IXBs (U-*109, 123*), four were IXCs (U-*66, 125, 128,
130*). It was incredible to him that large boats plainly unsuitable for
Gibraltar duty were being maintained there instead of being assigned
where they could do the most good. Only six, then, could sail on the
most dramatic cruise of the war, which—the same 10 December—
Dönitz christened Operation Paukenschlag—"Operation Drumbeat."[20] The code name was of a type favored by Dönitz. His nomencla-
ture for the most recent U-boat operational groups in the North
Atlantic had included *Mordbrenner* (Incendiary), *Schlagetot* (Hacker),
Reisswolf (Shredder), and *Raubgraf* (Robber Baron). Paukenschlag
was designed to inflict a sudden severe injury on the American enemy.
The blow would come like a thunderbolt—or like the percussion of a
timpani stick on the tightly stretched head of a brass-barreled drum.
Intended were quick, violent sinkings and resounding psychological
shock. By having all the boats strike their first targets on the same day
he would scatter and confuse the defending forces, such as they were.
Furthermore, the simultaneity of initial attacks would prevent one

boat's successes from either spoiling the chances of the others or triggering a trap for them. The plan pleased Dönitz. The number of available boats did not, particularly when he learned that owing to mechanical problems the sixth boat assigned to the mission, the newly commissioned U-*128* (Kptlt. Ulrich Heyse), would not be able to sortie in time. Now there were five.[21]

Dönitz broke off his walking reverie, called back the scampering Wolf, and joined Meckel in the command car for the ride back to Kernével. It was time to meet three of his commanders and give them their orders.

Hardegen and his colleagues heard the crunch of the admiral's car on the gravel driveway outside and looked at one another in anticipation. A few minutes later fragments of conversation drifted in from the area of Dönitz's private office. Hardegen had been in Dönitz's office twice, both times to go over his KTB following operational patrols that he commanded on U-*123*. He expected that all three commanders would now be ordered in. A door opened. Kapitän Godt entered the situation room and looked about expressionlessly. The commanders stiffened.

"Good afternoon, gentlemen. I am pleased that you have had this opportunity to study the kinds of things we do here. At the same time I am sorry that I could not spend time with you. Please continue at your ease. The admiral will see you in a few moments. Hardegen, come with me, please."

Hardegen's pulse quickened. What had he done now? He turned in behind Godt and followed him to Dönitz's office. A brief knock on the door and the two entered. Dönitz was seated at his desk. Hardegen drew to attention and saluted in naval style with right hand to eyebrow: "Heil, Herr Admiral!"

Dönitz stood and walked around his desk to take Hardegen's hand, his usual cold formality and stern visage turning to a warm smile and kindly diction. He used the familiar *du:*

"Are you feeling all right, Hardegen?"

"Yes, Herr Admiral."

Hardegen had cause to recall how fellow officers who knew Dönitz much better spoke of the Lion as a father. No father could be more demanding of his sons or more intolerant of less-than-peak performance than Dönitz, yet no father was more solicitous of his sons' welfare or more careful to attend to their leavings and their returnings. A fixture on the arrival dock at Lorient, Dönitz elicited a depth of personal loyalty from his U-boatmen, of all ranks, that was not only unprecedented in the Kriegsmarine but was of a kind accorded few military leaders in modern history. Hardegen's split-second memory journey went back to the summer of 1940, when he had first met Dönitz at the airport in Kiel. The recollection was reassuring as he faced the admiral now under more official, if not graver, circumstances.

Dönitz moved back behind his desk, sat down, and leafed through papers in a folder before him.

"I've been looking through your dossier today, Hardegen." He turned several pages. "There is one matter that bothers me here, something that I had not noticed before. From 1935 through 1939 you were a pilot in the Naval Air Force, before being assigned to U-boats. In 1936 you were seriously injured in an air crash. Because of lasting physical effects of the crash—internal stomach bleeding, a shortened right leg, it says here—your medical papers state, among other things, that you are 'not fit for service in U-boats.' It says so right here in your record. What, then, are you doing in the Ubootwaffe?"

Dönitz looked up, puzzled.

"My medical papers never quite caught up with me, Herr Admiral," Hardegen answered. "As I went from school to school they always came late enough for me to go on to my next assignment. Then, when I returned from my first patrol on U-*147*, the Flotilla Commander at Kiel told me that he had my papers and that they stated I was unfit for U-boats. He sent me to a doctor who confirmed the opinion. So I was sent away for a four-weeks' cure to another doctor at the naval recreational center in Spindelmühle. That doctor happened to be a good friend of mine. He wrote in my medical folder that I was fit for all surface ships but not for U-boats."

Dönitz now looked at Hardegen more in the manner of a schoolmaster than a father. He reached into the folder for a letter from his second in command, Admiral Hans-Georg von Friedeburg, at Kiel. Von Friedeburg, head of the large Organization Department of the U-boat arm, superintended the "endless belt" system that supplied new boats, commanders, and crews to the operational bases.

Dönitz held out von Friedeburg's letter for Hardegen to read. "The admiral writes, as you can see, that on your return from Spindelmühle he asked you if you were then fit for return to the Ubootwaffe, and that you answered yes, you were. Why did you lie?"

A look of disappointment was now plainly on Dönitz's face. Hardegen hastened to reply.

"Sir," he said, "the admiral asked me—and these were his exact words—'Are you fit to return to sea?' And I answered him honestly, yes, I was. He never said anything about U-boats. What he said next was, 'Then you are to fly tomorrow to Lorient and take command of U-*123*.' I jumped at the chance."[22]

Dönitz's face broke into a wide grin and he surprised Godt, who was standing to one side of the office, with a single loud guffaw.

"Hardegen," he said, "I knew you were aggressive, I just didn't know you were devious. I think the word for you is *ehrgeizig* (ambitious).[23] Yes, that's you. Well, you succeeded in getting yourself a large boat. But look at you! You're as pale as a boat's wake. If I didn't need you so badly right now I'd send you to a shore assignment straightaway. And that's precisely what I'm going to do just as soon as you get back from the next patrol. Do you understand?"

"Yes, Herr Admiral."

Dönitz nodded toward Godt. "You may bring in the others."

The other two commanders filed in, stood in a row alongside Hardegen, and saluted in the customary manner. As before, Dönitz walked around his desk to shake hands with each of them, speaking with the familiar *du* and remarking on special items relating to each. He then resumed his position behind the desk and, remaining on his feet, spoke to the three together.

"Gentlemen, as you might have anticipated, I am sending you together on the same mission. I could have let your Flotilla commander, Korvettenkapitän Victor Schütze, brief you on the patrol, as is customary. But this mission is so sensitive and so important to the future victory of the Reich that I choose to brief you myself.

"I have given the same orders to Ulrich Folkers whose U-*125* sortied yesterday. Later I shall speak to the fifth member of your group, Kapitänleutnant Bleichrodt. He should be ready to sortie in a few days. [Knight's Cross holder Heinrich "Ajax" Bleichrodt, commander of U-*130*, was the most successful to date of the five commanders, having sunk fifteen ships in 1940.]

"You will provision your boats for a long cruise. Take everything that you even imagine you'll need. Torpedoes. Food. Drinking water. Medicines. Tools and spare parts. Oilskins. Leathers for your binoculars. Check your potash cartridges. Everything.

"Test-dive your boats as soon as possible after departure. Make certain you can get below the surface in thirty-five seconds. On your transit of the Bay of Biscay to the Atlantic have your best lookouts on watch and your hand on the diving alarm. The British Sunderlands will come at you out of the sun. Too slow a dive and your part in this mission will be over. Your survival in the Bay of Biscay will depend on your ability to clear the bridge, dog the hatch, and submerge the boat in thirty-five seconds—no more.

"Once into the Atlantic the possibility of air attack will diminish. But not totally. Never become complacent. We do not know all that the enemy can do. Some commanders became lax once they passed the longitudes of highest danger. Some of them are no longer with us.

"Maintain the strictest discipline on board. I don't need to tell you in detail how to do that. You would not be commanders if you have not already learned how to lead men. On this mission I want optimum performance from every man. See to it that you get it.

"On 26 December you will receive a signal from me changing depth designations, so that sixty meters in transmissions will read A plus forty meters, thirty meters' depth will read A plus ten, and so on. Be alert to this signal and to others.[24]

"Sortie individually just as quickly as your boats are ready. Korvettenkapitän Schütze will hand each of you a sealed Operation Order on departure. As the instructions indicate you will open that Order and make it known to your officers when you cross twenty degrees longitude. As you approach your target area Korvettenkapitän Meckel will transmit attack data. Study the maps in your Order carefully. You will each be assigned a separate operational area. This is not a rake operation. There will be no patrol line. You will operate independently. However, there is one important sense in which you will act *in concert*. I emphasize this. You will all begin offensive operations against targets *on the same day*. That day will be transmitted to you by radio while you are en route.

"When you sortie into the bay take radio bearings on Saint John's and Cape Race, Newfoundland, and follow the Great Circle route. That will keep you on course until you open your orders and learn your exact destination. During your passage to the operational area, except for the initial short signal position reports, maintain absolute wireless silence. I will call you when I want you to transmit. For purposes of control I am naming U-*123*, *125*, and *66* as Gruppe Hardegen and *109* and *130* as Gruppe Bleichrodt.[25] Economize on fuel. The more fuel you save, the more time you will have on station. And when in place I expect you to move aggressively against all targets of opportunity. Because of the necessity of surprise you are not to attack any ships en route to your assigned areas unless you are convinced that the target exceeds ten thousand tons. We never let a ten-thousand-tonner go by.

"As you could see from the maps in our situation room, the number of combat boats in the main North Atlantic shipping lanes is smaller today than it was at the start of the war. Only five, and four of them are on passage to the Mediterranean.[26] We are going back into the Battle of the Atlantic, gentlemen. Your boats are the vanguard. We will beat the waters like a drum. This is Atlantic Order Number forty-six. I have named the mission Operation Paukenschlag. ["Drumbeat"]. Your five boats alone will constitute the force.[27] I intend this operation to succeed. And it will succeed if you live up to the charge contained in our U-boat motto: *Angreifen! Ran! Versenken!* —Attack! Advance! Sink!

"Do you understand my orders?"

"Yes, Herr Admiral!" the three commanders responded in unison. Dönitz walked around his desk, shook hands sternly with each man, and nodded to Godt, who opened the office door.

"This way, gentlemen," Godt said, leading the officers to the foyer, where they donned their coats and caps and then walked down the eight steps to the waiting cars.

The usually irrepressible Hardegen was subdued. "Well, I don't understand the orders at all," he said to his back-seat companions as their vehicle passed through the sentry gate.

"That's because he said nothing about America," said one. "We're not going to America. When he mentioned the St. John's and Cape Race beacons, that should have been your clue. I bet you're headed back to your fogs in the Strait of Belle Isle!"

Hardegen groaned. But then, he reasoned, he was lucky to be going anywhere at all.

In the days immediately following Pearl Harbor, Adolf Hitler's mind was pulled in two contrary directions. On the one hand he denigrated U.S. military power and considered the average American fighting man incompetent if not cowardly. On the other hand—though OKM endeavored to erase such memories—the Führer was aware that the United States' entry into World War I, in 1917, had been decisive in the resolution of that conflict, and that Germany's unrestricted U-boat campaign in that year had been the most important single factor leading to American intervention. Thus, ever since the previous June, when Germany invaded the Soviet Union (Operation Barbarossa) expecting to conquer the Russian defenders with a series of *Blitzfeldzüge* (lightning campaigns), Hitler had assiduously avoided any incident that might provoke U.S. entry into the war at that particular time; though from other evidence it is clear that he intended to make war on the United States after other, more immediate targets had been seized or neutralized. That caution was expressed on the very eve of the eastward plunge by Dönitz's superior, Grossadmiral Raeder: "Until the effects of Barbarossa can be seen, that is, for several weeks, the Führer wants every possible incident with the U.S.A. to be strictly avoided."[28] As events transpired that caution had had to be observed for months instead of weeks. On 9 July, anticipating victory in the east no sooner than September, Hitler told Raeder: "It is vitally important to put off America's entry into the war. . . . There must be no incidents with the U.S.A. before mid-October."[29] This policy, it must be acknowledged, required considerable restraint. The official animus of the United States toward what President Franklin D. Roosevelt called "the Nazi tyranny" was by this date overt to the point of undeclared war, and certain actions had been taken by the United States so that— under prevailing international law violated so frequently and so blatantly by Hitler—a case could be made by a dispassionate jurist that the United States had abandoned its long-declared neutrality and was now an avowed belligerent.

The first tentative U.S. step toward armed intervention could be discerned in the Third Neutrality Act of 1937, reconfirmed in 1939, which allowed that such commodities as copper, steel, aluminum, and lead, which could be used in the manufacture of weaponry and munitions, might be sold to other nations (read Britain and France) on a "cash and carry" basis. A proviso required foreign purchasers to haul the cargoes in their own ships. It was not expected that German merchantmen could pass through a British-French blockade, so the bias of the act was clear. In October 1939, the United States persuaded the other republics in the Western Hemisphere to sign the Declaration of Panama, establishing a Pan-American "security" or "safety" zone around the Americas, inside which, other nations were warned, no belligerent action should take place. The protected waters ranged from three hundred to one thousand miles offshore. (In December 1939, Roosevelt had to slap Britain on the wrist for her three-cruiser action that crippled the German pocket battleship *Admiral Graf Spee* a short distance off the Uruguayan coast.) The administration further directed that "planes or Navy or Coast Guard ships *may* report the sighting of any submarine or suspicious surface ships in plain English to Force Commander or Department"—action that plainly favored British antisubmarine patrols.[30]

In September 1940, with solid Gallup Poll backing (62 percent), the president agreed to transfer fifty 1,060- to 1,090-ton World War I vintage four-stack destroyers to Britain in exchange for six military bases under ninety-nine-year leases in the Bahamas, Jamaica, Antigua, St. Lucia, Trinidad, and British Guiana. At the same time, in a separate package, Britain ceded bases in Argentia (Newfoundland) and Bermuda as outright gifts. The destroyers were rusting "old iron" antiques, ten of which barely made it across the Atlantic. But even in decrepit condition they would contribute substantially to Britain's antisubmarine program, which, owing to the loss of destroyers at Dunkirk and to the fact that some 70 percent of the remaining destroyer force was laid up for repairs, was in desperate shape. In April 1941, the U.S. Navy delivered to the Royal Navy an additional ten 250-foot Lake-class Coast Guard cutters that were well armed and suited for escort of convoy. (Washington may have worried that the U.S. Navy might need these destroyers and cutters in its own coastal waters a short time later, but Britain's was the current emergency.) There was no question in any one's mind, least of all in Germany, that the warship transfers constituted explicit breach of the neutrality provisions generally honored in international law since the Hague Conference of 1907. British Prime Minister Winston Churchill would write nine years later that the destroyer deal "was a decidedly unneutral act by the United States" that would have "justified" Hitler in declaring war.[31] In Berlin at the time there was great indignation over the deal, which was seen as plainly threatening Germany's U-boat war against Britain. Hitler himself, however, remained silent. He would save this incident, along with others, for use in a scathing list of particulars delivered to the Reichstag fourteen months later.

Roosevelt's "arsenal of democracy," as he called the U.S. industrial base, moved even closer to armed participation in the war with the adoption by Congress of the Lend-Lease Act of March 1941. Under this act the U.S. abandoned "cash and carry" transactions in raw materials for a direct transfer to England of finished weapons and munitions on a deferred return, or lease, arrangement—a specious future possibility that Roosevelt rationalized to the American people by citing the homespun example of lending a length of garden hose to a neighbor whose home was on fire. Despite bitter isolationist objection, Gallup Polls showed that this new experiment in "short of war" interventionism had support from 71 percent of the population. During February and March, Washington seized German and Italian ships and those from German-occupied countries in U.S. harbors "to prevent their sabotage"; froze German and Italian assets in the United States; pledged to train eight thousand Royal Air Force pilots at U.S. airfields, mostly in Florida; and out of three destroyer squadrons and four flying-boat squadrons, used since 1939 as an Atlantic "neutrality patrol," created a Support Force of twenty-seven destroyers to escort merchant ship convoys from North America as far as Iceland. This force, together with two aircraft carriers, three battleships, five heavy cruisers, and four light cruisers, was designated Atlantic Fleet effective 1 February and its commander, Rear Admiral Ernest J. King, was promoted to admiral, commander in chief Atlantic Fleet (CINCLANT). The shortening of "short of war" gained momentum during April and May when Roosevelt authorized the transfer of additional battleships, light cruisers, and destroyers as well as the carrier *Yorktown* from Pearl Harbor to the Atlantic. On 9 April the United States signed an agreement permitting the establishment of U.S. military bases and meteorological stations in Greenland. Nine days later, in the manner of Pope Alexander VI drawing his famous line of demarcation to distinguish between the New World property rights of Spain and Portugal, Roosevelt drew a line that extended the Western Hemisphere, thereafter the Pan-American Security Zone, to about west longitude twenty-six—the meridian that passes some fifty miles west of Reykjavik, Iceland. The new zone extended 2,300 nautical miles east of New York, covered approximately four-fifths of the Atlantic, and included in addition to Greenland all the islands of the European Azores. On 7 July, as a concrete expression of these claims, a U.S. occupation force of 4,095 Marines steamed into Reykjavik harbor; and on the fifteenth Roosevelt revised his reading of the Western Hemisphere eastward to twenty-two degrees west longitude, to include Iceland. The United States was edging into the Battle of the Atlantic, as both Churchill and the *New York Times* were now calling the ocean struggle. When in September the U.S. Navy assumed full responsibility for escorting Britain-bound convoys as far as a mid-ocean meeting point (MOMP), or "chop" (Change of Operational Control) line, south of Iceland, where British escorts from Western Approaches Command took the guard, the odds greatly increased out on the deep that despite Hitler's still-tight leash on the Ubootwaffe one of Dönitz's boats would tangle with one of Admiral King's destroyers.

There had been incidents at sea before September. In the first, on 10 April off the coast of Iceland, the destroyer USS *Niblack* rescued three boatloads of survivors from a torpedoed Netherlands freighter, and in the process made sound contact with what was thought to be a submarine, range closing. *Niblack* dropped depth charges—the first American shots fired in World War II—but the lack of visible result combined with the absence of any account of the incident in German archives leads to the presumption that *Niblack*'s was a false contact. More certain and serious was a second incident, on 21 May, the sinking of a 5,000-ton American freighter, SS *Robin Moor*, on the edge of the Pan-American Security Zone in the South Atlantic. The ship carried a general cargo and flew the American flag. After sailing hundreds of miles in open boats the thirty-eight member crew and eight passengers were rescued. Two years later, an unrepentant Kptlt. Jost Metzler, commander of the attacking boat, U-*69*, justified his actions in a propaganda book as motivated by suspicion that the *Robin Moor* was a Q-ship (armed decoy vessel).[32] He was never disciplined by BdU. Roosevelt called the sinking "ruthless" and on 27 May declared an "unlimited national emergency." The State Department demanded compensation from Germany for the *Robin Moor*. Berlin defiantly rejected the demand. Hitler remained silent.

On 20 June, though the incident was not known until after the war, U-*203*, commanded by Kptlt. Rolf Mützelburg, attempted to attack U.S. battleship *Texas* in the Western Approaches to Britain. After a sixteen-hour pursuit U-*203* was not able to overtake *Texas* and obtain a favorable attack position.[33] There is no record to show that Mützelburg, either, was held to account for violating the Führer's strict directive against "incidents," and Dönitz seems to have accepted his commander's explanation that he thought the battleship, like the fifty destroyers, had been transferred to the British—a suspicion lent some credence from the fact that *Texas* was east of the Pan-American Security Zone and inside the announced German operational area surrounding the British Isles.[34] Dönitz issued new orders to all boats: "U.S.A. warships should not be attacked even in the blockade area, since the present [BdU] permission to do this does not seem to agree with the political views of the Führer."[35] Fearing that boat commanders might mistake a U.S. destroyer for one of the fifty former U.S. destroyers exchanged to Britain, on 21 June Hitler required BdU to signal all boats that, "Attacks on warships within and outside the blockade area" must until further notice be limited to "cruisers, battleships and aircraft carriers and only if these are definitely recognized as enemy [excluding U.S.] vessels."[36]

These last orders were particularly galling to boat commanders since it was the destroyers, corvettes, and frigates that provided the most effective curtain of protection to the U-boats' targets and it was the escorts, when aroused, that were the U-boats' most mortal threat. As a corrective to flagging U-boat morale, OKM issued a subsidiary order permitting a U-boat to defend itself against escorts when under attack, "but only while an attack on it was in actual progress."[37] Even with this proviso the new orders markedly favored the British antisubmarine forces, as Dönitz lamented: "Whenever a destroyer succeeded in locating a U-boat, it attacked it with depth charges or gunfire and destroyed it before it had time to reply."[38] Furthermore, the U-boats were hampered in their attacks on convoys because the surrounding screen of escort vessels was now untouchable. Throughout the remainder of the year resentment among commanders at the Hitler-imposed handicaps was widely shared and commented on. Germany, the commanders argued, was being forced to fight with one hand tied behind her back, and understandably they scorned American naval personnel for waging a war in which they could not be hurt. Despite the restrictions the North Atlantic remained a killing sea, although the records disclose that U-boat successes declined in number during the summer of 1941, and there were no further "incidents" until the first week of September, when the political and ostensible attempts by both U.S. and German governments to avoid exchange of fire, on the U.S. side by neutrality legislation, on the German side by restriction of U-boat operations, were overtaken by events.

At 0840 on the morning of 4 September USS *Greer*, a World War I twelve-hundred-ton flush-deck "four-piper" destroyer that the U.S. Navy had kept, was steaming independently toward Iceland at 17.5 knots with mail, freight, and military passengers when she received blinker signals from a British bomber. The plane reported that a U-boat lay submerged directly athwart her course about ten miles ahead. *Greer*'s officers sounded general quarters, rang up 20 knots, and took a zigzag course to the spot, where, after slowing, the destroyer's sound crew made contact and held it fast. Standing rules of engagement called for U.S. ships in such situations, where there was no U.S. or Icelandic-flag shipping to defend, to do no more than "trail and report." When this became clear to the bomber pilot who had remained overhead, he dropped his depth charges in a random pattern and headed back to base. Below the surface in U-652, Kptlt. Georg-Werner Fraatz had reason to believe that the exploding charges came from the ship above him with which he was maintaining his own sound contact. Accordingly, he came to periscope depth and, after identifying the destroyer as belonging to the same class that had been traded to Britain and concluding that OKM's subsidiary orders permitted him to defend himself in these circumstances, launched two torpedoes, ten minutes apart, at his pursuer. Both missed. Greer then responded with a pattern of eight depth charges, which, except for minor damage to U-652, also missed their mark. Greer subsequently broke off the chase ten hours after the first contact, and Kptlt. Fraatz repaired to less dangerous waters where, six days later, he took out two British merchantmen.

The exchange-of-fire "incident" had finally happened. Through miscalculation both Hitler's cunning caution and Washington's false neutrality had vaporized. From that date it can be stated that open naval war existed between the United States and Germany. An outraged President Roosevelt issued orders to "eliminate" the U-boat involved, which was hardly possible. To a news conference he described the attack on Greer as unprovoked, which he would learn later was not exactly true. In a "fireside chat" to the nation by radio on 11 September he spoke of the U-boats as "rattlesnakes of the Atlantic" and, though he did not use the phrase as such, indicated that henceforth U.S. warships would "shoot on sight" (as the press put it) all German and Italian vessels that endangered waters vital to American defense.

In a Navy Day address sixteen days later Roosevelt himself used the "shoot on sight" phrase to describe U.S. intentions. Conventional histories that treat of the subject maintain that this was the first operation order directing U.S. ships and aircraft to fire on German or Italian naval forces.[39] In fact FDR was merely articulating in public operation orders that Admiral King, with his tacit approval, had issued secretly months earlier. Documents found in King's command papers disclose that U.S. "neutrality" had been more of a pretense than was earlier believed and that, in fact, as long as six months prior to Pearl Harbor, U.S. Navy escorts in the Atlantic were under orders to initiate belligerent actions should enemy forces be sighted or sound-detected. Beginning in July, King issued a series of operation plans that contained such language as: "Destroy hostile forces which threaten shipping of U.S. and Iceland flag"; "my interpretation of threat to U.S. or Iceland flag shipping, whether escorted or not, is that threat exists when potentially hostile vessels are actually *within sight or sound contact* of such shipping or its escort [emphasis added]."[40]

The orders would obviously impact first on the perimeter forces, including the twenty-seven destroyers (DDs) of the Support Force, Atlantic Fleet. This force, which was also designated Northwest Escort Force and Task Force Four, was under the command of Rear Admiral Arthur LeR. Bristol, Jr., who was never in any doubt about the quality of his U-boat foes: "There is no doubt that they are a determined, bold and well-trained enemy with super-excellent material to work with."[41] On 19 July King issued Operation Order No. 6-41, which, given in the context of the base in Iceland, directed U.S. naval forces to attack any U-boats or other German or Italian warships found within one hundred miles of an American-escorted convoy to or from that island. "Shoot on sight" was formally adopted as U.S. policy at the Atlantic Conference of Roosevelt and Churchill at Argentia on 9–12 August. On 1 September the policy was implemented, effective 15 September, by U.S. Navy Operation Order No. 7-41 (Secret Serial 00164).[42]

Navy orders took a more concrete form on 5 November, in circumstances that, had occasion provided their being acted upon, might well have precipitated a German declaration of war. Acting on intelligence that German pocket battleship *Admiral Scheer* (or possibly battleship *Tirpitz*) was expected to sortie from its base in Norway, King deployed a battle fleet out of Iceland to prevent by force *Scheer*'s breakout into the Atlantic convoy lanes. Designated Task Force One and consisting of battleships *Mississippi* and *Idaho*, cruisers *Tuscaloosa* and *Wichita*, with three destroyers, the squadron took up attack positions athwart the Denmark Strait (between Iceland and Greenland). As it happened, machinery damage kept *Scheer* in port. Had the German raider entered the Atlantic as planned, it is not likely that she would have survived an encounter with the American fleet, and Hitler would have had no option but to declare war on the United States. According to German naval historian Jürgen Rohwer, the loss of fifty men in a U-boat could be kept quiet; the loss of a capital ship with one thousand hands could not. Pride, face, and anger would have forced the Führer's hand and moved his declaration forward from December to November, well ahead of Pearl Harbor.[43]

Whether the president personally had wanted such an incident as *Greer*/U-652 to occur so that the United States might throw itself more fully into the conflict on Britain's side has long been conjectured and debated. If that was indeed his wish he could gain assurance from the Gallup Poll of 2 October which showed that 62 percent of the citizenry supported the "shoot on sight" stance. In Berlin the Nazi press railed against Roosevelt the "callous liar." The Foreign Ministry condemned this latest charade of *die amerikanische Short-of-War Politik*. Admirals Raeder and Dönitz went to Hitler on 17 September. Dönitz proposed that if the United States was to be drawn into the war he wished to have ample warning so as to be able to station his forces off the American coast before war was officially declared. Hitler was not interested in such contingency plans, however, and, as though to say war with the United States was not contemplated, simply repeated his directive that all incidents with American ships were to be avoided.

A favorite tactic of Dönitz's, originally suggested in 1917 by Kommodore Hermann Bauer, flag officer for U-Boats of the German High Seas Fleet in World War I, first tested in Atlantic exercises in Spring, 1939, and many times since proven successful in actual combat, was to mass U-boats in a patrol line across the known or suspected path of a transatlantic convoy. The *Rudeltaktik*, or wolf-pack technique, as the British called it, required both a high degree of coordination among the available boats and effective wireless (radio) communications. The first boat to sight a convoy signaled its position, course, and speed to BdU, Dönitz's operations center at Kernével, then continued to shadow the convoy and report any changes. BdU radioed the information to all nearby boats and directed them into position for a concentrated night attack on the surface. In Dönitz's system U-boats did almost all their fighting at night on the surface, in the manner of oceangoing torpedo boats, diving only to evade enemy ships and planes or bad weather. Submerged attacks by periscope were the exception rather than the rule: Electric motor power under water could provide speeds no higher than six to seven knots, hardly enough for the maneuvering required to obtain and maintain attack positions on moving convoys. Another advantage was that British underwater detection gear (ASDIC, later called sonar) was useless for picking up nonsubmerged targets.

Learning of these surface tactics usually comes as a surprise to Americans who are more familiar, through books and motion pictures, with the periscope operations of U.S. Navy submarines in the Pacific; though, in fact, most U.S. submarine attacks on Japanese convoys from 1942 forward similarly took place on the surface at night. U.S. popular misconceptions of U-boat tactics in World War II were well demonstrated in the 1943 Warner Brothers film, *Action in the North Atlantic* (starring Raymond Massey and Humphrey Bogart), which depicted wolf packs attacking Allied convoys from underwater. The same film portrayed U-boat crews operating in spit-and-polish uniforms (!). On the surface German U-boats could take advantage of the darkness, of their low silhouettes with decks awash—this was particularly true of the Type VIIC, workhorse of the convoy battles— and of their high speed (seventeen to eighteen knots) under diesel engine power: On the surface U-boats could outrun the Flower-class corvette, one of the most numerous British armed escort type. With all boats in place the wolf packs pounced suddenly and swiftly. The resulting torpedo onslaught coming from many directions invariably broke up a convoy's disciplined columns and spread confusion among the escorts.

On the night of 15 October such a patrol line, or "rake," of U-boats was arrayed at fifteen-mile intervals across the route of slow convoy SC 48, which, with forty-nine loaded merchant ships in eleven columns protected by only four corvettes and a destroyer, was moving east at seven knots about four hundred miles south of Iceland. On an agreed signal the wolf pack struck from ambush and sank four freighters. The escort commander appealed for help to Reykjavik. The U.S. Chief of Naval Operations Staff ordered Destroyer Escort Unit 4.1.4. to disperse Westbound Convoy ON 24, which it was accompanying, and to proceed at once to the assistance of SC 48. After making twenty-three–twenty-five knots on course 009 in heavy seas, the escort unit intercepted the stricken convoy and took up stations: destroyers *Kearny*, port flank; *Plunkett* (flagship), center ahead; *Livermore*, starboard bow; and *Decatur*, starboard flank. The fifth destroyer of the unit, the now-famous *Greer*, arrived late on station because of low fuel and heavy seas. A British and a Free French warship also answered the summons. The following night, 16–17 October, brought worse havoc, however, as the wolf pack stood on the surface in a bow-attack position outside the protective screen and fan-launched torpedoes into the long lines of ships, hitting and sinking six.

In the melee one of the Iceland-based destroyers, the barely year-old USS *Kearny*, was discovered by U-*568* as a nearly motionless silhouette against the light of a fiercely burning freighter. Kptlt. Joachim Preuss decided that she was British, as he subsequently signaled Dönitz, and, even though the prohibition against attacking destroyers still stood, he put a torpedo into *Kearny's* starboard side. The stricken but tough new *Benson*-class destroyer was able to make the fleet anchorage of Hvalfjordhur at Iceland under her own steam, escorted by *Greer*, but the casualty list was high: eleven seamen dead, twenty-four wounded. For the first time American blood joined the Atlantic war. Two other incidents followed hard on the heels of *Kearny*. A German bomber sank the U.S. freighter *Steel Seafarer* 220 miles south of Suez on 5 September, with no loss of life. And on 19 October the U.S. freighter *Lehigh*, steaming in ballast off West Africa with its name, "USA," and two large American flags painted on each side of the hull, was sunk in daylight by U-*126* (Kptlt. Ernst Bauer). All thirty-nine crewmen were rescued. Reactions in Washington and Berlin were predictable.

That the U.S. Navy was now totally involved in the Battle of the Atlantic became clear in the last two days of October. On the thirtieth, while part of Westbound Convoy ON 28, the armed eight-thousand-ton fleet oiler USS *Salinas* took two torpedoes from U-*106* (Kptlt. Hermann Rasch). Quick and effective damage control prevented the ship from sinking, and Navy gunners on Number Four gun took the submerging U-boat under fire, though without known effect. Nearby destroyers drove the Germans off with depth charges. U-*106* signaled Dönitz that he had sunk the tanker.[44] *Salinas* would make port successfully, in Saint Johns, Newfoundland. Not so, however, USS *Reuben James*. At daybreak on the thirty-first this venerable "four-piper" was on escort duty with fast convoy HX 156 in the MOMP area about six hundred miles west of Ireland. Stationed some two thousand yards on the flank of the forty-four-ship formation, *Reuben James* was in process of turning to track a suspicious bearing on her direction finder when the warhead of a torpedo from U-*552* (Kptlt. Erich Topp) blew open the port side near Number 1 stack. A second, more violent explosion followed directly, probably from ignition of the forward magazine, and produced such energy that the hull lifted from the water and the entire forward section blew off aft of the Number 3 stack. The stern section remained afloat for about five minutes, then descended noisily beneath the surface. As it did so several on-board depth charges exploded killing a number of survivors who were clinging to rafts, life jackets, and balsa floats in the black oil and icy brine. Two nearby destroyers found alive only 45 of the ship's company of 160. They looked, rescuers said, like "black shiny seals." No officers survived. *Reuben James* was the first vessel of the U.S. Navy to be lost in World War II. Said U.S. Chief of Naval Operations Admiral Harold R. Stark: "Whether the country knows it or not *we are at war.*"[45] Though the bereaved families mourned the loss of more than a hundred bluejackets, the nation at large, noting that no draftees were on the casualty list and that death at sea was a risk taken by every career Navy man, showed more interest in the forthcoming Army-Navy football game. As playwright and White House familiar Robert E. Sherwood put it, "There was a sort of tacit understanding among Americans that nobody was to get excited if ships were sunk by U-boats because that's what got us into the war the other time."[46] One voice perhaps more sensitive to the human losses was that of balladeer Woody Guthrie, who sang:

> Tell me what were their names?
> Tell me what were their names?
> Did you have a friend
> On the good *Reuben James?*[47]

The following two months brought an unexpected lull in the Atlantic war. During November U-boats sank only fifteen ships, by far the lowest monthly total of the year. December's total was identical, but it included two U.S. merchantmen, *Astral* and *Sagadahoc.*[48] At Kernével a pained Admiral Dönitz entered his reasons for this decline in the BdU war diary: Over his strenuous objections Naval High Command had pulled increasing numbers of his boats out of the Atlantic battle line and placed them instead either in or just off the Mediterranean to attack British supply transports during the British winter offensive against General Erwin Rommel's Afrika Korps. What was worse, during November-December a precious eight boats were sunk off Portugal and the Strait of Gibraltar and another three in the Mediterranean. OKM had assigned a few other boats to weather missions. Dönitz could understand the emergency in North Africa. By 7 December the British offensive "Crusader," directed toward Tripoli, had Rommel reeling in his first retreat of the desert campaign. British support shipping had to be slowed (as it would be, starting at the turn of the year). Dönitz acknowledged that U-boats were required in the Mediterranean for political and strategic reasons, but by December the diversions to weather stations had thoroughly frustrated him.

"The *decisive* point of view, in my opinion," he recorded, "is that the U-boat is the *only* weapon with which we can conduct naval warfare against England *on the offensive*. If one considers the battle against Britain as decisive for the outcome of the war, then the U-boats must be given *no* tasks that divert them from the main theaters of this battle. The war in the Atlantic has been suspended for weeks now—the first objective must be to resume it with new forces as soon and as thoroughly as possible."[49] Lacking an air arm, BdU needed as many boats in the water as possible in order to discover the location of convoys. And then it needed as many torpedoes on location as possible if it was to have any chance at all to win the "tonnage war"—that is, to sink more ships than the enemy could build. Dönitz calculated that Germany would have to inflict a monthly loss of 700,000 GRT if England was to be brought to her knees. (Britain estimated that a 600,000-ton monthly loss would be enough to do her in. She relied on the Atlantic "bridge of ships" for much of her food, many of her finished weapons, most of her raw materials, and all of her oil.) If 1941 was any barometer of advance toward that goal, Dönitz had reason for concern: In May the harvest was 421,440 GRT claimed (367,498 actual); in June 441,173 claimed (328,219 actual); in July 227,699 claimed (105,320 actual); in August 168,734 claimed (83,427 actual); in September 399,775 claimed (207,638 actual); in October 601,569 claimed (370,345 actual); and in November 85,811 claimed (68,549 actual).[50] It was a tonnage contest that Germany was fated to lose, but at two critical junctures—the forthcoming massacre of shipping off the U.S. East Coast and the climactic battles between an enlarged Ubootwaffe and North Atlantic convoys in the spring of 1943—it was to be a near thing.

As for Adolf Hitler, the final provocation for which he had to summon forbearance was the U.S. war plan, Rainbow 5, or Navy War Plan 46, leaked by isolationist Senator Burton K. Wheeler of Montana to the like-minded *Chicago Tribune*, which gave it front-page play on 4 December beneath the largest headline typeface in *Tribune* history: FDR'S WAR PLANS! This plan had been drawn up by U.S. Army and

Navy strategists as a joint contingency understanding based on a strategic concept first put forward by Admiral Stark in a "Plan Dog" memorandum of November 1940. British military leaders had accepted the plan in the following March under what was called ABC-I Staff Agreement. The most notable revelations in the war plan, several times revised as to particulars, were that: (1) the Atlantic and European battle areas were the decisive theaters; (2) Japan and the Pacific theater should be held in check as second priority; (3) Britain and Russia alone could not defeat Germany; and (4) a massive invasion of the European continent in 1943 (in fact, it was 1944) by U.S. and British troops would be required for victory. The fundamental soundness of Rainbow 5 would be borne out in time.

For the moment, President Roosevelt was well aware that, having mustered margins of only thirteen votes in the Senate and eighteen in the House on 13 November to permit merchantmen to sail with armed guard detachments (Navy gun crews) into British ports, it was extremely unlikely that he would get a declaration of war through Congress if he wanted one. Still-strong isolationist feeling precluded it. Furthermore, many in the country feared that full-scale intervention on behalf of England would have the coincidental effect of saving Communist Russia, and thus of spreading communism in the wake of prevailing Soviet armies. These Americans thought that the wisest U.S. policy was to stand back and let the two totalitarian powers, Germany and Russia, destroy each other. The president was aware, too, of the provisions of the Tripartite Pact signed by the Axis powers, Germany, Italy, and Japan, on 27 September 1940, whereby each party pledged to come to the aid of the others should one of them be attacked by a power not then engaged in hostilities. By this pact Hitler was assured that Germany would not have to face alone an intervention by the United States, as had happened in World War I. What that meant for Roosevelt was that an American declaration of war against Germany would immediately involve U.S. forces in a two-ocean war, for which he thought the country unprepared. (As he would find out soon enough, the country was unprepared to take on Hitler alone in the form of Paukenschlag.) As December came the president hardened his intention to pursue for the time being the same policy of undeclared war. As December came, too, a carrier task force of one of the Axis countries was far out to sea, observing radio silence, bound for the Hawaiian Islands and about to decide things for everybody. Declarations of war were coming through the back door.

At Naval High Command (OKM) in Berlin, Grossadmiral Raeder and his Operations Staff followed developments in the United States with a wary eye. On 6 December the staff concluded that with the latest revisions to U.S. naval and merchant ship conduct in the Atlantic, the Americans had "now reached a point where an open declaration of war cannot make any appreciable difference." If American ships were to continue to be permitted to carry food and munitions to Britain without running any risk of U-boat attack, the chances of a successful war against Britain's supply pipeline would diminish in the proportion that American tonnage, certain to increase in numbers, replaced that of the enemy. "Therefore the Naval Staff considers the present instructions no longer tenable under which the United States, which is in fact an active participant in the war, receives more considerate treatment than a country which is actually neutral. . . . The Naval Staff renews its demand for permission to wage war within the entire Pan American Security Zone . . ."[51]

The staff, like the whole Kriegsmarine, was mindful at this juncture that among all the German naval forces available for action only the U-boat arm had permission to sortie and fight. The surface, or blue-water fleet, smaller than that of World War I, and far inferior in numbers to the British Home Fleet across the North Sea, was now little more than a fleet-in-being, effective as a menace in tying down British warships that might otherwise reinforce the Mediterranean fleets but otherwise bottled up in Breton, German, and Norwegian ports. Notable among its losses by this date were the pocket battleship *Admiral Graf Spee* (actually an armored cruiser of the *Panzerschiffe* class), scuttled in December 1939 off Montevideo, Uruguay, in an action that still shamed the Navy; *Blücher*, a heavy cruiser of the *Admiral Hipper* class sunk by Oslo shore batteries during the invasion of Norway in April 1940; the cruiser *Karlsruhe*, lost to British torpedoes off Norway the same day as *Blücher;* and the new heavy battleship *Bismarck*, which had dared to sortie from Norwegian waters on 18 May 1941 in search of Atlantic merchant tonnage and—though on her course she sank the British battle cruiser HMS *Hood* in twenty-four minutes—had fallen victim nine days after departure to a British combined air-sea force, going to the bottom with all but 110 of her crew of 2,000 officers and men. The losses had cast an enervating spell over Hitler. Although Raeder pressed him hard to release ships such as the new heavy battleship *Tirpitz* (at Kiel; after 16 January 1942, at Trondheim, Norway) and the battle cruisers *Scharnhorst* and

Gneisenau (at Brest, France) for forays against Atlantic commerce, the Führer remained obdurate: Capital ships must remain in port. An exception to the rule was permitted soon afterward, on 11–12 February 1942, when the *Scharnhorst* and *Gneisenau,* joined by the heavy cruiser *Prinz Eugen,* broke out of Brest and made a brilliant daylight run through the Strait of Dover to less-exposed harbors in the Elbe and at Wilhelmshaven. But the now-famous Channel dash was hardly offensive action.

With U-boats, the only dependable offensive weapons, withdrawn from the Atlantic and the symbolic might of the surface fleet immobilized by order from above, the Kriegsmarine was in a state close to suspended animation. No wonder the proud Naval Staff, hearing the news of Pearl Harbor the night of 7 December and dismayed that such a decisive blow had been delivered by the Japanese instead of the German Navy, expressed itself in plaintive terms: "It is that much more painful for the Naval Staff that the German Navy cannot be the one to deal the decisive blows whose historical significance is being felt already. . . . The Navy is not even in a position to exploit decisively in the Atlantic and the Mediterranean the great advantage which the war in the Pacific brings."[52]

Despite the attack on Pearl Harbor by Germany's ally Japan, despite even the numerous American provocations, it would still not appear to have been in Hitler's interests to declare war on the United States in December 1941—just at the time when Germany needed to focus all her resources, manpower, and energies, not to mention her concentration, against the Soviet Union in the East. The Führer's master plan required the conquest of Russia before all else. With victory in the East, an isolated England would futilely confront a continental colossus; with most of the German military might returned to stations in the West no invasion force such as the one envisioned in Navy War Plan 46 had a chance to succeed. The wisest course, it would have seemed at the time, was to let the United States exhaust her interest and energies in the Pacific war. That country's conflict with Japan, furthermore, could be expected to draw off naval escorts from the North Atlantic. Germany could then marshal all her armed services, sea as well as land and air, in the climactic struggle with Russia. This was all-the-more pressing a need on 7 December as the Wehrmacht divisions before Moscow that day, paralyzed by minus thirty-eight degrees Celsius temperatures and two-meter snowdrifts, were being forced into their first retreat of the war, and, as one result, a crisis was erupting in the Army Supreme Command (OKW). It was hardly a propitious time for new adventures, particularly with respect to an adversary whose industrial might alone portended great trouble, and the introduction of whose arms and propaganda in 1917 had helped decide the only previous war the two nations had fought against each other. Even Hitler's contempt for the "decadent" American military could not keep his eyes from certain of these realities.

The Tripartite Pact concluded with Axis partners Italy and Japan in September 1940 specified only that Germany would intervene militarily if either or both the other partners were attacked by another power, assumed to be the United States. In spring 1941, Hitler made verbal promises to Japanese Foreign Minister Yosuke Matsuoka to come in on the Japanese side if Japan initiated an attack, but those promises had not formally been signed. Hitler's real wish had been that Japan attenuate Britain's or Russia's war-making power by an attack on Singapore or Vladivostok.[53] In early December, however, while the Pearl Harbor attackers were approaching Hawaii, the Japanese demanded that Germany and Italy formally sign off on the Hitler-Matsuoka conversation, which would constitute a new tripartite agreement, to be kept secret until war had begun. The most important article in the agreement so far as Hitler was concerned was the one prohibiting any of the Axis powers from concluding a *Sonderfriedensvertrag*, a separate armistice or peace with England, the United States, or both.

Following the events of 7 December, except for deliberations with his foreign minister Joachim von Ribbentrop, Hitler pursued his options secretly, not bothering to consult even his military advisers. The first rent in the seamless policy by which he had sought by all means to avoid war with the United States came on 9 December when, whether by impulse or design—the records are unclear—Hitler released Admiral Dönitz from all prior restrictions on naval warfare against the United States, which was henceforth to be regarded as an enemy. With a relish quite at variance with the despondent expressions of the Naval Staff, Dönitz wrote in his war diary:

> The lifting of all restrictions regarding U.S.A. ships and the so-called Pan-American Safety Zone has been ordered by the Führer. Therefore the whole area of the American coasts will become open for operations by U-boats, an area in which the assembly of ships takes place in single traffic at the few

points of departure of Atlantic convoys. There is an opportunity here, therefore, of intercepting enemy merchant ships
under conditions which have ceased almost completely for
some time. Further, there will hardly be any question of an
efficient [defensive] patrol in the American coastal area, at
least of a patrol used to U-boats. Attempts must be made to
utilize as quickly as possible these advantages, which will dis-
appear very shortly, and to achieve a "spectacular success" on
the American coast.[54]

Immediately Dönitz requested OKM to release twelve Type-IX
boats for this mission. In order to make that number he advised that
some boats would have to be diverted from west of Gibraltar, where
the Type IX was not so well suited for operations anyway. The Type IX
was more complex in design than the more maneuverable Type VIIC,
because of its larger size was more easily located by British ASDIC,
and was more unwieldy in maintaining precise depth. Dönitz further
advised Berlin that the reassignment of the Type IXs would be balanced by a not-inconsiderable number of new Type VIICs that were on
stream and could easily be allocated to Mediterranean duty. Privately
Dönitz worried that, while the presence of Type IXs off Gibraltar and
VIICs in the Mediterranean had been "absolutely necessary" to prevent a collapse of the Afrika Korps, now there was a real possibility
that the boats he needed so badly for the American campaign "may be
trapped there one day and excluded from the Battle of the Atlantic."[55]
Lending credence to this worry was the fact that the British, as he
knew from B-Dienst decrypts of convoy-code traffic, had detected the
withdrawal of U-boats from the Atlantic and were moving their escort
vessels from the Atlantic into the areas directly east and west of
Gibraltar. To counter that move, as noted before, Dönitz decided to
send a VIIC boat into the North Atlantic to transmit dummy messages
simulating a large U-boat group.[56]
Though, understandably, Japan was now pressing him forward,
Adolf Hitler could well have concluded at this point that a formal
declaration of war was not necessary. The Japanese actions had had
the effect of blunting rather than sharpening the danger of American
intervention in Europe. Certainly Hitler could now decline Japan's
invitation to wage war against the United States in the same way Japan
had declined his suggestion that she attack the Soviets at Vladivostok.
He was under no obligations to Japan. The conversation with Mat-

suoka in April had been only that, a conversation. Why declare and thus cancel out the unexpected great advantage to Germany of the Japanese attack, namely its diversion of American attention from the Atlantic to the Pacific? As for a declaration from the other side, Hitler's embassy in Washington had informed him that Congress, its emotions directed solely at Japan, was in no mood to choose a two-ocean war. It was not too late to cancel the orders given to Admiral Dönitz. He had canceled U-boat orders before. Why should he not wait and examine later developments? A rational person might have chosen this course.

Instead, though for what precise reason still remains unclear, perhaps to guarantee (if any treaty the Axis members ever signed was a guarantee) that Japan would not make a separate peace before victory had been won in Europe; perhaps for vengeance pure and simple against Roosevelt, his false neutrality, and his destroyers; perhaps because, in his view, war with the United States was inevitable anyway, so he might as well seize this moment as, if not ideal, acceptable; perhaps because he saw this action as necessary to get Japan totally committed against his key enemy, England; perhaps because he relished the prospect of huge U-boat successes against U.S. naval vessels and merchant shipping; or perhaps because he agreed with his foreign minister that "a great power does not allow itself to be declared war on, it declares war itself"[57]—for whatever reason or reasons the Führer signed a revision of the Tripartite Pact that threw Germany into the war on Japan's side and extracted a promise from the Japanese to stay the course. The date was 11 December. Hitler instructed Ribbentrop to call in the American chargé d'affaires, the ambassador having been recalled in 1938 as a protest against the anti-Jewish pogrom carried out that year. The meeting took place at 2:18 in the afternoon at the Foreign Ministry on the Wilhelmstrasse and lasted three minutes. A standing, unsmiling Ribbentrop announced that Germany regarded herself "as being at war with the United States of America as of today."[58] At the same hour the German chargé in Washington delivered the identical message to the State Department. That night in Berlin the master of Europe went before the Reichstag in the Kroll Opera House and to a stamping, yelling house of deputies delivered a full-blown accusatory declaration. Here at long last the Führer vocalized his incriminating list of grievances: the "Neutrality Acts," the destroyer deal, the shadowing of German ships, Lend-Lease, *Greer*, the "shoot on sight" order, Rainbow 5, and the undeclared war in general, to which he had long turned the other cheek, but no more! In the peroration of his harangue Hitler read out the terms of the new three-power agreement signed earlier that day.

It would be argued later by historians that, next to Barbarossa, the 11 December declaration was Hitler's greatest mistake.[59] "Improvised and unnecessary," it doomed his war.[60] *Der Würfel fiel.* The die was cast. The Atlantic was now at formal issue between the two countries. And the single most destructive U-boat campaign in the war to date was about to begin.

4

A Fighting Machine

23 December 1941, 1400 hours Central European Time (CET). Position: Bay of Biscay, thirty nautical miles west of Lorient, course 275. Oberleutnant (Ing.) Heinz Schulz, the LI, looked about the *Zentrale,* or control room, master of the narrow space he surveyed, ten paces fore and aft by five across the beam, divided in the center by the stout rotary hydraulic hoist well for the periscopes and by the thin ladder leading up to the conning tower and bridge. The nerve center of a U-boat when under water, the control room occupied the interior space of the pressure hull midship directly below the tower. At the moment U-*123* was "on the march." Through the tower hatch Schulz could see a chalky cloud cover and hear faintly the waves that slapped against the hull. From aft came the sturdy hammering of the diesels as they drove the boat seaward. But any minute now, he knew from seeing the navigator's dead reckoning pencil cross the forty-meter curve on the chart table behind him, either the Old Man or Hoffmann, the number one, would order a shallow dive to trim the boat. Be on the ready, he advised his machinist mates, who flexed and unflexed their wrists on the BBC hydroplane hand grips and valve wheels.

Schulz bent and glanced forward through the hatch to the heavy green curtain that sealed the commander's cubicle on the port side. No motion. The Old Man must be busy with his log. And no sign yet from Hoffmann on the bridge. But any moment now, mates, he said as he braced himself before the gray enameled panels, illuminated gauges, and black and red handwheels on the starboard wall. Other officers and petty officers might have their torpedoes bow and stern, their diesels and E motors aft, their helm and periscope in the tower above, and others in the crew might share that special knowledge; but here in the control room Schulz alone was master. He alone had the knowledge. Even the Old Man conceded as much—Schulz had heard him say so—that he the commander did not know how every single gauge worked, or where every single pipe or cable led, or what every single valve controlled. But Schulz knew. He knew in excruciating detail. Before his mind the bowels of the boat spread out in perfect order and logical clarity. And everything required to dive and trim and surface the boat was within his reach: control buttons; large and small handwheels, facing and overhead; depth manometer; Papenberg column; pressure gauges; trim scales; and indicators for a myriad of functions from fuel to ballast to air supply. And add to that voice pipes, loudspeakers, and telegraphs, that enabled Schulz to know, and often to orchestrate, what every other crewman on board was doing in a dive condition, planned or emergency.

Suddenly the Old Man's curtain stirred, then pulled to one side, and Reinhard Hardegen stepped briskly into Schulz's domain. His Number 1 uniform now in the locker, Hardegen wore an open shirt, sweater, and trousers of unequal age and varying shades of blue and carried in his hand, as though not-quite-yet wanting to display the authority it represented, his *Schirmmütze*, or peaked officer's cap, with the tropical white cover that only U-boat commanders wore—though no regulations specified or prohibited it—in order to distinguish themselves readily, particularly on a bridge at night. As he paused first to look at Kaeding's chart on the table to port side and then at the *Lotapparat*, or fathometer, on the gray wall to starboard he unconsciously played his fingers across the cap's leather peak; woven mohair band; the red, silver, and black national cockade; and the gilt eagle and swastika now green with verdigris.

Abruptly he placed the cap on his head. "Chief," he said, "I'm going to pull the plug. Let's trim this boat."

"Yes, Herr Kaleu!," Schulz answered, as Hardegen bent to the voice pipe. "Number One," he called in a loud voice, "clear bridge for dive!"

"Yes, Herr Kaleu!" Hoffmann shouted back, and almost immediately the five-man bridge party began falling down the aluminum ladder into the tower and quickly thereafter into the control room.

Even in nonemergency dives bridge personnel were so conditioned to fast exits they always poured down the hatch at their best speed, the watch officer, Hoffmann in this case, pulling shut the hatch cover and wheeling the spindle home in its bed.

"Tower hatch secured, bridge watch below, Herr Kaleu!" Hoffmann reported as his boots hit the control-room floor plates with a loud pop.

"Very well, chief, take us down to periscope depth. E motors half speed. *Flood!*"

Schulz repeated the order, "Flood negative!," and hammered his fist against the dive bell, which rang shrilly throughout the boat to the accompaniment of flashing red lights. Immediately two dozen hands moved in unison at every corner of the control room and aft in the engine and maneuvering rooms, while various voices, fore and aft, reported by loudspeaker and Schulz sorted them out in the sequence his mind required:

Report: "Air vents open—one, two, three, five!" The vents on top of the ballast, or diving, tanks were cleared for the air they contained to escape, as it did now with a great roar.

Report: "Flood valves open!" As the air that filled the tanks for buoyancy vented, sea water flooded in to replace it, causing the boat to begin sinking.

Report: "Diesel air valve closed!" An overhead valve cut off outside air intake required for combustion in the diesel engines aft.

Report: "Diesel exhaust valves closed!" Two overhead wheels turned off the engine exhausts from the twin MAN diesels.

Report: "Diesels shut down and disengaged! Fuel levers switched to zero!" The engine room telegraphed "Ready to dive." All other departments signaled Ready.

Report: "E motors engaged to drive shafts! Half speed!"

Report: "Ventilators closed!"

Schulz leaned forward to his two hydroplane operators, who sat at bicyclelike seats facing vertically placed electric buttons, one for up, one for down, with hand grips. Each set of brass buttons sat within the spokes of a large black wheel that served as backup control. The buttons operated the movement of hydroplanes attached in pairs to the sides of the U-boat hull at bow and stern.

"Forward down ten," Schulz ordered in near simultaneity with all the other orders, reports, signals, and bells that resonated through the control room. "Aft down five."

The planesmen pressed the heels of their hands against the appropriate up or down buttons and watched the changes on the gauges. Like the stabilizers, or horizontal tail surfaces, on an aircraft the hydroplanes when tilted up or down directed the pitch of the boat underwater. As the twin rudders steered the boat from side to side, the four hydroplanes steered it up and down. Deployment of the bow planes helped provide initial down-angle on the dive, after which their use in coordination with the stern planes helped to maintain or change depth. Maneuverability depended on propellant power, however, and that was provided by the battery-driven E motors. While a U-boat could hover in neutral buoyancy condition at a particular depth without power for a short period of time its continued attitude and stability (or even keel) required, among other things, a steady forward movement.

With all the new weight on board and maldistributed as new weight always was—ammunition, torpedoes, fuel, four tons of food, an extra crewman—Schulz was not ordering hard-a-dive. This dive would be intentionally slow. An emergency drill for speed in descent could come later. On this first trial dive at sea his challenge was to nurse the weighty monster gently into the deep and then, with all the finesse in his prized special knowledge, to balance her out before *123* nosed over or bucked and broached the surface.

"Easy," he said as much to himself as to the planesmen. With them he watched the column of mercury in the periscope elevation indicator that, like the *Tiefenmesser*, or depth manometer, registered the depths the boat was passing through, but more precisely than the latter at shallow depths. "Five meters," reported the bow planesman.

"Five meters," acknowledged Schulz, who felt no need to shift his weight to accommodate the forward tilt of the boat since it was going down flat. "Just as I thought. This boat is badly out of balance, Herr Kaleu. Look at the inclinometer bubble. We're stern-heavy."

"Ten meters," sang out the operator. All else in the boat was quiet now as the conning tower, after one last cautionary slap from the sea, slid beneath the surface. The diesels' great gruntings and vibrations were stilled. The E motors hummed so faintly aft they could hardly be heard. The ventilator fans turned lazily to a stop. The surrounding sea noises, save for a distant gurgle of rushing water, were closed out. The crew, at their battle stations, observed the same silence in the trim drill as they would in an actual emergency.

"Forward up five." Schulz prepared to gentle the iron beast into level attitude at exact periscope depth, which the boat now approached on the depth-column scale lines.

The bow operator pressed his right button. "Twelve meters," he reported, "thirteen . . . thirteen-five!" Periscope depth.

Quickly Schulz ordered the controls neutralized: "Forward up five. Aft up five. Close flood valves. Close air vents. E motors slow ahead. Rudder amidships. Prepare to trim!"

The planesmen jockeyed the buttons on their own in an attempt to keep the boat constant at periscope depth by the planes and propeller thrust alone. Only so much could be done dynamically, however, and the stern began to go down.

Schulz looked to the mates standing by the bank of valves at the trimming station to the right of the stern planesman. "Pump six hundred kilograms from after trim to forward trim," he ordered.

Trimming, or balancing, was the most basic drill of any boat that would presume to be submersible. If dived out of balance a U-boat could plunge bow or stern down to the seabed, or else, like a whale, break the surface and expose its skin to enemy fire. Either could be fatal. The six hundred kilograms Schulz ordered forward was seawater housed in the after-trim tank at the extreme stern. Propelled by a dual-piston high-pressure air pump, the water moved the whole length of the pressure hull to a variable ballast tank, or trim cell, in the extreme bow. The transfer adjusted the boat's weight and tilting movement, but not, Schulz judged, enough.

"Pump one hundred kilograms from sea to forward trim."

As the new surge of compensating weight coursed through the interior pipes forward, Schulz watched intently the trimming scales. They showed that the boat was gradually settling into a static horizontal attitude, trim state zero.

"E motors ahead." Schulz was pleased that his estimates had been correct and that equilibrium had been achieved this quickly— though somewhat more than an hour had passed. No aircraft pilot carried greater responsibility or required greater mental and physical skill at his tasks than did an LI. The feat of trimming was akin to walking while trying to balance an ice tray full of water. And once again Schulz had done it.

"Satisfied with the trim, Herr Kaleu," he reported to Hardegen, who was leaning against the chart table behind him.

"Very well, chief," Hardegen responded, "but look to your mercury. We're rising."

Startled, Schulz peered at the depth column and saw that the boat, though level, was exhibiting more buoyancy than he thought possible and was now at 11.5 meters. The planesmen were looking back at him quizzically. In an attack situation, 11.5 meters would have placed the periscope, if fully extended, so high out of the water it could easily have been detected by an enemy vessel. Chastened, Schulz realized that not all his estimates had been correct and that he had concentrated so totally on the trim that he had neglected the possibility that his other estimates could be in error. He made a mental note not to permit the same lapse of concentration again — weight *and* balance had to be served.

"Pump three hundred kilograms from sea to regulator cells!" he ordered. These overall weight adjustment tanks sat in the overhead directly above the control room. As the ordered amount of outside Biscay water entered the sea cocks the mercury column moved back toward thirteen meters on the periscope graphic. A few kilograms more and Schulz had the boat "on the step," with a one-degree down angle that he favored as a protection against broaching in rough weather.*

"Does the commander wish to make an observation?" he asked Hardegen.

"No, chief," Hardegen said, "keep the periscope in the well. Continue your calculations. I'm going forward." Turning to Hoffmann from the circular bulkhead hatch he ordered, "Inform all hands: Secure from battle stations."

"Yes, Herr Kaleu," Hoffmann acknowledged and relayed the order by loudspeaker through the boat.

It was not three hours into the dive when Hardegen returned to the control room after inspecting the forward compartments. He smiled at his number one, Hoffmann, and said, "I just met our new crewman."

"Alwin Tölle."

"Yes. He seems like a nice enough sort, but clumsy. Of course the forward compartments are jammed right now and it's hard enough for a seasoned man to get around up there, but Tölle just has no sea legs at all. When I introduced myself he stumbled on a stanchion and fell flat on his back. And the boat isn't even pitching!"

Hoffmann laughed and said, "I'll look after him."

*See Appendix A.

"He asked me where we were headed," Hardegen continued, "and I told him Lake Constance. He didn't catch the humor. Seems pretty naive about geography and boats."

"I'll talk to him."

"Give him a tour. He needs to know where things are and where to go if we get into trouble. And be sure he stays out of the way of people who need to do their jobs. No photographs until after our first deep submergence."

"Yes, Herr Kaleu."

As Hardegen made his way aft to the engineroom, Hoffmann went forward through the narrow fore-and-aft passageway. He found Tölle sitting on the edge of a sleeping bunk in the forward crew room, his feet propped high on a crate of apples and his head half hidden by nets full of sausages and black bread. There was a look of total bewilderment on the photographer's face.

"I understand that you met our commander," Hoffmann said to him.

"Yes, sir. And I fell down."

"So I heard." He studied Tölle's tightly coiled legs. "Did you expect to spend your first Atlantic voyage in this fetal position?"

"No, sir."

"Well, it's going to be this way in here until we eat some of this food and especially until we launch some of our eels and free up the bunk space in the forward torpedo room. Sorry about that, but, as you can see, U-boats are war tubes, not cruise ships. Nothing here was designed for comfort. We're geared strictly for destruction. You'll learn to move about better as time goes on. If you can't walk, crawl. Now let's get up and see the insides of this boat while we're still submerged and riding easy. Have you memorized the steps for operating the head?"

"Yes, sir," Tölle replied.

Hoffmann smiled. "Very good." He turned to the mixers who were watching from their forward stations. "I hope you men did a good job teaching Tölle. I'd continue to be good to him if I were you. He'll take your photograph and make you famous." The mixers beamed broadly.*

Hoffmann directed Tölle's eyes forward to the bow torpedo compartment. Under the deck plates in long bunkers, he explained,

*See Appendix B.

were two reserve torpedoes, and below them was the forward trimming tank. Dead ahead, behind their white-painted caps, or doors, were the four forward launch tubes. Two reserve torpedoes were secured above the plates and two more in the space usually occupied by lower bunks. All but one of the eels in this compartment were type G7e, meaning Mark G, seven meters long, electric. They were the most dependable eels in service, and they left no wake. Targets could not spot their course and avoid them. Destroyers and other escorts could not "home" on them. There were more G7es stored in the after torpedo room. After two eels in the forward tubes were launched and the two reserves now in the bunk space were inserted in their place the crew could bring down the bunks that were now pressed flat against the hull and thus provide more space for sleeping and sitting. Not surprisingly, the forward technicians and seamen anxiously awaited the boat's first targets. Life afterward was always a bit easier.

Hoffmann swept his right hand across the heavy blue-and-white-check gingham sheets and pillowcases of one of the aluminum bunks with side rails in the seamens' compartment where he and Tölle stood. These berths, he said, were always warm from somebody's body. On the IXB there were eight bunks for twelve petty officers and twenty-four bunks for forty seamen and technicians. After each watch, whether two, four, or six hours, Tölle would see one man crawling out of a bunk and another crawling in to take his place. In fact, Tölle had better check with the torpedo-room petty officer to learn exactly where and what hours he would be allowed to sleep in this same bunk area. And count himself lucky he was on a IXB, Hoffmann said, because on a VII boat there were proportionately even fewer bunks. There was no laundry on board, Schulz went on, so Tölle shouldn't expect any clean sheets like those his wife or mother gave him every Sunday. These pretty blue-and-white checks that covered the leather mattresses would be stained and stinking after four weeks at sea. Only on completion of the outbound mission, when the boat was ordered home to base, would the sheets and pillowcases be reversed on the commander's order. Blessed indeed the first men to inhabit the clean sides![1]

At that point three crewmen preparing to go on topside watch when the boat surfaced entered the compartment and pulled down oilskins, scarves, long leather gloves, and binoculars from their stash amid the thick bundles of cables and pipes that ran fore-and-aft along the overhead. On their heads they wore the *Schiffchen*, or forage cap, made from blue wool with black lining. Everyone from now on, except the commander, if they wore caps at all would wear forage caps, Hoffmann explained to Tölle, and when heavy weather came the bridge watch would wear sou'westers over the caps. If anyone wanted to wear the pullover that grandmother knitted, or any other unconventional mufti, it was permitted. There was no dress code on a Feindfahrt. Most of the men wore standard naval blue-gray fatigues. Some wore British battle dress that had been captured at the Biscay ports. When the bilges started filling, Tölle would see the crew in felt-lined boots with thick cork or gum soles. Most of the underwear was knitted blue wool. As the outside temperatures fell Tölle should not count on any central heating system. There was none. The running diesels did little to warm the boat in wintry seas. Except in the vicinity of space heaters stationed here and there, temperatures inside the boat would be very close to those of the water outside. The principal thing Tölle would be spared inside was the wind. But even inside he would often feel himself to be outside because the constant soggy air created a visible interior fog. Very soon now Tölle would see the fog begin to form around the lights. And that was another thing: The lights would be on all the time. The U-boat interior operated full-time around the clock, which would remain on Central European Time throughout the cruise. Meals, too, followed German time, so that if *123* ended up in the Strait of Belle Isle, Tölle would have his lunch before daybreak. Inside the boat it made no difference if it was light or dark outside.

This compartment formed the principal living space for the crew. There was bunk space for petty officers and officers amidships, and sixteen crewmen shared eight berths in the after torpedo room, but this forward area, Hoffmann said, was what U-boat men called the "House of Lords"—from the nickname, Lords, traditionally given to naval ratings. These young men, eighteen to twenty-three years old, were mostly volunteers, as opposed to the officers whose assignment to U-boats was usually made by OKM. The ratings tended to come from the interior provinces—Hesse, Baden-Württemberg, Bavaria, and so forth—where romantic stories of the sea, together with good Ubootwaffe propaganda, led them to sign up. Tölle might have thought that these ranks would be filled mainly by youths from the seafaring cities like Bremen, Wilhelmshaven, Hamburg, or Kiel. But those boys had seen their fathers and uncles come home from the sea and had heard their woeful tales, and they knew better. They chose instead to join the Wehrmacht or the Luftwaffe. No, these U-boat

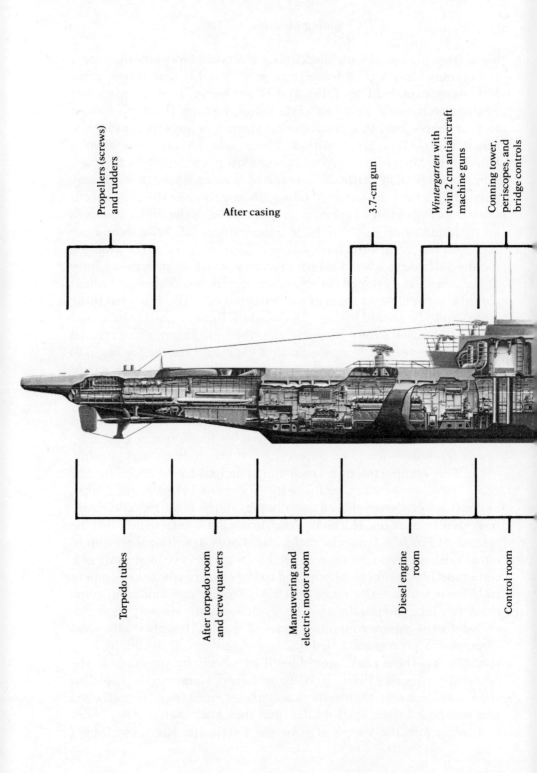

Propellers (screws) and rudders

After casing

3.7-cm gun

Wintergarten with twin 2 cm antiaircraft machine guns

Conning tower, periscopes, and bridge controls

Torpedo tubes

After torpedo room and crew quarters

Maneuvering and electric motor room

Diesel engine room

Control room

TYPE IXB U-BOAT
with Principal Exterior and Interior Features Shown

10.5-cm gun

Fore casing

Commander's cabin, radio (wireless) room, and sound room

Officers' wardroom and quarters

Galley

Petty officers' quarters

Forward torpedo room and crew quarters

Torpedo tubes

(Credit: from the book Great Campaigns of World War II)

ratings were country lads by and large, with one or two from families where a father or relative had been in the Navy, and they couldn't be farther away from home *or* from their dreams of the sea. Join the Kriegsmarine and see the world? Some of these men—and that is what Hoffmann called them because they did men's work and did it well—never saw the sea during an entire patrol. Their posts were belowdecks throughout. Some, like the engine room machinists, had no idea where the boat was or what it was doing except that it was diving, surfacing, or cruising on the surface—somewhere. A lot of romantic illusions about life at sea on a U-boat were long gone for many of these men. And yet they formed a happy comradeship.

Together the ratings knew that this steel hull was their common shelter and that the successful operation of its instruments and apparatus as well as the survival of all on board required that every man be able to depend absolutely on the performance of every other. They tolerated each other's peculiarities and subordinated personal habits to the team. In no other war machine, Hoffmann said, was the integral participation of every team member so vital—one hatch uncovered, one valve not turned, one battery array unchecked, one enemy aircraft not spotted, and the entire mission, boat, and crew were doomed. Confined together for long periods of time, every man visible to every other man, exposed to all the same disciplines, privations, perils, and fears, they coalesced naturally into a band of brothers. And fortunately for *123* every billet was filled by a seasoned hand.

Hard as life was on the tossing, relentless Atlantic, these young men had ample rewards, Hoffmann pointed out. Money, for one thing. Their base pay increased by 1.5 to 4 Reichsmarks each day that the boat dived, and once the boat passed twenty degrees longitude and became a *Frontboot*, a hazardous duty bonus in French francs about doubled that pay and made it possible on their return to Lorient—as the saying went—"to live like a god in France." Here on the boat, despite the long hours and sacrifices that crewing entailed, they had three hot meals a day, more than the poor footsloggers in Russia, Hoffmann ventured, and real bunks, also hot. Hoffmann laughed as he said it. For those interested in machine tools and technical careers the boat offered training in the use of some of the most advanced technology from Germany. Then, once they returned to base from a war patrol and went out on shore leave in groups, you could readily see the pride they had in themselves as members of the U-boat arm. The way they carried themselves, swaggered about in their marine uniforms with Iron Cross ribbons, and partied with keen abandon—all bespoke their awareness that the rest of Germans viewed them as an elite of the fighting forces. That status might be challenged by Luftwaffe crews, but Hoffmann doubted it now that Göring's boys had been bested in the skies over Britain. And certainly no surface naval crews could make such a claim, since all their ships were long frozen in harbor. And forget the Wehrmacht in Russia—God save those poor bastards this winter. No, these lads were Germany's favored heroic types, though Hoffmann was sure that that favor hardly extended to British opinion. The Tommies might salute our army and air officers when captured, he suggested to Tölle, and might sing "Lili Marlene" as lustily as any German seaman, but when it came to U-boat crews, British military respect and courtesy probably broke down, if one could judge from British propaganda, which uniformly portrayed U-boat crewmen as fanatical, vicious, sneaky, murderous villains. If the Tommies ever got their hands on us, Hoffmann speculated, they might not be able to restrain themselves. He didn't know about the Americans.

Did these men look like fanatical villains to Tölle? Hoffmann pointed toward a group of mixers crawling out of the forward torpedo room. Answering his own question, he said that these men were pretty much blank pages where villainy was concerned and not imaginative enough to be fanatical. And too young, probably, although Hoffmann had to correct himself on some of the ages. It was true that as a rule the ratings were eighteen to twenty-three years old, and that some of the officers were also quite young—von Schroeter, the commander's number two, for example, who knew the crewmen personally better than he, Hoffmann, did, was only twenty-two—but some of the men, particularly the petty officers, were a good deal older than twenty-three. Karl Latislaus, for example, chief diesel mechanic, whom the crew called Karlchen (Little Karl), was thirty and the oldest man on board. He had served on the pocket battleship *Deutschland*, where he once met Hitler. Almost all the petty officers and ratings had nicknames, by the way. Twenty-three-year-old Richard Amstein, one of the control room machinists, was Kraxel ("climber"). Petty officer Rudolf Fuhrmann was Kutscher ("coachman"). Seaman Second Class Max Hufnagl was Lackl ("roughneck"). Klinger was Icke ("I-guy"). He was from Berlin and had responsibility for cleanliness and hygiene on board. Holz was Kapitän, Biegerl was Groschengrab ("miser") and Karl Fröbel, the youngest on board, everyone called Langspleiss ("long splice"). So thin and six feet tall, he looked to everyone else like two lengths of rope spliced together. And no one had to duck more than he in order to keep his head from denting the overhead pipes and food stores!

Latislaus: I volunteered.

Amstein: Me, too, but not because I wanted to be a warrior. If I hadn't gone to the Navy, though, I would have ended up in the Army. And I didn't want to do that. In the Navy you had everything with you—the bunk, the food, the supplies—and you didn't have to walk or anything.

Latislaus: I also volunteered for the Navy, in 1928, because my father had been in the Navy, and my brother died in the Navy. And I was pleased to serve in that branch. I've got to admit, the highs and lows were frequent, but the highs out-weighed the lows.

Barth: I didn't regret that I went to the Navy. At the start of the war I was on a destroyer. We laid mines in the Dogger Bank. A lot of freighters and steamers ran into them. I didn't want to go to U-boats. And yet one day I ended up on a U-boat. I was simply sent to school. There was nothing you could do about it. But talking about *123*, about being confined in such a little area—a pipe—with fifty or so other men, and there you were for days, and weeks, you developed a cama-raderie, a forged unit that you can still see in us today. But I never thought that we would get together like this—still today.

Barth: We were young men. It was our job.

Latislaus: We were sailors. Just like career sailors all over the world. And we had no political direction whatsoever. We didn't even vote.

Lorenz: The relationships between crewmembers were very good.

Seigel: Yes, good, otherwise the boat would never have sur-vived the war.

Lorenz: Yes, we all got along well, no fights, and we all did our jobs.

Fröbel: We lived in close proximity on the boat for twelve weeks. The first weeks we'd have to go about on our knees in the forward torpedo room.

Kaeding: That was hard living. And naturally when we returned we celebrated with great parties. So it wasn't that we were hard men on board and mommy's babies on shore. We partied hard, too.

Fröbel: On shore we U-boatmen received special treatment. When we misbehaved the military police looked the other way.

Kaeding: Well, when you spend three months at sea, when we came home we partied, naturally. But I wanted to say something else. At that time we felt that we had to sail to serve our fatherland. We didn't think of Adolf Hitler. We didn't think about any specific political party. We simply thought that there was no other way—we had to go. This common experience, of course, held us together and helped us through the tough times. You must be clear on this: Serving on a U-boat was no easy task. And it certainly wasn't for those who had their hearts in their stomachs. To be a U-boat crewmember on an enemy mission—that was something!

Watch your footing and your head, Hoffmann cautioned Tölle as he led him aft over and around sacks and boxes and below the hanging hammocks full of perishables. Under these deck plates they were walking on, he told the struggling Tölle, was Battery Array Number 1. These and Number 2 storage batteries under the deck just aft supplied energy to the electric motors in the maneuvering room. Those motors were engaged now, propelling the boat forward at four knots—economy speed. The boat was putting out no exhaust and was completely independent of the surface atmosphere. The batteries made that possible. Each of the pasted-plate-type batteries had sixty-two cells. Switching panels enabled the electricians to use an individual battery, or batteries in series or in parallel, and to obtain voltages ranging from a low of 110 direct current for most on-board purposes to a high of 340 d.c. for powering the propulsion motors. The lead plates in the battery structures were an enormous dead weight, close to sixty tons. On a strictly observed schedule, battery technicians checked the batteries' acid levels and their possible contamination by saltwater in order to prevent buildups of chlorine gases that could lead to poisonous fumes or to explosions and fire. Here was another example of how the entire crew owed their safety to two or three men. Hoffmann could not stress the point enough: A U-boatman's first loyalty was to the rest of the crew. And that was why Tölle, with no essential boat duties to perform, could best serve the rest of the crew by simply staying out of the way, especially when the boat dived or came under attack. In an emergency dive, Hoffmann said, the LI and the chief bos'n might order all hands to the forward compartments to provide down weight to the bow. If that happened Tölle was to race to his bunk, climb in it, and stay there. Hoffmann did not want him to block the crew, nor did he want him killed in the stampede.

A few crouching steps more and Hoffmann took Tölle into the galley on the starboard side of the fore-and-aft passageway. Notice, he told Tölle, that everything in a U-boat was to port or starboard of one central, narrow, single-level gangway. Four bulkheads divided the gangway, but their hatches were always open, except—for reasons of noise—the one between the control room and the engine room. Here, then, was the realm of Hannes, the cook, who was off somewhere retrieving groceries. Hannes had a nice little Vosswerke stove, as Tölle could see, with two ovens and three hot plates, a short standing refrigerator, and a sink with hot and cold fresh water and a separate spigot for hot saltwater. Fresh water was taken on before departure, but distilling equipment on board could produce an additional 63.5 gallons a day from saltwater, which would be used for cooking, drinking, and servicing the batteries. None of it could be used for showering or shaving. If Tölle wanted to shave with saltwater he was welcome to try it, but most of the men found it too painful, so the result was that everyone grew a beard—except, of course, the youngsters who had nothing to shave.

Just aft of the galley were the petty officers' and then the officers' quarters. The officers' wardroom contained four private bunks, two on each side. The upper bunks could be folded back so that the lowers became seats. Here an attempt had been made by the nautical designers to present at least the facade of a home atmosphere. The walls were oak paneling. A cupboard contained porcelain dishes and cups. At mealtimes, when all officers except the one on watch were expected to eat together, a table leaf extended to provide a formal eating surface. It was always covered at mess with a white linen tablecloth, though as the voyage went on the white, like everything else on board, would turn to gray. Here, too, cream-colored overhead lampshades contrasted with the wire-guarded bare bulbs found elsewhere in the boat. If the boat was depth-charged, as she had been repeatedly on her last two patrols, Hoffmann said in an aside, Tölle might see a lot of smashed crockery about and officers eating out of metal mess kits like the rest of the crew! As for the commander, while he ate his meals here and joined the other officers in paperwork or board and card games at the wardroom table, he had his own private cubbyhole separate from the rest of the officers, here on the port side. Hoffmann pulled back the green curtain that provided Reinhard Hardegen's only privacy from the rest of the crew and showed Tölle the tiny oak-paneled compartment with its low bunk, personal effects locker, and washbasin under a hinged writing table.

On the starboard side directly across from the commander's cabin were the sound and wireless rooms. More often than not the commander left his curtain open so that he would always be in touch with either or both men. There had to be good chemistry for two very different elements, low-ranking technicians and a Kapitänleutnant, to mix together comfortably without anyone's feeling awkward or uneasy. Such was the chemistry here. The two radio/sound men were Petty Officers Fritz Rafalski and Heinz Barth. Both carried the same on-board nickname, Puster ("blower"). They had backups in two radiomen second class named Wälder and Beyer. When the boat was on the surface Rafalski and Barth switched off on watches of four hours, six, six hours, four, in the wireless room. When, as now, the boat was submerged one took the hydrophone and the other the wireless station, since both had to be manned in a dive condition. The commander would look into both side-by-side cubicles from his cabin, as he often did if the boat was submerged, since Rafalski and Barth were the only people on board who were in contact with the outside world. As Tölle could see, Barth in his small cupboardlike sound booth with its tongue-and-groove wood walls to deaden noise sat with earphones facing a control wheel and a glass-covered compass rose. A sweeping black indicator needle bisected the compass face. Barth's handwheel controlled hydrophone sensors, like microphones, that were arranged in arcs, twenty-three sensors on each side on the outer skin near the forward hydroplanes. Turning the wheel activated an electric pulse-timing compensator that ranged back and forth across all quadrants to pick up the distinctly different propeller noises of coal-fired steamers, diesel motor ships, and fast naval vessels such as destroyers and convoy escorts. The hydrophone could also pick up torpedoes, "ours and theirs," Hoffmann said, the breakup of torpedoed ships, the blowholes of breathing whales and porpoises, and various other sea noises. It took an experienced ear to separate out the sound sources and identify their signatures. By turning the handwheel Barth could obtain a crude directional sounding on a given source, estimate its range, and determine if it was approaching or receding. Tölle studied Barth's distracted look and watched him swing to a suspect noise bearing 015 degrees, then turn the wheel rapidly to its reciprocal.

"Anything?" asked Hoffmann.

"*Nein*," Barth replied laconically.

One step away on the starboard side was the adjoining wireless telegraph (W/T) room, which, with its several transmitters, receivers, electrical panels, Morse key bench, *Marine-Funkschlüssel-Maschine M* cipher machine, and phonograph, was twice as large as the sound booth. Here Rafalski, also with earphones, but one ear on and one off, moved a condenser pot across the long-wave frequency band. At this depth and down to twenty-five meters Rafalski could pick up Morse signals from Lorient keyed through the Goliath antennas in Germany. To the same question Hoffmann had posed to Barth the radioman answered "*Nein.*"

It was too early to expect any messages for *123*, Hoffmann explained to Tölle. But soon, probably tomorrow, Christmas Eve, she would get some traffic. Hoffmann told Tölle that he had to get into the control room, which was the next compartment aft, since a look through the hatch showed that the Old Man was back from his inspections and that an order to surface was probably upcoming. Tölle should spend some time talking with Rafalski, Hoffmann advised. Rafalski was very well known in the Ubootwaffe. He had been on U-*64* when she was sunk off Narvik, Norway, in 1940. He was the only man who ever escaped from a sunken U-boat without an escape lung. Tölle should talk with him. Then, when Tölle heard the order to surface, he could step into the control room and observe those operations. Stand by the chart table to port side, Hoffmann suggested, so that he was out of the path of the lookouts who would assemble to go topside. As for the engine, maneuvering, and after torpedo rooms, either he or Schulz would give him that part of the tour another time. And, Hoffmann said with a smile, not to worry, he and Schulz were not going anywhere.

"Yes, Herr Oberleutnant," Tölle replied.

With that Hoffmann grasped the bar over the circular bulkhead opening and threw his legs into the control room. Tölle looked back into the radio room and hesitantly tried to make conversation with Rafalski, who now busied himself with the innards of his shortwave receiver. To Tölle's questions about what he was doing Rafalski answered, as old hands were wont to answer new men on board, with more truth than they could handle, "I'm verifying the voltage levels—tubes nine and ten, cathode one-point-five volts, choke grid one-point-five, shielded grid five, anode one-thirty—tubes eleven and twelve, cathode one-point-one, choke one-point-one, shielded forty-five, anode one-twenty. That's what I'm doing."

Rafalski finished his task and replaced the cover on the receiver chassis. "Anything else you want to know?" he asked Tölle pleasantly.

Tölle mentioned what Hoffmann had told him about Rafalski's escape. "Would you mind very much telling me about it?" he asked, removing from a tunic pocket a notepad on which to record the account.

"All right," Rafalski said, with an inflection suggesting that he hoped this would be the last time he would have to tell the story on this particular voyage. "In the invasion of Norway we lost a lot of warships and transports to the British fleet that attacked our forces. We U-boats sank some of their ships, too, but not nearly as many as we should have because of torpedo defects. Anyway, on 13 April my boat U-64 was hit and sunk off Narvik by a Royal Navy fighter-bomber. I'm not superstitious, but that number thirteen had to mean something. Our boat had left base at Helgoland at thirteen-thirteen hours several days before and the Tommy plane hit us at exactly thirteen-thirty-five hours on the thirteenth! Anyway, we were in relatively shallow water close to shore. There was no way to raise the boat. We stayed with it for an hour and a quarter and then realized that we would have to flood the boat and try to float individually to the surface. What scared us most was not the escape—all of us had had to practice it in training—but the low temperature of the water. We worried about freezing to death. But every man reached for his *Dräger Tauchretter*—that's the escape apparatus with mouthpiece and nose clip, oxygen cylinder, breathing pipe, and life vest that we keep at our bunks—and the commander gave the order to open the hatches. As the water poured in I realized that my escape gear was missing. Everybody else had his apparatus on, but where was mine? Soon the water was up to the overhead. I held my breath and headed up the tower ladder in the middle of a group that half pushed me along. Just when I thought my lungs would burst I popped to the surface. Luckily, because the water was two degrees Celsius, we didn't have to tread water long. Some German infantry-men in row boats rescued us. I think I was in the water only five minutes. And that's the story. I went to U-124 after that—the Old Man was number two on board at that time—and then here to 123. I didn't ask to be transferred, I was just sent. But this is a good boat, except that the Old Man takes too many risks."[2]

Tölle scribbled rapidly in his notepad. "Too many risks?"

"Forget it," said Rafalski. "You better get into the control room like the lieutenant said."

Tölle ducked to take a look in the room. "Let's talk again later," he said to Rafalski. "Just one more thing. I see a ladder in there and some kind of well around the top of the ladder that has a framed photograph of the Führer on it. Did the commander put that up?"

"No," answered "Puster." "That went up at the time the boat was commissioned. It's standard issue. Every boat has the same photo in exactly the same place."

"Thanks."

Tölle stepped warily through the circular bulkhead hatch past the two-meter-high Christmas tree the Patenbattalion had decorated with tinsel and candles. Hoping not to be noticed, he walked to what appeared to be the chart table, as instructed, and waited to see what happened in this strange theater of dials, pipes, and levers, so unlike anything that he had seen before that it might easily be taken for the movie set of Dr. Frankenstein's laboratory.

The commander—the Old Man, as he should learn to refer to him—was engaged in conversation with IWO and IIWO Hoffmann and von Schroeter. The LI Schulz stood blankly watching the gauges until the Old Man called.

"Finish your data tables, Chief?"

"Yes, Herr Kaleu."

"All right, then, let's surface and build up some speed and time so that we can spend an underwater Christmas Eve tomorrow. Number One?"

Hoffmann leaned into the forward bulkhead opening and yelled, "Lookouts to control!" The same four seamen whom Tölle had seen equipping themselves with bridge gear swung into the control room. The Old Man ordered Schulz:

"Stand by to surface. E motors full ahead. Steer up. Blow out main ballast by diesel. *Surface!*"

Although Tölle would have no way of knowing it, the boat at periscope depth was so close to the surface there was no need to blow the ballast tanks underwater with compressed air—the usual procedure for surfacing. Blowing the tanks meant expelling the seawater that had been taken aboard and replacing it with air to restore buoyancy, causing the boat to rise. At this shallow depth, however, the boat could be steered dynamically to the surface, using E motors and planes. After surfacing, the engine exhaust from the refired diesels would be used to expel water from the diving tanks and thus save the boat's store of compressed air.

Schulz ordered the planesmen: "Bow up fifteen, stern up ten." As the boat rose up the mercury column, the chief planesman reported: "Ten meters . . . eight . . . six, five, conning tower clear!"

With that Hardegen and four lookouts behind him pounded up the ladder, wheeled open the hatch, stepped up to the dripping bridge platform, and swept all quadrants of the horizon with binoculars while Schulz, in the reverse of commands given on initiation of the dive, fed surface air to the diesels, shut down the E motors, opened the ventilators, neutralized the planes, and expelled the water ballast with exhaust. As air refilled the diving tanks the buoyant hull rose to optimum cruising depth.

Hardegen shouted down the voice pipe to the helmsman in the tower who had his hands on the engine telegraph as well as on the rudder buttons:

"Both engines *Grosse Fahrt*—full ahead—steady on course two-seven-five!"[3]

Schulz turned to Tölle, whom he recognized from the morning departure. "Now our screws are really digging holes," he said. "If the Old Man and the lookouts had spotted anything in their glasses—a warship or a plane—we could have dived immediately because we were still heavy. But there was no alarm and so we put both diesels on line. The Old Man must have a good sea up there if he's going *Grosse Fahrt*."

Against the noise that now filled the control room Tölle asked Schulz, "Do you think I can go up?"

Schulz walked over to the bridge pipe. "Herr Kaleu, Tölle requests permission to go topside."

"Granted," Hardegen returned.

"Go on up," Schulz said. "Watch your ass that you don't slip and fall. Don't stay too long, and don't get in anybody's way."

"Yes, sir."

As Tölle eagerly clambered up the ladder Rafalski called up his own radio shack pipe: "Herr Kaleu, permission to play Radio Berlin to the crew?"

With "granted" Rafalski tuned his Telefunken Type ELA/E1012 receiver to the 360-meter band and relayed its strong clear signal through the loudspeaker system. The time was exactly 1930 hours. A recording of the Potsdam garrison chapel carillon playing an eighteenth-century folk song by Ludwig Holty provided the signature background to Berlin's call sign:

"Here is Deutschlandsender on wave bands 360 meters, 410 and 492 meters. We bring music and news to comrades in the command areas West and Norway. And here is dance music, beginning with the popular Berlin music hall song, 'Es War in Schöneberg im Monat Mai.'"

As the catchy tune filled the boat the mixers forward, who knew the lyrics only too well, loudly chimed in with their own bawdy version:

"Ich war in Lorient in einem Puff . . ."
"I was in a brothel in Lorient . . ."

2150 hours. Tölle had been on the bridge for two and a half hours. To watch officer von Schroeter it was obvious that the guest from Propaganda much preferred the open air to the confined quarters below, even with the unsteady footing that came with mounting seas. The swells were breaking now into choppy waves, and as the boat passed from crest to trough she took on the pitch and roll that would characterize her movements for the rest of the passage. There would be no more phonograph playing belowdeck while the boat was on the surface: The needle would skid across the grooves. And the elephant dance would only become more pronounced as the boat approached, then entered, the storm-strewn Atlantic. While the four lookouts moved their binoculars across the horizon in never-varying rhythmic patterns looking for any black dot that might be more than a dot, von Schroeter's eyes took in a wider angle of sea and sky and his mind began to frame the report he would call below on the hour: "Wind northeast force two, sea running two, increasing, sky overcast, some moon to east, visibility eleven." His concentration broke the instant the lookout on starboard ahead disturbed the binocular ballet, and frozen in place, chopped his right hand toward ten degrees of the bow.

"Herr Leutnant!" he called. "Shadow off starboard bow!"

Von Schroeter placed the rubber-cushioned eyepieces of 7 × 50s against his eye sockets and looked ahead, slowly moving the lenses across the horizon where the lookout had indicated. There! A narrow black silhouette of some kind fell left and right against the night sky. He leaned to the voice pipe:

"Commander to the bridge!"

Moments later Hardegen stood alongside von Schroeter peering ahead through his own glasses.

"Yes," Hardegen said, "a superstructure, hull down, bow wake on our reciprocal. No masts. It's a U-boat, probably ours." To the pipe he ordered, "Port fifteen, both ahead slow. Gun crew stand by! Puster to the bridge with the blinker light!"

The voice of the helmsman in the tower acknowledged, and the shrill clang of his telegraphs came up the open hatch.

Barth reached the bridge with his shoulder-held signal light trailing a power cord from the tower.

"Challenge him, Puster," ordered Hardegen, who could now just barely see the tower of the approaching boat with unaided eyes. Barth flipped the blinker shutters giving the December code challenge: F-L-U-S-S.

"What's the recognition response, Puster?" Hardegen asked.

"BRUNO, Herr Kaleu," Barth answered. The seconds passed and there was no response. Hardegen ordered, "Open forward hatch! Forward gun crew to deck! Battle Stations!"

Just as the gun crew clambered up to man the 10.5 and gunnery officer von Schroeter made his way down the outside ladder to command them, yellow lights flashed off the bow to starboard: B-R-U-N-O— U-A.

"It's U*A!*" Hardegen exclaimed. "Gun crew stand down! Secure from battle stations. Puster, send blinker recognition U-*123.*"

Turning to Tölle, Hardegen said, excitedly: "That's Korvettenkapitän Hans Eckermann. His boat U*A* is on her way home to Lorient. I should have guessed it was U*A.* Flotilla told us the story day before yesterday." Hardegen went on to relate it.

U*A* had been on southern patrol off South Africa and there, together with U-68, received orders from BdU to rendezvous with refueling and supply ship *Python*. While the two boats lay nearby, *Python* was sunk by a British cruiser.[4] The German survivors in the water were unusually numerous since only ten days before *Python* had rescued the crew of the German surface raider *Atlantis*, sunk by another British cruiser.[5] UA and U-68 gathered the lifeboats and formed two tow groups. For the next five days, hauling 416 survivors, most in open boats, the two U-boats made five knots on a course of 330 degrees northward. On 5 December by prearrangement they rendezvoused with two other boats, *129* and Hardegen's old *Edelweissboot*, *124*, and divided up the tow. Most of the survivors were subsequently transferred to large Italian submarines, UA moving 50 of her 104 to the Italian *Torelli* off Freetown on 16 December. After taking the remainder inside her hull UA had twice the normal roster of a Type IXB, which she resembled in size.

As UA came into closer view and her dimensions materialized Hardegen explained to Tölle: "That boat was built originally in 1938 for the Turkish Navy. Her name was *Batiray*. When war came she was commissioned instead into the Kriegsmarine. Look at her come on. Fifty-plus extra men for ballast. They must be layered in there like anchovies. They'll open the tin tomorrow in Lorient!"[6]

"Why UA instead of a numeral?" Tölle asked.

"Any boat built for a foreign navy or captured from a foreign navy carries a letter rather than a numerical designation. Most of the boats we've captured were Dutch or Norwegian."

From UA by blinker: B-A-D—S-E-A-S—N-O—B-E-E-S.

Hardegen explained that "bees" meant enemy aircraft and that this information that UA had not encountered Sunderlands so far on the Biscay crossing was welcome news indeed. "Puster," Hardegen said. "Send message: WELL DONE. GREAT SEAMANSHIP. HAPPY CHRISTMAS." The Old Man and the bridge watch leaned on the bridge coaming and followed with fascination as the gallant boat passed on the starboard beam, her commander's white cap dimly visible above the tower, and then as, with her human cargo brought more than five thousand nautical miles, she receded from view in the black night aft.

5

Destination New York

0917 hours, Christmas Eve. Steering on the Nantucket Great Circle route used for reaching all six previously worked operational areas in the West Atlantic. "ALARMMM!" Hardegen's shout down the bridge pipe first stunned, then supercharged every muscle on board. *Brring! Brring! Brring!* In the *Zentrale* and aft a blur of well-trained hands whirred among the warren of valves and levers while the boots of the watch party, Hardegen in the rear, pounded on the floor plates, and Kaeding hollered over the loudspeaker: "All hands to the bow!" Down the fore-and-aft passageway every free hand, including the diesel machinists who had shut down their power plant, poured in a hunched running position through the compartments to whatever space they could find in the farthest points forward in the hull. Tölle, who had been asleep in a bunk, awoke to this bedlam of banged shins, crashing buckets, and seamen's obscenities and wisely stayed in place. With so much weight forward to assist the planes at hard-a-dive, *123* went down fast by the bow, her binoculars hanging crazily as pendulums.

"Rig for depth charge, rig for silent running," Hardegen ordered from his position at the chart table. To Schulz he said, calmly, "Go to fifty meters, Chief, then flatten your angle and steer down to A plus fifty." (A was the code for twenty meters, used in wireless transmissions to disguise reported depths. Seventy meters equaled 231.5 feet. The procedure of going no deeper than fifty meters at hard-a-dive and then gradually "steering in" to greater depths had only that month been decided on as safest for the boat by Ubootwaffe engineers.[1]) As the needle approached fifty on the depth gauge, Schulz ordered his planesmen, "Bow on ten, stern on five."

Hardegen looked over to Hoffmann. "Time on the dive, Number One?" With that question everyone in his hearing knew that the dive was a drill and not an actual emergency. Chests heaved and smiles flickered. "Thirty-seven seconds," answered Hoffmann. That was the expired time from the sounding of the dive order to the placement of ten meters of water above the hull. Thirty-seven seconds was not bad, but— "Regulation is thirty-five, Number One," Hardegen admonished. "Shave off those extra two and you may save our lives. Secure from depth charges. Crew return to their stations."

"Yes, Herr Kaleu." The admonition was meant as much for Schulz as for Hoffmann.

Hardegen followed the Tiefenmesser as the indicator passed the 60-meter mark. It was still well within the green range of the gauge, with caution amber starting at 100 and red, the danger zone, calibrated at 150 to 200. The Type IX was shipyard-certified to 200 meters (662 feet), but this "paper depth" below which water pressure theoretically would crush the hull had often been exceeded.[2] Even at maximum posted depth, Type IX commanders had been confident that they were safely below the deepest settings of British Wabos.[3] As the indicator reached 70 meters the LI Schulz neutralized the planes and trimmed the boat's attitude in the water. With a practiced ear he listened along with Hardegen to every small creak and moan in the hull, now tightly compressed against the outside water pressure.

"Let's stay here for a while, Chief," Hardegen said, "to see how good a job Keroman did on our valves and seals."

The "a while" lasted only seconds as, with a shattering blast, the water-depth gauge from the starboard diving bunker exploded, sending shards of glass across the control room.

"Not only that, Herr Kaleu," Schulz shouted, "we have a cutoff valve problem! Fuel followed by seawater is leaking into the main bilge! Recommend surfacing!" Hardegen approved. "Stand by to surface," he ordered. "Surface!" The boat went up at a moderate speed, broached bow-high, and settled down on the Biscay surface. While the lookouts scanned above, Schulz and his team made for the offending valve, which they found had not been properly installed. It was either negligence, Schulz reasoned, or a deliberate act of sabotage by French dockworkers at Keroman. With the machine shop equipment on board, together with the electric arc welder that operated off the portside main motor in the maneuvering room, Schulz and the control room machinist "Kraxel" remanufactured the valve housing and proved it watertight.

"Where are we now on the repairs?" the Old Man asked Kraxel after an hour and a half into the maintenance. Kraxel answered: "We're almost finished with installation of the valve, Herr Kaleu, and then we'll pump by hand to the regulating bunker. We lost some fuel. It was pumped out by the bilges when we surfaced. I estimate that we lost four cubic meters. And the chief found a problem with the main bilge pump and something on the periscope shaft that needs fixing, so I guess we'll be done in another half hour. The busted bunker depth gauge we can do without for now. We've cleaned up the glass."

"Very well. Carry on." Hardegen was not pleased by the loss of fuel. Four cubic meters was not a lot, but when a boat knew that it was probably going to the edge of the chart, any loss was a cause for concern. Was the faulty valve sabotage? There had been a number of incidents recently, such as water and sand discovered in the lubricating oil of some boats, and the tampering with diesel exhausts on U-*101* that had caused three crew deaths. There was no way of knowing, but Hardegen made a note to ask the appropriate questions when he returned to Keroman. For the noon log entry he examined Kaeding's DR line, wrote the numbers on a card, and handed it to Rafalski to type on the KTB form. Distance on the surface during the previous twenty-four hours: 222 nautical miles. Distance submerged: 24.5.

1230 hours. Hardegen could have stayed in port for Christmas Eve. Three of the Paukenschlag boats had not yet sortied, Kals (U-*130*), Bleichrodt (U-*109*), and Zapp (U-*66*). But Hardegen thought that if he had waited until after the Nativity festival to sortie, his men, still feeling the effects of Burgundy and Cognac, would not have been at their edge for the critical first day in the bay. So Christmas Eve was to be at sea. He dived the boat to twenty meters and addressed the crew over the loudspeaker:

"This is the commander speaking. Today we celebrate our Christmas Eve, the most solemn night of the year for us Germans. We could wait until the evening hours, as we would if we were home, but that is the time of day, as you well know, when we need to be on the surface making our best time. So we submerge now and spend a few hours in smooth running and peace and quiet. First, let me read to you a Christmas message, addressed to all boats, that has just been handed me by 'Puster' Rafalski: 'On this German Christmas, I am with you in heart and thought—you, my proud, tough, fighting U-boat crews.' Signed BdU, which means of course, Admiral Dönitz.[4]

"Now, since this is our War Christmas, I want to make it as joyous as possible. To that end I have a few surprises. So I ask every man who can leave his station to assemble now here in the control room."

Within minutes every crew member except Hannes, the cook, Barth on the hydrophone, Rafalski on the radio, and two electricians on the E motors, was crowded tightly around Hardegen in the *Zentrale*.

"You know," he then continued, "that our Patenbataillon has provided us with Christmas trees, enough for every compartment. They will be distributed in a few minutes by the petty officers. The largest of the trees, here in the control room, has been decorated with electric candles by the electricians. You know as well as I why we cannot use traditional beeswax candles. Those of you who have stations elsewhere in the boat are free to come here and to enjoy the large tree as long as we are submerged. It's from the Harz Mountains. I know that its scent evokes memories of home. Second, the Patenbataillon cooks have provided us with some cakes to go along with the pancake meal that Hannes is preparing for us. Now, here are the surprises. First, young people in many parts of Germany have sent you presents, and according to our Christmas Eve customs these will be distributed to the compartments by our own *Knecht Ruprecht* [St. Nicholas's helper], Herr Leutnant von Schroeter! But remember, if you have been a bad boy he will punish you! Next, a lot of mail has been received from your families at home. I will ask my two number ones to pass it out following the meal. I know that that is the most treasured Christmas gift of all, a Christmas message from your loved ones. Finally, the last surprise. You know that, unlike some other commanders, I never allow alcoholic beverages on my boat. Others may have their 'victory bottles' for successful attacks, and I do not judge them, it is simply not my operating procedure. But this one time, this one War Christmas, if you will, I have allotted a certain measure of red-wine punch to each man. The LI, who is so good at fluid levels, will distribute it!

"You also know that we do not have religious services on board, but it would hardly be appropriate to let this very special, sacred occasion pass without formally recognizing the religious faith that I suppose most of you profess. Therefore, if you would give me your reverent attention, I shall read from the Nativity account as it appears in the New Testament Book of Luke."[5]

When the brief reading was over, all hands repaired to their home compartments, where the duty stewards began passing out Hannes's Christmas pancakes and from their bucketlike food containers, called "long boats," ladling out beef and vegetable stew. Later, delivering a second course, they moved through the central gangway with fresh fruit and lemonade. For those who wished coffee, Hannes had prepared a brew less strong and more tasty than the usual bridge watch blend he provided the lookouts. The ratings with their mess kits sat where they could on boxes, bunks, or on the floor plates. In the officers' wardroom and petty officers' compartment, the mess was served on dishes placed on tables with racks, called "fiddles," secured to their edges to keep the crockery from sliding off. At the appropriate time the stewards returned with large slices of the Patenbataillon cakes together with Hannes's own Berliners (jelly-filled doughnuts). Finally, the LI passed through the compartments with large bottles of already prepared wine punch, which added luster to the warm glow left by what even the Old Man called *ein festliches Essen*—a holiday dinner.[6] Most of the men, knowing that this was their last drink for at least a month and a half—an unexpected reprise of "last drinks" taken at the Café les Trois Soeurs two nights earlier—slowly savored the taste from their cups and stretched their contents as long as they could. When the presents and particularly the mail came around, there was little doubt that Christmas sentimentality was very close to the surface among these men who, at other moments, cultivated a hard, soldierlike bravado. The presents from children were touching, but it was the mail from home that moved their hearts. Each man kept to his own self and emotions as he read, over and over, the news and Christmas greetings from family and girlfriends. In the control room Richard Amstein and von Schroeter took turns on Amstein's accordion, and familiar carols of the season filled the strange steel pipe in the belly of the sea: *"Vom Himmel hoch, da komm ich her," "O Tannenbaum," "In Bethlehem geboren ist uns ein Kindelein."* Since the Christmas tree was not only a uniquely German creation but for every man on board the most direct symbolic link with hearth and family, it was to be expected that crewmen accepted the Old Man's invitation and came, singly or in groups, to stand before the control room tree and allow themselves to be mesmerized by its scent and its lights. In each mind's eye no doubt was the fir tree at home decorated with real candles, with apples or blown-glass baubles, and *Kringeln*, pretzel-shaped Christmas cookies. Later this day, in the evening hours, the family would gather for the *Bescherung* when the candles would be lit and the presents distributed. Reinhard Hardegen, with his own small tree on his cubicle desk, pulled closed the green curtain and took out the photographs of wife Barbara and sons, two-and-a-half-year-old Klaus-Reinhard and one-year-old Jörg, while in the control room Amstein's accordion broke everyone's heart:

> *Stille Nacht, heilige Nacht*
> *Alles schläft, einsam wacht. . . .*

0700 hours, Christmas Day, boat on the surface, course 275, *halbe Fahrt*—both ahead two-thirds. Although Walter Kaeding was not the officially assigned navigator, he would end up, by his own choice, doing most of the work. The navigator of record was an Obersteuermann (chief helmsman) whose interests on the boat lay elsewhere. Kaeding (who later would make navigator rank himself) was listed on the boat's roster as petty officer second class and chief bos'n. Corresponding to Hoffmann's position as number one watch officer, Kaeding was the Old Man's number one among the noncommissioned crew members. With navigation his hobby, he had offered at every opportunity on earlier patrols to take readings and sightings as well as to keep the dead reckoning (DR) line on the Atlantic chart, and by the start of this latest patrol Hardegen was relying on him to assume those duties on a continuing basis.

Now Kaeding lifted the aluminum top of the chart case, removed the transparent celluloid cover, and with his pencil added a few millimeters to the DR line he had drawn on the extreme eastern edge of the ocean on paper known as *Karte Nr. 1870G Nordatlantischer Ozean*. With land features in green and water surfaces in white, the nautical chart was divided up into a mosaic of blue-lined squares, or grids, that bore specific letters and numbers. Naval staff had devised this system, by which each *Marinequadrat,* or naval square, covered a region of the North Atlantic approximately the size of France. Each bore a two-letter identifier, or digraph; for example, going west to Newfoundland a U-boat would pass through squares BF, BE, BD, BC, and BB. Each artificial square, about 486 nautical miles per side, was subdivided into many smaller squares identified by double-digit numerals, for example, from 11 to 99, and each smaller square was then subdivided nine times, then nine times again. The result was a fine screen that took the immense ocean down to a mesh no larger than six nautical miles per side and provided quick, near-accurate positioning by letter-number coordinates.[7] Thus, as Kaeding could readily see, U-*123* was positioned now at BF 4411.

With both U-boat and target convoy positions identified in this way, Admiral Dönitz had long feared that one of the grid charts might fall into British or American hands and provide the enemy with a means of locating U-boat stations, particularly if the naval code used in W/T transmissions had been compromised, something that worried him endlessly, though both B-Dienst, the German radio monitoring and cryptographic service, and Naval Staff had assured him repeatedly that British or American penetration of the code was impossible. Still, Dönitz had thought it prudent to camouflage the letter-number identifiers on the grid chart. Accordingly, on 9 September 1941, he sent a signal to all boats detailing a scheme that was to be adopted two days thereafter. It consisted of a contorted inversion of letters and numbers for certain specified naval squares. Knowledge of the new system was to be limited to the smallest possible number of personnel on each operational boat, and base personnel were to have no access to the system at all. The reception of this BdU signal by boats at sea caused widespread perplexity and miscalculation. One sentence toward the end of the transmission read: "If the foregoing is not clear send short-signal YYY."[8] It is said that Ys poured into Hans Meckel's telecommunications receivers at Villecresnes in great profusion.

To replace that admittedly cumbersome way of disguising grid positions, BdU in November introduced a simpler, published system called the Chart-Cipher *Adressbuch* (Address Book), and it was for that book, printed on saltwater-soluble paper, that Kaeding now reached in the confidential papers locker off the officers' wardroom. His DR line showed *123* fast approaching ten degrees west longitude, at which point outward-bound boats were required to send a short-signal report (*Kurzsignale*) to BdU confirming that they were still safely under way at such and such a grid position. (In the following year, when British aircraft—many of them equipped with airborne radar— became more active in the Bay of Biscay, causing boats to make most of their daylight transit into the Atlantic underwater, the reporting point would be changed to fifteen degrees west.) Short signals were brief transmission bursts designed to prevent enemy direction-finding

receivers from triangulating the boat's position; though here again
Dönitz had been assured time and again by Naval Staff that it was
impossible to obtain directional bearings on a shortwave transmission. Kaeding paged through the *Adressbuch* manual and found the
encryption for 25 December: the BF digraph was to be transmitted
that day as Holstenstrasse (Holsten Street), and the street number was
to be calculated off a value 2,500 less than the grid number, or in this
case 1911. Checking further Kaeding found that the camouflage that
day for 1911 was 2250. And U-boat number *123* that day translated to
the name Heinrich Krause. Beginning with two assigned Greek letters
to alert BdU that this was an outbound passage short-signal position
transmission, Kaeding's text now read: BETA BETA HEINRICH KRAUSE
HOLSTENSTRASSE 2250. He walked it through the hatch and handed it
to Rafalski.[9]

"This is ready to go, Puster," he said. "A Beta transmission."

Rafalski wheeled around to the wall bench and pulled forward
his *Schlüssel M* cipher machine. Resembling a portable typewriter
with raised keys, the black metal device occupied a lidded box eighteen by twenty-eight by thirty-three centimeters (seven by eleven by
thirteen inches). In addition to the keyboard, the four-volt battery-
powered machine had slots on the left rear top for the insertion of
three rotable drums, or rotors, and, in the front, a switchboard for the
insertion of plugs. Rafalski consulted his HYDRA cipher handbook
(prominently marked *Geheime Kommandosache!*—"top secret") for
the rotor and plug settings for 25 December and made the designated
connections and adjustments. This completed, he "typed out" Kaeding's already encrypted short signal on the keyboard. As he did so a
random series of letters appeared in glow holes on the top of the
machine, which Rafalski copied onto a pad and divided into letter
groups, which might have appeared as: JUZM RFTN XAELL HLQYM OEUCZ
CSRBB HTISD GUAWH IXMJA. This imponderable gibberish he then
tapped out on his Morse key, which connected through the "Ireland"
circuit, 4412 kilocycles, to Hans Meckel's receivers southeast of
Paris.*

0830 hours, Christmas Day, BdU, Kernével, France. After U-*123*'s position report passed through the receivers south of Paris and made its
way by land line to Kernével, it was handed to a naval cipher clerk in

*See Appendix C.

Meckel's three-story white communications building, itself a former château, adjoining Admiral Dönitz's headquarters. The clerk keyboarded the short signal through a *Schlüssel M* with rotor settings and plug pairs exactly conforming to Rafalski's, according to the cipher of the day. After decrypting, the signal was taken by messenger across a covered walkway that connected the two buildings and handed to the duty officer, Kptlt. Günter Hessler, the A-1, first operations officer and Dönitz's son-in-law. Hessler read the report and took it to the operations grid chart in the large situation room, where he affixed the numbers *123* to a small blue flag on a pin he stuck into the chart at the western edge of naval square BF. Learning of *123*'s safe passage to date, Hessler knew, would please the admiral at his morning conference. The Lion took a special interest in Gruppe Paukenschlag.

Promptly at 0900 Dönitz entered the chart room and, as was his habit, asked first for overnight attack reports, if any, and then for the disposition of all boats and convoys. Kapitän zur See Godt, assisted by Hessler, briefed him on both. There had been no night actions. Both the Atlantic and Mediterranean theaters were quiet. U-*653* west of Ireland had pursued two fast transports at seventeen knots, without result. Oncoming escorts had forced her under and she lost contact. According to intercepts of enemy Morse traffic a British gunboat, K-*196*, rammed a U-boat in the Strait of Gibraltar. This may have been U-*451*, which had not reported in. If lost, that would make six boats presumed lost just within the past several days—together with U-*127*, *131*, *434*, *567*, and *574*—all off Gibraltar.[10] U-*582* had been ordered to proceed to Trondheim at top speed to replace the stud bolts of her exhaust valves. And U-*653* had been assigned to special operations: She was to take up station in naval square AK southeast of Greenland and transmit dummy signals to give the impression of a large number of boats in the North Atlantic. That should distract enemy attention from the Paukenschlag boats and help to disguise their westward routes.

And what was the current status of Gruppe Paukenschlag? Dönitz wanted to know. Two of the Paukenschlag boats have already sortied, Herr Admiral, Hessler reported. Folkers in U-*125* had safely transited the Bay of Biscay and was in the open Atlantic, here—he pointed to a blue flag—at BD 58. Hardegen in U-*123* appeared on the chart for the first time—here—at BF 44. Zapp in U-*66* was scheduled to sortie that day. Bleichrodt in U-*109* and Kals in U-*130* would sortie two days hence.

Dönitz listened to the remainder of the briefing on convoy positions, W/T intercepts, and intelligence estimates. After his staff returned to their desks, he remained behind to brood over the chart. Two Paukenschlag boats were now at sea. Their mission and their positions must be guarded with scrupulous care. Maintaining radio silence at both ends of the communications link would ensure optimum security, but silence was not an option. Dönitz had long ago determined that success in the Atlantic war required that he personally coordinate the dispositions and attacks of U-boats by wireless. And that, in turn, required accurate position reports from the boats, also by wireless. The result to date was that BdU commanded the most complex, extensive, and efficient communications system in the history of military signals.[11] That the enemy would intercept his traffic was a known risk, but an acceptable one given the assurances Dönitz had received from Konteradmiral Ludwig Stummel, chief of the Second Department (Operations) of the Naval Staff at Tirpitz-Ufer in Berlin. Stummel, whose department superintended naval ciphers, including HYDRA, and who consulted regularly with the Berlin cipher firms Kurski & Kruger and Heimsoht & Rinke, had persuaded Dönitz that for an enemy to puncture the Schlüssel M/HYDRA system with its variable range and changes of settings—if the technical feat was possible at all with known methods of mathematical analysis—would require such a protracted time frame that any data developed by the penetration would be long out of date and operationally useless.[12] Dönitz usually felt better after his conversations with Stummel.

On the previous 19 November, concerned that to date convoys had been detected only by individual boats and not, with one exception, by patrol lines, Dönitz had worried in his war diary that the enemy might have decrypted HYDRA traffic and steered convoys around his "rakes." Armed with Stummel's reassurances, however, he added the notation: "This matter is being continually examined by the Naval War Staff and is considered as out of the question."[13] Just the day before, for that matter, on Christmas Eve, Naval Staff, commenting on the loss of Atlantis and Python, declared: "It cannot be assumed that the enemy was able to break our ciphers since the execution of numerous other operations gives no reason for such a supposition. In the opinion of the Naval Staff, U-Boat Division, our ciphers are safe. Conspicuous are recurring losses of ships while cooperating with U-boats. This might be explained by special concentration of enemy intelligence on U-boat warfare."[14] Stummel had argued that such losses were the result of chance-sighting reports from undetected reconnaissance planes, the activity of French agents, radio directional guesses, or brilliant deductions by the British Secret Service.

Perhaps. But Dönitz continued to fret that the cryptographic security of the HYDRA cipher might have been compromised and that U-*123*'s just-received position report, among others, was being read by someone "on the other side of the hill." Did the alternative explanations put forward by Naval Staff truly explain the losses of *Atlantis* and *Python?* (Dönitz did not think surface refueling and replenishing of U-boats would ever again be possible.[15]) How to explain, except by a breach of security, that in the wake of the sinking of the *Bismarck* seven months earlier the Royal Navy identified the positions of all eight tankers and supply ships that OKM had deployed to support *Bismarck* and the heavy cruiser *Prinz Eugen* and in the space of a month sank or captured seven of them? Had the *Prinz Eugen* remained at sea would she have been caught up in the same unprecedented sweep? Was it only striking coincidence that those supply vessels stationed at widely separated points in the Atlantic were so quickly located and disposed of? And was it not suspicious that three British submarines happened upon the controlled rendezvous of three U-boats in the Cape Verde Islands the previous September? More worrisome still was the Ubootwaffe's mounting failure in the past summer and fall to sight convoy targets in the North Atlantic and the U-boats' declining success rate against them.[16] It was manifest that convoys were methodically evading U-boat formations. And now in these last several days, the loss of six boats off Gibraltar! Was all this the result of conventional British intelligence and reconnaissance? Or—though a thorough investigation had failed to disclose a traitor—could it be treachery? Did it not suggest, despite Naval Staff's persistent effort to discount the possibility, that somebody in London was reading his mail?

The vexed admiral took one last look at the few blue flags and returned to his office.

2340 hours, 27 December, U-*123* on the surface, position BE 1976. There was a saying throughout the Ubootwaffe: The most interesting things to know on a boat were the things you were not supposed to know. To few crews at this particular moment was the import of that saying more telling than to the crew of U-*123*. The tantalizing wait for information began when Bootsmann Kaeding passed word to the other petty officers, who then relayed it to all ranks, that the boat had crossed twenty degrees west. That meant, first of all, that *Eins Zwei Drei* was once again a *Frontboot* with all the concomitant combat-duty bonuses in French francs thereunto appertaining. A whoop and a hurrah for that! In the second place it meant that the Old Man could now open his sealed orders, the news of which everyone now awaited with the usual high interest, particularly since wagers had been placed in the forward torpedo room. The boat's course, known to all, could lead to any number of patrol lines south of Greenland, east of Nova Scotia, or off the Newfoundland Bank. Just please don't send us back to Belle Isle Strait! one mixer mock-pleaded to Admiral Dönitz. (He need not have worried: Ice closed the Strait of Belle Isle to navigation from December to early July.) Since most of the enemy convoys formed up off Halifax, the general environs of that port city were the most popular choice of those who cared to make a guess or wager about the boat's destination. Sydney was a close second. Washington, D.C., was laughed out of the compartment—"It's not even a port!" When it finally did happen, word spread rapidly from fore to aft: The Old Man had opened his curtain, called for the officers, and closed the forward and control room hatches.

Hardegen began: "Gentlemen, we're part of a five-boat mission called Operation Paukenschlag [Drumbeat]." He named the other commanders and then placed the Operation Order folder on the wardroom table where his officers watched him slowly extract a chart—the same 1870G chart they carried on board. "Look familiar, gentlemen?" he asked with a smile. "This is as much detail as Flotilla can give us on our target area. Suppose you had never sailed into a particular shoreline or harbor before, knew nothing about its shoals and hazards and depths, much less about its navigational aids like lights and buoys. And all they gave you was this large-area small-scale 1870G. Would you feel very confident?"

"The scale is one to eight million," Hoffmann offered. "But you're smiling, Herr Kaleu."

"No sectional nautical charts," continued Hardegen, "no sailing directions, no list of light signals, nothing but this gross-scale 1870G. And I'll tell you why. Flotilla told me when he handed me the order folder. He said something like, 'Sorry we did not have all the supporting materials you might need.'"

Hardegen paused and, savoring the moment, smiled mischievously around the table. "Flotilla did not leave us totally empty-handed, gentlemen. I don't know where they found this stuff but it's better than nothing. We may not have sailing directions but we do have—" And he pulled out of his folder a slim tourist guidebook to New York City.

"New York!" said Hoffmann, looking blankly at von Schroeter. "New York," came an antiphonal response from Schulz. It was all that anyone could say—until Schulz added, "We can make it. We have the fuel."

"Yes, Chief," Hardegen agreed. "Now there are maps of New York City and some indication of its bays in this guide. But this second guide"—he lifted out a large garishly colored booklet—"this piece may actually help us."

Against a dark blue sky backdrop on the top half of the second guide's cover stood three towering emerald skyscrapers and a golden Statue of Liberty. The lower half presented a depiction of the sale of Manhattan to Dutch Governor Peter Minuit, the legend reading: "1626—Bought for Twenty Four Dollars. 1939—Valued at Twenty Four Billion!" Hardegen unfolded a large map from a pocket in the inside back cover.

"This shows all the ports and bays," he said. "And look at this"—he pointed to Lower Bay—"there's a ship's channel here marked Ambrose Channel and a lightship, the Ambrose Lightship. That tells us something, doesn't it?"

The officers compared the harbor to what they could make out of the irregular coastal features on the 1870G. As they did so they noticed that the 1870G had the Roman numerals I through VI drawn in ink alongside sections of the coastline from Cape Race to Hatteras. Did Hardegen know what the numerals represented? No, he answered, unless they were attack areas for the Drumbeat boats. Perhaps an F.T. to come would explain them.

"What I think happened here," Hardegen said, referring again to the guidebooks, "is that the war with America came on so suddenly and unexpectedly that BdU had no operational charts or other materials for that part of the world, and the only thing they could give us was these guide books. They probably found them in the Lorient or Brest municipal library."[17]

"You'd think that Naval Staff in Berlin would have sent something over," suggested Hoffmann.

"Well, they didn't, apparently," Hardegen said. "I was in New York City as a cadet in 1933 when my class made a round-the-world voyage on the cruiser *Karlsruhe*. I know our ship had to have had all the charts for the harbor at that time. Except for the lights and the tall buildings, I don't remember very much about the place."

"But is New York the only place we're going?" von Schroeter asked.

"Oh no," Hardegen said, pulling out the Operation Order itself. "Here is the full language of our order":

U-123 will proceed independently to naval square CA for initial operations in CA 28, 29, 52, 53. You will make attacks at and around New York Harbor on a day to be communicated by F.T. when all boats of Gruppe Paukenschlag are nearing assigned stations. It is imperative that attacks by all boats begin on the exact day designated. You will not attack any enemy ships encountered before that date unless *Gröner* [merchant ship silhouette identification handbook] shows them at 10,000 GRT or unless specifically permitted or directed to do so by BdU. You will maintain strict radio silence until after your attacks commence. Off the American littoral you will attack unescorted independently sailing coastwise merchant traffic of any kind and nationality, except vessels with clear neutral markings. Following initial attacks at destination New York U-123 will pursue targets south as far as Cape Hatteras. F.T. reports on sinkings, enemy defenses, weather, shore lights and radio beacons, and fuel remaining in cbms will be made on the schedule appended to this order. BdU-Ops.[18]

Hardegen passed the order around for his officers to examine. "So you can see, gentlemen, we're on a tight leash until some date a couple of weeks away. I must tell you that I am personally very gratified that we are going against the Americans. From the beginning I guessed that that was our mission. You remember our experiences off Freetown last spring. Well, now our day has come."[19]

There was certainly no problem making New York in time, he told his officers, whatever that time turned out to be. They and Folkers were at sea well ahead of three of the boats on the same mission. There was nothing in the orders about the stations assigned to the other boats, but Hardegen could report from his briefing by Admiral Dönitz that two other boats, U-125 and U-66, were to be parts of Gruppe Hardegen, so they probably carried orders to operate in the same square. The crew of 123 should feel proud that their boat had been named leader of this group. All the officers must be alert to the kinds of information BdU sought: beacons, lights, buoys, and especially defenses. The chief should be ready to report fuel remaining. The boat started with 250 cubic meters and average daily consumption had been 2.3 cubic meters at a daily run of 165–170 nautical miles. The chief should be ready to report to BdU in cubic-meter categories, but he, Hardegen, preferred to know fuel remaining in terms of days and hours. Now, before he addressed the crew he was required by a supplemental order in the folder to go over with his officers the enclosed "admonition" and "experience" messages. Most had to do with the avoidance of enemy aircraft and the appropriate response a U-boat should make when avoidance was not possible. Typical of the admonition messages were the following:

The greatest danger for the U-boat proceeding independently is enemy aircraft. Surprise attack may come (1) during the day with medium to heavy overcast sky or low-hanging clouds with medium to poor visibility; (2) during the night when there is clear, calm weather, bright moonlight, and phosphorescence.

Planes generally fly at low altitudes in the North Atlantic at about 2,000 meters, and therefore do not come into sight at the horizon but rather at an angle of 30–40 degrees. For the sector in which the sun is standing, use very dark glasses. When the sun is low have one lookout with glasses facing the sun, one without glasses away from the sun.

When proceeding on the surface have the antiaircraft guns always ready for use, that is, cocked and put on safety, magazine attached, and cranked to point high.

Allow only the most essential personnel on the bridge. The Commander will admit additional numbers in exceptional cases. No outside exercise programs are permitted.

For the boat to dive safely in an aircraft situation, the plane must be at least 8,000 meters distant. If in doubt remain surfaced. During a recent surprise attack on a group of three U-boats, one boat made the mistake of submerging. It was bombed while diving and lost. The surface defense of the others was successful. Moral: When surprised stay above and shoot. Diving is death.

There are still boats that during surprise aircraft attack

submerge at the moment the plane flies over the boat. This procedure is incorrect and mortally dangerous. Even the largest planes and flying boats are on the spot of the swirl again after a minute to renew the attack. In this length of time no boat can reach a safe depth, especially if a large number of men have been on the bridge for A/A defense.

Only those boats that constantly anticipate all possible defensive situations, plan their roles accordingly, keep practicing and improving them, and carry them out with unrelenting strictness will successfully overcome the enemy defense. On cruise out and cruise in the main task of the Commander is to get his boat through unendangered. Just passing the time of day is punishable levity.[20]

Hardegen looked about the wardroom to see his officers expelling breath through pursed lips. "As I can see from your demeanor, gentlemen," he said, "we needed to hear that. We've been lax. We need to tighten up. I don't want Tölle on the bridge any more until we reach the air-coverage gap in the central Atlantic. He would slow us up badly on an emergency dive. And besides, he's so clumsy he would probably break his neck. We need to improve our bridge discipline in every way, not just those mandated in these messages. In the days and weeks ahead, you may expect emergency-drill dives and attack simulations at all hours, and I want thirty-five seconds to be the norm and not the exception on submerging.

"Now one last 'experience' message—the chilling kind that you don't like to hear," Hardegen went on.

A U-boat was proceeding in seas force 4 and medium swell at high speed with following sea. The Commander's order to put on leather harnesses and attach them to the bridge brackets was not carried out by the watch officer since the bridge had remained dry for about 20 minutes. Then a heavy sea passed over the boat, the watch officer was washed overboard and not found again. Moral: Put on harnesses in plenty of time, especially with a following sea, even if the harnesses seem a disadvantage for crash diving.[21]

"A word to the wise is sufficient," said Hardegen as he returned the order material to its folder and took it to the confidential papers locker. "Study all this at your leisure. Number One, dive the boat to twenty meters and assemble the crew in the control room. For those who have to remain at their stations, I'll use the loudspeaker."

When the boat reached the ordered depth and most of the crew had jammed into the control room, Hardegen addressed them: "Men, I have opened our Operation Order and reviewed it with the officers. We are going against America. Our first destination is New York."

Hardegen enjoyed the silence that followed, but he observed that the surprise wore off quickly and that most of the crew accepted the news in a businesslike way. There were no expressions of shock, delight, or fear. The rows of impassive faces seemed to say simply, Well, *that's* a new operational area.

"I think we should have success there. Our targets are independently routed coastwise shipping of whatever kind or nationality. We are part of a five-boat attacking force called Operation Paukenschlag. One prong of the force formed by our boat and two others is called Gruppe Hardegen. The five boats will start attacking suddenly, all at once, on a day to be announced by F.T. The element of surprise favors us. The state of readiness of the American defenses is a question mark. Our patrol area is from New York to Cape Hatteras, which is a much-trafficked area some four hundred miles south of New York. The harbor at New York where we will begin is one of the busiest, if not the busiest, in the world. We should not lack for targets, and that will enable us to get even with the Americans who made fools of us off Freetown last spring.

"While waiting at Lorient, and expecting that America might be our destination this time, I asked my wife to send me my notes from the naval history course that I took at Mürwik eight years ago. German U-boats operated off the American coast in the war of 1914–18. But before America got into that war, one of our boats, an underwater freighter named U-*Deutschland,* made two peaceful voyages to that country carrying cargo and mail. A huge boat, 1,860 tons, bigger than we are, she had a complement of eight officers and sixty-five men. It was the commander of that boat, Kapitän Paul König, an old friend of my family's who lived for many years in our home after my father was killed in Flanders in 1917, who smoothed the way for me when I entered the Navy and applied for officer candidate school. In fact, when I was commissioned he gave me his Damascus steel officer's dagger, which I wear with my uniform today. It is a coincidence to say the least that he was the first U-boat commander to appear off the

American coast during the last war—though we were still at peace with America at the time—and now I am to be the first, or among the first, to appear off that coast in this war.

"Before hostilities were declared with America one of our fighting U-boats, U-53, destroyed six British, Dutch, and Norwegian vessels in American waters off Nantucket. And after American entrance into the war another of our fighting boats, U-151, crossed the Atlantic and sank American ships directly off their own coast. So you can see history repeating itself here, too. U-152 and U-117 were the most successful boats in American waters. Six boats in all, called U-cruisers, served in that operational area, and my notes say that in six months they accounted for a large number of ships sunk.[22]

"So you can see that our comrades of twenty-three years ago have led the way, marked the course, and set the standard. It is our duty to measure up. Let every man on board be mindful of his assignment. Constant discipline and steadfast attention to orders will bring us success. Keep your mind on what you're doing. And work together—always together—as a team! That is all. As you were. Return to your stations. Chief, maintain twenty meters for the time being."

Rafalski: The crew had not guessed we were going to the USA.

Barth: Our destination—we only discovered that underwater. But until that time we didn't know where we were going. We only found out in the middle of the Atlantic—"Destination New York."

Kaeding: It was no shock whatsoever. First, we were used to worries, and second, the Americans had really angered us on previous patrols.

Von Schroeter: Of course we recognized the possibilities because we were going into unexplored waters. We could hope that the enemy had not yet prepared for us.

Amstein: Before that we had been other places. It had nothing to do with America as such. If we were here or there, it didn't matter. We got the order and we went.

Barth: You have to admit, though, it was interesting to be going against America.

Sitting on the edge of his bunk where he could see Rafalski busy at his volume pots listening for W/T traffic, Hardegen idly perused the 1870G chart. He wondered if the Americans had learned any lessons from the last war. Were they expecting U-boats? If so, were they expecting them in winter? How many aircraft did they have on anti-U-boat patrol? How many destroyers, escorts, armed yachts? Had the enemy already organized his coastal merchant shipping into convoys? Had he secured port inlets with booms and nets? Or mines? How dangerous were the shoal waters along the littoral? Was there a black-out of coastal cities and towns as required in German home waters? Was there a dimout? Remembering the Strait of Belle Isle, were there fog signals? What was needed was current intelligence. But if BdU or Flotilla had it they were keeping it to themselves. U-*123* was sailing blind—except for one consoling fact: The St. John's and Cape Race radio beacons in Newfoundland were coming into Barth's directional antennas loud and clear. Not only did those navigational aids provide the boat with a midocean fix against which to check the D.R. positions, they suggested that all might still be normal on the North American coastline so far as beacons, lights, and signals were concerned.

Hardegen looked up to see Rafalski patiently holding aloft the F.T. and cipher logs for their every-two-hour signatures. Rafalski asked, "Herr Kaleu, if you plan to remain submerged for a few more minutes, may I play some records for the crew?" Hardegen remembered the just-read admonition about levity, but decided that the Puster's records were a help to morale, not levity. He checked first with Barth to make sure there was no surface traffic.

"Permission granted, Puster. Play the crew's favorite first."

"Yes, Herr Kaleu."

Rafalski hooked the turntable outlet into the boat's speaker system. Within half a minute fifty-one officers and men who had been in the process of assuming their duties, exchanging images of New York, or paying off francs in the forward torpedo room suddenly found themselves singing lustily along with the bright syncopation as their long, narrow tube of boilerplate and weld bored a hole through the dense Atlantic:

> Where's that Tiger! Where's
> that Tiger!
> Where's that Tiger! Where's
> that Tiger!
> Hold that Tiger! Hold
> that Tiger! Hold
> that Tiger! . . .[23]

The next few days passed uneventfully. Hardegen kept the boat on the surface, except for trimming and drill dives, alternating one and both engines on the line. With departure, Christmas, and the Operation Order behind him, and the day-by-day normality of midocean cruising, he had leisure to draw out OKM manuals and bone up on ship recognitions, attack solutions, coastal navigation, and escape procedures. His entries in the U-*123* war diary (KTB) and radio log became more spare and terse:

29 December
    1235. F.T. intercepted, BdU to Folkers (U-*125*) ahead of us. He is to slow and await other four boats in naval quadrant BD. Bleichrodt and Kals sortied on 27 December.

30 December
    1200. In the middle of a low front, shifting winds, rough, inconsistent seas, visibility 14 nautical miles.
    1503. Submerge. Attack drill.
    1610. Surface.

31 December
    1200. A second low, weather the same. Photographer guest crewmember Tölle broke his left index finger in rough seas.
    2300. Incoming New Year in North Atlantic. The U-boat can look back on a successful year, and we are all going into the New Year confidently, hoping for new successes that will lead to the decision of this war.
    2340. F.T. intercepted, U-*701* in BC south of Greenland to BdU: Second Watch Officer Lieutenant Weinitschke lost overboard today at 1849.[24]

Then, on 2 January at 0400 hours, dots and dashes addressed to U-*123* filled Barth's earphones and notepad. Except for Christmas greetings from Admiral Dönitz and New Year's felicitations from Admiral Raeder, this was the first signal to the boat that either Barth or Rafalski had received on their watches. When the Schlüssel M decrypt revealed the first word in the transmission to be *Offizier*—"officer"—meaning that only Hardegen or another officer could continue with the signal, Barth called for Hoffmann who took the cipher machine and the signal to the wardroom table and began punching out the decryption:

OFFICER. TO HARDEGEN U-123. ON 1 JANUARY EVENING IN SQUARE BC 4335 GREEK SHIP DIMITRIOS INGLESSIS REQUESTED TUG ASSISTANCE OWING TO DAMAGED RUDDER. YOU MAY ATTACK IF NOT FARTHER THAN 150 MILES FROM POSITION GIVEN. BDU OPS.[25]

Hoffmann crossed over to Hardegen's bunk and roused the commander from sleep. Within seconds the two men were huddled under the lamp over Kaeding's grid chart computing distances and times and checking out the Greek vessel in *Gröner*.

"She's 5,275 GRT, Herr Kaleu," said Hoffmann, putting *Gröner* back on the shelf.

"Not exactly a ten-thousand-tonner," answered Hardegen. "But since BdU says we can have her, I'd like to go for it. The problem is the distance. BdU says we can attack if the target is within 150 miles. But the Greek position is 360 miles, somewhat to the northwest, approximately here"—he pointed to Virgin Rocks on the Grand Banks where the least depth was 6.75 meters (fourteen feet) over rock. "I don't know. Let's keep steady on 270, both engines at three hundred RPM, and see what develops."

At 1745 hours the next day, following another practice drill underwater, a second signal from BdU arrived. This time the message was more detailed. St. John's had sent a rescue tug, *Foundation Franklin*, out of Halifax, to assist the Greek ship, which had been part of convoy SC 63. The rudder damage had resulted from a fierce sea storm. If the tempest permitted *Foundation Franklin* should be on the scene by 5 January.[26] At 1800 Hardegen made his decision. Even though it meant a fuel loss, and even though it meant disobeying BdU, which he had done once before with great success in the *Aurania* attack, he determined to catch this wounded prey and add her to his bag. Rafalski picked up an SOS directly from *Dimitrios* on the six-hundred-meter band: RUDDER LOST X NEED HELP IMMEDIATELY X APPROXIMATE LOCATION 48–39 N, 48–21 W.[27] At 2000 hours Hardegen and Kaeding calculated that from U-*123*'s current position at BC 6143 they could intercept *Dimitrios* on a steered course of 283 degrees. Hardegen gave the order to the helmsman and directed the engine telegraphs: "Both ahead full!"

At 1530 on 4 January Rafalski and Barth were able to report that the Greek steamer was transmitting directional signals to the recovery vessel. With a cross bearing off St. John's, Hardegen now figured the Greek's position at 310 degrees in approximately BC 2746. He joined von Schroeter and the bridge watch in the visual search. A fog that had hampered visibility lifted for a brief while and the glasses could reach ten miles. Then, gradually, the fog closed in again and visibility went down to two hundred meters. Barth and Rafalski stayed busy below, taking directional bearings and monitoring the six-hundred-meter transmissions that passed from *Dimitrios* to *Foundation Franklin* to St. John's. Rafalski called up the pipe: "They're talking about various means of towing. The salvage vessel will reach the position at 2200." Now a second ship asked for a bearing, Rafalski reported, and a signal was agreed upon: the stricken steamer would give two blasts on her whistle. At 2256 Hardegen heard a foghorn ahead. He ordered the gun crew to battle stations.

"Both ahead slow."

Now there were two different foghorns, very close. In the darkness and fog the watch could see nothing during the next thirty minutes of approach. Then, at 2338, a lookout shouted, "Two lights, weak, port ten!" Hardegen peered through his 7 × 50s and confirmed the sighting. That had to be the steamer and the rescue vessel. But two additional foghorns now sounded in the night. Did we have more ships about than these two?

"Shut down both engines!" he ordered the helmsman. To the sound room he called: "Puster, try to get a count on propellers." As the boat lay to and bounced quietly from trough to wave at steerageway, Barth in his sound room wheeled back and forth across the compass card examining the hydrophone effect produced by propeller cavitation—the partial vacuum that forms and collapses about rapidly revolving blades. At 305 degrees he picked up the familiar *thump-thump-thump* of a commercial steamer, but its higher-than-normal pitch suggested a tugboat. He reported to Hardegen: "HE bearing Red three-zero-five, Herr Kaleu. One small steamer, probably a tug." Crossing 360 degrees to the Green side of the compass, Barth froze as he detected two slightly different sources, mixed, that resembled if they were not in fact the dreaded *swish-swish-swish* of—

"Destroyers, Herr Kaleu! Two in number, bearing Green zero zero four and zero zero six!" Barth was not certain but he would rather be wrong than dead. "Ranges—."

On the bridge Hardegen did not wait for the ranges: "Diesels, both back emergency full! Rudder amidships! Open bow caps, prepare tubes one, two, and four! Gun crew below! Rig for dive!" At just that instant he saw looming before him, not one hundred meters ahead, a large shadow, no doubt the steamer, from which a white blinker light was signaling in Morse. Another smaller shadow now plodded slowly abeam the steamer. Hardegen followed it with his glasses and identified it as a two-stack oceangoing tug. He thought of turning *123* for a bow shot at the large shadow, but as the rudder worked the turn the fog suddenly lifted and moonlight filled the seascape, illuminating the shadow, which turned out not to be the helplessly drifting steamer but a destroyer! He had been within a soccer field's length of a destroyer!

Another destroyer lay five hundred meters off at starboard fifteen, rising and falling on the now-silver water. It was a good thing, Hardegen reflected with a shake of the head, that he had not opened fire with his gun. *Eins Zwei Drei* would have been no match for the barrels of two destroyers. As *123* disengaged, *Dimitrios* and *Foundation Franklin* came into view passing lines preparatory to towing. Hardegen held his breath as *123* backed out of the moonlight. So far, lookouts on both destroyers had failed to detect his nap-of-the-water silhouette. The security of fog finally embraced the boat, and, killing sternway, Hardegen struggled to decide what was his best course of action. While he pondered, the tug took storm-battered *Dimitrios* in tow and set out slowly toward St. John's 450 miles away on a course of three hundred degrees. The two destroyers took positions astern. Should *123* advance and attempt torpedo launches at the steamer and both destroyers? Or at the steamer alone? A submerged attack was out of the question: Despite the nearly full moon it was too dark for the attack periscope, which had poor light transmission qualities. He considered a surface attack. The problems here were several. First, because of the now-bright moonlight, he would have to launch from a great distance out, reducing accuracy. Second, he would have to go for the destroyers first—*Dimitrios* and the tug not being able to escape or do him harm—and from a distance the destroyers presented small, frisky targets; success was doubtful. Third, the fathometer in the control room was showing only sixty meters' depth under the hull, which meant no escape from depth charges should the torpedoes miss and even one destroyer bring her ASDIC to bear. Fourth, he should be saving his torpedoes for "Drumbeat." As this line of reasoning reached its end, a deep fog swirled in again. With visibility down to one-to-two-hundred meters, new circumstances made the question of attack moot. Such, one could say, was the nature of naval warfare in the wintry North Atlantic.

That was not what Reinhard Hardegen would say. In composing his war diary during the next hour and a half he reproached himself bitterly for not having attacked at all. "Attack, Advance, Sink!" were the words of the Lion. Hardegen had failed for the first time in his naval career to pursue an enemy, attack him aggressively, and sink him if possible. To the KTB he confessed: "Fundamentally, my behavior has certainly been wrong. I uselessly expended six cubic meters [1,600 gallons] of fuel. Only the coming weeks will disclose if my decisions are justified by 'Drumbeat.'"[28]

Deciding that he would never again permit this kind of ambivalence to develop, Hardegen determined that the next time imponderables threatened to overcome clean, direct military action he would attack first, at once, decisively, and let history sort out the consequences. Timidity, which is how he characterized his balancing of options and dangers, would never again cast an enervating spell over *123*. To hazards he would henceforth be indifferent. As boat and crew resumed their course for the United States, the commander braced his shoulders and hardened his face for the stern errand ahead.

6

Waiting for Hardegen

1100 hours, 2 January 1942. In the coastal township of Flowerdown near Winchester in southern England a motorcycle dispatch rider in battle dress sat lazily atop his Matchless G3L motorcycle waiting for a member of the Women's Royal Naval Service (WRNS) to bring him his packet. Towering above the Y Station hut where the Wrens worked were three rectangular radio antennas. The dispatch rider had no idea what the antennas were receiving. Neither, for that matter, did the Wrens, whose finely trained ears, plugged into RCA AR 88 super-heterodyne communications receivers with interference-cutting crystal gates, were in intimate, though hardly affectionate, contact with hundreds of German shortwave Morse senders, the fastest keyers in the world. The Wrens knew many of them as soon as their transmissions began, whether from stations on land or at sea, for each of them had his own distinctive keying style, or "fist." The BdU fists were unmistakable, like old family friends. And some of the U-boat senders, too, who had been at sea on numerous patrols, came into Flowerdown like regular club members. The Wrens gave them names like Handlebar, Wagner, Menjou, or Moselle. Where they were surprised by a new, idiosyncratic fist they ran a recording of the signal on an oscillograph that provided an operator signature called TINA. By RFP, or radio fingerprinting, they could identify a transmitter and its power supply. And by triangulating with other Y Service stations at Scarborough on the east coast and at Hvalfjord, Iceland, they could estab-

149

lish the intersection, or "cuts," of bearing lines and acquire a generally good "fix"—sometimes within a dozen miles, more often within thirty to fifty miles—of a given transmitter's geographical location. The system, called High Frequency/Direction Finding (HF/DF, or "Huff Duff"), zeroed in on a shortwave transmission from the moment the first dot or dash left the operator's hand. Not a boat at sea escaped the Wrens' net. What *did* escape them was the meaning of the intercepted signals. It would have been nice to know what Handlebar and Wagner were saying. But the five-letter groups were all gobbledygook to the Wrens as they prepared the sheaves of papers for the forenoon dispatch packet.

With the packet in its waterproof case slung across his shoulders, the rider kicked his starter and set out with a racket on country roads north through Hampshire and Berkshire Downs to Newbury, Oxford, and Stony Stratford. After four hours of riding, which he was under orders not to interrupt for any reason including calls of nature, he entered the outskirts of a Buckinghamshire railway-junction town called Bletchley, some fifty miles northwest of London and halfway between Oxford and Cambridge. Following its narrow streets he came to a guard gate outside a red-brick mansion in pseudo-Tudor-Gothic style with manicured lawns and a swan pond. The place was called Bletchley Park, though since 1939 the edifice itself had assumed the name—mostly fictitious—Government Code and Cipher School, GC & CS, called also BP or, by code name, Station X. After passing sentry inspection, the rider wound around to the back of the building, where thousands of men and women, in and out of the military services, worked around the clock in single-story white-frame Nissen huts that were scattered about the spacious grounds. His destination was Hut 8. There he handed his packet to the duty officer, signed the dispatch ledger, and headed for the WC and kitchen in the sentries' canteen. In two hours he would be on the road back to Flowerdown.

Inside Hut 8 the duty officer passed the packet of intercepts to the Wren in charge of naval cryptanalysis on the afternoon watch. She, in turn, assisted by a battery of other servicewomen, copied the intercepts, signal by signal, onto tapes and fed them into an eight-foot-tall "copper-colored cupboard" called *"Bombe."* At Bletchley Park (BP) the German Schlüssel cryptographic machine (as well as its product) was called "Enigma": the *Bombe* was an electromagnetic scanning machine constructed from a series of Enigmas yoked together. The *Bombe* had been conceived in 1934 by Polish Intelligence Service mathematicians who were in possession of an early model of the German-invented Schlüssel and had contrived with partial success to defeat it. Only months prior to Hitler's invasion of Poland, they had passed on two copies of the basic machine to French and British Intelligence together with plans, drawings, and instructions to explain how their yoked series of six machines could explore the Enigma's range of alphabet and word possibilities far faster than the pace of human thought. At BP a young, eccentric Cambridge mathematician named Alan Turing, who had long been devoted to the theory of a universal calculating machine, made an original contribution that greatly increased the power of the *Bombe*. Though electromechanical rather than electronic, Turing's brilliant design anticipated the modern computer. By April 1940 the "copper-coloured oracle of Bletchley" spoke. First to shed its veils was Luftwaffe Enigma traffic, owing to its low-grade operators and slack communications discipline. Shortly afterward, Wehrmacht Enigma yielded to the penetrations of the *Bombe,* which rendered the five-letter cipher groups into their original German message forms. Reading was not always current: Sometimes 72 hours would pass before BP could produce a passable text, sometimes the process would take a week, and sometimes the *Bombe* failed altogether; except that BP could always count on the Luftwaffe's key for the day being available by breakfast.[1] Having the key, which meant having the rotor settings and the plug pairings for a given twenty-four-hour period, was the essential requirement if BP was to be able to read the W/T intercepts with any regularity. And that was why naval Enigma was the last to submit.

Kriegsmarine cipher discipline was the tightest of any in the German armed forces. The Ubootwaffe was particularly security conscious and had made a number of complicating modifications in the machine. The result was that for a long time U-boat HYDRA (which BP called DOLPHIN) was invulnerable. What BP needed was a full or current HYDRA handbook giving settings and pairings, and that meant a capture, or, as the British liked to say, a "pinch." On 23 February 1941, during a commando raid on the Norwegian Lofoten Islands, a Royal Navy boarding party discovered spare *Schlüssel-M* rotors, though no machine, on the abandoned German trawler *Krebs.* By March 1941, BP was reading much of HYDRA but with a month's lag time, too great for the data to be of operational value. Then, on 7 May, in a tightly planned operation, boarding parties of the Royal Navy captured cipher material from the German weather ship

München. Two days later, in an even more dramatic and critical pinch, three warships escorting convoy OB 318 southeast of Greenland depth-charged and crippled U-*110*, commanded by Kptlt. Fritz-Julius Lemp, notorious as the sinker of the Donaldson liner *Athenia* on the first day of war and one of two commanders—Hardegen being the other—known to have been required by Admiral Dönitz to falsify a KTB. To Lemp and his crew, as their boat lay helpless on the surface, the British called out: *"Boot hoch halten, sonst wird keiner gerettet!"*— "Keep your boat afloat or no one will be rescued!" Gas fumes drove Lemp and the panicking U-boat crew into the water, where all but Lemp were picked up and taken below by the secrecy-sensitive warship captains. As for Lemp, he attempted to swim back to *110* and scuttle her but was shot dead as he clambered onto the deck. In *110*'s interior a boarding party discovered her Schlüssel M with spare rotors; HYDRA handbook with daily settings and pairings and special settings for officer-only signals, all valid to the end of June; short-signal position codes; and other confidential papers. Heavily guarded, the godsend was transported at flank speed to home port, and thence to BP, where the capture was quickly recognized as one of the decisive intelligence breakthroughs of the war to date. Within days BP was reading naval Enigma much closer to the grain.[2]

Between 25 May and 21 June, BP supplied the position coordinates from Enigma that enabled warships to destroy seven of the eight German supply ships that had been posted at various points in the Atlantic to assist *Bismarck, Prinz Eugen,* and operational U-boats. Wary lest such a wide-ranging roundup be taken by the Germans as more than coincidence, the Admiralty backed off from further grand slams and concentrated instead on evasive routing of convoys from known positions of boats and patrol lines. One of the first examples of Enigma-assisted diversions occurred on 23 June when BP warned that ten U-boats lay athwart the route of Britain-bound convoy HX 133. From that date throughout 1941 and into early 1942, BP supplied enemy information that led to an ever-decreasing number of sinkings in the established convoy lanes of the North Atlantic, off Gibraltar, and in the Mediterranean.[3] Only the short-signal position reports after November caused serious cryptanalytical problems and delays owing to Dönitz's *Adressbuch,* which, still unresolved by Turing's *Bombe,* required continuous ad hoc research.

Now on 2 January the Wrens who served the engine patiently

watched its front wheels spinning and listened to its innards—
clickety-click, clickety-click, like a knitting machine—as for hours the
device considered one possible setting/connection after another
seeking the one mathematically elusive combination that fitted a prescribed group of letters. Suddenly the machine stopped. A printer
engaged. An elated Wren, sensing personal triumph, drew out a
printed text on tape. From Wren to Wren the text made its way thirty
yards outdoors to Hut 4, Naval Section, where it came under the care
and scrutiny of a donnish group of men, mostly civilians recruited
from nearby Oxford and Cambridge. Linguists, logicians, classical
scholars, they formed the translating and intelligence-processing
watch for all Kriegsmarine signals. Combining an exact and comprehensive knowledge of German with a newly acquired mastery of
U-boat and surface-ship technology, nautical terms, and military ab-
breviations, the twelve-man watch sat around a bare horseshoe table
in a forty-by-forty-foot room, where the number one of the watch,
seated in the middle of the horseshoe, assigned decrypts for translating. The latest example presented no problems. Very quickly one of the
dons joined or separated the German five-letter groups to form words,
phrases, and sentences, translated the result into English, and handed
the result to the number one, who inspected first the reconstructed
German text and then its English rendering: OFFICER. TO HARDEGEN
U-123. ON 1 JANUARY EVENING IN SQUARE WRANGELSTRASSE 1587 GREEK
SHIP DIMITRIOS INGLESSIS REQUESTED TUG ASSISTANCE OWING TO DAM-
AGED RUDDER. YOU MAY ATTACK IF NOT FARTHER THAN 150 MILES FROM
POSITION GIVEN. BDU OPS.

The identity of the naval square Wrangelstrasse would have to
be established, or guessed at, by the Submarine Tracking Room in
Operational Intelligence Centre in London. Otherwise, satisfied that
the signal had been accurately translated and that it required no
annotation or comment, the number one assigned the text medium-
rank priority of two Zs (on a scale of Z to ZZZZZ) and passed both the
German and English versions to the Wren head of the indexer shift,
who underlined the name of the Greek vessel with red chalk for
inclusion in the Naval Section card file. This done, the English text was
taken to a teleprinter, where one of a bank of "teleprincesses" typed
the HUSH MOST SECRET document into a secure circuit that led directly
from this quiet Buckinghamshire backwater to the Operational Intelligence Centre (OIC) in the "Citadel," a concrete blockhouse on the

northwest corner of the Admiralty nearest the Mall, which runs from Buckingham Palace to Admiralty Arch.

0600 hours, 3 January 1942. Lieutenant Patrick Beesly was still so new at his job that every morning when he entered the "Citadel" and descended to the underground Submarine Tracking Room (NID 8 [S]) of the OIC, he could anticipate learning something entirely new—and being strictly examined on it by the Tracking Room director, Temporary Commander Royal Navy Volunteer Reserve (RNVR), Special Branch, Rodger Winn. It was easy to feel intimidated by Commander Winn, whose formidable intellect not only prevailed over U-boat movements but carried weight beyond the Tracking Room into the other divisions and functions of the OIC: the Lower War Room for Operations, the Movements Section of the Trade Division, Surface Ship Intelligence, D/F Plotting, Anti-Submarine Warfare (A/SW), and the civilian-manned War Registry, which handled all incoming and outgoing signals. Thirty-eight years old, Winn held degrees from Cambridge and Harvard. He enjoyed a successful civilian career as a barrister and when war broke out volunteered as an interrogator of German prisoners. Somehow in August 1939 he ended up in the Tracking Room where, still a civilian, he demonstrated a quick mastery of U-boat tactics and, somewhat to the annoyance of his superior, a regular RN paymaster captain, who insisted that the feat was impossible, an uncanny ability to predict future U-boat movements. Subsequently, to no one's surprise in the OIC, he was promoted to temporary commander's rank in the volunteer reserve and appointed to replace his superior—an unprecedented promotion for a man who had not passed through Dartmouth naval college to regular line or executive officer status. That by dint of mind and will Winn had overcome childhood polio that left him with crippled legs and a humped back further burnished his reputation and influence among OIC colleagues, who, though they did not always find him an easy man to work with—particularly if their own performance seemed not to measure up to his demanding standards—nonetheless admired him enormously.

Patrick Beesly had come into the Tracking Room by a similarly circuitous route. Like Winn, he had dreamed as a boy of joining the Royal Navy but in his case poor eyesight frustrated that dream. After Cambridge he entered upon a career as an insurance broker with Lloyd's of London. With war on the horizon and eyesight no longer the gatekeeper it was in peacetime he was accepted, in June 1939, in the Royal Navy Volunteer Reserve, Special Branch, where he wore a green stripe on his sleeve to show (as the executive officers' lobby required) that he and other reservists had not passed through Dartmouth to executive grade. As a twenty-seven-year-old "Greenstriper," he went to the OIC in July 1940 and started as an assistant to Commander Norman ("Ned") Denning, who was in charge of Surface Ship Intelligence. With Denning he worked primarily on German raiders operating under merchant ship disguise, until December 1941, when Commander Winn asked for reinforcement of his seriously understaffed Submarine Tracking Room and Beesly was sent over to be deputy director. Thus, at the onset of 1942, two essentially civilian types, Winn and Beesly, presided over the whole of Britain's intelligence war against the Ubootwaffe and, what was more remarkable, made the principal *operational* decisions that sent executive officers on their A/SW missions.[4] To Winn and Beesly, too, fell the duty of advising their new full-time partner in hostilities, the United States Navy, of U-boat movements that might intrude on U.S. waters.

On this particular morning Beesly entered the Tracking Room through the guarded door off the Main Trade Plot and took his chair in the deputy director's glass cubicle-office that adjoined Winn's on the southeast side of a fairly large room, an irregular pentagon in shape, with cream-painted windowless walls that were covered with charts, graphs, pictures of U-boats, and—by Winn's order—a large photograph of a pensive-looking Admiral Dönitz, since Winn thought of this room as a shadow BdU. Dominating the floor space on the southeast side was the Main North Atlantic Plotting Table, its center just reachable by an arm's reach. It depicted latitudes and longitudes seventy-three north to five south and one hundred west to sixty east. Tabbed pins on the plot identified all known surface ships, Navy and merchant, all military and seaborne trade convoys, and all operational U-boats. As a precaution against security penetration, particularly when the cleaning women came in the morning or when visitors without proper clearance were brought in by high officials such as the First Sea Lord, the pin tabs bore number and letter codes. U-boat numerals were disguised by double letters: digraphs with initial letters A, C, E, and so on denoted VIIC boats; those of series B, D, F, and so on indicated Type IXs. Thus U-*123* might appear as BH on one patrol and NR on another. A key to the digraphs was kept under seal, though the main plot was so precisely imprinted on Winn's mind that he (unlike Beesly at this point) never had to consult it. To the northwest side of the room was a table of near equal size bearing a captured German naval grid plot. Farther on, at the northwest point, was a smaller D/F plot table. In the southeast corner sat an ASW observer. There was not a regular officer in the room. The southwest wall held offices for the remainder of the small, overstretched staff: four civilian-suited RNVR watchkeepers, and three women civil servants who provided clerical assistance. The "teleprincesses" occupied an adjoining room from which a Wren called the Secret Lady distributed "Z" messages from BP. In the Tracking Room, Z messages were known as "Z" or "Special Intelligence." When signals containing or based on their contents went out from OIC to headquarters, base, and fleet commanders, these became known as "Ultra."[5]

Beesly's first task was to prepare for the 0730 review of overnight developments with Winn and for the 0800 scrambler conference call with the commander in chief Western Approaches and the commander in chief Coastal Command. He began by calling for the Secret Lady, who brought him a sheaf of telegram-size sheets each containing a separate naval Enigma decrypt. There had not been much traffic overnight, but one signal intercept suggesting an imminent attack caught his full attention. His eyes moved rapidly across it: U-123 . . . DIMITRIOS INGLESSIS . . . DAMAGED RUDDER . . . 150 MILES FROM. . . . He knew what Winn would want to have in hand in order to evaluate this signal. He walked across to the file clerk and obtained from her the cards on U-123. Next he looked up Dimitrios Inglessis in Lloyd's Register of Ships and asked one of the teleprincesses to transmit an overseas cable teleprinter message to Naval Service Headquarters (NSHQ) in Ottawa alerting the Canadian Navy to the threat posed by 123 and asking for an immediate position and status report on Dimitrios. Finally, back in his office, he placed a scrambler phone call to "Professor Corduroy," as Winn liked to call Harry Hinsley, a twenty-year-old Cambridge undergraduate with long tousled hair and worn corduroy trousers who was the Tracking Room's regular close contact, along with Section Head Frank Birch, in Naval Section Hut 4 at BP.[6] To Hinsley, Beesly expressed the wish of the Tracking Room that he keep a special lookout for all intercepts mentioning U-123 or Dimitrios. By 0720, all his data in hand, he prepared his mind for the questions he was sure—after working three weeks with Winn—the director would ask him or expect him to anticipate in his briefing.

At precisely 0729 the bespectacled wizard Winn came through

the door with his pronounced limp, waved a good morning at everyone as far as the two D/F plotters at the end of the room, and hung his cap and coat in his cubicle-office, nodding at Beesly through the glass wall as he did so. Beesly went out to meet him, and the two men took positions on either side of the main plot.

"Good morning, sir."

"Good morning, Beesly." Winn assumed his customary half-crouched position, supporting his deformed back by leaning stiff-armed on his knuckles against the table. "What does Admiral Dönitz have for us this morning?"

Beesly began. There had been no night actions. From Special Intelligence important new information had arrived on U-*123* that he would present at the close of the briefing. The general situation that morning was unchanged from the evening before, except that five boats had continued their advance toward the western Atlantic and there were these several new developments: U-*701* reported sighting a convoy at 1045 hours in AM 3377. That would be HG 76. U-*134* reported sinking an independently routed vessel in AB 6337, but a check with trade plot showed no ships lost at that position or elsewhere in the last twenty-four hours. And a Royal Navy patrol reported sighting a surfaced U-boat at 0948 hours in AM 2633. He would guess that to be U-*333*, here (pointing to the spot). Repeated failures of U-*79* and U-*75* to answer wireless calls from BdU confirmed that those boats had been lost, at the hands, respectively, of *Hasty* and *Hotspur* on 20 December and *Kipling* on the twenty-eighth. And that was all there was on the morning plot.

The final figures for December sinkings had been tallied, he went on, and they amounted to sixty-two thousand tons, the lowest monthly total since May 1940. Twenty 500-tonners continued to operate in the Mediterranean.[7] No new *Rudeltaktik* against transatlantic trade had formed. Only six boats were on stationary Atlantic stations, all near the Azores, although there continued to be a strong advance westward by individual boats, which the Tracking Room could identify as five in number, U-*125, 123, 66, 109,* and *130.* All were 740-tonners, all out of Lorient, the last two of which sortied on 27 December. Additional boats have sortied from various Biscay bases in recent days, all 500-tonners, and those that have sent position reports at ten degrees west were following a westerly heading, 270 or 275, that would take them in the wake of the five boats whose pins were at various points of midocean on the plot.[8] The advance westward of the five 740-tonners appeared to have been the reason for the attempted wireless camouflage by U-653 in the North Western Approaches. The *ruse de guerre* collapsed quickly, as noted before, since BP intercepted the instructions for the dummy signals and the boat was quickly D/Fed as a single source at a more or less stationary position.

The new information just in on U-123 suggested a correction to her course and position. (Beesly handed the Special Intelligence decrypt to Winn.) The Tracking Room first learned of her sortie, position, and probable track on 25 December when she sent her first, and so far only, short signal. The position was disguised, of course, and though the enciphered square went unsolved, Tracking Room knew it was sent at ten degrees west and D/F acquired a good fix, which indicated a westerly heading. By advancing 123's pin with dividers at an average speed of ten knots, the Tracking Room had the boat closing that morning on the north Newfoundland Bank. This new signal would suggest that she was at a position somewhat to the south of the pin, or at least that Admiral Dönitz assumed she was to the south. NSHQ Ottawa just now teleprinted the *Dimitrios* position as 48-39N, 48-21W, which was the vicinity of Virgin Rocks. If 123 was anything like 150 to 300 miles from Virgin Rocks, she would be located within a circle thus. (Beesly drew a circle south of the U-123 pin.)

That would be farther south at that longitude than any boat had proceeded thus far in Canadian waters. Had Beesly notified Ottawa of 123's presence?

Yes, Beesly replied. St. John's had already answered the distress call with a seagoing tug and two destroyers. The "Wrangelstrasse" position disguise apparently represented the western edge of naval quadrant BC; would Commander Winn agree to moving the pin south to about here (again, Beesly pointed)?

Agreed, Winn said. He was familiar with this boat. It had recently completed a patrol in the Strait of Belle Isle and south of Greenland. En route it torpedoed the AMC *Aurania*. Its patrol prior to that was off Freetown. Who was its commander and what did the room have on him?

Beesly reached for his cards. Hardegen, he answered. Reinhard Hardegen. Born in Bremen, 18 March 1913. Joined the Kriegsmarine in 1933, made the usual round-the-world cruise as a cadet, and entered the Naval Academy at Mürwik in June 1934. After commissioning was assigned to naval aviation, became a pilot. Crashed in 1936, leaving him with a limp and a bad stomach. Transferred to Uboot-waffe in 1939 and was appointed directly after basic training to U-boat Commanders School. Afterward was assigned as watch officer to the 740-tonner U-*124* for two patrols. First command was a training boat, U-*147*. Took over U-*123* from Karl-Heinz Möhle in May 1941 and made his first patrol off Freetown in June, July, August. Sailed last October–November to Strait of Belle Isle and Greenland. So far as the room knew he had seven sinkings and one damaged to his credit. POW interrogations disclosed that his reputation in the fleet was one of marked aggressiveness, independent and impetuous action—he disobeyed explicit orders from BdU when he torpedoed *Aurania* in October, as BP learned from intercepts—and daring. That was all that was known, except that he had married Barbara Petersen in Wolfen on 22 June 1938 and had two sons, Klaus-Reinhard and Jörg.

Winn raised his eyes to look past Beesly at the steely gaze of Admiral Dönitz in the wall photograph opposite. What was the Lion up to? Winn's eyes bored through the photograph in an attempt to read the German's mind. He was satisfied that he already knew much from D/F and particularly from Special Intelligence, to which even the transposition of grid identifiers and the street-address ciphers had proved permeable. He knew far more from these sources than Tracking Room had ever learned from CX (French agents' reports), which were uniformly so late in arriving they were operationally useless.[9] But what he did not know was the admiral's current *objectives*. Why the sudden reversal of course? From pulling all his boats out of the convoy lanes, he had now sent at least five, and it appeared a good many more to follow, into the Atlantic. And all the Special Intelligence and D/F to date could not explain why. The Libyan campaign had not wound down. Dönitz had no more boats on operational status than he had two weeks before, and he had just suffered a series of disastrous losses off Gibraltar. It was a puzzle. Two facts stood out, though, in Winn's mind: First, a Z message of 29 December had ordered U-*125*, the first of the western boats to sortie, to delay its advance in naval quadrant BD until U-*123*, *66*, *109*, and *130* caught up. That could mean that the first boats were meant to form a patrol line. Or—his brow darkened—it could mean that the five boats were scheduled to begin independent operations at the same precise time. Second, the United States had just formally entered the war.

Lifting himself with difficulty from the table's edge, he said to

Beesly: "Be sure that the people upstairs keep Washington informed." Winn smiled wryly. He rather liked the fact that someone on the other side also had a limp and a bad stomach.[10]

At the beginning of 1942, while British Naval Intelligence Division stood at the near zenith of its powers, the reputation and influence of its U.S. Navy counterpart in Washington, D.C., lay at ruinous discount. Still stunned by the operational failure that was Pearl Harbor, riddled with recrimination, confusion, intramural feuding, and disaffection, and burdened furthermore by administrative structures that frustrated the evaluation, dissemination, and use of data acquired from German and Japanese sources, the Office of Naval Intelligence (ONI) in the sixth wing on second deck of the Navy Department at Constitution Avenue and 17th Street presented a shocking contrast to the OIC.

Intelligence as a branch or specialty in the U.S. Navy was held in nowhere near the regard it could claim in the Royal Navy. During the period before Pearl Harbor it was not considered a path of advancement for any officer who aspired to the command of a deep draft ship. Even a forceful personality, as that exhibited by Captain Alan G. Kirk, who became director (DNI) of ONI in March 1941, could not long withstand the withering derision of officers in Operations. "Everybody sort of thought Naval Intelligence was striped pants, cookie-pushers, going to parties and so on," he said in an oral-history interview after the war.[11] Kirk thought that ONI should emulate the OIC into whose mysteries he had been initiated while serving as naval attaché in London. But his efforts to establish such a center, with a respectable U-boat tracking room, were resisted by the Navy's dominant Washington personality, fifty-five-year-old, six-foot, lantern-jawed Rear Admiral Richmond Kelly "Terrible" Turner, Director of War Plans (OP-12) in Operations. Holding intelligence types in persistent contempt, Turner treated ONI as no more than a hallway drop-box, raided its data, made up his own estimates, projections, and warnings, which were frequently wrong (as for example, his warning that Japan would invade the Soviet Union rather than, as Kirk and his staff insisted, Southeast Asia), and provoked near mutiny on second deck.

"Kirk certainly wasn't any weak sister," said one of his aides, ". . . and he and Turner were on the mat all the time. The DNI was fighting to maintain the integrity of this section, but losing out."[12] By October, Kirk was ready to fight a different kind of war: He asked for and received command of a destroyer squadron in the Atlantic. The last indignities had been to learn that he had been spied on by a White House operative and that his assignment of a brilliant naval attaché to Cairo had been withdrawn for other duties by the Department of State. Kirk's replacement, Medal of Honor winner (Veracruz, 1914) Rear Admiral Theodore S. "Ping" Wilkinson, was the third officer to head the besieged ONI in a twelve-month period, and, more conciliatory than Kirk, he was made short work of by Turner, who continued unimpeded to arrogate to himself functions of naval intelligence about which he seemed to know little, while Wilkinson for his part showed lamentable lack of interest in the most fundamental data coming in from communications intelligence—to the point that, when asked by a congressional committee after the war if he had even discussed the possibility of a Pearl Harbor, he answered, "Unfortunately, no."[13] This situation, combined with a power struggle between ONI and the Office of Naval Communications (ONC) and a disturbing display of professional backbiting and jockeying for personal advancement, led to an environment in which it was understandable that no high-ranking officer in the sixth wing seemed to be awake to the significance of the Japanese high-grade J 19 and JN 25 operational ciphers, of the "bomb plot" decrypt, and of the "lights code" message—all familiar items of evidence to Pearl Harbor inquisitors of a later time—and could only stand by mutely as the undetected carrier fleet of Admiral Chuichi Nagumo steamed across 180 degrees longitude into the Western Hemisphere.[14]

While the top ranks of operations and ONI engaged in their bitter turf struggles, in the midst of which Pearl Harbor might be described as a mere contretemps, the rank-and-file naval intelligence community—uniform and civilian, male and female, cryptanalysts and translators, Morse senders and radio technicians—were achieving excellent results on a near par with the work of the British Y Service and Bletchley Park. Their activities had begun long before, in January 1924, when a young lieutenant picked from command of a Yangtze River minesweeper conceived, built, and first organized naval Communications Intelligence (COMINT), later to be designated OP-20-G in department argot. In his rumpled uniform and with hair like an unmade bed, Laurence F. Safford contrasted sharply with the crisp upper-deck Navy, but "Saffo," as his admiring colleagues called him, proceeded over the years to construct electronic interception, decrypting, and analysis systems that at the outbreak of World War II compared favorably in many respects with the best examples of British and German developments in the same fields. He had started interception activity in 1928, when he and his assistants recruited enlisted men to be Japanese-language Morse operators and trained them in four-month courses conducted in a classroom structure that he had erected secretly on the roof of Main Navy, leading the first graduates, who went on to man interception stations in the North Pacific and at Bainbridge Island near Seattle, to brand themselves the On the Roof Gang. By December 1941 there were eight interception stations in operation, including four on the Atlantic Coast, with 116 receivers. All included HF/DF capacity with directional antennas that could fix on target transmitters and plot bearings geometrically, diversity receivers to defeat selective fading, and syphon recorders for copying high-speed automatic transmissions. By 1939 "Huff-Duff" was tracking Japanese warships and merchant vessels throughout the Western Pacific. By May 1941 the East Coast strategic D/F net was having some success in identifying U-boat transmissions in the Atlantic and in exchanging directional bearings with OIC in London; although it must be said that U.S. technology in this field lagged behind that of the British, and as late as June 1942 the number of operators with solid bearing-computation experience was so small that U.S. Navy fixes were frequently offered with the qualifier that they might be "within two hundred miles" of the U-boat targeted, so that primary reliance on the British net and estimate continued.[15]

POLISH

As the British distinguished themselves in the cracking of German Enigma, so at the same time U.S. codebreakers enjoyed striking success penetrating the Japanese ciphers, which also originated on an electromechanical machine, known in Washington in its progressively sophisticated forms as "M1," "M3," "Red," "Alphabetical Typewriter 97," and finally, "Purple." In the late 1930s both Navy and U.S. Army cryptanalysts attacked the Japanese diplomatic (DIP) and naval (J 19 and JN 25) machine-based random ciphers. At Commander Safford's OP-20-G cryptology division in Room 1621, Main Navy (code named Station Negat), and at his basement branch office in the old Administration Building near Dock Ten Ten at Pearl Harbor (Station Hypo), the immensely talented duo of Mrs. Agnes Myer Driscoll (Negat) and Commander Joseph Rochefort (Hypo) had both succeeded by the beginning of 1942 in making partial manual penetrations of the naval ciphers. (Rochefort had not been authorized by Washington to work on the crucial JN 25 cipher prior to 7 December. It was Rochefort who, six months after Pearl Harbor, would make the single most important intelligence finding of the Pacific war when he correctly identified "AF" in JN 25 transmissions as being Midway, enabling Admiral Chester W. Nimitz to engage and defeat the major Japanese fleet en route to that island on 3–5 June 1942. A jealous Navy hierarchy in Washington, which had identified "AF" as the Aleutian chain, conspired to deny Rochefort the Distinguished Service Medal recommended by Nimitz for his accomplishment. Secretary of the Navy John F. Lehman, Jr., made the award posthumously forty-three years later, on 8 October 1985.) Meanwhile, the Army's Signal Intelligence Section (SIS), headed by the brilliant Lieutenant Colonel William F. Friedman, with a timely assist from civilian Leo Rosen, had achieved a prodigious breakthrough—though it put Friedman in Walter Reed Hospital with a nervous breakdown—by solving the wiring diagram (which employed telephone stepping switches instead of rotors, as electrical engineer Rosen discovered) of the Purple machine used for DIP. Safford generously acknowledged the feat ("The Army's solution of the Purple machine was the masterpiece of cryptanalysis in the pre-war era."[16]) and immediately offered the manufacturing services of the Washington Navy Yard for constructing analogs of the machine. The first two Navy-built copies cost $684.55 for hardware. Eight eventually were built, three of which went to Bletchley Park, but none was sent, by Navy brass decision, to Pearl Harbor. The omission may have been crucial: According to some students of the Pearl Harbor debacle, the Purple machine's product, the Japanese diplomatic exchanges that Washington called "Magic," could conceivably have provided Rochefort and his team with clues to the forthcoming attack.[17] This failure, if it was one, together with mental lapses by an overworked staff in OP-20-G and the preoccupation of Washington's top officers with internecine quarreling, led to the situation described succinctly by Gordon W. Prange: "Having brought off one of the most astonishing coups in the history of intelligence, the United States failed to take full advantage of it."[18] It was the situation defined provocatively in 1946 by the Joint Congressional Committee Investigation of the Pearl Harbor Attack: "Why, with some of the finest intelligence available in our history, with the almost certain knowledge that war was at hand, with plans that contemplated the precise type of attack that was executed by Japan on the morning of December 7—why was it possible for a Pearl Harbor to occur?"[19] The answer was: The failure lay not with the lower ranks in naval intelligence but with the higher ranks in naval *operations*. It was a failure about to be repeated, with even more damaging results, on the nation's Atlantic frontier.

That such a failure on the Atlantic was possible would never have occurred to the British Admiralty, which—as Patrick Beesly insisted to this writer a month before his death—shared *everything* it knew about naval Enigma, U-boat dispositions, and counter-U-boat operations with Washington in the pre–Pearl Harbor and pre-Paukenschlag periods. Despite the concern of some Britons about U.S. security practices, no secrets were withheld. In February 1941, at OIC invitation, two Navy and two U.S. Army intelligence officers (including the newly commissioned Rosen) with strong communications and cryptanalysis backgrounds sailed to England on the shakedown return of the new battleship HMS *King George V*. Their earnest of confidentiality was the gift, authorized by SIS, of a Purple machine, the first of three to be given to the British. For ten weeks they studied closely the technical activities and functions of the Y Service, the huts at Bletchley Park, and the OIC, including Winn's Tracking Room. As two of the team members reported on their return: "We were invited to ask questions about everything we saw, no doors were closed to us and copies were furnished of any material which we considered of possible assistance to the United States." The naval officers returned with a complete Marconi-Adcock HF/DF installation, representing Britain's furthest advances to date in that technology, which the naval team judged "to be far ahead of us in these developments."[20] In May the offer and reality of British assistance to U.S. antisubmarine warfare took a higher form, when—accompanied by later-to-be-famous Lieutenant Commander Ian Fleming RNVR, as his personal assistant—British Admiral John A. Godfrey, Director of Naval Intelligence, who superintended the OIC, visited ONI Director Captain Kirk in Washington and laid before him a detailed summary of every known fact, technique, and procedure that the OIC and BP had amassed in two and a half years of active anti-U-boat warfare. The "Most Secret" document undergirding Godfrey's briefing of Kirk was one of the most significant printed artifacts of the Battle of the Atlantic. Patrick Beesly, who was in possession of "Copy No. 8," showed it to the writer. It bore the formidable title: "The Intelligence Division. Naval Staff. Admiralty. Organization and Development of the Naval Intelligence Division, September, 1939–May, 1941. An account prepared in the first instance for the information of Captain Kirk, USN, Director of

Naval Intelligence, Washington. *Important.* The contents of this document are for the PERSONAL information of the recipient and may on no account be divulged to a third person. (Sgd.) John A. Godfrey, Director of Naval Intelligence, May 15, 1941."

The document began with a description of the various functions of the OIC under the headings: enemy surface vessels and raiders; enemy naval air operations; enemy U-boat tracking; enemy merchant shipping; enemy minefields and other navigational obstructions; D/F plotting; enemy W/T intelligence; and the W/T technical section. Godfrey then elaborated on the various naval intelligence sources developed by the OIC: sighting reports by warships and aircraft; photographic reconnaissance of ports and harbors; D/F plotting and study of enemy W/T traffic; reports from Naval Attachés and observers in neutral countries; and Special Intelligence. The strength of the OIC's U-boat Tracking Room, Godfrey pointed out, lay in the fact that *all* intelligence from whatever quarter came into that one Room. The last-named source, Special Intelligence, was of particular importance because in that same month, thanks to the "pinch" from U-*110*, BP was making its first large breaks into naval Enigma, and only months later Admiralty could begin sending Kirk daily and weekly summaries of U-boat dispositions throughout the North Atlantic. With OIC's U-boat estimates, transmitted from London via the Intelligence Section (NID 18) of the British Admiralty Delegation in Washington, Kirk's staff plotted all U-boat positions on daily situation maps.[21] Should U-boats move against the U.S. East Coast, these data from Special Intelligence and D/F bearings would alert Washington to the fact day-by-day. U.S. Navy Intelligence, London assumed, was prepared. By December 1941 and the January that followed, U.S. Navy warships had been publicly engaged with the U-boats for a quarter year, running the convoy escort war in over two-thirds of the Atlantic, issuing orders to Canadian warships as well as to their own, hence there was no reason for the Admiralty and its OIC to doubt at that date that U.S. operational forces, too, were alert to any possible U-boat threats to U.S. waters and that they were poised and battle-ready to repel them. As the U.S. formally entered the war after Pearl Harbor, it was unthinkable in London that U.S. defenses on the Atlantic would be caught off guard and asleep. But London had not counted on that other war that was being waged on the second deck of Main Navy (from which the knowledgeable Captain Kirk withdrew in defeat). Nor had it counted on the unpreparedness, shortsightedness, rigidity, arrogance, and dereliction of the U.S. Navy operational command. The United States was about to suffer a six-months-long massacre, compared with which the defeat at Pearl Harbor was but a rap on the knuckles.

As 1941 passed into 1942, chaos reigned at the two major military headquarters buildings, Army and Navy, in Washington. Constant streams of officers poured in and out of their main entrance doorways, many of them in ill-fitting uniforms that they had not worn for years in mufti-minded Washington. Three kinds of Army caps—garrison, service, and campaign—might be seen mixed with Sam Browne belts and uniform parts as antiquated as 1918 puttee leggings. The smells of cedar and camphor were everywhere.[22] Civilians could wander off the street into military offices without being challenged by a guard. Office furniture, typewriters, and filing cabinets piled up in the rear service areas for use in hastily devised new office spaces for staff or clerks assigned to handle this new responsibility or that. Inside, both service buildings were like anthills with their tops kicked off. Paper flew everywhere. After coming upon the scene at the Army's Munitions Building on Christmas Eve, Major General Joseph W. Stilwell wrote to his wife:

> My impression of Washington is a rush of clerks in and out of doors, swing doors always swinging, people with papers rushing after other people with papers, groups in corners whispering in huddles, everybody jumping up just as you start to talk, buzzers ringing, telephones ringing, rooms crowded, with clerks all banging away at typewriters. "Give me 10 copies of this AT ONCE." "Get that secret file out of the safe." "Where the hell is the Yellow Plan (Blue Plan, Green Plan, Orange Plan, etc.)?" Everybody furiously smoking cigarettes, everybody passing you on to someone else—etc., etc.[23]

At the Navy Department, the problems posed to orderliness by intraservice squabbling and blame casting, which surely must have diverted attention away from essential war tasks, were compounded by the sense of confusion among all ranks that came from the ascending curve of war losses in the Navy's special interest preserve, the Pacific: First, battleship row at Pearl Harbor; then the surrender of the U.S. river gunboat *Wake* at Shanghai and Japanese seizure of the 10,509 GRT U.S. freighter *President Harrison* loaded with Marines; the loss of the U.S. minesweeper *Penguin;* the fall of Guam, Tarawa, and Makin; the gallant death of Wake Island; the sinking of British battleship HMS *Prince of Wales* and battle cruiser HMS *Repulse,* both of which Prime Minister Winston Churchill had intended to send to Pearl Harbor to replace U.S. ship casualties; additional British naval and merchant losses in the fall of Hong Kong; and, on 2 January, the fall of the U.S. Cavite Navy Yard in the Philippines.

To the understandable tensions in the Department created by that litany of reverses were added the jitters of false contacts and alarms: On 9 December a report of a German air raid reached Naval Operating Base (NOB), Newport, Rhode Island, where the cruiser USS *Augusta* went to general quarters. On the same day the Navy's Bureau of Aeronautics warned Operations of its belief that Japanese submarines "will surface at night in Santa Monica Bay and Coronado Road and bombard the aircraft plants of Douglas and Consolidated respectively."[24] On the eighth and again on the thirteenth came word that San Francisco had been hit by an "air raid" and that an attack on Los Angeles was imminent. (Some of the West Coast panic was not unfounded: Months later Japanese submarines would shell Seattle, Washington; Astoria, Oregon; and Goleta, near Santa Barbara, California. Those attacks, more symbolic than real, combined with false alarms and racism would lead to the tragically misguided Civilian Exclusion Orders of 31 March that directed the evacuation of more than 100,000 Japanese American citizens and Japanese resident aliens to internment camps inland from the coast.) St. Louis, Missouri, weighed in with fears that Japanese battleships were coming up the Mississippi. On the Eastern Seaboard hallucinatory U-boat "sightings" poured into U.S. Navy and Coast Guard offices. On Christmas a U.S. ship sighted a periscope *and* a torpedo thirty miles off Savannah. On 29 December a Coast Guard pilot reported a submarine periscope "heading up Ambrose Channel between Buoy #3 and #5 [in New York Harbor]." The next day a periscope was sighted in Long Island Sound south of New London, and two days later Coast Guardsmen reported a periscope between Cushing and Ram Islands in Portland Channel off Maine. Soon afterward the Army Air Corps sighted "two [enemy] destroyers, two submarines, and two unidentified ships" at one position; and at another, "a large black submarine, large conning tower, gun forward on surface moving slowly NE."[25] The USN destroyer *Trippe* chose this alarm-filled moment to steam from Norfolk to Newport and was set upon by four U.S. Army Air Force planes whose four bombs missed their "enemy" target. In Washington, hysteria reached such proportions that a secret ONI document circulated, charging that many merchant marine radio operators were Communists and therefore disloyal—this despite the fact that, as events would show, radio operators were frequently the last men off torpedoed ships after heroically sending their sss [attacked by submarine] . . . sos.[26]

Meanwhile, at the White House, a calmer head looked for that one proven steady hand who could conn the Navy safely through the mounting tempest. President Roosevelt thought he knew the man: sixty-three-year-old Admiral, Commander in Chief Atlantic Fleet, Ernest J. King. *Life* magazine had just run a cover article on him (24 November): "King of the Atlantic: America's Triple-Threat Admiral is the Stern, Daring Model of a War Commander." King was the fighting Navy. He had been running the Atlantic war west of MOMP, or the "chop line," since September.[27] He had the experience of combat sea command. He also had a command personality born of years of active duty at sea. A native of Lorain, Ohio, he entered the Naval Academy at Annapolis, Maryland, in 1901 where he achieved the highest cadet rank and was commissioned fourth in his class. Years of sea experience followed, punctuated by marriage and one period of instructorship in ordnance and gunnery at the academy, years that included two difficult cruises under Captain, later Rear Admiral, Hugo Osterhaus, who mentioned in King's service record the young officer's propensity to whiskey, tardiness, and insubordination, with resulting punishments "under the hatches." Redeeming himself, King became a destroyer division commander in 1911–12 and during World War I served commendably (winning the Navy Cross) as assistant chief of staff to Admiral Henry T. Mayo, Commander in Chief Atlantic Fleet, in the process acquiring a deep dislike for the Royal Navy and all things British. During the peacetime years King went into submarines and took command of the submarine base at New London in 1923. He won two Distinguished Service Medals for directing the salvage of submarines *S-51* and *S-4*. At Pensacola he qualified as a naval aviator and during the 1930s made significant contributions to the development of carrier tactics. In 1939, by then a rear admiral, King, with a service record as diverse as it was successful, was passed over for chief of naval operations. Chosen instead was Harold R. ("Betty") Stark, the candidate of surface-ship admirals who (as King thought) mistrusted air and underwater sailors. It appeared that his next appointment, to the General Board, a twilight cruise for admirals on their passage to retirement, would bring to a close his naval career. A year later, however, President Roosevelt, disregarding persistent rumors that King drank too much and womanized with other officers' wives, agreed to the recommendation of Stark and Secretary of the Navy Frank Knox that King be assigned as commander of the Atlantic Squadron. One year later, in February 1941, the squadron was re-designated the Atlantic Fleet, and King, promoted to full admiral, CINCLANT, could break his flag in one of the top commands at sea. It was not a fleet command in the sunny, starched-white Pacific to which every Navy man aspired. It was second-drawer command in the dero-gated Atlantic, with its gray, cold seas. But it was tons better than a desk on the General Board. His own personal fortunes brightened, while at the same time the Navy's fortunes turned bleak and danger-ous. To King it was clear that war with the Axis powers lay ahead. When the *Reuben James* went down, he gave up alcohol for the duration.

Naval historian Samuel Eliot Morison, who knew King well, captured him in these finely chiseled words: "Tall, spare and taut, with piercing brown eyes, a powerful Roman nose and deeply cleft chin . . . he was a sailor's sailor who neither had nor wanted any life outside the Navy. . . . He had a firm grasp of naval strategy and tactics, an en-cyclopedic knowledge of naval detail, an immense capacity for work, and complete integrity. . . . He had no toleration for fools or weaklings . . . and was more feared than loved. . . . He cleared the deck ruthlessly at frequent intervals." In sum, Morison recalled, he was "a hard, grim, determined man."[28] Or, as one of his daughters remarked of him, "He is the most even-tempered man in the Navy. He is always in a rage."[29] FDR, who liked hardness in a man, quipped, "He shaves with a blow-torch,"[30] and decided to name him commander of the entire U.S. Navy. This, then, was the man who would be Grand Admiral Erich Raeder's counterpart in Washington. With King in charge, there would be no more surprises. He was a known quantity—100 percent. Not only would he scrape the hull clean, he would also keep the mainland United States inviolate against enemy attack. An old Army friend, a retired colonel, wrote King from Malden, Massachusetts: "There is going to be HELL, with all the trimmings, popping up soon BUT . . . with Ernie King at the helm . . . America can rest assured that there will not be any repetition of the unfortunate affair at Pearl Harbor."[31]

On 30 December King assumed the duties of Commander in Chief, United States Fleet, originally designated CINCUS; King quickly changed that unfortunate-sounding acronym to COMINCH. Responsible directly to the President, he exercised "supreme command of the operating forces comprising the several fleets of the United States Navy and the operating forces of the Naval Frontier Command." It is worth emphasizing that King assumed primary and direct responsibility for the coastal (Frontier) commands. In these duties he worked at first in an uneasy duumvirate with the Office of the Chief of Naval Operations, still held by Admiral "Betty" Stark, previously the highest operations office in the Navy. By March 1942, however, Stark, who according to Morison "looked more like a bishop than a sailor,"[32] was posted to London in an expediently devised capacity as Commander U.S. Naval Forces Europe, and King subsumed Naval Operations under his own office, thereby becoming COMINCH-CNO with unprecedented powers. (In unpublished "Random Notes" found in his papers, King suggested that Stark had been "fired" by Roosevelt because of Pearl Harbor. Alleging that the Army had been equally culpable for what happened on 7 December, King wrote: "I again repeat that I have never been able to understand how or why F.D.R. could fire Admiral Stark without doing the same to General [George C.] Marshall [Army chief of staff]. In my opinion one could not possibly be more suspect than the other." Stark's biographer maintains that the CNO freely offered his resignation and proposed the London assignment for himself.[33]) For whatever reason, Stark was gone and King held undisputed authority over the Department of the Navy, where he proceeded over the next months to do his own brand of firing. The casualties were those officers whom King himself considered defeatist or responsible (or suitable scapegoats) for Pearl Harbor. Wilkinson would go, along with the director of naval communications.[34] As for Captain Frank T. Leighton, whose daily situation maproom pins identifying surface ships and U-boats King called "little toys and other play things," he ordered one day: "I want him out of the Navy Department before four-thirty this afternoon."[35] Leighton's replacement was Commander George C. Dyer, King's flag secretary.[36] Operations survived relatively unscathed, and "Terrible" Turner became an assistant chief of staff. It was clear early on in King's reign that Operations remained in full charge, and that the war with Intelligence would not soon be over. To King ONI was no more than an archive and lending library, and he treated it as such, cutting it off from all OIC/London messages and estimates as well as from all operational data: ONI for example would not learn of the Battle of Midway (3–5 June 1942) until it was over—and from a reporter at that.[37] Meeting Admiral King in a department corridor, Captain John L. McCrea, naval aide to the President, said: "They tell me you were heard to say recently, 'Yes, damn it, when they get in trouble they send for the sons of bitches.'" "No, John," King answered, "I didn't say it. But I will say this: If I had thought of it, I would have said it."[38]

What coastal defense against U-boats the U.S. Navy had been able to muster by January 1942 was under the putative control of the North Atlantic Naval Coastal Frontier, established on 1 July 1941, and commanded by King's Annapolis classmate, sixty-three-year-old Rear Admiral Adolphus "Dolly" Andrews, with headquarters in New York City, where Andrews was also commandant, Third Naval District. The frontier's jurisdiction ran from the North International Boundary (Canadian border) off West Quoddy Head, Maine, to the lower line of Onslow County in North Carolina and comprised four naval districts: Boston, New York, Philadelphia, and Norfolk. The southern Sixth Naval District headquartered at Charleston would be brought into the Frontier Command in the first week of February, thus extending its jurisdiction south to the boundary between Duval and St. Johns counties in northern Florida. At the same time, the name of the defense zone would be changed to Eastern Sea Frontier (ESF), by which it would be known for the remainder of the war (hence its use hereafter in this narrative). Similar frontier force commands had been in place since 9 September for the Gulf of Mexico, the Caribbean (east and west), and Panama, accounting, along with ESF, for some seven thousand miles of coastal water. Within its littoral responsibilities, ESF embraced all harbors, ports, waterways, bays, inlets, and coastal shipping lanes seaward; that is, east, for a distance of two hundred miles. With the "local defense" forces of each naval district, as well as with warships and aircraft assigned to the Frontier Coastal Force, Admiral Andrews was charged with the responsibility of "coordinating the operations" of these forces as well as any that might be provided by the Army's Northeast Defense Command and First Air Force. Specifically, by order of the general war plan WPL-46, Rainbow 5, Andrews was to (1) defend the frontier; (2) protect coastal shipping; (3) support the Atlantic Fleet, of which Admiral Royal E. Ingersoll took command as CINCLANT, relieving King, on 1 January; and (4) support the Army and "Associated Forces" within the frontier.[39] In meeting this large order, Andrews asked his district commandants to make the following assumptions: that submarine activity may be expected with submarines operating against shipping with torpedoes, mines, or gunfire; that small enemy surface-raiding forces in the form of warships or disguised merchantmen may penetrate the coastal zone; that minor raids on the U.S. coast may be made by shipborne aircraft or small motor torpedo boats; and that "large scale attacks will probably not occur unless the enemy managed to obtain a base within operating distance of the Frontier."[40] There is no question that Andrews meant business—in the abstract. As early as two months before Pearl Harbor, he ordered forces in his command: "Destroy German and Italian naval, land, and air forces encountered."[41] The only questions were whether his forces could—or would—destroy anything.

A proposal set forth by Andrews on 10 July for an "Army and Navy Joint Control and Information Center" received strong support from both the Army's Northeast Defense Command (Lieutenant General Hugh A. Drum) and the chief of naval operations. Admiral Stark urged the rapid establishment of such centers in all frontiers in a dispatch of 31 December. By that date Andrews' center was complete and operational, occupying the central and west wing space of the fourteenth floor of the Federal Building, 90 Church Street in New York City. It was no OIC, of whose operations Andrews seemed unaware (if one can judge from the surprise with which news of Rodger Winn's work was received at the center in May [!] 1942), but it was an honest effort by Andrews and his Army counterparts to gather, share, and respond to information about enemy operations in the frontier zone with what technique they had at the time; though, curiously, the one example offered by Andrews' staff of how the center would operate focused on the possibility of "an enemy aircraft carrier off the coast"—this despite the fact that as surely must have been known, Germany had no operational carrier.[42] The Frontier War Diary contains both a verbal and graphic description of the center. The T-shaped space measured ninety by thirty-two feet in one direction and forty by twenty in the other. Navy space included a large "operations office" with two wall charts—one of the Atlantic Ocean and another of the two-hundred-mile offshore frontier zones; offices for Andrews' seven-officer staff; clerical help; and communications equipment. One officer was detailed to write the ESF War Diary. For the period December 1941–March 1942 that officer was Lt. (jg) Lawrance R. Thompson. The system of monthly narrative chapters followed by daily/hourly reports instituted by Thompson would be continued by his successor, Lt. (jg) Elting E. Morison, who took up those duties in May and reconstructed the diary from March forward. Morison would compose the diary until November 1943 when he was reassigned to Main Navy in Washington.[43] The Army had equal space that it devoted to air intelligence, operations, and support personnel. The purpose of the center was expressed in the war diary: "Maintain a running estimate of the military situation in the theater of operations by means of plotting information on operating charts and maps and maintain a digest of unplottable material." The plots covered merchant ships traveling off the coast, changed every hour; surface patrol vessels, changed every hour; air patrols, changed every half hour; enemy operations and contacts (if any), including warnings received from the Army Air Corps Regional Filter Center. It was not sophisticated. The systems betrayed no acquaintance with the war-won experience of the OIC, which Main Navy had simply not passed on or taken much to heart itself. But there was one OIC gift that COMINCH *did* pass on (circumventing ONI), though its exact source other than Britain was never identified to anyone in the center, including Andrews and his communications officer, thirty-five-year-old Lieutenant (jg) Richard H. Braue. Each day when the gift arrived in the center code room, Braue would struggle with the British cipher, which required two to four hours to render intelligible.[44] Placing the decrypt in a metal message case and strapping on a service .45, the six-and-a-half-foot brown-haired Braue would then walk up to Andrews' office on the fifteenth floor. There, removing the decrypt from its case, he would hold it out at arm's length for Andrews to read. After the admiral finished scribbling down the coordinates of forces that might affect his frontier, Braue would place the decrypt back in his case and return to the code room, where he would file the decrypt in a safe to which only he and the admiral held the combination. Andrews would then descend to the operations office and move magnetic markers on the Atlantic wall chart. What he was watching, thanks to London's daily U-boat estimate, was the day-by-day march of five U-boats from east to west. In just over a week, the markers for three of those boats would move from the Atlantic chart to the frontier chart, and "Dolly" Andrews would move from the abstract world to the real.

Born in Texas in October 1879, Andrews arrived at the Naval Academy in Annapolis nineteen years later without ever having seen a ship of any kind in his life. By contrast with his future adversary, Dönitz, he was graduated first in his commissioning class. First assignments as an officer presaged a successful and distinguished career, in which it may fairly be said he specialized in presidents and battleships. In 1903 as an ensign he went aboard the USS *Dolphin*, a yacht designated for use by the secretary of the Navy, and for two years he served as a White House aide to President Theodore Roosevelt. After brief service on Asiatic station with a Yangtze patrol, he began battleship duty successively aboard the USS *Michigan, Utah, Oklahoma*, and *Mississippi*, becoming commander in 1918 of the *Massachusetts*. After brief assignments to the Third Naval District, Naval War College at Newport, and the Atlantic Fleet, he returned to White House duty as commander of the presidential yacht *Mayflower* and naval aide to President Warren G. Harding, whose deathbed he attended. Continuing as senior naval aide to President Calvin Coolidge and learning how to court the favor of powerful politicians, he acquired a reputation among his Navy colleagues as a shamelessly ambitious officer, a reputation that later explained to many the vote he cast as chief of the Bureau of Navigation against promotion of his classmate King to a vice admiral's billet. First in his class, he apparently believed that he therefore deserved to be the first with three stars. A rear admiral on the eve of war, he could claim extensive battleship experience; diplomatic service on two brief assignments to Geneva; command of the submarine base at New London; chief of staff duties with the commander, Battle Force, and with CINCUS (predecessor to COMINCH); as well as command of the Atlantic Scouting Force with the temporary rank of vice admiral. In July 1941 he received joint command of the Third Naval District and the Eastern Sea Frontier. At the time ESF did not appear to be a prestigious assignment, and few in the service were likely to have expected that it, the Gulf of Mexico, and the Caribbean Frontier would for six months of 1942 become the most intense continuous theater of German naval operations.

Andrews was a formidable person who could hold his ground when pressed, as evidenced by an exchange of correspondence with King in November 1941, when the latter was still CINCLANT. As he told Andrews, "It is none of my business, and strictly speaking, it is not," but he had heard that the organization and readiness for mounting U.S. wartime transatlantic convoys in Andrews' ports *"do not exist."*[45] Within two days Andrews fired off a spirited, detailed response the force of which was to convey his own conviction that the districts in his command, though undermanned, were exceedingly well organized and ready for such duties. "I have no idea who told you that organizations, etc., do not exist," he replied to King, and suggested that such reports were "pure fabrication."[46] To this fine defense King replied that, "My informant . . . is in a position . . . to know whereof he speaks—it is evident that he did not—and I shall tell him so."[47] By Pearl Harbor, Andrews was one of the most widely known flag officers in the Navy, though often parodied for his stilted speech and pomposity of manner. Secretary of the Army Henry L. Stimson called him a "terrible old fusspocket."[48] More charitable, Samuel Eliot Morison called him "senatorial in port and speech."[49] That he lacked Dönitz's capacity to laugh at the incongruous is attested by an incident in Boston when, as ESF commander, he inspected the operation room of First District Headquarters at 150 Causeway Street. The staff had cleared the desks of dispatches and all hands were in proper uniform, but Andrews was two hours late, so discipline slackened and a young ensign named Pete Rollins leaned back against a window to smoke his pipe. At just that moment Andrews swept into the room with a flourish of gold braid and ribbons. Rollins, startled, tried to dump the burning dottle of his pipe into an ashtray, but it settled on the top of his desk instead, where the embers raised a cloud of varnish smoke. While Andrews fixed him with a wooden stare, Rollins swept the dottle into a nearby metal wastebasket, forgetting that it contained a loose pile of old dispatches, which quickly ignited. His next maneuver, under Andrews' unremitting stare, was to stomp the flames with his size-eleven foot, which promptly became wedged in the basket. As flames leaped up his trouser leg, Rollins banged the basket about the floor until, at last, the fire went out. Now at smoldering attention, he looked up to see that Andrews had not altered his fixed, bleak countenance. The great man then turned and departed. The inspection of the operation room was over. Staff officers crowded around Rollins to congratulate him. It was his first day on active duty.[50]

There were many chinks in Andrews' frontier armor, beginning with the most glaring—a sea and air force so antiquated, so unprepared, so untrained, and so deficient in craft and weaponry that it stunned the Germans and British when they saw it go to war—and *that* after two and a quarter years of Atlantic war. It embarrassed Andrews. For him to send these defenders out to battle was akin to meeting Panzer divisions with troops of mounted cavalry. He acknowledged the fact in writing two weeks after Pearl Harbor: "It is submitted that should enemy submarines operate off this coast, this command has no forces available to take adequate action against them, either offensive or defensive."[51] Incredibly, to protect nearly fifteen hundred miles of frontier coastline, Andrews had only twenty ships, not one with a fully trained crew, not one equal to a U-boat in surface speed or armament. "There is not a vessel available," Andrews stated, "that an enemy submarine could not outdistance when operating on the surface. In most cases the guns of these vessels would be outranged by those of the submarine."[52] His tiny tatterdemalion "fleet," under orders to "uphold the majesty and might of the United States in the nation's own coastal water,"[53] consisted of the following vessels:

One 165-foot Coast Guard *Argo*-class WPC Patrol Cutter, *Dione* (WPC-107), commissioned in 1934;

Three 200-foot Eagle Boats, PE 27, PE 56, and PE 19, all commissioned in 1919;

Six 125-foot Coast Guard *Active*-class WPC patrol cutters, *Active, Antietam, Dix, Frederick Lee, Jackson,* and *Rush,* all commissioned in 1927;

Four 110-foot submarine chasers (wooden hull), SC 102, SC 330, SC 412, and SC 437, commissioned in 1918–41.

Four 170- to 245-foot smaller converted yachts, *Sylph* (CPY-12), 1940; *Siren* (PY-13), 1941; *Coral* (PY-15), 1941; and *Tourmaline* (PY-20), 1941.

Two 200- to 328-foot gunboats, *Dubuque* (PG-17), 1905; and *Paducah* (PG-18), 1905.

The fastest ships in this motley collection were the *Dione* at 16½ knots and the Eagle boats at "a possible 15 knots," but the three Eagles were written off as "materially unreliable": Andrews would tell King that "they are constantly breaking down."[54] The reliability of the remainder of this fleet was revealed in a plaintive letter from Andrews to King two weeks after enemy operations began in his command: By that date only *five* vessels—the one 165-foot cutter, two 125-foot cutters, one Eagle, and the converted yacht *Tourmaline*—were "capable of keeping the sea and taking offensive action against enemy submarines."[55] Because of the overall poor seakeeping characteristics of Andrews' fleet, the distances they had to travel, and the unfavorable winter weather conditions that prevailed, at most only two or three vessels could be kept on station at a time. Thus, in January the paper fleet of twenty would quickly descend to a guard of *three*, and the seacoast door would fall open wider still. (Perhaps only in the Uruguayan Navy—in which three admirals commanded one antiquated gunboat plus a number of tugs and dispatch boats—could one find a greater disproportion of command to forces.) Of more immediate concern to the present narrative is the fact that in the week ending 12 January, which was the eve of Reinhard Hardegen's approach to New York Harbor, an ESF "Availability of Forces" chart showed only three vessels in ready status in the Third and Fourth Naval districts (New York and Philadelphia); seven other boats were on ready status in the Fifth Naval District (Norfolk).[56]

Two questions leap to mind: Were craft of this small size useful and effective in antisubmarine warfare? If so, why were many more of them not available for such service at war's start? The answer to the first question is yes. It is true that the destroyer (DD), as also later the destroyer escort (DE)—with its speed, armament, maneuverability, superior sound gear, and ability to keep the sea in conditions that drove small craft into port—was the deadly and traditional surface enemy of the submarine. But Andrews had no DDs. He had none because those that were still in the Atlantic (two squadrons of the newest, long-legged destroyers had been removed to the Pacific theater in late December) had been assigned to King's relief as CINCLANT, Admiral Royal E. Ingersoll, for cross-Atlantic convoy escort or for local duty in the Sixth and Seventh Naval districts as well as in the Gulf, Caribbean, and Panama frontiers and the Brazilian bases of Recife and Bahia. That there were not more destroyers as a category in commission was owed in part to their elimination (fifty-two had been proposed) from the Naval Expansion Bill of June 1940 for reasons of economy. Cutters and patrol craft of 165, 125, and 110 feet were not so much killers (though they carried a depth-charge rack) as good observers and harassers. Similar small craft had proved indispensable around Britain's shores in locating (for bombers) and in *keeping down* U-boats. The German attackers operated on the surface at night: The presence of any observed defender, be it ship or plane, regardless how small, had the effect, psychological if not material, of keeping a U-boat submerged, where its movements and therefore its effectiveness were greatly hindered. The small craft were always at risk since in a confrontation the U-boat would seem to hold all the cards. Yet it was unlikely that a U-boat would waste a torpedo on a sub chaser; and if it chose to duel with deck guns, where, as Andrews conceded, the U-boat would have the advantage, the U-boat if close enough would *itself* be at risk absorbing four-inch, fifty-caliber gunfire and thirty-caliber machine-gun fire, which, if they did no more, could clear a U-boat's deck of gun crew. The little boats were not entirely without resources, including, as a last resort, ability to ram. Furthermore, their value for observation and rescue of survivors from sunken vessels should have been obvious.

To the second question it can be answered, first, that the U.S. Navy failed to produce a sufficient number of small craft because, like their counterparts in the German Kriegsmarine, the Navy's Operations and General Board admirals were intent on fighting another Battle of Jutland—this time against the Japanese in the Pacific, where battleships and heavy cruisers "crossed the T" and concentrated main-battery salvos in a decisive blue-water engagement. It was the "gun club" at Main Navy that did not want to fiddle around with small craft, lest naval appropriations be diverted from the great-hulled, impregnable, rakish brutes that were the battle line of the fleets. There is even evidence, uncovered by Senator Harry S. Truman's Special Committee Investigating the National Defense Program, that before 1942 the General Board often acted in league with the big-ship lobby of the larger private shipyards, where profits were a factor of size and tonnage.[57]

President Roosevelt, who had been Assistant Secretary of the Navy (1913–20) when U-boats first operated in the Atlantic and U.S. waters, and who subsequently followed U.S. naval developments more closely than anyone else in civilian life, was devoted to small craft as an indispensable means for control of coastal waters. At one point, recalling with pride the mosquito fleet of 110-foot subchasers the Navy put in the water in 1918, he offered a prize for the best design of a similar-size antisubmarine patrol vessel. As U.S. involvement with the U-boat war in 1941–42 deepened in intensity, FDR had to contend not only with Navy Department indecision and inertia that resulted from a belief that patrol craft, if they were ever to be needed, could be extemporized and produced rapidly in small shipyards, but with the overt prejudice of the "gun club." "My Navy has been definitely slack in preparing for this submarine war off our coast," FDR would write Churchill. "As I need not tell you, most naval officers have declined in the past to think in terms of any vessel of less than two thousand tons. You learned the lesson two years ago. We still have to learn it."[58] In this prepossession U.S. officers differed little from their opposite numbers on the Kriegsmarine Naval Staff, who—to the disgust of Admiral Dönitz—preferred capital ships to U-boats because they "couldn't parade a band on the deck" of a U-boat.[59]

In one of his "Random Notes," written sometime after 1943, Admiral King stated that, "F.D.R. did not understand the fact that the Nazis had very much improved their U-boats; he believed that we could combat the submarines with small boats of 50–60 foot length and light airplanes. Despite this, Admiral Stark—backed by myself and others—argued for proper escort craft; length 250–300 feet, speed 25 knots, displacement 1000 tons or better."[60] In 1946 he would write, "The early months of 1942 gave abundant proof of the already well-known fact that stout hearts in little boats cannot handle an opponent as tough as the submarine."[61]

King's recollections appear to have been flawed. First, according to the record, FDR never proposed building patrol craft smaller than the 110-foot subchaser he personally favored. Second, as King does not acknowledge, within four months after Pearl Harbor, he personally was requisitioning hundreds of privately owned pleasure craft *smaller than* 100 feet for offshore antisubmarine patrol.[62] Third, by four months into the war King was authorizing armed flights by private aviators in light planes of the Civil Air Patrol over the threatened sea-lanes.[63] Fourth, in enlisting Stark's name as support for his views King ignored Stark's long though unsuccessful struggle, dating from at least October 1940, to secure small craft: "One of the hardest fights I have had," Stark wrote, "has been to obtain small craft. . . . We may wake up some morning and find . . . submarines operating at our focal points and all that goes in its train."[64] Fifth, King was apparently unaware that in June 1941 a list of "urgent and important shortcomings" prepared at Stark's request for the Secretary of the Navy included the request: "Authority to construct 101 smaller vessels. . . . In addition to 10 ocean going tugs, a large number of 165′ PC [Patrol Craft] and a few 110′ PC should be laid down. Reason: The War Plans show a very great need for patrol vessels for the Naval Local Defense Forces."[65] Sixth, on 15 December Stark urged the naval districts in the ESF to recruit small private vessels, crewed by naval personnel or by "undoubtedly loyal civilians," and to outfit them with either voice or Morse transmitters so that ESF might station them at fifty to eighty miles offshore where they could report on approaching enemy aircraft, surface vessels, or U-boats to the Army Aircraft Warning System.[66] (This farsighted suggestion would not be implemented until four months later, at about the time Stark was being eased out of Washington.) Seventh, on 12 February, one month after Gruppe Paukenschlag struck, Stark would propose "arming a considerable number of the Cape Cod fishing boats, particularly with depth charges, for antisubmarine operations on the Grand Banks and other fishing grounds in the North Atlantic, and employing them as a volunteer force under Naval control."[67] Eighth, that small patrol craft became more essential rather than less as the coastal war got under way was indicated on 20 January 1942, when Admiral Ingersoll cautioned Rear Admiral Bristol in a personal letter, "Until the new PC's begin to get in service, I think we are in for a beating from the subs."[68] Ninth, in April, Vice Chief for Naval Operations Frederick J. Horne acknowledged that, "the services of the new submarine chasers are urgently needed in the various sea frontiers. Every effort is being made by the Department to expedite the construction and delivery of these craft."[69] Tenth, in May, King himself sent a handwritten note to Horne that began: "Please make arrangement to *continue* the building of 173′ PC's . . . [emphasis in original]."[70] By the beginning of that month, thanks to a crash program for construction of small antisubmarine vessels, King had available thirty-three patrol craft and thirty-four sub chasers, most on the East Coast, enough (at last) to begin full-scale convoying of merchant traffic. Eleventh, Admiral Andrews' headquarters declared in the middle of July, six months after the U-boat campaign in American waters had begun: "The importance of the utilization on Eastern Sea Frontier of all small craft of various types cannot be overemphasized. These vessels are being used for rescue, patrol, for submarine observation, and the reporting of floating mines. When armed, they can take offensive action against submarines."[71] Finally, twelfth, "stout hearts in little boats" *did* handle "an opponent as tough as the submarine": 165-foot Coast Guard cutters *Icarus* and *Thetis* sank two of the first three U-boats destroyed in U.S. waters (see chapter 13).

Despite the above, King would reconstruct events according to the filters of his own memory. Both in June 1942 and at war's end (as will be noted in a later chapter), he would claim that he and his staff had very early improvised the use of small craft and light planes to meet the U-boat challenge—expedients that in fact he and his staff appear to have opposed at every turn with force and ridicule until at last rigor alone proved unavailing in the conduct of seaboard affairs and the impact of events themselves broke through a recalcitrant ego to demand level good sense and innovative action. Stark had been no fool, as those same events would prove. Small craft *were* necessary to the nation's defense. Somehow Stark had escaped the prevailing big ship-big gun arrogance of his own operations staff. He deserved to escape guilt by association with Admiral King's wrong-minded dicta. Roosevelt, too, would be proved right. If the President's knowledge and advice had been heeded, and more of what Samuel Eliot Morison called the "indispensable small craft for anti-submarine warfare" had been built, the Eastern Sea Frontier would have been better prepared to face invasion.[72] But Stark and Roosevelt were of no help now, in the opening dark wintry weeks of January 1942, when the magnetic markers on his wall chart told Admiral "Dolly" Andrews that everything he feared was beginning to happen, and that all he had on station at any one time were three lonely craft between Calais, Maine, and Jacksonville, North Carolina.

No less inadequate than Andrews' bathtub navy was his naval air arm, which consisted of 103 aircraft of varying capabilities, about three-quarters of them unsuited to the tasks of coastal patrol and antisubmarine defense. From Salem (Massachusetts) Naval Air Station (NAS) in the north to Elizabeth City (North Carolina), NAS, in the south, ESF could count the following planes: fifty-one trainers, eighteen scouts, fourteen utility, seven transport, six patrol, three torpedo, three fighters, and one bomber. Not one was capable of maintaining a long-range maritime patrol. Most were suitable at best for inshore scouting since carrying depth bombs greatly limited their radius of action. For certain aircraft the long time lags required for arming with depth bombs between the receipt of an alert and the moment of takeoff made their use impractical: To arm an XPBM-1 or PBY-5 "flying boat" with MK-XVII depth bombs at Norfolk NAS, for example, required six-hour notice (!).[73] Andrews doubted that Admiral Dönitz would be so accommodating. For anything approaching medium-search ranges he had to depend on the few PBMs and PBYs and Coast Guard amphibians available at Norfolk, Salem, Floyd Bennett NAS (New York), and Elizabeth City, as well as on two nonrigid lighter-than-air craft (dirigibles) from ZP Squadron 12 at Lakehurst (New Jersey) NAS. For the rest, lamented Andrews, his air forces "have no place in modern war."[74] Yet he passed on to all his aviators the best received wisdom from the British Royal Air Force (RAF) that had arrived in the last week of December by way of Admiral Stark. British analysis had disclosed that in 35 percent of air attacks on U-boats the target was still partially visible at the time of bomb release. In another 15 percent of cases the U-boat disappeared fewer than thirty seconds prior to the attack. The best recommended attack procedures, therefore, were the following:

(a) Use shallowest possible depth setting for charges and depth bombs.
(b) Close U-boat by shortest path at maximum speed, attacking from any direction.
(c) Use lowest release altitude consistent with existing instructions.
(d) Space charges or bombs 60 feet apart.
(e) Drop all charges or bombs in one stick.
(f) If U-boat surfaces after bombs are expended, attack repeatedly with guns.[75]

Thanks to his support relationship with the Army's Northeast Defense Command, as symbolized by the Army and Navy Joint Control and Information Center on Church Street, Andrews was able to turn to the Army Air Forces (AAF) for long-range seaward antisubmarine patrols of which his Navy craft were incapable. Accordingly, on the afternoon of 8 December 1941, units of the First Bomber Command of the First Air Force began search-out/search-back flights over water to the limit of their range. The range varied according to the type of aircraft. Divested of most of its premier planes and best-trained crews for missions on the West Coast and overseas, First Bomber Command scrambled three different types of "in commission"—that is, flyable twin- or four-engine aircraft: nine B-17 heavy bombers; six B-18 medium bombers, of which two could not fire or bomb; and thirty-one B-25 medium bombers. The Boeing B-17 "Flying Fortress" had been introduced in 1937 as "the best bombardment aircraft in existence, particularly for coastal defense."[76] The Douglas B-18 "Bolo," introduced the same year as the B-17 and the standard U.S. bomber when war broke out in Europe in 1939, had shorter range than the B-17 and just over half the latter's bomb load; it would see little service in the war. The North American B-25 would fight effectively in all theaters and be the aircraft of choice for the sixteen-plane Tokyo Raid of Lt. Col. James H. Doolittle on 18 April 1942. Seventy-three other aircraft were in or out of commission, mostly out, during December and January.

The First Bomber Command patrols flew their missions from airstrips at Langley Field, Virginia, Mitchel Field, New York, Westover Field, Massachusetts, and (after 11 January) Bangor, Maine. Weather permitting, two flights daily, averaging three planes each, from each of the four bases swept the sea approaches. The B-17s could reach a maximum distance of six hundred miles before turnaround; the B-18s had the least range. For the pilots the dangers of being aloft over the Atlantic in land-based aircraft during midwinter were daunting, all the more so since the partially trained crews, thrown together as hurriedly as was the flight line, had the barest experience in navigation over water. Further diminishing their effectiveness was the fact that none of the crews had received training in ship recognition: It was questionable that over the threatened sea-lanes they would know a U-boat if they saw one. With navigation and recognition skills at a minimum, it is not surprising that First Bomber Command flew only in the daytime, though this was the period when U-boat lookouts could easily spot them and give the diving alarm. The small number of aircraft available for search, the limited number of coastal sectors that could be patrolled at any one time, the intermittent flight periods, and the absence of nighttime sweeps (when a surfaced U-boat's position could be betrayed to the practiced eye by phosphorescence or wake) combined with thin training, which means faulty planning, destined First Bomber Command's long-range aerial reconnaissance for inevitable failure. Compounding the futility was the fact that none of the crews, which had been conditioned for land bombardment, was familiar with the techniques of attacking submarines at sea, and even if they had been, the demolition (not depth) bombs they carried on board would have been useless, in the absence of great luck, against such targets. Though First Bomber Command may not have been the most quixotic force ever to lift off in wartime it deserves mention all the same—in the same breath with the Navy PBY-5 Catalina squadrons at Pearl Harbor, which in December had patrolled all the sectors on the compass rose except the twelve o'clock sector, which was exactly the path down which Admiral Nagumo sent his carrier-based Mitsubishis, Nakajimas, and Aichis. It could be argued, of course, that limitations of air resources led to both failures, which is another way of saying: unpreparedness.

To augment further the limited functions of his naval air forces, Andrews could rely on the Army's First Air Support Command for close-in air scouting. To that end Army aviators assembled a polyglot force of some one hundred single-engine land-observation planes that one observer likened to Joffre's Paris taxicab army of 1914. Wrote Andrews on 14 January: "The Army First Air Support Command is operating during daylight hours patrols in single-motored land observation planes extending about forty miles offshore from Portland, Maine, to Wilmington, North Carolina. These planes are not armed and carry only sufficient fuel for flights of between two or three hours. The pilots are inexperienced in the type of work they are endeavoring to do. Not more than ten of these observation planes are in the air along the Coastal Frontier at any one time."[77] It was to the credit of both services, many of whose earlier attempts to work together had foundered on the rocks of interservice rivalry, that they successfully consolidated what resources they had in order to meet the present emergency. The airplane was the most dangerous foe of the U-boat, as the British had discovered, and the Army and Navy were correct to pool their forces, however feeble, untrained, and inappropriate they were. For such was to follow Admiral Dönitz's own principle: Do the best with what you have. Still, it did not appear that Gruppe Hardegen and the waves of U-boats that were in train ran much risk of discovery, much less attack, from the American skies.

Behind these dented shields and virgin swords lay other defenses, planned or in place, for bases and harbors. Some net-and-boom barriers were positioned across the entrances to naval bases by the beginning of 1942, but this type of defense, which required constant manipulation of pegtop buoys, mooring buoys, shackles, and mooring chain, was not practical for commercial harbors, which had to remain open for their constant streams of freighter and tanker traffic (although a modest amount of net material was in place at New York Harbor). Instead, the Army, which held jurisdiction over harbors and intracoastal waterways, laid contact-mine barrages in the approaches to Portland, Boston, New York, and Chesapeake Bay. Notices such as the following, dated 10 December, went out to all shipping companies: "A mined area covering the approaches to New York Harbor has been established. Incoming vessels will secure directions for safe navigation from patrol vessel stationed off Ambrose Channel Entrance."[78] U.S. Navy engineers were preparing a variety of sound detection devices that would alert a harbor defense post, such as the Joint Harbor Entrance Control Post, established at Fort Wright on Fishers Island for New York Harbor, to the presence of an underwater intruder. These included underwater magnetic indicator loops, sound-modulated radio sentinel buoys (sonobuoys), fixed supersonic echo-ranging and listening equipment controlled from shore, and shipborne underwater sound detectors. None of these devices, however, was fully tested and in place by the opening months of 1942: Only Argentia in Newfoundland outside the ESF had a working magnetic loop system.[79] Except for its mine fields, a sub chaser here and a scout plane there, New York Harbor remained vulnerable to enemy ingress; so exposed was it, in fact, that Mayor Fiorello La Guardia wondered if the Republic could guarantee the defense of Coney Island![80] In view of events to come it was a good question. (The same question must have worried six-year-old Allen Stewart Konigsberg, who was wont to stand at dusk on the Long Beach shore east of Coney Island and, in his mind's eye, watch a large black U-boat with white swastikas on its tower surfacing and diving in the waters off Long Island. He would recreate that scene forty-five years later when, as Woody Allen, he wrote and produced the motion picture *Radio Days*.[81])

Essential to any seacoast defense in World War II was the darkening of lights that revealed shore positions or provided sky glow against which seaborne targets could be silhouetted. Total darkening came to be called "blackout," partial darkening "brownout" or "dimout." The British, Germans, and Japanese all practiced seacoast blackout. In the ESF during the first three months after Pearl Harbor the United States practiced no darkening discipline whatever. Reprehensibly, not a single coastal commander—ESF, Naval District, or Army—seems to have called for so much as a dimout of waterfront cities as security against U-boats. In Washington in 1940 the Coast Guard considered, in the event of war, extinguishing such lighted navigational aids as lighthouses, buoys, and automatic lights and declared in a *semper paratus* memorandum on blackouts, "The Coast Guard will be fully ready if and when called upon to accomplish the desired result effectively and with the least possible delay."[82] But when war came the Coast Guard would leave all the lights blazing in what was nothing less than a brilliant invitation to the U-boats, which, certainly in U-*123*'s case, much appreciated the assistance. The U.S. Naval Academy at Annapolis on the Chesapeake was equally watchful in 1940, deciding that "a routine daily darkening of the station will be required as an intermediate step preliminary to complete blackout"; but such plans at the time were predicated on the "risk of attack from the air."[83] Possible German air attacks also occupied the attention of the Third Naval District, which issued an "Illumination Control Plan" that called for blackout of shore lights, New York City and surrounding urban lights, and all beacons, lighthouses, and aids to navigation—but only in the case of "air raids."[84] Except in air raids the lights would stay on, but for a few New Jersey boardwalk communities that responded positively to the "request" made to them on 18 December 1941 by the Army's commanding general, Second Corps Area, Eastern Defense Command, that they "consider" dispensing with boardwalk lights (though not city lights).[85] The majority of boardwalk communities chose to ignore the request and would continue to ignore it for three months into the war in favor of more important tourism, recreation, and business interests. Even Admiral Andrews, who surely on one or another of his battleship billets must have noticed another ship in the water silhouetted against the distant loom thrown up by urban or harbor lights, underestimated the advantage that sky glow gave even to U-boats operating some distance from shore. As late as 10 February 1942, in the midst of the tanker and merchant carnage in the waters of his command, Andrews would state: "The lights of beach resorts frequently furnish a background against which vessels running close to the coast may be silhouetted by others further seaward. This is objectionable, but inasmuch as submarines are reluctant to operate in waters less than about 10 fathoms in depth, this is not at present regarded as creating a problem requiring drastic measures."[86] Andrews was dead wrong. Shore lights revealed passing commerce to U-boats far out to sea. Furthermore, the Gruppe Hardegen boats and those that followed would operate in very close proximity to shore, particularly U-*123*, which gave no quarter to shoal water. Drastic measures were, indeed, required. Because Andrews foolishly supposed they were not, scores of merchant seamen would go to watery graves, and desperately needed raw materials, not to mention "bottoms"—ships—would litter the continental shelf.

In January 1940 Commander Edward Ellsberg, USN, gave a comforting interview to the *Montreal Daily Star*. Described as "a world authority on submarines" and recently famous for his role in raising the sunken American submarine *Squalus*, Ellsberg stated that to expect German U-boats to operate in any significant way in Canadian or American waters was "ridiculous." Hitler, he said, might send over two or three boats as a "gesture" to put a "scare" into the Canadian people, but serious naval operations that far distant from home bases were "hardly worth while from a military point of view." Germany would be better advised to concentrate her undersea forces in the North Sea. "I am certain," Ellsberg continued, smiling, "that Churchill would be only too pleased to subsidize the German Admiralty to send their U-boat fleet to this side." Anyway, he said, modern defense measures had greatly lessened the striking power of U-boats, which themselves had not been improved on very much since the last war. Furthermore, U-boat warfare against merchant ships "can never have any real effect on the outcome of the war." Commander Ellsberg's final conceit was to claim that the U-boat [U-*29*] that sank the British aircraft carrier *Courageous* in the Western Approaches on 17 September of the foregoing year never made it safely back to Germany. "I don't care what the Germans say," he asserted, "I know that no submarine could have lived in shallow water with all those destroyers round after taking a potshot at the *Courageous*. I'll wager that the submarine and her crew are lying on the sea bottom within a quarter of a mile of the hull of the aircraft carrier."[87] The assertion would have made interesting reading for the commander of U-*29*, Kptlt. Otto Schuhart, who went on to sink enough additional ships to win the *Ritterkreuz* (Knight's Cross).

Fortunately, such recklessness on the part of the USN's "world authority" on submarines did not reflect the thinking in the rest of his service, where one could find a healthy respect for the modern U-boat and a confident expectation that the Ubootwaffe would move into U.S. waters as quickly as possible following Hitler's declaration of war. The Eastern Sea Frontier staff faced the danger with knowing, open eyes. It was to be expected, the ESF war diary acknowledged, that U-boats would operate in the U.S. coastal shipping lanes, for two reasons: First, because "what the Germans had done with some success and with less efficient submarines in the last war, they would try to do again in this war."[88] One German boat, U-53, paid a "goodwill" visit to Newport in 1916 prior to U.S. entrance into that war; on the day of her departure she sank five British and neutral steamers. In April–November 1918 six other U-boats operating in U.S. coastal waters sank twenty-four commercial ships of two thousand to ten thousand GRT and seventy-six small schooners and fishing trawlers. The depredations of that earlier U-boat campaign had inflicted no serious lasting damage, certainly none that adversely affected America's ability to maintain coastal shipping and to wage war in Europe. Whether the United States would get off so lightly in 1942 gravely concerned many of the Navy's more thoughtful officers, who did not share Commander Ellsberg's improvidence.

The second and "more compelling reason" why the ESF staff expected to see U-boats in U.S. waters was that the convoy protection given to the cross-Atlantic lifelines of the United Kingdom had proved so successful that fall and winter that the enemy very likely, it was thought, would shift both the method and location of his attacks. "The German has always been quick to discover the weakest link," said the diary, and the weakly guarded sea-lanes of the eastern shore and Caribbean, where tankers and merchant vessels ordinarily sailed alone for the lack of escorts, provided an "excellent opportunity for Admiral Dönitz to reveal his gifts for improvisation." In frustration the diary added: "Those responsible for the security of sea-lanes have had to spend far less time in hunting for theories than in searching for forces."[89] A third reason why Admiral Andrews for one could soon anticipate U-boats on his doorstep, though a reason he could not write into the diary for security reasons, was his day-by-day receipt of the British U-boat estimate. It would have been hard for Andrews, looking with growing alarm at the decrypted messages held at arm's length in front of his face, to believe that Edward Ellsberg was a world authority on submarine operations. He would have felt reassured, though, to know that a top secret war plan presented to the President by a joint Army-Navy war plans team on 21 December had confirmed his own judgment that on the North American coast "we can expect frequent appearance of submarines" and that in ESF waters "the most pressing danger is from enemy submarines"; as he also would have been reassured to know that the appropriate "decision" rendered was: "Increase as rapidly as possible coastal forces for defense against submarines."[90]

By that date even Ernest J. King himself was concerned. Still commander of the Atlantic Fleet (CINCLANT), the flinty Anglophobe admiral, if he did not want to heed the secret estimates from London's OIC and the daily situation maps of his own ONI, could hardly blink the fact, as ESF's staff had deduced, that with shrinking success in the cross-oceanic trade routes combined with the dangling temptation of single-sailing unescorted war cargoes in the U.S. coastal lanes it was inevitable that Admiral Dönitz would send an attacking force to the Boston-Cape Hatteras line. Accordingly, King wrote to CNO Stark: "Enemy submarine activities in the North Atlantic are considerably reduced. The naval insecurity of the outlying bases [Argentia; Reykjavik-Hvalfjordur; Londonderry, North Ireland; Gare Loch, Scotland], their distance from *the U.S. Atlantic seaboard, the imminent probability of submarine attack in that area, and the weakness of our coastal defense force, make it essential that the maximum practicable number of our destroyers be based at home bases* [emphasis added]."[91] The importance of this decision cannot be overstressed. King was pulling Support Force DDs from distant bases as well as from convoy routes where U-boat activity had slackened, and he was committing them to defensive positions along the U.S. East Coast.

It is not recorded when this decision reached the eyes or ears of Admiral Andrews, who must have been enormously relieved and encouraged by it, but it was obvious that the decision was acted on since in the first two weeks of January the Atlantic ports from Casco Bay (Portland, Maine) to Norfolk filled up with ocean-tested destroyers from Destroyer Squadrons (DesRons) 7, 8, 10, 11, 30, and 31. All were equipped with Sonar (Sound-Navigation, Ranging) the U.S. equivalent underwater detection system to British ASDIC.[92] All were well munitioned with Mark-VI (three hundred-pound) and Mark-VII (six hundred-pound) depth charges—"ashcans"—on Y throwers. All were Atlantic hardened, on ready status, with steam up on one or two boilers. With no fewer, in fact, than *twenty-five* destroyers bracketing Gruppe Hardegen's approach course, it appeared that the seaboard was going to be protected after all! Paukenschlag was headed for certain disaster. Coiled at Anchor Watch on 13 January were six *Wickes-* and *Clemson*-class "flush deckers," three *Benham-*, four *Sims-*, three *Benson-*, and nine *Gleaves-* (the newest) class ships. The litany of their names evoked Rudyard Kipling's World War I minesweepers in the English Channel:

Dawn off the Foreland—the young flood making
　　Jumbled and short and steep—
Black in the hollows and bright where it's breaking—
　　Awkward water to sweep.
　　"Mines reported in the fairway,
　　Warn all traffic and detain.
Sent up *Unity, Claribel, Assyrian, Stormcock,* and *Golden
　　Gain.*"[93]

In this case the flotilla that could be "sent up" read: *Livermore, Bristol, Ellyson, Roe, Monssen, Lea, Dupont, Bernadou, MacLeish, Gwin, Dallas, Upshur, Gleaves, Kearny, O'Brien, Mustin, Trippe, Wainwright, Mayrant, Rowan, Ludlow, Lansdale, Ingraham, Hilary P. Jones,* and *Charles F. Hughes.*[94] It was a stirring list. To name them was to see them in imagination charging out their channels with flags flying and sirens whooping to meet the invader. All that was needed was to light off their remaining boilers, load ashcans on their Y-guns, weigh anchors, sound general quarters, and wheel their steel bows toward the enemy—whose position, it bears repeating, was known to fair precision. That was what any defender, United States or British, had a right to expect, what any German assailant had a cause to fear. It was right there, in print, page eight of Operation Plan 8-41, promulgated by Admiral King on 20 December: "TASK FORCE FOUR [Support Force] will: . . . when available, detail one or more suitable hunting groups to operate in connection with reported submarine concentrations."[95] One such concentration was only hours away. Doubtless not a salt in the Atlantic on either side, and in the know, would have anticipated that, instead of fighting, the squadrons would either hold in port or find other things to do.

7

Beat on the Kettledrum

1000 hours Central European Time, 0500 U.S. Eastern Time 9 January, U-*123* on the surface, both ahead half, position CB 3321, estimated 560 nautical miles east of Cape Cod, course 250, heavy snowstorm, wind northwest force 6, seas running 5. Distance covered in the previous twenty-four hours: 124 nautical miles. Total distance since departure: 2,597 nautical miles. Total distance submerged: 50 nautical miles.[1] On the bridge, Watch Officer von Schroeter strained in the predawn dark to see anything at all through the windswept snow that, mixed with sprays of icy saltwater, stung the eyes and cut the face. In his ears the surrounding howl meant that the seas must be climbing to ten meters. Every half minute, as though in confirmation, whole waves broke over the conning tower, leaving von Schroeter and the lookouts of the forenoon watch gasping and hanging on. With miserable regularity steep crests lifted the boat's bow high on the shuddering surface, then smashed it down and forward so that dark rollers from the moun-tainous water attacked across the foredeck and exploded against the tower. With one hand on their harnesses and their binoculars in the other, the lookouts stared futilely at the angled curtains of snow, acquiring, von Schroeter figured, no more than one hundred meters lateral visibility. Underneath their gray-green oilskins and sou'wes-ters that the wind alternately flattened and ballooned, the bridge watch wore their leathers with lamb's wool linings, sweaters, towels around the neck, wool caps, sea boots, and gloves. Upright wood slats fitted to the inside of the bridge prevented the oilskins or gloves from freezing fast to the steel surfaces. Around their cork-soled boots dark water rushed and foamed. With the upper hatch battened down to prevent flooding, their only communication with the rest of humanity was by voice pipe, into which the weaker angels of their natures felt time and again like crying for relief as the "bathtub" in which they stood pitched, rolled, and yawed in the riled-up seas, and yet another wall of unseen ocean crashed heavily against their necks. To von Schroeter who braced his back between the UZO post and the periscope housing, it seemed that all the violence of the war was directed at him personally. *Verdammter Atlantik!* Was it for this that he had been born? Aft the two diesel exhaust fumes profaned the snow with their answering refuse, and engine noise competed with the outcry from the ocean breast. Now and again smothers of foaming seas swept across the exhausts and caused the ports to cough and grunt. And when the bow, after hanging momentarily over deep troughs, plunged sickeningly downward, the stern lifted naked from the water and the twin bronze screws shrieked in their unaccustomed freedom.

The afternoon watch that came up at 1200 hours CET (0700 ET), and precisely on time since punctual watch relief was a matter of honor, knew full well what to expect from the tumult they had experienced belowdecks, where crewmen were being thrown about like puppets and some, nauseous from watching the inclinometer bubble or compass needle, were puking into buckets. The new watch were glad to see the men whom they relieved. Every lookout knew the story of U-*106* on a calm blue day in October 1941, just outside the Bay of Biscay, when an unexpected wave from a stern sea carried the unstrapped bridge watch overboard. When Kptlt. Hermann Rasch came up the hatch later for a look at the sky, he found the four men simply gone—vanished. Ever after Rasch grieved whenever he speculated how the men must have cried out to the unknowing boat, then called to one another, then in their fatigue and despair yielded to the choking waters. There were stories, too, of men thrown out of their safety belts by sudden seas, and of ribs crushed against the binoculars or coaming, and of faintings from the stress of facing the violent, implacable Atlantic. No new watch relieved its exhausted predecessor without a healthy measure of respect for the ocean and fear of its freakish wrath. And when a watch completed its assigned hours, they counted themselves lucky to be alive and under cover, which was how the bone-chilled forenoon watch felt now, when—after four straight hours of presenting their bodies to the punishing seas—they hung up their binoculars, doffed their dripping oils and boots, splashed Colibri on their salt-encrusted beards and eyebrows, warmed their feet and hands before an electric space heater, gulped a cup of Hannes's coffee, and then, otherwise fully clothed, climbed stiffly into bunks. Sodden clothing dried on the body as well as anywhere else on board, including the aft torpedo room, which some men used. But perfect dryness was never achieved in an environment that was now always humid, where fog glowed around all the lamps, and one had to cut away the mold before eating Hannes's bread. No matter; the watch fell fast asleep. Even the foul emanations of the boat's interior were a blessing after the fragrant hell they had endured outside.

The Old Man himself appeared on the bridge during the afternoon watch and was surprised to find visibility improving to eleven miles. Snow still fell thickly, ice splinters covered the bridge cowling, and wind continued to thrash at the unsteady boat. Watch Officer Hoffmann and the lookouts held tightly on to their harnesses lest they lose their footing on the slick deck with its snow and slush. The wind, still from the northwest, was slightly down yet strong enough that when Hoffmann turned to speak to Hardegen it blew the words out of his mouth and away. What most struck the Old Man was the seamless gray of the snowscape. There was no discernible horizon, only one disorienting curve of gray from sea to sky. The sense of being alone without reference in the middle of the day was unsettling, particularly since the upper hatch remained closed against shipped water and the showers of spume and spray; except that periodically the turret hatch would open and hands from below would take the binoculars in, turn and clean them with a leather or dry absorbent cloth, then hand them back to the lookouts as the bilges below pumped out the water that splashed through the opening. The only variation in this gray-shaded world of which U-123's paint scheme was a part was the white foam that boiled on the crests of breaking rollers, or scalloped from the bow wake, or poured from the limber holes along the sides of the hull casing. Hardegen leaned forward over the cowling to tell, if he could, how well if at all the twin front wind collars on the bridge fairwater were working. Their purpose was to turn the horizontal air currents upward and over the bridge. To Hardegen the fairings seemed to reduce somewhat the straight-ahead wind, and that was what they were designed for. Quarter and counterclockwise winds seemed to be unaffected. And that, too, was unexceptional. Hardegen looked at his wrist chronometer, shielding it against the snow and spray. The mixers had to pull torpedoes from the tubes and adjust them. *Eins Zwei Drei* was getting too close to U.S. sea-lanes to neglect that task any longer, but it was too dangerous to undertake while the boat was being tossed like a cork in a maelstrom. Hardegen cupped his hand to Hoffmann's ear: "Take the watch below!" he yelled. "I'm going into the cellar!"

As the boat slid under the angry surface, men exhaled audibly in relief. *Eins Zwei Drei* settled into a quiet glide. In his bunk Alwin Tölle thought that the war must have ended. He had never known such sudden peace. Moving gingerly with his splinted finger onto the floor plates he asked a steward who was passing through with a pail of lemon juice what was happening. "Mixers have to mix," he was told. Tölle had watched the procedure before, but too many men and too many groceries had obstructed his view of the torpedo mates at work. He wondered if he might have a better view in the after torpedo room. But that meant passing through the diesel and maneuvering rooms, to which Hoffmann had not yet introduced him. *Es macht nichts*—Well, it was probably all right. He would make the transit on his own. After reaching the control room he asked the LI, Schulz, if it was all right to open the engine-room hatch. It was, said Schulz matter-of-factly, but pull it shut after passing through. Tölle opened the hatch, entered in a bent position, and stood upright in a world of machinery that was strangely inert and silent given the constant hammering he had heard from it day and night. So these were the diesels. He looked down two rows of engines on either side of the gangway from which rose lazy spumes of heat smoke and a dense, sweet smell of oil. He would have gagged, he thought, had he not already had his fill of that smell which, with other scents, defiled the boat throughout. From his left materialized a face he recognized from the Christmas party but had not seen since.

"The photographer, aren't you?" said "Karlchen"—Karl Latislaus—the chief diesel mechanic in his black overalls, wiping his hands on a towel just as black. There was an edge to his voice, betraying the general disdain that seamen had for landlubbers and suggesting as well a certain irritation with his lot in life, or so Tölle thought. Thirty years old, Karlchen was the oldest man on board.

"You must want pictures of some real heroes," he said, smiling grimly.

"No, I don't have my camera," Tölle said. "I'm just passing through. But maybe I should learn—"

"Yes, you should learn something about *these* poor bastards," Karlchen said, pointing jerkily at the rest of the engine crew faintly visible through the foul gauze at the far end of the passageway. "Six hours on, six hours off, not knowing where the hell we are or what the hell we're doing, living by the klaxon of the control-room telegraph. None of these men has seen the sky for two weeks, and it's not likely they'll see it again until we get home." Karlchen then suggested that Tölle pay a little attention to what was really driving this boat. "Those electric motors that are on now—they're for rest and relaxation. These babies," he said, patting the cylinder heads of the two long, gray engines within near-shoulder reach of him on either side as he stood in the passageway, "these are the power plants that take us to war."

There were two diesels, he explained to Tölle, manufactured by Maschinenfabrik Augsburg-Nürnberg AG, which had made engines for 1914–18 boats and now provided updated power systems for both Type VII and IX boats. These MANs were each nine-cylinder, four cycle, supercharged and salt water-cooled. At maximum power setting they each developed 2,200 horsepower at 470 RPMs. In a good sea they could drive *123* at eighteen-plus knots.*

Karlchen escorted Tölle aft to the maneuvering and electric motor room, where he called attention to the bright, clean panels and floor plates of the E-motor space, which contrasted vividly with the oily, stinking world that he inhabited. "These two guys," he said, pointing to *E-maschine* mates Renner and Pleuser, "will tell you what an easy life they have running their little silvery toy machines." Karlchen withdrew through the hatch chuckling at his own sarcasm, while Tölle tried to make sense out of the sculpted panels, black gauges, and red switches that confronted him.

Pleuser explained that on either side of the passageway were twin dynamotors, or E motors, manufactured by Siemens-Schuckertwerke AG, model type ZGU345/34. Each E motor was rated at 500 horsepower. Power was supplied by storage batteries—2 by 62 cells 28 MAL 1000, one of the largest accumulator types used in the Kriegsmarine—most of which were positioned under the forward compartments to counterbalance the weight of the diesels. With bat-

*See Appendix D.

teries in parallel at 210 volts the motors could develop 500 horse-power, 275 RPMs, and 1,950 amps, but only for one hour's duration. Like the diesels, the E-motors clutched directly to the line shafts. Tölle could see the voltage and ampere gauges, the shaft RPM indicators, rudder angle indicators, and, by the hatch, the control room tele-graph. On the starboard side Pleuser and Renner identified for him a panel with controls for electric welding and a four-stage Junkers air compressor for filling containers of compressed air that the control room needed to blow water from the ballast tanks when the boat surfaced, to start the diesels, and to launch the torpedoes from their tubes.

Tölle thanked the two mates and exited through the aft hatch-way. It was too much to assimilate.

The aft torpedo room was not unlike the forward torpedo room, it seemed to Tölle. There were eight bunks for sixteen crewmen, though for the moment some were lashed up to the sides to allow room for the torpedoes. At the extreme stern there were two white-faced torpedo tubes. The mixers were busy at the arduous task of coaxing an eel out of its tube, with all the expected sexual expressions—of which the Old Man did not approve. The differences were minor: two tubes instead of four, and directly in front of them there stood a lathe for repairs and an auxiliary steering wheel in the event something dis-abled the helmsman's buttons in the conning tower. And the view was better. It was easier here for Tölle to follow the actions of the mixers as they tended to the torpedoes that sat both in and out of their launch tubes and required these every-three-to-five-day inspections and ad-justments to maintain launch condition. Ordinarily on an extended cruise one torpedo fore and aft was withdrawn from its tube each day, but heavy seas made that regular sequence of inspections dangerous if not impossible. Numerous accidents had occurred when torpedo mates in rough weather had used their body weight to prevent eels swinging in their harnesses from bumping structures and thus bend-ing propellers or throwing directional controls out of calibration. As Reinhard Hardegen himself would write, "Many physical injuries take place here because the crewmen would rather protect the torpedo by intervening with their own flesh and blood than allow a torpedo to be damaged."[2]

Now the mixers' gleaming muscular arms manhandled a grease-streaked eel from the Number 6 tube and onto hoist rings and chains suspended from an I-beam secured to pad eyes on the overhead. The thickly coated weapon assumed an ominous presence as it hung under wire-guarded lights before Tölle's fascinated gaze. How much money—forty thousand Reichsmarks [ten thousand dollars] he had heard—had been invested in this sinister thing? How many brains and man-hours? How many people would die from its awful self-immolation? Tölle's fascination increased as he watched the formal surgical procedure begin. One mixer unscrewed a small test plate near the warhead while another removed an entire panel from the electric motor housing near the stern. Soon additional plates and panels were spread on a floor cloth, and many of the eel's innards were exposed. A mate holding a checklist clipboard offered Tölle a running commentary on the procedure:

These G7e electric eels, sometimes called T-2s, required much more care and maintenance, he said, than the old G7a compressed air-driven type. The boat still carried a couple of G7as. In fact there was one in the adjoining tube. The Old Man probably would use them first to get rid of them. Their exhaust gases left a bubble wake and their warhead was smaller, 380 kilograms compared to 500 in the G7e. Since the wakeless, more destructive electrics were a better weapon their maintenance was worth the trouble. What the mixers were doing at the bow end was checking the gyropots and guidance system generally. They were looking at, among other things, the pendulum, hydrostatic diaphragm, and differential valve in the depth-keeping mechanism. That mechanism had to be exactly tuned. The Old Man liked to fix depth settings as shallow as possible, two to three meters, depending on seas and swells as well as on target draft, so the depth had to be maintained precisely if the torpedo was not to broach and betray itself. Later, he said, Tölle would see the men tilt the eel with gyros running and check the angles of the vertical and horizontal rudders. For now the inspections inside continued: bearings and axles, steering controls, motor armature, lubrication points, and so on. But arguably the most important task of all was recharging batteries. These light lead storage batteries were the sole source of power. If they failed, everything else in the torpedo failed. So, as Tölle could understand, the mixers were especially careful to ventilate the batteries and prepare them for charging by the diesels as soon as the boat surfaced. One last inspection of the structure remained, however, before the torpedo was partially reinserted in its tube prior to charge, and that was the mixers' examination of the Pi-G7H impact pistol that, upon impact with a target, caused the torpex warhead to explode. The problem with these pistols was that their zinc lever caps tended to corrode, and if the guard flap should deteriorate the pistol would be alive. One big jolt to the boat and—*boom!* The crew could forget their girls in Lorient. And deep in the recesses of every mixer's mind was fear of what might happen when the exterior tube caps were opened to the sea. Every torpedo was programmed so that its small nose propeller would revolve so many times—over about four hundred meters' distance—before a screw thread armed the explosive charge. Theoretically it was possible that when water rushed into the open tubes before launching that the flow against the pistol propeller could activate the device that controlled the torpedo's safety run and cause the eel to arm itself while still in the tube. In which case maybe—*boom!* No more drinks at the Café les Trois Soeurs.[3]

None of this reassured Alwin Tölle, who decided to return to his bunk.

After the boat resurfaced Reinhard Hardegen leaned against the lurching chart table and read the wireless and radiotelephone intercepts that Rafalski had brought him. Most were from merchant ships on the international distress six hundred-meter band. Others were from United States naval vessels. All were related to gale seas that tormented the lanes through which *123* had just passed. The transmissions told of merchantmen from convoys HX 168 and ON 52 battered and lashed by force 9 seas and force 10 winds. Hardegen smiled knowingly at one ship's weather report: "The numbers don't go any higher." He knew that for most on the bruising cold rollers that day the war had halted of its own accord. It was challenge enough to survive. Perhaps meteorology would make peace where men could not. He thought about that for a while until brought up short by the question, Where were the other boats of Gruppe Paukenschlag? How were *they* faring in this winter storm? He realized that he did not know, and, given rigid wireless silence, could not. It was 9 January, *123*'s eighteenth day at sea, the American East Coast coming up. There was nothing to do but press on alone and hope that all was well with Folkers and Zapp, Bleichrodt and Kals.

At 2300 hours (1700 ET) Rafalski handed him an F.T. marked *Offizier.* A signal from BdU! Hardegen stumbled toward the wardroom table where Rafalski had already laid out the Schlüssel M. As he pressed the keys and copied out the decrypt, adrenaline rushed through his bloodstream.

"Rafalski!" he shouted at the Puster. "Call for the officers! We begin our attacks on the 13th!" He bolted for the 1870G chart in the confidential papers locker.

Rafalski had not seen the Old Man so elated since the opening of the Operation Order two weeks earlier. He called for the officers as directed and watched them assemble around the Commander, who held out the decrypt for them to read:

OFFIZIER
1058/9/1/42
(1) OCCUPY FOLLOWING ATTACK AREAS. ZAPP ATTACK AREA ROMAN NUMERAL I. HARDEGEN II. FOLKERS III. BLEICHRODT IV AND V. KALS VI.
(2) FOLKERS HARDEGEN ZAPP CONTINUE ADVANCE 10 JANUARY EARLY. BDU COUNTS ON YOUR ARRIVING IN ATTACK AREA 13 JANUARY.
(3) BLEICHRODT KALS ADVANCE PROMPTLY ENOUGH FOR NEW AT-TACK AREAS TO BE REACHED ON 13 JANUARY.
(4) BOATS WILL FORM THE GROUP DRUMBEAT.[4]

Immediately the officers' eyes flashed from the decrypt to the chart.

"As you can see, gentlemen," Hardegen said, "Attack Area Two corresponds exactly with the initial target zone in our Operation Order—New York to Atlantic City. Nothing new there. Folkers and Zapp will be nearby, Folkers farther off New York and New Jersey, Zapp off Cape Hatteras. Kals will be in Cabot Strait off Cape Breton Island and Bleichrodt southeast of Halifax. So Group Hardegen will be the only boats to hit the U.S.A. as such, at least at the start. And our particular boat can go as far south as Hatteras if we wish. The really new information in this signal is the attack date. I've already informed the Puster. You have my permission to inform the rest of the crew. Now let's make sure we make our area on time. Chief, maintain the diesels at both ahead half. That's about the best speed that we can make in these hard head seas. Anything more and we'll start undercutting. Number One, check the DR line with Kaeding. We haven't had a star sight for days. Number Two, resume bridge watch and keep your eyes peeled. We're fast approaching coastwise traffic."

Earlier that day at 2000 hours (1400 ET), the bridge had sighted the two threadlike masts of a hull down sailing vessel, course 300°, that von Schroeter estimated at six hundred GRT. It was the first vessel that *123* had sighted since the *Dimitrios Inglessis* debacle. Following standing orders, von Schroeter took an evasive course. Now as the sky grew dark and the boat's log entered 10 January, German time, the snow, which had lightened somewhat earlier in the day, thickened and began to lay a heavy carpet of slush across the bridge deck. Von Schroeter decided to close the hatch. He and the lookouts stood alone with their 7×50 magnified images of snow and their fantasies, von Schroeter imagining New York skyscrapers looming out of the white wall forward. Belowdeck crewmen went about their tasks as best they could in the fusty, twisting compartments. "Langspleiss" guarded his head against the violent rolls. Hannes struggled to keep his pots on the burners. "Kraxel" and "Icke" cursed the damp rot. "Lackl" examined his hands, green from verdigris on the rungs of the tower ladder. Tölle kept an arm wrapped warily around the guard rail of his bunk. Rafalski stared hard at a photo of his girlfriend Wally and worried: 13 was not a good date at all.

0730 hours British Zone Time, 10 January, London, OIC, Submarine Tracking Room.

"Good morning, sir."

"Good morning, Beesly. I see in the *Times* this morning that the Board of Admiralty has released news of the loss of our cruiser *Galatea* off Alexandria three weeks ago—by U-*557*, wasn't it? I always worry that some newspaper liaison type upstairs will name the U-boat that caused a sinking and absolutely compromise our game. Let's not forward those identifications in the future unless First Sea Lord demands it. And you seem to have a lot of paper in your hand this cold morning."

"Yes, sir." Tracking Room could now conclude confidently, Beesly said, that the enemy had returned to the North Atlantic in great strength. Tracking had good data on the VIIC, or 500-tonner, group that was headed to previously worked operational areas, and as of that morning the room had first notice of the attack areas assigned to the five 740-tonners approaching the North American coast. First the twelve 500-ton boats. Intercepts revealed that they formed *Gruppe Ziethen*, and the data clearly suggested that they were destined for stations on the Newfoundland Bank and off Nova Scotia, as the chart pins displayed. The boats were U-*84, 86, 87, 135, 203, 333, 552, 553, 582, 654, 701,* and *754*. As noted earlier, they already had two sinkings on their outward passage. U-*87* sank *Cardita* west of Ireland on 31 December and U-*701*—that was the boat fresh from training that had sighted HG 76 and lost its second watch officer overboard on the thirty-first—sank *Baron Erskine* southeast of Greenland on the sixth. When all twelve boats were in place they could be expected to constitute a formidable rake.

"Recommendation?" Winn asked.

"Notify convoys to evade," Beesly replied.

"Of course. But it will be hard to divert our formations if Group Ziethen moves about. Now, the seven-hundred-forty-tonners?"

Beesly reported that Special Intelligence had come in over night on the attack areas assigned to U-*66, 109, 123, 125,* and *130.* The intercept also gave the group name for the first time. Curiously, the attack areas in the intercept bore Roman-numeral designations rather than *Marinequadrat* numerals. The anomaly suggested that the attack areas were so unlike previously worked areas that it was more appropriate to mark them off on a chart by that means.

Beesly handed the decrypt to Winn who placed it on the plot table between his knuckles and stared at it for a full minute, mumbling several times, "Paukenschlag." Then, looking up, he said to Beesly that the Roman indicators could mean that Admiral Dönitz was dealing with a coastline—not just with positions at sea—but with a coastline that included positions at sea. Winn studied the five 740-tonner pins that Beesly had been advancing at ten knots day by day in a cluster toward the Canadian and New England coasts. He pointed out to Beesly that without any transmissions from those boats, which obviously were observing wireless silence, the two of them would have to deduce position and destination from other sources. Now they knew where U-*123* had been on 3 January—here (pointing) off Virgin Rocks—because of the *Dimitrios* show. And that was too southerly a trajectory for anyone who was intending to follow the Great Circle to Newfoundland Bank. It was not too far south for someone intending to work off Halifax, however. But U-*123* would have been southeast off Halifax already by 10 January—that very day. So their next clue was in this present signal, item two, namely: FOLKERS HARDEGEN ZAPP CONTINUE ADVANCE 10 JANUARY EARLY. BDU COUNTS ON YOUR ARRIVING IN ATTACK AREA 13 JANUARY. "Advance" was the controlling word. Those three boats were probably together, or more or less so, and they were destined for contiguous attack areas: one, two, and three. Since he and Beesly knew of U-*123*'s position a week before, Winn suggested that it would not be difficult using a divider to calculate the point to which that particular boat might advance three days hence. And that position would then help put a fix on the other two boats.

Winn set the divider for a ten-knot advance over twenty-four hours and placed one pointer southeast of Halifax. Then, working from the intercept's time of origin in Central European Time, he advanced the divider westward across the intervening three-day time period. The result described an arc that included the Canadian and U.S. seaboards as far south as Delaware Bay. Hardegen certainly and probably also Folkers and Zapp would go at least as far as New York, Winn concluded, if they kept pushing at a ten-knot speed, and it was clear from the intercept that BdU was counting on their doing so. That would be Tracking Room's "working fiction." Admiralty should make certain, he said, that those trajectories made it onto the U.S. Navy daily situation maps in Washington. As for the other two boats, *109* and *130*, Winn was less sure of their courses because, unlike U-*123*, BdU had not provided a recent reference point. They, too, were ordered to be on station by the same 13 January. Did that mean that their assigned attack areas were nearby the others? A Z message of 29 December had ordered U-*125*, the first out of Lorient, to wait in square BD for the other boats to catch up. That was all that was known. There was just no way of deciding about *109* and *130*, Winn concluded, whether their stations would be shoreward or seaward. The only really hard recent information they had, he reminded Beesly, was on *123*. That boat was the key. No doubt about it. She at least was going as far as New York.

Winn stood up stiffly. "How's your German, Beesly? The language chaps at Bletchley Park have translated the code word for this group—*Paukenschlag*—as 'Drumbeat.' If that is a correct translation, and I have no reason to doubt that it is, the word may tell us something of the Germans' intentions. We'll have to think about that. In the meantime"—Winn glanced at Dönitz's photograph—"we have the Lion to thank for our fix on Lieutenant Commander Hardegen. His wireless to Hardegen about *Dimitrios* was most obliging. Either he or Hardegen may favor us again before the next three days are out."[5]

Beesly suggested that they needed all the favors they could get. Five more 740-tonners were now at sea—U-*103*, *106*, *107*, *108*, and *128*. The first two had advanced to square BD. The last had just sortied from Lorient.

Winn nodded and limped to his office for the 0800 conference call to Western Approaches and Coastal Command.

1200 hours (CET), 0500 (ET), 11 January, U-*123* on the surface, both ahead half, position CB 4332, south of Halifax and Liverpool, due east of a point between New York and Philadelphia, course heading 270. Winds from the northwest at 4–5, sky overcast, seas 4, visibility 12. Distance covered the preceding day: 183 nautical miles. The boat had passed through the worst of the storm. The ceaseless pounding was over. Seas continued to be brisk with high swells, but the once-driving head seas had diminished to confused waves that canceled each other out. The boat, which had shaken and strained and groaned for so long, resumed its usual elephant dance, while exhausted crewmen nursed their cuts and bruises and rediscovered their appetites. Now, as Hardegen sat on his bunk, he read one after another the distress signals and damage reports that Rafalski handed across to him. They came from ships that unlike *123* had been unable to defy the mauling winds and seas. Seven ships from loaded convoy SC 34 that had departed Sydney on 9 January were forced by weather damage to seek shelter at St. John's, Newfoundland. Three Canadian destroyers were battered so hard they had to be withdrawn from the escort force.[6] Two U.S. destroyers, fourstackers *Badger* and *Cole,* bound for rendezvous with a returning convoy in ballast, suffered badly. *Badger*'s mainmast snapped at bridge level, and *Cole* sustained structural damage to side plating and Number 1 gun; *Cole*'s deck log registered a port roll of sixty-eight degrees.[7] Still other ships, naval and merchant, were pleading for radio direction signals from Halifax, Nantucket, or New York. From the six-hundred- and eight-hundred-meter wavelengths, Rafalski picked up sos signals. The Russian *Nikolina Batkovia* lost her rudder in square AJ 68, and her crew had taken to lifeboats. Another steamer, *Africander,* sank from sea damage in BC 58. The pitiless Atlantic.

Hardegen would later remember: "A look into *Lloyd's Register* told us that these were old hulks built between 1904 and 1907. The enemy was apparently already forced to send cranky old boats like these across the North Atlantic, probably heavily overloaded. Well, that allowed us to draw interesting conclusions about the shipping situation. I think it was hardly necessary to lend a helping hand in this kind of weather. The ships would surely go into the depths by themselves, and we could keep our torpedoes for better targets."[8]

At 1600 Hardegen mounted to the bridge for a personal look around with binoculars. There was good late-morning light and visibility was ten. Hoffmann had the watch. The seamen lookouts, who were a different breed from the mixers and other technicians on board, practiced their own rhythmic, painstaking art. With rubber-cushioned eyepieces held tightly against their browbones they slowly swept the binocular lenses by fingertip control, left to right, across the sectors of the horizon assigned to them. At the end of each sweep they let the heavy glasses hang for a few seconds on their neck straps while they flexed their triceps and scanned the sky and horizon with unaided eyes. Then, glasses raised again, they resumed their magnified search, this time from right to left. The ritualistic vigil continued uninterrupted except when spray or, as frequently happened to the bridge watch now, mist covered the lenses, requiring the lookouts to call for leather or cotton wipers or to send the glasses below for cleaning. The lookouts were experienced enough by this Feindfahrt that they knew what to look for as they moved their lenses back and forth, inch by inch: thin smoke trails that usually were the first betrayals of a steamer; masts that ordinarily materialized at ten thousand to twelve thousand meters on a clear day; dots and specks that became aircraft faster than anyone could predict. They knew that in order to pick out the shadow of a blacked-out ship at night they had to look not where it might be but a little above the horizon. They also knew the tricks that seascapes played on the best of observers: deceptive cloud formations, mirages, floating logs, whale spouts, cloud shadows and phosphorescence at night, and momentary near blindness that afflicted those lookouts who had not prepared for night watches by wearing red goggles beforehand. Each seaman lookout was aware that his duty, no matter how mind-numbing and tiring to eyes and arms, was the most critical duty post on the boat if *123* was to find targets. And no one wanted more that the boat should find targets than the technical crew below who craved to be rid of the torpedoes on the floor of the bow compartment so that they could move about in something approaching comfort. The failure at Virgin Rocks had put the technicians on edge. Thus, even though the boat was not due to begin attacking until the thirteenth, every eye on the bridge hoped to find a target so tempting that the Old Man could not pass it up.

The M IV/1T Carl Zeiss 7 × 50 binoculars, without case, weighed two pounds, eight ounces, as compared with the other best 7 × 50s in the Atlantic at the time—the British Barr and Stroud Pattern 1900A, which weighed a full pound more. The Zeiss was seven inches long, the Barr and Stroud nine. The Zeiss internal glass surfaces were bloomed to reduce reflection losses, not so the Barr and Stroud. The diameter of objective for both was 50 mm. The Zeiss glass was striking for its high light transmission, 80 percent compared to 66 percent for the unbloomed Pattern 1900A. The Zeiss provided excellent eye freedom in that it was not necessary for the observer's eye to hold rigidly to one position in order to maintain the best optical performance. Movement of the observer's eyes across the axis had little or no effect on the quality of definition in the various regions of the field of view, whereas in the Pattern 1900A any slight movement of the observer's eyes across the axis resulted in serious optical deterioration. The distance between the eye point and the eye lens, which determined the ease and comfort with which the instrument could be used, was preferable in the Zeiss, providing better eye relief. In comparisons of watertightness, the Zeiss again was clearly superior: a Zeiss immersed in water for ten minutes showed no bubbling, whereas a Stroud and Barr bubbled within two minutes. A pair of loose didymium glass filters with a strong absorption band in the yellow of the spectrum could be fitted to the Zeiss eyepieces, enabling nearby boats to communicate with each other at night by yellow lights.[9]

At 1635 the starboard ahead lookout suddenly stiffened like a dog on point. When he saw it happen, Hardegen whipped his own binoculars to eye level and followed the lookout's lead.

"Herr Kaleu—" the lookout began.

"Yes, I see it," Hardegen interrupted him. A small cloud curled south against the horizon at two points to starboard. "Headed north, hull down, can't see the tops. We'll have to get the angle on him and investigate. Right full rudder! Come to zero-three-five! Both ahead full!"

The bridge rolled port as the helmsman's rudders resisted the sea on the starboard side and the diesels thundered away at full power. After an hour's chase, first the ship's funnel and then the forward-connected double masts came into view. At Hardegen's order Kaeding handed *Gröner* up through the hatch. Flipping through the pages Hardegen came to the silhouettes that fit. Smokestack higher than its masts, this had to be a British steamer of the Alfred Holt Shipping Company, Blue Funnel Line. And the double masts meant ten thousand GRT or better. The Lion said that the boats should not pass up a vessel that size, and here was one as big as life. Paukenschlag was going to start a little earlier than the thirteenth. Gradually, with *123* on a slowly closing near-parallel course, Hardegen was able to obtain a better image in the glasses. Course of the steamer 038, he estimated, probably bound for Sydney or Halifax. A slight zigzag. Speed nine knots or better. *Eins Zwei Drei* pushed hard to get in front. At 2400 (1800 ET) dusk fell, then winter darkness. It was time to break off the parallel chase and close range on a heading of 350. Hardegen gave the order. Hoffmann brought up the UZO (*Uboot-Zieloptik*) target-aiming binocular apparatus and attached it to the UZO post. These pressure-tight Zeiss, Jena UDF 7 × 50 309 torpedo-control binoculars, with swastika and eagle markings on fourteen-inch barrels, weighed fourteen pounds. One of the barrels, which were equipped with tubular sun and spray shades and rubber eyeguards, was fitted with a graticule (aiming line) that glowed at night, having been painted with a luminous compound. A dimmer operated by a small lever near the right eyepiece controlled illumination of the graticule line from *hell* (light) to *dunkel* (dark), at opposite ends of its movement. Provided the eye was fully dark-adapted the bright-line graticule could be seen against a maximum sky brightness of .00005 candles per square foot. (The brightness of a clear starlit sky was about .00001 to .00003 c/sq. ft.) Thus the graticule could be seen at all sky brightnesses as either a bright or a dark line.[10] It was the dimming lever that Hoffmann now operated back and forth in order to acquire optimal use of the aiming line in that evening's sky conditions.

"UZO is set, Herr Kaleu," he reported.

"Very well, Number One."

In the dark and haze Hardegen had difficulty following the target, which was traveling completely darkened on a zigzag course. Twice when he thought he had an optimum ninety-degree launching angle staked out he had to take a parallel course again in order to stay in front at an acceptable range.

"Target speed nine knots, Herr Kaleu," reported Hoffmann, basing his estimate on *123*'s own speed as well as on the target's ship type and bow wake.

"Yes, that's our problem," Hardegen acknowledged. "Helmsman, come to three zero zero."

Finally, at 0145 hours (CET), they had what Hardegen calculated was their best opportunity. Range to target was reduced from three thousand to fifteen hundred meters and the torpedo track angle was eighty-five degrees. He called for engines both ahead half and handed over the approach to Hoffmann, who had followed the target through the rough alignment sight atop the UZO barrels and now placed his eyes in the cups.

"Open bow cap three, target bearing three-five-six point five, range fifteen hundred," Hoffmann said loudly from his half-stooped position, "angle on the bow (the difference between the line of sight and the heading of the target) seventeen Green (starboard). *Folgen!*"

By *folgen* ("track") Hoffmann inquired if the bearing, range, and angle were being transmitted by the electromechanical UZO and by his own voice reports to the *Vorhaltrechner,* the Siemens-made deflection calculator in the tower, and by the calculator to the *Torpedo-Schuss-Empfänger* (torpedo launch receiver) in the forward torpedo room, which in turn fed the aim-off heading into the guidance system of the Number 3 tube G7a torpedo.

Von Schroeter at the calculator in the tower had cranked in the range and angle. The UZO line of sight was registering automatically in the calculator gauges. The lamp board corresponded to the Number 3 tube. The trigonometric solution of the aiming triangle was indicating. Von Schroeter called back, *"Folgen!"* From Bootsmaat (Petty Officer) Rudolf Fuhrmann in the forward torpedo room came confirmation of the torpedo launch receiver: *"Folgen!"* The torpedo gyro was humming in exact parallel with the calculator; now, no matter what change in course the U-boat might take, the gyro system would automatically correct the heading of the torpedo to target and activate the rudder vanes accordingly 0.4 seconds after launch.

Hoffmann shouted back a setting that the calculator did not handle: "Depth three point five meters!"

"Three point five!" the torpedo room acknowledged. The mixers cranked in the depth of run by hand. Fuhrmann placed his palm on the manual launch button in case the electrical launch system on the bridge failed.

At 0149, with the UZO graticule slightly forward of the target's funnel, Hoffmann hit the electromagnetic launch button and yelled *"Los!"* The torpedo room yelled back: "Failure!" Fuhrmann hit the manual button and yelled "Launched!" Four seconds had elapsed because of the failure. The torpedo should now hit abaft the funnel. The LI, Schulz, had already begun taking water into the regulator cells to compensate for the lost weight. From the time of manual launch, Hardegen and Hoffmann began counting down the estimated ninety-six seconds to target. Hardegen did not like launching from this distance. The chances for accuracy were fewer, and the wait was too long for his liking—over a minute and a half. But at ninety-seven seconds—

WHACK!

A black-and-white explosion cloud with a light streak of yellow fire rose directly aft of the tall smokestack. Immediately the heavily loaded steamer slowed in the water and began to settle by the stern with a slight list to port. Alwin Tölle came up to take photographs. "Puster" Rafalski called from the wireless room: "She's signaling SSS—struck by torpedo—on the six-hundred-meter distress band . . . name of vessel *Cyclops* . . . giving position now."

Hardegen called down the voice pipe: "Come to course three-two-zero!" He would go directly at the stricken steamer. "All gun crews to deck! Man guns!" When the C/30 machine-gun crew was in place and had cleared the barrel Hardegen ordered that gun: "Take out the wireless. Aim for the deckhouse below the antenna array. Commence firing!"

The angry *dacca-dacca-dacca-dacca* of the machine gun spat shells that, owing to their still-considerable distance from the target, fell in white spurts short of the ship. Rafalski reported that the SSS transmissions were continuing. Hardegen ordered cease-fire on the C/30, whose acrid smoke curled over the bridge. As he closed the target he could discern through the 7 × 50s an artillery piece, possibly four-inch, on the aft deck. Even though the steamer's list made it unlikely that she would be able to bring her gun to bear, he did not want to risk a gun duel. He altered course slightly in order to pass around the bow of the now-stationary steamer, figuring that the lampblack dark would cover him, also that if there were any guns on the foredeck—Bofors, Hotchkiss, Lewis, or whatever—the sharpening rise of the bow would make it difficult for a gun crew to train on him, particularly if the guns were set for high-angle fire. The calculation proved correct and at 0218 hours *123* took a position at steerageway six hundred meters off the steamer's port side. From there Hardegen saw that *Cyclops* was still reasonably afloat and that some of the crew who had gone into lifeboats were reboarding. He ordered a coup de grace. With the boat's stern pointed directly at *Cyclops* Hoffmann flooded Number 5 stern tube and launched that G7a on zero angle toward a point forward of the bridge. This time the electrical launch button worked properly. After a run of thirty-one seconds the warhead detonated in a fierce eruption of smoke and debris that went one hundred meters straight up. The large hull quivered, collapsed, and began a rattling death plunge as the remainder of her crew went into the boats and rafts or leaped from the deck into the icy water. The final throe sent the bow skyward, where it lingered briefly before, with a shudder, it slipped below the frothy surface. Hardegen marked the time at 0223, only five minutes after the second hit. Almost at once he heard two huge detonations underwater. The U-boat shook from the blasts, which had a metallic sound, much like that of Wabos, and certainly too strong for a boiler blowup. He decided that they were ammunition exploding.

There was nothing to be done for the ship's crew in boats and rafts that made their way slowly through the typical surface detritus of planks, doors, ropes, cork life preservers, clothing, and coal dust. The Lion's orders were emphatic: Commanders were not to pick up survivors ("We must be hard in this war"). Hardegen had violated the rule only once, when he needed Bertie Shaw to confirm his sinking of *Aurania*. Anyway, there was no room on board *123* for these poor fellows, not to mention the hundreds of others he expected to set adrift as Paukenschlag continued. Turning aside, then, from the spectacle of survivors venturing into the freezing darkness in search of a rescue vessel that might respond to their desperate wireless transmissions, Hardegen called for course 220, engines at 300 RPM. From first sighting to sinking the attack had consumed eight hours. He had to make up a lot of time in order to reach New York the next day, and it was not certain now that he could do it. He did steam with a great personal elation, however. He had begun Operation Drumbeat. Now he asked Rafalski in the radio room to look up *Cyclops* in *Lloyd's*. Rafalski reported a minute later: "*Cyclops*, twin screw, 9,076 GRT, constructed 1906, owned by Ocean Steam Ship Company, Limited, A. Holt and Company, Managers, length four hundred eighty-five feet, beam fifty-eight point two, depth thirty-nine point five. Home port Liverpool." Not quite 10,000 GRT, but close enough, thought Hardegen. Poor old *Cyclops* would never see home again. She was *123*'s twenty-fourth victim (not counting *Aurania*) and Hardegen's eighth.[11]

Leslie Webber Kersley was *Cyclops*' master. He had brought the vessel out of Panama on 2 January with a general cargo bound for Halifax. Ship's company was 30 Europeans and 151 Chinese, most of the latter being ferried to other ships' crews. At position 41-51N, 63-48W, or approximately three hundred miles east of Cape Cod, while darkened and zigzagging on Pattern 11, course 000 degrees, *Cyclops* suffered two torpedo hits, the first between Number 6 and 7 hatches on the starboard side. At the time of the first hit two officers were on the bridge and lookouts were posted on the crow's nest, Monkey Island, fore and after decks, and gun deck. The U-boat was not observed, though lookouts did sight the wake of the second torpedo. Marine Gunner Joseph D. G. Green was getting ready to go on watch when the first torpedo struck. Racing to the gun station, he tried to sight the attacking boat but could see nothing in the darkness. Water was spouting up all around him from openings in the after deck, so he went forward to the boat deck to assist at Number 5 lifeboat if needed. The master ordered him back to gun station but Green, finding the vessel settled by the stern, saw that it was impossible to stand by guns. A few minutes later the second torpedo into the port side blew him off his feet and into the water abreast of Number 6 hatch, where he watched the hull and her Samson Posts sink quickly below the surface.[12]

Senior Radio Officer R. P. Morrison was on watch in the W/T house when the first torpedo exploded, setting the switchboards loose from the top bolts. Immediately he keyed SSS . . . SOS and position on the distress frequency, but, fearing that the damaged switchboards were frustrating his signal, he started up the emergency equipment and repeated the call. When no coast station or vessel confirmed receipt, Morrison ran out onto the boat deck to make sure that the portable emergency transmitter and receiver in boat Number 4 were functioning. Satisfied that they were, he returned to the W/T house to try calling out again on the regular emergency system. This time the coast radio at Thomaston, Maine (Station WAG) acknowledged receipt of the call and repeated the whole message. Morrison reported receipt to the master, who ordered him to dump overboard in locked weighted bags the W/T secret codes while Kersley himself dumped weighted bags containing confidential books, ship's papers, general mail, and one safe hand envelope. Morrison went over the side when the second torpedo hit and joined the forward port raft from the water. Kersley followed overboard and joined the same raft.[13]

Morrison's distress signal had its hoped-for effect. Naval Operations Halifax dispatched a PBY Catalina flying boat and two Royal Canadian Navy (RCN) *Bangor*-class minesweepers to the scene, HMCS *Red Deer* and *Burlington*. Dockyard Halifax, which had been *Cyclops'* destination, received its first notice of the ship's distress from U.S. Naval Communications Station at Charleston, South Carolina, via Boston: FROM C. IN C. LANT ACTION C.O. ATLANTIC COAST (R.C.N.) HALIFAX

FOLLOWING INTERCEPTED 500 KC/S. FROM "CYCLOPS" (BR.) AT 0000 G.M.T. POSITION 41.51 NORTH 63.48 WEST S.S. "CYCLOPS" TORPEDOED. NOTHING HEARD FROM SINCE. U.S. NAVCOM.[14] Commander Laurence F. Safford's On the Roof Gang had proved their mettle. Theirs was the first Atlantic intercept connected with Operation Drumbeat and the first U.S. source to reveal, if anyone in the U.S. Navy was listening, that an enemy force was approaching U.S. waters. Nor was Commander Rodger Winn's OIC Tracking Room in London unaware of the sinking. The Thomaston (WAG) confirmation of *Cyclops'* distress signal was intercepted by Y Service at 0002 GMT.[15] The loss of *Cyclops* confirmed Winn and Patrick Beesly in their earlier estimation that U-*123* and possibly the other two boats associated with her, U-*66* and U-*125*, would be at exactly that longitude by the time indicated. Emboldened now to believe that his coordinates were correct, Winn set down the overall strategic calculations in his weekly "U/Boat Situation, Week Ending 12.1.42":

> The general situation is now somewhat clearer and the most striking feature is a heavy concentration off the North American seaboard from New York to Cape Race. Two groups have so far been formed. One, of 6 U-Boats, is already in position off Cape Race and St. John's and a second, of 5 U-Boats, is apparently approaching the American coast between New York and Portland. It is known that these 5 U-Boats will reach their attacking areas by 13th January. Five other U-Boats are between 30 deg. and 50 deg. W., proceeding towards one or other of the above areas, and may later be reinforced by yet another 5 westbound U-Boats, making a total of 21 boats. It was presumably with the object of covering this concentration that the W/T ruse in the N. Western Approaches was carried out as described last week. The U-Boat concerned U-*653* is now returning to a Biscay port.[16]

Based on more detailed position coordinates supplied by Winn and Beesly the Admiralty sent a coded cable on the same date to COMINCH (Admiral King) on third deck, Main Navy, Washington, D.C., where it was retyped for distribution by Operations (OP-38-W) and its information relayed to Captain Frank Leighton's daily situation map. For days Leighton's "little toys and other play things," as King disparagingly called the map graphics, had plainly shown the

German advance. Now the estimate of 12 January (not declassified by the U.S. National Security Agency until 3 February 1987) boldly projected the probable U-boat positions, which Leighton displayed on his map by means of four open circles. It read:

12 JAN SUB ESTIMATE × INFO RECEIVED INDICATES LARGE CONCENTRATION PROCEEDING TO OR ALREADY ARRIVED ON STATION OFF CANADIAN AND NORTHEASTERN US COASTS × 3 OR 4 BOATS NEAR 40N 65W [17]

The position 40N 65W at the latitude of Philadelphia was 430 nautical miles off the U.S. seaboard, which slants sharply southwest from Cape Cod. This was the latitude to which U-123 came immediately after sinking Cyclops. That sinking was duly noted in the same estimate: MERCHANT SHIP TORPEDOED IN 41-51N 63-48W AT 0002 GCT 12 JAN X. Leighton represented the sunk Cyclops at that position by a darkened circle. The sinking of Cyclops, if nothing else in this remarkably clear and exact (except for citing "3 or 4 boats" when 3 was more correct) intelligence estimate, should have alerted all U.S. naval forces to the impending assault. *Perhaps no more telling attack warning, in unmistakable language and numbers, had ever come to the military forces of the United States.* In no way resembling a cryptic "bomb plot" or "lights code" message such as would fascinate Pearl Harbor students decades later, the 12 January warning contained empirical, verifiable confirmation: Cyclops sunk. The U-boats were coming, and along a known corridor of approach. Although the twin plots at BdU and OIC, relying on dead reckoning, would have both U-66 and U-125 proceeding abreast of U-123 in their march to the eastern seaboard, Zapp and Folkers were in fact more than a day behind Hardegen. The stormy head seas had slowed their advance and, as a result, Hardegen, even with the Cyclops delay, would enter U.S. territorial waters first and alone. The warning went out to all Naval Coastal Frontiers Atlantic, which included Admiral Andrews' command; to All Task Force Commanders Atlantic; to CINCLANT "For Action"and to Admiral Bristol's CONVOYESCORTS WEST LANT, whose twenty-five destroyers lay at Anchor Watch across Gruppe Hardegen's attack course. With advance notice of this initiation of warfare within the continental limits of the United States one should have thought that Admiral King's friend, the retired colonel, was entirely correct when he said: "With Ernie King at the helm . . . America can rest assured that there will not be any repetition of the unfortunate affair at Pearl Harbor."[18]

Meanwhile, at sea, a drama was being played out that would have many repetitions ahead. Gunner Green of *Cyclops*, who had made it onto a raft with eight Chinese, drifted through the freezing night with little hope of rescue. When morning dawned he and his companions, most now suffering from acute hypothermia, tied on to a nearby third mate's raft. During the day four Chinese died from exposure, two more at night, and two the following morning.[19] On another raft nineteen-year-old Midshipman L. J. Hughes, from Vancouver, Canada, survived to say: "Some of the dead men we pushed overboard. The others we kept to give some shelter against the cold and the water which sprayed across the bows."[20] Finally, the Catalina spotted the survivors with their yellow flags and vectored *Red Deer* to pick them up. The small vessel looked so large and magnanimous to the half-frozen Gunner Green that in his debriefing he called the minesweeper "the Cruiser." His perspective was understandable. In U-*123*'s attack only two men had been killed directly, a gunner and the ship's doctor, but a huge number of lives had been lost to the temperatures: 5 out of the complement of 30 Europeans and 93 out of the 151 Chinese. It was a much-depressed list of survivors that *Red Deer* brought to Halifax Dockyard. The fruits of Paukenschlag were fresh-taken and bitter.

> I tell you naught for your comfort,
> Yea, naught for your desire,
> Save that the sky grows darker yet
> And the sea rises higher.[21]

8

New York, New York

At midnight beginning 13 January (CET), 1700 hours U.S. Eastern Time (ET) on 12 January, Walter Kaeding reported to Hardegen that *123*'s first star sighting in three days showed that the DR line was off by twenty-five nautical miles at a deviation of 79 degrees. The correction was duly entered on the overlay, and the boat pursued a 275 heading at both ahead full. *Eins Zwei Drei* was going to go at New York Harbor on the surface—not as a lurking, furtive, sneaky underwater intruder, but boldly on the surface as a proud and daring war machine. Hardegen counted the nautical miles to date: 3,379 since Lorient, of which only 55, or .02 percent, were underwater. The only submerging he would do now on his approach, be it daylight or night, would be to evade sighting by aircraft. Anything on the surface he would sink; except small vessels such as the two-masted sailing vessel the lookouts spotted to starboard at 1527 hours. *Eins Zwei Drei* did submerge twice briefly at 1800 and at 2157, when multiengined aircraft with navigation lights that Hardegen thought were commercial airliners crossed the sky, the first on a heading of 330, the second on 130. (The fact that air patrols of Eastern Sea Frontier did not fly after dark would indicate that they were not war planes.) Other than these two aircraft, Hardegen would see nothing in the approaches to New York to cause him concern, though by 2315 on the thirteenth it was clear that *123* was not going to make her assigned coordinates by the close of that day. She was now in Marinequadrat CA 38 directly south of Nantucket

Island and on her present course would make CB 28 and 29 the following day, the fourteenth. The Lion should not be too disappointed. The boat's delay making station was occasioned by the successful *Cyclops* diversion; and now also by the heavy sea state that *123* was encountering as the DR line showed her approaching Long Island. By midnight beginning the fourteenth, owing to mounting combers, Hardegen had to reduce power to both ahead half. Still, to look on the good side, there was no sign of a battle group to meet him—no destroyers or patrol craft. And nothing was flying. The night was his.

At 0448, as though to say that the United States welcomed him, Montauk Point Lighthouse sent out a friendly beam ahead to starboard. Barth had already taken a reading on its radio beacon signal: one dash, one dot, and two dashes for sixty seconds, then silent for 120. Hardegen corrected to a slightly more northerly course so as to pass about fifty miles south of the light, the easternmost navigational aid on Long Island. As he did so the sea state improved and visibility extended to ten miles. Hardegen surveyed the horizon from the salt-caked bridge. It was encouraging to discover that there was no blackout. The Americans were gracious hosts. Lacking charts for the coastal waters, he took heart that he could rely on shore lights to lead him from point to point. At 0724 (0024 ET), just before a band of fog descended cutting visibility to 2–4 miles, a lookout sighted moving lights at approximately four thousand meters to port ahead on a near-reciprocal course, bows on. Hardegen ordered the engines slow ahead while he and the lookouts kept a wary watch for the vessel now hidden in the gauze. This could be a destroyer or some other type U.S. Navy antisubmarine vessel, he thought. Keeping his hand close to the alarm bell he worried that he had very little water under him in case he had to dive. It was impossible to know the depths ahead without coast charts, but his soundings currently showed sixty meters. It was not much, and the water was certain to shoal as he approached the harbor channel. These were tight quarters for a U-boat. Now the black loom of the ship to port suddenly came sharply into view—and with all its lights and lanterns ablaze. Hardegen could not believe it. The vessel was clearing New York Harbor as though peace had been declared!

Hoffmann affixed the UZO and began calling data to the tower. It quickly became obvious that this was not a warship but a tanker or freighter—what kind was not immediately apparent although the lookouts scoured its silhouette for clues. Hardegen now swung to a southerly heading that would bring *123*'s course at right angles to the target's bearing. "Helmsman," he ordered, "come left to two-eighteen, engines slow ahead, make four knots." To Hoffmann he said, "That should give you about an eighty to eighty-five track." He raised his glasses to study the target ship now materializing in more distinct form. "It's a tanker, Number One. A huge one. Two torpedoes. Aim for bridge and aft mast. Permission to launch at eight hundred and seven hundred."

Hoffmann refined his numbers as *123* closed on the line of sight range: "Target's course zero-nine-six, speed ten, angle on the bow Red (port) nineteen." From below von Schroeter called back confirmation of a solution on the Vorhaltrechner, and the forward torpedo room sang out, *"Folgen!"* Tubes 1 and 4 were flooded. The two G7es they contained were gyro set for *Mehrfach,* or multiple launch. At 0835 (0135 ET) on an eight-second interval Hoffmann released the two eels: *Los! . . . Los!* The first was calculated to impact at forty-five seconds. Hardegen cautioned the lookouts to continue sweeping all quadrants lest a warship be guarding the tanker. He hoped there was none. If there was one, he would have to take it on since he was sure that he lacked sufficient diving depth to avoid Wabos. At forty-five seconds— nothing. Then, seconds later, WHACK! One violent detonation caused *123*'s frames to shudder.

Both eels had been set for four meters' depth. Since the second hit exactly where it had been aimed, at the aft mast, Hardegen concluded that the first had run deep: G7s had a tendency to do that; in the future he would set for 2.5 and 3. Now he watched as a fifty-meter-high flame column turned into a black, sinister mushroom cloud 150 meters high, and the fog-streaked sky took on an eerie orange cast. The tanker's hull sagged a little aft and listed to starboard, but it did not burn. The masts bent and the radio antennas fell crazily on their sides, but close as they were to shore they successfully carried an emergency call that Fritz Rafalski intercepted on the forty-one-meter band: SOS HIT BY TORPEDO OR MINE 40 MILES WEST OF NANTUCKET LIGHT SHIP X NORNESS.[1] Hardegen told Rafalski to look up *Norness.* The first torpedo if launched on time would have taken out the W/T house. Too bad it missed. And now this: The ship was not sinking. He maneuvered off for a second launch. Stern Tube 5, depth of run three meters, time 107 seconds: WHACK! Just where he wanted it, below the bridge. Another tall flame and flowering cloud. But, after a few minutes it appeared that the only effect of the second explosion, apart from silencing the wireless, was to set the ship back on an even keel! Because of their inner compartmentation, tankers had been known to make port safely with large holes in their hulls. Hardegen had Hoffmann ready Stern Tube 6. At 0902 hours that eel failed to explode. A miss on a stopped target was not possible! The eel must have run deep, despite being set for three meters.

Yet one more torpedo, this time from Forward Tube 2, sped toward the smoking target at 0924. Five torpedoes—what a waste! thought Hardegen. But he could not allow this prize to be towed to a nearby harbor. After twenty-six seconds: WHACK! Now, at last, the target ship collapsed and went to her knees. Making water fast by the stern, she raised her dark bow to the sky as though in supplication, then descended noisily in that position, bouncing her stern on the bottom and leaving the bow exposed for thirty meters of its length. If Hardegen needed any demonstration of how shallow the sea had become, he had only to contemplate the head of this dying giant, whose lifeboats milled around her in confusion. He gave a new course and went below to compose his KTB entry, which ended: "Continue toward Ambrose Channel." That was the dredged channel into New York Harbor itself, as shown on the tourist map. Obviously a large body of shallow and dangerous water lay ahead before he reached the channel. Alarm diving would no longer be possible, that is, with any expectation of protection, and travel underwater was precluded by the unknown nature of the bottom with, Hardegen assumed, numerous banks and shoals. *Eins Zwei Drei* would have to go in at night, on the surface the whole distance, straight down the throat of harm's way. Twice now Hardegen had thrown down the gauntlet, with *Cyclops* and *Norness*. If the enemy wanted to come out and fight, now was the time to show his fists. The U.S. Navy had all the advantage. The farther *123* penetrated toward the shoaling harbor approaches the more vulnerable—but feisty—she became.

Norness was a modern diesel single-screw motor tanker built in 1939 by a German yard, Deutsche Werft AG, of Hamburg (No wonder, Hardegen mused when he looked at *Lloyd's*, she took so long to go down). At 9,577 GRT, 494-feet long, with a 65-foot beam, she was owned by a Norwegian company, Tanker Corporation, which had moved its offices to New York after the German conquest of Norway, and sailed under Panamanian registry. The U.S. Navy Bureau of Ships had just two months before issued the ship one four-inch fifty-caliber gun and four thirty-caliber machine guns.[2] Her forty-man crew was

Norwegian. At 0135 Eastern Time on the fourteenth, while at 40°28′ north, 70°45′ west, or sixty miles southeast of Montauk Point, as twenty-five-year-old seaman Sverre Sandnes on the wheel was steering a course for Nantucket Lightship, a torpedo struck hard on the port side. The violent shock toppled men from their feet and tumbled others from their bunks. A shower of oil from the ship's cargo of petroleum in bulk splattered the exterior deck and tackle. In his pajamas, Captain Harold Hansen grabbed a cap and overcoat and raced to the deck to survey the damage. A lookout yelled that he could see a U-boat maneuvering to port. Hansen, who at first thought he had struck a U.S. Army mine, now realized that the U-boat might strike again. Deciding not to use his guns but to concentrate effort on saving lives he ordered Abandon Ship. The oil-slicked tackle made the task difficult. Sandnes and a pump man named Kaare Reinertsen worked together lowering Number 1 boat when the oil-drenched lines slipped from their hands and the boat fell to the water, where it capsized. Reinertsen went under and was not seen again. Sandnes grabbed a hove line thrown to him by Anton Slettebarg but repeatedly, while the waves beat at him, it slipped through his oily hands. Finally he managed to hang on long enough to be pulled back on board, where he and Slettebarg, the latter with a jacket, pair of bedroom slippers, and prized gold watch, made for another boat. Sandnes described the water: "Was damn cold."

Captain Hansen and seven men succeeded in lowering the ship's one motorboat, only to discover on reaching water that the engine did not run. The men paddled with their hands to get away from the stricken vessel. Twenty-four men made it safely into a lifeboat and six found refuge on a raft. Chief Engineer Henry Danielson, who had survived a torpedoed ship in the North Sea during the last war, had slept fully clothed except for shoes and hence was better prepared than most, who were half-dressed or in their underwear, to face the wind and spray. "Wind was blowing and was cold like hell!" he said later. Twenty-one-year-old Paul Georgsen, who had fallen into the water while attempting to enter the first lifeboat and had scrambled back on board ship, searched the compartments for a white-haired mongrel puppy named Pete that he had bought in Buenos Aires five months earlier. He found the pup shaking and whimpering in the messroom. In that condition Pete had no chance to survive a cold lifeboat, he decided. "So I said good-bye to him, then brained him on the deck," he said later in a choked voice. One more life would be lost.

Seventeen-year-old oiler Egil Bremseth, the youngest on board, who was still standing on the deck when the second torpedo hit, was blown off to his death.

From Captain Hansen's motorboat the men could see in the gloom the U-boat that had attacked them as it half-circled the dying *Norness*. At one point it came so close that they could hear the "guttural voices" of the Germans. Fearful that the U-boat might shoot at them with machine guns they crouched low in the boat. Third Officer Oivind Ask would later report, however, that the U-boat made no attempt to shoot any of the survivors. During the night and morning hours the lifeboats and raft became separated. The men suffered terribly from the cold. Those in Hansen's boat had to bail constantly to keep their tiny boat afloat, but the activity helped keep them warm. They hoisted a peajacket on an oar and hoped that it would be seen by someone since they were close to shore. Indeed, as Hansen would say later, "Nobody was expecting a submarine so close in American waters. I think we are just as safe there as in New York Harbor."[3] The survivors would drift for half the day, however, without anyone knowing of their plight. (Nowhere in the records is there any explanation why *Norness*'s SOS on the forty-one meter band received no practical response. Nor is there any evidence that it was even received except by U-*123*.) The men with Officer Ask were confident that they would be rescued. They sang songs to keep up their spirits, including a sea chantey, "Hej å hå jungman Jansson!" and the American "Jingle Bells."

Finally, twelve hours after *Norness* went bow up, a fishing trawler out of New Bedford, Massachusetts, named *Malvina D* happened to sight Hansen's boat. At first thirty-two-year-old skipper Magnus Isaksen, on his first voyage as captain, thought that the boat was a floating log. When he neared the object he saw what it was and immediately hove to. The husky blond survivors, half-frozen and exhausted, had to be helped on board; one of them, Trygen Merkesdal, had a broken kneecap. Isaksen wrapped them in blankets, fed them hot coffee, and made for New Bedford. He recounted later that Hansen and crew had little to say other than that they had been sunk by a U-boat. They simply seemed glad to be alive. It might have occurred to Isaksen to ask himself as he sped home, where was the U.S. Navy?

Some of the Navy was taking life slow and easy these days. It was good for a destroyer crew to have the pressure off. Home port, a little liberty, late-hour rising, routine training, back by supper. This was better duty than escort of convoy. On the morning of 14 January USS *Ellyson* (DD 454), flagship of DesRon 10, was moored starboard side to East Dock at Torpedo Station, Newport, on Narragansett Bay, Rhode Island, with six doubled six-inch lines out fore and aft. Boiler Number 2 was lit for auxiliary use. At 0800 the skipper, Lt. Comm. John B. Rooney, decided that it was a good brisk day for a little peacetime steaming, to noplace in particular, just around the patch and do a little test torpedo firing in the process. The wind was southwest by south, force 5; the temperature was expected to be forty-two degrees Fahrenheit by 1100 and the visibility thirty-five miles under cloudy skies. So the engine room lighted fires under Number 3 boiler while the executive officer handled the morning paperwork. Two men were absent over leave since 10 January. The Condition 2 watches needed assigning. The general mess inspected as to quantity and quality 110 gallons of milk fresh from Aquidneck Dairy, 600 pounds of bread from Ward Baking Company, and 60 pounds of cottage cheese from T. J. Murphy. At 1102 *Ellyson* made preparations for getting under way. At 1110 she cut in all boilers on the main steam line. At 1127 she was under way, steaming on various courses and at various speeds, the captain conning, the navigator on the bridge. After passing through the entrance nets *Ellyson* came to course 220, changed to full speed, twenty knots, 188 RPM. (By this time *Norness*'s crew had been in the water ten hours.) At 1156 *Ellyson* changed to flank speed, twenty-five knots, 255 RPM. At 1153 she changed course to 155 and made daily inspection of magazines and smokeless powder samples. Conditions normal. At 1200 she was steaming as before—until a radio call came in that sent the exec to the speaker system: "This is not a drill! This is not a drill! General Quarters! General Quarters! All hands man your battle stations!" A naval patrol plane had sighted the near-perpendicular bow of *Norness* and the remaining lifeboat and raft. Newport ordered *Ellyson* to pick up the survivors. It seems not to have occurred to anyone at Newport that *Norness* might have been torpedoed by a U-boat, despite the fact that Admiral Bristol commanding CONVOYESCORTS WEST LANT, which included *Ellyson*, was an addressee of the exact attack warning issued two days previous. Missing from the orders sent to *Ellyson* was: "Seek out the enemy and engage."

At 1324 *Ellyson* sighted the lifeboat and took on board its twenty-four men. She then commenced zigzagging and searched for the raft. Not finding it but sighting the pointed hulk of *Norness*, she turned back toward Newport with her freight of shivering survivors.[4] A Coast Guard cutter, *Argo* (WPC-100), later found and rescued the men on the raft. At the Tanker Corporation Office in New York a spokesman stated that the Navy had forbidden the disclosure of any information about *Norness*'s port of origin (New York) or destination (Halifax). For their part, Navy spokesmen observed with clinical detachment, "The leisurely attack on the *Norness* followed the same pattern as that employed in the sinking of a ship earlier in the week about 160 miles off the coast of Nova Scotia, with the loss of ninety lives."[5] This was, of course, *Cyclops*. The Navy's matter-of-factness about the sinking contrasted with the public's alarm, best represented by the full-page *New York Times* headline and lead the next day: "TANKER TORPEDOED 60 MILES OFF LONG ISLAND: The Battle of the Atlantic flared within 150 miles of New York City yesterday."[6] But after describing the grim details of the *Norness* "tragedy," the *Times* found comfort in the fact that there was a "powerful and numerous fleet of submarine chasers operated by the United States Navy on constant patrol" that made the German U-boat venture "extremely hazardous."[7]

On the fourteenth floor at 90 Church Street, the *Times* account of Eastern Sea Frontier's "powerful and numerous" force no doubt provided a few sardonic chuckles. The ESF staff were bone-tired from their lengthy vigil. They had been on alert of one kind or another since 7 December. Lt. Richard ("Dick") Braue's son Richard (Rick) remembers how on that Sunday afternoon he and his father were tossing a football in the yard of their home on Green Avenue in Middlesex, New Jersey, while half listening to a football game on the radio. Suddenly the lieutenant froze on hearing something, and the ball thrown by nine-year-old Rick hit him in the chest and bounced away. Lieutenant Braue raced into the house, changed into his uniform, and drove off. The family would not see him again for three months, after which he returned for a few days and told Rick and his sister Margaret (Peggy) that he had been sleeping on his desk and that he was in communication with "someone named King."[8] Now on 15 January, with the alert upgraded to Condition Red, Braue, the most junior member in rank of the small defense team at ESF headquarters, watched the drama developing on the Operations wall chart. He may well have wondered why Admiral Andrews did not send out every ship and plane he had at his disposal, however few and inadequate, to meet the enemy. Perhaps the other, more senior, staff officers wondered the same: Captain John

T. G. Stapler, USN (Ret.), chief of staff, and five lieutenant com-
manders: Louis C. Farley, USNR, Operations; P. P. Bassett, USNR, War
Plans and Army Liaison; F. W. Osburn, Jr., USN (Ret.), Routing; R. G.
Payne, USNR, Air; and a recent addition, C. F. McNamara, USNR. The
ESF war diary plainly acknowledges receipt of the attack warning, on
13 January: "Submarines may be expected off our coast at any time. At
least four were known to be about 300 miles east of Nantucket Light on
January 12, and are probably proceeding westward."[9] The most that
Andrews' command did to repel the aggressor was to close the ports of
Boston, Portsmouth, and Portland at 0012 on the 14th(!). Hardegen
struck *Norness* an hour later.

Standard tactical doctrine since the time of turn-of-the-century
American naval theorist Alfred Thayer Mahan held that in the face of
enemy attack one ordered everything afloat into the fray. Whether or
not one's own forces were equal to the enemy's was immaterial. The
accepted doctrine demanded that when one was defending a position
with inferior forces only an aggressive response was in order. "From
such a position," Mahan stated, "there is no salvation except by action
vigorous almost to desperation."[10] Desperate, certainly, but correct,
had been the action of the three outgunned British cruisers *Ajax*,
Achilles, and *Exeter*, which engaged the pocket battleship *Admiral Graf
Spee* and brought her to self-destruction at the River Plate in December 1939. It was slow, fabric-covered biplanes (British Swordfish torpedo bombers) that had crippled the rudders of the mighty *Bismarck*.
In that same spirit Major James P. Devereux's 500 U.S. Marines at
Wake Island had driven off a strong seaborne Japanese invasion fleet
before, unreinforced, they had to succumb. Under that doctrine, too,
six months later in the defense of Midway, forty-one ancient, lumber-
ing, outmatched Douglas TBD-1 Devastator torpedo bombers would
take off against the most powerful invasion fleet Japan had ever
assembled, from which only four would return to their home carriers.
The fact that both U.S. actions were futile was beside the point. It was
what navies should do, wrote Mahan: The "nation that would rule
upon the sea must attack."[11] But Dolly Andrews did not attack. He
covered up and waited for the other boxer's blows. And when *Norness*
went down he simply picked up survivors and sent out a cutter, a
minesweeper, a blimp, and a few planes to examine the derelict and
report its condition.

No less baffling was the fact that First Bomber Command of
Brigadier General Arnold N. Krogstad did not concentrate its search

aircraft on the fortieth parallel, along which the clear warnings specified the Germans were advancing and along which now the bomber crews had *Norness*'s sinking as direct confirmation. Even though the Army Air Force flew only in the daytime, its observations could keep a U-boat down and force it to slow its advance and consume its battery charge and air during the sunlit hours. Constant aerial reconnaissance over the harbor approaches in daylight would discourage a U-boat from presenting even the frothy feather wake of its periscope. This was the tactical doctrine that British Admiral Godfrey had impressed so strongly on U.S. Captain Kirk nine months before: constant observation and concentration of forces. Instead, Bomber Command dispersed its forces and in the face of the known German line of attack on the New York–Philadelphia sector fanned out its search planes in all directions from 0 to 180 degrees. This misuse of aircraft, combined with Andrews' failure to send so much as a subchaser to harry Reinhard Hardegen on the 40 latitude corridor, constituted a failure of will and tactics almost as grave as the failure of Admiral Bristol's twenty-five destroyers—of which more later.

Narrow, whale-shaped Long Island extends 105 miles eastward from New York's Lower Bay. The waters off its southern shore present the mariner with some of the most difficult navigation on the U.S. East Coast. Off-lying banks and shoals, the broken bottom, strong and variable currents, frequency of fog, turbulence of wind and sea in thick weather, and the dense volume of waterborne traffic combine to make the approaches from Montauk Light to New York a formidable piloting challenge. Generally, there is a southwesterly set to the current, with the larger velocities found in the shoaler parts. In storms the sea breaks on spots with ten fathoms (8.9 meters, sixty feet) or less. Generally, vessels do not shoal the depth to less than fifteen fathoms, and at night they take soundings regularly in order to avoid the shore where numerous wrecks have attested the dangers of passing too close. On inbound approach a ship or boat follows a base course of 265 degrees for the sixty-eight miles between Montauk Point to Rockaway Beach and the entrance to Ambrose Channel, which was dredged to a depth of forty-five feet (13.6 meters) in the 1930s to accommodate the British Cunard liner *Queen Mary*. From the Ambrose Channel Lightship a vessel would follow the precise channel course through the shallow Lower Bay at 296°54′ true. Traffic outside the egress of the channel could be congested: On 10 January the British motor ship

Continent, four hundred GRT, bound for Bermuda, sank after a collision five miles outside Ambrose with the tanker *Byron D. Benson.*[12]

Hardegen's intention was to go no farther than the lightship.
Inside the channel itself he could get trapped. Now, in the last dark
hours of 14 January he pursued the approach. Lacking coastal charts
but paralleling the lights on the Long Island shore—houses, streets,
automobiles, it was impossible to know their source—he followed the
general trend of the coastline at 247 degrees. In the predawn vapors,
moving seaborne lights suddenly materialized to starboard. He
slowed the engines to one-third and began an attack approach. Unfortunately, as he closed the target, a bright red morning sun rose behind
him and silhouetted the U-boat tower to any alert lookout. He decided
to stay on the surface a few minutes longer, which enabled him to
distinguish two steamer lanterns and to obtain a good range and angle
on the bow. At 1430 hours (0730 ET), he dived and continued the
approach submerged at two-thirds speed on the amperes. The
steamer's course was 96 degrees, *123*'s 0 degrees. A textbook approach,
the target looming large and clear in the periscope, range closing six
hundred meters . . . five hundred . . . four hundred. He could read the
Plimsoll mark and now the name—*Verdammt!* It was neutral Spanish:
Isla de Tenerife. Rafalski looked her up: 5,115 GRT. Too bad! There was
a great letdown in the tower, then later elsewhere in the boat, when
word of the abortive attack passed from mouth to mouth as far as the
diesel machinists and maneuvering-room electricians in their permanently blind imprisonment. Hardegen decided to bottom out where he
stood. It would be self-defeating to proceed farther on the brightening
surface. He gave the order to flood. *Eins Zwei Drei* disengaged for the
day. Thirty meters down the boat rocked noisily to rest on the uneven
mud. Here they would stay until nightfall, hoping that no deep-draft
ship would tear off their tower. The men could sleep, catch up on their
tasks, or read the dog-eared magazines that passed from bunk to bunk.
But first they would eat. Hannes was ready with the German version of
lobscouse, the sailor's hash. To the last of his fresh store of potatoes,
which he boiled and mashed, he added cubes of corned beef, strips of
cucumber pickled in spirit vinegar, and a little salt herring. He would
have placed fried eggs on top but the eggs were long gone. The stewards passed through the hatches with their pails. The men ate quietly.
The officers chatted about New York and the Americans. Between
mouthfuls Barth listened to traffic moving overhead. Rafalski turned
up the gain on his broadcast receiver and tried to make sense out of

"The Goldbergs" on WOR and "Missus Goes A-Shopping" on WABC, electing finally to settle back with the Gramercy Chamber Trio on WNYC. When, at nightfall (2351 CET, 1651 ET) the boat surfaced, Rafalski's antenna captured a shortwave broadcast from DNB, the German News Bureau in Berlin, which he handed to the Old Man on the bridge:

> Buenos Aires. For the first time on Thursday the U.S. Navy made public an announcement concerning the torpedoing of a U.S. tanker off the coast of Long Island. A notification issued by the Navy station stated that the 9577 GRT tanker "Norness" was torpedoed approximately 60 miles off Point Montauk on Long Island. According to reports from New York, the Commander of the Navy station in Newport, Rear Admiral Edward C. Kalbfus, declared that an enemy U-boat had attacked the tanker, which flew the colors of Panama. The torpedoes had exploded abaft. Two crew members had been killed, the other thirty-eight had been rescued.[13]

Hardegen read the account with satisfaction. Though his boat was not named, *123*'s American exploits were becoming known to millions in the homeland. Now he peered intently ahead as the throaty rumble of his diesels violated the clear night air and the U-boat's bow thrust deeper toward the Lower Bay. Rafalski received another message, this one an encrypted *Offizier* signal from BdU addressed to *123:* ACCORDING TO REPORT FROM B-DIENST ON 14 JANUARY 1530 HOURS AN UNKNOWN TANKER SUNK IN QU CA 3770. CREW IN LIFEBOATS. ONE MINESWEEPER, ONE PATROL BOAT, ONE DESTROYER, THREE AIRCRAFT SENT TO HELP. BDU OPS.[14] When shown the signal Hardegen deduced that *Norness*'s emergency call on forty-one meters had not been received and that the tanker's loss had only been discovered in the following daylight. He was correct. The first notification of *Norness*'s loss reached ESF at 1800 (ET) on 14 January, 16½ hours after the sinking.[15]

At 0144 still another message came in, an intercept on the six-hundred-meter band: A British steamer named *Dayrose* near Cape Race, Newfoundland, was sending SSS—ATTACKED BY SUBMARINE. This was the work of Knight's Cross–holder Korvettenkapitän Erich Topp in U-552 (which had sunk *Reuben James*), one of the Group Ziethen boats farther north off the Avalon Peninsula of Newfoundland. On 15 January at 0138 CET Topp sank the British merchantman at 46-38N, 52-52W. It took five torpedoes to do the job, not because 4,113-ton *Dayrose* was that formidable but because three successive torpedoes failed from eight hundred meters out. A fourth eel wounded her and a coup de grace buried her.[16] A brief signal from Topp to BdU about the sinking—DAYROSE SUNK OFF CAPE RACE X MUCH HEAVY WEATHER X LOW TEMPERATURES X TODAY TEN BELOW[17]—constituted the first notice that Admiral Dönitz had received about any successes of the western boats, either of Paukenschlag or Ziethen, except for the B-Dienst intercept about the "unknown tanker sunk" in CA 3770. As for Paukenschlag, Dönitz wrote in his KTB for 14 January: "The result is not yet established. Conjectures are as follows: (a) It is not known if the boats have reached their positions off the coast of the U.S.A. It is possible that they will arrive later than the estimated time because of bad weather. (b) U-*552* reports bad weather south of Newfoundland so that the boats must be having difficulty taking position, to say nothing of making attacks."[18]

Actually, Ernst Kals's Paukenschlag boat U-*130*, one of the two north of the U.S. seaboard, had already on 13 January sunk the second and third victims of Drumbeat, after Hardegen's *Cyclops*. If Kals advised BdU of his conquests there was no acknowledgment of the fact in the KTB's of either BdU or Naval Staff in Berlin. Hardegen's earlier sinking of *Cyclops* had not been signaled home, either. Kals's first kill came shortly after midnight (CET) on 13 January not long after having been surprised by two 250-pound charges from a Sydney-based Canadian Bolingbroke 9063 aircraft. The Norwegian steamer *Frisco* hove into view northeast of Scatarie Island in Cabot Strait, and Kals took her down to a fiery death with one eel forward of the bridge and a coup de grace. In his *Schussmeldung* (shooting report) he claimed 6,000 GRT when in fact she ran 1582, as similarly he named her a tanker when she was a freighter.[19] Later in the same day at 0948 (CET) Kals sighted the Panamanian freighter *Friar Rock* en route to Sydney. With a good track angle from ahead of the target he stopped the vessel's way with a first launch, suffered torpedo failure with a second, and put her underwater with a third. In this case he claimed 7,000 GRT when the real figure was 5,427.[20] Moving off from that triumph to a position in close proximity to Sydney itself, Kals and his men experienced unusually cold weather (minus 15 degrees Celsius) that coated their boat with ice and chilled the bones of the ill-prepared bridge watch. There they also found intense Canadian destroyer and

air coverage. Another problem was the absence of detailed navigational information: As in *123*'s case, Flotilla had not been able on short
notice to supply *130* with sailing directions or coast charts. On 17
January BdU signaled all the Paukenschlag boats that they were free
to change attack areas at their discretion: IN CASE CONDITIONS UN-
FAVORABLE FOR ATTACK KALS CHANGE OPERATIONS TO AREA BETWEEN
HARDEGEN AND ZAPP.[21] Kals decided to do just that and made revolutions south.

The same problems afflicted "Ajax" Bleichrodt, whose U-*109*
would reach station southeast of Halifax on the sixteenth, when temperatures were minus ten degrees Celsius and navigation with inadequate charts and data was equally dangerous. Bleichrodt would not
find a target to aim at until the nineteenth, when off Seal Island below
the main body of Nova Scotia he encountered a dead-in-the-water
freighter, 4,000–5,000 GRT he estimated, waiting in 55 meters depth
to enter Yarmouth harbor. In a can't-miss attack situation the Knight's
Cross ace expended five torpedoes without experiencing a single hit.
The night sky was overcast with seas force 5–6, winds west southwest
at force 6, visibility "hazy" but with a good view of the target.
Bleichrodt led with a G7e from 800 meters at 0453 (CET). When that
eel failed to explode he tried another from the same range, then a third
from five hundred meters, and a fourth from fifteen hundred utilizing
the UZO only, at a fixed angle, without the Vorhaltrechner. When that
eel, too, miscarried he pointed the bow of the boat at the target from
500 meters and used the jumping wire (net guard) as a cross hair.
When that torpedo also foundered Bleichrodt gave up in disgust and
withdrew.[22] He had wasted two hours and five eels. And his torpedo
woes were not over. Two days later, off Shelburne, Nova Scotia (BB
7744), he would have yet another dud attacking a six-thousand GRT
freighter from eight hundred meters.[23] To Bleichrodt it must have
seemed like the Norway debacle all over again.

During Germany's invasion of Norway in spring 1940, forty-two
U-boats engaged British and Norwegian warships and transports
from the Skagerrak to Narvik. Because of torpedo malfunctions—
including premature detonations, pistol misfires, and eels running too
deep, thus passing beneath their targets to explode without effect on
the other side—no fewer than thirty attacks failed. The reports of
returning commanders were filled with frustration and anger. U-*48*,
which had had 50 percent duds the previous October (the "torpedo
crisis" had loomed as early as the second month of the war), launched

a textbook salvo from close range against the British battleship *War-spite* with no result. Two days afterward the redoubtable Günther Prien in U-47 took aim at "a wall of ships," launched four eels submerged, then another four surfaced, and had not a single *Treffer*, or hit, among them; as he pulled back, *Warspite* came into view and, as though to test the fates, Prien launched two torpedoes, one of which detonated prematurely and the other beyond range. Understandably, on his return to base, the Bull of Scapa Flow railed against the quality of his weapons. To Dönitz he complained that he was being asked "to fight with a wooden gun." Other commanders made similar complaints, all of which Dönitz indignantly passed up to Admiral Raeder in Berlin, who to the U-boatmen's bitter satisfaction convoked a court-martial of the vice admiral commanding and two subordinates of the Torpedo Test Establishment at Eckernförde. The subsequent six weeks-long investigation revealed a number of uncorrected deficiencies in the G7 types. The first of these was the tendency of the G7s to run deeper than they were set for. The variable, sometimes quite high, air pressure that developed in submerged U-boats was found to throw the sensitive depth mechanism out of calibration. Trials Command had not taken any special pains to correct this because the G7a was equipped with a magnetic as well as a contact pistol: When the magnetic pistol was elected (which could be done while the torpedo was in its tube) the weapon was *intended* to run beneath its target and to explode under the thin, and in warships unarmored, bottom, thus breaking the vessel's back and causing rapid flooding. The magnetic proximity detonator was designed to be activated by the target ship's magnetic field. It was a brilliant concept that theoretically made possible "down the throat" launches when the U-boat was presented with a zero angle on the bow. The problems with the magnetic exploder were many, however. For one thing all the testing on it had been done in German latitudes and low sea states unlike those frequently encountered on operational patrols. For another, the magnetic pistol tended to respond to the natural magnetism of the ocean floor; this was particularly true during the Norwegian Campaign, in which the U-boats operated above deposits of iron ore close to the North Pole. A third problem was the growing British practice of degaussing, an operation by which the permanent magnetism of steel ship hulls was neutralized. Following the court-martial analysis of these findings the magnetic pistol was abandoned and would not be reintroduced until 1944.

During the investigation, problems were also discovered with the contact pistol, which seemed to work well against a sheer surface like the flat side of a hull, but, as the TVA had not tested for, it failed to impact against a curved surface such as the rounded underside of a hull.[24] As a remedy for this failure, which Dönitz styled "criminal," BdU replaced all its contact pistols with a simpler and more effective design copied from a British twenty-one-inch (530-mm.) Whitehead-type torpedo from the captured minelaying submarine HMS *Seal*. The court-martial found the TVA officers guilty of negligence and sentenced them to six months' imprisonment, after which they were allowed to return to armament duties. Dönitz meanwhile made personal visits to as many U-boat crews as he could in order to restore morale and confidence. (When the U.S. Navy submarine fleet entered the war it would experience all the same problems with its Mark XIV torpedo, which tended to run eleven feet [3.3 meters] too deep, and with its Mark VI magnetic exploder which failed to detonate on so many attacks that, as their Pearl Harbor commander wrote, "Submarine captains returned from patrol ready to turn in their suits."[25] Rather than discard the exploder as the Germans had done, however, the USN clung to it "like grim death to a dead cat" for many months.[26] Only the Japanese torpedo worked consistently well during World War II.) None of this history was of any help now to "Ajax" Bleichrodt as, unaccountably, his new and improved eels and pistols failed one after the other. Aware of continued failures in the Atlantic and elsewhere BdU sent an advisory to all boats: "When fitting the pistol it is important to be careful that the pistol is not pressed in. The pistol is properly set when the hairlines on the pistol and the nose [*Greifnase*] match in line."[27] The advisory must have been read by Kptlt. Gerhard Bigalk, whose VIIC U-*751* would arrive off Newfoundland at the end of the month and also experience six torpedo failures. Reinhard Hardegen was lucky: As of 14 January he had had only two duds, both against *Norness*.

At 0309 15 January (CET) Hardegen sighted a bright light ahead. Was it a lightship? It could not be Ambrose, which was still some miles away. According to the tourist guide they were off Long Beach, approximately. Hardegen moved toward the light, whatever it was. "Starboard ten." From below a call came from Kaeding, who was reading the fathometer: "20 meters under the keel!" Then: "fifteen meters . . . ten meters!" Hardegen, who should have been grateful for the warning, yelled down the tube: "Which idiot is depth-sounding? They can hear us on land!" He also worried that the roar from the diesel exhausts and the odor of their fumes might betray the boat's presence to a knowledgeable person on shore. What he failed to understand was just how close he was coming to that shore itself. "That's a lightship, not Ambrose, but a lightship ahead," he replied to a worried Kaeding.

"That's not a lightship, Herr Kaleu," Kaeding responded.

"Better get up here!" Hardegen ordered.

Kaeding, who had been wearing red goggles in anticipation of this order, bounded up the ladder. "Herr Kaleu," he said when he reached the bridge, "the DR line shows we're headed toward the beach. That's a light on land. We're going to ground on the beach!" Hardegen could not believe it and maintained his heading for five more minutes until, just ahead of him, he saw the white foam of breaking combers.

"Both back emergency full!"

Kaeding breathed a gasp of relief. They had almost beached. As the boat's way shuddered to a stop, he himself quivered from delayed fear as he stared at what appeared to be a hotel, shore lights, and sand dunes backed by low, dark woods. "You just imagine to yourself, America—and there it is."[28] He sank against the periscope housing.

Asking Kaeding to remain on top, Hardegen righted the boat on a course that took them slightly away from the shoreline and its deceptive sirens. Chastened by his near disaster, he determined to be more careful about lights, which now increased in number and density as he approached on starboard the more populated Rockaway Beach. To port ahead he began to make out the low, thin peninsula of Sandy Hook, which juts north from the New Jersey shore into the Lower Bay.

"This is getting dangerous, Herr Kaleu," Kaeding said as he reported the depth readings from below. "We just went from twenty-seven meters to seventeen."

"Both ahead slow," Hardegen told the helmsman. For the first time he worried about grounding. The big steamers knew the traffic lanes that avoided the sandbanks and mud flats. He knew nothing, and there was no ship entering at that hour that he could follow. Already he was beyond the point where he could submerge deeply enough to escape depth charges, and now he was pushing his chances to have water enough to cover his tower and simply hide, if need be. But this was not the first time he had been audacious beyond reason. With a fatalistic touch he made a note for the KTB: "U-*123* is prepared for immediate self-destruction."[29]

Where was the Ambrose Channel Lightship? The tourist map showed it to be a short distance dead ahead. But in the real world it was not there. And if the lightship had horns or bells in addition to lights these were absent, too. Had the ship been removed? (She had, temporarily, to Cape Cod.) Hardegen came to steerageway at two knots or less. He was almost at the former lightship station but he dared not navigate farther, staggered as he was by the luminous spectacle that unfolded before him. The sky at 330 degrees was ablaze from the incandescence of Manhattan and its neighbor boroughs. The huge silver scrim thrown up by a million lights dazzled the waning moon. Though from where they stood Hardegen and the forward bridge watch could not see any of the city's tall buildings—their boat was well below the Narrows—they sensed the presence of the sky-scrapers and neon-splendored avenues. Having seen the city once up close, Hardegen could appreciate better than anyone else on board the feat that they had just accomplished: they were an enemy force on the very front doorstep of the greatest city in the world. Later that year he would attempt to describe the moment on paper: "I cannot describe the feeling with words, but it was unbelievably beautiful and great. I would have given away a kingdom for this moment if I had had one. We were the first to be here, and for the first time in this war a German soldier looked out upon the coast of the U.S.A."[30] He wondered what form the life of the city was taking at that hour, 2200 (10:00 P.M.) Eastern Time. Were the Broadway shows just letting out? Were the jazz clubs just getting started? Were the newsboys hawking the last editions—or the first? In his imagination he fantasized how clever it would be to walk around Times Square and tip his cap to passers-by.

The moment was as poignant as it was triumphant, for it seemed a shame to have to bring harm to this place, so evocative of man's ingenuity and style. At the same time the city irritated because its lights glowed while Germany's were darkened. *Didn't the Americans know there was a war on?* Their arrogance was beginning to get under his skin when he looked around at the other members of the bridge watch and found them gazing with stupefaction and thrill at the same scene. For the moment, against all rules, the lookouts peered in the same one direction, their glasses hanging unused against their chests. What need was there for magnification? Hardegen decided to let them have this experience; they could describe it later to their mates below. And call Tölle up with his camera and fast film. He opened the tourist map and took bearings. Due north was Rockaway Beach, many separate incandescent filaments that had coalesced into a tight necklace of pale yellow lights. Farther on, slightly to the left, was Coney Island. There he saw automobile lights moving about and two tall structures, some kind of tower and a Ferris wheel (the 303-foot-high Parachute Jump and Wonder Wheel), silhouetted against the sky-glow backdrop. Behind Coney Island, it appeared, was Brooklyn. And that must be Staten Island ahead in the distance at about 280 degrees, with a vertical string of red lights that indicated a radio tower (WOR) beyond. Dead ahead and close was the tip of Sandy Hook, protruding from New Jersey and forming the southern cusp of the Lower Bay. A prominent navigation light defined its thin northern tip.

Putting the lookouts back on search duty, he wondered briefly, would he and his men ever get out of here alive? New York was widely known to have major naval installations. U.S. Navy warships had to be around somewhere. If there was a picket line or battle group to fight him he should start seeing it now. Would the enemy descend on his boat and tear it to pieces? Or was his visit a total surprise? Or was the U.S. Navy incompetent—or negligent? He had no way of knowing. He resolved to stand his water. He had come this far. He would not leave until he had found a target, a sizable target, not the little boats that the lookouts were now identifying to port and starboard. The water was aswarm with them: fishing trawlers, tugs, and pilot boats scurrying from point to point on their private missions, like so many water ants. Hardegen wondered, did these boats see *123?* Some passed very close. Did they take her for a stationary barge? Or did they see her for what she was, a submarine, and say simply, "She's one of ours"? Since they all sailed on different courses it seemed that the harbor approaches at this point were mine-free. Past Sandy Hook in the Lower Bay there might be mine fields, even nets, but the crowded water directly around him seemed safe. He lay to where he was to see if larger fish also swam the night waters.

But none appeared. The east-west approach route was empty of large vessels. Perhaps the Navy or Port Authority had stopped all merchant traffic temporarily in the wake of the *Norness* sinking. Freighters and tankers steaming north and south on the coastwise lanes might have been diverted to other ports. If so, Hardegen could be wasting time sitting here at Ambrose station, and inviting trouble besides. He leaned to the voice pipe: "Helmsman, come to one zero zero, both ahead one-third." He would retrace his movements and get outside New York to the Jersey shore. And so, as Hardegen went below and von Schroeter took the conn, *123* steamed east away from the metropolis, past the Long Island landmarks she had steered by earlier—East Rockaway Inlet, Long Beach, a lighted tower east of Jones Inlet, Great South and Mastic Beaches, Moriches Inlet, Shinnecock Inlet—when instead of the forward lookouts sighting a target, as von Schroeter might have expected, one of the stern watch, at exactly 0840 (0140 ET), called out, "Herr Leutnant, steamer lanterns astern!" Von Schroeter wheeled around with his 7 × 50s. Sure enough, there was a vessel *following* them out of the approaches. So east—west traffic was moving after all. If they had waited at Ambrose station they would have had this morsel within sight of the city itself. But better here than nowhere. "Commander to the bridge!"

Hardegen followed the point with his glasses. Yes, a ship, a tanker to judge from its beam and masts, a big one, clearing port bows-on, with peacetime lighting. "Both ahead slow, starboard twenty." He would make a gradual turn and wait for the target on a heading of zero degrees. "UZO to the bridge, steady up on zero, make four knots."

Hoffmann took his position and estimated the target's course at 96 degrees, speed at ten—eleven knots, range closing at three thousand meters. He had her clearly in the UZO. What a sight she was outlined against the now-faint city glow! On she came right into his barrels, 10,000 GRT and deep in the water with a full belly. Hoffmann asked the helm for a lateral shift. "Come to zero one four." The steamer's lanterns gave a good position check. With *123* well forward of the target's beam, with known course and speed and perfect track angle, this one would be by the book.

"Flood Tube One. Depth setting two-point-five. Speed ten-point-five, range nine hundred, angle on the bow Green twenty." Von Schroeter and Fuhrmann both confirmed, *"Folgen!"* Hoffmann aimed for the bridge.

"Range eight hundred . . . seven hundred eighty . . . seven hundred fifty—*Los!*"

The pneumatic jolt in Tube 1 was felt slightly on the bridge. Von Schroeter on the Vorhaltrechner called up the running time: fifty-eight seconds. Hardegen was confident that they had a perfect solution and launch. In the near minute's time of run he allowed himself the luxury of hoping that the fireworks would be seen as far away as Manhattan, although that was doubtful. Even here, some twenty-seven miles south of the Hamptons, he could not see the shore.

WHACK!

From the aft edge of the tanker's bridge a violent detonation blew yellow and red flame mixed with black oil, water, and ship's parts two hundred meters into the sky. With bright fire licking the night that high the U-boat's field of vision was illuminated as though it was day and one could read a newspaper by the torch's light. On the tanker itself the bridge burned fiercely, which to Hardegen meant no radio calls were going out, while all around the wounded frame falling fireballs turned the water into steam. The hull, which had slowed its way and listed to starboard where it had been holed, clung to the reddened surface on an otherwise even keel. Through the glasses Hardegen saw crewmen running to man a gun on the stern deck. This ship needed another hole and fast because 123 was starkly visible in the flame light from the bridge. Better give it a quick death. Hoffmann readied stern Tube Five. At 0959 he launched from eight hundred meters directly at the engine room of the now stationary vessel. After forty-five seconds the hull erupted in another fire column that flowered into a black mushroom cloud. Broken amidship, the tanker now went down fast and hard by the stern, which settled on the bottom in fifty-four meters of water while the bow remained awash at an angle of about 30 degrees, some of its deck gear carrying away and sliding overside. Hardegen claimed 10,000 GRT in his Schussmeldung and made the sarcastic comment: "The Americans had recalled some of their light ships. So it was a good thing that my wrecks were partly sticking out of the water. Otherwise how would other ships find the harbor? We had carefully laid a 'buoy line' for them."[31]

The tanker was *Coimbra*, British, 6,768 GRT, 422.8 feet long with a sixty-foot beam and a capacity of eighty thousand barrels of oil. Like *Norness* she had been built by a German yard, in this case Howaldtswerke AG, of Kiel. The captain and thirty-five of the crew were killed, six were wounded.[32] On the south shore of Long Island many residents saw the funeral pyre from their homes and alerted local authorities, including the police chiefs of Quogue and Hampton Bays as well as the Coast Guard, whose Quogue station later informed the press that one of its patrol planes had sighted survivors in a dory and on a raft about twenty-three miles off Shinnecock Inlet and had dropped food and whiskey to them. Coast Guard rescue vessels went out into the rough sea that was whipped by a cold northeast wind so severe that fishing boats remained in port. One boat from the Long Beach station was forced to return by a broken propeller blade. At 90 Church Street, Admiral Andrews refused to confirm the sinking, stating that he had "no information."[33] When at 1600 (ET) on the sixteenth the Navy Department in Washington announced that *Coimbra,* flying the flag "of a United States ally" had been observed "in a sinking condition" off Long Island, Andrews' ESF headquarters continued to insist that it had "no information."[34] An examination of the ESF war diary shows that it possessed that information by 0830 and in more detailed form by 1045 on the fifteenth: "Ship reported awash at eight-thirty hours, sixty-one miles from Ambrose Light, ninety-six degrees true, is torpedoed British tanker *Coimbra.*"[35] Why Andrews refused to confirm the sinking even after Washington's announcement is not explained in the records. Main Navy's communiqué warned that the U-boat menace on the coast was "increasingly serious."[36]

That was certainly Hardegen's intention, to be increasingly serious, as he withdrew from the *Coimbra* hulk at 1100 (CET) on a due-south course of 180. He had done what he had come to do in New York waters. He had humiliated the United States at its very front door. He had avenged his frustrations at Freetown. He had spilled tons of Allied oil and taken three bottoms out of the sea bridge. Somewhat to his surprise, but certainly to his pleasure, he had shown that the U.S. Navy was a paper fleet and that its commanders were either incompetent or negligent, or both. With six eels left he would exact still more tribute from the enemy. Like an unsated leopard he moved away from the last carcass in search of new prey. The southerly heading would take him along the New Jersey coast to Delaware Bay. He would stay on the surface as long as he could before daybreak two hours ahead. The sky was overcast and the water choppy. *Eins Zwei Drei* began to feel the sea again, ploughing and pitching at three hundred RPM. At 1410, shortly after sighting a fishing boat to starboard in the first gleam of the rising sun, Hardegen submerged on a course of 230 and told the officers that they would stay down for the day. Not until 2400, ending 15 January (1700 ET the fifteenth), did he surface at dusk. But no sooner did the foam run off the bridge and the lookouts take their positions when one of them spied a small shadow to port against the evening sky. ALARMMM! An aircraft had intercepted their course just as they surfaced. Hardegen saw it turn toward them just as, last man down, he reached for the hatch cover. "All hands forward!" he yelled from the ladder to Kaeding. "Hard angle down!" It seemed to take forever to get below the surface. Finally they heard the last of the choppy seas against the tower and the LI Schulz announced: "Ten meters and descending."

"Hold her at thirty meters, Chief," Hardegen ordered, "we don't know how deep it is here. I don't want to hit bottom nose first." The tower was under but their swirl would still be visible to the pilot. How had he sighted them in the darkness? Was it marine phosphorescence?

POW! POW! POW! POW!

Four bombs exploded to starboard but far to starboard. Bad aiming, Hardegen thought, the Yankees still had a lot to learn. "Port 10, half ahead." He moved to be farther away yet from the second run. He waited. Ten minutes went by. Twenty. There was no second run. The pilot must have expended his full load on the one attack. But he surely would have called in other aircraft which would be on the scene shortly because of the proximity of land. And, no doubt, he would have vectored destroyers to their position. That is, unless the pilot was not really certain that he had seen a U-boat and was simply bombing away at anything that looked like one.

"Chief, come to periscope depth and give me the sky scope." At fourteen meters the wide-angle observation scope came hissing up from its well. Hardegen adjusted the focus and looked slowly around the horizon. He saw nothing except sea and clouds. "Chief," he hollered down from the tower, "prepare to surface, but keep her heavy, decks awash. Lookouts to the tower. Stand by, gun crews. *Surface!*"

At 0042, with the roar of air blowing out the diving tanks, *123* broached the Jersey waters just enough for the bridge to be exposed and ready for a quick return underwater should that be necessary. Hardegen and the lookouts leaped above. A 7 × 50 sweep showed nothing. They peered intently toward shore seeking the narrow shadows of oncoming destroyers or patrol craft. There was nothing. "Anything on the wireless, Puster?" Rafalski called back that all he was getting was six-hundred-meter traffic from the Hydrographic Institute in New York declaring the area around Sandy Hook a danger zone until 31 January. So, Hardegen concluded, the air attack had been a fluke. There was no organized resistance here at all.

He was correct. The one errant bombing that evening would be the only military attack he would experience during the entire American patrol.

. . .

The ESF diary for 16 January listed this belated attack and one other on an unidentified target. They were the only attacks made to that date on the known submarine "menace" in U.S. waters: "1000–2100. Numerous contacts with submarines by Army planes, Navy planes and ZNPs [blimps]. Bombs dropped by an Army plane and by the K-G [blimp]. Results unknown."[37] To date one lone vulnerable U-boat had rampaged on the U.S. littoral unopposed except by one hapless bomber that stumbled upon it surfacing (and at dusk, which was not the normal flying time) and dropped as many bombs, and with the same effect, as another Army bomber had dropped against the American destroyer USS *Trippe* weeks before. So far U.S. defenses had expended about as much munitions against the enemy as they had against themselves. The residents of Long Island bungalows who walked their beaches finding encrustations of oil, life preservers, timbers, ropes, and other grim testaments to war's astonishing close presence might well have wondered, Where was the Navy? How could this have happened? If they had been privy to secret Navy orders, which of course they had not, they could have asked the more telling question: Where were Admiral Bristol's twenty-five Support Force destroyers that had been stationed on the coast *precisely to prevent this?*

The twenty-five destroyers had done other things. Some stayed in port, some went off for training, and some went back on convoy escort seeking a distant danger rather than the one that was already on their plates. Taking the diversion to escort duty first, it would seem that Vice Admiral Royal Eason "Budge" Ingersoll was the immediately responsible person for that decision. At Newport two weeks earlier Ingersoll had broken his flag as CINCLANT, replacing Admiral King, at the mizzen of the frigate USS *Constellation,* the oldest ship in the Navy. Described as short, sandy-haired, saturnine, Indiana gothic, unassuming, publicity shy (he had his magazines delivered to "Mr. Ingersoll"), a piano player and stamp collector, Ingersoll had served thirty-seven years in nearly every commissioned post the Navy had to offer, both ashore and afloat, including most recently deputy chief of Naval Operations under Admiral Stark, from 24 July 1940 to assumption of CINCLANT. In that last assignment he had to have been aware of King's decision to reassign Support Force (Task Force Four) destroyers to their East Coast home bases because of "the imminent probability of submarine attack in that area."[38]

On 5 January an order went out from Main Navy that U.S. Marines in Iceland and British forces in Northern Ireland were to be relieved by U.S. Army troops and that these were to be taken across the Atlantic in ten transports escorted by a task force consisting of battleships, cruisers, carriers, and destroyers. The troop convoy was designated AT 10 and the escort Task Force 15. On the following day Ingersoll directed Rear Admiral Alexander Sharp, commander, Battleship Division Five, to command the task force. Specifically, Ingersoll ordered that the movement "will proceed from New York on January 15, 1942." As the CINCLANT Administrative History (1946) records: "To supply enough destroyers he [Ingersoll] had borrowed from Commander Destroyer and from Admiral Bristol."[39] So, on 14 January, the day U-*123* was blowing up *Norness*, U.S. destroyers *Mayrant, Rowan, Trippe*, and *Wainwright* from Norfolk, *Roe* from Newport, and *Gwin* and *Monssen* from Boston were leisurely assembling at New York for the departure of AT 10. None of them sortied in search of *Norness'* attacker. On 15 January, the day U-*123* was blowing up *Coimbra*, U.S. destroyers *Livermore* from New York, *Charles F. Hughes* from Boston, and *Lansdale, Ludlow, Ingraham*, and *Hilary P. Jones* from Casco Bay were joining up for the same mission.[40] Thus thirteen battle-ready destroyers were vacuumed in a flash from the area where they were most needed. Amazingly, U-*123* did not encounter some of them on their passages. With a convoy forming and departing in the very harbor off which he operated, it is astonishing that Hardegen did not bump into some element of it. Even apart from the question, Should destroyers be diverted from what King called their "essential" assignment for this purpose at this particular moment, there is the disturbing one, Why would any commander send troop transports with their precious human cargoes directly into known U-boat waters? (The Navy was not sure how many "raiders" were operating outside the harbor.) Fortunate indeed were the twenty-two thousand Army troops whose transports *happened* not to cross the UZO of U-*123*. And reckless were the commanders who sent them directly into harm's way.

AT 10 could easily have been delayed. There was no pressing urgency for its departure. President Roosevelt wanted the symbolic presence of a U.S. expeditionary force in British Northern Ireland at the earliest possible date. But no impending campaign required the immediate exchange of troops. Indeed, five months later in Operation "Bolero," the build-up of U.S. forces in Britain for eventual land offensives against the Germans and Italians, COMINCH recognized that there was no great urgency in getting every AT convoy to sea on the exact day scheduled: "This can be varied a day or two either way for convenience or to avoid regular departure dates for security purposes."[41] For AT 10 with thirteen destroyers to depart when it did in the face of a known, route-identifiable enemy attack was akin to a defensive naval force at Hawaii embarking casually on a convoy to the Philippines while the Japanese were launching their attack on Pearl Harbor. It was inflexibility *in extremis.*

What of the other destroyers assigned to defend the East Coast when Paukenschlag arrived? Most of the remaining twelve remained comfortably in port, except for *Bristol,* which steamed for Casco Bay on the fifteenth for routine duty, and the previously cited *Ellyson,* which was ordered to New London for "training."[42] These orders probably came from Bristol. Thus the "maximum number" destroyer force that Admiral King had gathered as "essential" to repel the "imminent" submarine attack of the Germans was inert, assigned to training, or dispersed on missions that could have waited a more favorable departure date. Was Ingersoll to blame for these acts of omission and commission? Was Bristol? Of either man it could be said, simply, that he received his sailing orders and he sailed. Yet there was an underlying principle of command laid down by King himself that neither man seems to have observed. As CINCLANT, King promulgated Fleet Policies that his official biographer asserts he held to "then and later."[43] A principal article in the original version dealt with, "Exercise of Initiative":

> If subordinates are deprived—as they now are—of that training and experience which will enable them to act "on their own"—if they do not know, by constant practice, how to exercise "initiative of the subordinate"—if they are reluctant (afraid) to act because they are accustomed to detailed orders and instructions—if they are not habituated to think, to judge, to decide and to act for themselves in their several echelons of command—we shall be in sorry case when the time of "active operations" arrives.[44]

In a later version he added the instruction, in italics: "*Make the best of what you have.*"[45] (Admiral Dönitz on the other side had offered the same counsel to his own forces.) The King policy would appear to place both Ingersoll and Bristol in positions where they were expected to make independent command judgments according to the circumstances that faced them. Ingersoll, who "exercised complete responsibility for troop convoys,"[46] certainly could have delayed AT 10 long enough to meet the German attack and decisively defeat it—a result that Hardegen's exposure in the New York approaches fairly invited. Bristol, who held responsibility for the disposition of Support Force destroyers not "borrowed" by Ingersoll, certainly could have sent DD's to face the enemy that was marauding inside his gates. But neither did so.

Does the principle of "initiative of the subordinate" absolve King of personal responsibility for these command decisions? Hardly so, since he was in overall command and in possession at Main Navy of the "big picture"; since he was the one who had initiated the East Coast destroyer defense against the expected U-boat attack, who had every reason to be concerned for its success, and who could have overruled both Ingersoll and Bristol in the disposition and use of their forces. In the event, unaccountably, he did nothing. Even following *Norness* and *Coimbra*, he failed to take a single warlike action. On paper, with his Operation Orders and Fleet Policies, King had been impressive; but at the deckplate level "King of the Atlantic" was a dud. Like a faulty torpedo, he failed to detonate. At Pearl Harbor, Hawaii, the responsible Army and Navy commanders were relieved of their commands for less evident dereliction.

Admittedly, the U.S. military has not always done well in the first battles of the wars that it has fought, from Long Island in the Revolutionary War, to Bull Run (Union Forces) in the Civil War, to Pearl Harbor and the Kasserine Pass in World War II, to Osan in Korea and the Ia Trang Valley in Vietnam. But in the set-piece engagement presented by Operation Drumbeat the U.S. military chose not to make a battle of it at all. On Ernest King's desk as commander in chief must lie the final responsibility for this defeat, this embarrassment, this awful loss of blood and treasure, this failed chance to stanch a wound before it hemorrhaged. Tragically for his country, Ernest King's irresolution in the face of Reinhard Hardegen's ruthlessness laid America open to the greatest maritime massacre in her history. Where was the King of the previous July—"Destroy hostile forces which threaten shipping of U.S."—"Threat exists when potentially hostile vessels are actually within sight or sound contact"?[47] *That* King had a chance to bloody Hardegen's nose and deliver a crushing Drumbeat in reverse.

Admiral Dönitz would have been far more cautious thereafter in approaching America's shores if the eagle had lashed out first and in force. King, who had the opportunity to avert catastrophe, ended by inviting it. He would spend the next six months compensating for it— and dissembling in his excuses for it.

As in the case of the Japanese bombers at Pearl Harbor the success of the Drumbeat strike was not a failure of Intelligence; it was a failure of Operations. At OIC in London Rodger Winn and Patrick Beesly looked at each other with wild surmise. As Beesly told the writer: "We were really staggered."[48]

Now, as the third week of January began and Hardegen moved south while Zapp and Folkers reached their stations, the mauling of U.S. and Allied resources at sea were about to reach a crescendo. There was no halting it now. The wolves were marching boldly into the sheepfold. And there was no one with the will to stop them.

9

Where Is the Navy?

North and south for a distance of 120 miles (193 kilometers) a knuckle of Outer Banks guards the Atlantic coastline of North Carolina. Narrow sand reefs broken by bights and inlets, these barrier islands project three major capes into the ocean: Lookout, Fear, and Hatteras, of which Hatteras, the most seaward, poses the greatest danger to the coastwise vessel, for at its apex the warm northbound Gulf Stream collides with descending Arctic currents and creates winds and waves of such savage fury that only the most skilled captain or master can negotiate them. Nor should the wary mariner think that he has escaped harm by eluding the Outer Banks themselves, for reaching miles out from them underwater, like grasping tentacles, are the shoals—restive sand dunes that bear such names as Wimble, Lookout, and the dreaded Diamond.

Since colonial times coastal trade vessels plied this dangerous passage transporting agricultural products and raw materials from southern ports to the Chesapeake and to the manufacturing cities of the Middle Atlantic and New England states. When American commerce expanded and merchant shipping, both sail and steam powered, connected the industrial centers to South America, the West Indies, and the Gulf of Mexico, much larger vessels and many different national flags approached the perils of the Outer Banks. Whether antique or modern, small or large, U.S. or foreign, wary or careless, a great number of ships from 1526 into the twentieth century wrecked fatally in these shoal-fathomed lanes. Many met their doom in storms, others in ordinary sailing across the hazard-strewn bottom. From Cape Fear in the south up to Currituck Beach, the shore sands filled with relics of those disasters: ribbed wooden skeletons of sailing ships and rusted steel winches, funnels, and posts from steamers and tankers. Then, added to the natural perils of this "graveyard of the Atlantic," German U-boats worked the adjacent waters in 1918 destroying (by torpedo, mine, or driving aground) six tankers, a schooner, a bark, and the Diamond Shoals Lightship.[1]

Twenty-four years later on 16 January Richard Zapp arrived in the same waters commanding the Paukenschlag IXC boat U-66. Delayed and wearied by the punishing gales of early January, and assigned to an area that required steaming farther than Reinhard Hardegen, Zapp and his crew began patrolling in CA 84, just north of the operational squares CA 79 and 87 and DC 12–13 that were outlined in ink as their Attack Area I on the 1870G chart. Like Hardegen, Zapp was late on station for the original January 13 "beat on the kettledrum," but there was no doubt on his boat that ample target opportunity would soon present itself, since all north–south merchant traffic had to make the turn around Hatteras, where far out to sea to escape the shoals they exposed themselves to manmade danger of the sort that Zapp had in mind. From the south steamed ships deep in the water with cargoes of bauxite from the Guianas and Brazil, vital for the manufacture of aluminum used in aircraft; oil and gasoline from Curaçao and Aruba in the Netherlands West Indies, Venezuela, and the Texas ports of Corpus Christi, Houston, and Port Arthur (Great Britain alone consumed four tankers' worth each day); iron, tin, rubber, concrete, phosphate, lumber, and cotton; not to mention foodstuffs such as winter vegetables, sugar, coffee, and Florida citrus, from which British children received practically their entire daily allowance of Vitamin C. Some vessels entered the Caribbean and U.S. East Coast waters through the Panama Canal from as far away as Bombay, India, with such varied cargoes as manganese ore, sulfuric acid, and wool. Having discharged their "beans, bullets, and black oil," the coastwise vessels returned south with general cargoes or in ballast to reload, risking again the Carolina shoals that forced them to deeper water away from the saving shore.

On the new moon night of 18 January, a night as black as any that had blanketed U-66's Feindfahrt to date, in a mild sea with a light wind from astern, Zapp's boat raised the Winter Quarter Lightship northeast of Diamond Shoals. As she did so the totally darkened form of an approaching northbound tanker moved obscurely, black on black, before the lookouts' sensitive binoculars. It was close. Zapp estimated three miles. He slowed to seven knots and waited in a bow attack position like a night game hunter sitting without sound or movement in the blind. The target was shoreward of the UZO. Zapp's number one called out the numbers: target speed eleven knots; range 2,000; angle on the bow, 21. He decided, with Zapp's approval, on a multiple launch from Tubes 1 and 2. The Vorhaltrechner programmed one G7e on a heading of 282 degrees aimed at the bridge, the other at 283 degrees aimed to hit in the engine room. At 0833 hours (CET) with the range closed to 1800 U-66 entered the Battle of the Water's Edge. Though the sea was calm and both eels were set at normal depths, one at three meters, the other at four, unaccountably one of them en route to target broached the surface in a splashy jump that had to have been sighted by an alert lookout because the tanker, which had not been zigzagging, seemed suddenly to go hard left rudder, though not with sufficient effect to escape the 122- and 126-second torpedo runs. The first eel slammed into the starboard side forward of the bridge by the foremast and the second, four seconds later, aft of the deckhouse. Zapp's pupils narrowed before the bright ball of flame that arched over the mortally fractured victim, and he watched amidst the smell of oil and the sound of grinding steel as the forward end twisted off to port amidships and sank from view five minutes after the detonations. Ten minutes more, and the ragged, bleeding stern stump canted to starboard and disappeared, while fierce surface fires spread nearby a quarter mile around the site where ruptured oil tanks had poured their black viscous contents onto the sea. With no identifiable name or colors that Zapp's lookouts could sight, and the Puster reporting from below that the tanker had gotten off no wireless transmissions that he could hear, it was not possible to identify the kill. Zapp ordered the searchlight played on the lifeboats but he decided not to venture closer to interrogate survivors because of the fires. After twenty minutes he withdrew to resume patrolling and put the success down in his Schussmeldung as simply, "Tanker about 9200 tons."[2]

The *Allan Jackson*, built in 1921, was actually 6,635 GRT. The American-flag single-screw 435-foot-long Standard Oil of New Jersey tanker had departed Cartagena, Colombia, on 11 January with 72,870 barrels of oil bound for an unknown consignee at New York. On a recent southbound passage in December the master, Felix W.

Kretchmer, was told at Norfolk, Virginia, that two days before Pearl Harbor, Eastern Sea Frontier headquarters in New York had established "Coastal Sea Lanes" for the protection, in case of war, of coastwise shipping and that he would receive these routing instructions from the United States consul in Cartagena before his next sailing. When Kretchmer called for those instructions, however, the consul stated that he had no knowledge of them.[3] On his own Kretchmer decided to black out the ship on the northbound voyage even though, by his departure date, 11 January, there had been no reports of U-boat attacks off the U.S. East Coast. He also made certain that the lifeboats were well equipped with food, water, and signals. No guns had been swung aboard, so his only defense was the night, and he timed his voyage so as to make the turn at Hatteras when the night was blackest. Zigzagging he did not think necessary, since the new moon assured protective cover. Or so he thought. Kretchmer's crew numbered thirty-five, all Americans save for a Dutchman and a Russian. On the night of 18 January, with most of the off-duty crew turned in and the rest playing cards, *Allan Jackson* was proceeding at ten knots on a course of 356 degrees true and had reached position 35-47N, 74-20W, or seventy-five miles east of Cape Hatteras, when twenty-five-year-old Second Mate Melvin A. Rand on the bridge sighted the white spray from a broaching torpedo on the starboard side. He yelled the alarm, but before the helmsman had the wheel full over the first of two shattering explosions rocked the bridge. Knocked down, Rand scrambled to the quarterdeck, absorbing as he went the shock waves from the second torpedo, and made for his assigned lifeboat station. When that boat jammed in its skids he jumped overside and swam for his life as surface fires spread rapidly from the ignited cargo. Struggling on the red surface he looked back to see the tanker "fold up like a hinge" and sink in halves, while in the distance the eerie glare of a white searchlight swept the scene intermittently. Finally, after about an hour in the water, where he was repeatedly bumped by fish and bitten hard on one hand, Rand found a lifeboat section called a strongback and clung to it. He was soon joined by Third Mate Boris A. Vornosoff. The junior third mate, Francis Bacon, swam to the same strongback but, exhausted, could not hold on and drowned.

Captain Kretchmer was sleeping fully clothed (as he advised his officers to do also) in his cabin topside on the forward end of the deckhouse when the torpedoes hit and rolled him from his bunk. The explosions had twisted shut the cabin door, trapping him inside. After struggling futilely with the door and feeling it grow hot from the flames outside, he forced his body through the porthole. As he fell to the boat deck on the lee side, the forward end of the ship sank beneath him and he swam vigorously away from the suction, eventually finding a small round seat from a wooden stool that kept him barely above the water for the next six hours. There had been no opportunity to sound Abandon Ship or to dispose properly of the ship's wireless codes and confidential papers, though with the ship gone, he hardly had cause to worry about either. Paramount in his mind was staying afloat and awake.

Some of the crew were killed outright in the explosions. Others jumped overside. Some, like Ross F. Terrell, made the correct decision. When the torpedoes interrupted a belowdecks poker game as he held a hot hand with twenty-five dollars in the pot, "Shanghai" Terrell said, "To hell with the money," and raced for the Number 3 boat. Another crewman in a game on deck made a bad decision, electing to run belowdecks to rescue eighty dollars in a locker. When, later, rescuers found his body floating on the surface, his eighty dollars were intact, not even singed. Chief Engineer Thomas B. Hutchins, by contrast, left behind his upper and lower teeth in exchange for his life. There were clear-headed leaders when there had to be. Boatswain Rolf Clausen took charge of the only serviceable lifeboat, Number 3, the other three being wrecked, surrounded by flames, or jammed in the chocks. Clausen ordered the boat swung out from its skids and the boat fell smartly to the water, its lines whistling through the blocks with Clausen and seven others aboard. The water surface around them was dangerously aflame, but the still-functioning discharge from a condenser pump forced the burning oil away as Clausen unhooked the falls, cut the painter, and unlashed the oars. By the time the oars were manned the men saw to their horror that they were being sucked toward the whirling ship's propeller! With a strength born of the certainty of death if they failed, they bent their backs to the task of oaring for their lives. As the aft section of the ship listed to starboard they could clearly see the tops of the huge blades still grinding away at high revolutions. Pulled inexorably toward this lethal machine by the suction it generated, the men, armed by frenzied desperation, opposed it with human power alone, and at one point, when the blades cut loudly at the wood of the very boat in which they rode and the men cried out in their understandable terror, they pushed, and pushed again, against the tanker's plating with their oars and somehow cleared the awful screw, their boat carried safely away in the back-wash through the conflagration of burning oil astern.

Once past the backwash, however, the lifeboat had to make its dangerous way through the flames, from which at one point it rescued the frightened radio operator, Stephen Verbonic. Other crewmen they saw still on deck with their clothes on fire, but instead of throwing themselves into the quenching sea they fell dying where they stood. Clausen kept his oarsmen at their work for more than an hour until, safely past the fires, he raised the lifeboat's sail. The rigging kept them moving for another three hours, when the men sighted a vessel not far distant and Clausen fired a flare from a Very pistol, and after the flare extinguished he signaled a distress signal in Morse by focusing the beam of a flashlight on the white sail. The answering vessel lay to until morning's light, when Clausen's smoke-blackened boatload, the captain on his stool seat, Rand, Vornosoff, and one other—for a total of thirteen survivors out of the ship's complement of thirty-five—found safe haven. Eight were injured, five seriously.[4]

The next night Zapp and U-66 were 180 miles east of Hatteras athwart the route of a Canadian ship bound from Montreal to ports in the West Indies and South America. One of five "Lady" ships of the Canadian National Steamship Line, the 7,988-GRT, 419-foot-long, twin-screw, oil-burning liner *Lady Hawkins* was zigzagging south at fourteen knots through a smooth sea on the moonless night on 19 January with 212 passengers, mostly civilians, including women and children, and a crew of 109, when at about 0135 (ET) she was intercepted by two bright white lights to port. It was U-66 running along-side! The searchlights enabled Zapp to identify the ship for exactly what it was, a *Fracht-u. Fahrgastschiff*—cargo-passenger liner.[5] Zapp then steamed at his highest speed ahead of the ship's course, swung hard-a-port, and flooded both stern tubes. At exactly 0143 he launched two eels from twelve hundred meters out. Though the *Lady Hawkins* took emergency evasive maneuvers, both torpedoes found their marks after an eighty-second run, the first exploding in Hold Number 2 forward of the bridge, and the second in Hold Number 3 near the engine room bulkhead. The ship heeled over from the force of the two concussions, and virtually everyone who was on deck at the time was swept overside into the sea. The mainmast toppled with a frightening noise, and all the ship's lights extinguished. As the stricken hull made water, the passengers and crew groped their way in the darkness down the slanting companionways and decks to the six lifeboats, three of which were seen to get away, the remainder hanging in their davits because of the ship's list. From the U-boat Zapp watched the victim begin to go down with small fires arrayed along the decks "like fine flowers."[6] After twenty minutes the *Lady Hawkins* was gone.

For a brief while the three lifeboats remained in sight of each other; then they separated in the darkness, and two boats with their desperate passengers were not seen again. On the third boat fifty-three passengers and twenty-three crewmen were so closely crowded in a craft designed for a maximum of sixty-three they were forced to stand upright, which none minded since their lot was better than that of other men and women who clung to wreckage or swam vainly toward the boat, which had to steer away from them lest it be swamped. The anxiety of the survivors was not lessened when the U-boat cruised within five hundred yards of their bark and illuminated them with a yellow light that was, as one of them described it, "characteristically without glare." One of the passengers, held tight in her mother's arms, was a two-and-a-half-year-old girl named Janet Johnson, from Trinidad. Also on board were seventeen Americans, twelve from Saint Joseph, Missouri, all construction workers headed for defense bases in the West Indies; several British Royal Navy, Marine, and foreign service officers; missionary families; and residents returning to their homes in the British West Indies. Chief Officer Percy A. Kelly, of Halifax, to whose seaman's skills, calm courage, and tact the survivors would attribute their lives, rigged the boat's sail and dictated the daily regimen, including arrangements whereby some would stand while others would sit to sleep. As the days passed in a seaward lane where, as Kelly knew, there was little traffic, he distributed to each person a daily ration of one biscuit, two ounces of water, and a swallow of condensed milk served in the cap of his flashlight. The Gulf Stream kept temperatures moderate in the daytime, but the nights were chilly. Little Janet, wrapped in a greatcoat, remained amazingly cheerful and lively despite being doused by the continuous salt spray. During one night she ran a fever, and the Chief Officer allotted the tot a spoonful of brandy, which caused her to laugh continuously, with the result, as Kelly said later, that "we were all immensely bucked up." Their travail in the open boat would last five days. It was an experience, Kelly said, of "bravery and discipline, tears and laughter, alternate hope and despair." Using the boat's lantern as a scoop, the construction workers bailed water from the boat, joking with each other about which were the fastest. Mrs. Marian Parkinson, a Canadian missionary en route to Trinidad with her husband, led the group in hymn singing. Her ministry would be called upon in other moments when, to the great grief of all, five men and women, whose strength was unequal to the exposure and the strain, died before rescue. First to go was a seventeen-year-old black crewmember. Next was the ship's bartender, followed by an elderly man, a woman, and one of the construction workers. As each died Chief Kelly removed the clothing from the body so that it might be worn by another shivering passenger; then he lifted the corpse overside to float off in the waves.

Several times Kelly sighted wisps of smoke in the distance, but they receded from view. Finally, shortly past midnight on Saturday the twenty-fourth a large steamer appeared suddenly no more than two hundred yards away from the lifeboat. Kelly sent up flares, which brought the ship, SS *Coamo*, of the New York and Porto Rico Line, to their rescue. When debarked at San Juan, Puerto Rico, the survivors numbered 50 of the 212 passengers and 21 of the 109 crewmen. No trace of the other lifeboats was ever found.[7] It is not recorded what material losses occurred in *Lady Hawkins'* 270,000 feet of bale space for general cargo and 13,000 feet of space for perishables, but the toll in human lives taken by Paukenschlag to date reached over four hundred.

In the last, dark nighttime hours of 16 January Reinhard Hardegen was on the bridge of U-*123* pushing south toward Delaware Bay when Puster Rafalski handed up a sheaf of intercepts. According to one, off the six-hundred-meter band, the Barnegat Lightship and the Five Fathom Lightship ahead had been removed and replaced by light buoys. According to another, U-*123* had been sunk! The Army Air Force was announcing that the German submarine that had had the impertinence to sink two tankers in the approaches to New York Harbor had itself been sunk by an Air Force bomber.[8] So *123* was now a "ghost" submarine! With luck she would soon have the chance to launch a few phantom torpedoes. By 0400 (CET) the boat was approaching Five Fathom Bank, where Hardegen ordered engines dead slow ahead since soundings showed the water depth below the keel shoaling to eight meters. For the next nine hours, in clear sight of the brightly lighted Jersey shore to starboard, he vainly scoured the seaward horizon for ships on the Hatteras–Delaware Bay–New York routes. One lone fishing boat was all he saw. It was another sour-pickle time. At daybreak he decided to steam east to deeper water and bottom out for the day. At 1700 (CET) he submerged to bottom at depth A-25 (forty-five meters) and waited for the next night's cover of darkness. For the crewmen who stayed awake the daylight hours were filled with sounds. At their shallow depth, propeller noise from passing ships was clearly audible throughout the boat. At one point for ten minutes' duration the men heard soundings: one hundred impulses a minute, a ringing, hard tone. Perhaps, they thought, it was an American echo sounder like ASDIC. Hardegen considered that it might be a steamer taking soundings for the entrance to Delaware Bay, but he concluded that that was unlikely both because the pulsing lasted only ten minutes and the visibility upstairs was good. Shortly after the pulsing stopped the U-boat reverberated slightly from a single distant detonation underwater. Curious, Hardegen thought. Was Zapp nearby?

At 0042 (17 January CET) *123* surfaced in the new darkness and headed back to Five Fathom Bank. On the same station as before, Hardegen waited for a target to happen by. At 0200 (1900 CET) a star shell appeared to starboard. Von Schroeter, the duty watch officer, called the Old Man's attention to floodlights at Cape Henlopen on the south, or Delaware, side of the entrance to Delaware Bay. Where they stood, eight miles off Wildwood, New Jersey, von Schroeter was impressed by the fact that the cities and towns were brightly illuminated and that he could even see automobiles moving about on the streets and coastal highways.[9] Forty-three years later, in an interview, he would remember: "It was a special experience for us to be that close to the American shore, to be able to see the cars driving on land, to see the lights on the streets, to smell the forests. We were that close."[10] At 0635 one of the lookouts spotted a shadow to port, which on closer examination turned out to be a destroyer. As Hardegen noted later in his KTB, "Since I don't want to start anything in 15-meter depth I moved away to starboard. At 0713 destroyer out of sight."[11] The waiting continued for five hours until 1200, when lookouts sighted moving lights on the water to the north. *Eins Zwei Drei* began an approach. The narrative of what happened next must come from Hardegen's own hand, in his KTB and Schussmeldung (shooting report), since he records there that he approached and sank a four-thousand-GRT freighter whose loss is unaccounted for in the official USN lists of vessels sunk. In his comprehensive register of ships sunk or damaged by U-boats, German naval historian Jürgen Rohwer names the vessel sunk by U-*123* on this day (17 January), at this time (1304 CET), and at this position (naval square CA 5756) as the 1,932-net-ton American-owned United Fruit steamship *San José*. But that cannot have been the case, since *San José* was sunk that night farther to the north off Atlantic City in a "collision of saints" with the Grace Line freighter *Santa Elisa* (7,600 tons). The collision was attested to and described by the seventy-plus survivors of both ships involved in the incident. *San José*'s helmsman explained that his vessel was running blind at the time, with running lights only, by permission of the U.S. Navy. *Santa Elisa*, which burned for six hours, made it to New York Harbor with the assistance of tugboats despite a twenty-foot hole on the port side forward from the water line to the deck.[12]

Hardegen's KTB reads as follows:

> Approach! A short while later I recognize a freighter of about 4000 GRT, four holds, heavily loaded. It carries only one lantern on its fore mast. The position lamps are turned off. Course 130°, speed eleven knots. Too bad that the sun is coming up. I position myself in front of the target and close the range. Determined to get it, I close to 600 meters and launch my last stern torpedo on a track angle of 90°. After 57 seconds there is a mighty detonation and a huge, pitch-black explosion column. The hit was under the bridge. With its high speed the steamer ran itself under water. When the smoke lifted only the mast tops were still visible and shortly afterwards they disappeared, too. The water depth is 45 meters. We move with top speed to the east because I need more water under the keel during the daylight hours. The ocean is calm and cloudless, so I stay on the surface in order to make my best speed to Cape Hatteras since, according to a wireless intercept, traffic is piling up there.[13]

In Hardegen's shooting report the diagram depicting the relative courses of the two vessels, U-boat and target, shows that the torpedo hit on the target's port side. The accompanying narrative repeats the data in the KTB except to say that the vessel went under in thirty-five seconds(!). There is no mention of survivors in either account. What "ghost" ship this was that was sunk by the "ghost" U-boat is a mystery. Could Hardegen have been mistaken in claiming the sinking? He had been mistaken once before, in the case of *Aurania*. But that sinking he had not witnessed. This one he did, as also did IWO

Hoffmann, who cosigned the shooting report. No notice of a missing ship in the geographical vicinity or of a ship's failure to make a port of destination in this general time period is on file in the pertinent archives. Is there a wreck at that position, CA 5756, which corresponds to map coordinates 37-50N, 74-10W? The *Wreck Information List* compiled by the U.S. Hydrographic Office in 1945 contains no unidentified wreck at that or nearby coordinates.[14]

Another ghost ship stood just over the horizon.

HARDEGEN BLEICHRODT SCHUG [U-*86* with Group Ziethen] REPORT SITUATION. BDU-OPS.[15] The F.T. came into Rafalski's long-wave receiver (twelve thousand to twenty thousand meters) by way of the Goliath transmitter at Calbe. BdU must have thought *123* was bottoming in shoal water, Rafalski thought as he handed the decrypt to Hardegen sitting on his bunk across the passageway. And why not? At Kernével they knew it was daytime on the U.S. East Coast. Actually, *123* was thundering along on the surface in broad sunlight, in sight of shore, destination Hatteras. It was a bold thing for the Old Man to do because they were proceeding directly past the major U.S. Navy anchorage and air station at Hampton Roads–Norfolk on the Virginia coast. "Too many risks," Rafalski muttered to himself. Hardegen had shifted the watches so that the best eyes in the crew were on the bridge during the daylight run. Five times in the course of the day the sighting of aircraft forced the boat under. Except for one land plane the aircraft were identifiable USN types: the Consolidated PBY-5 Catalina and the Vought-Sikorsky OS2U-3 Kingfisher. While the good eyes on top kept their coastal sprint safe from discovery and harm, Hardegen drafted ideas for his report to BdU: "Operational Area II normal . . . area from CA 2849 to 2793 [Long Island to Sandy Hook] free of mines . . . although area CA 54 [Delaware Bay] has medium air and destroyer patrols it appears free of mines . . . three tankers and one freighter sunk so far . . . still have five electric torpedoes . . . fuel remaining 90 cubic meters . . . Position CA 8145 [directly alongside Hampton Roads]."[16] When this information was put into final form, encrypted, transmitted, and received at BdU together with other Paukenschlag and Ziethen reports, Admiral Dönitz recorded his enthusiastic acknowledgment in the BdU KTB: "Reports from the coast of U.S.A. and Canada show that activities of U-boats can be successful much longer than was expected. Report from U-*123* indicates that this boat has had success far above its expectations."[17] The Lion would have been even prouder of his "unfit for U-boats" Kptlt. Hardegen had he been aware that U-*123* was on a coastal dash passing Hampton Roads in broad daylight. That was the kind of defiance that Dönitz admired—the defiance that an entire German nation would applaud three and a half weeks thence (11–12 February) when in Operation Cerberus the battleships *Scharnhorst* and *Gneisenau* together with the heavy cruiser *Prinz Eugen* broke out of Brest and made their Channel dash through the Strait of Dover under the derelict guns of the Royal Navy. At least the Royal Navy, when belatedly aroused, fought gamely against the dashers. The U.S. Navy let *123* dash splendidly unimpeded.

At 0833 hours (0133 ET) on the eighteenth U-*123* stood at the western edge of naval square CA 84, twenty nautical miles due east of Kitty Hawk, North Carolina. To port side seaward Hardegen and the lookouts sighted a bright red flash on the horizon, and immediately afterward heard two explosions. The Old Man made a note for his KTB: "That must be U-*66*."[18] (It was; the victim was *Allan Jackson.*) Rafalski called up the voice pipe to report a lot of traffic on six hundred meters. Apparently numerous ships had sighted the red glare of the same ship's fire that *123* watched for forty-five minutes. One of those vessels, surely, would make an appearance in Hardegen's field of vision. Nearly four hours later at 1210 (CET) the bridge lookouts defined a shadow on the port side. Hardegen studied it for a while and in the first glow of dawn identified it as a tanker. The sun was going to ruin his chances, he knew, as he began a surface approach. Sure enough, the tanker turned suddenly to starboard. He had been spotted. A submerged attack had not been possible because of his distance from the target. Now two more sets of steamer lanterns appeared on opposite courses, but again they were at ranges too long to permit a submerged approach. What bad luck! The sun coming up with three good-size targets concentrated at the same position! Hardegen winced, but he took heart from the fact that these Outer Banks seemed to be great waters for hunting. If there were that many ships today there would likely be as many tomorrow—unless they got scared off by the sinking. He ordered Hoffmann: "Come to course nine zero, proceed to deeper water, put the boat on the bottom at A-plus twenty-five."

U-*123* mounted to the surface at 0046 hours beginning 19 January (CET). As the warm Gulf Stream water ran off the bridge and deck and poured in white torrents through the limber holes, and the diesels startled the night air with their roar, the Old Man, refreshed by a long day's sleep, stretched his arms and surveyed an evening custom-made for U-boats: sea state 1, wind from the south-southeast at 2, one-tenth cloud cover, and visibility 14. He headed at both engines full toward Cape Hatteras, fifty nautical miles to the south. In his KTB he noted that the hydrophone had picked up evidence of numerous steamers in that general vicinity: "I want to stay close to the coast at Cape Hatteras. Again it's starry and the sea is calm. I should get rid of my five torpedoes tonight."[19]

He *would* get rid of them, in the most violent night of his career.

At 0304 lookouts sighted a northbound light to starboard between *123* and the Outer Banks just north of Oregon Inlet (which was shown on the 1870G chart). As he closed range Hardegen identified it as a freighter, about 4,000 GRT with four holds, heavily loaded, course 340, speed nine–ten knots. With a bow attack position and a clear night for Hoffmann's UZO, *123* launched the first of her five remaining G7es in textbook conditions from eight hundred meters out. But after some twenty seconds Barth's Hydrophone Effect showed that the eel (No. 32774) was not following the 240 heading cranked in by the Vorhaltrechner and T-Schu receiver.

"She's off course port ten!" Barth called up the pipe.

"Damned G7s!" Hardegen responded. After the estimated time of run it was obvious that Barth was right. The eel had swung aft of the target. The first good ship of the night had escaped—for the time being.

"Helmsman, come to three six zero! Both ahead full!" He would chase this freighter down. "Schroeter, check your launching data!" The Number Two on the deflection calculator was already double-checking the numbers. Hoffmann reconfirmed his data. The launching triangle was faultless.

"We had a perfect solution, Herr Kaleu," von Schroeter called up the hatch. "It had to be the eel that fouled up."

"Very well," Hardegen acknowledged. "We're gaining on that guy. I recommend that we take the same position and launch again with the same triangle as far as that is possible. We can then show in the shooting report that the fault lay with the torpedo and not with us."

"Yes, Herr Kaleu."

It did not take long to overtake the northbound freighter and pass it on the latter's starboard side, back north as far as Kitty Hawk.

At position CA 7668, with a triangle similar to that on the first launch except that *123* launched from only 450 meters out, Hoffmann pinned his hopes on G7e No. 15967, which in fact behaved very much better than its bow mate. "Running hot, straight, and normal on the HE!" reported Barth. After thirty seconds the warhead exploded below the aft edge of the funnel. The fierce detonation crippled the steamer at once. The stern sagged as ship's parts of various sizes splashed in the water around *123* or banged loudly on her deck. Hardegen looked around to see the bridge watch cowering behind the cowling, and he had to laugh at the sight of them peeking out again.

"You don't like it up close, do you?" he said, and redirected his attention to the mortally wounded vessel, which quickly capsized, the stern sinking over the sternposts within ninety seconds of the hit and the bow poking out from the twenty meters' depth of water. Hardegen added this to his shooting report: "The [first] torpedo failed to run straight. Proof of the correctness of our firing data is the hit after the second attack."[20] In neither the KTB nor the shooting report did Hardegen identify the vessel sunk. He did not interrogate survivors in lifeboats, if there were any, since, as will be seen, he had to move off immediately to take advantage of several steamers passing on a reciprocal course. That he did not identify the sunk vessel leaves the reader of his documents with another "ghost" ship. Jürgen Rohwer names the ship as *Brazos*, an American steamer, 4,497 GRT, sunk "off Cape Hatteras." Unfortunately for this identification, the public record establishes that *Brazos*, a steamer of the Atlantic, Gulf, and West Indies Line, sank six days earlier in a collision with another vessel 150 miles southeast of Hatteras. The student of Operation Drumbeat is left with another mystery sinking to whose reality both Hardegen and his number one attested as witnesses. Again, for whatever reason, no vessel answering the description in Hardegen's KTB was reported overdue. Naval square CA 7668 corresponded to map coordinates 36-06N, 75-24W.[21] The *Wreck Information List* gives only one unidentified wreck (Number 273) at the gross coordinates 36N, 75W, but that was deleted in the corrections supplement of 1946.[22]

Immediately Hardegen turned back south to chase three ships' lanterns. The navigable water close to the Outer Banks was well marked by light buoys. *Eins Zwei Drei* ran along the string of buoys until, at 0700 (CET), she sighted ahead the wake and lights of a steamer that the Old Man estimated at about four thousand GRT with four holds, speed 10. Soon both the hunted and the hunter would be raising

Wimble Shoals Lighted Whistle Buoy, which meant that the steamer would change course seaward to avoid the shoals and Cape Hatteras. Hardegen asked the engine room for all the revolutions they could give him. He noted the depth beneath him: 7–8 meters. This was not U-boat country. Now at 0845 hours he was abreast of the target and pulling ahead. The shoal buoy was abaft. He wanted perfect frontal position before the vessel turned. By 0909 he had it, and Hoffmann, who had a perfect silhouette of the target against lighted beaches, released the third of the last eels. If the bridge watch thought the last launch had been up close and dangerous, this one was from only *250* meters out. The Number 2 Tube torpedo, set at only two meters depth to prevent it going aground in the shoals, leaped from the water twice during its fifteen-second run. The violent concussion that followed, in the target's stern section, sent shock waves that stunned the watch and jarred even the crewmen below. Again the lookouts ducked as ship's parts whistled past overhead and splashed all around. The steamer sank quickly beneath its black explosion cloud, the stern going down first, listing the entire vessel to port and eventually rolling it over so that its stack and upper works lay flat on the water even before losing headway. Hardegen did not wait long to see the final agonies. He had two torpedoes left, and there were bound to be more targets around the cape. A course slightly to seaward took him away from the latest ship to die in the United States. And of that one's name there would never be any doubt. It was Hardegen's lone case of tonnage underclaiming.

The *City of Atlanta*, 5,269 GRT, was long familiar to passengers on the Savannah–New York run, although she had not been in passenger service for several years. General cargo was the ship's business now, and the 1904-vintage vessel was still a prime property of the Ocean Steamship Company of Savannah. On the night of her doomed passage, her crew comprised forty-seven men. Only three would survive: thirty-four-year-old Second Officer George Tavelle and two oilers, twenty-two-year-old Robert S. Fennell, Jr., and thirty-year-old Earl Dowdy. When the German warhead struck at 0209 (ET) *City of Atlanta* was proceeding south from Wimble Shoals, two and a half miles inside. Her lights were dimmed according to wartime regulations (although she had just sighted a brightly lighted northbound vessel outside the shoals that seemed oblivious to the regulations). Her speed was 11.75 knots on a slightly choppy sea under light clouds. Cape Hatteras and the beach lights were clearly visible. The master, forty-eight-year-old naturalized U.S. citizen Lehman Urquart, was in his cabin. The second officer and two men were on the bridge. Thirty-three men were in their bunks. The torpedo's explosion at the Number 3 hold in the aft engine room bulkhead killed three men outright, destroyed the radio shack, blew out the bridge windows, and threw on all the bridge lights. Immediately the ship listed to port, where she had been holed. Some of the aroused crewmembers stopped the engines and turned off the lights, while others rushed to launch the starboard boats, though this last endeavor proved fruitless because of the list. When it appeared that none of the boats would make it down the davits and the U-boat showed itself by means of a blinding searchlight—eight inches in diameter and two hundred candlepower, the survivors estimated—the on-deck crew lined the rails and cursed the U-boat with raised fists. Then the ship's keel turned abruptly up and all the men went overside. The last Tavelle and Fennell saw of the master, he was on deck giving orders to get the lifeboats down.

Tavelle barely escaped being crushed between two jammed lifeboats as he washed over. The water was cold and choppy—the sea lane was inshore from the Gulf Stream—but he managed to catch hold of a dining saloon door frame that added buoyancy to his lifejacket. From that handhold he looked around and counted eighteen other men clinging to pieces of the vessel, some singly, others in groups. Fennell, for one, was lucky to be among them. Asleep when the torpedo struck, he threw on some clothes and was almost to the deck when he remembered the eight by ten portrait photograph of his wife Marie. He returned to his bunk, removed the picture from its frame, folded it twice, and stuck it in his shirt pocket. He also donned a heavy sheepskin coat that, along with the rest of his belongings, had been blown out of his locker onto the floor. The coat would nearly be his undoing. Once on deck he labored fruitlessly to free up one of the lifeboats, in the process catching the back of the coat's belt on a rail. He was still struggling to release himself when the ship went under. Now underwater, he managed to break the belt knot on the jacket front and swim free, gasping to the surface, where he found a floating skylight and grabbed hold. The ship sank only a few feet away from him but, to his relief, it created very little suction. Later he spotted a bench from the crew's dining room and transferred to it. Finding some of the other crewmen nearby, he joined in their general shouting to one another, but as the cold numbed the men, one by one they fell silent, uncurled their hands from the flotsam, and gently surrendered to the corpse-ridden sea. After a while Fennell saw men in their lifejackets bobbing by face down in a macabre dance. At daybreak six hours later Tavelle, Fennell, and Dowdy were the only men left alive to reach for the lines thrown to them by boats from *Sea Train Texas,* a northbound freighter that had sighted, first, littered wreckage, and then the survivors, twelve miles south of Wimble Shoals Buoy. The ship's chronometer read 0830.[23]

Three hours later *123* was set up again for a UZO attack. After passing a small coastal vessel that was not worth one of his last two torpedoes, Hardegen watched with high anticipation as five larger vessels with lanterns lit advanced south along the buoys in a straight line ahead. With the beach lights providing a luminous backdrop, he need only keep the ships to shoreward, sit back, and launch away at the silhouettes. What a war! Too bad the Tommies were not as accommodating as the Americans. Here one could take a camp chair like a Prussian deer hunter and wait for game to be driven in front of the gun.[24] Von Schroeter would later relate: "I remember Cape Hatteras where ships going to and from New York were steaming with full lighting. We cruised slowly and observed them passing: 'There's one—no, it's too small. He doesn't make it into the frying pan. There—we'll take that one.' Steaming with their lights on. Really, totally crazy, that situation, something I never experienced elsewhere during the entire war."[25]

Everyone was at battle stations as the first ship in line came into view, a disappointingly small four-thousand-tonner, as Hardegen estimated it. He was hoping for six- to eight-thousand-ton targets. He hesitated as the black form of the ship, a tanker, passed against the lights. Then, he suddenly realized that he could still keep his last two eels but cripple and possibly sink this tanker by artillery.

"Gun crews to action stations!" The 10.5-cm crew vaulted into place on the fore casing, the aimer bringing up with him the sensitive optical sight, which he affixed to an L-shaped bracket on the port side of the gun. The layer took his station on the same side while the loader removed the tampion (watertight muzzle plug) to a storage hole on the gun pedestal, then took his firing position at the breech. Three ammunition ratings passed the heavy shells that came up the tower hatch by hand from the magazine of 180 rounds under the floor plates belowdecks. IIWO von Schroeter, commanding guns, ordered the first round loaded and the breech closed. The aimer focused on the stern of his target, and the layer turned his elevation and traverse wheels to the correct barrel position. Although a U-boat deck did not provide a stable gun platform, the seas at force 1 were relatively calm and von Schroeter was confident of good shooting as he reported: "Forward gun ready to fire, Herr Kaleu!"

Hardegen leaned forward to the voice pipe: "Helmsman, port ten, both ahead slow. LI, just so everyone will know what we are doing, the boat is going to slip into a line of steamers. We will come up on the wake of a tanker proceeding south and disable it, perhaps sink it, with artillery alone. Then we will pivot and use our last two torpedoes on the second and third ships in line. Distance to tanker one thousand meters."

Hardegen told Hoffmann, who was standing up by the UZO: "This is going to be tricky. I've never had a course in artillery, so I don't know how effective artillery alone will be. We're making the turn into the tanker's wake now. Range about five hundred meters."

To the helmsman: "Steady up on one-nine-five. Both ahead two thirds." The U-boat was now positioned directly astern the target and gaining on it. Hardegen picked up the megaphone and leaned across the bridge fairwater. "Permission to fire at two hundred meters! Ten rounds!"

Then Hoffmann spoke up: "Herr Kaleu, we're boxed in fore and aft by steamers. We're bound to be seen. If any one of them is armed we could be receiving fire as well as giving it, and at this range we're more vulnerable than the steamers. They can catch fire, but we can be sunk. It's a real risk."

"Thank you, Number One. I believe in my luck, which has never failed me. The bolder you start something the more bewildering it is to others. When the first shots hit home not only that ship but the others in line will lose their heads. I want to exploit that moment of confusion."[26]

Hardegen was well aware of the risk, also that he was violating standard U-boat rules. But audacity seemed the virtue of the moment—

CRACK! It had been a long time—the sinking of *Ganda*, in fact, eight months before—since Hardegen and his men had used the 10.5 Bootskanone, so they were startled both by the report and the brilliant muzzle flash of the first shot. The second, third, and fourth shots got off in quick order, then the remaining six followed at a slower rate since the crew passing the heavy shells from below, long unaccustomed to the drill, were unable to maintain an unbroken flow.

Hardegen counted the hits, starting with the first projectile, which exploded in a bright red-and-white ball on the tanker's bridge. Then three—four—five—more hits out of ten shells fired. Not bad. Debris blew up from the bridge and stack. The tanker lost headway. Was the engine room also hit? Fires spread along the deck.

"Cease firing! Forward gun crew stand by gun! All gun crews look alive!"

With the tanker losing way and *123* still with both engines ahead two-thirds, the U-boat was catching up to the target.

"Port ten!" Hardegen intended to pass on the port side. Von Schroeter joined the Old Man and Hoffmann on the bridge just in time to have a good view of the wounded tanker as they came abreast and passed.

Damn! It was huge! Much larger than the bridge had estimated, maybe as much as eight thousand tons. They had misjudged it because it lay very deep in the water. Hardegen surveyed the decks with his glasses. "Look for guns!" he yelled, now frightened by the realization that a ship this size could easily be armed and, if so, *123* at this range could be blown out of the water with one good shot.[27]

"No guns, Herr Kaleu!" the lookouts reported.

Hardegen looked at his officers and expelled air between pursed lips. Von Schroeter essayed in a dull tone, "Herr Kaleu! *Mit die Dummen ist Gott!*—God stands by fools!"[28]

"Yes, yes," Hardegen agreed. "Hard-a-port! Look aft!" The officers lifted their glasses toward the line of ships astern, which were turning off their position lights and dispersing. "They've seen the tanker's fire. We'll come back and finish it off with our last eel. First, let's make an approach on one of the first two ships in line. Both engines slow."

After making a turn to the north and west on 282 degrees in order to place the next ship, an advancing freighter, against the shore lights, Hardegen realized that he had miscalculated the target's speed. Making an unusual time of fourteen to fifteen knots, the freighter passed in front of *123* before Hoffmann could get a setup. Too bad, Hardegen thought, because it appeared to be a six-thousand-tonner. All right, they would wait for the next one. While they waited a darkened northbound steamer stumbled by to seaward, but fast, and before Hardegen could get turned around for a bow shot—the only two torpedoes left were in Tubes 1 and 4—that target, too, moved out of range on an oblique heading.

At that point two things happened. First, Rafalski called up with an intercept from the shelled tanker. She was SS *Malay,* signaling that she had been attacked by a submarine's artillery and asking repeatedly for help from the U.S. Navy station at Norfolk. Rafalski had looked her up: 8,207 GRT, owned by the U.S. firm Grosvenor-Dale Company, Inc., 464.4 feet long, capacity seventy thousand barrels, launched 1921. From another intercept Rafalski reported that a passing steamer, the Swedish *Scania,* lay alongside to assist with its fire extinguishing equipment which it transferred by lifeboat. The second thing that happened was a break in the major cooling water pipe of the port diesel. The LI, Schulz, reported to the bridge that the engine had to be shut down until the pipe could be disassembled and welded. Great! Hardegen thought. Here he was with steamers all around and *123* was a lame duck, her surface maneuvering power cut by half. He need not have worried, however. In the confusion that he had predicted a large southbound shadow appeared suddenly on a 160-degree course within five hundred meters of where they lay. With hardly enough time to collect launching data, Hardegen steadied the boat on 253 degrees and Hoffmann punched the trigger on Tube Number 1. The next-to-last eel popped out at point-blank range of 450 meters for a 32-second run. Time of launch: 1201 (CET), 0501 (ET), two hours before sunrise, but anyone on the bridge could have thought it was sunrise from the incredibly bright fireball that exited from the freighter's port side.[29] The explosion's concussion waves buckled the knees of *123*'s crew belowdecks, where, as soon as they recovered, men said matter-of-factly to one another: *Wieder eins* — "another one." Hardegen noted for his KTB: "Our boat has now conquered over 200,000 tons and I, myself, over 100,000."[30] That was the figure at which commanders began to get "neck itch," since one hundred thousand was the tonnage that usually qualified for the Knight's Cross, which was worn around the collar.

This latest conquest was a Latvian freighter, *Ciltvaira,* 3,779 GRT, with a crew of thirty-two Latvians, Estonians, Finns, Danes, Swedes, Dutch, one Rumanian, and a mess boy from British Guiana. Most were asleep as the thirty-eight-year-old cargo ship plodded along at eight knots in the predawn hours nine nautical miles abeam of Hatteras Island and ten miles south of Wimble Shoal Buoy. She was not darkened; nor did she zigzag because news of other sinkings on the southern coast had not reached her before departure; nor had she received routing instructions from the Navy at Norfolk, whence she set out the day before with a load of paper for Savannah, Georgia. The burning *Malay* was not yet in sight to warn her of imminent danger, when a torpedo slammed into the port side of the engine room, pierced the boilers, and flooded the Number 2 hold. Two firemen were killed outright, the only casualties in the sinking. A coal passer, Friederich Lusis, might have been a third fatality had he not chosen that moment to go on deck for a breath of fresh air. Nick Creteu, the Rumanian, was standing near the galley door and was knocked straight off his feet about two feet into the air. Latvian radio operator Rudolph Musts leaped from his bunk at impact to find the lights gone, the door to his compartment jammed shut, and the interior space filling with hot steam. A mighty heave against the door with his shoulder gave him release and he raced to the boat deck which was already listing to port. There he found the master, Karl Skerbergs, and the other officers directing the crew into a large starboard lifeboat. Most of the men were in their underwear. One had rescued a pet cat named Briska and another a puppy named Pluskis. The master and officers followed down the falls in a smaller boat, taking with them the ship's log and manifest. In the daylight three hours after their orderly abandonment the survivors saw that *Ciltvaira* was not going down, and the master with eight volunteers reboarded to secure passports, ship's papers, and warm clothing. They also hoisted a distress-signal flag over the vessel, which, though broken in two and capsizing as far as the guard rails on the port side, was still stubbornly afloat. Back in the boats the survivors waved down the U.S. tanker *Socony-Vacuum* and the Brazilian freighter *Bury,* both of which lay to and took them on board. *Bury* also attempted a tow, but three manila lines and one steel cable parted, and the derelict had to be abandoned. Notice went out about the drifting menace to navigation, which was last seen, awash, two days later far out to sea at 35-46N, 74-37W. No one on board *Ciltvaira* had seen the U-boat that sank her. Nonetheless, Radioman Musts, described as a bushy-browed man with a ready smile and a thick Latvian accent, said on reaching Charleston, South Carolina, aboard *Socony-Vacuum:* "We couldn't fight back this time, but probably our next ship will be armed. It will be different then. You will see what we can do when the devils attack." The master reported a strong odor of phosphorus after the torpedo's explosion, which he thought had a surprisingly low intensity given the fact that the rupture it caused in the hull was only four feet in diameter at a point six feet below the waterline. But, of course, he allowed, four feet were suffi-cient since the warhead was expertly placed.[31]

The ordeal of *Malay* was far from over. After torpedoing *Ciltvaira*, Reinhard Hardegen returned at reduced speed toward the wounded tanker south of his position while Schulz and his mechanics worked furiously on the broken water pipe in the port engine. On the bridge the lookouts searched vainly for fire licks from the tanker's deck on which to home the boat. Hardegen guessed that with the Swedish ship's help, *Malay*'s crew had been able to extinguish the blaze, and he proceeded south using the nearby coast as reference. After a while Hoffmann told Hardegen that he could smell burning wood. Hardegen sniffed several times and agreed. They would follow their noses against the wind. After navigating in this fashion for about ten minutes the lookouts sighted two stationary shadows dead ahead. The time was shortly after 1230 (CET), or 0530 (ET) with sunrise an hour and a half away. Hardegen studied the shadows through the 7 × 50s as he closed. *Malay*'s exterior fires were out, but several interior fires glowed through the portholes and doors. These must be under control, he reasoned, since the vessel was putting out boiler smoke and getting underway. Hardegen watched as she wheeled to starboard and took a reverse heading, no doubt to her port of origin or to a repair yard. He turned his attention to the rescue freighter, which was haul-ing up its boat. The freighter was a sitting duck, an easy mark for the last eel. But the tanker was more valuable a prize, and she was already injured. He estimated her new course at 340 degrees. Ordering the starboard engine ahead slow, he called for right rudder to 280 degrees so that Hoffmann could set up for a good track angle. While they waited for their prey to come into optimum range the sky to starboard was suddenly illuminated by star shells fired by *Ciltvaira*'s survivors. In the shells' bright white light Hardegen could see the hull of his last victim rolled to portside and collapsing in the center. At 1244 Hoffmann had *Malay* where he wanted her: speed a surprising eleven knots, range 400, angle on the bow Green 21.[32] *Los!* The last G7e left for a twenty-eight-second voyage, but Hardegen did not stay idly by to watch its immolation. The water was shallow, twelve to fifteen meters, and with all of *Malay*'s emergency calls to the U.S. Navy at Norfolk, *123* might very quickly find herself under attack by destroyers or aircraft and unable to dive. Schulz was reporting that they had just enough hours of fuel remaining to make it home to Lorient at economy cruise.

Hardegen paused for a moment, reluctant to leave these bonanza sea-lanes, then, bowing to reality, he called down the pipe: *Ruder hart steuerbord. Kurs Heimat!*—"Hard-starboard. Course home!"[33]

Malay had departed Philadelphia in water ballast after pumping oil she had brought from Port Arthur, Texas. Her crew of thirty-four were Americans except for a Portuguese, a Norwegian, and a Mexican, but fifteen of the complement were new to the ship. Proceeding at night with running lights on a true course of 193 degrees in a line of four ships off Hatteras, she was struck in port wing of the bridge by an exploding shell. Seconds later another shriek and crash carried away the after port lifeboat. On the bridge Second Mate William A. Green gave the order for hard right rudder to take the ship inshore, rang the general alarm, stopped the engines, and switched off the running lights. Three more shells smashed into the crew's after quarters, one of them piercing the bulkhead over the bunk of Second Cook Adams J. Hay. Badly burned, Hay would die later in a lifeboat. Some crewmen raced on deck to fight fires that were spreading wildly, while others filed along the catwalk toward the lifeboats. In one they placed a crewman with a broken back, but the forward lines fouled, the boat capsized, and the injured man with three others drowned. The forward port boat successfully lowered with nine men including the fatally burned Hay. After an hour the master, John M. Dodge, who had remained with the ship, ordered the boat's occupants back on board to assist with the fires. In the meantime the wireless had been active signaling the SSS call—"attacked by submarine"—and asking for Navy assistance. That help never came, despite the fact that shore station WBF in Baltimore acknowledged the call and notified the Navy of the tanker's plight. The passing *Scania* did lay to and sent fire-fighting equipment by boat. The SS *Coamo* was also seen to pass, but that vessel, which five days later would rescue survivors from *Lady Hawkins*, did not stop. Finding that structural damage to the *Malay* was slight, the master ordered steam up again and the vessel resumed headway at half speed, turning north toward Hampton Roads. After raising speed to eleven knots, at 0544 (ET) the tanker suffered a torpedo detonation on the starboard side, just aft of the mainmast, at about Number 7 tank. The explosion caused a gaping hole three to four feet below the water line, pierced a hole through the opposite, or port, side, and ripped a tear upward through the main deck that nearly took the mast down. As a precaution the master threw overside in a weighted bag the ship's secret wireless code and routing instructions, but the empty, buoyant compartmentation kept the ship afloat. Dodge determined that the tough old tanker was still seaworthy and capable of making way. Shortly after daybreak Coast Guard vessels arrived on the scene to take off Hay's body and a number of crewmen with painful injuries, including broken leg, collarbone, and fingers. Boatswain Walter Bruce, with injured hands, commented: "The next time I go to sea it will be in an armed ship. You can't fight off subs with potatoes." Others, less bellicose, were simply glad that the oil tanks were empty and that they had not roasted on a flaming pyre.

At 0945, her engines started once again, the redoubtable *Malay* made way at defiant speed to Hampton Roads, which she entered the next day under her own power and anchored at 2145 off Newport News, the first U.S. merchant ship to survive combined shelling and torpedoing by an enemy submarine. Her master praised the crew "for the courageous way they did their duty under fire," and added, "I hope the *Malay* will keep her good luck."[34] The *New York Times*, in reporting the attack on *Malay*, stated: "The Navy, engaged in a ranging hunt for the submarine pack responsible for the attacks, continued to veil any successes it may have had behind strict censorship."[35]

Though brightly confident in public, the Operations staff at Main Navy in Washington wore worried expressions in private. Tanker and freighter losses to U-boats in U.S. waters were reaching serious proportions. The war effort would soon be affected if sinkings continued at the same pace of the last five days. Logistics experts calculated the long-range effects on war matériel: The sinking of two six-thousand-ton freighters and one three-thousand-ton tanker with their cargoes meant the equivalent destruction of forty-two tanks, eight six-inch Howitzers, eighty-eight twenty-five-pound guns, forty two-pound guns, twenty-four armored cars, fifty Bren gun carriers, 5,210 tons of ammunition, six hundred rifles, 428 tons of tank supplies, two thousand tons of stores, and one thousand tanks of gasoline. The loss of the freighter's cargo equaled the loss of goods carried on four trains of seventy-five cars each. If, on the other hand, the two freighters and one tanker successfully made port and discharged their cargoes the amount of enemy force required to destroy those goods in dispersal would approximate three thousand air-bombing runs.[36] The military advantages of getting loaded merchant ships safely to port were manifest.

Of equal concern to Naval Operations was the fact that U-boat dominance of the Atlantic seaboard was rapidly becoming a public relations disaster. For six months the Navy had presumed to hold sway over four-fifths of the Atlantic as far east as Iceland and the Azores, and here the United States was having its nose rubbed publicly in the Navy's own front yard. The obvious question was spreading rapidly among the public and, not unexpectedly, was put to Franklin D. Roosevelt at the President's Oval Office press conference on 20 January: *Where was the Navy?* The President's response could not be directly quoted under press rules existing at the time. The *New York Times* version ran: "Mr. Roosevelt asserted that the only answer would be to take such people [who asked that question] into a White House room where there were maps showing the location of every naval ship. This, he added, he could not do." The paper added that Mr. Roosevelt implied that units of the fleet and its air arm were busy elsewhere.[37] This has been the usual answer since of Navy apologists. In fact, one CINCLANT advocate, writing as recently as 1975, stated: "In the time of slaughter the public asked, 'Where is the Navy?' The Atlantic Fleet was fighting the Battle of the Atlantic."[38] While that answer may not have appeared fatuous in 1942, when the data were lacking, it will hardly serve today. There *was* no "Battle of the Atlantic" elsewhere during January (or February through June) to divert forces from the Battle of the Atlantic that was being waged directly on America's doorstep. The cross-oceanic convoy routes became so quiet in early 1942 that merchant seamen on those routes became careless about showing lights.[39] During the first four months of 1942, in fact, only one convoy, ON 67 in late February, experienced significant enemy contact, losing six ships to torpedoes off the Newfoundland Bank. By that same date (22, 24 February) *sixty-two* ships had been lost in waters closely abutting the U.S. and Canadian shorelines; and *nine* more in the Caribbean. In March a total of seventy-nine Allied and neutral vessels would be sunk worldwide; of that number seventy-four went down in the Atlantic; all but four of the seventy-four were sunk in the coastal or offshore waters of North America west of 50 degrees west. During the same period—one of "comparative safety of the sea lanes to England," noted the ESF war diary for March—519 ships completed the passage from the New World to the Old. Yet USN destroyer strength was distributed as though just the opposite was true: In the Northern Convoy Waters (Halifax, Argentia, Hvalfjord, Londonderry sectors) where 6.33 percent of tonnage was lost 41.7 percent of destroyer strength was stationed; while in ESF waters, where 49.3 percent of tonnage was lost (thus where shipping was most endangered), only 4.9 percent of destroyer strength was assigned.[40] The plain fact is that from January forward the bulk of U-boat forces were operating off, proceeding to, or returning from North America. For the Atlantic Fleet not to have concentrated defensive units where the enemy was, and not to have gone after him where, thanks to the British Tracking Room, the Navy knew him to be, is the mystery that no amount of smoke will explain.

A cacophony of voices sounded in Washington. Senator Tom Connally of Texas, chairman of the Foreign Relations Committee, argued that the "wanton raids" by the Nazi "assassin" were timed to intimidate the twenty-one American republics that were meeting in an Inter-American Conference at Rio de Janeiro, Brazil.[41] President Roosevelt rejected that interpretation, stating that he knew the reason why the U-boats had come, but he declined to say what it was.[42] Meanwhile, the Navy was spoonfeeding news of merchant ship sinkings to the public, keeping details of the carnage to a minimum while fostering the notion that the coastal sinkings were of no special importance.[43] On the twenty-second, in an attempt to cover the Navy's failures to that date by a carefully crafted suggestion that naval forces had sunk one or more of the U-boats offshore, a Navy spokesman in Washington declared "emphatically" that there would be no announcements of submarines sunk and that newspapers were forbidden to publish reports of such successes "as part of the security program."[44] The *New York Times* headlined the statement: "NAVY HIDES ITS BLOWS."[45] That the Navy had in fact destroyed U-boats in the preceding week was further suggested by a statement (totally false) that had been made two months before by Secretary of the Navy Frank Knox. On 21 November, referring to pre–Pearl Harbor convoy warfare, Knox had declared to the press: "After careful weighing of the evidence, I can now state that in the Atlantic Ocean United States naval forces have up to the present time probably sunk or damaged at least fourteen enemy submarines."[46] (To this brash claim a classified internal Navy history would retort that, "There was no positive proof that [the Navy] had knocked out even one U-boat during 1941."[47]) In the last weeks of January, with desperate need for a good press, the Navy made no effort to discount widespread rumors that captured U-boats were being towed into Navy ports from Maine to Florida.[48]

The Navy's plight, in fact, led it to abandon the "hidden blows" strategy only two days after it was announced. On 23 January, in one of the more regrettable (and, in retrospect, laughable) propaganda efforts of the war, the Navy announced for front-page consumption that during the preceding nine days it had liquidated an unspecified number of U-boats off the East Coast, saying sarcastically of these "excursionists," as it called them, that "some of the recent visitors to our territorial waters will never enjoy the return portion of their voyage." The Navy spokesman detailed to sustain this fiction appealed to U.S. citizens who might "have seen a submarine captured or destroyed" to keep silent. "The Nazis think themselves pretty clever," he went on, but by regarding "secrecy as his own personal antisubmarine weapon" the U.S. citizen could be cleverer still. It was not explained how that was so, but everyone was invited to play the "game": "This is a phase of the game of war secrecy into which every American should enter enthusiastically." The Navy will "take care" of enemy submarines; the public can help by "keeping quiet." The press and radio can make the same "great, patriotic contribution."[49] Thus the Navy effectively put the muzzle on the people's wonderment. It was the Big Lie, nicely handled, in a cynical and meretricious sort of way. The Atlantic Navy's image as sub-busters was restored. And no one would know that the only place where CINCLANT actually took the offensive was in public relations. If there were doubters they seem not to have broken the muzzle, even after "Dolly" Andrews, on 29 January, offered two hundred dollars to each naval crew that sank a U-boat, which must have seemed a curious inducement given the Navy's already potent success against "excursionists."[50]

In reality the Navy had not made a single planned attack on the Paukenschlag boats, and the only U.S. shots fired in the vicinity of one appear to have been the four bombs dropped harmlessly against U-*123* on the fifteenth when a bomber chanced to sight the surfacing U-boat. On that occasion there had been no follow-up by air or sea, and so far as the Eastern Sea Frontier was aware, the action was no different from a number of other reported attacks on targets, real or imaginary, where no one stayed around to pick up the commander's cap. The kill board at ESF was still empty by the date that Reinhard Hardegen set *Eins Zwei Drei* on a homeward course, and it would remain empty for *three long months;* although it should be noted for the record that Fast Minesweeper *Hamilton* (DMS-18), a converted flush-deck destroyer, did its level best to post a trophy. On the night of 26–27 January off the coast of Florida, *Hamilton* was patrolling astern of Troop Convoy BT 200 bound from New York to the Panama Canal Zone. The seven transports with their screen were zigzagging south at fourteen to fifteen knots under a first-quarter moon when, at 0500 hours, *Hamilton* sighted a vessel on her starboard hand that looked like a submarine on the surface. Going to general quarters, she fired a gun across the bow and came to a collision course. When very close aboard and bearing down at full speed with crew bracing for the impact, *Hamilton*'s skipper noticed that the "U-boat" was a small darkened freighter! He called for emergency back full and rudder put hard over, but it was too late. In a screech of torn and twisted metal the minesweeper slammed into the freighter's portside. The 1,946 GRT American motorship SS *Green Island* survived the "attack." After repairs she would go to sea again, only to be sunk south of Cuba three months later on 6 May by Ulrich Folkers, who was on a second American patrol in U-*125*. After her ramming attack *Hamilton* was detached from the convoy and sent into Key West for repairs to her starboard bow, which took ten days.[51] Shortly afterward, she was removed from patrol duty and converted to Miscellany Auxiliary (AG). It was embarrassing.

Convoy BT 200 was not the only naval force that cruised along the infested seaboard in the last days of January. On 28 January, Battleship Division Six, consisting of *North Carolina* (BB 55) and *Washington* (BB 56) with the carrier *Hornet*, escorted by seven DDs and a cruiser, departed Key West for home yards Norfolk and New York. Cruising in two columns, the force zigzagged during both day and night except in the darkest hours. Speed was kept high to outdistance U-boats, fifteen to twenty-three knots, which strained the capabilities of the destroyers, especially the twelve-hundred-tonners, which hurt in the strong head seas. One, the *Clemson*-class flush-decker *Noa*, damaged herself at twenty-two knots and had to put in at Charleston. The destroyer screen kept a close lookout, maintaining stations ahead and on each bow, distance three thousand to four thousand yards, and abaft and on the beam, distance twenty-five hundred yards. One DD swept astern at night. On reaching home port the screen commander reported, "Although the route lay along the Atlantic coast and submarines were numerous no sound contacts or depth charge attacks were made."[52] Actually, U-boats along the route were not numerous, and never had been. The most that operated off the East Coast at any one time in January was three: U-*123*, U-*66* (Zapp), and U-*125* (Folkers) for most of the period; U-*130* (Kals) descended into New England waters by the twenty-first when *123* was heading home; and U-*106* (Kptlt. Hermann Rasch) replaced Kals at the end of the month, with the result that the number continued at three. U-*106* was the first of a new wave of five IXB and IXC boats that Admiral Dönitz had sent to the U.S. coast even before learning of any Paukenschlag successes (see chapter 6). During the first week of February four of those boats (U-*103, 106, 107, 108*) would operate at the same time in U.S. waters. The fifth, U-*128*, which had originally been assigned to Paukenschlag, would make five boats together when she took up station off Florida in the third week.

During the last ten days in January eight ships went down between New England and the Carolinas. Kals (U-*130*), who on the seventeenth had received BdU's permission to change his operation area from Cabot Strait to a position between Hardegen and Zapp, steamed south as far as Georges Bank east of Nantucket Island by dusk on the twenty-first, where he sighted the Norwegian motor tanker *Alexander Höegh*. A submerged launch of two eels added 8,248 GRT to his total.[53] The next day, Zapp, who was south of Hatteras and the Outer Diamond Shoal, sank the small (2,677 GRT) U.S. freighter *Norvana*.[54] By dark on the twenty-second Kals was off Albermarle Sound approaching Hatteras, where he sank *Olympic*, a Panamanian tanker, 5,335 GRT.[55] Zapp had quick back-to-back kills off Hatteras on the twenty-fourth (CET). The first, the four-month-old motor tanker *Empire Gem*, bound for Britain via Halifax with a cargo of 10,600 tons of gasoline from Port Arthur, had just crossed ahead of the U.S. ore carrier *Venore* while both were raising Diamond Shoal Light buoy. At 0240 (CET) she took two torpedoes from Zapp in the after tanks on the starboard side.[56] The roaring flames that quickly enveloped her illuminated the ore carrier abaft, and only three minutes later Zapp struck *Venore* forward on the port side. *Empire Gem* burned down to the water line. Of her all-British crew of fifty-seven only the master and two radio operators survived—the worst human toll since *City of Atlanta*.

Venore, with 22,300 tons of iron ore from Chile, suffered little damage or water intake from her hit, but twenty members of the multinational crew, panicking at the sight of the ignited tanker on the starboard quarter, lowered lifeboats even though the ship was still making headway. All were lost. One other crewman, from the engine room, ran to the stern and jumped to his death. At 0324 (CET) a second torpedo from Zapp exploded in the Number 9 ballast tank just forward of the fire room, and *Venore* listed forty-five degrees to port.[57]

The master ordered Abandon Ship and twenty-one men in one boat got away safely, though neither the master nor the radio operator was among them. The survivors rowed and sailed toward land eighty miles to the west, subsisting on rations of sea biscuits and water. Thirty-nine difficult hours later they were lifted aboard the tanker *Tennessee*. A U.S. Navy report on the twin sinkings commented: "The apparent ease with which the enemy U-boat sank both vessels was alarming and it is presumed that the same U-boat was also responsible for the triple sinking off Wimble Shoals Buoy four days previous." The report meant to say two ships sunk (*City of Atlanta* and *Ciltvaira*) and one damaged (*Malay*)—actually the work of U-*123*. The same report noted that *Empire Gem* had a four-inch gun and that both ships were steaming with their running lights on under a bright moon at the time of the attacks.[58]

Kals, meanwhile, had headed back north where on the twenty-fifth U-*130* found the Norwegian *Varanger* thirty-five nautical miles east of Sea Isle City, New Jersey. The 9,305 GRT motor tanker was carrying a capacity cargo of fuel oil from Africa and the West Indies to New York. Kals caught her amidship on the portside at 1002 hours, then put three coup-de-grace torpedoes into the stricken hull at 1007, 1013, and 1024. The last entered the engine room and exploded the boiler. The shock rattled windows in Sea Isle City and was heard as far away as Atlantic City, twenty-five miles to the north. The entire forty-man crew survived, the first instance when a Paukenschlag attack off the U.S. coast caused no human fatalities. The crewmen, who were so thickly coated with black oil they had to be given kerosene baths, managed to save a dachshund puppy, but the mother went down with the ship.[59]

Ulrich Folkers (U-*125*) got his first-ever sinking the following night after a series of disappointments that included one ship damaged (U.S. steam tanker *Olney*) and six misses or duds. In a surface attack off Cape Hatteras at 0604 (CET) Folkers launched two G7es eight seconds apart at the southbound *West Ivis*, a U.S. freighter. The first exploded below the bridge, the second in the engine room—classic hits—and the steamer sank inside fourteen minutes. Thirty-five men died including the master.[60] *West Ivis* would be Folker's lone sinking on the Paukenschlag patrol, a disappointing performance in his own eyes and in those of the Lion. He would later go on to higher achievements, however, winning the Knight's Cross in March 1943, the last of the Drumbeat commanders to do so. Two months afterward he and his boat would be sunk with the loss of all hands by HMS *Vidette* south of Greenland.[61] The souls of *West Ivis* would have their revenge.

The final Drumbeat sinking in U.S. coastal sea-lanes came on the night of 27 January (0943 CET, 0243 ET) twelve nautical miles southeast of Winter Quarters Light Vessel, off Chincoteague, Virginia. U-*130*, which had headed south again, placed one devastating warhead in the port side, aft of the amidship deckhouse between tanks Numbers 4 and 5, of the northbound Atlantic Refining Company tanker SS *Francis E. Powell*.[62] Seeing the amidship section awash, and the radio antenna, twenty-five feet of catwalk, and much of the port rail carried away, and worried about the menacing odors released by eighty thousand barrels of gasoline and furnace oil aboard, the master, Thomas J. Harrington of Baltimore, ordered Abandon Ship, which was effected within five minutes' time. Three lifeboats were put over the side and two managed to get away. For some reason the master reboarded, possibly to throw over codes and confidential papers. When next seen Harrington was attempting to climb down a rope into the third boat when a sudden lurch of the tanker caused him to be crushed between the hull and the lifeboat. Crewman John D. Alexson, of Bayonne, New Jersey, was in one of the lifeboats: "We started rowing. We ran almost headlong into the submarine. The conning tower and catwalk were out of the water. They seemed to be waiting for us in order to shell us, but they didn't. We swerved the boat around and pulled away from the submarine as fast as we could." The boat that carried Alexson and ten others drifted for seventeen hours in constant cold biting rain before being found by the Coast Guard. Seventeen survivors in the other boat were rescued by a merchant ship.[63] The master and three others were dead, one of the smallest casualty figures of the Paukenschlag campaign. In Canadian waters "Ajax" Bleichrodt, who had been bedeviled by duds, broke the string with a successful launch from four hundred meters against *Thirlby*, a British steamer, 4,887 GRT, south of Yarmouth, Nova Scotia.[64] Bleichrodt then steamed south to rendezvous with Kals (U-*130*) north of the Bermudas and take on fuel from the latter's larger (IXC) bunkers for the voyage home.[65] On the way to the rendezvous Bleichrodt sank two vessels far out to sea, the British freighter *Tacoma Star* (7,924 GRT), east of New Jersey, on 1 February, and the sizable Canadian motor tanker *Montrolite* (11,309 GRT), east of Hatteras, four days later.[66] The final January sinking in U.S. waters was posted by the new arrival Hermann Rasch (U-*106*), who caught the U.S. tanker *Rochester* (6,836 GRT) off Cape Charles, Virginia, on 30 January.[67]

Understandably, the stories of merchant seamen who survived these attacks received far greater coverage in the press than did accounts of cargoes and bottoms lost, though to the strategists on both sides the latter weighed more prominently in the scale, since in wartime seamen were the more easily replaced. To more sensitive observers who happened also to be aware of the British OIC submarine plot, the sinking of *Rochester* signaled more than the arrival of a new wave of IXB and IXC boats to replace the Drumbeat fleet, more even than the loss of yet another ship and cargo: With three crewmen killed by the torpedo blast and four more men dead weeks later from wounds suffered in the explosion, the sinking meant that the hemorrhaging of human life offshore was going to continue, particularly since the U.S. Navy had thus far proved unable to stanch it. Already in nineteen days' time more than 500 seamen and civilians had lost their lives to Drumbeat—one-sixth the U.S. Navy fatalities at Pearl Harbor; a larger toll than that taken in any of America's previous coastal battles since colonial times; the largest concentrated loss of merchant mariners' lives in that service's history; and the greatest Atlantic coast disaster since 8 September 1934, when the luxury liner *Morro Castle* burned off Asbury Park, New Jersey, with the loss of 125 passengers and crew. More yet were to die as Reinhard Hardegen (U-*123*) made his way back across the Atlantic. And a frightful loss was looming ahead as the post-Paukenschlag fleets, finding the stable door still open, arrived to increase the number of operational boats on the bloodied coast. (Meanwhile, up to 31 January, in their own version of unrestricted submarine warfare, U.S. Navy S- and Fleet-class boats in the Pacific had sunk fifteen Japanese ships of all descriptions with an unknown number of fatalities.)

It was estimated that an Atlantic merchant seaman's chances of surviving if a ship sank under him were fifty-fifty. American survival equipment was not yet as effective as British devices, which by 1942 included lifejacket lights, protective clothing, and manual pumps for expelling water from lifeboats. Working against survival for many crewmen in the Drumbeat waters was the number of lifeboats that were destroyed by the upward blast of torpedoes or that became unusable because of the ships' rapidly developing lists to one side or the other. Unlike British vessels, on most of which guns had been swung aboard, the typical U.S. freighter or tanker in coastwise traffic had as yet no U.S. Navy gun crew, or Armed Guard, as such units came to be called. Excepting the passengers lost from *Lady Hawkins*, the deaths at sea occurred among men committed to the sea and to its dangers. As seaman-novelist Nicholas Monsarrat said of them, "Some men died well . . . some men died badly . . . some men just died."[68] But of those who survived it may be said that they exhibited a notable courage and tenacity in hiring on to other tankers, freighters, and troop transports as soon as they could. Sizable bonuses for the riskier routes were a significant incentive, but something more than money seems to have motivated many of the ordinary seamen, firemen, oilers, electricians, stewards, cooks, and jacket men (formerly waiters on the now defunct or diminished passenger ship trade) who in late January filled the hiring halls of the National Maritime Union at 346 West Seventeenth Street in New York City. "It's like this," said one survivor matter-of-factly. "If your house burns down, you move to another house. If a sailor loses his ship, he gets another ship. That's his house. That's the way it is."[69] In another vein a "tanker stiff" explained his motive: "Good dough. You don't think about torpedoes. You figure if one's got your number on it, that's too bad. If it hasn't it won't get you."[70] Some others, though, worried about the torpedo addressed, "To Whom It May Concern." One Canadian chief steward in the British merchant navy, who had been torpedoed four times, complained to New York reporters about the "loose talk" of his American counterparts. "I wouldn't be a bit surprised," he said, "if some of the present torpedoings so close to your shores were due to fifth-column work. New York is full of loose talk."[71] Although a major U.S. propaganda campaign would shortly be launched in support of the steward's allegation, under the general title "Loose Lips Sink Ships," there is no evidence that the interception of sailing information played any role whatever in the German U-boat campaign in American waters during the first months of 1942. There were so many unescorted ships blithely sailing in perfect target formation that no U-boat commander in the period, even if he possessed "loose lips" information, and it is not certain that any of them did, had need of data other than the fat images steaming one after the other against a bright background into his UZO lens.

· · ·

In Washington, meanwhile, public relations officers at the Department of the Navy agonized over the uncontrollable stream of survivors' tales. Perhaps it was not enough after all to imply that the Navy was taking care of the U-boats by asking the public to keep quiet about the boats that it had seen "destroyed" or "captured." Perhaps some more-active strategy was required. Accordingly, when it was learned on 28 January that a Navy pilot, Chief Aviation Machinist's Mate Donald Francis Mason, had dropped bombs on a "U-boat," the prior "secrecy" policy, only five days old, was abruptly abandoned. Mason was too good to pass up. Whether he sank the U-boat or not was beside the point. An enlisted man besting a German commander was dynamite copy. The basic facts: Mason, a PBY-Catalina pilot in Atlantic Fleet Squadron 82 out of Argentia, Newfoundland, sighted what he thought was a U-boat and dropped a brace of bombs. That was the full report he made by radio to base. In Navy public relations hands the report was transmuted into language that had Mason compared in the next morning's *New York Times* and elsewhere to Oliver Hazard Perry at the Battle of Lake Erie (1813), who had sent the terse and memorable message: "We have met the enemy and they are ours." The finely crafted message prepared for Mason was no less terse or memorable. It not only won front page play in newspapers across the country but, more important, it won rapid acceptance into the national locution. Few Americans who were alive at the time will not remember the immortal, sibilant, and alliterative words: "Sighted sub, sank same." A nation was thrilled. Mason was embarrassed. The Navy wordsmiths breathed a sigh of relief. For a few more days the pressure was off.

10

Course Home!

When Reinhard Hardegen turned away from the smoking *Malay* and set course for home he had every reason to believe that this last victim of U-*123* was headed for the bottom. The ship's emergency radio calls were increasingly desperate. Hardegen recorded one of them, in the original English, in his KTB: "SOS sinking rapidly, next ship please hurry, torpedoed, sinking"; and he added his own comment in German: "Well, we finally cracked this one, too."[1] On a 90-degree heading *123* made her fastest one-engine speed east out of the ten-meter water into depths where she could dive if need be. At 1300 (0600 CET) one hour before dawn, and while Kraxel was still welding the port cooler pipe, Hardegen sighted a large shadow on the port bow—a very large shadow, larger than he had ever seen at sea, except for capital ships and liners, and it was only four hundred meters away! And cutting across his course! God in Heaven! "Hard-a-starboard! Hard-a-starboard! *Starboard ahead emergency*! LI, give me every turn you've got! Maximum load! Push it!" Barth started shouting up wireless intercepts from the mammoth apparition: "She's *Kosmos II*, Norwegian whaling factory.... Calling nearby ships.... Now saying there's 'something wrong' about us.... Now calling the Navy to send planes! ... Now says she's going to ram!"

Stocky, thirty-six-year-old Einar Gleditsch, a native of Sandefjord, Norway, prior to the war the world's leading whaling port, had been at sea for eighteen years, always on whalers, and his biographical folder in the files of the Norwegian Shipping and Trade Mission in New York described him as "always a fearless, almost foolhardy, courageous fellow," very much like the characterization commonly made of Reinhard Hardegen—from whom he was now separated by only four hundred meters. Master since the year before of *Kosmos II*— reputedly at 16,966 GRT the largest cargo carrier in the world and now operating as a tanker—Gleditsch had sighted *Malay* burning between himself and shore, then had sighted a second ship or boat about which he signaled other nearby vessels, in English, that there was "something wrong" with it. He, the chief engineer, and the officer on watch studied the low black silhouette that was crossing his bow and watched it abruptly turn to starboard and away in the clear, smooth morning sea.

"It's a U-boat!" he decided. "Must have been the one that hit that tanker to shoreward. Give me 17 knots! Helmsman, stay on that boat's tail! Try to ram him!" With no gun on board, ramming was Gleditsch's only tactical weapon. He knew that if he could catch up his huge stem would splinter the German. Seventeen knots was the highest speed he had ever gotten from *Kosmos II* in ballast, but he ordered the chief engineer, if he knew any way he could force extra RPMs from the power plant, to do it quickly. "If the German can outrun us," Gleditsch said, "he's going to have to do it on the surface. If he tries diving that will slow him up and we've got him!"

On *123*'s bridge a shaken Hardegen yelled down the voice pipe: "LI, weld that pipe and install it or we'll be rammed! Do you understand?"

"Yes, Herr Kaleu!"

Schulz raced through the engineroom bumping Karlchen Latislaus aside as he went. "Karlchen, get ready to install the pipe— *emergency!*" When he reached the welding station in the aft torpedo room he hollered at Kraxel: "Finish it! Finish it! We're about to be rammed!"

Kraxel's torch raced along the fracture and when he was satisfied, he flung back his face shield, looked briefly at his work, and handed the pipe to Schulz. "It should hold, LI," he said in the wake of the disappearing Schulz who was already racing with the life-saving organ to the moribund port engine, where with pounding heart and little breath he assisted in the installation. In two minutes the port cylinder coughed to life, the temperatures held, and Karlchen clutched the engine shaft.

At once Hardegen on the bridge sensed the lurch forward. And none too soon! The whaler's blade was only seventy-five meters astern. But now they might be able to keep that distance. The thundering diesels bent to the task. The bow threw up a boiling wake. "Helmsman, rudder amidship!" Any turn, however slight, might slow them in their escape. With Hoffmann at his side he stared at the black giant bearing down on them. He did not need any reminding from Hoffmann: "Herr Kaleu," Hoffmann shouted over the diesels, "if we reach diving depth we still can't dive. Submerging will slow us up too much. He'll catch us. Even if we got the boat under, a deep draft ship like that would slice us across the top."

"Number One," Hardegen yelled back, "you better pray that the weld on the cooler pipe holds. If it goes out on us now we're finished." He paused and then added, "The water's too shallow for diving any-way. And we're headed south along the same depths. I'll turn seaward if we can open up some distance. If only we had two eels in the stern tubes! Our pursuer doesn't have any guns, I guess. He would have fired on us by now. We're sitting ducks." He turned to the voice pipe: "LI, what speed are we making?"

After a moment Schulz sang back, "Estimating eighteen-max with your freshening sea."

An edge of half a knot would be enough. Hardegen ordered the bridge watch to take a squatting position behind the fairwater in order to reduce the drag created by their heads and shoulders. It might be a futile gesture but everything, he reasoned, should be tried. The photographer Tölle, who always liked to be on the bridge with his camera when there was action, now made an appearance in the hatch opening. Hardegen angrily ordered him below.

Hoffmann said from a kneeling position, "Herr Kaleu, if she reaches our stern we can go rudder hard right and let the stern take the brunt with the rest of the boat flying off to starboard. Recommend moving all hands forward except engine crew and closing all passage-way hatches aft of the control room."

"Very well," Hardegen replied. "Order Schulz to get on it."

As movements and precautions got under way below Hardegen noticed that crewmen of the *Kosmos II* were standing on the bow watching them. He decided to wave to them, which he thought they would find disconcerting. Then he waved to port and starboard as though signaling other U-boats.[2] To Hoffmann he said, "Get Rafalski up here with the yellow signal light and have him simulate signals to other boats! And send up flares and the pistol!"

When Rafalski came up Hardegen bent below the cowling while the Puster went through the motions of his ruse. When it seemed enough Hardegen ordered Rafalski below while he looked up to gauge the distance between the hunter and the hunted. If he was not mistaken *123* had drawn ahead slightly. Just to gain a little more advantage he pointed the flare pistol at the hunter's bridge and fired. A brilliant flash of red light that must have blinded the Norwegian bridge poured cascades of incandescence down the ship's sides. Hardegen readied the pistol and fired again. The second flash, against the upper works, showed that the men who had stood on the bow had left that position, which was good, he thought, since he was relieved of the temptation to use the machine gun against them as a way of giving the ship's master second thoughts. Now it did appear certain that *123* was pulling away, meter by meter. The pulsing diesels were at their limits, and the limits seemed to be enough. *Eins Zwei Drei* probably had a one-knot advantage. Hardegen looked at his chronometer. An hour had passed. He ordered the bridge watch to their feet.

"Look alive," he said. "So far we have outdistanced the whaler. But she called for Navy airplanes an hour ago. We're cornered. If the Navy had come, by this time we might have been finished. They may yet come. Keep your eyes on the horizon, particularly to the west. At the first sight of aircraft I'll order up the AA crew. We'll have to fight it out on the surface unless we can make deep water first. The sun's coming up. We are vulnerable as hell until we can dive. There's enough distance now between us and the whaler for the boat to turn east and then north. I doubt that our enemy will want to go north. Number One, execute gradual ten-degree turn to the east and north."

"Yes, Herr Kaleu."[3]

By an hour and fifty minutes into the chase, *123* was on a northeast heading and the *Kosmos II*, left behind, had resumed normal navigation. At 1420 (0720 ET) Barth on the wireless heard the chatter of Navy aircraft taking off from nearby Norfolk. Alerted, Hardegen changed course to 90 degrees and deeper water. An *hour and fifty minutes* after the whaler had first sent out the alarm and position, a single Navy aircraft circled over the position where the U-boat had last been sighted, but by that time a rainsquall developed and *123* dived successfully to avoid detection. The aircraft, unable to find its quarry, gave up and returned to base. Even in a situation where the enemy was trapped the USN could not prevail.

Now, in the peace and steady state of submerged cruising, a greatly relieved Hardegen composed this entry in his KTB:

> *Die Nacht der langen Messer war beendet*—"The night of the long knives was over." A drumbeat [Paukenschlag] with eight ships [he counted the two "mystery" ships and *Malay*], including three tankers and 53,060 GRT [more like 40,898]. It is a pity that the night I was off New York we did not have two mine-laying boats along. And tonight we could have used 10 to 20 boats instead of one. Every boat would have gotten its fill. I have sighted no fewer than 20 steamers, some with their lights on. All of them hugged the coast, the darkened ones not visible until two or three nautical miles away. . . . Monitoring the 600 meter band proved a real boon since I learned not only about the removal of lightships but about the recognition signals of the buoys that replaced them. In addition, I received U.S. assistance from wireless bearings and reports about traffic density. After the first sinkings, though, wireless traffic became very restricted.[4]

When night fell Hardegen surfaced and sent a signal listing the number of ships and tonnage sunk by *123* to BdU at Lorient. Not many hours later he received acknowledgment from the Lion: TO THE DRUM-BEATER [PAUKENSCHLÄGER] HARDEGEN. BRAVO! YOU BEAT THE DRUM WELL. BDU.[5] As the boat made its way eastward on a course for home via Bermuda, Hardegen lay in his bunk savoring the recognition and composing in his mind the reports that he would make to the Lion personally on his return to base: Targets abound off the coast from New York to Cape Hatteras. . . . Most are lighted. . . . Only the British seem to have guns. . . . American defenses against U-boats almost nonexistent. . . . Sighted few destroyers or patrol craft. . . . Aircraft untrained and inefficient. . . . Norwegian whaler gave us our only real fight. . . . Coastal towns and cities fully illuminated. . . . Lighthouses, buoys, and beacons operating as in peacetime, though some lightships have been withdrawn.

Close by his head Hardegen could hear the slap of the surface rollers against the port side plating while his bunk pitched and yawed with the rest of the boat's interior, now a much more relaxed environment than at any time since Christmas. Officers and crewmen moved through the passageway with a lighter, slower step, their conversations, for a long while past edged with the baritone of tension and fatigue, now taking on a bright tenor sparkle, punctuated by frequent loud laughter. With permission Rafalski played swing music from WBT, Charlotte, North Carolina, through the loudspeakers: "Perfidia," "The Hut-Sut Song," "Chattanooga Choo Choo." In the galley Hannes banged his pots around in time with the music while "Icke" the galley mate flattened empty tin cans to the same beat. Other duties were being performed with the same animation, born of the knowledge that for a while the war was over and everyone was going home. There was a nimbleness to the movements of the bridge watch as they mouse-squeaked by in their gum boots, of the hands detailed to dump trash and garbage overside in weighted sacks, and of the stewards as they passed through the compartments with the obligatory daily ration of lemon juice. Not only the need but the desire of the men for exercise was manifest. Calf muscles had gone soft and slack. And everyone anticipated the day when he could emerge from this eternally soggy fug into dry, bright sunlight. It had been twenty-eight days since *123* left La Rade de Lorient, and all hands felt the physical effects of the patrol. Psychologically, though, they seemed not to have suffered much. Where other crews on long patrols were known to have developed *Blechkoller,* the tin-can neurosis that came from prolonged nervous strain in a U-boat's unnatural enclosure, this crew's mental state was holding up quite well, it seemed to Hardegen. No doubt the boat's huge success was one reason. And now the anticipation of dry land, baths, girls, Beck's, Martell, and Iron Crosses lifted spirits further. Certainly of this boat, Hardegen thought, the old sea saying was true: *Je länger die Fahrt, um so besser die Kameradschaft* — "The longer the voyage, the better the crew's spirit."

In the torpedo rooms fore and aft the mixers, with no more eels to mix, passed the time playing skat, or reading, or telling stories, or sleeping. With the eels gone the bunks were in down position fulltime, and more than the usual number were occupied since, on turning for home, the Old Man had ordered the sour-smelling sheets and pillow cases turned to their clean sides. With the pressure off, sleep came easily, especially to the strains of swing music mixed with the harmonic throb of the diesels. When not on watch the officers now spent a large amount of time playing chess and the board game Mensch ärgere Dich nicht.[6] With his sextant and chronometer Walter Kaeding was often on the bridge to catch a round of stars or sun lines; then, in his own high state of anticipation, he would go below and step off four-hour positions on the chart track home. In the engineroom Karlchen Latislaus nursed his "babies" along, the starboard clutched to the screws, the port to the dynamotors, for charging the batteries. Every hour he lubricated the rocker arms and entered the cooling water temperatures in the engine logs. He hoped he would not again have to strain his babies to escape whalers. A member of the bridge watch had described the close call to him. What an impertinence, Karlchen thought, a factory ship pursuing a U-boat! He whistled through his teeth, however, when he recalled how near the boat had been to having one engine down because of the broken cooler pipe. If Kraxel had taken any longer than he had *Eins Zwei Drei* would be history in the mouth of that slavering Leviathan.

Hoffmann and von Schroeter huddled in the control room debating whether it would have been wiser for the Old Man to have turned toward shore instead of holding to a straight course south to evade the whaler. Hoffmann thought that the boat should have risked the small loss of speed in a turn to the west since the whaler would not have pursued them into shoal water where she was certain to run aground. Both officers ended up agreeing that the Old Man's decision was the correct one, however, since it succeeded. They laughed when they both spoke together the same line, now a commonplace on board: "Well, he pulled it off again!"[7] The LI, Schulz, half listening nearby, was having some fun with Tölle, telling the photographer the kinds of things, Schulz knew, that Tölle did not like hearing. When the dynamotors charged the batteries, as they were doing now, Schulz told him, a high level of hydrogen built up in the battery compartments. If any spark got to that hydrogen from any source, be it motor, wireless, or strike of metal against metal, it would cause an explosion and fire, and that in turn would fill the hull with chlorine gas, and Tölle knew what that meant, did he not? As Tölle nodded sickly, Schulz was confident that he could identify the one person on board who wanted to be back home more than anyone else.

22 January. 2400 to 0400 (CET), Hardegen made a reconnaissance of the coast of Bermuda on his passage eastward, noting for the KTB that the towns of Hamilton and Saint George were as brilliantly lit as coastal cities and towns on the U.S. seaboard. Indeed, the night defenses here seemed to be based on illumination. Floodlights swept the harbor entrances, and twice the bridge sighted star-shell barrages at Hamilton Harbor. Flashing buoys were everywhere. Mount Hill light-

house was out but was visible as a silhouette against the night sky. One could easily see hotels, single homes, the radio station tower, and other lighted features. There was no sign of mines or of nets. Hardegen did add, however: "A very strong tidal current prevails here. U-boats will have to navigate very carefully."[8] The next day BdU transmitted these observations to all Atlantic boats.[9]

The KTB for the next day's travel recorded only one practice emergency dive and a cleaning of the 10.5 gun. But for 24 January two short entries over Hardegen's signature represented major moments in his life. The first, at 1600 (CET), recorded: "We just listened to the special shortwave announcement [from Germany] about the successes of U-boats in American waters. Our ship was mentioned by name."[10] The second, six lines long, recorded the realization of one of Hardegen's chief professional goals. At 1740 (CET), he walked into the control room to find it tightly crowded with most of his officers and crewmen. What was going on? LI Schulz, with a broad grin, addressed the Old Man.

"Herr Kaleu! Your officers and men salute you! On this war cruise you have left standing orders that all wireless signals addressed to this boat are to be brought to you instantly after decrypting. This one time we have disobeyed you long enough for Kraxel to manufacture something in the aft torpedo room. I have the honor now to read to you two F.T.s received by our boat. The first: TO HARDEGEN. I EXTEND TO YOU AND YOUR BRAVE CREW MY HEARTIEST CONGRATULATIONS ON THE AWARD OF THE KNIGHT'S CROSS. SUPREME NAVAL COMMAND. Shortly after Admiral Raeder's signal the following arrived from Admiral Dönitz: TO HARDEGEN. HEARTY CONGRATULATIONS ON THE KNIGHT'S CROSS. BDU.[11]

"Herr Kaleu, the officers and crew decided that you should not have to wait until reaching *Isère* to receive your Ritterkreuz. And so Kraxel here has fashioned our own version for you to have in the meantime. You will notice that on the reverse side we have engraved the number of ships, sixteen, that the boat has sunk since you took command, together with the tonnages. Congratulations, sir."

Schulz then placed the Ritterkreuz copy with its attached ribbon around the Old Man's neck while the *Zentrale* rang with cheers. Hardegen energetically shook the hands of Schulz, Hoffmann, von Schroeter, and the petty officers, then joined in the general merriment as Amstein's accordion struck up sailors' songs.

·   ·   ·

1431 hours (CET), 25 January, position CC 7927, boat on the surface in state 4 seas under mostly cloudy skies, winds at 4 from the southwest, daylight visibility twelve miles, course 070 degrees. The voice pipe barked: "Commander to the bridge!" Hardegen bounded up the ladder with his 7 × 50s and trained them along the starboard lookout's point. "Steamer on starboard bow, Herr Kaleu," one of them said. "Yes," Hardegen responded, drawing out the word. "Our Sunday dinner." He called down the pipe: "Number Two to the bridge!" When von Schroeter arrived Hardegen showed him the mast tops and said, "I estimate it at nine knots, course two twenty, crossing to port of our reciprocal. We'll submerge and wait for it. Have your gun crews stand by. With no eels left we'll have to take this one out by artillery. You, Schulz, and I will need to coordinate. Meet in the control room. Now let's get under. *Alarm!*"

When Schulz had the boat at periscope depth and trimmed, the Old Man held his conference. They would attempt to sink this vessel by artillery alone, he said, and employ machine-gun fire at the bridge and at any sighted gun positions. If the target was unarmed, von Schroeter was to direct his cannon fire at the waterline below the stack since that was where the engine room would be. He was to use both the 10.5 forward and the 3.7 aft. If the steamer turned out to be armed, von Schroeter would have to concentrate his fire on the gun or guns and neutralize them before disabling the steamer's hull and power. He reminded the two officers that in a daylight artillery duel the U-boat would have nowhere near the advantage it had in a surprise torpedo attack. A gunfight meant hand-to-hand battle. It meant finding out who had the better training, the better aim on a tossing deck, the stronger nerves, and the greater luck. He asked them to remember that the goddess of fortune always smiled on them when they refused to give up.

"LI," he said, "you take charge inside the boat. Have every man ready for damage and fire control. Be sure that the ammunition chain works efficiently and safely. Number Two, have your gun crew steadied down. With the swell upstairs it's going to require cool minds and level hands to load and aim. Be sure the aimer, layer, and loader are strapped in. I'll navigate at a speed that will wet you the least, and I'll maneuver against the wind so that your sight will not be hindered by our own powder smoke. Have Tölle come up last. All right, everybody, stand by!"

As the gun crew gathered in the control room von Schroeter

talked to them as an athletic coach might speak to his players, calming them down, reminding them of their assignments. He and they would be first up the ladder after the Old Man. In the passageway forward the petty officers were forming up the party that would hand-cradle the shells through the tower to the bridge and from there down to the two guns. Hardegen climbed up the ladder to the periscope saddle, where Hoffmann had been tracking the steamer's approach at high-power magnification. As the Old Man placed his right eye into the lens cup Hoffmann reported, "It's armed, Herr Kaleu. I can make out a deck gun aft and automatic weapons on the bridge. I estimate three thousand GRT, a freighter, and since it has guns, British."

"Yes, that's about right, Number One. I see it has a hoop around the bow for attaching minesweeping equipment. Heavily loaded—sheds on deck. A five-centimeter gun, it looks like, with a shield, on a circular platform aft. Machine guns on the bridge. Number Two, go after their machine guns with ours. We can't have them hurting our men on deck. Now here comes someone—a sailor with a load of wash that he's hanging on a line. Maybe he won't have to take it down."

As tension built in the control room Hardegen continued to watch intently as the target came on in the bright daylight. "One thousand meters . . . We'll surface at six hundred . . . Use E motors and planes, LI . . . nine hundred . . . eight hundred . . . Stand by to surface! . . . seven hundred . . . *Periscope down! Surface!*"

"*Turmluk ist frei,*" Schulz sang out. "*Boot ist raus!*" "Hatch is free. Boat is up!" The gathered deck force clambered noisily up the ladder, the Old Man in the lead. Hardegen took in the scene with his glasses while the gun crews took their positions and the two guns received their first shells from the crew chain. What must emotions be like on that steamer? he wondered. No doubt its seamen shuddered inside to see this huge metal shark suddenly break the surface and bare its teeth. "Permission to fire!" Hardegen called fore and aft through the megaphone. The target was now four hundred meters distant. With a sharp clang the 10.5 breach closed, and a second later the muzzle erupted with the first shot, which cleaned the barrel. It fell well aft of the target. The second shot hit below the bridge, the third below the stack. From von Schroeter's gun dense brown cordite smoke trailed aft across the conning tower. But now the enemy gun crew was training its weapon in *123*'s direction, and an incoming shell plunged into the water to port of the U-boat sending up a large column. "Take out that gun crew!" Hardegen yelled to the 2-cm machine-gun crew behind him, but they yelled back, "Herr Kaleu, the firing pin is broken!" Now four more incoming shells ricocheted off the water sending some fragments banging against the U-boat's hull and others whistling past Hardegen's head on the bridge. One puncture of the pressure hull, Hardegen worried, and *123* would not be able to dive anymore. The enemy gun crew had continued to fire while von Schroeter's gun was pounding away at the hull beneath them—Hardegen would say later: "It must have been awful for that gun crew to feel our explosions just below them. I have to show my respect to the enemy: They stuck to their battle stations."[12] But finally the U-boat's aim and range combined to hit squarely on the target's gun pivot, destroying the gun and killing the crew. Von Schroeter's 10.5 crew raised their arms and cheered. A few more shots set the bridge on fire and silenced the machine guns. The freighter blew off steam, slowed, and began settling by the stern. The surviving crewmen went into lifeboats while the wireless operator, among the last to leave, put out repeated SSS signals. On *123* the belowdecks crew one after the other were invited to the bridge to see the dramatic picture of a burning, sinking ship. Karlchen enjoyed the fresh air more than the scenery, before which his darkened eyes narrowed and blinked. Meanwhile the 2-cm gun crew replaced the firing pin and set the firing chamber for one shot to test the weapon.

POW! The barrel exploded! A fragment entered the back of Tölle's skull, and the photographer collapsed, bleeding badly, near the aft periscope where he had been taking photographs. Hannes, the cook, who was on the machine-gun crew, was hit, but not seriously, by a fragment in the left thigh. Blood poured from Tölle's head and he began vomiting. Hardegen ordered the wounded men taken below. A crewman picked up Tölle's camera and continued taking pictures while Hardegen returned his attention to the steamer, which was making water heavily by the stern. Navigating at dead slow he approached the lifeboats and asked their occupants the name of the victim. "*Culebra,*" an officer answered, "three thousand forty-four GRT out of Liverpool with a general cargo." He went on to say that their boats were full of water and they had only one bucket, which was punctured. Hardegen ordered the forward gun crew below to round up a few buckets, some bread, lard, sausages, canned foods, and a knife for opening the cans. The survivors said that they probably had sufficient water. Kaeding then plotted their precise position, 35-30N, 53-25W, and gave them a course to the Bermudas. Hardegen observed in his KTB: "They were all very thankful and waved to us when we left."[13] It was the kind of solicitude that Hardegen could take time to show, seaman to seamen, in the mid-Atlantic "air-gap," where he was unlikely to be surprised by enemy defenders.

Unexpectedly, *Culebra*'s ammunition and flares magazine exploded and the U-boatmen and survivors alike were treated to a daytime fireworks display that included descending parachute flares. Hardegen ordered von Schroeter to shoot more holes into the waterline, after which the mutilated vessel sank over her sternposts, and cargo stored in the sheds on deck broke loose and slid overside. The "general cargo" turned out to be disassembled warplanes with RAF wing markings—red, white, blue, and yellow roundels. Finally, *Culebra*'s bow went vertical and she disappeared with all her mice. Hardegen resumed normal surface navigation, course 070, both engines half, and went below to assume the role of doctor. With Rafalski's help he managed after a long while to stop Tölle's profuse bleeding, but the photographer had suffered a serious concussion and the barrel fragment could not be removed without surgery, for which the Old Man and Rafalski were untrained and unequipped. On *123*'s patrol to Freetown the year before a doctor had been on board. Would that they had one now, Hardegen reflected, especially as treatment of the large skull wound became as unpleasant as it was delicate. Hardegen gave Tölle injections of morphine to ease his pain. The five-centimeter thigh injury to Hannes required only a dressing. For the first time in Hardegen's career as a commander he experienced the hurt of war. He had often stood where the bitter wind of death blew across the waves, but this was the first time that that wind had even touched his own boat and crew, causing, fortunately this time, only the loss of blood, yet at the same time offering a somber, ghostly counsel that bade him remember how many mariners who had lived by the sword died by the same blade.

The Old Man noticed that on board some of the light step and lilt of voice of the last several days had vanished. He could have passed up *Culebra* and sustained a pleasant, uneventful homeward cruise. But the Lion would have expected better, so long as there was ammunition for the guns. And that, he determined, would be his mind if he encountered anyone else across his course.

Life had never been easy for tanker motorman Wilfred Larsen, of Bergen, Norway. Raised by a foster mother who beat him as regularly as she fed him, Wilfred escaped to sea when he was seventeen, first on board the training ship *Statsraad Lehmkuhl*, then on the cargo ships *Grana* and *Salta*. In April 1940 the *Salta*, together with six other Norwegian vessels, was interned at Dakar in French Senegal on the coast of West Africa. During the long internment many of the Norwegian crewmen became half-crazed on board their ships in the intense heat. Many engaged in fistfights at the slightest provocation. Many escaped and were captured. Finally, after thirteen hot months, nineteen-year-old Wilfred succeeded with several others in rowing four days in a lifeboat to the British colony of Gambia, and from there he made his way as a seaman to the United States and a new ship. She was *Pan Norway*, a Norwegian motor tanker, 9,231 GRT, built in 1931, owned by Per Holm Shipping Company in Oslo but chartered since the German occupation of Norway by the Allied company Nortraship. On 27 January 1942, the tanker, with Wilfred aboard, was en route in ballast from Halifax to Aruba in the Dutch West Indies to load aviation gasoline for Britain. Like the rest of the all-Norwegian crew, Wilfred feared the "underwater" menace posed by the German U-boat. To him the presence of a 1918-vintage 12-cm gun on the tanker's aft deck provided only the barest comfort. Wilfred knew from the SSS received from *Culebra*, news of which passed swiftly to all hands, that a U-boat was nearby, and he feared its sinister presence— deep down in the ocean as he imagined it—feared that its "beastly" and "bloodthirsty" crew would at any moment turn *Pan Norway* into one huge iron casket. "All we could do," he remembered forty years later, "was to prepare ourselves to abandon ship. We placed extra water tanks in the lifeboats, extra food and cigarettes." The crew, he said, had a near palpable sense of the U-boats. "We were completely surrounded. We could not see them, but we could sense their presence—a feeling that is impossible to describe. We stood double-watch at the gun. We stared into the night until our eyes hurt."[14]

Just off watch that evening, while he was having supper, Wilfred's nightmare took form as an earsplitting bang and blinding flash filled the mess room. An artillery shell had smashed into the tanker's starboard side. With the brilliant light followed by total darkness, Wilfred could not see anything for a while as he groped his way toward the gun deck. There, after his eyes adjusted to the dark, he saw the U-boat of his fears, a single sharklike form moving boldly on the starboard surface. Fascinated and terrified at the same time, he watched the assailant's foredeck gun spit red flashes as it loosed one, two, three more exploding projectiles at his ship's side. The engine room took one of the hits, slowing way, and then the stern erupted in flames. It was no longer possible to man the gun, but Wilfred observed that machine guns on the bridge had taken the attacker under fire. He watched the U-boat circle astern of the tanker and come up on her port side. Then, knowing that Abandon Ship had been his only hope from the beginning, he raced for a starboard lifeboat. As he climbed into it the bridge machine guns were taken out by answering fire from the U-boat, and the bridge signalman began sending SURRENDER in Morse on the signal lamp. The U-boat's gun ceased fire for ten minutes, apparently to allow the lifeboats to get down and away.

Only two boats put out successfully, the rest having been damaged by the shelling. Wilfred succeeded in holding his boat's descent on the davits until his best friend climbed in. They had had their photograph taken together on deck just the day before. Where had he been? The friend refused to say, even to speak. Obviously traumatized, he sat in the boat looking blankly, mutely ahead. Only many years later did Wilfred learn from his friend's wife that, when the first shell struck, his friend had dashed below to the cabin they shared to rescue something precious and, while he was there, a second shell hit, jamming the cabin door. As his friend struggled to get out a third shell exploded against the ship, unjamming the door. In the lifeboat he was simply unable to handle the incongruity that the U-boat commander had both imprisoned him and released him. The lifeboat descended successfully down the falls. Wilfred was unconcerned that he had left behind eight hundred rare stamps and a prized sweater that he had just purchased in Halifax. To save himself was enough. Later, congratulating himself on his discretion, he would learn that only the steward failed to get away in a lifeboat or life jacket. (He had gone below to save a picture of his wife and was not seen again.)

Wilfred's lifeboat pulled away from the starboard side of the doomed ship. Other men, not so lucky, clung to preservers and wood planks in the water, kicking hard with their feet to escape the tanker's death throes, while on the opposite side to them, unseen, the U-boat's artillery began pounding again at the port waterline. After a time the U-boat came around to their side, where Wilfred could see the energetic Germans at their deadly work. The bombardment, which was incredibly loud, continued for two and a half hours before *Pan Norway*, by then a sieve, lifted her bow skyward and began a macabre dance, forty meters up, twenty meters down, each time expelling air from her interior, until, at last, a grotesque ballerina in the footlights of flaming oil, she passed below the dark water. At that instant the U-boat turned toward the survivors, causing Wilfred and his companions to shout in fear. He knew that now it was their turn to die. "I was petrified when the U-boat came toward us," he said forty years later. "The sight of that dark monster I shall never forget. Nor will I forget the emotions that filled me during those long seconds when I felt sure I was about to die. I was barely twenty years old. I had not seen enough of the world. I had not had many experiences. It did not seem fair that I should die at that moment."[15] But, just as abruptly, to the Norwegians' huge relief, the U-boat veered off at high speed toward the northeast.

From the time of his first shots at this unfortunate tanker that chanced to intersect his course, Reinhard Hardegen had noticed another ship, fully illuminated, about three nautical miles to the northeast. He guessed—correctly—that it was a neutral. He intended to investigate the vessel when he finished with *Pan Norway,* whose name he could clearly see from the range, 250 meters, where he fired the 10.5. Before the tanker's machine guns were disabled, the Norwegians had managed to make numerous hits on the U-boat's conning tower and deck, but lacking the punch of artillery, the bullets had been no more than bee stings on the steel. *Eins Zwei Drei* did suffer one casualty when a cartridge case fell down the bridge hatch into the control room where it struck one of the control room machinists in the face. Hardegen sutured the man's split upper lip, but his broken teeth would have to wait for a dentist's chair in Lorient. After two hours of firing, ammunition for the 10.5 gave out and Hardegen peppered the tanker with the 3.7. At last the riddled hull went under, and Hardegen turned his glasses on the lighted ship in the distance. It lay to as it had for several hours, as though not wanting to miss any of the long-drawn-out punishment that *Pan Norway* was absorbing. Hardegen decided to go after it, not to shoot, since, one, he was out of shells, and two, the ship was obviously neutral, but in order to direct the ship to pick up survivors. It was in that spirit rather than in the one Wilfred Larsen feared that the commander of U-*123* approached the Norwegians. He wanted to check on their condition, which he could do easily by the light of the oil flames. Satisfied that they could stay afloat until his return, he then called for both engines ahead full and raced after the neutral. What happened next Hardegen described after the action in his KTB. It is a moving account. Perhaps, later, back in Lorient, the Lion—he who had said, "We must be hard in this war"—reacted to this entry when he read it with mixed emotions, but nearly five decades later the reader of the German text is glad to have the chance, amid so many depictions of carnage and destruction, to acknowledge humanity and compassion in a protagonist when it appears:

The previously mentioned light was a neutral ship, waiting three nautical miles away. We sailed up to it and to our surprise it took to its heels. We pursued at full speed and, using our blinker light, we asked it to stop, which it did. It was the Greek *Mount Aetna* sailing under a Swiss flag. We approached and asked that she pick up the survivors. She turned to do so and we led her to two lifeboats that we had observed previously. Then we went back to the site of the sinking, where we found a sailor floating in the water and we picked him up. Since he was injured by shell fragments and exhausted from struggling several hours in the water it was difficult to question him. Besides, he spoke only Norwegian.

This seaman informed us that the crew were caught by the war in an English port and were forced to sail for the English. The captain was English, the crew Norwegian. They had just sailed from England to Halifax and now they were en route to Aruba. When we confronted him with the fact that their position and course hardly corresponded to an Aruba run he said that the ship had taken a circuitous route in order to avoid U-boats. They had not sighted us. After the first of our shells hit panic broke out on board. The crew fought each other for space in the lifeboats. This man was already in a lifeboat when a "friend" punched him in the face and knocked him overboard. The blow cost him his front teeth and the lifeboat passed him by in the water. So he was lucky that we found him, and he was very thankful.

We then noticed that the Swiss ship was leaving the scene. We pursued her, stopped her with our blinker light, and handed over this survivor. The Swiss had picked up 29 men and that group told the captain that they were the entire crew. We knew that [*Pan Norway*] had a crew of 51. It turned out that those already taken on board were afraid that we would sink the *Mount Aetna*, too, and so they had persuaded the captain to steam off. We, however, had seen many more survivors of the tanker clinging to debris in the water, and we ordered the captain to return and save them, which he did. He thanked us warmly for not sinking his ship and for allowing him to rescue the others. We turned [back to our] course 070°. All the survivors lined the rails waving and wishing us luck for the voyage home.[16]

Something had to be done for Tölle. His wound was festering, draining blood and pus, and he was in and out of delirium. The poor man needed a physician. Was there perhaps a German surface ship or U-boat nearby that had a doctor on board? Hardegen asked Rafalski to sift through his sheaf of intercepts. There was one possibility, Rafalski suggested, a German blockade runner named *Spreewald* that was proceeding north under the Norwegian camouflage *Elg*. Some days before she reported having reached *Punkt* (position) *Specht*, and her latest orders, also intercepted by *123*, directed her to rendezvous with U-*575* (Kptlt. Günther Heydemann) at *Punkt Sperber* for escort into Bordeaux. The rendezvous date was 29 January, just over a day away.[17] Hardegen huddled with Kaeding to check the navigational code book for these reference points: *Punkt Specht* was northeast of South America, *Sperber* was mid-Atlantic in square CD. *123* was already entering the southwest corner of CD. There was no doubt they could make *Sperber* in time. But did *Spreewald* have a doctor? Hardegen drafted a signal to be sent to BdU: HAVE JUST SUNK PAN NORWAY IN CC8691 BY CANNON. OUT OF AMMUNITION. NET 66135 GRT. SURVIVORS PUT ON MOUNT AETNA. IN CASE PHYSICIAN IS ABOARD SPREEWALD REQUEST HIS SERVICES. HAVE ONE SERIOUSLY AND ONE LIGHTLY WOUNDED. PROPAGANDA CAMERAMAN TÖLLE HAS SPLINTER IN BACK OF HEAD, MUCH LOSS OF BLOOD, CONCUSSION OF BRAIN. CAN BE AT RENDEZVOUS BY 29 JANUARY. FROM THIS POINT WILL KEEP WIRELESS SILENCE AND PROCEED ACCORDING TO INSTRUCTIONS. 40 CUBIC METERS FUEL REMAINING.[18]

A preliminary response came in during the early morning hours of 28 January directing *123* to steer for CD 3800: FURTHER INSTRUCTIONS FOLLOW. Although Hardegen would have no way of knowing it, *Spreewald,* a 5,083 GRT cargo-passenger motor ship of the Hamburg-American Line, was one of a sizable number of German merchant vessels that had been caught unawares in distant waters when war broke out in 1939. Most steamed to neutral countries, where they were interned. *Spreewald,* which was off the U.S. West Coast at the time, proceeded to Japan and thence to Manchuria, where she remained for two years. In December 1941 she was pressed into service as a "rubber transport." Her holds were filled with desperately needed raw rubber from French Indochina, also with tin, tungsten, and quinine; and the German naval attaché in Tokyo arranged to have her passenger space occupied by British merchant seamen–prisoners whose ships had been intercepted in Asian waters by the German auxiliary cruiser (Raider G) *Kormoran*. Several aliases and disguises were provided the ship, including the names *Elg* and *Brittany* (British). She sailed in mid-December and followed an independent course along the loneliest routes that Naval Staff in Berlin could devise. (Her chances of proceeding undetected were good: Between April 1941 and May 1942 twelve of sixteen blockade runners from the Far East arrived safely in French ports, including the Italian *Cortelazzo*, which made Bordeaux on the same day that *123* sunk *Pan Norway* with 5,238 tons of cargo, including rubber, peanuts, edible oils, fats, tea, hemp, and sisal.)

Late on the twenty-eighth (CET) Hardegen received a lengthy signal addressed to both him and Heydemann. In it he learned that *Spreewald* did indeed have a physician on board and that he had been advised of *123*'s medical needs. The signal went on to inform the two commanders that *Spreewald* was adjusting her speed down from 9.8 knots in order to make point *Sperber* no earlier than on the morning of the thirtieth, for rendezvous on that date or on the thirty-first. It was not expected, since the position selected was in the British-U.S. "air gap," that three vessels meeting together posed a special danger. However, if the ship and U-boats failed to meet as planned, *Spreewald* was to continue on her assigned course forthwith, without waiting, without searching, and without transmitting. As for Hardegen, he was not to tarry at the position any longer than 1 February. When two hundred nautical miles distant from *Spreewald*, taking into account the vessel's direction of advance and speed, he was to report results of the encounter to BdU.[19]

At 1131 (CET) on 30 January, *123* reached the assigned point and reduced speed to steerageway. U-575 was not observed, nor was *Spreewald*. Hardegen waited. And waited. Almost exactly twenty-four hours later he wrote laconically in the war diary: " 'U-Heydemann' in sight. I approach and heave to alongside. We exchange information and ideas. He has been here for three days. Last night at 2330 he saw a wake and heard engine noises. Since I lay to at the time with engines down it could not have been I. He suspects an enemy submarine. We line up and wait for *Spreewald*. At 1900 an F.T. arrives announcing that

Spreewald was torpedoed today in BE 7142. We take a heading to that position to hunt for survivors."[20]

This stunning news left the Old Man and his officers wondering what in the world had gone wrong? *Spreewald* was sunk two whole marine squares away to the east-northeast! How had she ended up *there?* Hardegen reckoned that he could not reach that position before dawn on 4 February. And who had sunk her? A vexed BdU wanted to know the same. Rafalski handed the Old Man a signal from Lorient: REPORT AT ONCE WHO TORPEDOED A SHIP IN BE7140 AND GIVE DETAILS.[21] By perverse coincidence Kptlt. Peter Cremer, commander of U-*333*, was at that very moment originating a proud transmission to BdU: IN BE7114 JUST SANK A COMBINED PASSENGER AND FREIGHT STEAMER 8000 GRT WITH MY LAST STEAM TORPEDOES. TWO HITS AT 350 METERS. PROBABLY LOADED WITH AMMUNITION SINCE A BIG EXPLOSION AFTER SECOND HIT. APPEARANCE DARK GREY HULL WHITE SUPERSTRUCTURE ONE STACK TWO SLIM MASTS WITHOUT CROSS TREES. FIVE BIG HATCHES TWO BIG POLE MASTS IN FRONT OF BRIDGE. ROUND DECK. NO FLAG NO NEUTRALITY MARK. ONE CANNON ON STERN. ZIGZAGGING ON COURSE 060.[22]

When Cremer's signal arrived at Kernével, Admiral Dönitz was not impressed. Naval Staff in Berlin were furious: A tart entry in their war diary for that day read: "This loss was extremely painful and was caused by an unforgivable error, which should not have happened under any circumstances. The lost cargo of 3,365 tons of rubber and 250 tons of tin is irreplaceable, and of great consequence given the dire raw materials situation."[23] The British, too, learned of the sinking, not only from Bletchley Park's decrypt of Cremer's success report, but also from reception in the clear of *Spreewald*'s distress signal on the six hundred-meter wavelength: receivers at Land's End were surprised to hear an unknown "British" ship named *Brittany* transmitting "SOS . . . sunk by submarine . . . position 45N 25W." At sea not only U-*123* and U-*575* went to the scene but Lorient vectored seven other nearby boats, including Cremer's, to search the area for survivors. Dönitz, however, specified: "Shipwrecked personnel and those in lifeboats are not to be told that a German U-boat was responsible for the sinking."[24] U-*105* found twenty-four German merchant seamen and fifty-eight British prisoners aboard three lifeboats and three rafts on 1 February. U-*123* was hampered in making the search area in time to help by her low fuel state and need to proceed no faster than seven knots economy cruise if she did not want to be towed into Lorient; and Hardegen was not about to have that kind of humiliation compromise his triumphant return to base. Subsequently he learned that most of the *Spreewald* crew and passengers had been rescued.[25] On 3 February he could record: "Tölle's condition slightly improved." Four days later he heard on a radio broadcast that the *Pan Norway* survivors had been landed at Lisbon.

As for the unfortunate Cremer, when he returned to the U-boat base of La Pallice near La Rochelle on the French coast at the end of a forty-five-day patrol, he was not met with any of the usual bands, flowers, girls, or other homecoming trappings that a boat on an extended Feindfahrt had a right to expect. Instead, filthy and unshaved, KTB and wireless log in hand, he was whisked away by an official car on the long drive to Kernével, where Dönitz's duty officer informed him that a court-martial was there assembled to try him on the charge of "disobedience in action, manslaughter, and damage to military property." Before the court Cremer successfully argued that it was *Spreewald*'s fault she was sunk, not his. Before his departure on patrol he was told that he should exercise care in approaching vessels within certain naval squares, since those were squares used by transiting German blockade-runners. Square BE, however, was not among the squares thus proscribed. Furthermore, the vessel conformed exactly to a British type, so much so that she even used an English ship name and the English language in sending a distress signal. Finally, he argued, he had learned through wireless intercepts that *Spreewald* was under orders to have been in square CD on the date she was sunk, not hundreds of miles removed in BE. So the fault lay with the blockade-runner, not with U-333. When Kptlt. Günter Hessler, Dönitz's son-in-law, supported Cremer's line of argument, the court voted acquittal. No explanation for *Spreewald*'s alteration of course and failure to rendezvous with U-123 and U-575 in square CD has appeared.[26] Cremer went on to conduct successful operations off the Florida coast in May 1942, eventually won a Knight's Cross, and served as commander of Dönitz's bodyguard battalion when the latter became head of the German Reich following Adolf Hitler's suicide in 1945.

The same night (6–7 February) that "Ajax" Bleichrodt took on fuel from Kals (U-130), he scored with one hit and two misses on the 3,531-GRT Panamanian steamer *Halcyon*. With that action, the last torpedo launchings by the combined force of U-123, 66, 125, 109, and 130, Operation Paukenschlag came to an end. As the boats steamed home their crewmen sewed and labeled success pennants to fly from the attack periscopes when they reentered their base. *Eins Zwei Drei*'s crew labeled ten pennants for a total claim of 66,135 GRT. The actual number of ships put in the locker was nine, if one accepts the two "mystery" ships; *Malay* was damaged not sunk. The actual estimated tonnage, using the *San José* and *Brazos* numbers for the two "mystery" ships, and excluding *Malay*, was plus or minus 53,173. U-*130* (Kals) was the second most successful boat with six sinkings and 43,583 GRT claimed; the actual numbers were six and 36,993. U-*66* (Zapp) sewed pennants for five ships sunk and 50,000 GRT; the actual numbers were five and 33,456. U-*109* (Bleichrodt) claimed four ships (excluding the 6,082 GRT *Empire Kingfisher*, which Dr. Rohwer gives him) and 29,330 GRT; the actual numbers appear to be four and 27,651 GRT. U-*125* (Folkers) returned with only one pennant, claimed tonnage 7,000, actual 5,666; *125* also had one ship damaged.

Altogether the Drumbeat boats accounted for twenty-five ships sunk for a total actual tonnage of (probably) 156,939. Lower by one ship and 30,902 GRT than the numbers claimed, the actual figures are not only respectable—they compare favorably, for example, with the 152,000 GRT sunk by eight boats in the famous "Night of the Long Knives" in October 1940—they fully justified the characterization later made by U-boatmen of the Drumbeat operation and the American campaign launched by it as "the Second Happy Time" and "the Great American Turkey Shoot." More than that, they established for the time being German naval supremacy over the United States Navy in that force's home waters. The Ubootwaffe had tweaked the USN's nose, had dared it to come out and fight, which it did not, and had destroyed masses of vital Allied war matériel often within sight of U.S. coastal cities and shoreward towns. This first strike, the beginning of America's Atlantic Pearl Harbor, had exceeded even Dönitz's expectations. Add to that the concurrent successes of the twelve Group Ziethen VIIC boats in Newfoundland-Canadian waters, and it was clear to Dönitz, Godt, and their BdU staff that Kernével could sustain a mass destruction network three thousand and more miles from the French bases—a network that, given enough U-boats, could conceivably take Great Britain out of the war.[27]

As German domestic broadcasts touted the distant successes, particularly the "spectacular sinkings off the coast of the United States," "elation" and "great joy and surprise" over American "loss of prestige" swept the German nation, which, after the recent

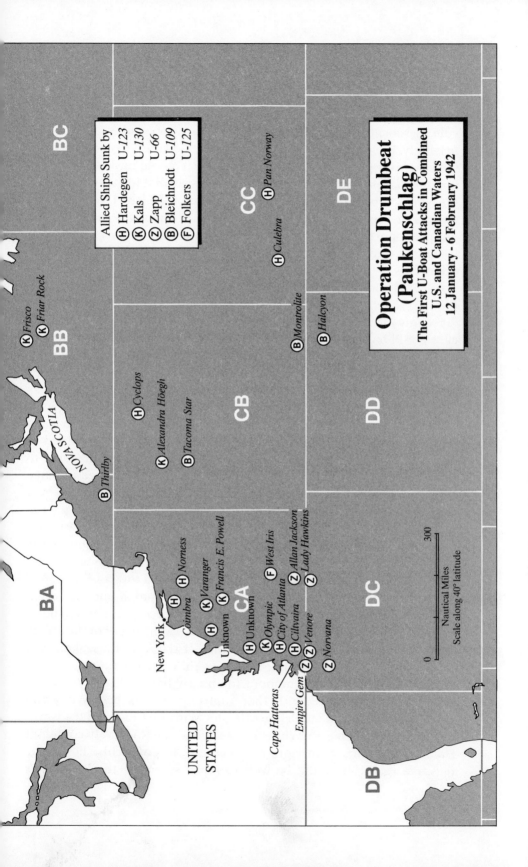

BA

BB

BC

NOVA SCOTIA

(K) Frisco
(K) Friar Rock

(B) Thirlby

(H) Cyclops
(K) Alexandra Höegh
(B) Tacoma Star

CB

CC

(H) Culebra

(H) Pan Norway

(B) Montrolite

(B) Halcyon

New York

Coimbra
(H)
Unknown (K) Varanger
(K) Francis E. Powell
(H) Unknown (F) West Iris
(K) Olympic (Z) Allan Jackson
(H) City of Atlanta (Z) Lady Hawkins
(H) Cilwira
(Z) Venore
(Z) Norvana

CA

UNITED
STATES

Cape Hatteras

Empire Gem

DB

DC

DD

DE

Allied Ships Sunk by

(H) Hardegen   U-123
(K) Kals   U-130
(Z) Zapp   U-66
(B) Bleichrodt U-109
(F) Folkers   U-125

0   300
Nautical Miles
Scale along 40° latitude

**Operation Drumbeat
(Paukenschlag)**
The First U-Boat Attacks in Combined
U.S. and Canadian Waters
12 January - 6 February 1942

Wehrmacht reverses before Moscow, badly needed some good news. Buoyed by the reports, Hitler celebrated the ninth anniversary of his rule by scornfully dismissing Roosevelt as "a poor idiot."[28] Not surprisingly, the perfectionist Karl Dönitz found cause to complain and lament: "It is perfectly clear that 'Drumbeat' could have achieved far greater success had it been possible to make available the twelve boats for which U-boat Command asked, instead of the [five] by which the operation was carried out. Good use, it is true, was made of this unique opportunity, and the successes achieved have been very gratifying; we were, however, not able to develop to the full the chances offered us."[29]

In London at month's end Patrick Beesly was still stunned by the U.S. Navy's abject failure to meet and repel the German invaders. "It seems inconceivable now," he would write later, "that the Americans could have been so completely and totally unprepared as was in fact the case." He was confident that the Navy knew precisely, day by day, that the Paukenschlag fleet was headed their way; and USN documents, declassified in 1987, fully support that confidence. "It was all the more galling," he wrote, "because this holocaust could have been largely avoided if only the U.S. Navy had been prepared to learn from the bitter experience of the British and Canadians, gained in nearly two and a half years of war and freely and fully imparted to them since 1940. The Navy Department, however, preferred to make its own mistakes and learn in its own fashion. There seemed to be a feeling that 'we've got the ships, we've got the men, we've got the money too, and we don't need a bunch of Limeys to teach us how to run our war.' "[30] For his part Rodger Winn recorded the dimensions of the mounting danger in his weekly "U-Boat Situation": "The number of U-boats in the Atlantic has now reached the record total of 53. . . . It is apparently intended that the far western campaign should be extended . . . inspired by the not inconsiderable successes achieved notably off Cape Hatteras and Hampton Roads. . . . The brunt of the attack has continued to be borne by shipping off the Atlantic seaboard of U.S.A. between North Carolina and New York. . . . The tonnage lost in January will be found to amount to an ugly figure."[31]

When presented with that "ugly figure," as best Winn and Beesly could compute it, Prime Minister Winston Churchill transmitted an urgent cable to White House aide and Roosevelt confidant Harry L. Hopkins. Sent while *123* was still on slow cruise home, the message read: "It would be well to make sure that the President's attention has been drawn to the very heavy sinkings by U-boats in the Western North Atlantic. Since January 12, confirmed losses are 158,208, and probable losses 83,740."[32] Churchill did not make a point of the fact that eleven of the ships lost to Paukenschlag and Ziethen were British and that two were Canadian, or that the loss of bottoms was more grievous than the loss of cargoes. FDR replied the next day: "Harry gave me your message about sinkings in the Western Atlantic. This matter is being given urgent consideration by Stark King and me."[33]

The procedures for returning to base at Lorient were precisely set forth in the Operation Order. Thirty-six hours out *123* sent an Epsilon (inbound) short signal giving her location. After receiving a F.T. acknowledgment and further instructions from BdU she proceeded along the approach corridor marked *Tannennadel*—"pine needle"—though, owing to DR errors and trouble with direction-bearing equipment, she was not, as Hardegen learned later, on course. This fact, together with the need to proceed at a creeping speed in order to conserve their rapidly dwindling fuel, caused the boat to arrive three hours late at Point L2 (47-38.15N, 03-34.3W) where a Räumboot escort was awaiting her. The rendezvous with escort and final approach were timed so that a returning boat would arrive inside La Rade de Lorient during the period two hours before to two hours after high tide. With the three-hour delay, *123* had to join her escort in a high-speed approach in order not to miss the high water—and the official reception that awaited her—which placed an unexpected burden on the fuel supply. The Old Man became concerned that *123* might have to be towed into port after all. He need not have worried. *Eins Zwei Drei* persevered.

During the final days of the return voyage the crew had completed the success pennants and run them up the periscope standard. In addition, at the Old Man's suggestion, they had painted appropriate emblems and numbers on the conning tower: on the sides two representations of the Knight's Cross, one for Möhle who earlier had won his on this boat, the second for the Old Man; a large kettledrum with a stick; and the total tonnage claim of both commanders: 224,805. For old times' sake they had mounted atop the fairwater the fins of a shark that the men had caught off Freetown the year before. Now, as the cranes over Keroman materialized in the eastern haze, Hardegen donned his blue uniform and ordered the petty officers to form up the crew on the deck at parade rest. Soon Hardegen could make out the ocher battlements of the venerable Fort Saint Louis and the harbor itself, with red-sailed fishing boats working the outrunning tide, and a half hour afterward he was passing to his port the admiral's headquarters château at Kernével and the cavernous, dark bunker openings of Keroman II. Slowing down to harbor speed, and leaving behind the escort whose crew stood at the rails waving and cheering this first of the Paukenschlag boats to return, Hardegen conned *123* up the Scorff River to old *Isère*. As the pontoon boat came into view the bridge could clearly hear the welcoming martial strains of the *Englandlied*. A huge crowd of U-boatmen and base and dockyard workers had assembled, overflowing *Isère*'s deck to cover most of the quay to either side. Hardegen had stood at dockside himself witnessing the arrival of new Knight's Cross winners. Now he maintained the conn and brought the boat in himself. If this was to be the end of his last patrol in U-boats he was determined to relish command to the very last. Deliberately, then, he averted his gaze from the ramrod figure of the admiral, who stood in the foremost position before the banks of naval officers on *Isère* and kept to the business of bringing *123*'s manila lines into position to throw. When the engines were shut down and the brow was put across, Hardegen and his officers descended the outside ladder and walked to the foot of the brow where they came to rigid attention, faced the Lion, and saluted smartly: *"Heil*, Herr Admiral! I respectfully report *Eins Zwei Drei* back from action against the enemy!" Dönitz responded, *"Heil, Eins Zwei Drei,"* and came across the brow to shake Hardegen's hand and place around his neck an authentic Ritterkreuz, making him the youngest wearer of the award in the Kriegsmarine. Hardegen would write later: "It was a proud and unforgettable moment."[34] The Lion spoke privately with him a few moments, shook the hands of the other officers, and then informally walked the pallid, haggard, filthy ranks assembled on the fore and aft decks, speaking at least a word to each man and tousling the long hair of one. Then he led the happy, bearded U-boat officers across to *Isère*. The ratings followed and fell in smartly on the quay. Meanwhile, base medical corpsmen gently lifted Tölle through the forward hatch, placed him on a stretcher, and carried him to a waiting ambulance.

The newsreels taken that day show *123*'s officers surrounded by women base workers in bright white aprons thrusting huge bouquets of flowers into their hands and placing a boutonniere in Hardegen's left lapel, then Hardegen in uniform and tall sea boots reviewing his crew with a wide, proud smile. In the background a military band energetically clashed and boomed, but it was not from the Paten-bataillon; that unit had been sent to the Eastern Front while *123* was at sea. When the ceremonies ended and the cheering ceased and the band packed up their instruments, the officers and ratings were led into the Flotilla canteen, where both groups enjoyed their first mail and Beck's in forty-eight days. Hoffmann asked Hardegen if he wished to share what the Lion had said to him after presenting the Knight's Cross. Hardegen looked around and said quietly: "He told me not to lose my mental edge. That he needed me for one more patrol. That we would have a fast maintenance turnaround. And that he would tell more when he went over my KTB." The officers smiled. "Back to America!" whispered Schulz. "I would think so," said Hardegen. They raised their steins. "Back to America!"

The next day awards were distributed to members of the crew, whose freshly washed and shaved appearance and clean uniforms made them barely recognizable to Hardegen. This day they wore their navy blue melton wool trousers and pullover tops. Behind their necks fell large blue collars edged with three white bands and a black silk. On the right breast they displayed the eagle and swastika national emblem in yellow cotton embroidery and on their left sleeves the rank and trade badges. A navy wool peakless cap with Kriegsmarine in-scribed across the front of the tally ribbon completed their uniforms. After the ceremony the men swaggered off, bedecked with red-white-black Iron Cross ribbons, to spend their accumulated francs, some to "live like a god in France" in the cafes and houses of the city or in the newly built *Ubootsweiden*, U-boat "pastures," rest centers, in the coun-tryside. Other crewmen, with leave papers, took fast trips home on the *BdU Zug* (headquarters train) that ran through Le Mans, Paris, and Rotterdam, where the men could find winter flowers in the station to bring home, to the German cities Bremen, Hamburg, and Flensburg. Civilian trains took them where they wanted from those stops, and most were home within two days of setting out.

Back in Lorient, Hardegen and Rafalski finished typing the final copy of the KTB. Underneath the last date, 9 February, Hardegen wrote: "Total distance: 8,277 nautical miles. Total submerged: 256." Schulz completed his own logs, and whistled pointedly when he showed the numbers to Hardegen: "Fuel remaining: 80 liters [21 gallons]."

The Lion questioned Hardegen closely the next day at the for-mal debriefing, and Kapitän Godt took copious notes. After Hardegen was dismissed, the admiral appended a last sheet to the KTB that read: "A very well-planned and executed operation with excellent success. The Commander has superbly exploited our first appearance off the North American coast with his pluck and his toughness. Dönitz."

11

Last Patrol

The weather on Thursday morning, 19 February, in Washington, D.C., was overcast, gusty, with temperatures in the low forties, as Admiral Harold S. Stark, in mufti, drove his personal car downtown to the Riggs National Bank. On the passenger seat beside him, in a nondescript black briefcase with straps and buckles, was $500,000 in high-denomination currency. There was much to think about as Stark wove through the crowded streets, including an editorial in that morning's *Washington Post* warning that gasoline rationing was imminent, since "submarine warfare along our coasts" had made "alarming inroads" on eastern petroleum stocks. "The threat to our water-borne transportation of petroleum," the paper had concluded, "is painfully immediate."[1] At Riggs the short, silver-haired, cherubic man who presented his briefcase to a bank officer was unlikely to be recognized as a chief of Naval Operations in his or any other Navy. With the not-inconsiderable deposit Stark opened a joint account in the names of F. J. Horne and/or W. S. Farber with the understanding that he, Mr. Stark, might at times transfer funds from the account to other names, as indeed he now did, requesting that half the deposit be credited to three different companies:

Atik Shipping Company, E. T. Joyce
Treasurer—$100,000

Asterion Shipping Company, K. M. Beyer
Treasurer—$100,000

Eagle Fishing Company, L. F. Rogers
Master—$50,000

Stark then drove home, changed into his uniform, and took his sailor-chauffeured staff car to Main Navy. Everything was now in place for Project LQ to proceed on schedule. The project had not been the Navy's idea, as officers were quick to point out then and later. It had been the President's idea. But when Franklin Roosevelt gave orders, and when he sent his Naval Aide, Captain McCrea, with the cash to back the orders, the Navy had little choice but to follow through.

What did Admirals King and Stark think about Queen Ships? FDR had asked them one day, the same 19 January when U-*123* was rampaging off Cape Hatteras. Not much, the admirals confessed. Queen, or Q, ships were U-boat traps that had been employed with spectacular success by the British in World War I, but eight advanced versions commissioned by the Royal Navy in 1939 and 1940 had had no success, and two had been sunk. The principle was well known, especially to the Germans, and that was the problem. A Q ship was a freighter or tanker converted in everything but appearance to naval use. Behind collapsible false structures and tarpaulins, it hid a bristling array of heavy and light guns. The Q ship's strategy was to deliberately lure a U-boat into making a close-in torpedo attack. To prevent the decoy ship's sinking from the invited torpedo explosion, its holds were filled with a buoyant cargo such as pulpwood or empty drums. When the explosion settled, half the crew, forming a "panic party," would go into lifeboats. The ruse was designed to bring the attacking U-boat to the surface in order to finish off the still-floating target with artillery. At that point the other half of the crew, standing by hidden guns, threw down the hinged bulwarks and exposed the U-boat to withering fire from four-inch barrels and machine guns.[2] It was still a brilliant concept, thought FDR, and since the Navy did not seem to have anything else to throw at the U-boats he suggested that it throw Q ships. McCrea would supply the money. The project was to be shrouded in the deepest secrecy. There were to be no formal requisitions and no accounting of funds. Any absolutely necessary written records of the shipyard conversions or of the missions undertaken were to be kept in a secret safe in the CNO's office. Every other communication was to be made by word of mouth.

The next day Admiral King sent a coded dispatch to Admiral Adolphus Andrews at Eastern Sea Frontier headquarters on Church Street in New York City: "Immediate consideration is requested as to the manning and fitting-out of Queen repeat Queen ships to be operated as an anti-submarine measure. This has been passed by hand to OpNav for action."[3] Andrews could hardly have missed the hand as being that of his old patron Roosevelt, and he loyally threw himself into the work-up of a plan. It took him, however, nine days to respond with a four-page analysis in which he argued that Q ships should succeed since the U-boats' "most prevalent method has been a night attack on the surface from close range." Thus, there was no need to entice a U-boat to surface: the enemy was already exposed. The best decoy, Andrews thought, was a tanker, since the enemy so far had concentrated on that type of vessel. To be consistent with its character, such a tanker should travel north in a deep condition, south in a light. Empty oil drums would make the best flotation cargo, he thought, and there should be three well-separated guns on each broadside and one astern so that a single torpedo could not knock out all that could be brought to bear on a side. The entire crew and officers should be hand picked and should wear merchant-style clothing. If those conditions were followed the plan had "a reasonable chance of success."[4] Not aware, apparently, of either the urgency or the highly secret character of the enterprise Andrews sent his report in plain language by mail.

At the Department of the Navy, Operations could not wait on Andrews, and a decision was made to invest in two old coastwise cargo vessels of the three-island type (raised forecastle, midship structure, and an enclosed superstructure at the stern) and in one Boston diesel trawler. Participating in the decision were King, Stark, and the two men for whom bank accounts had been opened, Vice Admiral Frederick J. Horne, vice chief of Naval Operations, and Horne's assistant, Rear Admiral William S. Farber. A staff officer, Commander Thomas J. Ryan, Jr., was directed to obtain the vessels and to supervise their conversion. On 27 January, armed with a memorandum from Stark granting him extraordinary authority, Ryan arranged for the U.S. Maritime Commission to acquire on bareboat charter two steamers, sister ships SS *Carolyn* and SS *Evelyn,* from the A.H. Bull Steamship Company in New York City. Each was thirty years old, 3,209 GRT, 318 feet in length, with a 46-foot beam. From a fishing fleet in Boston Ryan obtained the 133-foot beam trawler MS *Wave*. All three ships there-upon were delivered to the Portsmouth (New Hampshire) Navy Yard for conversion to AK (cargo ship) status. The two cargo vessels underwent extensive overhaul, the *Evelyn* having to be substantially rebuilt. Their holds were filled with pulpwood for flotation, since steel drums were all but unobtainable. The pulpwood caused some worry since, if left dry, it could become explosive, and if kept too damp its rot might lead to fire. The old Scotch boilers delivered a maximum speed of 7.5 knots. On the deck behind false works the Navy installed on each of the two larger ships four four-inch, 50-caliber guns, four 50-caliber machine guns, six "K" guns—depth-charge throwers—and numerous small arms and grenades. The trawler received slightly less armament. All three vessels were equipped with extra Abandon Ship equipment and with the latest electronic and communications gear, although antennae had to be disguised, with the result that the transmitter range was limited even in favorable conditions.[5]

The work of conversion proceeded at the fastest possible pace, making maximum use of shifts, overtime, Sundays, and holidays. When certified seaworthy, equipped, and fully armed, the three ships were transferred to Admiral Andrews' command. His new chief of staff, Captain Thomas R. Kurtz, USN (Ret.), consulted with Commander Ryan in the development of an Operation Plan. Meanwhile, on 5 March, the ships were formally commissioned into the U.S. Navy, *Carolyn* becoming USS *Atik* (AK101), *Evelyn* becoming USS *Asterion* (AK100), and *Wave* becoming USS *Eagle* (AK132), thus accounting for the names of the dummy companies on the books at Riggs National Bank, used to mask the arming of the vessels. None of the commissionings, however, was made a matter of record in the Department of the Navy.[6] *Atik* and *Asterion* each received a complement of six officers and 135 enlisted men. *Eagle* had proportionately fewer. Originally only the commanding officers, who volunteered for the hazardous Q-ship duty, knew the nature of their missions: Lieut. Comdr. Harry L. Hicks, USN, of *Atik*, Lieut. Comdr. Glenn W. Legwen, USN, of *Asterion*, and Lieut. Comdr. L. F. Rogers, USNR, of *Eagle*. Before shakedown all other officers and ranks were informed of the Q-ships' hazardous assignments. The news could not have come as too great a surprise to the ships' companies since numerous civilian yard workers were familiar with the conversions and, as the wife of one *Atik* officer reported, the ships' purpose was the subject of common talk in several

Portsmouth boardinghouses.[7] Every man other than the three commanding officers was given an opportunity to decline service without prejudice to his career. None did so. It is not recorded, however, whether the crews of *Atik* and *Asterion* were told that neither ship was expected to survive at sea longer than one month after commencement of assigned duty.[8]

On 11 March at Admiral Andrews' headquarters the *Atik* and *Asterion* skippers received their orders for sailing on shakedown. Until departing Portsmouth no sign was to be given that the ships were anything other than armed vessels regularly commissioned in the Navy. Once having cleared port and beyond shore observation, their crews were to erect the false bulwarks and other concealments, remove the identification numbers from the bows, break out false merchant warrants, and take down the U.S. flags and commissioning pennants. If challenged on their course by friendly ships or aircraft they were to respond with their original commercial names, SS *Carolyn* or SS *Evelyn*. If challenged by the enemy *Atik* was to respond: "SS *Vill Franca*, Portuguese registry, call CSBT." *Asterion* was to respond: "SS *Generalife*, Spanish registry, call EAOQ." In the shakedown orders care had been taken to direct both ships along routes known not to have been frequented by U-boats. Commander Ryan remembered: "My memory is very clear on the fact that there was great pressure on all concerned from the highest authority [Roosevelt] to get these ships to sea on everybody from the CNO down to Ryan including the various Flag officers in between. We did not, any of us, feel that the ships were in top fighting trim when they sailed and . . . we hoped their sailing orders for about the first two weeks would take them clear of any enemy subs."[9] Accordingly, *Atik* was assigned a cruise area some 300 nautical miles east of Norfolk, Virginia and *Asterion* 240 miles to the south of her. The two expendables sailed at 1300 hours on 23 March. The next day an unnamed officer on Stark's staff wrote, "It's gone with the wind now and hoping for a windfall."[10] If he was thinking of *Atik* alone it was a false hope, though no one could have known that from Roosevelt down to Ryan. On 1 February the Kriegsmarine had introduced a fourth rotor to the Schlüssel M machine. Bletchley Park worked mightily to defeat it but the new TRITON code (called "Shark" at BP) proved impermeable, and it would remain so for ten long months. Rodger Winn's OIC Tracking Room suddenly went semiblind.[11] So, too, therefore did Washington. No one in the U.S. capital could have known in the last week of March that east of Norfolk was the least safe place to be in the entire Western Atlantic. It had been chosen by BdU as the route for the return of Reinhard Hardegen.

By the beginning of March, when U-*123* had been refitted, reprovisioned, and rearmed for her next Feindfahrt, Admiral Dönitz had a fairly accurate picture of conditions on the U.S. East Coast. The data had come from the five Paukenschlag commanders and by wireless from the replacement boats that were on station during February from the Gulf of Maine to Florida (U-*103, 106, 107, 108, 128, 432, 504, 564, 578, 653*). Amazingly, four of those boats (U-*432, 564, 578, 653*) were Type VIIC, which had not previously been thought capable of such extended missions. But their commanders, eager to participate in the "second happy time," had persuaded Dönitz that by filling various auxiliary tanks with fuel and by cruising at seven knots on one diesel they could make the distant coast, maneuver, and return. Most succeeded in reaching the United States with twenty tons of fuel for use in operations, thereby far exceeding the Type's theoretical radius of action. Dönitz did worry, however, about the enthusiasm of some crews, which gave up some of their drinking-water tanks to the diesels' thirst. The first four VIICs sank five ships. BdU also had good information by this date about defensive measures in waters farther to the south, where the U.S. Navy protected a Caribbean Sea Frontier so extensive it had to be divided into East and West divisions. Rear Admiral John H. Hoover commanded the CSF from headquarters in San Juan, Puerto Rico. During February BdU had five IXC boats (U-*67, 129, 156, 161, 502*) in the vicinity of the oil- and gas-rich Dutch islands of Curaçao and Aruba or off the harbors of Port of Spain, Trinidad, where the bauxite trade and other South American shipping passed. During February in the waters guarded by the two frontiers, Eastern Sea and Caribbean, U-boats sank a total of forty-eight vessels, nearly half of them tankers, amounting to 281,661 GRT, 68 percent in the ESF. In addition, seven ships were damaged.[12] U-*156* (Kptlt. Werner Hartenstein) shelled the Lago Refinery on Aruba, but without serious effect.

From all reports received at Kernével by the close of February it was clear that the U.S. Navy had tightened up shoreline and island defenses. Destroyers no longer sailed on patrol schedules so regular that U-boats could predict and discount them. Small patrol craft were more visible. Air activity was up all along the U.S. littoral, and blimps could be observed at numerous high-traffic points. In all other respects the Americans were continuing to act as though there was no war: The beaches and towns were still a blaze of lights; lighthouses and buoys still operated as in peacetime, though some were dimmed; shipping moved singly instead of in escorted convoys; traffic traveled straight ahead from point to point rather than follow zigzag courses on sheltered sea-lanes; merchantmen used their wireless without discipline, particularly on the six-hundred-meter distress wavelength; many proceeded with lanterns lit; and U.S. Navy and Army antisubmarine air forces, through inexperience and poor training, still failed to follow up initial attacks, with the result that in shoal water, where they stood a good chance of succeeding, they abandoned their attacks too early and withdrew. By contrast, the Canadians to the north had learned from the British example and never let up on the pressure. Kals in U-*130* had been so bedeviled by constant air and destroyer surveillance in Cabot Strait—surveillance as intense as any that he had experienced in the English Channel—that he moved south into U.S. waters.[13] Bleichrodt, too, off Halifax, had been frustrated by the same relentless coverage.[14]

If U.S. defenses posed no serious threat as yet to U-boats grazing in the western pastures, the same cannot be said for threats in the other direction, as the story of one of the ships lost in February demonstrates. In the early morning of 28 February the *Wickes*-class flush-decker destroyer USS *Jacob Jones* (DD 130) was proceeding south from New York on patrol about five miles off the line of lighted buoys. *Jacob Jones* was the size warship that ESF had long pleaded for. To Admiral Andrews' delight CINCLANT had loaned her to coastal duty for an unspecified period. During February several other destroyers had been permitted to serve ESF patrol functions if they happened to be within frontier limits on escort duty or for repair and overhaul, but *Jacob Jones* was the first to be assigned on a regular basis. The old (1919) DD was the namesake of a U.S. destroyer that had been torpedoed by a U-boat in the Western Approaches to the British Isles in 1917. On that occasion numerous survivors in the water had been killed by depth charges that exploded as the destroyer sank. At 0500 on the twenty-eighth the "new" *Jacob Jones* was off the Delaware Capes, making fifteen knots in a calm sea under a full moon, when two torpedoes, arriving almost simultaneously, blew apart everything forward of a point just aft of the bridge and carried away the after part of the vessel above the keel plates and shafts. On the center section, which remained afloat, the twenty-five men who survived the blasts tried vainly to break the boats out of their cradles. With the deck and lines slippery from spilled oil it was impossible to get purchase, and they resorted to the rafts. As the parts of *Jacob Jones* sank, the depth charges exploded and some of the men on the rafts were killed by the concussions. Five hours after the attack a Navy observation plane sighted twelve survivors and vectored USS *Eagle 56* to pick them up and take them into Cape May. One more crewman died on the way. *Jacob Jones* was the first man-of-war sunk by enemy action in American coastal waters.[15] The trophy belonged to Korvettenkapitän Ernst-August Rehwinkel in the VIIC U-*578*.

Admiral Dönitz needed more boats on American patrol to take advantage of these incredible opportunities. The American "shooting season" could not be expected to last very much longer. Eventually the Yankees would start listening to the British and the season would end. Convoying was the logical next step. It was bound to happen. What advantage the U-boats still possessed must be seized on at once. And yet, maddeningly, Adolf Hitler was frustrating the U-boat fleet's last great chance to exploit this undefended frontier by his insistence that no fewer than twenty boats be placed on permanent station off the coast of Norway to prevent an Allied invasion of that country. Dönitz thought it very wrong minded of the Führer to expect an attack on Norway, although there had been minor British raids during 1941, and in April 1942 Churchill would seriously consider a landing in strength, from which he was dissuaded by his chiefs of staff. Actually Dönitz was fortunate that Hitler took away only twenty of his boats. On 22 January the Führer expected "unconditional compliance" with his orders that "all U-boats be transferred to Norway." But the next day he relented, "in view of the successful operations of our U-boats along the American coast," and limited the Norwegian detail to eight.[16] During February, when the American hunt club was most inviting and Dönitz was forced to the expedient of using overstressed VIICs, Hitler upped the Norwegian ante to twenty boats. Dönitz protested that the tonnage war on shipping, which was the only offensive means Germany had left to defeat British arms, was gravely compromised by the diversion of U-boats to static duty. British naval historian Roskill agrees: "Inevitably the weight of the offensive off the American coast declined just at the time when it had proved highly profitable. . . . The small total [of boats] available early in the year, combined with diversions to unprofitable purposes, now seems to have been a decisive factor in the Atlantic battle."[17] Another of Hitler's "intuitions" led to a mighty blunder affecting the sea battle on which the entire course of the European war depended.

Lorient, France, Tenth Flotilla, 2 March. U-*123*'s departure from *Isère* on her second American patrol was much like that on her first, with a large crowd of well-wishers present from the base and a spirited brass band playing the usual send-off music. There were certain differences, too. For one, the mooring lines fell away under floodlights at a dark 1930 in the evening. For another, instead of Christmas trees women base workers presented bouquets of flowers to the officers. And there were several new men on board: IIWO Wolf-Harald Schüler who took over the functions of von Schroeter, who moved up to Number One replacing Hoffmann, who was reassigned; an LI in training named Mertens to assist Schulz; a young midshipman named Rudolf Holzer whose assignment was to get a first taste of war; a seaman second class named Walter "Laura" Lorenz; and a new propaganda photographer named Rudolf Meisinger, whom the crew quickly dubbed "Schöner Rudi" (Handsome Rudi). He replaced Tölle, who had recovered well from surgery and had returned in good health to his home in Germany. There was one other difference: This time both the crew and the crowd knew full well the boat's destination. The Lion was hurling every boat that was not tied down off Norway against North America and the Caribbean. There was no secret about it at all. So the cheers of bystanders carried a certain specificity as they counseled *123* on how to deal with Roosevelt.

When the freshly scrubbed boat stood out to sea the bridge watch threw the flowers overboard—an old sailors' custom—and peered ahead into a rapidly descending fog. Reinhard Hardegen, holding the conn, groped cautiously along the buoys. With the fog deepening he soon could not make out his own bow, much less the Räumboot escort that was waiting outside the harbor. A strong low-tide current made it doubly difficult to hold course in the narrow channel. Then—a *crunch* forward! They had run aground! *"Both back emergency full!"* Quickly the boat disengaged from the bottom. The Old Man thought it was a rock. Then the stern ran up a sandbank! Were they trapped? Again the engines worked them free. The Old Man now cut the engines, ordered out the anchor, and rowed ashore in the boat's dinghy. This was embarrassing. To be stranded directly in front of the harbor entrance—and he an experienced traveler to the States—it was not the proud moment that he had envisioned. At Flotilla a surprised duty officer gave Hardegen permission to continue his advance if the fog lifted, which it did shortly after he reboarded at 2210. With good visibility under a full moon *123* worked herself free, came alongside the appointed escort, and proceeded safely through the channel and mine field. In the early hours after midnight the Old Man and the bridge observed that rarest of nighttime phenomena, a full eclipse of the moon. They took it as a good omen after the humiliating adventure just past.

At 0855, with her escort and 129 nautical miles behind her, *123* made her first trim dive with Mertens carefully studying the practiced technique of Schulz. The Old Man took a turn through the boat to check on the readiness of all stations. When the boat was submerged no one as a rule was allowed to go forward or aft, since to do so disturbed the trim. Anyone who was required by duties to move positions had to advise the LI, as the Old Man did now, tapping with his knuckles the belowdecks *Kreiselgeräte* (gyrocompass) as he stooped to pass through the forward hatch. At the outset of every Feindfahrt it was difficult moving through the passageway, with food cans and boxes squirreled away in every deck-level cranny and bulging hammocks filled with sausages, bread, potatoes, and other perishables hanging low from the warren of overhead pipes and valves. To both sides and above the Old Man looked to be certain that everything was lashed and secured for the hard Atlantic they were about to enter. Someone else's word, no matter how well proved, was not enough. He had to see for himself. He also looked into the eyes of every man at his station to reassure himself that every Jonah was fully alert in this steel-ribbed whale, and every man responded with a respectful smile and a nod. They were still fresh faced and shaved, these companions of the deep. Soon enough they would have that familiar U-boat pallor and, all but those too young to grow one, beards as fearsome as any pirate's. The still-clean U-boat interior sparkled, and the delicious aroma of Hannes's hot rolls wafted through the compartments. Even in the engine room (where the hot-roll essence was unlikely ever to penetrate) "Karlchen's" hot engine blocks wore a bright blue-gray exterior. The Maneuvering Room, as usual, was spotless. Satisfied that everything was in order, and that the men were ready and eager to fight this boat again, the Old Man retired to his half compartment and pulled shut its green curtain. He did not catch Fritz Rafalski's worried look across the gangway as he did so. Like everyone else on board,

Rafalski thought that the American shore offered easy successes. But he followed wireless chatter and base gossip closely enough to know that most of the U-boats that had been lost to date were either on their first patrols or were led by bold, aggressive, tenacious commanders. And the man behind that curtain was no slacker.

Hardegen sat at his small tip-up desk and reviewed his Operation Order. This time he did not have to wait until crossing 20 degrees west to know his destination and mission. Both Dönitz and Flotilla had already told him plainly what he had on the paper before him: "Take a direct course to the United States East Coast. Make your descent through naval quadrant CB opposite Norfolk and steer for Hatteras in QU.CA. On or about 22 March BdU will instruct you by F.T. on further maneuvers. During transit sink any enemy vessels of appropriate tonnage." To assist him in working off the United States this time BdU and Flotilla had supplied him not only with a full set of coastal charts but also with sailing directions—*Handbuch der Ostküste der Vereinigten Staaten* (*Handbook of the East Coast of the United States*)—that had been abstracted from U.S. and British publications and printed in German between seafoam green covers. With his dividers he estimated 3,600-plus nautical miles to Hatteras Light, or twenty-five days of unobstructed steaming. He would have to check the numbers with Kaeding. The Atlantic could be a boring passage— day by day grinding away the degrees while some staff officer back at Kernével slowly advanced a blue flag across the green baize table. He would try to keep the crew razor sharp with emergency dives, practice approaches, and qualification tests. Sometimes the Atlantic had its own way of keeping a crew alert.

13 March, 1200 hours (CET), position BC 9827, boat on the surface, total miles traveled 1,660, skies overcast, gale force winds at 8 from the north-northwest, sea state 7, visibility 18. The implacable Atlantic had them again in its challenging envelope, testing the limits of their capacity to endure. It was a test for humans only. The boat itself was a real sea keeper; there was no need to worry about their craft. *Eins Zwei Drei* sliced through the mountainous crests in a workmanlike way, sea-sledded with a rising stern as though it was her preferred way of march, plunged casually into the steel blue pits, and took the full force of the foaming torrents that she divided. There was never any worry about the boat—only that now and then power should be reduced to prevent undercutting and the waste of energy against the crashing seas. It was the human cargo that needed attention. Could

flesh withstand what high-tensile steel threw aside with a laugh? Walter Kaeding:

> On the bridge, the bathtub, you stood in a meter of water. I used to cut drainage holes in my boots. Standing there in gale seas was horrible. It was like being tied fast to a delivery truck. And that truck drives across potholes half a meter deep at thirty to forty kilometers per hour. And let's say every thirty seconds someone throws a bucket of freezing cold water in your face, another person takes a hose and squirts you, yet another throws ice at you. Then the truck occasionally tips toward one side, maybe thirty degrees, and then careens thirty degrees toward the other side, and sometimes the driver goes straight through a river and you're standing on the bridge, lashed to it by a safety belt, and these mountains of water roll over you, fifteen meters high, and one breaks right on top of you. And there you stand gulping for air. Not even the old Vikings experienced such things.[18]

On the seventeenth the Atlantic relented. The boat passed on to a nearly pacific surface with winds and seas no greater than force 1. The crew, stinking in damp clothes and numbed by the fatigue caused by bracing themselves against the elements, stretched their limbs and necks. Those coming off duty slept deeply. The mixers who had fallen behind on their torpedo checks now put their gleaming, oily arms to the work of extracting the G7s onto rattling tracks and chains. Rafalski listened to Goodwill Service messages from Kiel to other boats: "Seaman Second Class Buchholz. Brother Matthias fell 10 March Eastern Front. Otherwise all well. Family wishing you all the best. . . . Petty Officer Heinz Müller. On 15 March wife Frieda delivered small sailor with periscope. Frieda, Irmgard, Kurt, and family send greetings. . . ." In the galley Hannes expressed his relief at finally being able to hold down his pots by preparing a favorite stew and pastries. With his broad cheeks, short chin, and shock of black hair Hannes was by consensus the most likable man on board. Nothing seemed to affect his cheery disposition, not even the complaints from some when violent seas caused outbreaks of testiness that he was serving up "dead dog" or "chopped missionary." Of no one on board was more inventiveness and flexibility required. If he was in the middle of frying pork cutlets and the dive alarm rang, Hannes had to pull the meat from the fire lest smoke drift through the compartments causing red eyes and coughing. In such moments he would reach under the reserve "eels" for sausages that only needed warming up or he would open cans of sardines in oil. Later, when the boat was back on the surface, he would reheat the cutlets and give them a little moisture by mixing them with sauerkraut. For the Old Man, whose bleeding stomach required bland foods, Hannes varied the flavors of the oatmeals and gruels that the steward delivered to the commander's place at table. And when everything else on a Feindfahrt had been eaten and all that was left was macaroni—what the crew called "Mussolini asparagus"—Hannes invented different sauces to make it palatable. Everyone knew him affectionately as *Unser Hannes*—"our Hannes." No one could know that one year later on another boat, less lucky than *123*, Hannes would go down to a watery grave.

Much of the off-duty crew time in the days ahead would be spent reading and telling stories. A small library in a locker next to the Old Man's cubbyhole contained both serious and light reading, but most of the ratings preferred the magazines and detective or adventure novels they had brought on board themselves, which they passed, dog-eared and oily, from bunk to bunk. The Old Man's only concern was that this literature not be pornographic or salacious. Hardegen subscribed to the Lüth school in these matters. Korvettenkapitän Wolfgang Lüth, who had won the Knight's Cross in October 1940, held that during the monotonous days of a long sea passage it was important for the maintenance of morale that "iron will power" be exercised where sexual appetites were concerned. "To be sure," he would write, "I have not permitted the men to hang pictures of nude girls on the bulkheads and over their bunks. If you are hungry, you shouldn't paint bread on the wall."[19] Though the Old Man also had the petty officers monitor the men's conversations for lewd content, it was unreasonable to expect young, unmarried seamen's banter to be entirely devoid of sexual allusions, and much of the laughter on board came in response to quips in that area.

The younger men were as yet too inexperienced in life to have many stories to tell, so the crew turned to men who had had numerous previous adventures, such as Rafalski, and particularly thirty-year-old "Karlchen," when he could be coaxed forward from his engines. Everyone except the new crewmembers had heard "Karlchen's" stories before, but they pressed him to tell them as though hearing them for the first time. "I met Adolf Hitler personally once," he would say. "I was on the Panzerschiff *Deutschland* for two years. In 1935 the Führer came on board with much fanfare. General Werner von Blomberg was with him and we could observe them every day. You can't imagine the deference paid him. The general walked with Hitler on the after deck. Up and down they went, and when Hitler turned to walk the other way the general jumped to his left side. And when they went belowdecks the general said, '*Bitte schön, bitte schön*,' and Hitler walked first through the hatch, his head erect. I sat directly across from him once when we had afternoon coffee, and we were permitted to ask him questions. I asked him what was going to happen in the Kriegsmarine. He asked me back, 'How many Panzerschiffe do we have?' I told him, 'Three—*Scheer, Deutschland*, and *Graf Spee*.' 'What?' he said. 'Only three? We must have twenty. The English must be made to quiver.'"

"When was that, did you say?" asked Barth.

"Maybe it was thirty-four. Yes, Hindenburg was still living then. I can tell you it was awful being on the *Deutschland*. Even when Hitler was not on board they had fanfares all day long—da-da, da-da! All day long. We had more freedom on a little ship, like the torpedo boat I'd been transferred from. And then one day the Ubootwaffe started up and I applied. The number of men rejected was very large. I was lucky to be sent to school where I was taught everything there was to know about U-boat mechanics, and then I went to sea in a training boat. Our first crew had wonderful camaraderie on board and a great commander. He's died in the meantime. In port we went bowling on Fridays. And on Saturdays we fooled around a lot. . . ."

"Tell us about Saturdays," one of the seamen would ask—at just about the time a petty officer showed up to listen in.[20]

22 March, 1047 hours (CET), position CB 8342, course 270. "Commander to the bridge!" The steady, questing eyes topside had found a faint, black smoke column on the port beam. Hardegen decided it was worth a look. "Hard left rudder, come to one eight zero." After a short while mast tops and then a stack materialized. Hardegen estimated the ship's course at 345 degrees. It was coming to them. "Our Sunday dinner," he said to von Schroeter standing alongside. "It seems to happen that we get a morsel every Sunday." When the bow wake finally came into view, Hardegen guessed a ship's speed of seven knots.

The target seemed to be on a zigzag course, but Hardegen thought that that might be due to yawing, since the sea was rising and von Schroeter had readings of 4–5. The sun was also up, so this attack would have to be made underwater. *Alarm!*

After dogging the hatch Hardegen took his position on the saddle of the Standzielsehrohr in the upper tower and waited for the lens to come hissing from its well. At 13.5 meters Schulz called up the ladder: "Periscope depth!" Hardegen placed his right eye in the lens cup and checked the visibility. "Bring her up to thirteen, LI!" he ordered Schulz. "I have a lot of wave action up here." With better clearance of the surface Hardegen put pressure on the left foot pedal to train the lens around toward the target. Now he had it in the cross hairs. He could set up the solution. "Speed greater than I thought," he said to Schüler, manning the Vorhaltrechner. "Crank in eight-point-five knots. Range one thousand. Angle on the bow nineteen. Let's set up for a sixty-degree track. Helmsman, come thirty degrees to port so our eel runs lateral to the waves. Number Two, flood Stern Tube five. Let's get rid of that G7a. Set depth at three meters. I'm having a lot of trouble holding position here. When I'm not under I can see only the two mast tops." Although the hydroplane operators below were doing their best to anticipate the rise and fall of the boat as registered in the Papenberg column and make the necessary adjustments to keep the exterior periscope lens at a steady height above the surface, the IXB boat, with its wide flat upper deck, simply did not hold periscope depth as well as the VIIC in rough weather. Hardegen therefore was not blaming the control room for the lift and dip or for the fact that his lens was underwater as often as it was out. And the worsening seas were another factor: Not only did they throw blinding waves at the periscope, they also placed the target in troughs so deep that much of the time all that Hardegen could see were the masts. He ordered a slight change in course to acquire the stability of a beam sea.

"Range seven hundred. Folgen?"

"Folgen?" von Schroeter repeated.

"Folgen," the petty officer on the stern tubes replied to the tower. The T-Schu receiver was feeding the solution into G7a (ATO) torpedo No. 13516.

"Range six-fifty . . . six hundred . . . *Rohr los!*"

The boat seemed to shoot forward slightly, and also up, in reaction both to the discharge of the eel and to the loss of weight on board. Schulz worked quickly to take in 1,600 kilograms of seawater to make good the loss and maintain trim, while above the Old Man and his number two counted down the seconds.

At the end of the eighteen seconds estimated for the run there was a short, high-pitched metallic bang that sounded like a dud—a torpedo hitting without exploding. That close, Hardegen expected a vigorous detonation, and he had withdrawn his eye from the sight fearing that the concussion would bruise the flesh around his brow bones. Now, though, he returned to the sight and saw to his surprise a black detonation column rising exactly between the masts where he had aimed. The hit probably occurred low in the engine room, where its sound was muffled, Hardegen concluded. Ordering the boat to surface, he climbed out onto the dripping bridge platform to see the vessel with its stern already deep in the water. Soon, as the stricken ship's crew went overside, the bow rose full out of the water and the stern disappeared. After sixteen minutes the bow, too, went under, and no trace of the ship remained save for a spreading silver ring of oil slick and several rafts struggling to get away from its edges. Hardegen approached the rafts and asked the dozen or so men the identification of their ship. "*Muskogee*," one of them answered, "United States flag steam tanker, 7,034 GRT, bound from Venezuela to Halifax with a cargo of Bunker C crude." Rafalski looked her up: built in 1913 at Danzig. An old ship. No wonder she sank so fast, the Old Man wrote into his KTB.[21]

None of the thirty-four members of *Muskogee*'s crew was ever found.[22]

U-*123* resumed normal navigation.

At 2000 hours BdU transmitted the boat's further operation orders: UNRESTRICTED HUNTING FROM HATTERAS TO KEY WEST.[23]

The Old Man was delighted. Freedom to roam anywhere he pleased, seeking whom he might devour, from the Outer Banks to a semitropical paradise, was a U-boat commander's dream. He could not have asked for better duty. But other targets like *Muskogee* no doubt would intervene before he reached the operational area, since, at his present position north-northeast of Bermuda, he was already crossing the eastern edges of the heavily trafficked north–south sea-lanes. At 1823 the next day, in confirmation of that prospect, the port ahead lookout sighted two threadlike masts. In his 7 × 50s Hardegen watched the masts for a long while, deciding at last that the hull-down vessel was on a very irregular zig-zag course on *123*'s reciprocal, apparently not a part of the north–south traffic at all, but on an independent, unescorted route directly to England. Very daring, Hardegen thought, and the reason therefore it was making such erratic maneuvers, now zigzagging for half an hour on a mean course of 0 degrees, then on a mean of 30 degrees, then on 90 degrees. *Ein gewiegter Bursche*—a very clever fellow. Hardegen had trouble maintaining contact, which was exactly the purpose of the zigzag. Just before dusk, when the upper works and bridge screen came into view, he was able to identify the vessel as a modern tanker like *Norness* with short masts and a low, thick funnel. He estimated 9,500 GRT, speed 10.5 knots. After darkness fell the groping of the hunter after the hunted became even more difficult, and hours passed as Hardegen tried to guess which way the wily tanker master would turn next. When a bright moon broke through the clouds it was both a help and a hindrance—a help because the lookouts could keep the weaving target in view, a hindrance because *123*'s own surface silhouette and wake became visible. Finally the tanker zigged when it should have zagged, and a large storm cloud crossed below the moon. The combination led the tanker directly in front of the hunter's bow tubes. Von Schroeter had flooded Number 3 tube, and Schüler had a quick solution on a track angle of 70 degrees. When the huge black target loomed at six hundred meters, Hardegen gave permission to launch. At that distance success was certain. Immediately after von Schroeter hit the launching lever, Hardegen conned the boat hard to starboard for a second launch from the stern. Von Schroeter flooded tube Number 5. During the turn, with the tanker for a few moments only three hundred meters away on a near-parallel course, Hardegen identified a 8.8-cm gun on the stern and two 6.6-cm guns with shields on either side of the stack, also machine guns and searchlights on the bridge. So it was British! None of the guns was manned, though. Had he not yet been sighted?

Von Schroeter turned from the voice pipe to report: "Herr Kaleu! The eel never left the tube! It's stuck!"

"Damn! Eject the eel!" Hardegen ordered. "Use the mine ejection device! Get it out of there!"

Just then the pipe barked again, and von Schroeter reported: "Tube Number Five has launched!"

"*What?!*"

"The petty officer in the stern reports a mixer thought he heard an order to launch manually and he hit the lever."

"Great! A torpedo lost. Just what we need, one of our priceless eels running around out there somewhere, and to what purpose? Do we have panic down there? Put that man on report and keep him away from the tubes!"

Hardegen was furious. With malfunctions and stupid errors like these, that tanker was going to get away from them, particularly since, as he saw now, a thunderstorm was sweeping over the water, giving the target unexpected cover.

"Come to zero-nine-zero," he told the helmsman, "both ahead full!" He had the speed to catch up if he could keep the target in sight. Rafalski called up to say that the tanker had now definitely sighted them and had transmitted an SSS submarine warning. She gave her name as *Empire Steel*, British. The data in *Gröner* had her at 8,150 GRT, built in 1941. Her transmitted position at 37-45N, 63-17W was, according to Kaeding, just ten miles south of his DR position. Hardegen acknowledged the message and reflected on how easy it was to overestimate the tonnage of tankers since they had fewer reference points than freighters. But this was a brand-new ship, built during the war, everything modern, nothing improvised. He wanted her.

Empire Steel was now off to the east in the dark and the rain zigzagging for her life. Hardegen estimated that she had increased speed to twelve knots. With his own eighteen-plus knots he managed to keep her in view, but he had no desire to come too close to the enemy's guns.

"I'm going to keep our bows dead on," he told von Schroeter, "to present the smallest possible target to her guns. It's odd that they haven't manned them, even though they know we're out here. I'll bring you in to within nine hundred meters. Permission to launch from that distance. Use a spread of two eels."

Von Schroeter ordered open the bow caps to tubes numbers 1 and 4, and with the track angle established on the calculator he hit the launch switch. The time was 0300 on the twenty-fourth (CET). At precisely the same moment Hardegen saw the tanker slow her headway and turn to starboard. In his glasses he watched British crewmen race across her deck to man the guns. Evidently the master had decided that his only chance in this deadly encounter was to stand and fight it out. But Hardegen noticed that it was taking the gun crews an awfully long while to load and train. They only had sixty-one seconds in all if the Vorhaltrechner was correct, and it usually was. There still had been no muzzle flashes when—

WHACK!

A tall black geyser of smoke, water, and debris shot up from the forward mast, and seconds later the entire forecastle shuddered from a violent, bright yellow explosion. Gasoline! Two more similar explosions and everything forward of the bridge was a sea of flames such as *123*'s bridge had seen only a few times before. After five minutes, when on all other counts she seemed to be doomed, the tanker was still afloat on an even keel and Rafalski reported that she was still putting out distress signals. The bow was burning; so also were the upper deck and structures on the stern, but the fire extinguishing system seemed to be limiting the principal blaze to the forecastle. Now the wind was helping by blowing the forward gasoline flames away from the rest of the ship. There was a lesson here, Hardegen told von Schroeter: Not every exploded tanker is in the locker. He leaned forward to the voice pipe: "Battle stations gun crews!"

Schüler pounded up from his calculator station and took the exterior tower ladder down to the 10.5 gun, the rest of the gun crew and ammunition train following him. After the second artillery shot hit home in the engine room area, Hardegen ordered, "Fire for effect!" and six more shells penetrated the engine room and stern bunkers. Those bunkers held diesel fuel, Hardegen reasoned, since they erupted in red flame with dense, curling black smoke. Now the ship's ammunition magazines began exploding in a riot of sparks— ammunition that, surprisingly, was never brought to bear on *123*. Poor observation and poor training, thought Hardegen. There was no need to continue the bombardment. This tanker had enough holes. Though at a distance, as opposed to what he imagined hand-to-hand fighting to be like, he was able to maintain a clinical, military detachment from the human suffering that he and his boat had caused, it did worry Hardegen that no lifeboats or rafts were seen to get away. Was the master going to go down with his ship? Was the wireless operator, who had stayed at his post? Were the gunners? The other crewmen? In his imagination Hardegen attempted both to comprehend and to erase the disaster. The fires were turning deck paint to black smoke and water to steam. Burning wood from the deckhouse gave off white smoke. Hardegen knew that the men still alive on board were competing with the flames for oxygen and that those who threw themselves into the sea faced being fried in the gasoline film, suffocating in the surface smoke, or lingering in a kapok jacket until starvation and dehydration brought about the same result, though more slowly. Hardegen stood transfixed before the appalling spectacle, the heat and glare so intense on his face that he dared not approach closer even if there were something he could do. The inferno roared as it soared. The belowdecks crew, with his permission, came up, one by one, to experience the display. Finally, five hours after the torpedo hit, the fore part of the ship stood straight up, revealing the jagged torpedo hole that ran from the keel to the rail fifteen meters from the bow. Then the tons of hot metal went down in a cauldron of bubbles and steam. No lifeboats, rafts, or other signs of survivors were visible. But as *123* withdrew on a heading of 260, the lookouts could see for well over an hour tongues of red fire that flickered where the Union Jack had vanished. Like the Old Man they would never forget what they called thereafter the night of the *Tankerfackel*—the "Tanker Torch."[24]

24 March, 1027 (CET). The boat sighted the first U.S. "bee," a flying boat, probably PBY-Catalina, and dived to escape detection. No bee had been sighted this far out on the first patrol. Hardegen took its appearance to mean that American defenses were now better organized and more venturesome. He decided to stay down for a while. The weather upstairs was worsening, winds force 7–8, headseas 6–7. In such conditions he probably could proceed faster underwater. He took the occasion to mete out punishment to the inattentive mixer who had launched the No. 5 eel, deciding on three days of "hard lying"— sleeping on the floor plates. (He would lift the punishment the next day.[25]) *123* surfaced at 1800, to find the weather improving somewhat, and remained on the surface making knots the rest of that day, all of the twenty-fifth, and into the twenty-sixth when she entered the southeastern grid numbers of Marinequadrat CA, about three hundred nautical miles off Norfolk and Virginia Beach. At 1903 (CET), with daytime visibility twelve miles, the starboard lookouts made an unusual sighting: several smoke clouds in a line such as one would see in a convoy. Had the Americans started routing their merchant traffic in protective convoys? Hardegen followed the smoke columns until, at dusk, he was able to reassure himself that all the smoke, seemingly in dense bursts, was coming from just one ship. But why, he wondered, was the ship making so much smoke? And why, after darkness fell, did the amount of smoke diminish? Curiously, too, the ship then began zigzagging when her daytime course had been straight ahead on 215 degrees. Hardegen kept his glasses on the strangely behaving vessel, and when the hull materialized he identified it as a normal freighter

with a low forecastle and a smooth stern. Structures aft of the stack were unusually high, unlike any he had seen before.

"The target will come from the starboard quarter, Number One," he said to von Schroeter, "and cross our course on a diagonal. Its mean course is two-one-five. I'll maintain two-six-four and slow to five knots. There is no sign yet that he's seen us." Then to the voice pipe: "*Auf Gefechtsstationen!*" — "Battle stations!"

A heavy cloud cover hid the moon. The seas continued brisk. With the engine room on starboard slow ahead, the bridge could hear the other boat sounds that the diesels normally overwhelmed: the snorting and snuffling of the induction valves sucking air into the diesels, the squish of gumboots on the bridge plates, and the sibilant rush of water through the limber holes on either side of the upper casing. The lookouts could soon also hear the high splash of the blacked-out freighter that came from the starboard quarter and began its pass very close by. Their glasses swept the deck and staffs but descried no flag.

"Range seven hundred," von Schroeter recited, "speed ten, angle on the bow Red nineteen. Folgen?" He had flooded bow tube Number 2 and its menacing occupant, electric eel Number 9031. "Permission to launch," Hardegen said when Folgen came back. At exactly 0237 hours (27 March CET) or 2037 (26 March ET) with a perfect track angle of 90 degrees at six hundred-meter range von Schroeter hit the lever. "*Los!*" He turned to Hardegen: "Forty-eight seconds, Herr Kaleu. Depth Setting three."

"Very well, Number One."

The two men stood together silently waiting until von Schroeter said, "Three . . . two . . . one . . ."

WHACK! There was a good clean hit at the front edge of the bridge but a weak detonation with a short debris column. That was surprising. The vessel began to lose way. Hardegen now saw that it was a small prize, perhaps 3,000 GRT. It would be pointless to waste another eel on it. Rafalski sent a message slip up the tower ladder: "Herr Kaleu, it's signaling: LAT 3600 N LONG 7000 W CAROLYN BURNING FORWARD NOT BAD." Two minutes later Rafalski sent up another slip: "Now signaling: SOS SSS SOS SSS SOS SSS BT OON 7000 W APPROX SS CAROLYN TORPEDO ATTACK BURNING FORWARD REQUIRE ASSISTANCE."[26]

"Stand by, gun crews!" Hardegen ordered. "Have the Midshipman Holzer come to the bridge!" Young Holzer should see something like this. "Helmsman, come right ten." Before manning guns he would cross the target's wake and close on her starboard side. As he came around he saw two lifeboats, one on each side, filled with men in typical merchant-ship clothing going down the falls into the water. That was fast, he thought. Why did they abandon so soon? The steamer was still making way. In fact, the steamer now began a tight turn to starboard. Hardegen straightened out his course. The steamer continued turning. It was not going down. It was picking up speed! And coming right at them!

"Emergency full ahead!" Hardegen yelled below. With the greater speed he would escape being rammed, but suddenly there were other things to worry about: the steamer's bulwarks fell away, structures aft of the stack collapsed, tarpaulins were pulled aside, the Stars and Stripes were run up the hoist staff, and one large deck gun and two machine guns began fast firing at the retreating U-boat! The artillery was first short, then long. Geysers of water from the impacts showered over the bridge. A hail of machine-gun iron rattled against the tower and stern casing. Hardegen yelled to the bridge party: "Get down!" He slammed his fist against the cowling: *Eine U-Bootfalle!* — "a U-boat trap!" He wondered how he could have been fooled like a schoolboy!—like a damned beginner!

Eins Zwei Drei was widening the distance, but the American fire persisted—artillery shells that whooshed overhead; red, white, and green tracer fire from machine guns; and now huge depth-charge canisters hurled in their direction. The surface of the sea quaked all around them, and the concussions staggered the boat, momentarily cutting out the engines. But then the enemy shot started falling short as *123* pulled out of range, Karlchen's engines again running at flank speed. For the moment the danger was behind them. The appropriate thing to do was to dive as soon as possible, but Hardegen wondered if the boat was capable. The upper deck had taken hits (he would later count eight) and the explosions of the Wabos underwater could have caused fissures in the hull.

He called down the pipe: "LI, run a low-pressure test to see if we're still leakproof!" Then he turned to see Holzer lying wounded on the bridge platform. The sight stunned him. He had not seen the youth fall. Quickly he saw how badly he was hurt: A projectile that had passed through the double-plate steel cladding had exploded in his right thigh and ripped the leg open from the hip joint to the knee. Apparently the bone was shattered; when the lookouts took him in their arms to lower him down the tower ladder the leg seemed to hang by pieces of skin. Conscious throughout, the midshipman made no complaint about his pain. Hardegen followed down and directed that Holzer be laid before the wireless room, where he applied a tourniquet with Kaeding's belt to the upper leg and attempted to stanch the flow of blood with a clean towel from the boat's stores. He also brought morphine from the secure medical locker and gave Holzer a maximum dose. Then, directing Barth and "Laura" Lorenz to stay by the lad, he returned his attention to the boat. Schulz reported that the hull appeared to be intact, no vital systems were damaged, and the trim was adequate for submerging. *Eins Zwei Drei*'s impudent luck continued to hold. The Old Man, by this time visibly angry both for having been taken in by the trap and because of the injury done to Holzer, dived the boat and began setting up for a submerged torpedo launch. The men around him shared the Old Man's outrage and his fury and more than one expressed the intention to kill *Carolyn*'s entire crew—the same intention, machinist Horst Seigel reminded others, that *Carolyn*'s crew had had toward them. This was war and they were getting their first bitter sight of it inside their own boat. Tölle's wound had been an accident. Holzer's was from a shot fired in anger.

Through the attack periscope Hardegen could barely see *Carolyn* about two thousand meters off, where she stood stationary taking the "panic party" back on board. With her flotation cargo apparently unaffected by the torpedo she stood on an even keel. To sink her Hardegen would have to penetrate the engine room. That should not be too difficult, he reasoned, since the target was not moving—a fatal mistake, he thought. The trap's commander should have left his panic party to pick up later and sped away from the scene while the U-boat was submerged and greatly limited in speed and endurance. Was the commander perhaps fearful of what the U-boat might do to his men in the lifeboats? Did he have some kind of pact with them?—a promise to pick them up regardless? The *Carolyn*'s commander should have known that if he invited a second torpedo it certainly was not going to be wasted on the holds. Now *all* his men were put at risk. As *123* advanced von Schroeter flooded Number 1 tube and, at the Old Man's instruction, set the G7e's depth at a shallow 2.5 meters. Hardegen wanted the boilers.

The setup was a zero-angle launch sighted through the fixed-angle night lens, on a course of 150 degrees at three knots, range five hundred. After a twenty-four-second run the eel struck precisely in the engines. This time there was a normal detonation column. So much for this trap. But Hardegen knew that it would take a long time to go down. He was willing to wait, submerged, in order to be sure. The sea state began to worsen as he lay to. After a while the *Carolyn*'s forecastle sank as far as the bridge, and she began to list to portside. The crew, this time all, went into lifeboats. The stern came out of the water, exposing the now-dead screw. Hardegen began moving off. An hour and twenty minutes after the second torpedo the vessel, still awash, was wracked by fierce explosions that filled the periscope lens with smoke clouds and waterspouts. Hardegen thought it was depth charges and ammunition going off, less probably the boilers because of the force. By that time *123* was sufficiently distant not to be affected. He wondered, though, about the lifeboats.

The Old Man came down into the control room to inquire about Holzer. Lorenz reported that he was dead. He had remained conscious and brave until the end, which came about the time of the second torpedo, at 0430 hours. His last words, according to Barth, were: "When I get home again everything will be all right." Everyone on board was greatly affected. There had been nothing any of them could do to relieve the shock or stop the bleeding. The Old Man directed that the body should be wrapped in canvas for burial. He surfaced soon afterward in the still black night and, while his men at reverent attention held the midshipman's remains on the after casing, he recited aloud against the wind the words of the burial service in his Evangelical Christian tradition. "We now commit his body to the deep. . . ." Then, as the body was consigned to the dark water and the waves closed over the sailor's grave, Hardegen led the boat's company in the "Our Father."[27] Amstein's accordion played, *"Ich hatt' einen Kameraden"* — "I once had a comrade." Holzer's tearful comrades wished him Safe Mooring. And the Old Man wrote his resting place for the record in the KTB: 35-38N, 70-14W.

To take the men's minds off their loss, their commander set them to work transferring two replacement torpedoes from upper-deck containers to the pressure hull below. *123* had sortied with fourteen torpedoes belowdecks, ten fore and four aft. On Type IX boats it was possible to carry ten extra torpedoes in pressure-tight containers housed between the pressure hull and the upper deck. The central part of the deck was steel plating. The lateral surfaces were teak planking for ease of removal. These the crew now lifted to remove, one on each side, the two extra torpedoes, all that *123* had been assigned. By means of a winch that was difficult to operate on the tossing ocean surface the crew manhandled the eels below. When the arduous task was completed the Old Man took course 270 toward a point fifteen nautical miles east of Diamond Shoals. The weather thickened and high swells became breakers that swamped the bridge. The heavy seas and bright moonlight greatly hampered a surface attack that Hardegen attempted at 0434 hours on the thirtieth against a tanker, later identified by wireless intercept as the U.S. 9,511-GRT *Socony-Vacuum*. The G7e went awry, "made a bayonet," as Hardegen described it, and detonated on the shallow (thirty meters) bottom. Because of the tanker's high speed, thirteen knots, it was not possible to position for a second attack.[28] *Schade!* Too bad! But soon the KTB recorded, "Cape Hatteras light is in sight, just as in peacetime, our old acquaintance from the last voyage."

The two emergency wireless messages from USS *Atik* (SS *Carolyn*) were received by the Third Naval District receivers at Manasquan, New Jersey, and Fire Island, New York, and direction bearings taken by each station established her location at the intersection of 150 degrees and 146 degrees, respectively, or east by south of Norfolk.[29] Neither station knew what to make of the messages, however, other than that they represented yet another in a long March litany of merchant vessels torpedoed. When the messages reached the ESF Army and Navy Joint Control and Information Center, on Church Street in Manhattan, the duty officer, who had not been briefed on *Carolyn*'s secret identity and mission, simply forwarded the messages as information items to COMINCH in Washington. Several hours later an alarmed officer who was in the know at Operations in Main Navy telephoned the ESF duty officer to inquire if either Admiral Andrews or his chief of staff Captain Kurtz had been notified. When told no, the operations officer said that they should be, *immediately*. Both Andrews and Kurtz were in Norfolk that night, so the duty officer rang up ESF Operations Officer Captain John T. G. Stapler, USN (Ret.), at his home. The result was that early the next morning, about nine hours after *Atik*'s calls, a U.S. Army bomber, the destroyer USS *Noa*, and the tug USS *Sagamore* were sent to the attack site. The bomber returned without finding a trace of either *Atik* or her crew. A second Army flight that day and a sweep by a Navy seaplane from Bermuda similarly were unsuccessful. Unable to keep the heavy seas, *Sagamore* was recalled on the twenty-eighth; *Noa* searched the area without result until the thirtieth when, low on fuel, she was forced back to New York. On the thirtieth, too, two Army aircraft and a PBY-5 out of Norfolk reported sighting wreckage about ten miles south of *Atik*'s position, but the next day an Army bomber and a seaplane from Bermuda examined the area without any notice of survivors. On a hunch, Navy investigators boarded the Norwegian freighter SS *Minerva*, which had passed through the same area, when that vessel reached Saint Thomas, Virgin Islands. None of her crew, however, reported sighting survivors.[30]

A thorough search was also conducted by *Atik*'s sister ship *Asterion*, whose log provides a good indication of the weather conditions in which *Atik*'s lifeboats would have struggled. During evening watch on the twenty-sixth, 150 miles north of Bermuda in a heavy-running sea, *Asterion* intercepted *Atik*'s distress call and immediately made for the coordinates given. Lieutenant Commander Legwen, USN, recorded:

> March 27. Passed lifeboat with stern stove in and about half submerged. Looked as if it had been in the water a long time. Could make out no identifying marks. Definitely not one of ATIK's boats.
>
> March 28. Continued westerly course. Wind had increased to gale force. Made good about two knots over ground. No signs seen of ATIK.
>
> March 29. Steering gear jammed. Shifted to hand steering and removed two shackles from steering chain. Wind force nine. . . . During storm bottom of hot well sprang several leaks and began to use more water than we could make. Discontinued search for ATIK and set course for Hampton Roads.[31]

Legwen concluded that, "In view of the state of the wind and sea, all hands perished with the ATIK."[32] Further news of *Atik*'s fate came from a Berlin, Germany, radio broadcast on 9 April: "The High Command said today that a Q-ship—a heavily armed ship disguised as an unarmed vessel—was among 13 vessels sunk off the American Atlantic coast and that it was sent to the bottom by a submarine only after a 'bitter battle.'"[33] (This information, of course, had come by F.T. from U-*123*.) Admiral Andrews then expressed his belief "that there is very little chance that any of her officers and crew will be recovered" and recommended that if no further information was forthcoming by 27 April they be considered missing in action and that next of kin be notified. Such notification went out on 6 May, although on the hope that some of the men had survived, perhaps as prisoners, files were kept open until May 1944, at which date the families were notified that the *Atik* men were presumptively dead. The Navy Department posthumously awarded the ship's skipper, Lieutenant Commander Hicks, the Navy Cross.[34]

At war's end captured U-boat commanders were interrogated closely on whether they had seen or rescued any of *Atik*'s men. None could provide help.[35] Navy records at the highest levels do not disclose that information was sought from either Reinhard Hardegen or Admiral Dönitz specifically; nor do they indicate that any attempt was made to study the pertinent KTBs, then in British possession. On 10 January 1946, the *Washington Post* published the first public account of the *Atik* incident. For the families of the lost officers and crew, the article provided their first knowledge from any source of the nature of vessel on which their men had served.[36] Not publicized were the Navy's findings in the winter of 1943 that *Atik* probably never had a chance to withstand a U-boat attack. In January of that year *Asterion*, which fortunately had not encountered a U-boat on six missions in the Atlantic and Caribbean, put into the New York Navy Yard for overhaul. The next month inspectors from the Bureau of Ships, Damage Section, pronounced the *Atik*'s sister ship "unseaworthy" and raised doubts that, because of her three large holds, she could remain afloat if hit by a single torpedo. The ESF war diary commented on this finding: "Undoubtedly this weakness had been demonstrated several months earlier and was responsible for the rapid sinking of the sister vessel, USS Atik."[37]

After eight months of costly reconstruction of her bulkheads and replacement of her pulpwood cargo by 16,772 empty steel flotation drums, *Asterion* stood out to sea on a seventh cruise that proved to be as unproductive as those before. In October she was withdrawn from Q-ship service and a short time later was converted for use as a North Atlantic weather ship. The several cruises of the former beam trawler, *Wave*, originally commissioned USS *Eagle* (AM 132) and later changed in name and classification to USS *Captor* (PYC 40) were just as fruitless. Encountering no U-boats off Boston or on Georges Bank, she ended the war as a regular, nonsecret, armed patrol craft. Admiral Andrews had his Q-ship wishes fulfilled in July 1942 when COMINCH approved the arming and commissioning of a tanker, SS *Gulf Dawn*, as USS *Big Horn* (AO 45). With thirteen officers and 157 enlisted men *Big Horn*, disguised as a fleet oiler, made numerous coastwise cruises and two Atlantic convoy runs (playing the role of a straggler) but not once sustained the attack she invited. In early 1944, her complement replaced by Coast Guard officers and crew, she was retired to join *Asterion* as a "rainmaker" on weather patrol.

The last of the Q-ships to be fitted out was a twenty-three-year-old, 144-foot, wooden three-masted Canadian coasting schooner, *Irene Myrtle*, which was commissioned USS *Irene Forsyte* (IX 93) and sent to sea duty with a volunteer crew in late September 1943 under, alternately, Portuguese and Spanish flags. Not only was her first and only cruise as barren of results as those of her predecessor decoy ships, but caught in a hard storm east of Bermuda she nearly went down from opened seams. Displeased that the vessel had been allowed to sail in such unseaworthy condition, the naval inspector general, COMINCH, characterized the schooner's conversion "an instance of misguided conception and misdirected zeal" that cost the Navy nearly half a million dollars and a serious waste of effort. He recommended appropriate disciplinary action in view of the "unprofessional incompetence on the part of the officers concerned." With this debacle the practice of authorizing frontier commanders to arm and commission decoy vessels came to an end. British naval historian Stephen Wentworth Roskill, agreeing with his American counterpart Samuel Eliot Morison, has lamented: "The Americans . . . certainly seem to have been slow in putting much of our experience to practice. They first tried every conceivable measure—except convoy and escort. Even 'Q Ships' were sent out, and one cannot but agree with Professor Morison's description of them as 'the least useful and most wasteful of all methods to fight submarines.'"[38]

30 March, twenty-eighth day at sea, daylight hours. U-*123* submerged on the bottom off Hatteras Light in twenty-five meters of water. Total distance covered to date: 3,895 nautical miles, of which 207 were submerged. Forced down earlier in the dawn than expected by a patrol craft, Hardegen was surprised by the number of small pickets that now patrolled the Outer Banks and by the frequency of overhead flights by Army and Navy reconnaissance aircraft. This was not going to be a vacation cruise like the first patrol.[39] Waiting for nightfall he heard six steamers pass over or near his position and wondered if the

Shown in center is Admiral Karl Dönitz's headquarters château (BdU) at Kernével near the mouth of the harbor at Lorient, France. (Credit: Michael Gannon)

The U-boat bunkers, or "pens," at Pointe de Keroman, near the harbor entrance at Lorient, where U-123 was refitted for her two American patrols. Entrance to the bombproof bays was to the left. The seven-meter-thick roofs were never penetrated by Allied bombs. (Credit: Michael Gannon)

Oberleutnant zur See Horst von Schroeter, second watch officer, playing carols on accordion at Christmas tree in the control room during the first operational cruise to New York Harbor, 24 December 1941. The photograph of Adolf Hitler on the tower ladder well was standard issue on U-boats. (Credit: Horst Bredow, U-BOOT-ARCHIV)

Crewmen Franz Loosen and Ke "Karlchen" Latislaus (oldest man board) open presents on Christmas E 1941 en route to the U.S. East Coa (Credit: Horst Bredow, U-BOO ARCHIV)

Walter Kaeding, navigator. (Credit: Horst Bredow, U-BOOT-ARCHIV)

tz Rafalski, radio operator. (Credit: Horst edow, U-BOOT-ARCHIV)

Richard "Kraxel" Amstein, control room machinist, on first cruise to the U.S. East Coast. (Credit: Horst Bredow, U-BOOT-ARCHIV)

Left, *Max Hufnagl, diving planes operator.* Right, *Heinz Schulz, chief engineering officer (LI). (Credit: Horst Bredow, U-BOOT-ARCHIV)*

(L-R) *Rudolf Hoffmann, first watch officer; Hardegen; Horst von Schroeter, second watch officer. The UZO post in center held the target-aiming binoculars used for surface attacks. (Credit: Horst Bredow, U-BOOT-ARCHIV)*

Johannes "Hannes" Vonderschen, the co *who doubled on the machine gun crew. (Cre* *Horst Bredow, U-BOOT-ARCHIV)*

TEXT 12 JAN SUB ESTIMATE X INFO RECEIVED INDICATES LARGE CONCENTRA-
TION PROCEEDING TO OR ALREADY ARRIVED ON STATION OFF CANADIAN

AND NORTHEASTERN US COASTS X 3 OR 4 BOATS NEAR 4ØN 65W X 5
OR 6 SOUTH CAPE RACE PROBABLY NORTH OF 43N X 8 MORE WEST OF

3ØW PROCEEDING WEST IN FOLLOWING APPROX POSITIONS X 56N 32W X
55N 38W X 48N 33N X 47-3ØN 32W X 47-3ØN 44W X 48N 42W X 52N

42W X 52-3Ø 41W X MERCHANT SHIP TORPEDOED IN 41-51N 63-48W AT
AT ØØØ2 GCT 12JAN X ONE NW SCOTLAND X ONE NW MALIN HEAD X 2

ENTERING 3 LEAVING BISCAY X SIX VICINITY GIBRALTAR TO WESTWARD
X ONE WESTBOUND 46N 2ØW

DISTRIBUTION

38W....ORIG
12....38S....380....COMINCH....DOO...FILES...2ØOP...CONVOY FILE
   2OG

                              1. Card...........
                              2. U.S............
                              3. Foreign.........
                              4. Submarine........
                              5. Raider..........
                              6. Convoy..........
                              7. Info...........
                              8. File...........

Thanks to British Admiralty decrypts of German Navy radio (wireless) messages, a daily Sub Estimate (intelligence summary of U-boat positions and courses) was prepared in London and sent daily to the U.S. Navy Department in Washington, D.C. The first three lines of the "12 JAN SUB ESTIMATE" shown here clearly warned the U.S. Navy that three or four U-boats on the latitude of New York-Philadelphia were proceeding toward the U.S. Coast. It was, says the author, perhaps the most telling attack warning ever received by the military forces of the United States. All Atlantic coastal commands (upper right boxes) were notified, including "For Action CINCLANT [Commander in Chief Atlantic Fleet]." Yet the U.S. Navy did nothing. (Credit: National Archives and Records Administration)

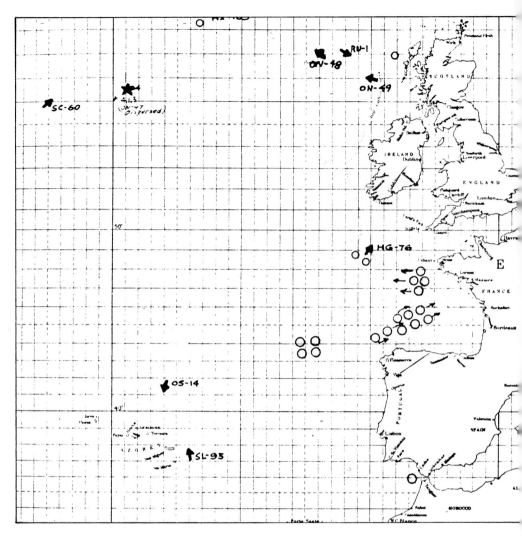

From "Ultra" decrypts of German Enigma wireless traffic, transmitted to Washington by the British Admiralty, U.S. Navy Intelligence knew that U-123 and other Drumbeat (Paukenschlag) boats were heading from their Biscay bases toward Canada and the U.S. East Coast. Their progress across the Atlantic was plotted day-by-day. Above, the USN Daily Situation Map for 24 December 1941 shows the departure of the U-boats from France. Note the group of U-boats to the south returning from Gibraltar. Right, the USN Daily Situation Map for 12 January 1942 shows the approach of Hardegen's group to the New England and New York coasts. The German attack, which has already begun with U-123's sinking of SS Cyclops, would carry as far south as Cape Hatteras. Despite this detailed advance warning the U.S. Navy did nothing to resist the attackers. Five Paukenschlag boats sank twenty-five ships in the space of twenty-six days. (Credit: Operational Archives, Naval Historical Center)

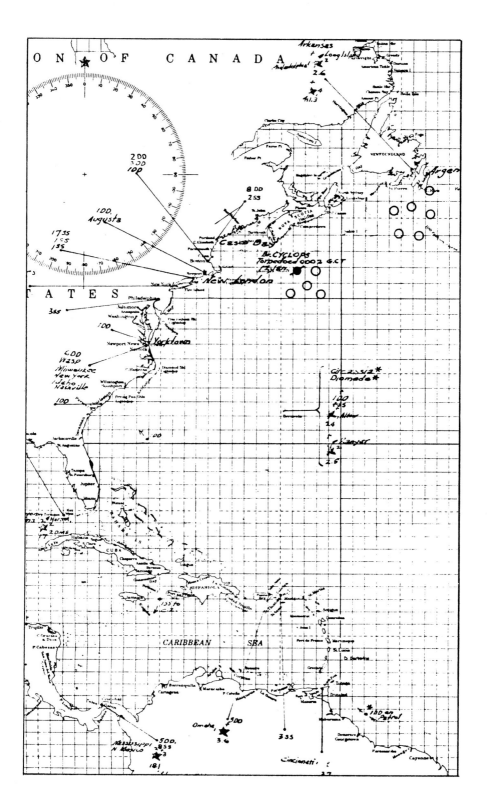

Out of torpedoes, U-123 engages in a mid-Atlantic surface gun battle on 25 January 1942 with the armed British freighter Culebra *during her return to base after the first American patrol (Paukenschlag). Not before or since, the author believes, was U-boat artillery used with such effect as it was by Hardegen on his two American patrols. The British crew, who were transporting disassembled aircraft parts, made a spirited defense before their vessel was fatally holed. The U-boat photographer who began this sequence of pictures, Alwin Tölle, was badly injured during the battle by an exploding machine gun barrel. In the final picture, taken by another crewman, Hardegen's men hand survivors bailing buckets, bread, lard, sausages, canned foods, and a knife. They also gave them a position plot and a course to Bermuda. (Credit: Reinhard Hardegen)*

This detail from Hardegen's 1870G Chart of the North Atlantic that he carried on board U-123 during his first American patrol (Drumbeat) shows his approach to New York Harbor, including his sinking of Norness *in naval square CA 37 and of* Coimbra *in CA 28. (Credit:* Michael Gannon*)*

The British tanker Coimbra *awash and sinking twenty-seven miles south of the Hamptons off Long Island, New York. Her eighty thousand barrels of oil erupted in fire columns that were easily seen by residents of Long Island. Hardegen torpedoed the vessel in the early morning hours of 15 January 1942, his third victim in Operation Drumbeat. (Credit:* New York Times*)*

On return from first U.S. patrol Hardegen (center) and Seaman Karl "Langspleiss" Fröbel (left), youngest man on board, prepare pennants showing claimed tonnages of ships sunk. These were then hoisted on the attack periscope (right) before entering home port. (Credit: Horst Bredow, U-BOOT-ARCHIV)

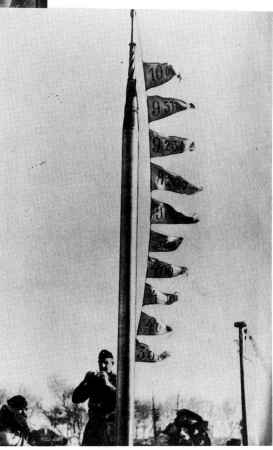

nnage pennants fly from U-123's tended periscope as boat enters Lorient rbor following first U.S. patrol. redit: Horst Bredow, U-BOOT- RCHIV)

Hardegen (left) on bridge of U-123 as U-boat prepares to enter Lorient base after the first American patrol. Device on conning tower casing at left is the wounded badge described in the text. A kettledrum and drumstick are shown at center, symbolizing Operation Drumbeat (Paukenschlag). Officer front and center is Hardegen's second in command, Oberleutnant zur See Rudolf Hoffmann. Crewman at lower right is painting the U-boat's total tonnage claim (224,805 GRT) under her two commanders, Möhle and Hardegen. Also displayed, above the wind deflector, were a representation of the Knight's Cross and two fins of a shark caught off Freetown, Africa, the year before. (Credit: Horst Bredow, U-BOOT-ARCHIV)

Hardegen wears the Knight's Cross of the Iron Cross after its award to him by Admiral Karl Dönitz on U-123's return to Lorient following the boat's first American patrol (Paukenschlag). (Credit: Horst Bredow, U-BOOT-ARCHIV)

apitänleutnant Reinhard Hardegen, ommander U-123, on second operaional cruise to U.S. Coast, 1942. (Credit: orst Bredow, U-BOOT-ARCHIV)

*At his Rastenburg headquarters in East Prus-
sia Adolf Hitler awards Oak Leaves to the
Knight's Cross to Hardegen following the
U-123 commander's second successful U.S.
patrol. (Credit: Horst Bredow, U-BOOT-
ARCHIV)*

*Admiral Karl Dönitz, creator of Operation
Drumbeat, is shown (center) in the situation
room of his U-boat headquarters (BdU). To his
left is Chief of Operations Konteradmiral
Eberhard Godt and to his right staff officer
Kapitänleutnant Adalbert Schnee. This photograph was taken in 1943 when BdU had been
moved from France to Berlin. (Credit: Martin
Middlebrook)*

*Fleet Admiral Ernest J. King, Commander
Chief United States Fleet (COMINCH) a
Chief of Naval Operations (CNO) from 1942
1945. (Credit: Official U.S. Navy photogra[*

unusually relaxed Vice Admiral ...lphus Andrews, Commander East-...Frontier, is shown in his office at 90 ...urch Street in Manhattan congrat-...ting Hans Nielson, master of the Nor-...gian freighter Reinholt, *which ...vived a gun battle with U-752 (Kptlt. ...l-Ernst Schroeter) on 23 April 1942 ...t of Delaware Bay. (Credit: U.S. Naval ...titute)*

... Schlüssel M (Enigma) cipher ...chine of the type carried on board ...23. The metal lid has been raised. ...wn in front are the plugs. On top are, ...rder, the keyboard, the glow holes, ... three rotors. The machine was por-...e in an oak box 7 x 11 x 13 inches. ...dit: Imperial War Museum)

U-123 crew members from the 1942 American patrols gather at Bad König/Odenwald, West Germany, in 1985 to recall their experiences. Left to right are Walter Kaeding, Richard Amstein, Max Hufnagl, Karl Latislaus, Karl Fröbel, Rudolf Meisinger, Heinz Barth, Reinhard Hardegen, Fritz Rafalski, Hans Seigel, and Horst von Schroeter. *(Credit: Herbert Bubenik)*

Reinhard Hardegen in 1986 stands before his portrait painted in 1942 and an inscribed photograph of Admiral Dönitz that hang in his home in Bremen-Oberneuland, West Germany. (Credit: Michael Gannon)

Americans had wakened to the fact that the safest time for seaborne trade to make passage in deep water around the Carolina shoals was in the daylight. If so, his pickings here no doubt would diminish in number. At dusk, 2145 hours (CET), he surfaced to take a quick look around. While Kaeding checked their DR position against the Hatteras Lighthouse, lookouts spotted a U-boat surfaced about 3,500 meters to shoreward, with its periscope standard extended. Hardegen assumed that it was one of theirs.[40] After it disappeared he consulted his coastal charts and sailing directions and steered southwest toward Buoy 14 off Cape Lookout, where, after a night's travel, he sighted a shadow to starboard sailing on a 057 degree heading at eleven knots.

With daybreak coming he submerged for a Stern Tube 5 attack and waited until the target, a loaded freighter about 6,000 GRT, came before the lens at a 90-degree track angle and so close that it filled half the periscope at a magnification of 1.5. With textbook numbers a miss was not possible. And yet, for the second straight time, a G7e went askew. Barth reported from the sound room that the eel took a heading twenty to thirty degrees off course and maintained it until going aground. No explosion was heard. Hardegen ordered the guidance systems of all remaining eels checked and double-checked. It was a frustrating night and morning, as was the next night, 1 April, when all that was sighted were patrol craft and search planes, and *123* spent indolent hours on the bottom ten nautical miles abeam Buoy 14 light and whistle. Surfacing at 2128—diving at 2131 when a "bee" showed on the horizon—and surfacing again at 2205, *123* sighted another likely target. The blacked-out shadow approached rapidly at an estimated twelve knots on a zigzag base course of 220 or 230 degrees. Because of the brightness of the moonlit night Hardegen decided to launch an attack underwater. But everything went wrong. The night periscope lens fouled; the Vorhaltrechner broke down; when he turned for a zero-degree-angle stern attack Hardegen saw that the target's speed was eleven not twelve; the electrical launch mechanism failed, and the Tube 6 torpedo had to be launched manually three seconds late; and after forty seconds at the end of its six-hundred-meter run the eel simply died. How could it have missed? At a range of five hundred meters the target covered the whole periscope field of view on low magnification. The track was a classic 90 degrees. Was the target's speed off? *Gröner* showed her to be the U.S. tanker SS *Liebre*, 7,057 GRT, speed in the range of ten to eleven knots. If the eel bottomed, why did it not explode? Hardegen guessed that the ship had nets of some kind hung below the waterline. (She did not, and a more likely reason for the miss was that Hardegen misread *Liebre*'s course and speed: Survivors reported later that their course was 273 true and speed was nine knots.[41]) Whatever had happened, Hardegen was not going to let this one get away.

"Surface! Battle stations gun!"

The forward gun began firing from the 2,500-meter range at a rate of two shells per minute against the tanker's port side. There were numerous misses, but hits showed up on the flying bridge, the midship house, crew quarters, deck erections, and hull. One shell exploded the ship's signal rockets in a brilliant pyrotechnic display. The illumination enabled Hardegen to see that the tanker was steaming in ballast and he ordered IIWO Schüler, commanding guns, to aim for the waterline and engine room. After more pounding *Liebre* blew off steam and lost way. Soon her crew were seen going into lifeboats. Rafalski reported up the pipe that a SOS . . . SSS had gone out and had been acknowledged. Holding his fire while *Liebre*'s crew abandoned ship and his own men passed the spent shell casings down the tower, Hardegen worried that shellfire might not be enough to cause this tanker, with her empty bunkers, to sink. Another eel might be required—a thought interrupted by a lookout's cry: "Patrol craft starboard beam!" Hardegen raised his 7 × 50s to see a narrow shadow with a frothy white wake bows-on. It could be close enough to ram!

"*Alarm!*"

The boat went down quickly enough to avoid a ramming, but just barely, and Hardegen could hear the propellers pass overhead. A ramming would certainly tear up a small craft's bow, thought Hardegen, but the impact could also separate the plates of a U-boat's hull, which would be worse. The American up there had guts. Hardegen ordered periscope depth and rigged for Wabos. "She's turning back, Herr Kaleu," Barth called up the pipe as Hardegen took his place on the saddle in the upper tower.

"Up periscope!"

It was a risk poking the scope above the surface on a small sea in moonlight with unlimited visibility at close quarters with the enemy, but he took it. There—at 265—a small patrol vessel in a turn. With his *Weyer* identification manual Hardegen identified it as an *Argo*-class WPC patrol cutter. (He was wrong: It was British Motor Torpedo Boat *332*, on loan to the U.S. Navy, with a Canadian crew.[42]) For a few minutes there seemed to be no inclination on the enemy's part to press the attack. There was no ASDIC pinging. He reasoned that the enemy crew were uncertain in which direction the submerged U-boat was traveling.

"Down scope. How much depth do we have here, LI?" he asked Schulz below.

"The fathometer reads thirty meters, Herr Kaleu."

"All right, if we have to dive, go to twenty."

Hardegen hoped he would not have to take Wabos in water this shallow. The explosive power of the charges would be greatly enhanced by the reflective hydraulic pressure wave off the bottom. He ordered the scope raised again and saw the enemy vessel which was facing him at a zero degree angle immediately accelerate. Damn! It had seen the scope!

"Dive! Dive! Down scope! Brace for Wabos!" he yelled as he fell down the ladder into the control room. Moments later the boat lurched violently from a single Wabo inexpertly dropped too far from the hull to cause damage. Barth reported that the vessel was turning for another pass. "Screws coming on!" he sang out. Again the men held on. The propellers crossed overhead. But nothing happened. Strange. Barth reported the vessel moving off toward the stricken *Liebre*. Was it a trick? When Barth reported the vessel had stopped, probably at *Liebre*'s position, Hardegen ordered the boat to periscope depth and confirmed the fact by eye. The enemy had simply given up when it had them fairly well located, and in shoal water. Was it because they lacked ASDIC? How much good luck did *123* deserve? Better not push that luck too far, he thought, since there were bound to be more patrol craft assembling here soon in response to the tanker's distress call. With regret, and some anger at himself for not getting off a coup-de-grace eel at *Liebre*, he moved slowly away from the scene underwater. An hour and a half later, under a bright moon, he surfaced and resumed his descent of the coast south toward Florida on the two-hundred-meter curve. The ploughshare of the bow sliced into the western edges of the opposing Gulf Stream, dividing the warm black masses that retarded their progress. Eventually, like the southbound merchantmen he had observed on his first patrol, Hardegen hugged the shore to avoid the three-knot currents. To the KTB he confided: "To what extent [*Liebre*] will fill up with water from holes at the waterline is hard to say, but from my experience it is quite possible that she will sink. In any case, no one will be happy with her condition now."[43]

Liebre had sailed in ballast from New York on 30 March, bound for Beaumont, Texas. She was seventeen miles east of Cape Lookout Outer Buoy, blacked out and zigzagging on Navy Plan No. 2, when the first shells arrived on the port side. The crew counted forty rounds fired but only ten to fifteen hits. An SOS . . . SSS went out, the first time the radio had been used since departing New York, and a strong "R" was received from a shore station, probably Charleston. The engine room hit disabled the starboard generator, plunging the ship into darkness. Thinking the damage greater than it was, the master, Frank C. Giradeau, ordered closed the main stop valve from the boilers to the main engine, which killed way and enabled lifeboats Numbers 1 and 4 to be safely lowered. Of the thirty-four-man crew, two had been killed outright in the engine room and seven others, panicking at the bewilderingly sudden attack, had jumped overboard and drowned. The boats pulled away and lay to until daybreak. Some crewmen reported seeing a craft of some kind approach *Liebre* and show lights on her, which probably was Canadian motor torpedo boat *332.* In the ensuing daylight the survivors saw that the mangled tanker was still riding steadfastly afloat. They were rowing back to board her when rescue vessels arrived, some to take them in to shore and others, a tug and a trawler, to tow the tanker into Morehead City, North Carolina. In subsequent developments *Liebre* was reconstructed at Baltimore and returned to service on 19 July, and Master Giradeau was criticized by naval authorities for not having removed the confidential papers, which included both British and American codes, although there was no sign that these had been molested. (Reinhard Hardegen never boarded a ship that he had torpedoed or shelled.) Fifth Naval District at Norfolk speculated that since no torpedo attack had taken place (so far as anyone knew), and it was ordinarily the policy of U-boats to finish off targets with torpedoes when shelling alone failed to sink, it "cannot be overlooked in the case of the *Liebre*" that the attack "might possibly have been made by a surface raider."[44]

Leaving behind this tantalizing hypothesis as his calling card Hardegen on the night of 8 April, the Wednesday after Easter, was making knots in a slight sea south, along the coastal barrier islands of Georgia. Here there were few lights on shore since the broken land chain, storied as the Guale, Golden, or Sea Islands, was thinly populated, most residents being gulls, herons, wood ibis, clapper rail, an occasional feral hog, Spanish horse, or three-hundred-pound sea turtle waddling ashore to lay eggs. Passing St. Catherine's, Blackbeard, and Sapelo islands, U-*123* came upon St. Simons Island where lookouts spotted two shadows under the quarter moon proceeding north-bound in tandem three miles apart on an inshore routing two miles off buoys. Hardegen put a torpedo into each of them, 52 minutes apart, the shock waves rushing across the dark water to rattle among the sand dunes and sea oats. The first in line, SS *Oklahoma,* was a 9,264-GRT Texaco, Inc., tanker with a cargo of one hundred thousand bar-rels of kerosene, gasoline, and diesel oil from Port Arthur destined for Providence, Rhode Island. The second was SS *Esso Baton Rouge,* a 7,989-GRT Standard Oil of New Jersey tanker, bound from Baytown, Texas, to New York with seventy thousand barrels of lubricating oil and twenty thousand barrels of heating oil. Hit in the engine room, *Oklahoma* made water quickly astern and her master, Theron P. Davenport, ordered Abandon Ship. Eighteen men went overside in boats, but the master and three others reboarded when they heard screams from the vessel and found one critically wounded officer, who subsequently died. Eighteen more men were apparently trapped be-low in or near the flooded engine room, and could not be saved. Shortly after the boarding party returned to the boats they saw their attacker surface about three points off the port bow and begin shelling the carcass in its now-grotesque posture with stern against the bottom (depth twelve meters) and funnel, bridge, and forecastle above the surface. The survivors had a clear view of the U-boat and later de-scribed in detail how it fired about twelve rounds and then made off at high speed toward the *Esso Baton Rouge.* A G7e below the waterline between bunkers and engine room of the second tanker set her fuel oil ablaze and the engine, fireroom, and crew quarters immediately flooded causing the stern to sink to the bottom in a reprise of *Okla-homa*'s plight, the decks at ten-degree list to starboard and the bow draft reduced to seventeen feet. Two men on watch in the engine room were killed by the torpedo's explosion. A third crewman, a naturalized German, unaccountably jumped overboard in a rubber suit and was not seen again. One survivor reported hearing a voice from the U-boat say in broken English, "Come over here and we will save you," but there is no mention of the incident in Hardegen's KTB. Thirty-five men successfully abandoned ship in Numbers 1 and 3 lifeboats. Hardegen fired a few shells into the bow to release the air giving buoyancy, after which he pronounced the ship a *Totalverlust!*—"total loss!"[45] Joining up with the boats from *Oklahoma* the survivors were eventually towed into Brunswick by a USN patrol boat. The two tankers remained awash and drifting, the oil from their bunkers fouling wilderness beaches until the week following, when it was decided by naval and shipping investigators that the two sunken hulls could be raised and refloated. After preliminary salvage both tankers were towed to repair yards and returned to ocean service seven months later. So, U-123's last three tanker kills were illusory.

In Hardegen's view he had sunk them all. *Liebre* he had left a helpless derelict. These last two tankers he had brought as low as they could be brought. In his mind they were legitimate sinkings. "We seem to be specializing in tankers," he wrote in his KTB.[46] If the ships had gone down in deeper water certainly they would have been lost for good. But a stern bumping on the bottom could keep the bows full of air, and thus, technically, one could deny Hardegen the trophies. Or one could backdate claims, since both tankers would be sunk again, and that time for good—the first, *Esso Baton Rouge,* on 23 February 1943, when U-202 (Kptlt. Günter Poser) caught her 100 miles due south of the Azores; the second, *Oklahoma,* late in the war on 28 March 1945, when U-532 (Fregattenkapitän Ottoheinrich Junker) got lucky in mid-Atlantic.[47]

After spending the daylight hours of 8 April on the Georgia seabed *123* rose like a sea monster at nightfall twelve miles southeast of St. Simons Sound light buoy. Shortly afterward the lookouts sighted a northbound vessel that Hardegen quickly identified in the ample moonlight as a fast (thirteen-knot) cold storage motor ship named SS *Esparta,* property of the United Fruit Company. Even though it was small, only 3,365 GRT, Hardegen considered it a valuable prey because of its sophisticated refrigeration system; besides, its food cargo was also a fuel of war. Taking a position four hundred meters off the target's course and slowing to three knots *123* launched G7e Number 9283 from Tube 1 on a course of 305 degrees. Von Schroeter's data called for a hit at forty-two seconds. Right on time, WHACK!, and a dark detonation column rose above the aft mast. Within a short time the stern to the front edge of the funnel submerged. Under the glare of red and white emergency flares Hardegen could see that the ship had a smooth deck with almost no superstructure, conforming to the silhouette in *Gröner,* where he also learned that she was 101 meters long with a 7-meter draft. Certain that she would sink—and this time he was right—Hardegen resumed navigation south. On *Esparta,* meanwhile, several men jumped overboard to escape the fumes released from twelve hundred pounds of ammonia gas used in the ship's refrigeration system, while most of the rest of the forty-man crew abandoned ship in Numbers 1 and 3 starboard life-boats and forward raft. After throwing codes overboard in a weighted bag and sending distress signals, the master and radio operator jumped into the water alongside the raft. Only one crewman, who panicked, was lost, by drowning. The rest were rescued seven hours later by Navy Crash Boat USS *Tyrer*.[48]

At 0924 CET (0244 ET) on the ninth *123*'s lookouts sighted a large flying boat dead ahead and coming straight at them. Hardegen dived the boat, worried about the marine phosphorescence in his wake and swirl. When nothing happened he decided that the aircraft was a commercial Pan American Clipper, since the Americans would not be using flying boats on coastwise patrols. He decided to stay underwater where he was. Daylight was a few hours off. He wanted solid darkness when he passed the Naval Section Base at Mayport on the mouth of the St. Johns River. That station was just a comparative few miles away, he saw on his charts. From the locker in his cubicle he pulled the paper-bound *Handbuch*, Part II, on American coastal landmarks and began studying closely the features described there: "*Andere gute Land-marken sind ein roter, kegelförmiger, nicht mehr als solcher benutzter Leuchtturm bei dem Ort* Mayport, *1¾ sm westlich von* St. John Point, *sowie die Gebäude in den Seebädern* Atlantic Beach *und* Jacksonville Beach, *3¾ und 6¾ sm südlich von dieser Huk. . . .*"[49]

12

The Navy Stirs

By mid-March, after sixty days of tragically unnecessary blood and brine, even the imperturbable Ernest J. King was starting to panic. "The submarine situation on the east coast," he wrote to a flag officer, "approaches the desperate."[1] The imperious Anglophobe admiral who had resisted every piece of Britain's hard-won advice on fighting U-boats, and who ridiculed President Roosevelt's predilection for "small boats" and "light airplanes," was forced finally to a volte-face. It was about time, thought the exasperated British, Winston Churchill in the lead. "It is surprising indeed that during two years of the advance of total war towards the American continent more provision had not been made against this deadly onslaught," the Prime Minister observed. Of course the naval war in the Pacific pressed hard on the resources of the U.S. Navy. "Still," he exclaimed, "with all the information they had about the protective measures we had adopted both before and during the struggle, it is remarkable that no plans had been made for coastal convoys and for multiplying small craft."[2] Churchill had put his finger on two of the principal reasons for the U.S. failure. Others in Britain were less gentle in their expressions. Captain Brian B. Schofield, whose Admiralty Trade Division superintended British merchant shipping in all the world's sea-lanes, found the "inadequate" state of U.S. Navy defenses in the American lanes to be "quite incomprehensible."[3] Having to count staggering losses of British-controlled shipping, particularly of tankers, as well as an enormous slaughter of human life in waters where the Admiralty's writ did not run, Schofield found it "extremely difficult to be polite about it."[4] As Admiral Sir Percy L. H. Noble described the situation to the First Sea Lord, Admiral Sir Dudley Pound: "The Western Approaches Command finds itself in the position today [8 March] of escorting convoys safely over to the American eastern seaboard, and then . . . finding that many of the ships thus escorted are easy prey to the U-boats . . . off the American coast or in the Caribbean."[5] No doubt it jarred the Admiralty to read Bletchley Park's decrypt of Adolf Hitler's reaction to the massacre (as quoted in a transmission to Tokyo by Japan's ambassador in Berlin, Baron Hiroshi Oshima): "I myself have been surprised at the successes we have met with along the American coast lately. The United States kept up the tall talk and left her coast unguarded. Now I daresay that *she* is quite surprised."[6] The official historian of the Royal Navy called the sinkings on the U.S. seaboard a "holocaust."[7] Patrick Beesly, who watched the holocaust day by day on the OIC plot, told the present writer that in his opinion the U.S. Navy's delay in providing appropriate protection to coastwise merchant traffic was "criminal."[8] In a cable to Roosevelt aide and confidant Harry Hopkins on 12 March Churchill exploded: "I am most deeply concerned at the immense sinking of tankers west of the 40th meridian and in the Caribbean Sea. . . . The situation is so serious that drastic action of some kind is necessary. . . ."[9] Roosevelt called King to the White House to discuss the Prime Minister's concerns and replied seven days later with what Churchill suggested might have been "a touch of strain" but more likely was the influence of King's acid quarterdeck style: "Your interest in steps to be taken to combat the Atlantic submarine menace as indicated by your recent message to Mr. Hopkins on this subject impels me to request your particular consideration of heavy attacks on submarine bases and building and repair yards, thus checking submarine activities at their source and where submarines perforce congregate."[10] This Ciceronian attempt to turn blame back on his reprover ill became FDR, though it was quite in character with the frosty King. More to the point, it ignored the fact that where U-boat bases were concerned, as the British knew, no bomb in the Allied arsenal was capable of penetrating the seven-meter-thick carapaces of the Biscay bunkers. Churchill gallantly did order bombing raids on U-boat yards in Germany but, as the postwar data showed, they were inconsequential. The proximate and answerable causes of British losses were not to be found in Brittany or Germany. They were to be found on the American main.

In an extraordinary move, Britain's proud career executive admirals dispatched the layman Commander Rodger Winn to Washington. No man, save Dönitz himself, knew more about the U-boat war than did the director of the OIC's Submarine Tracking Room. Moreover, Winn had studied at Yale and Harvard, thus there was an assumption at the Admiralty that he knew how to deal with Americans. Winn's specific mission, as Beesly remembered it, was to persuade the U.S. Navy to institute coastwise convoys at the earliest possible moment, to impose shoreline blackouts, and to establish a U-boat tracking room on the OIC model.[11] Thus one of the most vital emissary responsibilities of the war was laid on the deformed shoulders of this volunteer reserve backroom operator. Arriving at Main Navy, Winn found that it took three long days of show-and-tell before he could make headway with Commander George C. Dyer, head of the ONI Information Room, a clearinghouse for strategic data. Despite the fact that Dyer's intelligence background was minimal, in the end he recognized the sense that Winn was making and arranged for him to see Rear Admiral Richard S. Edwards, King's deputy chief of staff, who oversaw USN antisubmarine warfare. To Winn's earnest presentation Edwards replied that "the Americans wished to learn their own lessons and that they had plenty of ships with which to do so"—King's doctrine in a nutshell.[12] Stupefied and offended at this response, the outranked Winn remonstrated: "The trouble is, Admiral, it's not only your bloody ships you are losing: A lot of them are ours!"[13] Edwards, brought up short, grudgingly agreed that Winn had a point, and he suggested, "You had better see Admiral King." To Winn it seemed, when he was finally led into King's austere third-deck office, that the obdurate and forbidding Navy chief had been well briefed on the Admiralty's line of argument and that the logic of Winn's case had broken through, since, to his surprise, King seemed very willing to discuss the issues in an open, even friendly, way. The result was reassurances from King that he was moving forward as quickly as he could to institute coastal convoys, that he would develop with the Army a plan for darkening the coastline from Maine to the Keys, and, of most immediate importance to Winn, that he would create a Submarine Tracking Room to which all naval information of whatever kind would be directed. Winn was satisfied. He declared his mission accomplished and rushed off to New York to convert Admiral Andrews.

In sign of COMINCH sincerity on the last point—a belated and stunning concession of Operations to Intelligence—King instructed Edwards to appoint an officer who would learn the tracking room business at Winn's elbow in London and then become Winn's USN counterpart in Washington. The officer Edwards selected for this critical position was not a Washington hand but Kenneth A. Knowles, a regular who had retired from active duty in 1936 because of eyesight disability but after Pearl Harbor had returned at lieutenant's rank to serve as ROTC adviser at the University of Texas, Austin. Plucked from this obscurity in May, Knowles went to Washington, where he received two and a half stripes and was sent almost immediately to London for an intensive two-week immersion in the OIC Tracking Room. "Winn was quite a man," Knowles recalled to the writer. "He was a hunchback but that didn't deter him. What impressed most was his mind. The atmosphere in the room was very controlled and businesslike. There was never any panic despite the fact that at that time there were great losses off the U.S.—the loss of bottoms being more deplored than their cargoes—and very few U-boat casualties."[14] Rather than being blinded entirely by the newly adopted U-boat Atlantic TRITON cipher, Winn and Beesly had been only sorely inconvenienced. From long acquaintance with HYDRA they knew Dönitz's mind, the U-boat routes, the boats' average speed of advance, their endurance at sea, the nature of their communications, and the style of their commanders. The length and position of W/T transmissions of boats to Kernével provided valuable clues as to course and destination, even if the full meaning of the transmissions escaped Bletchley Park's wizardry, as it would continue to do until the following December.

All this insight into Ubootwaffe stratagem and ambuscade Winn and Beesly passed on to Knowles, as they also instructed him in the use of conventional sources of intelligence and of two extremely valuable technical tools that still remained: D/F fixes and the TETIS cipher. D/F (Huff-Duff) readings were still less accurate and dependable on the American side than they were on the British, but the OIC D/F staff taught Knowles how to interpret the "cuts" he would get from USN W/T intercept stations at Winter Harbor, Maine; Amagansett, Long Island; Cheltenham, Maryland; Poyners Hill, North Carolina; Charleston, South Carolina; Jupiter, Florida; and San Juan, Puerto Rico. TETIS, on the other hand, was a cipher long since penetrated by BP and still in use by U-boats training in the Baltic.

Through TETIS Winn and Beesly could track a boat from first commissioning through work-up and training until it finally departed for an operational base. At the Biscay bases R-boat escorts that accompanied outward- and inward-bound U-boats through the swept channels still employed HYDRA (an unaccountable German oversight), thus the Tracking Room could deduce when a new boat came into service as well as assess the number of boats at sea and their probable distribution. Pledging to share all these data with Knowles when he got set up, Winn and Beesly suggested that if access to the Atlantic cipher had to be lost, this was the best possible time for it to happen, when everybody knew where the boats were proceeding anyway—at, to, or from the U.S., Canadian, and Caribbean shorelines; when there was little regular BdU-to-boats wireless to monitor; and when, in the Western Atlantic, at least, there were no rakes around which to divert shipping.

On his return to Washington, Knowles organized an Atlantic Section, Intelligence Center (OP-20-G, later F-21) on the sixth wing of Main Navy that operated as an exact clone of Winn's Tracking Room and exchanged all its data with the parent organization. The start-up marked the beginning of a transfer of U-boat tracking from a frontier (local) to an Atlantic scale. Even King came to appreciate the value of what he had belatedly set in motion. As one admiral recalled (from a later date, when F-21 was known also as the "Secret Room"): "I had a particularly outstanding lieutenant commander who would brief King every morning at 0900. He emphasized the locations of the various German submarines as if he knew exactly where they were, as I think he usually did."[15] The American Winn, like his mentor, would finish the war as a captain.

If Britain's dander was up, so, too, was that of the oil industry. On 4 March in Washington worried members of the Tanker Committee of the Petroleum Industry War Council met with service representatives from the Navy and War departments. By that date sixty-five ships had been sunk in Maine–Florida and Caribbean waters, twenty-seven of them tankers. If the sinkings continued at the same rate throughout the remainder of 1942, the industry spokesman argued, by the following January 125 of the 320 tankers available on the coast would be destroyed. (Their fears were well-founded: During March vessels of all kinds went down at an average of more than one a day, and during April the East Coast was, as the ESF war diary described it, "the most dangerous area for merchant shipping in the entire world."[16] Insurance companies ceased writing policies on merchant vessels.) Unless the U-boat attacks were checked, the spokesman said, the supply of oil would sink to levels "intolerable" both for the domestic economy and for any projected continuation of the war effort, by the United States or its Allies. Furthermore, the lives of three thousand seamen would be lost.[17] Daunted by the appalling losses of the past seven weeks, merchant seamen who in the first weeks of war had proved eager to sign on for new sailings after being torpedoed were now increasingly demoralized by the sinkings, especially engine room men on tankers, who were leaving in troubling numbers. In the past chief mates complained about men who got drunk in port or were hard to handle; now they complained about not finding enough men to make a crew. One master reported that on reaching home port thirteen of a crew of thirty disappeared. Aggravating the problems of deteriorating morale and crew shortages was the belief of some Navy and shipping officials that certain crewmen were Axis sympathizers who had been induced by enemy agents in various New York and Brooklyn bars (Highway Tavern, the Old Hamburg, and Schmidt's being named) to divulge sailing times. But most Navy officials dismissed this possibility as irrelevant since, as one said, "The submarines could lie off focal points up and down the coast and await the arrival of ships without having any previous knowledge of sailing times."[18]

The oil industry committee made numerous positive suggestions for improving the situation, chief among which were: (1) swinging guns aboard all tankers, as the British had done, and crewing them with highly trained USN Armed Guards; (2) engaging the services of the Civil Air Patrol, private pilots with their own light airplanes, to force down U-boats in the sea-lanes (an idea endorsed by Admiral Andrews); and (3) suppressing bright shore lights showing to seaward against which it was obvious U-boats silhouetted their targets. (These eminently sensible recommendations, be it noted, came from laymen.) For the Navy's part COMINCH agreed to look into the question of Armed Guards. One of the first tankers to be so equipped was the Gulf Oil Corporation's just-launched SS *Gulfamerica*. As she took on ninety thousand barrels of fuel oil at Port Arthur, Texas, for her maiden voyage to New York at the beginning of April the deck aft presented one four-inch 50 SP Mark IX Mod. gun and bridge nests held two 50-caliber Browning Mark II machine guns. Seven Naval Armed Guard crewmen officered by a reserve ensign manned the weapons. As for private pilots and light planes encroaching on the Navy's airspace

King would have none of it (for now), answering that the idea had too many "operational difficulties."[19] The Army, whose aircraft dominated offshore search operations, had no objection to civilian help.

Where coastal blackouts were concerned the two services vacillated, despite the fact that since the President's Executive Order 9066 of 19 February the services had authority "to assume control over all lighting on the seacoast so as to prevent the silhouetting of ships and their consequent destruction by enemy submarines."[20] Their reluctance to take action came principally as a result of intense pressure exerted by coastal business interests such as beach resort operators who did not want to "inconvenience tourists." In the meeting of 4 March it was decided by the military representatives that control of coastal lights was "a Navy function."[21] Accordingly, five days later—and two months after the date when, it might be argued, he should already have acted decisively and on his own initiative—Admiral King sent out a halfhearted "request" to Andrews in New York: "It is requested that the Commander Eastern Sea Frontier take such steps as may be within his province to control the brilliant illumination of Eastern Seaboard amusement parks and beaches in order that ships passing close to shore be not silhouetted and thereby more easily exposed to submarine attack from seaward."[22] An additional five days later, on 14 March, King made it clear that what he was requesting was not a blackout but a "dimout"; blackouts "were not considered necessary" since only the glare of the brightest lights posed a danger to shipping. This tragic misjudgment, repeating an error that Andrews had made on 10 February (see chapter 5), would lead by omission to further loss of lives and treasure.

On the very day that King was rejecting blackouts, the 7,610-GRT American freighter SS *Lemuel Burrows* was torpedoed and sunk by U-*404* (Korvettenkapitän Otto von Bülow) off Atlantic City, New Jersey. Twenty crewmen died. The second engineer, who arguably had a better picture of the situation from his lifeboat than King had from his desk, reported that the lights of a New Jersey beach resort doomed his vessel and that they would "continue to cause daily torpedoings until a blackout is ordered along the coast." The engineer added: "We might as well run with our lights on. The lights were like Coney Island. It was lit up like daylight all along the beach. . . . We're going to lose boats every day if they don't do something about it."[23] On 19 March Third Naval District advised the Commanding General, Second Corps Area, U.S. Army, that even with dimout vessels were silhouetted as much as ten miles out to sea against the sky glow cast from ground light on haze or low-lying cloud banks. It recommended "a complete blackout of all communities within approximately five miles of the coastline," but this would never be done.[24] Tests at sea in April found that patrol boats twenty-five miles out could discern the New York glow even with dimout.[25] In May, Army studies concluded that dimout was still so dangerous to shipping that "like targets in a shooting gallery our ships are moving in off a backdrop of hazy light."[26] And as late as 7 July when the 8,141-GRT British freighter *Umtata*, under tow, was torpedoed and sunk off the south Florida coast (at 25-35N, 80-02W) by U-*571* (Kptlt. Helmut Möhlmann), the *Umtata*'s second officer blamed the sky glow of Miami ten miles to the northwest. "We could see the loom of Miami 35 miles out to sea," he reported. "The glow of light is just what those subs want."[27] The glow came from street and automobile lights, resort and house windows, dog tracks and other amusement areas. On 8 July the *Miami Herald* reported that motorists on the Overseas Highway between Homestead and Key West were driving with high beam lights, and, in a related story, cited the experience of a U.S. naval vessel that found the loom of Key West so clearly visible from thirty-one miles at sea that it silhouetted any ship that passed before it.[28]

During the time of slaughter no general blackout was ever declared on the U.S. East Coast. While the British and German coasts, which were quiescent in the same period, practiced total light elimination, the endangered U.S. littoral remained lighted. Dimout and shielding was as far as King would go. The Army concurred. So did the general public, which wanted business and pleasure as usual. Civilian avarice and carelessness must take their places on the list of agents accountable for the U-boat triumphs.

The USN destroyer (DD) with its speed, maneuverability, firepower, sound gear, and ability to keep the sea in thick weather, was everybody's ship of choice against the U-boat. It was also during March and April the most maldistributed weapons platform in the Atlantic fleet. Of seventy-three destroyers assigned to the Atlantic, ordinarily fifteen on the average were laid up for repair and overhaul. Of the remainder, 42 percent were stationed at sea along the arc that ran from Casco Bay, Maine, through Argentia and Hvalfjord to Londonderry, Northern Ireland, where during March only 6 percent of Allied world tonnage lost to U-boats could be counted. It bears repeating that, by contrast, inside the Eastern Sea Frontier protectorate that ran five hundred miles seaward from the U.S. shoreline, where 49 percent of Allied tonnage went down in the same period, only 5 percent of destroyer strength was apportioned. In other words, where ships and cargoes were most endangered the least destroyer strength was available.[29] Admiral Andrews had struggled futilely to correct this imbalance, beginning in February when he realized the mounting threat to shipping off the Jersey shore, the Delaware and Virginia Capes, Wimble Shoals, and Diamond Shoal. To King he defined fifteen full-time destroyers as his minimum need.[30] But in response only one DD, *Jacob Jones*, was assigned full-time to the frontier and she was sunk on the twenty-eighth. Eleven other DDs were assigned to ESF part-time during the same month, but none remained long before being whisked away to the convoy arc, with the result that there was much lost motion and little defensive contribution by the DD squadrons. On 8 March CINCLANT (Admiral Ingersoll) made the modest concession that while his destroyers made passage through frontier waters to and from repair and overhaul yards, they might be employed for the protection of merchant shipping. By these means Andrews was able to call on the services of two DDs, on average, each day in March—a month in which the U-boat campaign in the frontier reached its full fury.[31] By the end of the month either King or Ingersoll, or both, finally noticed the dislocation of destroyer strength and assigned eight DDs to the frontier on temporary service; but only nine days into April all but two were vacuumed away for the "essential escort of convoys."[32] Then on 16 April King swung the other way again and ordered CINCLANT to assign three DDs to ESF "at once" and a total of nine as soon as possible.[33] When the promised nine came on station at the end of the month a harried Andrews held his breath; but to his relief, during May sixteen DDs patrolled in the frontier, some for as many as twenty-one days, some for as few as two.

Andrews began receiving help from other quarters in the same period. In a reversal of the 1940 fifty-destroyer deal, Winston Churchill sent across twenty-four antisubmarine trawlers with trained crews. COMINCH accepted the gift graciously. Following overhaul the coal-burning trawlers with their nine- to eleven-knot speed were put into service beginning the last week of March. They bore such names as HMS *Lady Rosemary*, *Bedfordshire*, and *Northern Duke*.[34] In face of what he now recognized as "the desperate submarine attack situation along the Atlantic coast,"[35] King began to change his mind about the usefulness of small craft. As early as 7 February he authorized Andrews to employ "at sea anywhere within your Frontier" seventy-, seventy-five-, eighty-, and eighty-three-foot Coast Guard cutters and to arm them immediately with depth charges and guns (one pounders and machine .50 caliber).[36] By the end of March sixty cutters would be on patrol in the ESF sea-lanes together with other small craft: ten PC and PY patrol vessels, five SC chasers, five PE Eagle boats, two gunboats, and the British trawlers. Andrews also converted five yachts varying in length from 75 to 175 feet to patrol use. The number of combat ships and craft advanced to 150 by the end of June, to 156 by the end of July. Some of these were new PCs and SCs produced in a "sixty vessels in sixty days" program of small-craft construction begun in April.

Slight increases of surface strength could be observed in ESF's neighboring command, the Gulf Sea Frontier (GSF), which ran from the Duval–Saint Johns County line (above Saint Augustine, Florida) south around the Keys, past the Mississippi River Passes, and down the coasts of Texas and Mexico as far as Belize in British Honduras, where yet another USN sea frontier, the Panama, ranged south and east to Punta de Gallinas, Colombia. Included in the GSF protective area were the Florida Coast and Straits, most of the Bahamas, half of Cuba, the entire Gulf of Mexico and the Yucatan Channel. Until mid-May the GSF barely existed as an independent command, but operated as an extension of the Seventh Naval District (Miami). Key West was the first GSF headquarters as such, though a very unsatisfactory one because of its isolation and poor communications: In order to respond to a U-boat sighting off Cape Canaveral, for example, GSF had to make a commercial telephone call to the Third Army Bomber Command at Charleston in order to request a search by Army aircraft based at nearby Miami![37] The first entrance of U-boats into GSF waters took place on 19 February, when U-128 (Korvettenkapitän Ulrich Heyse), which had originally been scheduled as the sixth boat of Paukenschlag, sank the 8,201-GRT American tanker SS *Pan Massachusetts* twenty miles off Cape Canaveral. Thereafter Floridians on their beach-cottage decks and tourists on hotel balconies became frequent witnesses to offshore violence. Between 19 February and 14 May sixteen ships were sunk inside Florida territorial waters. Four others were damaged. One loss, that of the neutral Mexican-flag tanker *Portrero del Llano* eight miles south-southeast of Fowey Rocks near Miami on 14 May, precipitated Mexico's declaration of war on Germany.

First notice of the entrance of the enemy into the Gulf of Mexico came on 4 May when U-507 (Korvettenkapitän Harro Schacht) sank the 2,686-GRT American freighter *Norlindo* west-northwest of Key West. During May ships went down in the Gulf itself at a rate approaching one a day, most off the muddy Passes of the Mississippi.[38] The onslaught caught the frontier both surprised and ill-prepared. In London, Rodger Winn observed that half the number of U-boats that appeared inside the Gulf during May did so without previous warning: They had not been detected on their departure from France nor on their transatlantic crossings. It occurred to Winn that these might be boats that had been followed across on earlier passages and that now were being supplied and refueled at some isolated site on the south coast of the Gulf, or, less likely, in the Western Caribbean.[39] Admiral Andrews' staff had earlier theorized that U-boats might be making rendezvous with neutral-flag tankers operating out of Mexico, Honduras, Nicaragua, Colombia, or Venezuela.[40] Neither hypothesis was correct. At no time in the American campaign did U-boats refuel or provision from surface vessels, coasts, or islands.[41] What many of them did do, however, accounting for what Winn concluded were unusually lengthy periods on station both in the Gulf and Caribbean, was to rendezvous with newly constructed U-boat tankers of a new type (XIV) immediately dubbed by U-boat men *Milchkuh* (milch cow). Through aerial photography Winn and Beesly had spotted the first of these, U-459, on her departure from Kiel in April. From her size (1,688 tons surface displacement) and broad beam Winn deduced at the time that she was a minelayer. Lacking access to Special Intelligence because of the TRITON blackout, Winn could not know that northwest of Bermuda in early May, U-459 refueled no fewer than fifteen boats from her stores of seven hundred tons of oil.[42] The Type XIV, of which ten were built, carried no torpedoes and mounted only AA guns. "Clumsy," Dönitz called them—none survived the war—but their capacity to refuel and revictual extended the cruise time of Type IX boats by eight weeks and that of Type VII boats by four, thus producing the equivalent of a marked increase in the number of boats on operational patrol at one time. Dönitz noted that with the supply boats his radius of action extended now to "the Gulf of Mexico and off Panama or down to Cape Town and Bahia." He also observed that "U-boat losses are now extraordinarily small."[43] Winn counted nearly thirty boats in the Western Atlantic during May, from Nova Scotia to Florida, the Gulf of Mexico, and Caribbean. By the time he and Beesly discovered the reprovisioning activity, three tankers were tending pump at assigned grid positions in the Western Atlantic. Soon there would be six.

To meet the enemy fleet the Gulf Sea Frontier had available two four-piper destroyers, *Dahlgren* and *Noa,* two 165-foot Coast Guard cutters, two Treasury-class cutters, four 145-foot cutters, one 125-foot cutter, sixteen 83-foot cutters, three converted yachts, and a small assortment of PCs, SCs and YPs ("Yippies"), the last of which were 75-foot yard-patrol craft originally built to Coast Guard specifications in 1924–25 for interception of Prohibition rumrunners. In the Caribbean Sea Frontier (Rear Admiral John H. Hoover commanding at San Juan de Puerto Rico) surface forces were in far shorter supply, despite the fact that the Dutch islands of Curaçao and Aruba were rich sources of gasoline and oil derivatives, that all the bauxite trade and much of the rest of shipping to and from South America sailed past Trinidad, and that the Vichy French governed in Martinique and Guadeloupe. Naval Operating Base (NOB) Trinidad boasted two 500-ton converted yachts, two Yippies, and, after June, one 110-foot sub-chaser. Bases at San Juan, Curaçao, and Guantánamo (Cuba) were no better equipped. The Gulf and particularly the Caribbean fleets were heavily over-matched by the southern U-boat dispositions, now reinforced by at-sea support. Little wonder that during May and June more shipping vanished in those two frontiers, sixty-five and eighty-two vessels, respectively, than had gone down the world over in any previous two-month period.

Naval air strength showed some improvement through the first six months of the year. In the ESF long-range air patrol seaward continued to be the responsibility of the Army's First Bomber Command, which flew almost as many hours in March as it had in the previous two months combined. While the bombers made relatively few attacks, and there were no authenticated kills during the six-month period, their expanded patrol flights had the effect of keeping U-boats submerged for increasing spans of time. It was the Navy that badly wanted a kill. Early in January, Andrews had begged COMINCH for "at least one squadron" of long-range patrol planes from the shore-based Fleet squadrons at Quonset Point, Rhode Island, and Norfolk, but CINCLANT (Ingersoll) objected that he could not make such craft available until Atlantic Fleet Patrol Wing needs had first been satisfied.

The shortsightedness of Ingersoll's turf protection was glaringly apparent on 25 January when, grudgingly, he informed ESF that he would make available Fleet aircraft "for emergency assistance in the combat of enemy submarines" provided that such emergency use did "not interfere unduly with scheduled training operations[!]." As the ESF war diary acidly comments, "Unfortunately, emergencies were the order of the day."[44] Driven by exigencies that incredibly escaped the notice of Ingersoll, Andrews looked in a different direction and found twenty long-range PBY-5 Catalina flying boats manufactured for the Royal Air Force sitting idle at Elizabeth City, N.C., NAS for lack of crews to man them. Why not assign the "Cats" temporarily to ESF? he suggested, but he was turned down in January and again in February.[45] Finally, in the last week of March, when he identified seventy idle Vought-Sikorsky OS2U-3 aircraft similarly assigned to the British, Andrews won his point. ESF and Gulf Sea Frontier jointly acquired the planes at a rate of four per day. A grateful Andrews wrote to Secretary of the Navy Frank Knox: "I can assure you that no grass will grow under my feet as long as I am in this command."[46] Popularly called the Kingfisher, the OS2U-3 was a two-place (tandem) seaplane, powered by a single 450-horsepower Pratt & Whitney R-985 engine, with a top speed of 177 m.p.h. Designed as an observation plane to be launched by catapult from battleships and cruisers, it had a range with depth bombs of three hours, thus it was useful only for limited coastal patrol.[47] Still, for ESF, the "step-child of the Fleet,"[48] it was something. And by dribs and drabs additional military aircraft came under ESF command in the months following with the result that by the end of May the frontier had a total of 172 aircraft available in various states of readiness (up from 126 in April) and by the end of June 209 available including blimps in a Fleet Airship Wing.

In the Gulf and Caribbean frontiers the numbers of aircraft also advanced, though more slowly, and as spring turned to summer it was these southern waters, to which Admiral Dönitz was shifting the weight of his offensive now that ESF had begun to button up, that most desperately needed air coverage. For a long while the Gulf command had tried to get by with nineteen unarmed Coast Guard planes, fourteen 0-47 Army observation planes that flew out of Miami armed only with .30-caliber machine guns, and two ancient B-18 "Bolo" bombers that were described as "practically falling apart."[49] By the end of June, however, there were fifty-one depth bomb-equipped OS2U-3s at Banana River, Miami, Key West, San Julien (Cuba), St. Petersburg, and Biloxi, Mississippi, together with a sprinkling of Martin PBM Mariner flying boats and utility amphibians. In an emergency, training aircraft could be scrambled from air stations Banana River, Miami, Key West, Pensacola, and Corpus Christi, Texas. At Municipal Airport, Miami, an Army Air Task Group based twelve B-25, ten B-34, four B-18, and two A-29 bombers. Smaller numbers (one to two) of bombers flew out of Key West, Fort Myers, New Orleans, Louisiana, and Houston, Texas. For emergency use the Army could call on training forces at Tampa (MacDill Field), Sebring and Shreveport, Louisiana.[50] In the Caribbean Frontier air strength continued to be much less impressive as the U-boat war reached the six-month mark—only a handful of PBYs and PBMs were added to those forces—and the inadequacy of coverage was one factor leading to losses that would occur throughout those waters long after the U-boats were contained (temporarily) in ESF and the Gulf.

It took Admiral King an uncommonly long time to recognize the truth that in warfare the weaker side must learn to use the weapons that weakness imposes. The Kriegsmarine had recognized this long before: With its surface blue-water fleet frozen in port, the U-boat was the weapon that weakness imposed. King came to realize not only that there was a place for small naval craft after all, but that his weak position imposed as well the use of weapons even less commanding or Navy-like. By March, provoked to act by the British as well as by events, King looked with favor for the first time at civilian yacht clubs and power squadrons. To his desk on the seventh of that month came a letter from the representative of the British Ministry of War Transport in Canada, forwarded by way of Admiral Sir Charles C. J. Little, a member of the British Joint Staff Mission in Washington. In it the suggestion was made that, as the British had done at Dunkirk, the Americans might want to press into service a volunteer fleet of private small craft that could assist the Navy with patrolling and rescue. King directed Admiral Stark, who was still on board at the time, to "advise Admiral Little that the seriousness of the situation on the Eastern Seaboard is fully appreciated and that all possible steps are being taken. As to the small craft mentioned . . . if your office will arrange for the organization of such a voluntary fleet I will see that they are employed."[51]

King had come a long way. At COMINCH direction Admiral Andrews scoured the harbors south to Jacksonville for almost anything that could float. To Naval District commandants he ordered on 15 March: "Vessels in your district that can be purchased and are capable of carrying depth charges and guns and are fit for sea patrol report at once."[52] A large inventory of private power craft under one hundred feet was thus assembled and enlisted in the Coast Guard Auxiliary. Eventually no fewer than 1,716 suitable craft under one hundred feet were identified, 317 of which from the New York ports and harbors could have played a decisive role in sighting Hardegen's U-*123* on her first approach in January.[53] On 2 April COMINCH distributed the first "Manual of Anti-Submarine Warfare for Small Craft" and later, on 2 June, printed the collected doctrine for minor patrol craft in an illustrated "Sub Chaser Manual."[54] By 17 June ("Finally," wrote the exasperated writer of the ESF war diary), now a devoted convert to the place of small craft, whose importance in antisubmarine warfare, Andrews stated that month, "cannot be overemphasized,"[55] King issued the following order to Andrews and to his counterpart Rear Admiral James L. "Reggie" Kaufman, new (since 3 June) Commander Gulf Sea Frontier, whose headquarters moved to Miami from Key West on the same date: "It has been directed that there be acquired the maximum practicable number of civilian craft that are in any way capable of going to sea in good weather for a period of at least 48 hours at cruising speeds. These crafts will be acquired and manned by the Coast Guard as an expansion of the Coast Guard Reserve. They will be fitted to carry at least four 300-pound depth charges and be armed with at least one machine gun, preferably 50 caliber; and will be equipped with a radio set, preferably voice."[56]

The armed civilian craft were duly assigned to patrol stations spaced along the fifty-fathom curve of the Atlantic and Gulf coasts in what the Navy called Coastal Picket Patrols. Some Main Navy staffers worried that the small craft might blow themselves to pieces if they dropped three hundred-pound depth charges too near themselves, and COMINCH followed up with cautions that (a) the charges should never be set to less than 50 feet, (b) the speed of the boat should never be less than 10 knots, and (c) charges should never be dropped in water less than one hundred feet in depth since little was known about reflective effect of the explosive wave off the bottom. One message the Navy did *not* want to receive was, "Sighted sub, sank self." After a few unhappy experiences proved the point of the cautions, arming of Coastal Pickets was limited to the .50-caliber machine gun. By 12 July the first 49 craft of the 143 armed and available were on station in the

Eastern Frontier, where their principal value, apart from rescue operations, was perceived as keeping the U-boats underwater where the
enemy's speed and maneuverability, hence fighting effectiveness,
were greatly retarded.[57] On a number of occasions during the months
that followed U-boats were seen diving on their first sight of a picket
boat, for the same reason that U.S. submarines dived at the sight of a
Japanese auxiliary sampan in the Pacific: The submersible did not
want to waste a torpedo or to give away its position by staying on the
surface to shell. The same deterrent role may have been played by
offshore fishing boats, which in the same catch-up game had been
organized as radio-reporting vessels during April.

The original impetus for a civilian coastal patrol had come not
from the British but from U.S. fishermen and sportsmen. As early as
30 June 1941, the owner of a large swordfish fleet at Wakefield, Rhode
Island, wrote to the Navy Department suggesting the installation of
radio telephone equipment on his and similar fleets for offshore observation ("oilskin intelligence") and patrol work. The then-acting CNO
Ingersoll turned the idea down. It would be revived and supported by
CNO Stark on 12 February 1942, but King withheld support and the
plan died again. In the summer of 1941 another initiative came from
the New York–based Cruising Club of America, which offered to loan
the Navy fifty- to seventy-five-foot sailing yachts with experienced
skippers and crews for offshore antisubmarine patrol. (The term *auxiliary* was used to denote a sailing vessel with an auxiliary gas or diesel
engine.) On 23 February 1942, at a time when an increasingly critical
public thought that the Navy should make more aggressive use of
small craft, both power and sail, the Cruising Club renewed its offer. If
Main Navy's admirals had at first looked askance at "Crunch and Des"
cabin cruisers, one can only imagine the dismay with which they
viewed the pleasure fleet of the white-flannel set. Yet the Cruising Club
proposal made some sense. Although lacking in speed and maneuverability to take on U-boats directly, a sailing vessel running silent
under a sheet of canvas could observe U-boats or their periscopes
without giving warning of its presence. As one devotee of sail, who had
served on sub-chasers in World War I, wrote King, "You can creep up
on 'Jerry' with a stitch of canvas."[58] Then, too, a sailing vessel hove to
(headsails backed, helm up) made a steadier observation platform
than other patrol craft; and a lookout aloft in the hounds, forty to
sixty feet above the deck, had a height of eye equal to that on the bridge
of a large patrol vessel. Washington was not convinced. Typically,

King's staff at COMINCH reacted negatively, arguing that sail's lack of speed and maneuverability outweighed the advantage of silent running.[59] In New York, however, where the maritime tradition was strong and rugged, blue-water yachtsmen knew their way around the angriest northern waters, Admiral Andrews seized on the offer as a godsend. Assigning his chief of staff and intelligence officer to the project, and appointing yachtsman Commander Vincent Astor, USNR, to superintend it, Andrews introduced thirty-six of the seagoing yachts into the Coastal Picket Patrol in June to the accompaniment of wide public approval.[60] The sail fleet and power craft alike were officially known under the Coast Guard title, "Corsair Fleet." But nobody called them that. The men who served aboard the civilian craft were privileged amateur admirals, businessmen, professors, college boys, deep-sea charter operators, Ernest Hemingway out of Cuba, ex-bootleggers and rumrunners—anyone who, as Samuel Eliot Morison put it, could "hand, reef and steer"—and the term by which they knew themselves was the Hooligan Navy.

Ironically, by the time the Hooligans were on station in force (June and July) the U-boats had shifted the brunt of their operations southward to the Caribbean and back to the trans-oceanic convoy routes. Thus, the Hooligan Navy would not be tested in full-scale combat conditions. But its members had their moments: U-boats forced down by the civilian boats' presence, aircraft (in a test) detected (missed by naval vessels and shore stations), and torpedoed merchant seamen rescued. They also had their hard times, for example, motor cabin cruisers unable to hold the sea; and, it must be said, their embarrassing moments, as when off Florida a U-boat surfaced alongside a sport cruiser and its commander yelled in excellent American: "Get the hell out of here, you guys! Do you wanna get hurt? Now scram!"[61] The Coastal Picket Patrol was gradually reduced in force during 1943 after it was decided that the U-boat menace had subsided, and as part of the draw-down the Hooligan Navy was disbanded. The maritime minutemen would have had a more critical role at sea, one may suppose, had they been called to service in the time of greatest need, when the U-boats first arrived. But that call would have required of the Navy more imagination and flexibility and less apathy and arrogance than, unfortunately, it displayed in January and February 1942 or earlier. Years later, in his semiofficial history of the Navy in World War II, Samuel Eliot Morison memorialized the Hooligans: "The Coastal Picket Patrol is another of those things which should have been prepared before the war came to America. . . . More of the Dunkirk spirit, 'throw in everything you have,' would not have been amiss . . . when regattas were being held within Chesapeake Bay while hell was popping outside the Capes. The yachtsmen, or some of them, were eager to stick their necks out; but at the time of greatest need, the Navy could not see its way to use them."[62] When the Navy Department finally decided that the private craft were a good thing after all, the public relations staffers were ready: They announced to the press that twelve hundred small craft were already conducting antisubmarine patrol in coastal waters during July. The actual figure was 143.

The idea of the civilian fleets was one of a large number of ideas presented to the Navy by the general public after it became clear that the Navy did not have the U-boats under control as it earlier had boasted. Some ideas were of the crackpot variety but others had merit, such as this suggestion, found in the King Papers, submitted by Robert K. Miller, of Rahway, New Jersey: "I had a thought last night that probably isn't worth a damn, but I thought I would pass it on to you. . . . Why couldn't tankers leave in the night, then at some secret rendezvous, pick up one of those 'Mosquito' boats and let the tanker tow it. The 'Mosquito' boat would be hard to see and if they are equipped with listening devices, they could pick up the submarine and be ready for her. . . . I hope some young lieutenant will not take it upon himself to throw this in the waste basket. If he is so inclined, I hope he will remember of [sic] the lieutenant who refused to do anything when the private at Pearl Harbor reported he heard planes in the listening device." Rear Admiral Willis A. Lee, Jr., Assistant Chief of Staff, answered for King: "The particular measure suggested by you is already in hand together with many other methods which we are exploiting in our effort to combat the submarine menace."[63] One of the better ideas floated before the Navy had been the use of Civil Air Patrol (CAP) aircraft proposed by the Tanker Committee of the Petroleum War Council on 4 March. At that meeting the chief War Department representative, Major General Carl Spaatz, of the Air Force, expressed no objection to the idea, but Navy opinion, particularly King's, was cool. The Civil Air Patrol, composed entirely of civilian volunteer pilots from every state, many with their own planes, had first organized a week before Pearl Harbor with expectations of being useful in coastal patrol, rescue, and ferrying service. The Army Air Force showed interest early on, and at Atlantic City the 112th Squadron Army Ground Air Support Command offered to experiment with CAP participation in overwater patrols. Accordingly, on 8 March a variety of civilian craft—Luscombes, Cessnas, Stinson Voyagers, and Waco cabin jobs—lifted off on the first CAP antisubmarine flight. No interest in their patrol services was forthcoming from the Navy. On 12 March Admiral Andrews attempted to turn his service's mind around with a well-reasoned letter to King in which he proposed that the general aviation fleet be organized into what he called a Scarecrow Patrol. Such a coastal patrol, if numerous enough, would force U-boats underwater at more frequent intervals than at present, thus restricting the range and cramping the operations of the enemy.[64] When King asked his staff for reactions, Rear Admiral Donald B. Duncan, Assistant Chief of Staff, argued that the proposal was no more than "a scheme promoted by the builder of pleasure aircraft," and Deputy Chief of Staff for Operations Rear Admiral Richard S. Edwards contended that, "It will serve no useful purpose except to give merchant ships the illusion that an adequate air patrol is being maintained" while at the same time leading to false contact reports, clogged communications, and "the probability that lost amateur flyers will require the use of anti-sub vessels to look for them."[65] King answered Andrews that the "Scarecrow Patrol" was rejected on grounds of "operational difficulties."[66]

The CAP forged its first official relationships with the Army's First Air Support Command (later with First Bomber Command, finally with the Twenty-fifth Wing of the Antisubmarine Command). Under those auspices from March forward the CAP maintained a continuous air patrol over coastal shipping lanes within sixty miles of shore during daylight hours. Fifty percent of all aircraft carried either one 325-pound depth charge or two 100-pound demolition bombs, together with a simple garage-built bombsight. Frequently pilots had to saw off a bomb fin in order to taxi and lift off. The CAP flew in every kind of weather, even the foulest when military pilots were grounded. Coastal residents and fishermen became accustomed to seeing the low-flying, brightly colored red, blue, and yellow one-engined planes—mostly high-winged, with red or white pyramid insignia—pass overhead. For their part, U-boat commanders cursed the persistent presence of what they called the "yellow bees." CAP pilots, whose rules forbade them to claim draft deferment, wore specially devised uniforms in the event of capture. The Army supplied the aviation fuel but the pilots had to provide their own maintenance and hangars. By and large these men were not from the wealthy set associated with sailing yachts, and often the money to keep going came hard or had to be begged. There are few finer examples in the war of civilian generosity and intrepidity than those found in the CAP units, of which twenty-one eventually were established from Bar Harbor, Maine, to Brownsville, Texas. Typical were the units based in Florida, which flew two-plane patrols continuously, daylight to dark, during June and July 1942. Fifty percent of the planes were equipped with bomb racks and bombs. From Daytona Beach, twenty-three planes covered the sea-lanes from Melbourne to Jacksonville; from Lantana, fifteen planes surveyed the water from Melbourne south to Riviera Beach; and from Miami, twenty planes scouted the sector from Riviera Beach to Molasses Reef in the Keys.[67] As CAP activity increased King and the Navy grudgingly accepted the value of the civilian units and began to make use of them, their first modest use coming shortly after 26 March 1942 when all offshore air patrols, Army as well as Navy, came under the overall command of the Sea Frontier Commanders. On 16 November, by which date U-boat activity had significantly diminished in the various frontiers, King reduced the scale of CAP flying. And on 18 May 1943, in a letter that began, "The Commander in Chief, United States Fleet appreciates the valuable contributions rendered by these civilian aircraft in Sea Frontier operations," King peremptorily ordered the deactivation of all remaining CAP patrol operations. Even the ESF war diary noted the "bluntness" of the directive. As though to make amends the diary writer officially saluted "the interesting record of service" achieved by the CAP Coastal Patrol:

Missions flown:	86,685
Hours flown:	244,600
Radio reports on submarine positions:	173
Vessels reported in distress:	91
Irregularities observed at sea:	836
Special investigations made at sea or along coast:	1,046
Floating mines reported:	363
Dead bodies reported:	36
Bombs dropped against enemy submarines:	82
Enemy submarines definitely damaged or destroyed:	2
Special convoy missions performed at Navy request:	5,684
Airplanes lost:	90
Fatalities:	26
Personnel seriously injured:	7[68]

• • •

Since the first quarter of the sixteenth century numerous European invaders had showed their flags off Florida. The original native peoples of the Timucua, Calusa, and Apalachee tribes who inhabited the peninsular shoreline—the Seminoles being latecomers to Florida and invaders themselves in the 1700s—saw the likes of Juan Ponce de León, Pánfilo de Narváez, and Hernando de Soto, would-be conquistadors with terrifying armies, horses, works, and pomps. The Spaniards' ocean-going galleons and caravels with their tall masts, sails, and pennants flying must have made their own alarming impressions. Over the space of two centuries the Spaniards themselves became natives of *Tierra florida*—the land of flowers—where twice each year they watched with pride the columned march of stolid black-and-green-colored hulls of the plate fleets that sailed north with the Gulf Stream burdened with gold, silver, precious gems and minerals from Peru, Mexico, and the distant Philippines. They were the first armed convoys of modern times, precursors of British convoys in the Napoleonic Wars, World War I, and World War II. After the first appearance of the Spaniards, Florida beheld invading navies, successively, of the French, the English, the Union (in the American Civil War), and, finally, in the nineteenth and twentieth centuries, the tourists. But when in the winter and spring of 1942 U-boats first appeared in these same semitropical waters—gray spectral menaces to the playground of sunbathers, boatmen, and anglers—it may fairly be said that, since the arrival of Ponce de León in 1513, the Germans were the most unexpected hostile force ever to approach Florida's shoreline.

Reinhard Hardegen and U-*123* were not the first, as has been noted. U-*128* (Heyse) entered the Straits of Florida in February and sank two tankers, the first off Cape Canaveral, the second north of Bethel Shoals. In the same month U-*504* (Fregattenkapitän Fritz Poske) similarly sank two tankers in Florida waters, the first three miles off Jupiter Inlet, the second 12 miles northeast of the same site. Since February, however, no German nationals crossed the Florida state line until, on the night of 9 April, Hardegen and fifty-one companions slipped past the St. Marys River border and the northernmost Florida city, Fernandina, which was as brightly lit as a welcome station. Ahead, according to the charts and the *Handbuch,* was the mouth of the St. Johns and the U.S. Navy base at Mayport. As predicted, the St. Johns River Lightship anchored five miles east of the river jetties came into view. Its surprisingly intense light worried

Hardegen, who thought that *123*'s profile might become visible to an
alert lookout on shore. Since the chart showed an anchorage inside the
jetties, Hardegen gambled further on detection by closing the mouth
of the river with the lightship to port. When, finally, he could look into
the river's mouth, he saw no vessels of any kind, naval or merchant,
though red warning beacons atop the few structures on the south bank
suggested that there was an airfield nearby. (There was not, and there
would not be until 1943.) The whole scene had a silent, sleepy cast to it,
leading Hardegen to conclude (correctly) that Mayport was not the
major military threat he had expected it to be. Moving south of the
river and out of the lightship's glare, Hardegen conned the boat close
to shore where he recognized resorts and cabañas, a pier, a roller
coaster, other amusement rides, and beach houses. That had to be
Jacksonville Beach, he reasoned. Everything was richly illuminated
and automobiles with bright headlights cruised incredibly back and
forth on the beach itself, throwing white reflections on the dancing
waves to starboard. Hardegen had risked detection enough for one
night and there was no steamer traffic to keep him on the surface, so he
came to 150° and, nearing daybreak, put the boat on the bottom three
miles offshore.

At 1400 hours local Eastern War Time (2000 CET) on 10 April
123 rose from her sand bed as far as periscope depth. In his saddle
Hardegen scoped the sunlit horizon and saw nothing. He wanted to be
off St. Augustine Lighthouse by dusk, but a surface run in daylight
might be too dangerous now that American search patrols apparently
had intensified. He decided to proceed underwater and wrote in his
KTB: *Unterwassermarsch nach St. Augustin*—"underwater advance to
St. Augustine." In her near-four hundred years of existence the city
of St. Augustine, oldest in the country, had been sailed against by
numerous foreign hostile forces, but none underwater. This would be a
first for a city that boasted of many. By late afternoon the slow-moving
boat, 13.5 meters down, had a periscope view of the radio tower of St.
Augustine's local 250-watt station WFOY. Rafalski had its powerful
signal on the earphones. Though the Puster had no way of knowing it,
the tower's radial copper ground wire lay underwater on the marsh
shore, accounting for the unusually strong carrier wave that traveled
to *123*. Rafalski listened with curiosity to the strange American banter: "Yes, that's Tommy Dorsey's *Boogie Woogie* announcing another
Touchton's Telequiz, brought to you by Touchton's Rexall Drug Store,
Forty-seven King Street, in downtown Saint Augustine. As usual we'll

play two mystery tunes, and if we call you and you can identify the tunes, you'll win today's giant jackpot of eleven dollars, yes, eleven dollars!"[69] As *123* came abeam the city, which—except for the Exchange Bank Building, the Cathedral campanile, and the twin Spanish-Moorish towers of the Ponce de León Hotel—was hidden by the north end of a large island, Anastasia, that ran fifteen miles down the coast, Hardegen decided to surface. The sun was red and falling slowly behind the black-and-white-banded St. Augustine Lighthouse when, with a roar that startled the gulls and mullet, *123* broached the surface dripping brine, and a bridge detail in short sleeves mounted watch in the warm April air. Hardegen and the lookouts trained their glasses carefully across all quadrants. They were clear. No defenses. *Eins Zwei Drei* seemed to be alone. Coming up on starboard was St. Augustine Beach. Hardegen would write in the following year: "The coast was clearly visible. Houses, trees, the dunes of the beautiful beach, the slender lighthouse beyond it, everything could be seen without binoculars. One of my bridge lookouts suddenly said, 'Herr Kaleu! Can you see the little girl in the third beach chair from the left?' He was kidding, but if there had been beach chairs we would have seen them. We were that close to the shore."[70] It was an idyllic experience to savor on the eve of what would be one of the most dangerous nights of Hardegen's career.

As dusk came *123* moved twelve miles offshore and patrolled south as far as Marine Studios (Marineland) below Anastasia Island, then back north as far as Vilano Beach above St. Augustine, always keeping within sight of the lighthouse while searching for targets. At 1945 local time the boat was on a northbound leg when the port-ahead lookout picked up what appeared to be two separate shadows proceeding north between them and the shore. Hardegen followed the lookout's point and established that the superstructures and masts belonged to a single vessel. It appeared to be two because of its indistinct contrast with the coast at dusk. "A tanker, northbound," he said to von Schroeter, whom he called to the bridge. "It's huge, heavily loaded, must be 12,500 GRT. And fast—maybe twelve knots. It's hugging the coast. We'll have to turn screws to catch it."

To the helmsman he shouted: "Come to three four zero, both ahead full!" The diesels responded to the telegraph and soon high bow waves scalloped back as *123* noisily raced after her prey. An hour passed, and they had not caught up, but Hardegen reduced speed because of the great amount of marine phosphorescence they were generating in their wake. Not only the target could sight them in that condition, but any passing aircraft would be able to make them out easily. He began to realize that catching up completely might not be possible and that they might have to make a launch from astern on an obtuse angle. Von Schroeter at the UZO checked and rechecked his numbers as the tanker passed Ponte Vedra and came up on Jacksonville Beach. "From the second bow wave I measure it at twelve point five knots, Herr Kaleu," he told the Old Man. "Track angle one-two-one, range twenty-seven hundred."

"The range is too great as yet," Hardegen answered. "Wait until you reach two thousand." Hardegen worried about the eel not covering the distance accurately. An attack from astern meant that in addition to the range at the time of launch, one had to add the meters the target would have traveled ahead by the time of expected impact. It was axiomatic that the accuracy of the run diminished as the range increased. It had been a long while since he had considered a launch at such a range. But the G7e had a range of five thousand meters and a thirty-knot speed. It had the capability. Hardegen had only this and one other eel left, plus ninety rounds of artillery.

"Coming up on two thousand, Herr Kaleu," von Schroeter reported.

"All right, Number One, reduce speed, open bow cap. Permission to launch at two thousand." Hardegen saw that the target was now directly off Jacksonville Beach, perhaps four nautical miles from shore.

"Open Number One!" von Schroeter called.

"Number One bow cap open!"

"Folgen?"

"Folgen!"

Two porpoises surfaced and snorkeled through their blowholes on the port side.

"*Rohr eins—los!*"

Von Schroeter clicked his stopwatch and stood up straight to check the second hand while Hardegen found that, because of the phosphorescence and the perfectly calm sea, he could follow the wakeless eel through the first part of its run. While he waited von Schroeter entered launch data onto the Schussmeldung form: torpedo depth three meters; U-boat's speed at time of launch nine knots;

own course 307 degrees; target's course 350.5 degrees; torpedo's course 318 degrees; water depth fourteen meters; time of launch 0422 [11 April CET].[71]

"How big do you think the tanker is, Number One?" Hardegen asked.

"I'm guessing a hundred sixty meters in length, Herr Kaleu, since it filled three-quarters of the UZO." Both men stared at the large fast-moving shadow now sharply outlined against the brilliant Jacksonville Beach lights. They said nothing more to each other until two and a half minutes had passed since launch, when von Schroeter noted quietly, "One hundred fifty seconds." Twenty-five seconds later he added, "Two . . . one . . . *impact!*"

But there was no impact.

Damn! Hardegen reproached himself for having wasted his second to last eel on such a desperate attempt. Now he would have to go all the way around the St. Johns River Lightship and make another attack north of it, that is, if he could ever catch up with the tanker without betraying himself. But just as he bent to give a new course to the pipe the western sky suddenly erupted in a blinding red-and-yellow explosion! A hit! What had happened? Was it a timing mistake, or a fortunate aiming error? Who cared? Hardegen thought, as he watched the tanker torch break apart in the middle and its photoflash illumine the beach as brightly as though it were noon. In the incandescence he saw people on shore pour out of their hotels, homes, and places of entertainment. "A rare show for the tourists," he wrote in the KTB, "who probably were having supper now." It was 10:20 P.M. local time, which was a little late for American supper, but the bars, dance halls, drive-ins, and amusements were still going strong, since it was the end of the week and the beaches were crowded with sailors from the training base, Jacksonville NAS, twenty miles inland from Mayport on the St. Johns; soldiers in basic training from Camp Blanding in the interior; and high-spirited youths and civilians of all walks and ages to whom Friday night in Florida was party time.

Not satisfied that the tanker with its compartmentation would sink when its cargo burned out, Hardegen ordered the deck guns manned and approached the broken vessel with the intent of holing her fatally with artillery. When he saw the large number of spectators on shore, however, and noted the proximity of the beach homes to the point of attack, he worried that the shells he fired from seaward might overshoot and hurt innocent people and their property.[72] He therefore made a turn around the victim's stern and came up on its shoreward, or port, side, where any errant shells would pass harmlessly out to sea. The tactic created four problems for him: One, *123* was silhouetted against the fire's glare and thereby became vulnerable to any onshore weapons. Two, the shallow depths in which he now swam forced Hardegen to take a position only 250 meters from the fiercely blazing target. Three, as he closed the target he saw that it was equipped with a four-inch gun on a platform aft, though for some reason it was not yet manned. And, four, when *123*'s forward gun crew pulled the lanyard on the first shot the muzzle flash ignited the sea of spilled oil around them! Only the fortunate circumstance of a wind blowing away from the boat prevented the gun crew and bridge watch from being roasted alive. At point-blank range every shot was a hit, and soon the target hull was aground. There was no return fire. Two large concentrations of oil now burned independently, giving the appearance of two ships ablaze. Hardegen began a fast withdrawal south on a course of 165 degrees. He wrote: "All the vacationers had seen an impressive special performance at Roosevelt's expense. A burning tanker, artillery fire, the silhouette of a U-boat—how often had all of that been seen in America?"[73]

On shore, it was true, frivolity quickly turned to horror as the shocked revelers beheld the funeral pyre at sea and the U-boat itself bombarding the fiery corpse. Their faces red from the glare, the witnesses stood in stupefaction, endeavoring to comprehend how a war they considered so officially remote from their daily lives could suddenly appear in front of them. By telephone they spread word of the experience to family and friends in nearby communities, including Jacksonville, Florida's most populous city at the time; and soon the highways to the beach were clogged with the automobiles of the curious. Most were stopped and turned back by military police. At St. Augustine, thirty miles distant, a man who had heard the report walked into the lobby of the Alhambra Hotel and related it to the night manager, Miles "Zig" Zeigler, and seventeen-year-old Edward Mussallem, son of the hotel owner. Zig and Eddie looked at each other and said, "Let's go!" Driving across the Vilano Bridge to the ocean highway A1A, they were stopped by military police who informed them that A1A was closed to traffic. Instead, the two drove up U.S. 1 and took a narrow road through Palm Valley that came out at a point on the ocean highway where there was no barrier. Almost directly in front of them as they drove north was the tanker spitting twisted red columns like a volcano. Other, smaller, oil-fed conflagrations rode the waves. A pall of black smoke rubbed out the stars. It was the most frightening thing that Eddie had ever seen. Even Zig, who had flown rum into the Everglades during Prohibition and had seen it all, was impressed.[74]

The curious were not alone in racing to the scene. No more than five minutes after the torpedo struck PBY-3s from NAS Jacksonville were over the area dropping magnesium flares in an attempt to sight the U-boat. They were quickly joined by North American B-25 Mitchell bombers armed with MKXVII depth bombs from the Army 106th Observation Squadron, based at the Jacksonville Municipal Airport. No attacks were made using bombs, but the constant use of parachute flares and star shells enabled rescue craft to locate survivors. These vessels came from Mayport. Too small to have been spotted by Hardegen when he passed by the St. Johns, they were Mayport's total fleet of two converted yachts, one the 125-foot *Tyrer*, which had rescued survivors from *Esparta* two nights before, one minesweeper, and two Yippies. The vessels made trip after trip to bring in survivors and bodies. Emergency medical care was given in the base Administration Building, which was transformed into an emergency sick bay.[75] The dead were placed on the lawn outside. Many were charred beyond recognition. George W. Jackson, a reserve ensign commanding Yippie YP-32 (which had been a World War I sub-chaser), remembers reaching into the burning water to rescue a seaman only to have the man's flesh come off the arm as he seized it. For him and his twelve-man crew it was the grisliest experience of their young lives.[76]

SS *Gulfamerica* at 8,081 GRT was not quite the monster that Hardegen supposed, but was still a good-sized, spanking-new vessel. Owned by the Gulf Oil Co., she was steaming toward New York on her maiden voyage from Port Arthur with ninety thousand barrels of fuel oil when she had the misfortune to encounter Reinhard Hardegen. Forty-one merchant crew and seven naval Armed Guard formed her complement. Oscar Anderson, the master, had her on course 352 degrees true, speed fourteen knots (higher than von Schroeter's estimate), all lights out, radio silent, two lookouts on top of the pilothouse and two more, from the gun crew, on the poop deck. At 2022 EWT a torpedo approaching at 35 degrees from stern to starboard exploded in the after-bunker Number 7 tank, which blew oil skyward and caused an immediate fire. Anderson, like all the other survivors, would report that a second torpedo, quickly following the first, struck in the engine room at after mast about ten feet below the waterline. This must have been a secondary explosion, perhaps of the boilers, since only one torpedo was launched. Anderson ordered engines stopped and Abandon Ship. Radio Operator William M. Meloney, who had been torpedoed on another ship 30 days before, put out distress calls on 500 KC while Anderson threw confidential codes overboard in a weighted bag and those members of the crew who were capable lowered the lifeboats. Abandonment was orderly until the U-boat began shelling from the port side and elongated red trails of machine-gun tracer fire curved overhead seeking the mainmast and radio antenna. In the confusion that followed twenty-five men threw themselves overboard, many of whom were lost, and Number 4 lifeboat capsized. Two other boats made it safely down the falls. One of the last men to leave was fifty-seven-year-old Chief Engineer Vasco R. Geer, a native of nearby Jacksonville, who with Second Pumpman Glen W. Smith and Third Mate Oliver H. Gould lowered the Number 2 boat on the starboard side. The three circled to the port side looking for men in the loathsome-smelling water but had to withdraw when oil flames threatened to engulf them. Geer saw the men from one boat go overboard while the U-boat was firing in the apparent belief that the Germans would shoot at the lifeboats. But, he reported, "there was no attempt to shell or molest survivors in the boats."[77] Rescue craft picked up twenty-four (including the master, with a shell splinter in his arm, and the radio operator) of the forty-one merchant crew, five of the seven-man Armed Guard, and twelve bodies. Geer told USN interrogators, "I only wish we had a chance to use the gun against them [the Germans]."[78] No explanation is given in the records for the failure of the Armed Guard to use either the four-inch or the two .50-caliber machine guns with which *Gulfamerica* was one of the first U.S. tankers to be equipped. The U-boat's position was clearly revealed by muzzle flashes and tracer fire when it began its surface attack. The official USN Armed Guard report reads: "The 4" after gun was manned and loaded but no defensive fire was offered."[79] Perhaps the four-inch could not be trained because of list. Perhaps the gun crew obeyed the Abandon Ship order before it had a chance to sight the U-boat on the surface. Or perhaps the gun crew panicked. The Navy's public announcement stated simply, "The crew had no opportunity to fire at the attacking submarine."[80]

Of those who were rescued alive the longest time in the water was spent by a man named McCollum, described as a "winter visitor," who, more gallant than wise, put out in a small rowboat from Jacksonville Beach to aid in the rescue work. Assisted by the offshore wind he quickly reached and then passed the flaming tanker. When found the next day at noon he was twenty miles out to sea.[81]

Realizing that backlighting from the Jacksonville Beach shore had enabled the U-boat to sight its target Florida Governor Spessard Holland on 11 April declared a "screenout" of all lights showing to seaward in coastal and beach communities. The regulations and their enforcement would never be adequate, however, to prevent silhouettes at sea.[82]

Four days after the *Gulfamerica* attack a Requiem Mass was sung at the Cathedral of St. Augustine for several of the dead crewmen who were Roman Catholic. Young Eddie Mussallem sang in the choir.

On 16 April, *Gulfamerica*, which had settled by the stern with a 40 degree list to starboard, finally rolled over, bubbled, and sank from view, her maiden voyage now completely ruined.

On the same day COMINCH issued an order halting all further oil tanker traffic on the East Coast. Molasses could travel from the Gulf to Port Everglades. But as far as oil was concerned Hardegen's attack on *Gulfamerica* had been the last straw. No oil would move in tanker bottoms for the remainder of the month. The Allied war effort would have to live off its capital.[83]

Early morning on 9 April the *Clemson*-class flush-decker destroyer USS *Dahlgren* (DD 187), Lt. Comdr. R. W. Cavenagh Commanding, slipped her six manila lines at Pier Baker, NOB Key West, and with all four boilers cut into the main steam line, full stores from Busy Bee Bakery, but Fireman Second Class M. Podoll, USN, absent over leave since 0630 (EWT), proceeded through the main ship channel and steamed on a general course north along the Atlantic coast Florida shoreline. The next day and evening *Dahlgren* proceeded on various base courses, zigzagging on Plan No. 9, and making speeds from fifteen to twenty knots. At 1633 on the tenth, GSF headquarters at Key West ordered her to sweep for a U-boat between St. Augustine and Fernandina.[84] By midnight she was off St. Augustine Light bearing 292 degrees, distance twelve miles. At 0215 (11 April) an aircraft came overhead and dropped a flare. At 0235 another plane dropped several flares around the DD, which went to general quarters. The planes and flares were *Dahlgren*'s only indication that there might be a U-boat nearby, since no notice of *Gulfamerica*'s plight had been sent by Key West. Another nearby vessel probably did see the U-boat being sought by the aircraft. It was, of all vessels, *Atik*'s sister Q ship *Evelyn* (USS *Asterion*), which at 0133 sighted a U-boat surfaced at 29-40N, 80-56W, or southeast of St. Augustine, and reported it by radio.[85] Hardegen read the intercept and was sure the sighting was of *123*. In the KTB he wrote: "We have just heard on 600 meters that the steamer *Evelyn* has transmitted a U-boat sighting at precisely our position [DB 6781]. She must have seen us by the last parachute flare. It's about time to clear out of here and head to sea."[86] *Dahlgren* also intercepted the report and closed on the position. The destroyer and the U-boat were about to engage, as Hardegen wrote in his diary account for that night:

> Suspicious shadow on portside. Doesn't look like a freighter. Lies almost stopped or at very slow speed, northbound. Now, after three hours, the fire of the burning tanker is out of sight and we can see only the red glow in the sky. A southbound shadow on starboard which I can attack. As I turn to do so an airplane drops a parachute flare astern that fully illuminates us. Then I detect a second airplane sending Morse Code light signals to the ship which we had sighted as a suspicious shadow earlier. Now I can see it much more clearly and it seems to be a destroyer. It transmits a longer response back to the airplane which we cannot decipher. The airplane blinks acknowledgement. The flare is still burning when I see yet another airplane, without lights, on our starboard. I stop and hope that it doesn't see us. But then it suddenly dives and attacks us! *Alarm!* We never had such a crash dive. When I fell through the hatch the plane was almost on top of us—a single-engine, low-wing plane like our Heinkel 70. At 20 meters we hit bottom. No bombs dropped, but we definitely had been seen. Now we hear propeller noise from the destroyer. We start creeping underwater toward "deeper" water (30 meters) on a course of 120°. The propeller noise, directly astern, increases. Distinctly destroyer propellers. This fellow runs exactly above us, not very melodious, and drops six Wabos. The boat takes a terrible beating, the crew members fly about, and practically everything breaks down. Machinery hisses or roars everywhere. We break out

the escape apparatus. The destroyer turns back for another run. We are now on the bottom at 22 meters. I have turned everything off. We listen with our bare ears.[87]

Hardegen swept his flashlight beam around the control room until he found von Schroeter's face. "Number One," he whispered, "prepare to destroy Schlüssel-M rotors, cipher books, and all confidential papers. Pass the word in whispers fore and aft to don escape gear. Have all hands move quietly toward the control room. This time I don't think we're going to make it."

"Yes, Herr Kaleu."

The officers spoke sotto voce in the likely case that the American pursuer had hydrophones.

"And prepare to set the timer on the scuttling charge. And check on injuries."

"Yes, Herr Kaleu."

When he found Schulz the Old Man walked over the cracked instrument glass and placed his hand on the LI's shoulder. "What's our damage so far, Chief?" he asked.

Schulz whispered back: "All the head valves have burst open, Herr Kaleu. We're losing air. You can hear it bubbling to the surface. The destroyer's got a big bubble patch upstairs to home on. I don't hear any ASDIC pinging. He must not have the equipment. But he has our bubbles. Also the tower hatch cracked open, but we got it closed. I'm waiting for the Maneuvering Room to send someone forward with a report. We could have been hurt bad back there."

The Old Man winced and looked up, unseeing, at the menacing *swish-swish-swish* of the oncoming destroyer's screws. This was not the place to be for a depth-charging. With only twenty-two meters of water above their heads there was no place to hide. If they survived this next pattern he would order Abandon Ship.

SWISH-SWISH-SWISH. The American was overhead and crossing. Now the deadly canisters would roll from his fantail. Or perhaps he had throwers.

"Hold on!" the Old Man counseled loudly, not concerned for the moment about silence since on the destroyer's final approach it had to run at high speed in order to avoid the blasts of its own explosives, and its hydrophones during that period would hear only the destroyer's high revolution propellers. Every man in the control room reached for a wheel or stanchion. Bound together in a fraternity of commonly shared danger they awaited the mauling that they all would receive equally. Officers and ratings stood side by side where no visible distinctions in insignia existed and where the only man who counted was the man who did his duty. Here no one could jump aside and find cover when the bomb exploded. No wounded could be carried behind the lines.

Every man stood alone with his thoughts or prayers. Flashlights beamed down in white cones. Someone coughed. Another exhaled air.

SWISH-SWISH-swish. Hardegen looked up. *Swish-swish-swish.* . . . "He's passed us," he whispered. "He didn't drop a thing!" Why? he wondered. The American had them dead on. Did he lose his confidence at the last minute? Did his bomb rails or throwers malfunction? Did he miss his mark? For whatever reason, it was bizarre good luck. But how long could that kind of luck hold? The screw noises receded and took what seemed to be a stationary position a short distance off. The Old Man waited a few minutes to see if the destroyer was making another approach. When the sound continued at the same distance he ordered on the emergency red lamps.

"All right, Chief," he said to Schulz quietly, "let's try our systems and get some damage reports. We have to know our status even if it means making noise. If the destroyer lacks ASDIC he certainly must have some other form of sound detection equipment. So he will hear us no doubt. But he already knows where we are from our bubbles. So this is a risk we must take."

Schulz moved quickly through a checklist in his head, ordering on and off the E motors, blowers, and ventilators. He checked the battery charges, fuses, and wiring connections. To the hydroplane operators he gave specific test instructions and, with them, watched for responses on the gauges.

"Karlchen" from the engine room and Renner from the E motors, both wearing their *Dräger Tauchretter,* came into the control room and met the Old Man's eyes. Hardegen motioned them in the direction of Schulz and stood by to listen.

"Oberleutnant," Karlchen said, "the port engine is down. We can only blow tanks five and seven with the starboard. We might be able to blow the rest with compressed air, except for one and eight where we have air escaping. The head valves are bent. And I may have busted pipes."

"Thank you, Karlchen," the LI acknowledged. "Renner?"

"Oberleutnant, most of our batteries are out. We can't go very far with what we have left. When Pleuser and I clutched our remaining power to the shafts we got a hellish noise from the shafts and screws. I asked Karlchen to come aft and listen with me, and he agrees, we have bent shafts, perhaps screws, too."

"All right, Renner, thank you." Schulz turned to the Old Man. "There are also problems with the hydroplanes, Herr Kaleu. Probably it's the stuffing boxes. I fear we could not control the boat even if we got her under way, and Renner's report about the batteries and the shafts is not good."

The Old Man looked hard at Schulz, then at Latislaus and Renner, testing the cut of their faces under the harsh red light. He lifted his ear to listen for any change in the destroyer's position. *Swish-swish-SWISH*. It seemed to be heading their way again!

"So," he said to Schulz, "you're saying that even if we escaped from this attack we would probably not reach Lorient."

"That's correct, Herr Kaleu," Schulz said. "If we managed to get to the surface we probably would not get far with deformed shafts. With two burst tanks and questionable electric power I'm not sure we would be able to dive safely. In other words, we would be sitting ducks for whatever distance we could travel."

Hardegen weighed the options carefully, although his ability to concentrate was limited by the approaching tormentor upstairs. In a few moments the American would be on top of them again—

Swish-Swish-Swish
SWISH-SWISH-SWISH
Swish-swish-swish. . . .

But again, no Wabos. The destroyer passed directly over their position. And did nothing! What *is* he up to? Hardegen wondered, and then, as his heartbeat settled, he returned to the options at hand. The more he considered them the more clearly he concluded that, since it was unlikely that they would make it home, either because of the boat's mechanical failure or because they could not defend themselves successfully against enemy attacks—and the hunter upstairs without question was calling in every available nearby ship and plane to make certain this trapped prey was killed—the best course to take for the welfare of his men was to order their immediate escape to the surface, here, where the depth was shallow, where St. Augustine and the beaches were nearby, and a ship was on the scene to pick them up. As he put it in writing a year later: "So this was the end. Now we would get to know Mr. Roosevelt's hospitality after all."[88]

Hardegen ordered in a loud voice: "Prepare to abandon ship!"

He stepped past the crewmen who were crowding the passageway forward to his cubbyhole, where he took the photographs of his wife and children from their frames, placed them in his shirt, and donned the escape apparatus, with its mouthpiece and noseclip, oxygen cylinder, breathing pipe, and life vest, that had been stowed under his bunk. Then he returned to the control room and placed his right foot on the bottom rung of the ladder. On a U-boat, unlike a surface ship, the first man to abandon ship was the commander. If there was any hazard on top he would be the first to face it.

To von Schroeter he said, "As soon as I begin flooding, set the timer on the scuttling charge. Place the confidential papers where they will dissolve. Stick the rotors in your pockets so that you can dump them randomly. Be sure the men are out of their shoes and any heavy clothing. Now turn off all electrical power and circuits! *Alle Männer aus dem Boot!*"

As he mounted the ladder the Old Man caught the eye of Fritz Rafalski, who had been through all this before, except that this time the Puster had his gear on. Rafalski wore a look that said that this was exactly what he had expected.

When Hardegen reached the tower hatch he braced himself with one arm around the ladder so that the onrushing water would not carry him down, and positioned the mouthpiece and nose clip. He knew that the men below, who had been through many escape drills, were similarly beginning to draw their air from the bottles. Now he reached up and slowly began turning the hatch cover wheel to the open position. The spindles disengaged. He wanted only to crack the hatch so that water would fill the interior gradually. When water completely filled the boat and the pressures inside and out were equalized, then the men, Hardegen in the lead, could make their individual exits, relying on the buoyancy of their bodies to carry them to the surface. (Water temperature at surface was sixty-six degrees F.)

With the wheel now in the full open position Hardegen pressed against the sea pressure that bore down upon the hatch cover. Water immediately poured down his neck, frightening him. He immediately reclosed the cover. A few moments later, overcoming his fear (he thought), he cracked open the cover again, this time wider. A burst of water hit him full in the face and he winced again, pulling the cover closed. Now he heard the *swish* of the destroyer once more closing the U-boat position. The *swish* became *SWISH*. "Suppose," Hardegen thought, "I successfully get out of here and that destroyer drops Wabos. Their concussions will kill me. And my men, too, if any of them are in the water with me."

The *SWISH* diminished in intensity as again, unaccountably, the destroyer passed overhead without dropping charges. Hardegen now realized that he was paralyzed by fright. It had never happened to him before. He had no way of knowing at the time that, ironically, his fear would save his boat, and for the moment he was humiliated by what he thought was unmanly dread. (In later years he would say, as he did to this writer, "Only because I was too scared was I not captured."[89])

Without stating his fear to the others, much less trying to defend it, he wheeled the cover tight, pounded down the ladder, and announced: "I have decided that we are going to save this boat! Power on! Emergency lights on! Belay scuttling charge! Stow escape gear! Every man to his station! Chief, get to work!"

For the next hour, while the destroyer's screw noises faded and Barth, with power restored to his hydrophone, reported, "HE bearing Red three four zero and receding," Schulz and his repair crews worked prodigiously to secure the integrity of the diving tanks that were still serviceable, to restore battery power, and to free up the movements of the hydroplanes. Driven by a newfound hope of saving their boat as well as themselves, the men made enough gains for Schulz to report to the Old Man:

"I have half the batteries back, Herr Kaleu, but not enough to run the E motors any distance. And much of the power will be expended running the compressors to blow tanks. If we can surface I can recharge—that is, if the starboard engine works. The electricians will continue to hunt for possible broken connections. The battery crew are under the floor plates. As far as the planes are concerned, we have them functioning well enough for emergency use. Even without tanks one and eight we should be able to lift off the seabed without any trouble. If we can start the engine after getting on top I may be able to give you enough propulsion to creep away from here at dead slow. But the drive shafts worry me. I don't know how far we would get."

"I understand, Chief," the Old Man said. Then he smiled. "Heinz, you may prove both of us wrong about this boat. I hope so. Let's prepare to surface."

It was one thing to get their boat on the surface and running again. It was another to have to face a formidable foe in their wounded state. Though it was still dark on top, and destroyer's *swish* had not been heard for some time, there could be planes, with flares. Add to that the damnable marine phosphorescence and a U-boat surfacing should stand out like a full moon. It was a chance he had to take. There were no other options. His fear had brought them this far. Now he would have to exchange one fear for another.

"*Auf Gefechtsstationen!* — "Battle stations! Gun crews prepare to man guns! Number One, flood Tube Number 4! Chief—*surface!*"

The LI's pipe-and-valve team spun their wheels and pumped their levers. The roar of the compressors expelling water from the tanks filled the boat with hope. Prayers, exhortations, good luck charms, tightly closed eyes—every device known to desperate men was called upon by the crewmen not involved in the attempted ascent. After two minutes cheers erupted in the compartments when the hull lifted briefly, screeched and groaned, bounced on the bottom, then lifted again and became buoyant. Sausages and binoculars swung back and forth. On the *Tiefenmesser* (depth gauge) Schulz confirmed the steady rise: "Twenty meters . . . eighteen . . . sixteen . . . periscope depth . . . tower hatch clear!"

Hardegen and the bridge watch scrambled up the ladder followed by the gun crews. He flung open the hatch cover with an abandon uncharacteristic of his earlier behavior and stepped out onto the dark bridge, sweeping his 7 × 50s in a full circle as he did so. There was no sign of the destroyer. To starboard four to five miles distant two aircraft were dropping flares. The magnesium was too far away to present a threat. Just as the forward gun crew took their positions the starboard engine ignited with thunderous detonations, and Hardegen called to the helmsman:

"Hard right rudder! Come to one five zero! Starboard ahead dead slow!" From astern he heard what Renner had described: a hard metallic grinding of shaft and screw. "Stand down, forward gun! Antiaircraft stay alert!"

He would creep toward deeper water while Schulz and the electricians tried to build up battery strength. They might have to stop propulsion at some point, lie to, and let the engine do nothing but charge. Until that point Hardegen wanted to place as much distance as possible between himself and his pursuers. He was elated to see that no naval vessels were advancing after him. With a quarter moon, phosphorescence, and twelve miles visibility the destroyer certainly would have seen him had it stayed in place. But *123*'s amazing luck prevailed again. Later in the day he wrote the following as part of a lengthy KTB entry about this night:

> I'm surprised that the enemy was not tougher, using depth charges in these shoal waters when he had us. He had only to drop a series of patterns on the same spot that was marked by air bubbles and we definitely would have had to abandon the boat. We were about to destroy all our secret documents. That the enemy didn't wait for the Commander's cap as proof of their kill was totally incomprehensible. During the day they could have held us. It shows how inexperienced the defense is. They probably thought we were finished when they saw the air bubbles and didn't hear anything from us. . . . When considering the behavior of the destroyer I can only say, *selbst schuld!* — "it's your own fault."[90]

Hardegen went on to discuss the "riddle" of how the destroyer could have made such a precise first depth-charge run on his submerged position. He decided that just as he had been able to track his G7es (ETOs) in this shoal water filled with phosphorescence, so the aircraft had been able to track *123*'s course underwater from the air and to vector the destroyer onto the exact target area. "The precise approach can hardly be explained otherwise," he wrote. The *Dahlgren* log, however, does not reveal if her officers were that confident about the target location. Noting that she "made sound contact" and that she "made attack," the log goes on to state: "No evidence that an underwater depth charge contact had been made."[91] Thus, the Schulz-Hardegen theory of an air-bubble patch giving evidence of injury to the boat was not confirmed by *Dahlgren*. Rafalski, for his part, stated the German thinking on board *123:* "The crew were very surprised when the destroyer moved off. A British destroyer would have worked over the area repeatedly for a regulation thirty-six hours."[92] *Dahlgren* called in no help, either surface or air. At 0358 (EWT) she secured from general quarters and steamed off northeast at eighteen knots.

During the daylight hours of 11 April, while the boat proceeded on a base course toward Cape Canaveral, diving and surfacing as needed by the repair crews, Schulz managed to restore full power from the battery array and to complete repairs on the planes. Now the boat could make an alarm dive if emergency required it. On the surface in calm seas the boat maneuvered well on tanks five and seven. The starboard shaft continued to rasp and whine, which worried Schulz, but it performed efficiently enough to move the boat south while Karlchen and his crew welded and repaired damaged structures on the port engine. Fortunately for the boat only one aircraft was sighted and that after it was too late to dive, but it passed by without incident. At 1225 CET (0625 EWT) on the next day, off New Smyrna, Hardegen placed the boat on the bottom for the daylight hours and gave his exhausted, though immensely relieved, crewmen a chance to rest. Men looked at photographs of their sweethearts with new appreciation now that they had good reason to think they would see them again. Most slept the sleep of the redeemed. Others read or talked quietly. Hannes prepared treats that he had been saving for the return voyage. Hardegen went through his records on the attacks he had made since first assuming command of the "canoe" U-147. Altogether he counted forty-nine torpedoes that he had launched as a commander. That meant that the eel in Tube Number 4, his last on board, would be the fiftieth if he could find a target. A tanker would make a fitting last prize, he thought.

At 2000 hours he came to periscope depth and proceeded on underwater cruise toward the Cape. At 2209 in late daylight he surfaced and straightaway found a ship. It was not the tanker he hoped for but a freighter, northbound, approximately 5,500 GRT. His first inclination was to let it pass, but, as he wrote in the KTB, "I can't let this one go or fortune will punish us!"[93] It took seven hours with one engine still down to maneuver into a position for launching. Finally, at 0511 (CET, 13 April), when 3.5 miles southeast of Hetzel Shoals gas buoy and within sight of Cape Canaveral Light, von Schroeter released the last torpedo of Hardegen's naval career. Appropriately, it hit its target forty seconds after launch and a high, dark detonation column rose from the freighter's starboard side abaft of amidships. Hardegen watched the now-familiar scene. The stern settled while the rest of the vessel listed heavily to starboard. Two lifeboats lowered and rowed away. After fifteen minutes the stern was on the thirty-one-meter bottom and the bridge underwater. It was a fine trophy. But it was not a tanker. *Eins Zwei Drei* had no more eels, but it did have ninety rounds of artillery. Hardegen decided to get a tanker with the gun before heading home to the barn.

SS *Leslie* was small, at an actual 2,609 GRT. American-owned, chartered to W. R. Grace & Co., she was en route, unarmed, from Antilla, Cuba, via Havana to New York with 3,300 tons of sugar, course 360 degrees true, speed six, radio silent, zigzagging, no lights burning, when Hardegen's last-ever torpedo exploded in Number 3 hold blowing open the bulkheads, rupturing the overhead domestic tanks, and flooding the shaft alley with sugar and water. With a rapidly developing starboard list, the master, Albert Ericksson, saw that there was no hope of saving the vessel. He put the engine astern and ordered Abandon Ship. No distress message went out because the explosion had knocked out the radio. Of the crew of thirty-one and one consular passenger, twenty-seven men, carrying one body picked out of the water, rowed in two lifeboats to land a short distance north of the lighthouse. Another, rescued by SS *Esso Bayonne,* was put ashore at Key West the next day. Three persons were missing. Survivors reported that about five minutes after their ship settled the U-boat sent up a reddish orange flare that illuminated a large area. About two hours later, they said, they saw and heard gun flashes about four miles to the southward. They counted ten to twenty rounds.[94]

This was U-*123* at work. Hardegen had found his cannon fodder south of Cape Canaveral Lighthouse. He described the target as "a fully loaded northbound tanker of about 8,000 GRT." It was nothing of the kind. In the sinking of *Empire Steel* three weeks before he had acknowledged how easy it was to overestimate the tonnage of tankers because of their few reference points. In the present case Swedish Motorship *Korsholm* was not only 5,353 tons smaller than Hardegen's estimate, it was not a tanker. Chartered to the British Ministry of Shipping, *Korsholm*, a freighter, was en route from Port Tampa, Florida, to Liverpool, England, via Halifax with a cargo of 4,593 tons of phosphate. At the time of Hardegen's sudden bombardment from the starboard side she was on a northerly course, blacked out but not zigzagging, radio silent. The first incoming rounds "exploded" the bridge, wrecked the starboard lifeboat, and decommissioned the radio transmitter. (Rafalski remembered the Old Man's predilection for gunfire: "He loved it. He would stand on the bridge with arms akimbo, pushing his elbows up and down saying, 'Give 'em another one!' "[95]) After ten minutes the shelling stopped and the crew began abandoning ship. A second volley began while the port lifeboat was still being lowered. Fire then broke out amidships and spread rapidly. The one lifeboat rowed safely away leaving twelve men still on the hulk. Aircraft from Banana River NAS arrived on the scene shortly after 0400 EWT and dropped life rafts and flares. Vectored to the wreck by the planes, the Dutch SS *Bacchus* rescued two men who were still on board. The American SS *Esso Bayonne,* which had performed the same service for *Leslie* only shortly before, picked up a survivor from the water. One body washed ashore. Eight others including the master were missing. Perforated methodically along the waterline, Hardegen's "tanker" went down.[96]

"*Ruder hart backbord! Kurs Heimat im Golfstrom!*" — "Hard to port! Course home in the Gulf Stream!" While von Schroeter conned the boat on a new course zero degrees, and Rafalski looked anxiously at the clock to see how many hours remained to 13 April, Hardegen went below to draft his patrol-end report to BdU. By his reckoning he had sunk ten ships for a total of 74,815 GRT, or, as he boasted in the KTB: "We have broken the record of our last voyage. With 300,141 GRT U-*123* is the second German U-boat to pass 300,000 tons during the war."[97] (Giving him *Oklahoma* and *Baton Rouge* [but not *Liebre*], which by every standard were "sunk" except that, awash in shoal water, they could be refloated and salvaged, his actual total was nine ships sunk. His tonnage total, as usual inflated for most vessels, was a still respectable 52,336.) It remained now to relay these data to BdU. Hardegen composed his report in verse:

> *Sieben Tankern schlug' die letzte Stund'.*
> *Die U-Falle sank träger.*
> *Zwei Frachter liegen mit auf Grund*
> *Versenkt vom Paukenschläger!*[98]

For seven tankers the hour has passed,
The Q-ship hull went down by the
    meter,
Two freighters, too, were sunk at last,
And all of them by the same
    Drumbeater!

13

Final Reckoning

At the Department of the Navy on 1 April the same public relations officers who gave America "Sighted sub, sank same," announced that, as of that date, twenty-eight German U-boats had been "sunk and presumably sunk" off the U.S. coast, four by Army bombers and twenty-four by the Navy.[1] A patriotic national population wanted to believe the Navy. It would have pained the public to learn that the guardians of the shore were equating sub sightings with sinkings, or that the word "presumably" in the Navy's communiqué ought to have been italicized. But the fact was that, as of that date, not a single U-boat had been sunk in U.S. or Caribbean waters. In the war against the Ubootwaffe so far only the brash lie had succeeded, and then only in the heartland. Residents of the water's edge knew better. To them it seemed that the U-boats were more numerous than ever. Night after night the seaward horizons were red from the tankers' fires. Morning after morning the beaches filled with the freighters' sodden debris. The sea-lanes claimed by the PR victors in truth presented a scene of total defeat: melancholy graveyards where hundreds of ships' carcasses lay buried; where the canted bows, foretrucks, and masts of other, half-submerged wrecks formed hazards to navigation inside the ten-fathom curve. Only Admiral Dönitz could draw satisfaction from such a catastrophe: "Our U-boats are operating close inshore along the coast of the United States of America," he told German war correspondent Wolfgang Frank, "so that bathers and sometimes entire coastal

378

cities are witnesses to the drama of war, whose visual climaxes are constituted by the red glorioles of blazing tankers."[2]

Although there were many rumors of it happening, no one, military or civilian, could give a positively authenticated account, much less provide a photograph, of a captured U-boat being towed into an American port. Other rumors, even more widespread, held that U-boatmen were coming ashore to purchase fresh groceries and to attend the movies. Despite persistent stories to that effect in various coastal communities at the date of this writing—a commonly heard Florida story holds that a sunken U-boat recently entered by divers was found to contain Holsum Bakery bread wrappers—no U-boat crewman is known to have gone ashore on the American coast, and surviving commanders like Hardegen firmly deny that it ever happened. U-*123*'s propaganda photographer on the second patrol, "Schöner Rudi" Meisinger, asked Hardegen off Florida if he might go ashore in the dinghy to take pictures but was refused. Standing BdU orders forbade anyone to leave the boats. The only exceptions were to permit visits to other U-boats at sea on official business or to land saboteurs on enemy shores, as would happen twice on the U.S. East Coast during the six-month period under study.

In what Abwehr II, the German Military Intelligence Corps, code-named Operation Pastorius, after a seventeenth-century German settler in Pennsylvania, U-*202* debarked four men with explosives and U.S. dollars at Amagansett, Long Island, on the night of 13 June, and U-*584* placed another four men, similarly equipped, ashore at Ponte Vedra, south of Jacksonville Beach, Florida, three nights later. The U-boat oarsmen returned at once to their boats in each instance, though not before scooping up sand as souvenirs. The saboteurs' mission was to blow up aluminum-manufacturing plants, power plants, waterworks, bridges, and railroad systems. Nonprofessional misfits, they were poorly trained and the details of their cover were badly bungled. Worse (for them), one of the northern group immediately betrayed both landing parties, with the result that the Federal Bureau of Investigation captured all eight, six of whom were electrocuted by the Army in Washington, D.C. on 8 August, the informer and one other receiving long prison terms. The story of the would-be saboteurs has been told before.[3] It figures little in this account since it does not bear on the U-boat war as such—the ESF war diary for June (chapter 6) spoke of the "Amagansett Incident"—and the effect of Pastorius was totally inconsequential alongside the U-boat onslaught against seaborne trade. As a training manual prepared by NAS Quonset Point, Rhode Island, put it, "The massacre enjoyed by the U-boats along our Atlantic Coast in 1942 was as much a national disaster as if saboteurs had destroyed half a dozen of our biggest war plants."[4] Not on land but in the coastal water—*that* was where the sabotage was being done.

The first sinkings of U-boats by U.S. servicemen took place off Newfoundland during March. Naval Reserve Ensign William Tepuni piloting a Lockheed Hudson with Patrol Squadron 82 (VP-82) out of Argentia on 1 March dropped depth bombs on a crash-diving U-*656* twenty-five miles south-southeast of Cape Race. Oil and deck parts rising to the surface gave Tepuni the right to claim a kill, which was confirmed by postwar checks of BdU records. The second sinking was claimed on the fifteenth by none other than Chief Aviation Machinist's Mate Donald Francis Mason. In a PBY-3 belonging to the same squadron, Mason sighted U-*503* southeast of Virgin Rocks and, this time without PR assistance, sank same, thus redeeming his self-esteem and earning an instant ensign's stripe. Like Tepuni's, Mason's kill was later confirmed. The first U-boat sinking in U.S. waters came in the following month, when two U-boats succumbed to patrols of the Fifth Naval District. Headquartered at Norfolk, 5ND by this date was the best organized and trained antisubmarine warfare (ASW) force in the ESF. Its ships and planes patrolled a jurisdiction of nearly twenty-eight thousand square miles of water that lay between the thirty-eighth and thirty-fourth parallels (Chincoteague Inlet, Virginia south to New River Inlet, North Carolina), through which, at any one time, forty-five to fifty merchant vessels proceeded on their lawful occasions, all of them forced to deep water out to sea to avoid Hatteras and the Shoals on the most dangerous legs of their journeys north and south. After 1 April, when it announced a new, aggressive "hunter-killer" doctrine, 5ND maintained all its available craft, surface and air, on intensified ocean patrol.[5] The British-like exertion quickly yielded results.

At midnight beginning 14 April the *Wickes*-class flush-decker destroyer USS *Roper* (DD 147) was operating east of Nags Head, North Carolina, on course 162 degrees true, speed eighteen knots. At 0006 she made radar contact bearing 190 degrees at 2,700 yards. New radar installations on ASW vessels gave them an edge over surfaced U-boats, this one being U-*85* (Oberleutnant Eberhard Greger) proceeding off the coast on various courses. The contact may have been made by purest chance, but 5ND Operational Intelligence later contended: " 'ROPER' did not stumble on the U85 by chance. The finger of 5ND Operations, on the basis of accurate intelligence reports, skillfully and unerringly directed the 'ROPER' to the location of the first contact."[6] Whichever the case, the radar finding was confirmed by echo ranging on propellers and, shortly afterward, lookouts sighted the suspect vessel. The skipper (Lt. Comdr. Hamilton W. Howe) called his crew to general quarters and went over to the attack. As the faster *Roper* (twenty knots) closed the vessel, which fled on constantly changing bearings, she held slightly to the starboard quarter so as not to catch a stern torpedo. It was a wise decision. When the range had closed to seven hundred yards a torpedo indeed passed down the port side of *Roper* close aboard. At three hundred yards the destroyer's twenty-four-inch searchlight picked out U-*85*'s distinctive Type VIIB tower, enabling the executive officer on the flying bridge to make a positive identification. The U-boat made a hard turn to starboard, which placed it inside the turning radius of the destroyer, perhaps seeking an opportunity to dive.

Holding her light on the German, *Roper* commenced firing, first with the Number 1 machine gun, which accurately cut down the U-boat's gun crews as they raced to their stations. The Number 5 three-inch gun was under the command of a gun captain who had never before been in command of a firing. He acquired the range quickly, however, and placed a shell directly on the tower. Before *Roper* could get off a torpedo of its own the U-boat went down, either by choice or as a result of artillery damage. About forty German crewmen abandoned the boat as it submerged. Choosing not to rescue them, but determined to assure a U-boat's destruction in ESF waters after three months of humiliating failure and frustration, *Roper* dropped an eleven-charge barrage across the swirl of the diving boat. The charges destroyed the boat. Their concussions also killed the men in the water. *Roper* lay to until daybreak, when a PBY dropped a depth bomb over an oil slick and assorted floating debris, and *Roper* added two more. By 0830 seven aircraft, including a blimp, were overhead and a British trawler, HMS *Bedfordshire*, arrived to assist in recovering bodies. Twenty-nine were found, some with personal diaries (a forbidden practice) that described the boat's last days. Not only 5ND but also the beleaguered Eastern Sea Frontier headquarters on Church Street in

Manhattan finally had something to cheer about. The U-boats were beatable after all. Destroyer men in the frontier were particularly well pleased with themselves.[7]

Not to be outdone, the small craft, too, would have their day. On the afternoon of 9 May the 165-foot cutter *Icarus* (WPC-110) was proceeding alone from New York to Key West when, off Cape Lookout, she acquired a "mushy" sound contact about nineteen hundred yards at 15 degrees on the port bow. As the contact came abaft the beam it increased in definition and the skipper, Lt. Comdr. Maurice D. Jester, USCG, was called to the bridge. At 1629 EWT, nine minutes after the first echo return, a fierce explosion was "seen, heard, and felt" some two hundred yards on the port quarter. It was a torpedo either misfiring or detonating on the shoal bottom that had been launched by U-*352* (Kptlt. Hellmut Rathke). The warhead's geyser corresponded in location with the screw noises heard by the cutter's hydrophones. Jester therefore decided to drop a diamond pattern of five depth charges directly over the swirl left by the explosion. It was a good decision because Kptlt. Rathke had made a bad decision: He grounded his boat in 120 feet (36 meters) of water at exactly that position, thinking, as he said later, that that was the least likely place for the cutter to drop charges. The rain of Wabos that hit him at 1631 hours caused immense damage as well as killed his number one. *Icarus* returned to drop three more charges in a V pattern at 1645. Two charges later, at 1709, U-*352* broached the surface stern-down by 45 degrees.

Icarus immediately swept the decks with machine-gun fire to prevent guns being manned while three-inch gun pointer Charles E. Mueller earned himself a promotion to Chief Boatswain's Mate by ricocheting his second round off the water into the tower and placing six more rounds into the now mortally wounded hull. During the bombardment the U-boat crew abandoned ship through the tower hatch in order of seniority, or as *Icarus* reported, "in clock-like precision." Some were caught in the gunfire, which ceased at 1714 when U-*352*, broken and punctured, sank from view with twelve of her crew, one dead, still aboard. Thirty-three survivors bobbed in the water, one with a severed leg whom the commander assisted by fashioning a tourniquet to stop the bleeding. Another held up the stump of an arm in supplication to the Americans not to shoot them; later the same man, in great pain, would beg, in English, to be shot. Jester was not at all sure how to manage such a large number of prisoners on his small craft, and he sent a plain-language radiotelephone message to shore stations asking for instructions: HAVE SUNK SUBMARINE. 30 TO 40 MEN IN WATER. SHALL ICARUS PICK UP ANY OF MEN? Sent repeatedly, the transmission elicited no response for thirty-six minutes until, finally, Sixth Naval District directed Jester: PICK UP SURVIVORS. BRING THEM TO CHARLESTON. Despite their ordeal the Germans, except for the wounded, seemed to be in excellent physical and morale condition when brought aboard the cutter. Commander Rathke imposed silence on his crew, going so far as to caution them to avoid the company of any German-speaking girls to whom they might be introduced on shore. At 2250, before reaching Charleston, the crewman who had lost his leg died.

Two days later Naval Intelligence interrogated the German officers and crew, who had remained under the martinetlike discipline of the thirty-two-year-old Rathke. Even had they been willing, the Germans could not have divulged much about the U-boat war as such, since their boat had not a single sinking to its credit since being launched the preceding summer. About tactical, technical, and mechanical details the crew remained obediently silent. The most that Navy questioners learned was that during the last four days off the Outer Banks the boat dived repeatedly to avoid patrol aircraft and that the crew much enjoyed the "jazz" from U.S. broadcast stations that was played over the boat's loudspeaker. Other marginal data obtained included the names of the best bars for enlisted ranks in Lorient, Brest, Saint-Nazaire, Kiel, Flensburg, and Gotenhafen. In order to obtain more substantial information, including, if possible, a TRITON cipher book and rotors, an attempt was made to raise the U-boat. The tug USS *Umpqua* (ATO-25), with deep-water diving equipment sent down from New York, departed Charleston on the nineteenth and next day found British trawlers HMS *Northern Duke* and *Northern Dawn* standing by a buoy they had planted to mark the wreck site. On the twenty-third a diver found the U-boat lying on its starboard side at an angle of 60 degrees. Every attempt by the tug, assisted by the trawlers, to raise the wreck failed, and on the twenty-ninth the project was abandoned. A second effort in August similarly was abandoned after grapnels succeeded in bringing up no more than one 20-foot section of "upper deck grating."[8]

Five other U-boats were destroyed by U.S. forces in the various frontier waters during the close of the "second happy time," 14 January–15 July. The first of these was the victim of another small craft, the 165-foot cutter *Thetis* (WPC-115). Lt. (jg) Nelson C. McCormick USCG and his crew were part of a GSF hunter-killer group out of Key West. At 1550 EWT on 13 June they dropped seven depth charges on a sound contact in the Gulf, which resulted in the destruction of U-*157*. Huff-Duff bearings fixed U-*158* at 130 miles west-southwest of Bermuda on 30 June enabling Lt. Richard E. Schreder USNR in a PBM Mariner of Navy Squadron VP-74 to drop a depth bomb that, amazingly, stuck in the U-boat's tower and detonated when the boat submerged. U-*701*, which was on her third war cruise out of Brest (and had been the source of a "man overboard" intercept at Winn's OIC in January) was fatally bombed by a Lockheed Hudson from U.S. Bomber Squadron 396 while crash-diving 30 miles off Diamond Shoals Lightship on 7 July.[9] On 13 July USS *Lansdowne* (DD 486), in combination with Bomber Squadron 59, dispatched U-*153* off Panama. The fifth and last U-boat to be destroyed during the six-month-long concentrated U-boat campaign in American waters was U-*576*, sunk on 15 July off Diamond Shoals by a joint force of two Navy aircraft from Squadron VS-9 based at Marine Corps Air Station, Cherry Point, North Carolina, and the Naval Armed Guard of the merchant ship SS *Unicoi*.[10] Clearly Eastern and Gulf Frontier defenses had stiffened by midsummer. More surface and air forces were coming on line. U-boat tracking was adopting British standards of precision and sophistication. At ESF headquarters in New York two new reserve officers brought analytical expertise to the team—Harry H. Hess, a professor of physics at Princeton, and Robert Wolf, a statistician for a New York brokerage firm. Training greatly improved over the preceding January, when skill levels had been demonstrably low.[11] Three major ASW schools began turning out thousands of skilled sea personnel: the Naval Local Defense Force School, equipped with British-style mechanical "attack teachers," at Boston; the Fleet Sonar School, at Key West, for instruction in hydrophones and sonar; and the Submarine Chaser Training Center, at Miami, where young officers—older men could not take the strain—learned how to handle the now-desperately-wanted SCs and PCs, called elsewhere in the service the "Donald Duck Navy." A civilian Anti-Submarine Warfare Operations Research Group (ASWORG) applied scientific and mathematical data to the improvement of operational doctrine. And Admiral King was finally getting around to instituting coastal convoys.

·   ·   ·

What really broke the back of the U-boat campaign in U.S. waters was the coastal convoy. And what made the convoy system possible was the multiplication of small craft. The responsible Navy commanders had not been blind to the need for convoys. As early as 20 January, in a personal communication to Support Force commander Admiral Bristol, Admiral Ingersoll had stated: "The sub situation on the Atlantic coast will result in demands for coastal escort vessels and antisubmarine vessels. Converted vessels will not yield much and until the new PC's begin to get in service I think we are in for a beating from the subs."[12] Through a similar personal letter channel King himself wrote to Ingersoll on 4 February: "The increasingly serious scale of attack on shipping in the North American eastern seaboard points, in my view, to the desirability of extending the convoy system to cover this area." He then proposed releasing twenty-one short-legged destroyers for use in establishing an interlocking convoy system up and down the seaboard.[13] Ingersoll, who assiduously guarded his transatlantic properties, was sympathetic to the proposal but not so far as to give his DDs to it. Eight days later, King asked Admiral Andrews to canvass the ESF district commandants for ideas and to "submit a plan for a convoy system to protect coastal shipping in this Frontier."[14] In varying degrees commandants advised against the immediate institution of convoys for lack of adequate escort forces. Though the ESF war diary noted certain advantages a coastwise system possessed that a transatlantic system lacked—principally, capacity for merchant vessels to lie over in sheltered harbors during the most dangerous nighttime hours and air coverage afforded by planes operating from shore bases—Andrews recommended to King "that no attempt be made to protect coastwise shipping by a convoy system until an adequate number of suitable escort vessels is available." He added that, if a system *had* to be established at once, the first leg should be that south of Hampton Roads.[15]

King accepted Andrews' judgment particularly since each day by Andrews' count there were 120 to 130 merchant ships proceeding within the boundaries of the frontier, and all that ESF could offer for escort of convoy were nineteen vessels with speeds of twelve to fourteen knots, and they were all small craft. When King thought of convoys he thought of destroyers. Lacking destroyers on the seaboard he thereupon announced his doctrine: "Inadequately escorted convoys are worse than none."[16] A British historian has recently commented: "The senior American commanders, acknowledging the lack of small craft, instead of striving with might and main to remedy the evil in 1941, used it as an argument against convoy just as alarmists in the Admiralty had done twenty-five years earlier. So the fatal doctrine was propounded that 'a convoy without adequate protection is worse than none.'"[17] This was the exact opposite to all that British experience had taught in the second world conflict and, indeed, as late as 19 March the First Sea Lord (Pound) advised King that, on the contrary, convoys with weak escorts were a superior tactic to no convoys at all, and that the introduction of convoys was a matter of "urgency."[18] King's resistance to the tactic may have been the result of persistent Anglophobia. It may have derived from the U.S. Navy's long tradition of the *offensive* as against the passive role of warships having no more splendid duty than that of shepherding seaborne trade to safe and timely arrivals: One should not forget that King and his generation were shaped in the dream of great fleet actions and in the glory of single-ship enterprise. Moreover, he no doubt genuinely feared that concentrating attractive ill-defended targets in convoy invited rather than repelled attack. But that was precisely the point, the British argued. Convoys drew U-boats to warships. Instead of fruitlessly searching for the elusive Germans—"hunting the hornets all over the farm," Woodrow Wilson called the practice in World War I—the escorts had the U-boats in known positions where they could attack them. Conversely, convoying had the effect of mathematically reducing individual ship targets, since if a U-boat was not correctly positioned to attack a convoy it would miss all the ships that formed it, and it would have a long wait for another target opportunity.[19]

Exactly when and under what circumstances King changed his mind is not clear. Perhaps it was the influence of Andrews' growing conviction that patrol and search violated the two great principles of war, "conservation of energy" and "concentration of force," and that the more economic and effective method of combating U-boats was the coastal convoy.[20] Certainly one sees a change in King by 16 March, before the date of the First Sea Lord's communication, when COMINCH called for a meeting to take place in four days' time of representatives of the Eastern, Gulf, and Caribbean Frontier commanders for the purpose of discussing the institution of an East Coast–Caribbean convoy system. A report from that meeting on the twenty-seventh proposing such a system was approved by King.[21] On 1 April, Andrews inaugurated a partial convoy arrangement, labeled the "Bucket Brigade," whereby ships moved only in the daylight hours and took cover in protected anchorages by night, including a patrolled anchorage behind Cape Lookout. Elaborate plans were put under way to inaugurate a full coastwise system no later than 15 May. The most pressing question was escorts. The minimum strength thought necessary was five escorts per convoy of forty to fifty ships. Where would they come from? Only nine destroyers permanently assigned to ESF duty were available. But to them could be joined nine new 173-foot-class PCs, four 165-foot-class Coast Guard cutters, seven new and old gunboats, two Eagle boats, and twelve British-manned trawlers. Also the District Local Defense Forces were stripped of all small craft available, especially seventy-five- and eighty-three-foot Coast Guard cutters, PC-452 and SC-453 classes from the 60-60 program, and seakeeping vessels then engaged in laying mined anchorages for the protection of independently routed vessels, which, because of speed or lack of it, were not expected to join the convoys. 5ND contributed forty small craft to the escort pool, among them twenty eighty-three-foot cutters, which, though originally thought "of very limited usefulness," proved to be the short-leg workhorses of the New York–Delaware run. Thus, the much denigrated small craft, against which King himself had animadverted, proved to be the key to the solution of the escort deficit.

The first southbound convoy sailing, designated KS 500, left Hampton Roads on 14 May. The next day northbound KN 100 departed Key West. The plan called for a forty-five-ship convoy to run the gauntlet in each direction every three days, following precise sea-lanes drawn on the trackless water. Sailings were timed so that the formations would be in daylight when they steamed from Cape Lookout to the Chesapeake past Hatteras, where the narrowness of the continental shelf had for so long enabled the U-boats to operate in deep water close inshore at night with marked profit and relative impunity. Later in May a northern link, New York–Halifax, was added to the chain; and in August and September a Galveston-Mississippi–Key West link made the coastal system complete. The Caribbean routes required more complex coverage with fewer resources, but a subsidiary set of convoy links was established in that Frontier beginning in July, thanks in part to the dispatch of a number of British and Canadian destroyers and corvettes from the northern transatlantic routes (to the joyful relief of their crews).[22]

The Caribbean would take some time to show the effects of convoy practice, but the effects in the Eastern and Gulf Frontiers were nearly immediate. In the Eastern Frontier sinkings fell in number from twenty-three in April to four in May. They rose to thirteen in June (when, as part of their last-gasp effort on the East Coast, U-boats sowed mines in the ship channel at the Chesapeake, where on 15 June near Buoy 2 CB, two ships from northbound convoy KN 109 sank from collisions with the explosive charges, and another was damaged).[23] June figures were encouraging to President Roosevelt, who noted the disparity between the number of convoyed vessels sunk and the much larger number of independently sailing vessels sunk. He wrote to King, "I think it has taken an unconscionable time to get things going . . ."[24] In July, sinkings dropped to three, and then to zero for the remainder of the year. On 19 July, Admiral Dönitz withdrew the last two U-boats that operated off Hatteras, U-754 and U-458, and eight days later he transferred the main effort in the U-boat war away from the seaboard and back to wolf-pack attacks on shipping in the mid-Atlantic air-coverage gap. The Battle of the Atlantic was back where it began.

In the Gulf Frontier, sinkings declined sharply after convoys became the routine mode of passage in late summer, and the last ship to go down in the Gulf itself was sunk on 4 September. The Caribbean continued to be a problem area throughout the summer and into the fall, but the concentrated campaign in U.S. waters was over. Ships would continue to be sunk here and there along American shores: There would be a U-boat semi-*blitz* against East Coast and Caribbean shipping in the period April–December 1943, as well as sporadic nuisance attacks until the very last month of the war in Europe, but after the institution of convoys the American coastline for the first time could be declared secure. On 21 June 1942, speaking in the hyperbole of the convert, Admiral King stated: "Escort is not just *one* way of handling the submarine menace; it is the *only* way that gives any promise of success. The so-called patrol and hunting operations have time and again proved futile."[25] The promise was not that the escorts would actually sink U-boats but that the U-boats, recognizing the hazard that the convoys posed to them, would abandon American waters, which happened. What sinking of U-boats occurred came in every instance, paradoxically, at the hands of hunter-killer groups or of single aggressively patrolling ships or planes, contrary to King's dictum.

The end of the six-month period of maximum destruction left nearly four hundred hulks on the seabeds of the Eastern, Gulf, and Caribbean Frontiers. By frontier, they numbered 171 (ESF), 62 (GSF), and 141 (CSF). An additional twenty-three vessels were sunk in the Panama Frontier—an aggregate of *397 ships sunk in U.S. Navy-protected waters*. And the totals do not include the many ships damaged. Overall, the numbers represent one of the greatest maritime disasters in history and the American nation's worst-ever defeat at sea. For Germany this was the most successful sustained U-boat campaign in the whole course of the war. In exchange for negligible losses of men and boats the Ubootwaffe had carried off a triumph that was fully the equivalent of victory in a major battle on land. For America's chief ally Great Britain, the losses proved so grievous they imperiled that trade-dependent island nation's ability to continue as an effective contributor to the war. For the Soviet ally it cast doubt that the West would be able to deliver the weapons required to defeat the Wehrmacht's eastern operations. For the United States, in terms of raw resources and matériel, Paukenschlag and its aftermath constituted the costliest defeat of World War II. Most calamitous of all was the toll in human lives, which can be estimated at hardly fewer than 5,000 souls—U.S., British, Norwegian, and other merchant seamen; U.S. and Royal Navy officers and men; and civilian passengers. Whether shot, drowned, scalded, set on fire, frozen, smothered, crushed, starved, or maimed by sharks, they rested now everlastingly on the bed of the sea.

The Pacific Pearl Harbor lasted two hours and ten minutes on a Sunday morning. The Atlantic Pearl Harbor lasted six months. The American people understandably were stunned and angered by what happened at Hawaii, where the naval losses included proud, allegedly impregnable battlewagons and the lives of thousands of young men, though the full account of ships sunk and damaged and the full enumeration of human casualties (2,403 dead, 1,178 wounded) would not be released until after the war. Compounding the shock of those losses was the abhorrent nature of the Japanese tactics, which, carried out while her diplomats were still negotiating in Washington and without prior declaration of war as required by international law, were widely condemned in this country as a "treacherous" "sneak attack" that "hit below the belt." Yet any close examination of the fleet losses at Hawaii discloses that they were not nearly as severe as popular opinion held them to be. No aircraft carriers were in the harbor on the day the attackers struck. Together with all the heavy cruisers and more than half the fleet's destroyers, they were off elsewhere on missions. The anchored victims were mainly aged, slow, obsolete battleships that had no role in the immediately forthcoming carrier battles with the Japanese. By the date when heavy guns were needed for shore bombardment of invasion beaches much of the Pearl Harbor battle line had been rebuilt. Four battleships disabled on 7 December, USS *California, West Virginia, Tennessee,* and *Maryland,* participated in the U.S. naval victory at Surigao Strait on 24–25 October 1944. The repeatedly holed *Nevada,* which managed to slip her moorings during the attack on Pearl Harbor and beach herself on Waipo Point, supported the Marine landings on Iwo Jima in February 1945. Ironically, those battleships and other warships that were raised from the muck of Pearl Harbor and restored to action would probably never have survived to fight again had they been off soundings instead of at their anchorages. Another piece of luck that the Navy enjoyed was the incredible failure of the Japanese attackers to hit the three targets that *would* have taken the Navy out of the Pacific war for at least twelve months: (1) the Navy fuel farm in the hills beyond Pearl City; (2) the port installations, including repair yards; and (3) the submarine base with five submarines on manila lines. The judgment of Morison persuades: "One can search military history in vain for an operation more fatal to the aggressor."[26]

Though the public had no way of knowing it, the German assault on U.S. coastal shipping was far the greater disaster for the United States and her allies. Here for a long while the losses were irremediable. Unlike Hawaii, where the undamaged fleet units were able to take the offensive almost at once after 7 December and to score the major victory at Midway just six months later, in the Western Atlantic, Gulf, and Caribbean sunken bottoms and lives, not to mention cargoes, could not that quickly be made good. Some U.S. military leaders, like Army Chief of Staff George C. Marshall, were late in realizing the magnitude of the catastrophe. On 19 June Marshall wrote to King:

The losses by submarines off our Atlantic seaboard and in the Caribbean now threaten our entire war effort. The following statistics bearing on the subject have been brought to my attention: Of the 74 ships allocated to the Army for July by the War Shipping Administration, 17 have already been sunk. 22% of the bauxite fleet has already been destroyed. 20% of the Puerto Rican fleet has been lost. Tanker sinkings have been

3.5% per month of tonnage in use. We are all aware of the limited number of escort craft available, but has every conceivable improvised means been brought to bear on this situation? I am fearful that another month or two of this will so cripple our means of transport that we will be unable to bring sufficient men and planes to bear against the enemy in critical theaters to exercise a determining influence on the war.[27]

To this memorandum King responded two days later in more detail than can be repeated here, but with this particular answer to Marshall's query about "every conceivable improvised means":

We had to improvise very rapidly and on a large scale. We took over all pleasure craft that could be used and sent them out with makeshift armament and untrained crews. We employed for patrol purposes aircraft that could not carry bombs, and planes flown from school fields by student pilots. We armed merchant ships as rapidly as possible. We employed fishing boats as volunteer lookouts. The Army helped in the campaign of extemporization by taking on the civil aviation patrol.[28]

The reader is left to reflect, in view of the foregoing chapters, how "rapidly" on the "large scale" King extemporized his defenses. In 1946 the admiral published his official wartime reports to the Secretary of the Navy under the title, *U.S. Navy at War, 1941–1945*. In a chapter called "The Atlantic Submarine War," he wrote that directly upon the outset of hostilities the Navy "accelerated its program of acquiring such fishing boats and pleasure craft as could be used and supplied them with such armaments as they could carry. For patrol purposes we employed all available aircraft—Army as well as Navy. The help of the Civil Air Patrol was gratefully accepted."[29] It is not recorded how Marshall accepted King's dissembling or whether he knew it to be a cover. King was not well regarded at the Munitions Building. A bright brigadier general in charge of War Plans had confided his opinion of the admiral to a personal diary entry for 12 March. Wrote Dwight David Eisenhower: "One thing that might help win this war is to get someone to shoot King."[30]

To balance the record it must be stated that after July 1942,

King and the Navy performed creditably in the creation and operation of an antisubmarine force that became so formidable, sophisticated, and well trained that, in concert with the British during the following year, it overwhelmed the U-boats in every quadrant of the Atlantic. In May 1943, King organized all ASW warfare units and personnel, surface and air, into what he called the Tenth Fleet, with himself as commander and Rear Admiral Francis S. ("Frog") Low as chief of staff. In a stroke he eliminated most of a large number of organizational problems and conflicts that had bedeviled the frontiers and CINCLANT, not to mention the Army Air Force, with which Navy relations were periodically strained. (The writer has not engaged in any lengthy discussion of these organizational conflicts, for example, should the Army or the Navy have primary control over land-based ASW aircraft, or should CINCLANT authority intervene in sea frontier operations, or should district commandants be expected both to run their districts and to conduct ASW operations at sea? A thorough airing of these and other command-relations problems is given in the Eastern Sea Frontier war diary for April and July 1942 and April and July 1943.) Navy fighting effectiveness in 1943 and after was helped by the addition to convoy lanes of new-class destroyers, and particularly, the new destroyer escorts (DE) which, with their high reserve buoyancy and freeboard, excellent compartmentation, and easy working space, immediately became recognized as the ideal escort vessels. That they could be built for just over half the cost of a *Benson*-class destroyer did not go unnoticed by Congress. (After the war King charged that construction of the much-needed DEs had been frustrated by President Roosevelt's "predilection for small antisubmarine craft." Documents in the Bureau of Ships refute this charge, proving instead that FDR was one of the DE program's earliest advocates, from June 1940.[31]) Convoy escorts bristled with new armament, including a fast-sinking six hundred-pound Mark IX torpex depth charge and two versions of a British-invented throw-ahead contact bomb projector, called "Hedgehog" and "Mousetrap," which fired patterns of small rocket projectiles at a submerged U-boat while the attacking vessel maintained sonar contact with the target. Sonar equipment and operator training improved, and uniform use was made, finally, of British tactical doctrine. A significant addition to the Atlantic Fleet was the Escort Carrier Group (CVE), the first of which was organized in March 1943 around the small carrier USS *Bogue*. With four flush-deck destroyers operating as a screen for the carrier, Grumman F4F-3 Wildcat and TBF-1 Avenger aircraft followed radar and Huff-Duff bearings to surfaced U-boats in daylight hours and, because of their high speed, bombed or strafed the boats before they could completely submerge. Eventually eleven carrier groups would operate in the Atlantic, five chalking up enviable records as "hunter-killers" of unwary U-boats. From Spring 1943 forward to the end of the war it would be British and U.S. "hunter-killer" groups of various sea and air compositions, and not convoy escorts, that would be the great destroyers of U-boats; thus challenging Admiral King's convert belief that convoy was "the *only* way" of defending against the U-boat menace. Not the least of new advantages afforded both the Americans and the British was the penetration, at last, of the U-boats' TRITON ("Shark") cipher. Bletchley Park announced the triumph on Sunday, 13 December 1942. Patrick Beesly took the call. Winn had collapsed from overwork.

Arguably the most valued American contribution to the Atlantic war apart from the CVE was the Consolidated Liberator four-engine bomber, known to the Army Air Force as the B-24 and to the Navy as PB4Y-1. The British had converted one of its three bomb bays to auxiliary fuel tanks, which gave the aircraft up to twenty hours continuous flying time. This VLR (very-long-range) Liberator with RAF Coastal Command crews patrolled the North Atlantic convoy routes from bases in Northern Ireland and Iceland. The western half of the Atlantic, or the Greenland Gap, went for many months unprotected, however, due to Admiral King's procrastination over basing some of the Navy's Liberators in Newfoundland. At the January 1943 Casablanca Conference of Roosevelt and Churchill together with their nations' Combined Chiefs of Staff, it was agreed that the defeat of the U-boat was the first priority in the battle for Europe, and that to achieve that goal eighty VLR aircraft should be deployed immediately to cover the Greenland Gap. King, who was a participant in the conference and had 112 Liberators at his disposal, did nothing to meet this charge until 18 March when, after the previous day's losses of sixteen merchant ships in Atlantic convoys HX 229 and SC 122, Roosevelt asked him where all the Navy Liberators had been. Once the Greenland Gap was closed beginning in April and May by Liberators from Newfoundland, U-boats surfaced at their peril in the western North Atlantic. Acknowledging the probability that VLRs would eventually plug that remaining Air Gap, Admiral Dönitz anguished to his

BdU war diary as early as the foregoing August: "These developments will lead to irreparable losses and to the end of any chance for a successful conclusion of the U-boat war."[32]

USN training and tactics improved to the point that Admiral Dönitz's successor as BdU, Konteradmiral Eberhard Godt, stated after the war that in the years 1943–45 any distinction between U.S. and British combatant skill was not observable.[33] The Royal Navy complimented USN ships on their engineering plants, armament, cleanliness, and generally superior standards.[34] Where antisubmarine equipment was concerned the British seem to have been the more originally inventive, while the Americans were the more successful at development and perfection; although the Americans did have their inventive moments, as, for example, with "Fido" (Mark 24 Mine), a deadly airborne torpedo that homed in on a submerged U-boat's propeller cavitation. The British came up with two airborne devices that in combination succeeded so well in detecting U-boats on the surface that they veritably took the night away from the Ubootwaffe. The first was the Leigh Light, a twenty-four-inch searchlight devised for placement in the lower turret of a Wellington bomber by Squadron Leader Humphrey de Vere Leigh, RAF. These lights, and later more powerful ones of U.S. design, enabled aircraft to sight surfaced boats, particularly when used in tandem with airborne radar. Although the use of early radar sets of long wavelength type could be counter-detected by a U-boat employing a search receiver ("Metox" or one of four successor systems), U.S. improvements to a British design resulted in the airborne installation of microwave (ten-centimeter) radar equipment (ASV) that for a long while the Germans had great difficulty detecting.

Thus, beginning in 1943, ASV-equipped Liberators and Leigh-Light Wellingtons achieved near-total control of the ocean's surface and made the Bay of Biscay in particular a killing sea. The Germans countered with the *Schnorchel* (a dialect word for nose), a prewar Royal Netherlands Navy invention that enabled a U-boat to travel and charge batteries on diesels underwater by "breathing" the air needed for combustion and expelling exhaust through a double pipe that extended above the surface of the water. Float valves on the pipe closed automatically when the boat submerged to use electric power alone. The advantage provided by the *Schnorchel* was that boats could thereby escape both lights and radar. Disadvantages were that underwater speed on the diesels was not high, and the effect on crews of both leaked carbon-monoxide-laden exhaust gases and of sudden interior oxygen loss to the engines when the pipe closed owing to surface turbulence or to miscalculation by the planesmen could be very unpleasant, not to mention dangerous. Even the *Schnorchel* was defeated eventually by American development of a 3-cm radar that picked up the head of the U-boat's pipe. In the end the microwave radar was one of four major reasons cited by Admiral Dönitz for Germany's loss of the U-boat war, the others being: (1) Hitler's radical reduction of U-boat construction in favor of tanks during 1940; (2) the appearance in mid-Atlantic of ASV-equipped VLR aircraft; and (3) the phenomenal output of new merchant vessels by America's shipyards, which completely frustrated the touted "tonnage war." The attempt to sink more ships than the enemy could build was doomed from late 1942 forward, but not without one last transcendent effort by Dönitz to avoid that fate.

Dönitz and his staff greatly underestimated the capacity of America's ninety-nine shipyards to replace and then exceed the number of bottoms lost to U-boats. In October 1942 a "Liberty" category ship named *Joseph N. Teal* came off the ways only ten days after her keel was laid. Faster records would be set. Construction of prefabricated "Liberty" and "Victory" ships, conceived by shipbuilder Henry Kaiser and put together by "Rosie the Riveter," proceeded at such a pace that the 7.75 million deadweight tons of merchant shipping produced in 1942 increased to 19.2 million tons in 1943.[35] In the same period naval construction also multiplied dramatically. Thus, it has been estimated that if every major unit of the entire U.S. Navy had been destroyed at Pearl Harbor, and if Japan had been able to complete its own construction program unimpeded, the newly built U.S. fleet would outnumber the Japanese fleet by mid-1944.[36] Plainly, American industrial power won World War II.

Still, one could not overlook the fact that Germany for its part was building U-boats at a furious rate, and faster than the British, Canadians, and Americans could sink them—121 built as against 58 sunk in the last six months of 1942. At the onset of the critical year 1943 Admiral Dönitz had 212 operational boats out of a total of 393 in service compared with the numbers with which he began the previous year—91 operational and 249 in service. The stage was set in winter–spring 1943 for a climactic and decisive collision of the enlarged forces at sea, which through March seemed to go the Germans' way. In that one month alone U-boats sank 97 Allied ships in twenty days, about twice the rate of replacement, while losing only 7 boats and gaining 14 more placed in service. At that pace the Germans would win the Atlantic. The crescendo was reached in midmonth (from the seventeenth to the twentieth) when more than 40 boats engaged east-bound convoys SC 122, HX 229, and HX 229A in the still-existing western Air Gap. Twenty-two merchant ships were sunk for the loss of one boat, U-384. The Germans expended 90 torpedoes, the Allies 378 depth charges and bombs.[37] Berlin radio broadcasts called it the greatest convoy battle of all time. The British Admiralty ruefully conceded that "the Germans never came so near to disrupting com-munication between the New World and the Old as in the first twenty days of March 1943." Official Royal Navy historian Stephen Went-worth Roskill reflected thirteen years later: "For what it is worth this writer's view is that in the early spring of 1943 we had a very narrow escape from defeat in the Atlantic; and that, had we suffered such a defeat, history would have judged that the main cause had been the lack of two more squadrons of very long range aircraft for convoy escort duties."[38] To Admiral King inevitably would have gone the primary blame for that defeat, although it must be said that the British were of no help in the matter either: Bomber Command, obsessed with the generally futile area bombing of Germany, stub-bornly resisted the call to divert Liberators to maritime operations.

Shortly after the March disaster the trial of strength turned in the Allies' favor. The Air Gap closed and the lethal combination of American and British carrier groups, escorts, Support Groups of British hunter-killer destroyers, frigates, and sloops, Leigh-Light Wellingtons, and ASV-equipped Liberators bore down hard on the U-boats that returned to sea after refitting. The cracked TRITON cipher betrayed U-boat movements. During what the Germans called "Black May" forty-one U-boats were destroyed. Kills in June and July brought the three-month total to ninety-five. The Bay of Biscay, which now had to be transited underwater as far as 18W, if it could be transited at all, filled with iron coffins. The long-awaited introduction at this time of a new generation of "electro-boats" Types XXI (1,600 tons) and XXXIII (250 tons) which, with submerged speeds as high as 18 knots, transformed the U-boat from a diving boat to a true subma-rine, came on stream too late, owing to Allied strategic bombing of U-boat construction and assembly yards, to avert total defeat. Had these Types been available in significant numbers but one year earlier they might well have frustrated the Normandy invasion and turned the Atlantic campaign around in Germany's favor. The Biscay massacre continued through August 1944, when, after the Allied invasion of France and the entrance of the U.S. Third Army into Brittany, the U-boats were forced to operate from Norwegian bases, with the result that their operations became limited to an area north of the Gibraltar-Hatteras line where Allied naval strength could concentrate with increased economy of forces. All the while the experience level of commanders declined sharply, a not-inconsiderable factor while skill levels and confidence among crewmen also deteriorated markedly. In these circumstances morale (though not courage) inevitably faltered. The Ubootwaffe would stay at sea, with commendable determination, but never again would it be the effective fighting force that was once the scourge of the ocean. Dönitz shifted his dwindling units to various suspected "soft spots" in the Atlantic, including, again, the American shore, but for the next two years no such spots existed. The titanic struggle was decided. Poignant, unanswered wireless calls went out repeatedly from BdU to boats: "U-____ report position. . . . U-____ report situation." The huge hostile ocean stood ominously silent. The attempt to wage unlimited war with limited means was over. As Dönitz wrote simply in his memoirs: "We had lost the Battle of the Atlantic."[39]

Upon final surrender of German forces in May 1945, Dönitz bade farewell to his U-boats by wireless: "My U-boat men: six years of war lie behind us. You have fought like lions. An overwhelming material superiority has driven us into a tight corner from which it is no longer possible to continue the war. Unbeaten and unblemished you lay down your arms after a heroic fight without parallel."[40] In the same month the United States Navy and British Admiralty announced jointly that there would be no further armed convoys: "Merchant ships by night will burn navigation lights at full brilliancy and need not darken ship."[41]

In a war's-end report Kenneth Knowles, who as the USN's Rodger Winn observed the progress of the U-boat war more closely than any other American, declared: "The Battle of the Atlantic was the most important single operation in World War II for upon its outcome rested the success or failure of the United Nations' Strategy in all other theaters of operation."[42] Morison concluded that the battle was "second to none in its influence on the outcome of the war."[43] These were certainly correct judgments. They reaffirmed the soundness of the "Germany First" strategic assumption adopted by American planners, principally Admiral Stark, before U.S. entrance into the war—

namely, that the defeat of Germany ensured the defeat of Japan, but not vice versa. Not only the Normandy invasion but the success of the Soviet armies in the East depended on weapons and supplies carried over the Atlantic bridge, and therefore on British-American mastery over the U-boat. After victory on the Eurasian landmass the total weight of Allied strength, east and west, could be brought to bear on the less-advanced military machine in the Japanese islands. (Admiral King, whose interests lay primarily in the Pacific, seems never to have understood this.) The Germans' attempt to rupture Allied sea communications was the longest battle fought during the Second World War, beginning on 3 September 1939, and ending on 8 May 1945. It was also, overall, the most complex battle in the history of naval warfare.[44] In understanding the battle one could do worse, as German naval historian Michael Salewski was quoted in the Prologue to this book, than to study one single heavily engaged U-boat, which, *pars pro toto*, "mirrored at once both the greater strategy of war and its everyday horror." Few individual boats served that purpose better than U-*123*.

14 April 1942. U-*123*'s forty-fourth day at sea. Position DB 6329, due east of Savannah, on new home course 55 degrees. Boat on the surface in a small sea, port engine back on line, both *langsame Fahrt* (slow ahead) so as not to overstress the twisted shafts which were performing noisily but well, and to conserve fuel. For Reinhard Hardegen the war at sea was ending early. He doubted that there would be any more reprieves. This was the end of his last patrol. So it was with a sense of finality as well as accomplishment that he read the signal that emerged at 1200 from the Schlüssel M: BRAVO HARDEGEN! THIS TOO WAS A DRUMBEAT. COMMANDER IN CHIEF.[45] Two days later a similar congratulatory signal arrived from Grossadmiral Erich Raeder.

Hardegen found occasion to give one last rap on the drumhead. While still daylight at 2200 hours (CET) on the sixteenth, at DC 2361 about 260 miles east of Cape Hatteras, lookouts sighted two steamers athwart the U-boat's course. Hardegen selected the target steering 150 to 160 degrees, which turned out to be a freighter, and changed heading to place himself in front. A half hour before dusk he submerged and waited for the freighter to close, finally getting a good look through the periscope from three hundred meters range. About 5,000 GRT, he estimated; speed, eleven knots; no heavy armament; hinged loading arms flapped upward on the masts; trucks and huge yellow-painted gas or water tanks on the upper deck, four fore, four aft—a worthwhile target. There were no torpedoes left, of course, but he did have twenty-nine rounds, eight of which were wet, for the 10.5 Bootskanone and plenty of rounds for the 3.7 cm and the 2 cm. After the freighter passed he pursued the target on E motors until dark when he was able to surface, speed past the vessel, and take a bow-attack position as though he was making a torpedo approach by the book. When the freighter's starboard beam was four hundred meters distant and 90 degrees off the 10.5's muzzle, Hardegen gave permission to fire.

CRACK! The first shot cleared the barrel, and eight of the next nine shells exploded against the bridge and engine room. Hardegen steered to the vessel's portside where the 3.7 and 2 guns set about rending and tearing the decks and upper works. After five minutes of this fusillade Hardegen ordered a cease-fire and withdrew to the starboard side to study the situation. As he did so the freighter, which was still running at top speed, turned starboard directly at him! Was this another trap? He decided no when the vessel continued the turn past him and offered no fire. To Hardegen's surprise it made several complete 360-degree turns at high speed. Its rudder must have blocked. It was spinning now like a child's top, and fires on the bridge spread rapidly as winds, because of the turns, blew jagged orange flames in all directions. Despite the vessel's speed, two lifeboats and a raft went overside, which was a feat of seamanship. Rafalski called up an intercept from the stricken ship's wireless: POINT BRAVA [a former name of the vessel, now named SS *Alcoa Guide*, and apparently used by mistake in the excitement] FROM NORFOLK TO GUADALOUPE. MASTER INJURED. CREW IN LIFEBOATS.[46] "That's what we needed to know," Hardegen would write in his KTB—that all the crew were safely off the ship and he could now press his bombardment at point-blank range, directing the fire of all guns at the engine room and waterline of the hull, though it was no easy task firing at a rapidly turning target from a high-speed outer circle. Finally, the mangled engines shut down. The freighter slowed to a stop and listed sharply to starboard. The yellow tanks carried overside and floated on the surface. Haregen's guns ventilated the hull plates. At 0530 CET (17 April) the tortured vessel, in a billow of hissing fire-fed steam, went down hard by the stern and sank from view. Gunnery Officer Schüler counted up the ammunition expended: 27 rounds of 10.5, 86 rounds of 3.7, and 120 rounds of 2. The Old Man added 4,834 GRT to his total tonnage, while the LI, Schulz, worried that they had consumed too much of the fuel needed to get home.

Alcoa Guide had departed Weehawken, New Jersey, on 11 April with military cargo for U.S. Army bases in the West Indies and flour for delivery at Point-à-Pitre, Guadeloupe. A U-boat warning caused her to seek protection briefly at Hampton Roads anchorage. At 2150 (ET) on the sixteenth she was again en route independently on a true course of 162 degrees, speed ten knots, blacked out but not zigzagging, with two lookouts on watch in good visibility conditions under bright stars, no moon. At that moment Ordinary Seaman Francis Martens, lookout on the monkey bridge, was startled by an explosion on the starboard side of the saloon deck. Putting the wheel hard right, Martens left the engines running while he raced to his boat station. On deck there was great confusion among the crew as successive shells from a submarine that was clearly visible off the starboard beam exploded against the side. The master, Samuel Leroy Cobb, was throwing codes and confidential papers in a weighted sack from a wing of the bridge when an exploding shell close by knocked him off the bridge and onto the deck winch at Number 3 hatch. There he was found by Second Assistant Engineer Charles E. McIver and placed in the port lifeboat, which lowered safely during a respite in the shelling. Radio Operator M. E. Chandler got off a distress signal that was acknowledged by WSC, Tuckerton, New Jersey. Black smoke and the "burnt acid" odor of the explosions hung over the ship as the starboard boat made it down the falls and a raft with four men also got away, after which shelling resumed. The crew watched the vessel's last torments as they distanced themselves from the violence. For two days the lifeboats steered toward land but the badly burned and wounded master and an injured fireman died at sea on the nineteenth. Later the same day the twenty-seven survivors in lifeboats were picked up by USS *Broome* (DD-210) and landed at Norfolk.

The raft on which able seaman Jules Souza, the chief engineer, a fireman, and a black Virgin Islands seaman escaped became separated early from the lifeboats. At one point it was nearly cut down by the wildly circling freighter, which had not lost steerage (as Hardegen thought) but had been left hard-a-starboard, full ahead, by the bridge. As the freighter passed for the last time Souza saw standing on the poop deck, the only part of the ship not yet aflame, his Filipino seaman cabinmate, fully dressed, holding a suitcase. Souza wondered about him; he had always thought him "too well educated for his job," as he later told investigators. Had the Filipino tipped off the submarine about the freighter's sailing time and route? Was he now waiting to be picked up by the grateful submarine? Whatever the likelihood of a conspiracy, Souza had more immediate problems to worry about. He and his companions were alone on the open sea with marginal amounts of food and water and no sail or oars. All they could do was drift. Two days later, the date when their companions in the lifeboats were rescued, a passing aircraft sighted the raft and signaled, but no vessel arrived as a result. On the twenty-first a zigzagging freighter came within a mile of the raft and even stopped to take a look, but incredibly proceeded on. Now the men became desperate. They had made profligate use of their cask of drinking water, anticipating an early rescue, and more water was lost one day when the spigot on the cask was accidentally left open. The food supply was down to malted milk tablets. On the night of the twenty-third the chief engineer died from exposure. The fireman succumbed the next day. Souza and the black seaman kept the bodies on board hoping, with rescue, to return them to their families. Eight days later the odor of decomposition forced them to give the bodies to the waves. On 12 May, twenty-six days after their ship went down, the two men tasted the last drops from their cask. On the seventeenth, after drinking two quarts of salt water a day, the black man died. Souza, who drank a quart a day, survived into the next day, when a British cargo vessel SS *Hororata* sighted him and took him aboard. Hospitalized for exposure, malnutrition, and sunburn at Cristobal, Canal Zone, he fully recovered to tell his grim story.[47]

From Hardegen's KTB:

23 April
    1700. For the first time U-*123* received a wireless signal from the Führer. The Commander has been honored with an Oak Leaf Cluster [to the Knight's Cross]. Everybody was delighted because everybody had earned it. A homemade Knight's Cross with Cluster was presented me in a festive ceremony in the control room.

26 April
    1600. I am ordered by F.T. to rendezvous with U-*107* at 1400 on the 28th in Qu BE 7188 and hand over to her my *Adressbuch*. Since I would reach that position 12 hours

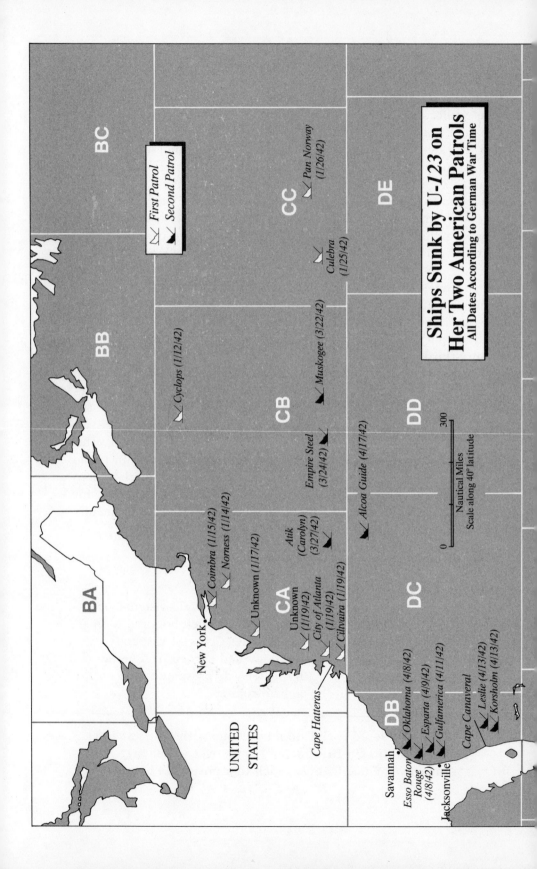

Ships Sunk by U-123 on
Her Two American Patrols
All Dates According to German War Time

First Patrol
Second Patrol

BA

BB

BC

CA

CB

CC

DB

DC

DD

DE

UNITED
STATES

New York

Cape Hatteras

Savannah

Esso Baton
Rouge
(4/8/42)

Jacksonville

Cape Canaveral

Coimbra (1/15/42)
Norness (1/14/42)
Unknown (1/17/42)
Cyclops (1/12/42)
Unknown (1/19/42)
City of Atlanta (1/19/42)
Ciltvaira (1/19/42)
Atik (Carolyn) (3/27/42)
Empire Steel (3/24/42)
Muskogee (3/22/42)
Culebra (1/25/42)
Pan Norway (1/26/42)
Alcoa Guide (4/17/42)
Oklahoma (4/8/42)
Esparta (4/9/42)
Gulfamerica (4/11/42)
Leslie (4/13/42)
Korsholm (4/13/42)

Nautical Miles
Scale along 40° latitude
0   300

earlier I suggest a different meeting point in BE 7289 at 1000.

28 April

1000. I am six miles west of the meeting point.

1100. At the meeting point. I transmit direction bearings since U-*107* is not in sight. U-*107* then responds with her position. I steam on 120° to meet her.

1150. U-*107* in sight.

1230. I am on U-*107*'s beam prepared to throw the *Adress-buch* across in a watertight tin can with rope attached. U-*107*, however, breaks out her rubber dinghy because she wants to thank us with a case of eggs. That was just what we needed this far from our base. She also gives us some mail and we discuss our latest U.S.A. experiences by megaphone.

1245. Course home—85°. Both engines 300 RPM.

1302. U-*107* out of sight.[48]

1 May

0240. BF 4852. Two fishing vessels with lanterns on starboard.

0740. Alarm! Three large aircraft ahead, possibly our own, southwest heading.

1010. Surface. Since we had no problems from the aircraft I continue, surfaced, along the exact approach route into Lorient, frequently checking position because of the mine fields.

1807. A German aircraft HE 115 closes from the northeast. We exchange recognition signals.

2300. We reach outer range of entrance channel *Bogenlampe* [Arc Lamp].

2 May

0700. We reach Point Two.

0730. R-boat escort takes us under guard.

1050. We tie up at Lorient. Total nautical miles covered on patrol: 8918. Total submerged: 310.

As *123* made her way into La Rade de Lorient, the familiar Keroman bunkers and Fort Saint-Louis appearing to left and right, the diesels suddenly coughed and died. What Schulz had feared had happened. They had run out of fuel. In the silence Hardegen could hear martial strains from the welcoming band on *Isère* in the distance. This was embarrassing. The R-boat escort that had brought them to the harbor entrance, observing their difficulty, made inquiries by wireless and asked if Hardegen wished to have the Flotilla engineer send out an oil barge. Hardegen said no. He would complete the voyage on E motors. The boat's pride was at stake. His might be the quietest arrival ever heard at *Isère*, but it would be done on Hardegen's own two feet.

Slowly, silently, the boat made her approach. The crew stood at stiff parade rest on the decks fore and aft. Hardegen had stand alongside him on the bridge two officers who had been promoted during the last days at sea: von Schroeter, who was now Oberleutnant zur See, and Mertens, the LI in training, who was now Oberleutnant (Ing.). On the periscope above their heads fluttered eleven pennants with tonnage numbers boldly painted on each, while forward the photographer Meisinger had hung from the cannon barrel enlarged photographs of the five ships that *123* had sunk by gunfire alone. As *Isère* came into view Hardegen sighted not only Admiral Dönitz front and center but also—an unexpected honor—Grossadmiral Raeder. The crowd seemed even larger than after his first American patrol. Among them, as before, were *Blitzmädel* and Red Cross nurses with large bouquets of flowers and numerous U-boat *Kameraden*.

After the hawsers were secured Admirals Raeder and Dönitz crossed over the brow for the arrival formalities. Hardegen would receive his Oak Leaf Cluster personally from the Führer, Raeder told him, pointing out that he would be only the eleventh commander so honored, and the eighty-ninth soldier from all the German services to have the cluster. Dönitz gave Hardegen his own earnest congratulations. The grand admiral, who happened to be in Lorient on an inspection, announced to the officers that he would personally review the crew the next day and at that time present Iron Cross decorations to those whom Hardegen recommended. With that said, Raeder dismissed the crew so that they might rush for beer and mail while he and Dönitz took Hardegen to a new terrace dining room of the base officers' quarters where they were joined for lunch by Commanders Erich Topp (U-*552*), who had been awarded Oak Leaves twelve days before Hardegen; Karl-Friedrich Merten (U-*68*), who would win the Knight's Cross in June and Oak Leaves in November;

and Helmut Witte (U-*159*), who would win the Knight's Cross in October.

The next day, following formal dress ceremonies for the crew, Hardegen had his usual debriefing with the Lion, but at Flotilla, not at Kernével: Dönitz had abandoned Kernével on Hitler's orders on 29 March following a major British commando raid on St. Nazaire, and with Godt and staff was now directing U-boat operations from an apartment complex on the Avenue Maréchal Manoury in Paris. Pleased with Hardegen's report, Dönitz endorsed the boat's KTB in these words: "A superbly executed operation. With the fullest use of his equipment and with an exemplary spirit of attack, the Commander has achieved outstanding success, which to this date, without a resupply of torpedoes at sea, is unique."[49] Indeed, probably not before or since was U-boat artillery used with such effect as it was by Hardegen in his two American patrols. Dönitz asked Hardegen to write up the principal advice and caution that he would give a U-boat going to America. *Eins Zwei Drei*'s commander obliged with two single-spaced pages. Among his admonitions were the following:

West of 55° continuously monitor the 600 meter wave band. It is the most important resource for successful operations. Not only when being attacked but also when sighting U-boats or "suspicious craft" or "mysterious lights" ships give their positions and often their courses and speeds. By carefully entering these positions on a chart one can get a good overall picture of ship routes. Then, sailing along those routes guarantees a target.

Once you find a target and it is between you and the coast you can easily measure its speed by steaming about 4000 meters parallel and adjusting your speed to its. Type and size can be determined when it passes in front of coastal lights or lightships.

The most dangerous feature of American waters is marine phosphorescence at night, which is particularly strong off the coast of Florida. If you have to dive in shallow water, that is, within the 20 meter curve, because of aircraft or destroyers, be aware that if you then travel at periscope depth vortices off your screws and cannon will show up as phosphorescence and betray your position.

Since I never had contact by ASDIC I assume that the Americans rely on sound detection. In that I believe they do a good job. When approached by one of their vessels it is best to lie on the bottom and "play dead." Granted, it is not your normal experience to lie there at 20 or 22 meters and have destroyers and subchasers cruising overhead. You have to have good nerves. The opponent is not tough. He leaves if he doesn't hear or see anything. When that happens surface immediately and clear out.

The small submarine chasers are dangerous because of their small silhouettes which often don't show up in the periscope. On the surface they can be detected by their wake but not by their shadow. If they should ever learn to patrol at slow speed they would be fatal.[50]

Several days later, Hardegen and the twenty-eight-year-old Erich Topp took a Junkers transport flight from Lorient to Rastenburg in East Prussia. There a command vehicle with armed escort took them through the Görlitz forest to the *Wolfsschanze,* Adolf Hitler's field headquarters. In an anteroom to the Führer's office the two officers stood stiffly in dress blues with gray gloves and daggers. Hitler entered smiling in his usual dove gray tunic and black trousers, Iron Cross on his left breast, and eagle with swastika on his upper left sleeve. The two officers saluted. Hitler shook their gloved hands and offered some polite words of congratulations as an aide opened two ornate leather cases each containing the *Eichenlaub zum Ritterkreuz des Eisernen Kreuzes* with a hand-lettered parchment certificate. The Führer placed the ribboned decorations around the commanders' necks, shook their hands again, and invited the two "aces" into his private dining room for dinner. Numerous Wehrmacht and Luftwaffe general officers were assembled at the table.

Hardegen sat at Hitler's right. During the vegetarian meal Hitler commented on the Air Force insignia that Hardegen wore on the left breast of his tunic. Hardegen explained that he had been in the naval air arm before it was disbanded and he was assigned to U-boats.

"It was a great mistake abolishing the naval air arm, my Führer," Hardegen said.

"What?" Hitler asked, surprised.

"The Ubootwaffe desperately needs air coverage of its own—

Folke-Wulf 200 *Kondor* long-range reconnaissance planes to find convoys at sea, and the new Heinkel HE-177s, which not only have the range and fighting power to join us in attacking the convoys but also have the guns to take on the English aircraft over the Bay of Biscay."

"I don't think you quite understand our military priorities, young man—" Hitler began.

"Another thing, my Führer. We never would have lost the *Bismarck* if you had allowed our aircraft carrier *Graf Zeppelin* to be completed. Its planes would have turned back the English attackers."

"Hardegen!" one of the generals at table interposed.

"And Navy planes can drop torpedoes," Hardegen continued. "Look at what the Italians did in the Mediterranean, and the Japanese at Pearl Harbor."

A brief silence followed. When Hardegen resumed every fork was frozen in hand and every eye was on this aviation authority from underwater—all except Topp who stared straight ahead in mortal embarrassment.

"You will forgive me, my Führer," Hardegen lectured, "if I say that you make the mistake of looking only to the east, while the war will be won or lost in the west—at sea."

Hitler turned red in the face. He placed his fist on the table and spoke slowly: "Reichsmarschall Göring is enjoying great success with our air forces. He has our aviation strategies correctly in hand. We will have no more talk about these matters."

Following the meal Hardegen was taken aside by a furious General Alfred Jodl, head of the OKW Operations Staff. "What impertinence!" he said sharply. "Who do you think you are talking to the Führer like that?"

"Herr General," Hardegen answered," the Führer has a right to hear the truth, and I have the duty to speak it."[51]

On his return to Lorient, Hardegen was informed that the Keroman repair facilities did not have the heavy equipment required to replace his bent drive shafts and that he would have to take his boat north around the British Isles to drydock in Stettin by way of Kiel. What he was not told was that the English had installed the first metric airborne radar sets in their Sunderlands and Wellingtons, so that he had no explanation for the constant stream of aircraft that forced him down time and again during the passage. On one occasion he and the crew narrowly escaped death when a Sunderland, not sighted until it was too late, came out of the clouds and pounced on the boat's swirl as she dived. Through the sky scope Hardegen could see every detail of the aircraft including the faces in the cockpit. And yet nothing happened because of *123*'s unimaginable luck. The one bomb dropped was a dud. Hardegen, whose spine shivered in the after chill, decided not to tell the crew on how thin a thread their lives had dangled. North of Scotland their passage became particularly treacherous because of the few hours of actual dark, which were really more like dusk than night, and everyone was greatly relieved to make harbor safely in Norway. For the approach to Kiel, Hardegen raised on both extended periscopes forty-five pennants representing the total number of ships claimed by the two-year-old *123* under himself and predecessor Commander Karl-Heinz Möhle, and on the tower's front he painted the boat's overall tonnage claim under both men: 304,975. When he finally tied up at the Blücherbrücke at Kiel the officers were met by their wives. Hardegen's Barbara had heard him describe triumphal arrivals; this was the first time she had witnessed one. Admiral Hans-Georg von Friedeburg, who had almost short-circuited Hardegen's U-boat career, was also present to meet the boat, which Hardegen accepted as a delicious irony. He listened with acute pleasure to the admiral's welcoming speech about the achievements of *Eins Zwei Drei* and her Oak Leaves commander.

And then it was time to take leave of treasured officer-comrades and loyal crewmen. To Admiral Dönitz, Hardegen had argued successfully that only Horst von Schroeter was qualified to command his beloved *123*. To the young number one he now transferred the boat that for the past eleven months had encapsulated his life and, with Barbara, he left for his new assignment as an instructor with the Training Flotilla at Gotenhafen (née Gdynia) on the Gulf of Danzig (née Gdańsk). Apparently he had been relieved from active sea duty at just the right time, since at his new station he was frequently in the hospital with stomach bleeding. His shore career took him later to Torpedo School at Flensburg-Mürwik, to Kriegsmarine headquarters (OKM) in Berlin where he worked on new acoustic and wired torpedoes, and when the Berlin facilities were destroyed by Allied bombing he moved with its staff to Neubrandenburg where he served from October 1944 to January 1945.

In the last desperate months of the war, like other shore-based Navy officers, Hardegen was assigned to land warfare. In field gray uniform he commanded a Marine infantry unit against British troops south of Bremen. The ground forces suffered huge losses and most officers were killed. Hardegen owed his survival, so he has stated, to the fact that he was hospitalized with a severe case of diphtheria and missed the worst of the fighting. In the last days before surrender he served on Dönitz's staff at Flensburg-Mürwik where, one night, he heard the fatal shot that felled his U-boat comrade and friend Wolfgang Lüth, who had won the Knight's Cross with Oak Leaves, Swords, and Diamonds (one of only two commanders so honored): While walking home from headquarters Lüth had failed to hear a German sentry's challenge and was shot. At the end of July, following the surrender, Hardegen was arrested and imprisoned by the British who mistook him for one Paul Hardegen, a member of the Waffen SS (*Schutz Staffeln*, the virulently Nazi ground divisions). Although he carried a military passport that certified to his naval service and current rank of Korvettenkapitän, the British, who apparently could not see beyond his field gray uniform, placed him in a political prison camp for SS where he remained for a year and a half. Hardegen finally was able to persuade a Dutch interrogator to write a letter to his wife, who had been found alive in November 1945 in the Soviet-occupied zone of Germany. She could provide photographs and news clippings proving that he was not SS but a U-boat officer. When Barbara responded with these articles Hardegen was released. The date was November 1946. No apology was ever made for the mistake, and Hardegen was obliged to report every week to an occupation officer until he was "de-Nazified," certification of which came through after six months. Reunited with Barbara and their four children, he began a new life.[52]

Afterword

It has become common among historians to assign great lapses or errors in wartime decision making to external circumstances that envelop and overwhelm the individuals responsible. Increasingly in such discussions one speaks of the "fog of war," or of the "confluence of individual and organizational breakdowns," or of the surrounding "noise" of irrelevant signals and messages. Thus Samuel Eliot Morison, twenty-two years after the event, decided that the defeat at Pearl Harbor resulted from the combination of divided responsibility between Army and Navy, false operational assumptions, and "noise" that "overwhelmed the message" coming in from excellent intelligence. He held no individuals as such responsible.[1] Roberta Wohlstetter's thoughtful analysis of the Pearl Harbor documents and testimony, which she published a year before Morison, drew much the same conclusion, though she gave a higher place to the importance of "noise" that caused strategists in Washington to feel secure in their own (false as it turned out) expectations of Japanese actions. Wohlstetter also was the first to stress the damage done to intelligence analysis by the internal naval rivalry that existed between Operations and Intelligence, a rivalry later (1985) examined in detail by Rear Admiral Edwin T. Layton, USN (Ret.), who as intelligence officer of the Pacific Fleet at the time suspected that radio intelligence (data not declassified in time for use by Morison and Wohlstetter) was disclosing Japanese intentions, and that those data were being misinterpreted and misrepresented in Washington.[2]

Did "fog," "noise," false assumptions, divided responsibilities, or intraservice rivalry contribute significantly to command failures at the start, in January, of what this book has called the Atlantic Pearl Harbor? Were Admirals King, Ingersoll, Bristol, and Andrews perhaps to be excused for their failure to resist Paukenschlag by extraneous circumstances? Although Elting E. Morison and Kenneth A. Knowles both told the writer that when they assumed their duties in May of that year, Morison at ESF, Knowles at Main Navy, there was still much confusion and uncertainty about the best means for combating the U-boats, there is no evidence in the written record for saying that any kind of "fog" obscured the patent fact in early January 1942 that Germany was sending U-boats to the U.S. coast. The daily British submarine estimate and Captain Leighton's daily situation maps based on the estimate plainly displayed the attacking force and its progress westward day-by-day. No "noise" obfuscated the clear intent and meaning of the incoming British intelligence, which, as recently declassified (1987) messages show, was transmitted to all pertinent commands, including those of Ingersoll, Bristol, and Andrews. Furthermore, it would be hard to say, given these clear warnings (which at the last included the sinking of *Cyclops*) that either Main Navy or its Atlantic sea commands was misdirected by false assumptions about the German intentions.

When divided responsibility is considered one may find that there was division of a kind that could conceivably have encouraged false assumptions about what individual U.S. commanders might do. The semiautonomous Ingersoll, for example, could have assumed, while he organized military convoy AT-10, that Andrews had the approaching U-boats under control, though one must wonder with what forces; Bristol could have assumed, since Ingersoll gave no indication otherwise, that the U-boats were being taken under attack by someone else, so that he could leisurely dispose his destroyers for convoy AT-10 and training; Andrews could have assumed that the twenty-five destroyers amassed by King precisely for the purpose of opposing the U-boat advance were taking up battle positions under orders from Ingersoll, or Bristol, or both; and King for his part could have assumed that Ingersoll and Bristol, employing "initiative of the subordinate," would deploy their destroyer force to stop the U-boat invasion when it came. All those assumptions are in the realm of possibility, though they are not likely.

It is hard to credit external circumstances with altering knowledge and judgment so completely that Ingersoll would not know that destroyers assigned to home port by King expressly to resist U-boats would not be available for that duty if they were diverted to convoy AT-10. It stretches credulity to think that Bristol could not be jarringly aware of the same conflict and of the fact that someone had made a conscious decision to choose AT-10 over U-boat defense. Can Andrews truly be thought to have assumed that Ingersoll and Bristol were deploying the destroyers against Paukenschlag when many of the same destroyers were assembling in New York (Third District) water for convoy duty? An irrational foulup is theoretically possible, to be sure, but more probable is the explanation that some one person decided on the priority of the tasks that would be undertaken and on the disposition of forces that would be employed. Ingersoll comes first to mind since it was he who received COMINCH's order to arrange escort for AT-10. But Ingersoll's decision not to deploy any of the destroyers against the U-boats could easily have been overturned by King. All the strings ended in King's hands. And they were not disinterested hands. As pointed out in chapter 8, King had more at stake in this decision than anyone else since it was he who had devised the destroyer defense. Thus, though no "smoking-gun" order has turned up to document the point, it is difficult to avoid the conclusion that if that defense was to be abandoned it would be abandoned only with King's deliberate say-so and approval; unless, alternatively, King experienced a *lapsus mentis:* Lulled into inattention by the recent months' decline in U-boat activity, or by an underestimation of the U-boat as a naval weapon, or by an arrogant disregard of British warnings, or by a repugnance for intelligence estimates in general and for Captain Leighton's "little toys and other play things" in particular, or by a preoccupation with the war in the Pacific, or by all of the above, King may simply have failed to act in a timely and decisive way, like a sentry asleep at his post.[3] In either event, whether by commission or omission, King was the final responsible agent who allowed Drumbeat, and Hardegen in particular, to enter the nation's gates unmolested. King it was who caused the Navy to miss the only chance it would have to bloody the German nose at the outset and to persuade Admiral Dönitz that he would pay a heavy price if he attempted to have his way with the American shoreline. Probably not since Günther Prien's U-47 entered Scapa Flow in the Orkneys to sink the *Royal Oak* had a U-boat commander made himself so exposed and vulnerable to destruction as did Reinhard Hardegen on his approach to New York Harbor, coolly daring—inviting as it were—U.S. Navy ships and aircraft to attack. But King would not fight him. In the event, Dönitz, encouraged by Drumbeat's surprising successes, took the Atlantic Coast away from the United States, and proceeded to inflict a six-month punishment that spread to the Gulf of Mexico and Caribbean. King's subsequent efforts to cover for the massacre, beginning with his decision not to mention in correspondence or in print that in January he had available twenty-five destroyers with which to render a Drumbeat in reverse, did him and his service no credit.

There was an adage in the Navy that a sea dog deserved "two bites"—two mistakes. Admiral Husband E. Kimmell, the Navy commander at Pearl Harbor, was not allowed a second. But Admiral Richmond Kelly ("Terrible") Turner was allowed his two: first, at Main Navy, when he insisted that the Japanese would open the Pacific war by striking at Russia, and second, when by dogmatic miscalculation he presided over the Navy's worst sea battle loss to the Japanese, at Savo Island on 9 August 1942. By contrast, Ernest J. King had at least six bites: first, when he failed to deploy the destroyer defense he himself had devised to oppose the expected U-boat offensive; second, when he refused to apply British tactical doctrine and to heed OIC and ONI intelligence; third, when he failed to take timely action to construct small antisubmarine craft, which he contemned, though they later (after the loss of much flesh and steel) made coastwise convoys possible and accounted for two of the first three U-boat kills; fourth, when he failed to establish a coastal blackout; fifth, when he rejected, until forced to it, the proffered patrol assistance from private boats and airplanes; and sixth—the reason why his excessive allowance of bites never became widely known in or out of the Navy—when he dissembled in explaining how Drumbeat and the six-months' massacre could have happened.

The exact form of King's culpability might have been established had an exhaustive investigation been conducted at the time or later, similar to the Roberts Commission, Hart Inquiry, Navy Court, and congressional hearings that were convoked to explain Pearl Harbor. No such proceedings took place. The principal witnesses are now deceased. And the documentary record, already polished by King's redaction of events, may long ago have been sifted for paper that did not substantiate the official COMINCH account. Enough paper remains, however, to suggest that the naval record for the period deserves closer scrutiny and that, absent "fog" and "noise," one individual person must be assigned final responsibility for the U.S. Navy's failure to prevent America's worst-ever defeat at sea.

After seeing the U.S. Navy through to victory against Japan in the Pacific, where his heart and mind were always preponderantly fixed, Fleet Admiral King resigned as COMINCH and CNO effective 15 December 1945. His replacement was Fleet Admiral Chester W. Nimitz. Various honors followed, including a gold star in lieu of a third Distinguished Service Medal from the new President Harry S. Truman, a Joint Resolution of appreciation from the 79th Congress, a similar message from the British Chiefs of Staff, and an honorary degree from Harvard. He died on 25 June 1956, at the age of seventy-eight.

Admiral Harold R. Stark returned to Washington in 1945 after service as Commander, U.S. Naval Forces Europe, which included the planning and supervision of the Allied seaborne invasion of Europe. Rather than finding honors awaiting him he learned that King had formally censured him for negligence in the Pearl Harbor attack and had recommended that he be relegated "to positions in which lack of superior judgment may not result in future errors."[4] King recanted a part of his censure in 1949, at which time Stark received a third Distinguished Service Medal for his service in London (for which King, inconsistently, had recommended him in 1945). Stark died at age ninety-two on 20 August 1972.

Admiral Adolphus Andrews retired from the Navy as Commander of the Eastern Sea Frontier in November 1943. He had taken on the frontier defense when, without aid from Ingersoll, it was a near-impossible task. Except for two costly errors, failing to throw everything he had at Hardegen when the German first arrived and refusing to douse coastal lights, particularly those of resorts, he acquitted himself well in the difficult post. Upon his retirement he was immediately recalled to active duty as chairman of the Navy Manpower Survey Board at the Navy Department in Washington. He died on 19 June 1948. Admiral Ingersoll was relieved as CINCLANT in November 1944 and served as deputy CNO until his retirement in April 1946. He died on 20 May 1976. Rear Admiral Bristol, Commander Task Force Twenty-Four, formerly Task Force Four, formerly Support Force, died from a heart attack on 30 April 1942 and was succeeded by Vice Admiral R. M. Brainard.

Deservedly, Rodger Winn, to whom Allied victory in the Atlantic may be attributed as much as to any other single individual, received at war's end two of his country's highest decorations as well as the American Legion of Merit. His final rank of captain was unusual recognition for a volunteer reserve officer. After demobilization he returned to the Bar and rose to the position of Lord Justice of Appeal. He died in 1972. Patrick Beesly, his Tracking Room deputy, died in 1986.

Karl Dönitz succeeded Erich Raeder as grand admiral, commander in chief of the Kriegsmarine, in January 1943. On 30 April 1945 he succeeded Hitler, who had killed himself, as Reichspräsident. In that capacity he was arrested at Flensburg-Mürwik by British forces on 23 May 1945. His U-boats had sunk 2,775 Allied merchant ships, amounting to 14,573,000 tons. At the same time 754 U-boats had been sunk, a high 87 percent of all operational boats. Dönitz himself had lost two sons in the war at sea. At the International Military Tribunal at Nürnberg in 1946 (where he contended under oath that Lemp's U-*30* KTB was the only one that had been altered during the war) he was convicted on charges of "waging aggressive war" and committing "crimes against peace." His ten-year sentence at Spandau prison in West Berlin might have been harsher had he been convicted on another charge—that of conducting unrestricted submarine warfare—but Fleet Admiral Nimitz, USN, in an affidavit to the tribunal testified that the U.S. Navy submarine fleet had conducted exactly the same kind of warfare in the Pacific. It was the only instance at Nürnberg where *tu quoque* was accepted as a valid defense. Rebecca West has written: "That submarine warfare cannot be carried on without inhumanity, and that we have found ourselves able to be inhumane . . . This *nostra culpa* of the conquerors might well be considered the most important thing that happened at Nuremberg. But it evoked no response at the time, and it has been forgotten."[5] Dönitz served his full sentence and died on 24 December 1980. Grossadmiral Erich Raeder, convicted at Nürnberg of "waging aggressive war," was sentenced to life imprisonment but was released in September 1955. He died on 6 November 1960. Admiral Hans-Georg von Friedeburg, acting for Dönitz, signed the document surrendering all German forces in northwest Germany to British General Bernard Montgomery; on 23 May 1945 he committed suicide by taking poison.

Of the five Paukenschlag commanders only one, Ulrich Folkers, was lost in action at sea, on 6 May 1943, south of Greenland, at the hands of convoy escort HMS *Vidette*. All aboard U-*125* were killed. Folkers was twenty-eight years old. Heinrich Bleichrodt (U-*109*) continued at sea until October 1942, when he was assigned to shore duty, and ended the war as Korvettenkapitän commanding the Twenty-second U-boat Flotilla at Gotenhafen/Wilhelmshaven. Ernst Kals (U-*130*) and Richard Zapp (U-*66*) also ended the war at Korvettenkapitän rank commanding flotillas, Kals at Second Flotilla, Lorient, and Zapp at Third Flotilla, La Pallice. Bleichrodt died on 9 January 1977, aged sixty-seven; Kals on 8 November 1979, aged seventy-four; and Zapp on 17 July 1964, aged sixty. All five Paukenschlag commanders received the Knight's Cross during their careers, Hardegen and Bleichrodt with Oak Leaves.

Horst von Schroeter, who at age twenty-three had been jumped over numerous senior officers to command of *123*, because, as Hardegen argued to Dönitz, "he has such rapport with the crew they will fight the boat better for him than for any other commander," took *123* to further successes, in the process winning his own Knight's Cross. True to the seaman's superstition, the boat's only unsuccessful cruise was its thirteenth, in March–April 1944. Von Schroeter ended the war in command of a new generation electroboat Type XXI. In the postwar years he was recalled to service in the new German Navy (Bundesmarine), and as commander of all NATO forces in the Baltic he rose to vice admiral, the highest rank in the peacetime Navy. He lives in Bonn.

Like many others in the crew who had served under Hardegen, Fritz Rafalski eventually ended up on another boat, in his case the minelayer U-*233*. Off Halifax on 5 July 1944, this boat was sunk by U.S. Destroyer Escorts USS *Baker* and *Thomas* from an escort group centered around the carrier USS *Card*. Thirty-one of Rafalski's crew were killed. He and twenty-nine others were rescued and taken to the United States aboard *Card*. He spent the remainder of the war picking cotton as a POW at Camp McCain in Mississippi, where he says he was well treated. He lives in Bonn.

•   •   •

U-*123* was decommissioned at Lorient on 19 August 1944. The boat was later recommissioned in the French Navy under the name *Blaison*. She was scrapped in 1957.

In volume 4 of Winston Churchill's *History of the Second World War*, published in 1950, the former Prime Minister wrote: "The U-boat attack was our worst evil. It would have been wise for the Germans to stake all upon it."[6]

For thirty-nine years tanker motorman Wilfred Larsen of the *Pan Norway* was unable to shake the mental picture of the man who had been both executioner and savior on that night at sea, 27 January 1942, when his ship went down. Permanently fixed in his memory was the sight of the U-boat commander, binoculars in hand, scanning to see if Wilfred and his companions were all right, then steaming off to hail the *Mount Aetna* and ensure that every man in the water was rescued, even when some of the Norwegians themselves attempted to persuade the Swiss master to depart prematurely. For thirty-nine years Wilfred felt himself in terrible debt to the German who had transmuted the Atlantic from a battlescape to a sea of mercy and thus given him a life he would not otherwise have had. Back in Bergen after the war, he bought a home, married, and continued the life of a seaman. At age fifty he began to experience nightmares about his escape from death, and his nerves became so raw that he jumped at any unusual noise. When medication failed to help his condition he decided that the only remedy was to meet the man whose memory presided over his every day, waking and sleeping. Perhaps then he could lay to rest some ghosts, some debts, and some ill-understood resentments.

On a railroad siding in Bremen, Germany, in December 1981 the short, roundish Wilfred excitedly took the outstretched hands of a tall, athletic-looking, gray-haired man. As the two men later drove through the streets of Bremen in the Mercedes with its *123* license plate, Reinhard Hardegen explained that after the war ended he began a marine oil company that proved to be very prosperous, enabling him to enjoy a life that included thirty-two years of service in the Bremen Parliament (*Landtag*) as well as lots of "golf, swimming, and lawn-mowing." Wilfred was impressed by the large Hardegen home on Kapitän-König-Weg in Bremen's Oberneuland suburb. There he met Barbara Hardegen and a neighbor, Walter Kaeding. Long, friendly conversation ensued over coffee and sandwiches before a blazing hearth, German and Norwegian taking the measure of each other, Wilfred gradually getting over his initial tensions, and both agreeing, "We were seamen at that time. Enemies yesterday, friends today." They passed over matters of blame and justification. Hardegen told his new friend: "After the war my family was impoverished in a bombed-out Germany. We had nowhere to live. We were cold. I was out of work. I started from zero as a businessman, first on a bicycle, then on a motorcycle, finally in a car. In 1952 I started my own oil company, which I still run today. Hard work has given me and my family a beautiful home and security. This I am proud of."

Hardegen took Wilfred out onto his extensive lawn and garden at the rear of the house. He pointed out the various ornamental bushes that he had planted. In the distance stood a deer. It was idyllic, Wilfred thought. It was a day when he was truly glad to be alive. As the two men walked the old U-boat Commander noticed that one of Wilfred's shoelaces had become untied. He knelt in the grass to tie the sailor's shoe.

When Wilfred returned home to Bergen he said: "I shall tell you what made the deepest impression on me. When the German U-boat commander knelt down and tied my shoelace, at that moment I felt that, at last, all that had happened to me long ago was gone and forgotten."[7]

Flaunt out O sea your separate flags of nations!
Flaunt out visible as ever the various ship-signals!
But do you reserve especially for yourself and for the soul of
    man one flag above all the rest,
A spiritual woven signal for all nations, emblem of man elate
    above death,
Token of all brave captains and all intrepid sailors and
    mates,
And all that went down doing their duty,
Reminiscent of them, twined from all intrepid captains
    young or old,
A pennant universal, subtly waving all time, o'er all brave
    sailors,
All seas, all ships.[8]

APPENDIX A

Maintaining Trim

After achieving trim the LI and his team recorded on paper all the volumes and levels in the trim and regulator cells. From those benchmark readings all subsequent readings would be measured. For the moment the weight of the boat, which included the weight of the water taken into the large exterior diving, or ballast, tanks at the initiation of the dive, equaled more or less the weight of the water the boat displaced. Any change in that weight, however slight, would either cause the boat as a whole to rise or sink in depth or cause the bow or stern alone to move up or down. Minor changes such as the movements fore and aft of individual crewmen could be compensated for by the planesmen, but major changes such as the accumulated consumption of fuel, food, and fresh water over time required alterations of the water levels in the trim and regulator cells. So did changes in the specific gravity of the seas through which the boat passed, and changes owed to varying depths, currents, temperatures, sun times, salt contents, and levels of marine life. Particularly critical were torpedo launches since those events, leading to sudden weight losses of 1,600 kilograms per torpedo, required immediate additional flooding to make good the losses. In attack situations the LI had to calculate in advance how much seawater he would have to take on and then check the sudden buoyancy an instant after each torpedo left its tube. When the launch occurred underwater stabilization had to be achieved with unusual quickness lest the boat, which was only at periscope depth, surge through the surface and betray itself. The chief hydroplane operator carried the responsibility of constantly re-calculating weight and balance, using written data supplied him regularly by one of the control room machinists. For these calculations even the cook had to report each day the number of food cans used in preparation of meals, from which point in the boat the cans had come, and how much garbage he had had to jettison. And every second, third, or fourth day the commander would order a shallow dive to check the trim and weight against the numbers.

APPENDIX B

Operation of the Head*

Cabin H, the head (toilet), was on the forward port side opposite the galley. Type IXB boats had six torpedo tubes; crewmen called Cabin H "Tube Seven." It contained one of the most complex mechanisms on board, the use of which was governed by three rules. The first was not to attempt use when the boat was submerged below twenty-four meters, since outside water pressure made the system inoperable. The second was never to use the head when the boat was submerged and under attack, since, it was believed, an enemy soundman could pinpoint the pumping noise. The third was that the first action of a crewman on passing through the narrow steel door into the confined space of Cabin H should be to sign his name, date, and time of entry on a clipboard, so that, in the event of backup, everyone would know whom to call for clean-up.

When a crewman finished his business he observed the following sequence of actions. First he checked to see that the safety lever on the valve from the intermediate chamber to the outside chamber was closed and that the lever from the bowl to the intermediate chamber was open. Then he used the pump lever to transfer the contents of the

---

*This description of the head's operating system relies on former Oberleutnant Otto Giese (U-*181*) in a letter to *KTB 49* (March 1988), a monthly newsletter published by Sharkhunters, Harry Cooper Enterprises, Tampa, Florida. Cf. Gasaway, *Grey Wolf, Grey Sea*, pp. 37–38.

bowl to the intermediate chamber. Next he closed the lever from the bowl to the intermediate chamber and opened the valve from the chamber to the outboards. Then he pumped the contents of the chamber to the outboards and checked to see if anything had returned to the bowl; if it had he repeated the two pumping actions. Finally he returned the levers to their original positions, filled the bowl with water using another hand pump, and signed his departure time on the clipboard. Various examples of nautical verse usually made their way onto the clipboard pages as well.

APPENDIX C

Operation of the Schlüssel M (Enigma) Machine

The cipher handbook for a specific day directed the operator to select a specific three of eight available rotors, for example, wheels A, C, and G, and to place them in the machine slots in a certain wheel order, for example G,A,C. The rotors were each 1.27 cm. (a half inch) wide with serrated rims so that as they sat in their housings with the edges barely visible the operator's fingers could rotate them manually. As the operator did so letters of the alphabet that were inscribed on the rotors would appear consecutively in small round glass holes. The operator then rotated the wheels so that they presented that day's settings, for example, E,L,Q. Next, the handbook prescribed that pairs of connecting plugs resembling those on a telephone switchboard be inserted into specific plug holes, each representing a letter of the alphabet, the usual number of pairings being six to ten.

This completed and the Schlüssel M set for the day, the operator could begin the actual message encrypting. He selected at random three letters to constitute the preambular key, such as SHB, which would identify this message as different from all others that he might encrypt and transmit on the same day. With this key embedded in the message he "typed out" the message. As each key engaged—the resistant key action was hard on the fingers, slowing the punching process—a number of permutations took place inside the electromechanical device. For each key (letter) depressed the right-hand rotor advanced one position. Around the rotor rim, twenty-six to a side, were fifty-two electrical contacts. Movement of the rim caused a constantly changing series of current intersections. Once twenty-six character keys had been punched, the middle rotor, with a completely different wiring pattern, would also begin to advance, adding yet further complexity to the network of electric pulses in Schlüssel M's entrails. In long messages all three cylinders would be in movement, allowing the machine to encipher $26 \times 26 \times 26$, or 17,576, characters before the cylinders returned to their original positions. By rearranging the selection and order of the cylinders the possible combinations increased six times to 105,456. Further complicating the route the electric pulses followed were the plugs in the switchboard that operated independently of the mechanical operation in the rest of the machine and provided additional circuits and loops to the tortuous passage of the cipher maze, whose number of possible permutations approached one hundred and fifty million million million, a number maintained by German cipher authorities to be beyond solution. Without knowledge of the day's selection and order of the three rotors, the settings of their rims, and the plug pairings, an enemy cryptanalyst, even if he possessed the machine, would face, it was believed, an impossible task making sense of the alphabet gibberish that emerged.

Exactly replicating the keyboard, individual glow holes lit up as the operator punched the keys one by one. If he depressed M in the first word of his message, the R glow hole might light up, which letter the operator took down on his pencil pad; when he depressed the second M in the first word the F hole might glow, and so on as the machine transposed letters in seemingly random fashion. The final step was wireless transmission of the message in its encrypted form. The intended receiver then decrypted the message on an identical machine with the same rotor and plug settings prescribed for that day: The gibberish that the receiver "typed out" on his machine appeared in the glow holes as understandable German.

The HYDRA cipher used by Atlantic boats was originally called HEIMISCH ("home waters") but is best known in the intelligence literature as HYDRA, hence that term's use here. The cipher was known at Bletchley Park as DOLPHIN.

APPENDIX D

The Engine Room

The MAN engines provided numerous options. For turning the boat in close quarters, as for example in port waters, the RPMs of the port and starboard crankshafts could be varied. Or, one engine only could be clutched to the crankshaft and screw while the other at half speed was coupled to a dynamotor that, acting as a generator, charged the storage batteries. German boats differed from the boats of other navies, particularly from American fleet submarines, in that the diesels were shafted directly to the screws, whereas in American boats the diesels each had a generator attached at one end and electric motors alone, with power from the generator or batteries, turned the propulsion shafts in the manner of a diesel-electric locomotive. Fuel for the engines was contained in saddle tanks, or bunkers, on the two flanks of the boat outside the pressure hull. The bottoms of the tanks were open to the sea. The fuel floated on the top of saltwater, and as the fuel was consumed water took its place. Seawater was heavier, so that on the way home a boat would ride a little lower on the surface. From the bunkers the fuel was pumped into a smaller tank in the overhead and then into the cylinders for combustion by compression. Air for combustion was sucked through ports in the exterior of the conning tower and fed to the engines by superchargers. Any water that might get in with the air was splashed into the bilges. Exhaust gases went out through ducts in the hull to ports aft between the pressure hull and the superstructure.

Anything that got into the engine room atmosphere, such as gases or heat fumes or excess diesel odor, was mostly removed by two large ventilators. Ventilation was never really satisfactory, however. A man could easily get sick in the engine room, and many did on their first extended patrols. The main and auxiliary blowers used up considerable fuel on the surface and much battery water when submerged. On very few occasions, as on surfacing to get the CO_2 out—carbon dioxide could rise to levels as high as 2.5 percent inside the boat—were both mains and auxiliaries operated together, and then only for a few minutes. Some of the CO_2 was absorbed by chemicals. *Sauerstoff-laschen*—oxygen bottles—were available for emergency use. There were no hydrogen detectors on board, but hydrogen levels were quite high when batteries were being charged. One man lighting a cigarette could blow the boat apart. Many thought there ought to be an indicator of some kind, like a canary in a coal mine. And there was always the threat of saltwater from the bilges mixing with the battery acid to form chlorine gas that could kill everyone on board. The entire crew followed ventilation discipline religiously, though the interior fug remained generally unpleasant and unhealthy.

NOTES

Acknowledgments

1. Reinhard Hardegen, *"Auf Gefechtsstationen!" U-Boote im Einsatz gegen England und Amerika. Mit eimen Geleitwort von Grossadmiral Dönitz* (Leipzig: Boreas-Verlag, 1943).

Prologue

1. National Archives and Records Administration, Washington, D.C. [hereafter NARA], Modern Military Branch, Military Archives Division, Record Group [hereafter RG] 457, "German Navy Reports of Intercepted Radio Messages" [*X.B. Berichte*] Nr. 50/41, p. 8

2. The War Diary of the Operations Division, German Naval Staff, *Kriegstagebuch der Seekriegsleitung* [hereafter KTB-1/Skl] noted under the date 7 December 1941: "The attacks on the U.S. bases in the Pacific and against Singapore were a complete surprise." This KTB is in the Operational Archives, U.S. Naval Historical Center [hereafter OA/NHC], Washington Navy Yard, Washington, D.C. All German war diaries (*Kriegstagebücher*) are hereafter cited with the prefix KTB.

3. NARA, RG 242, PG/30301a/NID, KTB-BdU., 9 December 1941.

4. "The British have detected the complete withdrawal of German U-boats from the Atlantic. . . ." Ibid., 23 December 1941.

5. Karl Doenitz, *Memoirs: Ten Years and Twenty Days*. Translated by R. H. Stevens in collaboration with David Woodward (Cleveland, Ohio: World Publishing Company, 1959), p. 202.

6. See chapter 13 notes.

7. Michael Salewski, "The Submarine War: A Historical Essay," in

Lothar-Günther Buchheim, *U-Boat War,* translated by Gudie Lawaetz (New York: Alfred A. Knopf, 1978), appendix, n.p.

8. Winston Churchill, *The Second World War,* vol. 1, *The Gathering Storm* (Boston: Houghton Mifflin Company, 1948), p. 17.

9. Hitler's frequent expression was: "I have a reactionary army, a Christian navy, and a National Socialist air force." Alfred Jodl, in *Trial of the Major War Criminals,* vol. 15, p. 194; quoted in Walter Ansel, *Hitler Confronts England* (Durham, N.C.: Duke University Press, 1960), p. 14. That Dönitz himself was a Nazi, if not in 1941–42 then later, is argued in Peter Padfield, *Dönitz: The Last Führer* (London: Panther Books, 1985); an earlier statement of the argument appears in Michael Salewski, *Die Seekriegsleitung, 1939–1945* (Munich: Bernard & Graefe, 1970–75). Although naval personnel were not permitted to join the party, some U-boat officers sympathized with Nazi politics and accepted the *Führerprinzip.* One such, it appears, was Kptlt. Ernst Vogelsang (U-*132*) who incorporated the swastika into the insignia painted onto the fairwater of his boat's conning tower.

10. That "courage and patriotism can surely be admired whichever side a man fought on" in the Battle of the Atlantic is the view of British historian Martin Middlebrook, *Convoy* (New York: William Morrow, 1976), p. x; and of Edward L. Beach, Captain USN (Ret.), "Foreword: An Appreciation by an American Contemporary," in Herbert A. Werner, *Iron Coffins* (New York: Bantam Books, 1978), p. xiv.

11. *New York Times,* 15 March 1989.

12. KTB-1/Skl, 16 December 1942. When Reinhard Hardegen read in this manuscript the accounts of survivors of the ships he sank he commented: "It was a terrible emotion for me to learn the fates of the crews of the ships I sank. War is cruel indeed." Hardegen to writer, Bremen-Oberneuland, West Germany, 20 September 1989.

13. Clay Blair, Jr., *Silent Victory: The U.S. Submarine War Against Japan* (Philadelphia and New York: J.B. Lippincott Company, 1975), pp. 383–86.

14. Ladislas Farago, for example, writing in 1962, imagined that, "The flamboyant skipper of the U-*123* observed dancers on the gayly illuminated roof of the Astor Hotel in midtown Manhattan," an error repeated in numerous publications since; Ladislas Farago, *The Tenth Fleet* (New York: Ivan Obolensky, Inc., 1962), p. 65. New errors about U-*123* and Paukenschlag mar Homer H. Hickam, Jr., *Torpedo Junction: U-Boat War Off America's East Coast, 1942* (Annapolis, Md.: Naval Institute Press, 1989). Other books of American origin in which Hardegen and U-*123* are mentioned include: Theodore Taylor, *Fire on the Beaches* (New York: W.W. Norton and Co., 1958); Edwin P. Hoyt, *U-Boats Offshore: When Hitler Struck America* (New York: Stein and Day, 1982); and Gary Gentile, *Track of the Gray Wolf: U-Boat Warfare on the U.S. Eastern Seaboard, 1942–1945* (New York: Avon Books, 1989).

1. U-Boats Westward

1. U-*125* (Folkers), the first of the five boats out, sortied on 18 December. *123* (Hardegen) would be next, on the 23rd, followed by U-*66* on the twenty-fifth and *109* and *130* together on the twenty-seventh.

2. KTB-BdU, 23 December 1987. Schütze's command, *Second U-boat Flotilla,* would become *Tenth U-boat Flotilla* in January 1942.

3. This account is based on Hardegen, *"Auf Gefechtsstationen!",* pp. 102, 165.

4. The reconstruction of Schulz's briefing is based on technical data about Type IXB boats, on the fact that Tölle had to receive such a briefing, and on the assumption that the LI would have been the logical person for the task. The LI's guess about *123*'s destination is meant to convey the fact that no member of the crew knew where the boat was headed; interview with Fritz Rafalski, Bonn, West Germany, December 1986. For comparison the Type IXB boat was twenty feet longer than the fuselage of the most recent Boeing jumbo jet, the 747-400. Again, for comparison, the typical U.S. fleet submarine of WWII was 312 feet long. The USS *Bonefish*, one of four diesel-electric submarines still operated by the U.S. Navy, built in 1959 and scheduled for decommissioning in 1990, is 219 feet in length, somewhat shorter than the Type IXB. The Soviet Union has approximately one hundred diesel-electric submarines in service at the date of this writing. As a U-boat type the German IX series boats sank more tonnage per boat than any other type, including the better known VII series. The IX series was produced in the following numbers: IXA (8), IXB (14), IXC (143), IXD (2), IXD2 (30). The VII series, one of the most numerous ever built of any warship, was produced in these quantities: VIIA (10), VIIB (24), VIIC (691), VIID (6), VIIF (4).

5. A.L.P. Norrington, ed., *The Poems of Arthur Hugh Clough* (London: Oxford University Press, 1968), poem no. 52, untitled, p. 104.

2. Down to the Seas

1. Hardegen, *"Auf Gefechtsstationen!"*, p. 18; William A. Wiedersheim, III, "Officer Personnel Selection in the German Navy, 1925–1945," *United States Naval Institute Proceedings* (April, 1947), pp. 445–449. Hitler Youth leaders fared poorly in this selection process. Found emotionally unstable, uncooperative, unintelligent, or overbearing, many were not considered good officer material.

2. The actual presentation of oak leaves to Lehmann-Willenbrock would come on 31 December 1941. His boat, U-*96*, and he himself as commander, were portrayed in a postwar German novel (and motion picture) as notorious for its technical errors and misrepresentations of officer and crew behavior as it was justly celebrated for its dramatic sequences: Lothar Günther Buchheim, *Das Boot* (Munich: R. Piper, 1973). Lehmann-Willenbrock died in April 1986.

3. Konteradmiral was equivalent to rear admiral in the U.S. Navy. Dönitz was promoted to that rank in October 1939. He would be promoted to full admiral in March 1942.

4. The account of Hardegen's early U-boat experiences given in this chapter is drawn from or based on *"Auf Gefechtsstationen!"*, pp. 13–165; on the war diaries: KTB U-*124*, NARA, RG 242, PG/30,114/1-13/NID, 11 June 1940–16 August 1941; KTB U-*147*, NARA, RG 242, PG/30,137/2/NID, 16 April 1941–11 May 1941; KTB U-*123*, NARA, RG 242, PG/30,113/6/NID, 12 May 1941–23 August 1941; PG/30,113/7/NID, 24 August 1941–22 November 1941; on the *Schussmeldung für Überwasserstreitkräfte und U-Boote* ("shooting report") for each of the attacks cited in the war diaries; on KTB-BdU (*Befehlshaber der Uboote*—Commander in Chief U-boats [Dönitz and staff]); and on the writer's interviews with Hardegen and Fritz Rafalski.

5. This attack by U-*124* took place on 25 August 1940, twenty-three nautical miles north of the Hebrides. The four vessels belonged to convoy HX 65A. Gross Register Tons (GRT) is the measurement of all the enclosed spaces

in a ship expressed in hundreds of cubic feet (2.8317 cubic meters per 100 cubic feet). As a rule the GRT is more than the weight of the ship alone (light displacement tonnage) but less than the weight of the ship fully loaded (loaded displacement tonnage). As will be noted later in the text of this chapter U-boat claims were not always exact, and where not were usually exaggerated. Compare KTB-BdU, 25 August 1940, and Jürgen Rohwer, *Axis Submarine Successes, 1939–1945*. Introductory Material Translated by John A. Broadwin (Annapolis, Md.: Naval Institute Press, 1983), p. 26.

6. *Kommandant an Kommandant:* Commander to commander.

7. After the war Schéhérazade became the favorite nighttime haunt of Arthur Koestler, Albert Camus, Jean-Paul Sartre, and Simone de Beauvoir, who together dominated French intellectual life in the late 1940s and 1950s.

8. The massacre began with *Trevisa* at 0350 hours Central European Time (CET) on 16 October 1940 and continued to 0504 on 19 October. Where he speaks of the "Long Knives" event in *"Auf Gefechtsstationen!"*, pp. 55–58, Hardegen credits Kretschmer [U-99], Endrass [U-46], Frauenheim [U-101], and Bleichrodt [U-48] with 173,000 GRT sunk, when their actual total was closer to 75,000; and where in the same source he gives 325,000 GRT as the two-nights total of all boats, the actual tonnage sunk by all boats (eight in number) was 152,000 GRT. See Jürgen Rohwer, *Axis Submarine Successes,* pp. 32–34, and *The Critical Convoy Battles of March 1943: The Battle for HX.229/ SC122* (London: Ian Allan Ltd., 1977), p. 17. Hardegen was merely repeating the tonnage numbers reported by the commanders to BdU where Dönitz accepted them uncritically as a "colossal success"; KTB-BdU, 20 October 1940.

9. E. B. Gasaway, *Grey Wolf, Grey Sea* (New York: Ballantine Books, 1985), p. 77.

10. Rohwer, *Axis Submarine Successes,* pp. 34–35.

11. The sinking of *Augvald* took place at 2212 CET on 2 March 1941, at 150 nautical miles northwest of Loch Ewe; ibid., p. 45.

12. The boats that accompanied Hessler to the African coast were U-*38, 69, 103, 105, 106,* and *124.* The first boat to have worked the West African sea lanes was Hardegen's old *Edelweissboot,* U-*124,* under Schulz, in March 1941. Prior to that date Africa was the assigned area of Italian submarines.

13. The victim was *Ganda,* 4,333 GRT, sunk at 2019 CET on 10 June 1941, at 34-10N, 11-40W.

14. KTB U-*123,* 25 June 1941. Spain was officially neutral but aided German warships in much the same way that the U.S. aided the Royal Navy. Other U-boats that refueled from the supply tanker *Corrientes* in the Canaries during the same period were U-*124* (4 March 1941), U-*105* (5 March 1941), U-*106* (6 March 1941) and U-*69* (30 June 1941). See Timothy Mulligan, ed., *Records Relating to U-Boat Warfare, 1939–1945: Guides to the Microfilmed Records of the German Navy, 1850–1945: No. 2* (Washington, D.C.: National Archives and Records Administration, 1985), pp. 39, 46–47, 50. The refueling and victualing operation in the Canaries was stopped by British diplomatic action in July 1941; see Captain Stephen W. Roskill, DSC, RN, *The War at Sea, 1939–1945,* two vols. (London: Her Majesty's Stationery Office, 1954, 1956), vol. 2, p. 479.

15. Rohwer, *Axis Submarine Successes,* p. 58.

16. ASDIC was an acronym standing for Antisubmarine Detection Investigation Committee, which had initiated the British detection system in 1917. Overconfidence in the operational efficiency of ASDIC had caused the

Admiralty to cut funds for convoy escorts in the 1930s. Dönitz in great part frustrated the system by fighting on the surface at night. ASDIC did have its successes when U-boats were trapped underwater and could not escape the "Pingers," as the Antisubmarine Branch of the Royal Navy were called.

17. Crew interviews, Bad König/Odenwald, West Germany, 8–9 November 1985.

18. "Loaded merchant cruiser Río Azúl sunk. Continuing pursuit." KTB-*123*, 29 June 1941. On his return to port Hardegen would fly a red pennant from the periscopes signifying that he had sunk a warship. He was mistaken, however, in calling *Río Azúl* a *Hilfskreuzer*—an armed merchant cruiser. With an armed guard and deck guns, a common British merchant defense, *Río Azúl* was a Defensively Equipped Merchant Ship (DEMS). See Rohwer, *Submarine Successes*, p. 58. Two other ships from SL 76 were sunk the same day, 29 June, by *Fregattenkapitän* Richard Zapp (U-*66*), who later would accompany Hardegen to the U.S. East Coast in Operation Paukenschlag.

19. "Jedesmal wenn ich diese Flagge sah, hoffte ich deshalb, dass auch wir noch einmal den Tag erleben würden, wo wir es den Yankees heimzahlen konnten"; Hardegen, *"Auf Gefechtsstationen!"*, p. 125.

20. KTB-BdU, 25 August 1941.

21. KTB-*123*, 18–24 June 1941, pp. 7–10; Bibliothek für Zeitgeschichte [hereafter BFZ], *Schussmeldung für Überwasserstreitkräfte und U-Boote* [hereafter *Schussmeldung*], U-*123*, 20 June 1941, No. 4292, page 18; No. 4293, page 2; No. 4293, page 6.

22. Padfield, *Dönitz*, p. 505.

23. *"Auf Gefechtsstationen!"*, p. 152.

24. BFZ, *Schussmeldung* U-*123*, 21 October 1941, No. 4295, p. 2.

25. Public Records Office [hereafter PRO], Kew, England, Admiralty [hereafter ADM] 1/11903, "Torpedoing of H.M.S. AURANIA, 21/10/41."

26. Rohwer, *Axis Submarine Successes*, p. 70.

27. Hardegen's record of the prisoner interrogation is in an appendix to the KTB-*123*. Date and time of the torpedoing were 21 October, 0420 CET. Hardegen quoted Shaw as the crewman who gave the order to abandon ship.

28. On 3 November east of Belle Isle Strait U-*202* (Kptlt. Hans-Heinz Linder) sank two ships and hit two others from convoy SC-52. U-*203* (Mützelburg) sank two and U-*569* (Kptlt. Hans-Peter Hinsch) sank one from the same convoy. The three boats belonged to a newly formed pack code — named *Gruppe Raubritter*.

29. *Lloyd's Register of Shipping, 1942–43* and *1945–46* (London: Society's Printing House, 1942, 1945).

30. *"Auf Gefechtsstationen!"*, p. 165.

3. "We Are at War"

1. "Hatte ich persönlich doch eine Mordswut gerade auf die Amerikaner . . . ," Hardegen, *"Auf Gefechtsstationen!"*, p. 165. Hardegen's experiences with American ships are described on p. 125.

2. See ibid., p. 146, where Hardegen speaks bitterly about the Strait location: "Ich selber hatte eine nach meiner Ansicht völlig aussichtslose Position zu besetzen und schimpfte innerlich sehr, dass ich keinen besseren Platz erwischt hatte." Cf. Michael L. Hadley, *U-Boats Against Canada: German Submarines in Canadian Waters* (Kingston and Montreal: McGill-Queen's University Press, 1985), pp. 25–26.

3. Telephone interview with Hans Meckel, 20 October 1987.

4. Holger H. Herwig, *Politics of Frustration: The United States in German Naval Planning, 1889–1941* (Boston: Little, Brown and Company, 1976), pp. 42–63.

5. Ibid., p. 223. See Jochen Thies, *Architekt der Weltherrschaft: Die "Endziele" Hitlers* (Düsseldorf: Drost, 1976), pp. 136–48.

6. Herwig, *Politics of Frustration*, p. 214.

7. Ibid., pp. 214–15. In 1941 the U.S. Navy developed its own contingency plan for occupation of the Azores; OA/NHC, "CINCLANT; Jun.–Sep. 1941." U.S. Navy Intelligence anticipated a possible *Luftwaffe* strike at Key West, Hampton Roads, or New York Harbor, possibly from a base on Vichy-controlled Martinique, but did not explain how German bombers would be transported to that island or to any other nearby base; Jeffrey M. Dorwart, *Conflict of Duty: The U.S. Navy's Intelligence Dilemma, 1919–1945* (Annapolis: Naval Institute Press, 1983), pp. 184–85.

8. KTB-1/Skl, 22 March 1941, cited in Gerhard L. Weinberg, *World in the Balance: Behind the Scenes of World War II* (Hanover, N.H., and London: University Press of New England, 1981), p. 85 and n. 17. The writer is indebted to Dr. Weinberg for additional insight into the meaning of this plan, by personal communication.

9. Quoted in Padfield, *Dönitz*, p. 91.

10. Ibid., pp. 91–92.

11. Quoted in John Costello and Terry Hughes, *The Battle of the Atlantic* (London: Collins, 1977), p. 62.

12. OA/NHC, Box 1045, "Hyman-Idaho, 1945," re: sinking of U-*352* by USS *Icarus* on 9 May 1942, Lieut Comdr. J. T. Hardin to Commanding Officer ASW Unit, U.S. Atlantic Fleet, n.d. but 1942. For Admiral Nimitz's testimony at Nürnberg see Document Dönitz-100, "Interrogation of Fleet Admiral Chester W. Nimitz, U.S. Navy, 11 May 1946, *Trial of the Major War Criminals Before the International Military Tribunal, Nuremberg, 14 November 1945–1 October 1946* (Nuremberg: Allied Control Authority for Germany, vol. 40, 1949), pp. 108–11.

13. Padfield, *Dönitz*, pp. 76–191, passim, 538. The brief sketch of Dönitz's early career given here relies primarily on Padfield.

14. This list of forces is taken from Costello and Hughes, *Battle of the Atlantic*, p. 35. Different versions of the list are given in Jak P. Mallmann Showell, *The German Navy in World War Two* (Annapolis: Naval Institute Press, 1979), pp. 23–24; and in Edward P. Von der Porten, *Pictorial History of the German Navy in World War II*, Revised Edition (New York: Thomas Y. Crowell Company, 1976), pp. 29–37; and elsewhere. "Z" stood for *Ziel*—"target." The target date was sometimes rendered 1946.

15. This did not mean that by December 1941 Hitler had given up on surface fleet construction. He simply postponed its final completion until a date following the conquest of Russia, and possibly that of England also, when he could strike across the Atlantic at the U.S. with a huge fleet that included eight aircraft carriers and battleships larger than the USS *North Carolina*. See KTB-1/Skl, 31 July 1941, cited in Weinberg, *World in the Balance*, pp. 89–90.

16. Wolfgang Frank, *The Sea Wolves: The Story of U-Boats at War*, translated by Lieutenant Commander B.O.B. Long, R.N.V.R. (New York: Rinehart & Company, Inc., 1955), p. 121. After the war Dönitz told Allied interrogators: "The war was in one sense lost before it began. Germany was never prepared for a naval war against England.... A realistic policy would have given Germany a thousand U-boats at the beginning"; quoted in Samuel Eliot

Morison, *History of the United States Naval Operations in World War II*, vol. 1, *The Battle of the Atlantic: September 1939–May 1943* (Boston: Little, Brown and Company, 1964), p. 4. Winston Churchill would state at war's end: "The U-boat attack was our worst evil. It would have been wise for the Germans to stake all upon it"; *The Hinge of Fate*, p. 125.

17. KTB-BdU, 30–31 December 1941.

18. This enumeration is based principally on KTB-BdU, 1 January 1942. Cf. Dönitz, *Memoirs*, p. 197, who adds: "Thus at the beginning of 1942, after two and a half years of war there were never more than ten or twelve boats actively and simultaneously engaged in our most important task, the war on shipping, or something like a mere 12 per cent of our total U-boat strength." Naval Staff counted 98 boats at operational status on 27 December; KTB-1/Skl, 27 December 1941, as against Dönitz's count of 91 in the same month.

19. "The Commanding Admiral, U-Boats, requests immediate release of the large U-boats [Type IX] now at sea and of those which will be able to leave port in the next few days, in all twelve U-boats. Plan: Operation Paukenschlag off the American coast. Medium U-boats [Type VIIC] can fulfill operational requirements in the Gibraltar area. Naval Staff is releasing six large U-boats which are to be taken from those now leaving their bases. Release of the large U-boats already in the operational area west of Gibraltar is out of the question." KTB-1/Skl 10 December 1941.

20. KTB-BdU, 10 December 1941. Hitler would learn of Paukenschlag two days later from Raeder; "Führer Conferences on Naval Affairs," Rear Admiral H. H. Thursfield, ed., *Brassey's Naval Annual*, 1947 (New York: Macmillan Co., 1947), p. 245.

21. U-*128* was assigned to Paukenschlag while still at sea west of Ireland. BdU ordered her to "proceed at maximum cruising speed" to Lorient which she entered on 25 December. Needed repairs delayed her departure and made her participation in Paukenschlag impossible. She would sortie finally on 8 January 1942. See KTB-BdU, 19 December 1941. Dönitz continued to push for additional boats, naming U-*107, 108*, and *67* as boats he wanted Naval Staff to assign to the American operation; KTB-BdU 19 December 1941. Naval Staff obliged on 20 December, adding, "All other large [Type IX] U-boats will also be used in this area as they become available"; KTB-1/Skl 20 December 1941. One problem faced by Naval Staff and Dönitz alike was a marked disparity between the number of U-boats of all types in service (235) and the number on operational status (91). Staff gave as reasons for this "unusually unfavorable balance" that seemingly was not helped by the commissioning of twenty-plus new boats in both November and December the following four: (1) the great shortage of torpedo recovery vessels for training new boats and crews; (2) the repeated failure of practice warheads on torpedoes used in training; (3) delays in final fitting operations; and (4) delays in training caused by direction of resources to the Russian campaign; KTB-1/Skl 9 December 1941. The Paukenschlag strategy was described by Dönitz in KTB-BdU, 10 December 1941, where he added: "It is only regrettable that there are not sufficient boats available to strike a truly 'spectacular blow.'"

22. The writer's reconstruction of the events and dialogue at Kernével are based on the interviews with Hardegen; and Dönitz's KTB and *Memoirs*. While not claiming to be historically exact the reconstructed conversations and discourses do, the writer believes, accurately represent the men, their histories, and the events surrounding the start of Paukenschlag. One

surviving member of Dönitz's staff remembers Hardegen at the time; see n. 23.

23. This was the general impression of Hardegen at Kernével; telephone interview with Hans Meckel, 20 October 1987.

24. NARA, RG 457 (National Security Agency), "German Navy/U-Boat Messages Translations and Summaries"; Box No. 7, SRGN 4774-5513; BdU to all boats, "*Offizier*," 26 December 1941.

25. KTB-1/Skl, 25 December 1941. Naval Staff erred in its enumeration of boat numbers.

26. Dönitz makes this statement in KTB-BdU, 2 January 1942. In the previous September he had had as many as twenty boats on Atlantic station.

27. Hardegen is insistent that only U-*123, 109, 130, 66,* and *125* constituted Paukenschlag. Other boats designated to follow them to the North American coast, such as U-*107, 108,* and *67* (see KTB-BdU 19 December 1941 and KTB-1/Skl, 20 December 1941), as well as those that actually did follow in January 1941 (U-*552, 203, 86, 103, 106, 107,* and *108* and [finally] *128*) did not constitute Paukenschlag, either "first" or "second waves" so-called. The designation of those boats as being part of Paukenschlag either as original force or as subsequent waves is in error. Hardegen is confirmed in this by Jürgen Rohwer, interview, Stuttgart, Germany, 16 December 1986. He is also confirmed by the Naval Staff which spoke of "the *sudden appearance* of German U-boats in the American safety zone (operation 'Paukenschlag')" [author's emphasis]; KTB-1/Skl 25 December 1941. Dönitz clearly meant by Paukenschlag a sudden, first-time blow.

28. Gerhard Wagner, ed., *Lagevorträge des Oberbefehlshabers der Kriegsmarine vor Hitler 1939–1945* (Frankfurt am Main: Bernard und Graefe, 1972), p. 263.

29. Ibid., p. 286.

30. Quoted in Thomas A. Bailey and Paul B. Ryan, *Hitler and Roosevelt: The Undeclared Naval War* (New York: Free Press, 1979), p. 41. Also useful for the U.S. "belligerent neutrality" period are Patrick Abbazia, *Mr. Roosevelt's Navy: The Private War of the U.S. Atlantic Fleet, 1939–1942* (Annapolis, Md.: Naval Institute Press, 1975); William L. Langer and S. Everett Gleason, *The Undeclared War, 1940–1941* (New York: Published for the Council on Foreign Relations by Harper & Row, 1953); and Morison, *Battle of the Atlantic,* chaps. 2–5.

31. Churchill, *The Second World War,* vol. 3, *Their Finest Hour* (1949), p. 404.

32. Jost Metzler, *Sehrohr südwärts! Ritterkreuzträger Kapitänleutnant Jost Metzler erzählt; niedergeschrieben von Otto Mielke* (Berlin: W. Limpert, 1943), pp. 138–48. Cf. KTB U-*69,* NARA, RG 242, PG/30066/1-16, 27 May 1941.

33. Morison, *Battle of the Atlantic,* p. 73.

34. Doenitz, *Memoirs,* p. 189. Cf. KTB U-*203,* NARA, RG 242, PG 30191/1-11. 19–20 June 1941.

35. KTB-BdU, 20 June 1941.

36. Ibid., 21 June 1941.

37. Doenitz, *Memoirs,* p. 190. Also, Hitler told Admiral Raeder on 25 July 1941, "He will never call a submarine commander to account if he torpedoes an American ship by mistake. After the Eastern Campaign he reserves the right to take severe action against the U.S.A. as well"; "Fuehrer Conferences on Naval Affairs," Thursfield, ed., *Brassey's Naval Annual,* 1947, p. 222.

38. Doenitz, *Memoirs*, p. 190.

39. See, most recently, Waldo Heinrich, *Threshold of War: Franklin D. Roosevelt & American Entry into World War II* (New York: Oxford University Press, 1988), p. 167; and William K. Klingaman, *1941: Our Lives in a World on the Edge* (New York: Harper & Row, Publishers, 1988), pp. 370–71.

40. NHC Library, Rare Books, Operation Plans Nos. 4-41 and 5-41 (1 July and 18 July, 1941, respectively), in MS dated 1946 CINCLANT, Administrative History No. 139, "Commander Task Force Twenty-Four," pp. 61–62. Confirming copies of the same orders are found in OA/NHC Box CINCLANT (June–Sept. 1941), Operation Plan 5-41, Serial 00120, 15 July 1941; NARA RG 80, Records of the CNO Headquarters COMINCH 1942, Box 11, cited in Task Force Fifteen, USS *Idaho*, Flagship, Secret Serial A4-3/(005), 29 August 1941; and Washington National Records Center Suitland, Maryland [hereafter WNRC], RG 313, Box 108, CINCLANT, cited in Task Force Three, USS *Memphis*, Flagship, n.d. but presumed July 1941. Thus Roosevelt and King went to war six months before a formal declaration of war in the same way that Dönitz would go to war against the United States two days (9 December) before *his* country's declaration.

41. WNRC, RG 313, Box 108, Bristol to CINCLANT, USS *Prairie*, Flagship, 3 November 1941. The term Support Force was abolished on 12 March 1942. At the same time the other title of Task Force Four was changed to Task Force Twenty-Four.

42. Operation Orders Nos. 6-41 and 7-41 are in OA/NHC, Box "CINCLANT, Jun.–Sep. 1941."

43. Interview with Jürgen Rohwer, Stuttgart, Germany, 16 December 1986. Dr. Rohwer described the *Admiral Scheer* incident in Jürgen Rohwer, "Die USA und die Schlacht im Atlantik 1941," Jürgen Rohwer and Eberhard Jäckel, eds., *Kriegswende Dezember 1941* (Koblenz: Bernard & Graefe Verlag, 1984), pp. 81–103. At the time it was unclear to British Naval intelligence if it was the *Scheer* or the battleship *Tirpitz* that intended to break out. Postwar access to German records has revealed it was the *Scheer*, which had sunk nineteen merchant ships on a foray into the Atlantic in autumn 1940. To Roosevelt's "shoot on sight" order Adolf Hitler responded on 8 November: "I have commanded German ships, whenever they see Americans, not to shoot thereupon but to defend themselves as soon as they are attacked . . . and our torpedoes will strike"; *New York Times*, 9 November 1941.

44. KTB-BdU, 30 October 1941.

45. Stark to Admiral Thomas C. Hart, 1 November 1941, *Hearings Before the Joint Committee on the Investigation of the Pearl Harbor Attack, Congress of the United States, Seventy-Ninth Congress* (Washington, D.C.: Government Printing Office, 1946), part 16, p. 2121.

46. Robert E. Sherwood, *Roosevelt and Hopkins* (New York: Harper & Brothers, 1958), p. 382.

47. *New York Times*, 1 November 1941.

48. Rohwer, *Axis Submarine Successes*, pp. 71–73.

49. KTB-BdU, 29 December 1941. This is a recurrent theme in Dönitz's log beginning in November: "Further dispersal of U-boats for secondary duties should be avoided. These tasks are certainly excellent in themselves but compared with the gaps they create in the Atlantic battle they are most injurious to our cause"; 9 November 1941. He was particularly nettled by the assignment by Naval Staff of four boats to weather reporting and eight to escort the battleship *Tirpitz* on an intended sortie. Of the newly commissioned

Tirpitz he said, acidly, "It can hardly be hoped that this detrimental effect will be offset by comparatively large successes being scored by this ship"; 10 November 1941. In his official history of the Royal Navy in World War II, Captain Roskill states that the small number of U-boats available to Dönitz at this general period, "combined with diversions to unprofitable purposes, now seems to have been a decisive factor in the Atlantic battle." *War at Sea,* vol. 2, p. 104.

50. Rohwer, *Axis Submarine Successes,* pp. 50-72.

51. KTB-1/Skl, 6 December 1941. Admiral Raeder had long pleaded with Hitler for permission to wage unrestricted warfare against American shipping, throughout the winter of 1940–41 and especially after Roosevelt's "shoot on sight" order. As early as 10 October 1939, Raeder expressed his willingness to risk war with the U.S., which he thought was inevitable. "Führer Conferences," Thursfield, ed., *Brassey's Naval Annual,* 1947, pp. 46, 161, 177, 183–84, 192–93, 232–33.

52. KTB-1/Skl, 7 December 1941. Adding to the Navy's grief, *Gneisenau,* already damaged by an English mine during the Channel dash, was soon afterward bombed in the Kiel shipyard, thus rendered *hors-de-combat* for the rest of the war. These and other reverses of the heavy ships are described in Grand Admiral Erich Raeder, *My Life* (Annapolis, Md.: United States Naval Institute, 1960), pp. 361–74. Two advantages to having the still serviceable heavy ships in North and Norwegian Sea ports were (1) their deterrent to British amphibious operations against Norway, and (2) their use against PQ convoys to Murmansk; Jürgen Rohwer to author, 17 February 1987.

53. Eberhard Jäckel, *Hitler in History* (Hanover, N.H.: Brandeis University Press and University Press of New England, 1984), pp. 70–73. The chapter, "Hitler Challenges America," pp. 66–87, is a recent treatment of what Jäckel calls the "still unclear" reason why Hitler declared war. Cf. Bailey and Ryan, *Hitler vs. Roosevelt,* pp. 238–39.

54. KTB-BdU, 9 December 1941.

55. Ibid., 18 December 1941. An account of Dönitz's numerous discussions and lengthy teleprinter correspondence with OKM on this point is given in Doenitz, *Memoirs,* pp. 159–63.

56. KTB-BdU, 23 December 1941.

57. Ernst von Weizsäcker, *Erinnerungen* (Munich: Paul List, 1950), p. 328, cited in Weinberg, *World in the Balance,* p. 69. Certain of the foregoing reasons for Hitler's declaration are drawn from Weinberg, pp. 69, 91–92.

58. Jäckel, *Hitler in History,* p. 66.

59. Norman Rich, *Hitler's War Aims: Ideology, The Nazi State, and the Course of Expansion* (New York: W.W. Norton & Company, Inc., 1973), calls it "the greatest single mistake of his career" — "a monumental blunder" that "sealed his fate"; pp. 237, 245. Cf. Peter Loewenberg, "Nixon, Hitler, and Power: An Ego Psychological Study," *Psychoanalytical Inquiry* 6, 1 (1986): 31–46. Loewenberg, a practicing psychoanalyst as well as historian, addresses what he calls Hitler's impulsive, self-defeating, and megalomaniacal decision to declare war against the United States at just the moment when his armies were reeling in Russia: "His judgment was now impaired by grandiosity and defensive manic omnipotence in order to combat the fears of deterioration and disintegration from within." Weinberg, however, finds that there were no oral or written dissents from this decision on the part of Germany's political, diplomatic, or military leaders. If Hitler was "impaired," so, it could be argued, was everybody else. "There is curious irony in a situation where the

leaders of a country were united on war with the one nation they were least likely and worst equipped to defeat." *World in Balance,* p. 95.

60. Fritz Stern, *New York Times Book Review,* 12 May 1985, p. 7.

4. A Fighting Machine

1. U-boat berths for both officers and crew were four inches shorter and four inches narrower than standard berths on U.S. Navy fleet submarines of the same period.

2. Interview with Fritz Rafalski, Bonn, West Germany, 21 December 1986. The trim dive sequence and the briefing given Tölle by Hoffmann in the foregoing pages are reconstructed from the crew interviews as well as from the war diary, standard operating procedures, and technical data about Type IXB boats.

3. Details as minute as these are given in U-*123*'s unusually thorough KTB.

4. On 1 December HMS *Dorsetshire* closed on *Python,* which scuttled herself, the crew and passengers abandoning to lifeboats.

5. *Atlantis* (sometimes cited in German documents as *Schiff* [Ship] 16) was sunk by bombardment from *Dorsetshire*'s sister ship HMS *Devonshire* on 22 November. Her crew were first picked up or towed by U-*126* and then transferred to *Python.* Roskill, *War at Sea,* vol. 1, pp. 470, 480, 545–46.

6. U*A*'s adventures on this rescue mission are recounted in KTB-BdU, 1, 5, 11, 12, 16, and 24 December 1941. A synopsis of U*A*'s war diary is given in Mulligan, ed., *U-Boat Warfare,* p. 196. Tribute to the accomplishment of U*A* and the other rescue boats was paid by British naval historian Roskill, *War at Sea,* vol. 1, p. 546, who called it "a rescue for which the enemy must be given full credit." U-*123*'s sighting of U*A* on her outward passage is noted in KTB-*123,* 23 December 1941.

5. Destination New York

1. NARA, RG 457 (National Security Agency), "German Navy/U-Boat Messages Translations and Summaries"; Box No. 7, SRGN 4774-5513, BdU to all boats, "*Offizier,*" 26 December 1941. This signal reported the change in A from earlier values that had ranged as high as eighty meters. Also see NARA, RG 457, SRH 201, "A Collection of German U-Boat Admonition/Experience Messages (1943–1945), OP-20-G."

2. Gasaway, *Grey Wolf, Grey Sea,* p. 73, states that the deepest dive recorded by a IXC boat (U-*126*) was 750 feet. Middlebrook, *Convoy,* p. 69, on the basis of interviews conducted with former U-boat officers in the 1970s, places the record for a IXC at 1,020 feet.

3. As late as early 1943 the maximum depth setting for British depth charges was 550 feet; ibid., p. 69.

4. NARA, RG 457, Box 7, SRGN 4774-5513; BdU to all boats.

5. This reconstruction of Hardegen's words is based on the Hardegen interviews, on the crew interviews, on KTB-*123,* and on the account in "*Auf Gefechtsstationen!*", pp. 168–70.

6. Ibid., p. 169.

7. Similar grid charts existed for the other world oceans. Since they were drafted to Mercator's projection the large squares differed in size, becoming smaller as they approached the equator. The Luftwaffe had grid maps

of its own but the grids did not coincide with the naval squares, leading to frequent foul-ups in attempted Air Force-Navy joint operations.

8. KTB-BdU. The order of 9 September occurs in the KTB following the diary entry for 15 September. Prior to 9 September and as early as 16 June BdU had tried other methods of disguising its dispositions; see F. H. Hinsley et al., *British Intelligence in the Second World War: Its Influence on Strategy and Operations*, 3 vols. (New York: Cambridge University Press, 1979–88), vol. 2, pp. 171, 681–82.

9. For Dönitz's assurances about shortwave transmissions see Jak. P. Mallmann Showell, *U-Boats Under the Swastika* (Annapolis, Md.: Naval Institute Press, 1987), p. 59. The peculiar transmission properties of shortwaves at the time, most of whose energy was deflected upward into space, are described in Rohwer, *Convoy Battles*, p. 37. The *Adressbuch* continued in use for the remainder of the war, and a copy of the book was not obtained by the Allies until the capture of U-*505* by the U.S. Navy off Cape Blanco, Africa, on 4 June 1944.

10. KTB-BdU, 25 December 1941; also see 24 December. U-*451*, whose fate was not known for certain at BdU on 25 December, had been sunk on 21 December, not by ramming but by aircraft bombs, with forty-four killed and one captured. All boats reported as presumed lost at the Christmas Day briefing were in fact lost. The loss of U-*567* with all hands on 21 December cost the Ubootwaffe one of its greatest aces, Knight's Cross holder Kptlt. Engelbert Endrass.

11. Hinsley, *British Intelligence*, vol. 2, p. 551. Dönitz discussed the pros and cons of wireless control in *Memoirs*, pp. 142–43.

12. Peter Cremer, *U-Boat Commander: A Periscope View of the Battle of the Atlantic* (Annapolis, Md.: Naval Institute Press, 1985), pp. 134–36.

13. KTB-BdU, 19 November 1941.

14. KTB-1/Skl, 24 December 1941.

15. KTB-BdU, 1 December 1941.

16. This was so much the case that the British Admiralty concluded on 20 December 1941, that, "the primary object [of the Kriegsmarine] seems, at least temporarily, to be no longer the destruction of merchant shipping"; quoted in Hinsley, *British Intelligence*, vol. 2, pp. 175–76. That the German cipher had been penetrated might have occurred to anyone who knew, as Dönitz did, that B-Dienst was reading the main Royal Navy Cypher No. 2 on a daily basis and was beginning to read the new British Naval Cypher No. 3, which carried the bulk of North Atlantic convoy information. But Dönitz never seems to have acknowledged that HYDRA itself was vulnerable, and he resisted the possibility as late as the date of his memoirs in 1958. See Doenitz, *Memoirs*, pp. 324–25; and Hinsley, *British Intelligence*, vol. 2, pp. 177–79. In Patrick Beesly, *Very Special Intelligence: The Story of the Admiralty's Operational Intelligence Centre 1939–1945* (London: Hamish Hamilton, 1977), the author writes (p. 70): "Even as recently as 1973, Dönitz, in an interview with Ludovic Kennedy, was apparently still loath to accept that most of his ciphers had been consistently and thoroughly penetrated for four years of the war." See Ludovic Kennedy, *The Spectator* (London), 3 January 1981.

17. Hardegen does not recall the titles of the guidebooks referred to in the reconstruction of this scene. Hardegen was not the last military commander forced to rely on tourist guides. For the hastily mounted U.S. invasion of Grenada in October 1983 the Army 82nd Airborne and Rangers were provided tourist maps on which an improvised grid system was imprinted the

night before the operation began. *Wall Street Journal,* 15 November 1983, p. 1; Richard A. Gabriel, *Military Incompetence: Why the American Military Doesn't Win* (New York: Hill and Wang, 1985), p. 174.

18. The Operation Order is reconstructed from the orders transmitted subsequently by F.T. to U-*123* from BdU on 28 December 1941, 2, 3, 9, and 17 January 1942; NARA, RG 457, Boxes SRGN 4774-5513, 5514-6196. The dialogue of Hardegen with his officers is based on interviews with Hardegen, May 1985 and December 1986. *Gröner* was the merchant fleet handbook, with silhouettes of all known merchantmen class ships of all nations, compiled by the German nautical authority Erich Gröner.

19. Hardegen, *"Auf Gefechtsstationen!",* pp. 125, 165, 168.

20. NARA, RG 457, Box 39, "Admonition and Experience Messages."

21. Ibid.

22. Hardegen, *"Auf Gefechtsstationen!",* pp. 18, 170–171. On cargo U-boats and the U-cruiser (*U-Kreuzer*) class boats see Eberhard Rössler, *The U-Boat: The Evolution and Technical History of German Submarines* (London: Arms and Armour Press, 1981), pp. 67–87; and Bodo Herzog, *60 Jahre Deutsche Uboote 1906–1966* (Munich: J.F. Lehmanns Verlag, 1968), p. 54. Cf. Kapitän Paul König, *Die Fahrt der Deutschland: Das erste Untersee-Frachtschiff* (New York: Hearst's International Library Co., 1916); the writer is grateful to Robert Bartlett of the University of Chicago for this citation as well as for a copy of a personal letter carried to Baltimore via *Deutschland.* Cf. also Dwight R. Messimer, *The Merchant U-Boat: Adventures of the Deutschland, 1916–1918* (Annapolis, Md.: Naval Institute Press, 1988); and Henry J. James, *German Subs in Yankee Waters: First World War* (New York: Gotham House, 1940). Most of the boats and ships sunk by the U-cruisers were schooners and steam trawlers from fishing fleets, 18 to 53 tons, together with a number of steamers, 3,875 to 7,127 tons. Cf. Hadley, *U-Boats Against Canada,* pp. 5–9.

23. On the Edelweissboot U-*124,* where Hardegen and Rafalski served together, the crew favorite was Irving Berlin's *Alexander's Ragtime Band;* Gasaway, *Grey Wolf, Grey Sea,* p. 168.

24. KTB U-*123,* and NARA, RG 457, Box No. 7, SRGN 5514-6196.

25. PRO, ADM 223/103, "F" Series, Admiralty Signal Messages, October 1941–February 1942, DEFE-3 [hereafter cited PRO, DEFE-3], 2 January 1942. The decrypt erred in giving the *Dimitrios* position at PF 7335; the correct transmitted position was BC 4335, as found in KTB-*123,* 2 January 1942.

26. NARA, RG 457, Box No. 7, SRGN 5514-6196. Cf. Hadley, *U-Boats Against Canada,* p. 60. The story of *Foundation Franklin's* rendezvous with *Dimitrios Inglessis* is given from the tug's point of view in Farley Mowat, *The Grey Seas Under* (Boston: Little, Brown and Company, 1958), pp. 235–38.

27. KTB-*123,* 3 January 1942.

28. Ibid., 6 January 1942. The principal BdU Operations adjutant to Kapitän zur See Godt, Korvettenkapitän Victor Oehrn, wrote in the margin of Hardegen's KTB at this point: "*Fraglos richtige Überlegung"* — "blameless, appropriate caution." Hardegen believes that his caution in the *Dimitrios* incident belies the reputation for risk-taking attributed to him by crewmen Rafalski, Barth, and Amstein (chapter 2).

6. Waiting for Hardegen

1. Development, operation, and utilization of the *Bombe* are described in numerous sources among which may be mentioned: Hinsley, *British Intel-*

ligence, vol. 1, Appendix I, pp. 487–99; Ronald Lewin, *Ultra Goes to War: The First Account of World War II's Greatest Secret Based on Official Documents* (New York: McGraw-Hill Book Company, 1978), passim; Peter Calvocoressi, *Top Secret Ultra* (New York: Ballantine Books, 1980), passim; Beesly, *Special Intelligence,* pp. 63–75; Rohwer, *Convoy Battles,* pp. 235–40; and Costello and Hughes, *Battle of the Atlantic,* pp. 243–44. For Luftwaffe and Wehrmacht Enigma Huts 6 and 3 corresponded to naval Enigma's Huts 8 and 4. By 1 January 1942, BP had acquired sixteen *Bombes,* of which twelve were operational. Most were not at BP, where a single bomb of another kind could wipe out BP's entire cryptographic capability, but in various towns in the surrounding countryside.

2. Captain Stephen W. Roskill, *The Secret Capture* (London: Collins, 1959); Costello and Hughes, *Battle of the Atlantic,* pp. 153–55; Hinsley, *British Intelligence,* vol. 1, pp. 337–38; Lewin, *Ultra Goes to War,* pp. 205–7.

3. By the end of 1941 BP had read 25,000 naval Enigma signals; Calvocoressi, *Top Secret Ultra,* p. 98.

4. Interview with Patrick Beesly, Lymington, England, 9 July 1986; Beesly, *Special Intelligence,* pp. 57–61, 102–5.

5. This description of the Tracking Room comes from the interview cited above, fn. 4; and to a lesser extent from a telephone interview with Kenneth A. Knowles (Captain, USN, Ret.), 12 July 1986, who served a two-week stint in Winn's Tracking Room in May 1942.

6. This is the same Hinsley as F. H. Hinsley, co-author of the three-volume *British Intelligence in the Second World War* that has been cited in these pages. See Richard Langhorne, ed., *Diplomacy and Intelligence During the Second World War: Essays in Honour of F. H. Hinsley* (Cambridge: Cambridge University Press, 1985).

7. *Five hundred-tonner* and *740-tonner* (standard displacements) were the terms used in the OIC to designate the Type VIIC and IX boats, respectively. The U.S. Navy used the same terminology, with slight variations, for example, 517 and 750.

8. These new departures were twelve VIIC boats (U-*84, 86, 87, 135, 203, 333, 552, 553, 582, 654, 701, 754*) that would form Gruppe Ziethen on the Newfoundland Bank and off Nova Scotia.

9. Dönitz's persistent fear that French chambermaids, prostitutes, and dock workers were feeding vital operational data to London was generally ill founded. What CX information did reach London had little operational value because of the time delay. Of far greater value to London were CX data on technical matters, for example, new-type antennae, diving depths, repair and maintenance schedules, and so on. POW interrogations were another prime source of technical data.

10. This briefing sequence has been reconstructed primarily from the interview with Beesly; also from PRO ADM 223/92, No. O.I.C./S.I./40, U/Boat Situation, Week ending 20 December 1941; ADM 223/15, No. O.I.C./S.I./5, U/Boat Situation, Week ending 27 December 1941; KTB-BdU, 2, 3, January 1942; *The Times* (London), 3 January 1942, pp. 110–11. The first orders from BdU to the ruse boat, U-*653*, designed to camouflage the transit of Operation Drumbeat, were intercepted on 24 December. Decrypted by BP, they read in part: "Task is to carry out according to a pre-arranged plan a W/T ruse in order to mislead the enemy into assuming the appearance and operation of numerous boats in that particular area. Instructions for carrying out this plan will follow separately every day." PRO, DEFE-3, 24 December 1941.

11. Rear Admiral Alan G. Kirk, Oral History Transcript, Oral History Office, Low Library, Columbia University, p. 183.

12. Commander Arthur H. McCollum, Far East section chief, quoted in Rear Admiral Edwin T. Layton USN (Ret.), with Captain Roger Pineau USNR (Ret.), and John Costello, *"And I Was There"*: *Pearl Harbor and Midway— Breaking the Secrets* (New York: William Morrow and Company, Inc., 1985), p. 98. Cf. the account of the same conflict in Dorwart, *Conflict of Duty*, pp. 157–61.

13. Quoted in Dorwart, ibid., p. 181; see also pp. 187–88. See Layton, *"And I Was There,"* pp. 20, 96–100, 142. Dorwart contends that Turner had performed creditably in intelligence-gathering in the Philippines, Japan, and along the China coast in the 1920s; p. 157. From Washington, Turner went on to direction of Pacific amphibious operations from Guadalcanal to Iwo Jima; Kirk to decorated command of naval forces in Normandy invasions; Wilkinson, relieved six months after Pearl Harbor, resumed sea duty and as vice admiral commanded the Third Amphibious Force in the recapture of the Philippines.

14. Ibid., passim. Layton's is the most revealing study of ONI at the time of Pearl Harbor and Midway. Its orientation is strictly to the Pacific. For various interpretations of the Pearl Harbor attack and its causes the Library of Congress lists more than one hundred book titles.

15. NARA, RG 457, SRH 149, Laurence F. Safford, "A Brief History of Communications Intelligence in the United States," March 1952; SRH 305, Safford, "History of Radio Intelligence: The Undeclared War," November 1943. For U.S. Navy HF/DF capability in June 1942 see OA/NHC, War Diary, Eastern Sea Frontier [hereafter ESF], July 1942, p. 30.

16. Safford, "Brief History," p. 16. On 4 October 1940, the day he learned of Friedman's achievement, Safford wrote: *"Army did a swell job."* NARA, RG 457, SRH 355, Part I, Captain J. S. Holtwick, Jr., USN (Ret.), "Naval Security Group History to World War II," June 1971, p. 401.

17. This is the argument, for example, of Layton, *"And I Was There,"* pp. 137, 140–41, 160, 218. See Gordon W. Prange, et al., *At Dawn We Slept* (New York: McGraw-Hill Book Company, 1981), p. 82, for a different view. On the general role of "Magic" see Ronald Lewin, *The American Magic: Codes and Ciphers and the Defeat of Japan* (New York: Farrar Straus Giroux, 1982). When Secretary of the Navy John F. Lehman, Jr., made the posthumous award of a Distinguished Service Medal to Rochefort it was on the strength of evidence amassed in Layton's book; *Foreign Intelligence Literary Scene* 4, 6 (December 1985): 4.

18. Prange, *At Dawn We Slept*, p. 84.

19. Quoted in Safford, "Brief History," p. 16, with the comment that, while "the White House and State Department used this information [intelligence] with consummate skill," "the General Staff and Naval Operations [failed] to profit from the same information." It should be acknowledged that Safford was an interested party and had his own case to make. The same qualification should be placed on other in-house histories in the NARA SRH series.

20. NARA, RG 38, Box 14, Collection of Memoranda on Operations of SIS, Intercept Activities and Dissemination, 1942–1945; Captain Abraham Sinkov and First Lieutenant Leo Rosen, both of U.S. Army Signal Corps, to Assistant Chief of Staff, G-2, "Report of Technical Mission to England," 11 April 1941. The naval members of the team were Lieutenant Robert H. Weeks and Ensign Prescott H. Currier. Another account of this research trip, based on

an interview with Sinkov, is given in Thomas Parrish, *The Ultra Americans: The U.S. Role in Breaking the Nazi Codes* (New York: Stein and Day, Publishers, 1986), pp. 61–66. Parrish errs in stating that the U.S. team was "not given any hardware to take back home in return for the Purple machine," p. 65. Hinsley, who seems not to have been aware of the Sinkov-Rosen trip or of the Godfrey mission to Kirk's ONI, wrongly states that Britain was reluctant to share Enigma secrets with Washington at that time; *British Intelligence*, vol. 2, p. 55. Hinsley's asseveration is taken up and repeated by Warren F. Kimball, ed., *Churchill and Roosevelt: The Complete Correspondence* (Princeton, N.J.: Princeton University Press, 1984), vol. 1, pp. 214–15.

21. The originals of these are preserved in bound volumes in the OA/NHC. The ESF war diary acknowledged that, "The Admiralty was able to furnish daily reports of submarine movements to the Navy Department in Washington even before our entry into the war. . . . Shortly after the Axis declared war on the United States, British submarine tracking enabled Cominch to send warnings of probable submarine activity off the eastern coast of the United States." ESF, July 1942, p. 27. Winn and Beesly sent out a daily noontime signal, "U-Boat Situation," which in 1941 and 1942 "presented a fairly accurate representation of our plot in the Room"; Beesly to the writer, Lymington, 13 July 1986. The first notice of the receipt of U-boat positions at Washington appears on the USN Daily Situation Map of 25 August, OA/NHC, "Submarine Position as Estimated by Admiralty for 24 Aug. '41." From at least August forward Ultra could be employed by the U.S. Navy to route convoys around known U-boat rakes. Thus, it could be argued, President Roosevelt by these means avoided rather than invited incidents. Again, one might argue that Roosevelt could safely push the Kriegsmarine in July (by King's belligerent orders to the Atlantic Fleet) because he knew from other Ultra sources that Hitler did not want war with the United States at a time when his attention was absorbed in the Russian campaign. The writer has no hard evidence to support either of these speculations, however.

22. An account of Washington in this period is given in David Brinkley, *Washington Goes to War* (New York: Alfred A. Knopf, 1988), p. 91.

23. Quoted in [Admiral] Ernest Joseph King Papers [hereafter King Papers], Container 35, Manuscript Division, Library of Congress [hereafter LC].

24. NARA, RG 80, (Records of the CNO) Headquarters COMINCH 1942, Box 59, Rear Admiral John H. Towers [Chief of the Bureau of Aeronautics] to Chief of Naval Operations, 9 December 1941.

25. ESF, 29 December 1941; January 1942, p. 61.

26. NARA, RG 80, COMINCH, Box 245, Op-20-WP, 5 December 1941. The charge of Communist was made on the slim grounds that merchant operators belonged to the American Communication Association, identified by the House Un-American Activities Committee, chaired by Martin Dies of Texas, as "more predominantly communistic than any other union."

27. See chapter 3.

28. Morison, *Battle of the Atlantic*, pp. 115–16.

29. Quoted in Eric Larrabee, *Commander in Chief: Franklin Delano Roosevelt, His Lieutenants, and Their War* (New York: Harper & Row, Publishers, 1987), p. 155.

30. Quoted in Layton, *"And I Was There,"* p. 355. King's reputation as a hard drinker and womanizer, which must have concerned FDR, is cited in Robert William Love, Jr., "Ernest Joseph King, 26 March 1942–15 December

1945," in Love, ed., *The Chiefs of Naval Operation* (Annapolis, Md.: Naval Institute Press, 1980), p. 140.

31. LC, King Papers, Container 8, Colonel, U.S.A. (Ret.), A. T. "MacDuff" Rich to King, 11 December 1941.

32. Morison, *Battle of the Atlantic*, p. 41.

33. LC, King Papers, Container 35, undated; B. Mitchell Simpson III, *Admiral Harold R. Stark: Architect of Victory, 1939–1945* (Columbia: University of South Carolina Press, 1989), p. 126. The usual published sources for King are: Thomas B. Buell, *Master of Sea Power: A Biography of Fleet Admiral Ernest J. King* (Boston: Little, Brown and Company, 1980); Ernest J. King and Walter Muir Whitehill, *Fleet Admiral King: A Naval Record* (New York: W.W. Norton & Company, Inc., 1952); and Fleet Admiral Ernest J. King, *U.S. Navy at War, 1941–1945: Official Reports to the Secretary of the Navy* (Washington, D.C.: United States Navy Department, 1946).

34. Layton, *"And I Was There,"* p. 367; Dorwart, *Conflict of Duty*, p. 193.

35. Buell, *Master of Sea Power*, p. 175. Cf. ESF, July 1942, p. 28. Leighton went on to serve as Commandant Eighth Naval District, New Orleans, and was promoted to rear admiral on 27 June 1942. He died on 23 November 1943.

36. Buell, *Master of Sea Power*, pp. 175–76.

37. Dorwart, *Conflict of Duty*, pp. 189–92. Buell mentions the "animosity between the operational planners and the intelligence specialists"; *Master of Sea Power*, p. 175; and he concedes, "The intelligence staff seemed particularly vulnerable"; p. 231. Layton contends, "This war within a war raged on through the first half of 1942"; *"And I Was There,"* p. 510.

38. LC, King Papers, Container 35, "History of Headquarters, COMINCH."

39. ESF, December 1941, p. 5.

40. Ibid., p. 5.

41. NARA, RG 80, COMINCH, Box 222, North Atlantic Naval Coastal Frontier Force Operation Order No. 5-41, 30 October 1941.

42. NARA, RG 80, Box 50, Sec Nav/CNO Secret Correspondence, "Army and Navy Joint Control and Information Center," 10 July 1941. The hull (Hull "A") of Germany's first planned carrier, *Graf Zeppelin*, was launched on 8 December 1938 but the vessel was never completed.

43. After the war Thompson went on to a distinguished academic career at Princeton, which included authorship of a much-noted three-volume biography of Robert Frost. Morison, a second cousin once removed of Samuel Eliot Morison, who had interrupted his graduate education to receive his Navy commission, also went on to a distinguished career as a teacher and author at Massachusetts Institute of Technology, where he is Killian Professor of Humanities. He makes his home in Peterborough, New Hampshire, where he kindly granted an interview to the writer on 17 July 1989.

44. As late as July 1942, ESF complained to COMINCH about the length of time, two to four hours, it was taking to decipher each day's U-boat Estimate in the British Ultra code. Why, it asked, could the Estimate not be transmitted by Main Navy to ESF in the U.S. Mark II ECM cipher which would be handled "in about twenty minutes"? A COMINCH staffer replied that [ESF's suggestion] "will not be done for reasons which I do not feel free to discuss"; ESF, July 1942, p. 29.

45. LC, King Papers, Container 8, King to Andrews, USS *Augusta*, 17 November 1941.

46. LC, King Papers, Container 8, Andrews to King, New York City, 19 November 1941.

47. LC, King Papers, Container 8, King to Andrews, USS *Augusta*, 21 November 1941.

48. Quoted in Larrabee, *Commander in Chief*, p. 177.

49. Morison, *Battle of the Atlantic*, p. 208.

50. Alexander W. Moffat, Captain USNR (Ret.), *A Navy Maverick Comes of Age, 1939–1945* (Middletown, Connecticut: Wesleyan University Press, 1977), pp. 48–50.

51. ESF, 22 December 1941.

52. Ibid.

53. Commander Walter Karig, USNR, et al., *Battle Report: The Atlantic War* (New York: Farrar and Rinehart, Inc., 1946), p. 91.

54. NARA, RG 38, COMINCH, Box 110, Andrews to King, 20 May 1942.

55. NARA, RG 38, COMINCH, Box 110, Andrews to King, 27 January 1942.

56. ESF, 31 January 1942.

57. Farago, *Tenth Fleet*, p. 75. A battle of battleships and cruisers, in the Jutland tradition, would not occur until the engagement of U.S. and Japanese fleets at Surigao Strait in the Battle of Leyte Gulf, 24–25 October 1944, in which four battleships disabled at Pearl Harbor took part: *California, West Virginia, Tennessee,* and *Maryland.*

58. Kimball, ed., *Churchill and Roosevelt*, Washington, 18 March 1942, vol. 1, pp. 421–22. Historian Morison quotes one naval officer: "We were just plugging along to find out what sort of antisubmarine craft we wanted in case we needed them, and then all of a sudden, by God, we were in the war!" *Battle of the Atlantic*, p. 230.

59. Jochen Brennecke, *The Hunters and the Hunted* (New York: W.W. Norton and Company, 1957), pp. 10–12; also Mallmann Showell, *German Navy in World War II*, p. 34.

60. LC, King Papers, Container 35, undated but after 1943.

61. King, *U.S. Navy at War*, p. 80.

62. See chapter 12 notes.

63. Ibid.

64. NARA, RG 80, COMINCH, Box 241, Stark to Rear Admiral William T. Tarrant, Commandant, First Naval District, 3 October 1940. The same bias against small craft surfaced forty-seven years later in 1987 when, owing to their disdain for small vessels as lacking prestige, glamour, and career advantage, another generation of admirals was embarrassed to find itself without minesweepers (seventy-six to three-hundred-forty-one feet) when those craft were desperately needed to protect U.S. and other tankers traversing the Persian Gulf.

65. NARA, RG 80, COMINCH, Box 51, unsigned "Memorandum for the Chief of Naval Operations," 3 June 1941.

66. ESF, December 1941, pp. 17–18.

67. Ibid., March 1942, p. 9, Stark to Tarrant, 12 February 1942.

68. NHC Library, CINCLANT Administrative History No. 138, MS, "Commander in Chief, U.S. Atlantic Fleet," vol. 1, 1946, pp. 279–80.

69. NARA, RG 80, COMINCH, Box 110, Vice Chief of Naval Operations [Rear Admiral Frederick J. Horne] to Naval Districts, 22 April 1942.

70. NARA, RG 80, COMINCH, Box 110, King to Horne, 3 May 1942.

71. ESF, July 1942, "Coastal Picket Operation Plan No. 11–42."

72. Morison, *Battle of the Atlantic*, p. 230. Sixteen months after war began the ESF officers would readily acknowledge, "When the U-boats hit our coast in January we were caught with our pants down through lack of anti-submarine vessels." Captain W. A. S. Macklin, quoted in Morison, ibid., p. 254. Morison suggests: "Small craft were neglected because, it was believed, they could be improvised and rapidly produced in quantities at small shipbuilding yards. But if the President's wishes and recommendations had been followed, the Navy would have been better prepared to meet the U-boats"; ibid., p. 230. When asked in 1938 his opinion of Roosevelt's proposals for production and use of the 110-foot SC the then CNO Admiral William D. Leahy answered, "They weren't worth a damn." Robert C. Albion, "Makers of Naval Policy, 1798–1947" (ms., Harvard University Library, 1950), cited in Thomas B. Buell, et al., *The Second World War: Europe and the Mediterranean* (United States Military Academy; Wayne, N.J.: Avery Publishing Group, Inc., 1984), p. 217.

73. ESF, 31 January 1942. Cf. ibid., Andrews to King, New York City, 14 January 1942.

74. Ibid., December 1941, p. 15.

75. NARA, RG 80, COMINCH, Box 51, Stark to CINCLANT and Commander in Chief, U.S. Pacific Fleet (CINCPAC), 22 December 1941.

76. Wesley Frank Craven and James Lea Cate, *The Army Air Forces in World War II*, volume 1, *Plans and Early Operations, January 1939 to August 1942* (Chicago: University of Chicago Press, 1948), p. 68.

77. ESF, Andrews to King, 14 January 1942.

78. ESF, December 1941, p. 17.

79. NARA, RG 80, COMINCH, Box 245, Op-20-WP/an, 5 December 1941.

80. Abbazia, *Mr. Roosevelt's Navy*, p. 91.

81. *Radio Days*, a Jack Rollins and Charles H. Joffe Production, written and directed by Woody Allen. Copyright 1987 by Orion Pictures Corporation.

82. NARA, RG 80, COMINCH, Box 50, Commandant U.S. Coast Guard to All District Commanders, Washington, D.C., 26 October 1940.

83. NARA, RG 80, COMINCH, Box 50, "Air Raid Defense Bill," 11 September 1940.

84. NARA, RG 80, COMINCH, Box 51, Third Naval District Illumination Control Plan, 24 January 1941.

85. OA/NHC, ESF, "Suspension of Dimout Regulations," November 1943, pp. 28–29.

86. Ibid., p. 29.

87. The *Montreal Daily Star*, 31 January 1940, p. 1. The writer is grateful to Michael L. Hadley for a copy of this newspaper page.

88. ESF, January 1942, p. 64.

89. Ibid., January 1942, pp. 65–66.

90. NARA, RG 80, COMINCH, Box 243, "Brief Joint Estimate of the Military Situation of the Associated Powers," 20 December 1941, p. 9.

91. WNRC, Box 108, CINCLANT, King to CNO Stark, U.S.S. *Augusta*, Flagship, undated but after 14 December referred to in the message and before 30 December when King left *Augusta* to become COMINCH.

92. Vice Admiral Sir Arthur Hezlet, *The Electron and Sea Power* (London: Peter Davies, 1975), p. 212.

93. *The Collected Works of Rudyard Kipling*, vol. 20: *The War. A Fleet in Being* (New York: AMS Press, 1970), p. 211.

94. OA/NHC, Command File World War II, Daily Location of Ships and

Aircraft, 13 January 1942. By ports the DDs were stationed as follows: At Casco Bay—*Ludlow, Lansdale, Ingraham,* and *Hilary P. Jones;* at Boston—*Monssen, Charles F. Hughes, Lea, Dupont, Bernadou, MacLeish, Gwin, Dallas, Upshur, Gleaves,* and *Kearny;* at Newport, Rhode Island—*Ellyson* and *Roe;* at New York—*Livermore* and *Bristol;* at Norfolk—*O'Brien, Mustin, Trippe, Wainwright, Mayrant,* and *Rowan.* The list does not include three additional DDs at Charleston (*Jouett, Somers, Moffett*); thirteen submarines at New London, Connecticut, three at Philadelphia; three battleships (*Texas* at New York, *Idaho* and *New York* at Norfolk); six cruisers (four at New York, two at Norfolk); or the carrier *Wasp* at Norfolk, which was thought effective enough as a deterrent that she was dispatched the next day (14 January) on antisubmarine escort-of-convoy (A-10) but far from the present danger (see chapter 8). Destroyers bore names of distinguished officers and enlisted men of the Navy and Marine Corps, of secretaries of the Navy, and of a few civilians who helped the Navy. Where two or more bore the same surname first names and initials were used and places in the alphabetical listing of a class were determined by the first names.

    95. OA/NHC, Box CINCLANT (Oct 1941–Dec 1942), Operation Plan 8-41, Serial 00311, 20 December 1941.

7. Beat on the Kettledrum

    1. All operations of U-*123* described in this chapter are drawn from the KTB, the *Schussmeldungen* (shooting reports), Hardegen's *"Auf Gefechtsstationen!"*, Kaeding's chart overlays from the Bundesarchiv/Militärchiv in Freiburg; and from interviews with the commander and crew. Technical details are drawn from: OA/NHC, U.S. Naval Technical Mission in Europe, Technical Report No. 307-45, "Living Conditions and Accommodations Aboard German Submarines," August 1945; OA/NHC, U.S. Naval Technical Mission in Europe, Technical Report No. 303-45, "Submarine Main Propulsion Equipment and Arrangement," August 1945; also, from Rössler, *The U-Boat, passim;* and *The Story of the U-505* (Chicago: Museum of Science and Industry, 1981), pp. 20–21. The dialogue has been reconstructed by the present writer.

    2. Hardegen, *"Auf Gefechtsstationen!"*, p. 93.

    3. NARA, RG 457, SRMN-054 (Part 2), OP-20-GI, Special Studies Relating to U-boat Activity, 1943–1945, pp. 33–46. Again, the dialogue has been reconstructed by the present writer.

    4. This decrypt is found both in PRO, DEFE-3, "Intelligence from Enemy Radio Communications 1939–1945" [hereafter DEFE-3] 10 January 1942, and in NARA, RG 457 (National Security Agency), "German Navy/U-Boat Messages Translations and Summaries," Box No. 7, SRGN 5514-6196, 9 January 1942. The KTB-BdU, under date 9 January, provides the actual grid identifiers represented on the U-boat charts by Roman numerals: "Distribution of attack areas off the American coast: U-66—CA 79 and 87 and DC 12-13; U-123—CA 28, 29, 52, 53; U-125—CA 38, 39, 62, 63; U-109—area between points BA 9633–CB 1577–BB 7355–BB 8575; U-130—BB 51, 52, 54, 55, 57, 58." A key to these assignments is given in the KTB-BdU two days later, where the "enemy situation" reports include "heavy single ship movements" off U.S. coasts and "at the assembly points on the Halifax-Sydney Line."

    5. The dialogue of Winn and Beesly has been reconstructed from the interview with Beesly; also from PRO, DEFE-3, 10 January 1942; PRO, ADM,

223/15, No. O.I.C./S.I./57, U/Boat Situation, Week ending 12 January 1942; KTB-BdU, 10–11 January 1942; J. Rohwer and G. Hummelchen, trans. Derek Masters, *Chronology of the War At Sea, 1939–1945, volume 1: 1939–1942* (New York: Arco Publishing Company, Inc., 1972), pp. 177 ff.; Rohwer, *Axis Submarine Successes*, p. 73; and the London *Times*, 10 January 1942. The codeword "Ziethen" appeared jointly with "Paukenschlag" in an Enigma signal from BdU intercepted on 7 January: "To 'Ziethen' and 'Paukenschlag' Groups. Offizier Cypher. Remember these new regulations concerning offensive action. Merchant vessels are considered to be darkened even when, although travelling with steaming lights showing, neutral markings are not clearly lit up." PRO, DEFE-3, 7 January 1942.

6. Hadley, *U-Boats Against Canada*, pp. 58–59.

7. Abbazia, *Mr. Roosevelt's Navy*, pp. 379–80.

8. Hardegen, *"Auf Gefechtsstationen!"*, p. 172. When this stormline reached Iceland on 11–17 January, it carried winds as high as 120 knots. Much damage was done to U.S. aircraft and to ships, a number of which, dragging anchors, collided with each other in the harbor. Remembered in the Navy as "the famous blow," the storm was the worst in Iceland since 1925. NHC Library, Administrative History No. 138, p. 276.

9. PRO, ADM 1/15124, "Comparison (Nov 1941–Feb 1942) of the German M IV/1 T Carl Zeiss 7 × 50 binoculars and the Barr and Stroud Pattern 1900A 7 × 50."

10. Ibid.

11. The attack on *Cyclops* is described in detail in BFZ, Schussmeldung U-*123*, 12 January 1942, No. 4792, pp. 12, 16; also in KTB-*123*, 12 January 1942. For a technical description of the Type IXB torpedo launching mechanisms see OA/NHC, "Records of U.S. Naval Technical Mission in Europe 1944–1947," Box 27, 01045, Technical Report 239-45, "Torpedo Fire Control System for the Type IX German Submarine," 21 pp.

12. Directorate of History, Department of National Defence, Ottawa, Canada [hereafter DHIST], Statement of J. D. J. Green, R.M., Chatham 22820, 13 January 1942, in "Particulars of Attacks on Merchant Vessels by Enemy Submarines," Naval Control Service, NS 1062-13-10. The writer is indebted to Michael L. Hadley, Chairman of the Department of Germanic Studies, University of Victoria, for a copy of this report.

13. Ibid., Statement of Senior Radio Officer R. P. Morrison, n.d.

14. Ibid., NSHQ Naval Message, Charleston to Boston to Halifax, 12 January 1942, TOR 0547Z.

15. Ibid., NSHQ Naval Message, O.I.C. via Camperdown, 12 January 1942, TOR 0205Z.

16. PRO, ADM 223/15, 100820, No. O.I.C./S.I./57, U/Boat Situation, Week ending 12.1.42 (12 January 1942).

17. NARA, SRMN-038, "Functions of the 'Secret Room' (F-21) of COMINCH Combat Intelligence, Atlantic Section Anti-Submarine Warfare, WW II (Undated)," Naval Message 121716, 12 January 1942. Three weeks before his death Patrick Beesly wrote to the present writer: "I have been thinking about our conversation and it does seem to me that a most important point in your book will be to establish, if possible, that the U.S. did receive advance warning of Paukenschlag"; Lymington, Hampshire, England, 13 July 1986. The above cited message, based on the O.I.C. daily plot, together with the Daily Situation Maps of 12 January and before clearly establish receipt of advance warning.

18. See chapter 6, n. 31.

19. DHIST, "Particulars of Attacks," Statement of J. D. J. Green.

20. Quoted in Hadley, *U-Boats Against Canada*, p. 62.

21. Gilbert Keith Chesterton, "The Ballad of the White Horse," D. B. Wyndham Lewis, ed., *G. K. Chesterton: An Anthology* (London: Oxford University Press, 1957), p. 205.

8. New York, New York

1. KTB-*123*, 14 January.

2. NARA, RG 38, CNO Armed Guard Files, "Norness," Naval Message, NYNYK to BUSHIPS, *et al*, 11 December 1941.

3. This quotation and the survivors' accounts are drawn from the *New York Times*, 16, 17 January 1942.

4. OA/NHC, Microfilm Reel NR-A 40-3, "Deck Log of USS *Ellyson* (DD 454), Dec 1941–March 1942," 14 January 1942.

5. The *New York Times*, 16 January 1942.

6. Ibid., 15 January 1942.

7. Ibid.

8. Interviews by telephone with Richard H. Braue and Margaret Classe, 17, 18, September 1987.

9. OA/NHC, ESF War Diary, p. 2, January 1942.

10. Alfred Thayer Mahan, *The Influence of Seapower upon History 1660–1783* (1890; reprint, New York: Sagamore Press, 1957), p. 351.

11. Ibid.

12. Jeannette Edwards Rattray, *Perils of the Port of New York: Maritime Disasters from Sandy Hook to Execution Rocks* (New York: Dodd, Mead & Company, 1973), p. 215.

13. Quoted in Hardegen, *Auf Gefechtsstationen!* p. 177.

14. KTB-*123*, 15 January.

15. OA/NHC, ESF War Diary, 14 January 1942.

16. Hadley, *U-Boats Against Canada*, p. 65.

17. Ibid, translated by Hadley.

18. KTB-BdU, 14 January 1942.

19. BFZ, *Schussmeldungen* U-*130*, 13 January 1942, Nos. 5122, 5123, pp. 17, 1. See also Hadley, *U-Boats Against Canada*, pp. 63–64.

20. BFZ, *Schussmeldungen* U-*130*, 13 January 1942, No. 5123, pages, 5, 9, 13. See also Hadley, *U-Boats Against Canada*, p. 64.

21. NARA, RG 457, Box SRGN 5514-6196, 17 January 1942.

22. BFZ, *Schussmeldungen*, U-*109*, 19 January 1942, Nos. 5125, 5129, pp. 16, 20, 3, 7, 9. Rohwer credits Bleichrodt with a sinking, naming the vessel the British motorship *Empire Kingfisher*, 6,082 GRT; *Axis Submarine Successes*, p. 74. However, *Empire Kingfisher* was not sunk by enemy action. The Royal Canadian Navy reported: "S.S. Empire Kingfisher struck a submerged object in clear soundings south of Cape Sable. H.M.C.S. LYNX anchored her near Bantam Rock where she later sank." DHIST, "Halifax Local Defence Force Monthly Report January 1942," p. 1.

23. BFZ, *Schussmeldung* U-*109*, 21 January, 1942, No. 5129, page 15.

24. U.S. Navy torpedoes in the same time period had the exact opposite problem: "Torpedoes that hit their targets squarely generally failed to detonate; only those that hit glancing blows on the hulls of their victims would

explode!" Admiral Ignatius J. Galantin USN (Ret.), *Take Her Deep! A Submarine Against Japan in World War II* (New York: Pocket Books, 1987), p. 42.

25. Vice Admiral Charles A. Lockwood USN (Ret.), *Sink 'Em All: Submarine Warfare in the Pacific* (New York: Bantam Books, 1984), p. 78.

26. Ibid., p. 10.

27. PRO, DEFE-3, 16 January 1942.

28. Interview with Kaeding, Bad König/Odenwald, November 1985.

29. KTB-*123*, 15 January 1942.

30. Hardegen, *"Auf Gefechtsstationen!"*, pp. 174–75.

31. Ibid., p. 178.

32. Rattray, *Port of New York*, p. 210.

33. *New York Times*, 16, 17 January 1942.

34. Ibid., 17 January 1942.

35. ESF, 15 January 1942.

36. *New York Times*, 17 January 1942.

37. ESF, 16 January 1942.

38. See chapter 6, n. 91.

39. NHC Library, Rare Books, MS No. 138 dated 1946, Naval Administrative History "Commander in Chief, U.S. Atlantic Fleet," vol. 1, p. 280; MS No. 139 dated 1946, "Commander Task Force Twenty-Four," vol. 2, p. 106. The Order from Ingersoll to Sharp (Operation Plan, Serial 003) is in OA/NHC, "CINCLANT, Jan–Mar 1942."

40. OA/NHC, "Command File World War II, Daily Location of Ships and Aircraft, January 1942," pp. 13–16, January 1942.

41. WNRC, RG 313, Box 109 "Bolero," Headquarters Memorandum COMINCH, Rear Admiral Richard S. Edwards, Deputy Chief of Staff, to Ingersoll, 19 May 1942.

42. OA/NHC, "Command File World War II, Daily Location of Ships and Aircraft, January 1942," p. 15, January 1942.

43. King and Whitehill, *Fleet Admiral King*, p. 324.

44. LC, King Papers, Container 36, "CINCLANT SERIAL (053) OF JANUARY 21, 1941, Subject: Exercise of Command-Excess of Detail in Orders and Instructions."

45. LC, King Papers, Container 36, "Annex B to CinClant's Annual Report for the period 1 July 1940 to 30 June 1941."

46. Morison, *Battle of the Atlantic*, p. 118.

47. See chapter 3, n. 40.

48. Interview with Patrick Beesly, Lymington, England, 9 July 1986.

9. Where Is the Navy?

1. David Stick, *Graveyard of the Atlantic: Shipwrecks of the North Carolina Coast* (Chapel Hill: University of North Carolina Press, 1952), pp. 193–208.

2. BFZ, *Schussmeldung U-66*, 18 January 1942, No. 4778, p. 8.

3. OA/NHC, "War Record of the Fifth Naval District, 1942," pp. 30–33: "The S.S. *Allan Jackson*, Tanker, First Victim of Submarine Campaign in Fifth Naval District."

4. Survivors' reports are in OA/NHC, "Fifth Naval District, District Intelligence Office," pp. 30–32; *New York Times*, 20, 21 January 1942; and Captain Arthur R. Moore, *A Careless Word . . . A Needless Sinking* (Kings Point,

N.Y.: American Merchant Marine Museum, 1983), n.p., ships listed alphabetically. Cf. ESF, December 1941, pp. 21–23.

5. BFZ, *Schussmeldung* U-66, 19 January 1942, No. 4778, p. 12.

6. Ibid. *Lady Hawkins* was the second "Lady" ship to be torpedoed. An Italian submarine sank the *Lady Somers* east of the Azores on 15 July 1941.

7. Survivors' reports are in the *New York Times*, 29, 30 January and 6 February 1942; and in OA/NHC, "Fifth Naval District, District Intelligence Office," pp. 31–32.

8. Hardegen, *"Auf Gefechtsstationen!"*, p. 170.

9. Hardegen reports on the city lights and moving vehicle lights in KTB-*123*, 17 January 1942.

10. Crew interviews, Bad König/Odenwald, November 1985.

11. KTB-*123*, 17 January 1942.

12. *New York Times*, 18, 20, 21 January 1942.

13. KTB-*123*, 17 January 1942.

14. *Wreck Information List Compiled by the U.S. Hydrographic Office from All Available Sources, Corrected to March 10, 1945* (Washington, D.C.: Government Printing Office, 1945), pp. 28–36. There may have been a witness to the mystery sinking. A young Navy ensign on shore reported seeing a small freighter sunk at the location (apparent) and on the day and time (apparent) recorded by Hardegen. The ensign furthermore reported that a small Coast Guard rescue vessel put out to the position of the freighter, described as the "San José," about 1,000 yards from shore. This is according to Hickam, Jr., *Torpedo Junction*, p. 10 and n. 15.

15. NARA, RG 457, Box SRGN 5514-6196, 17–18 January 1942.

16. Ibid. and KTB-BdU, 17 January 1942.

17. KTB-BdU, 17 January 1942.

18. KTB-*123*, 18 January 1942.

19. KTB-*123*, 19 January 1942.

20. BFZ *Schussmeldung* U-*123*, 19 January 1942, No. 4794, pp. 12, 16.

21. Das Bundesarchiv/Militärarchiv, Freiburg, West Germany, "Wegekarte U-*123*," the DR overlay on the 1870G chart.

22. *Wreck Information List*, p. 38; "Corrections and Additions as of 30 September 1946 to H.O. Wreck Information List of 10 March 1945," p. 2.

23. Survivors' reports are in OA/NHC, "War Record of the Fifth Naval District, 1942," pp. 36–38: "S/S City of Atlanta Torpedoed Off Wimble Shoals"; "Fifth Naval District Intelligence Office," pp. 32–34; *New York Times*, 22 January 1942. Eleven bodies of the dead were eventually recovered and taken to Norfolk.

24. This simile is drawn from Karig, *Battle Report*, p. 93.

25. Crew interviews, Bad König/Odenwald, November 1985.

26. Hardegen, *"Auf Gefechtsstationen!"*, p. 181.

27. Hardegen later wrote: "[e]rschrak ich doch"—"I was frightened"; ibid., p. 182.

28. Ibid., p. 182.

29. KTB-*123*, 19 January 1942; BFZ, *Schussmeldung* U-*123*, 19 January 1942, No. 4794, p. 20.

30. KTB-*123*, 19 January 1942. Hardegen was calculating his total on the basis of claimed tonnage, which, counting the *Aurania*, *Ganda*, and the two "mystery" ships that he claimed at 4,000 GRT each, amounted to 102,502 GRT. The total also included *Augvald*, sunk on his first command, U-*147*, 2 March 1941. The actual tonnage sunk, *Augvald* through *Ciltvaira*, giving him two

"mystery" ships at 3,214 GRT each and excluding only *Aurania,* was 71,215 GRT. This degree of discrepancy between claimed and actual tonnage was not unusual in the Ubootwaffe and as a rule Admiral Dönitz accepted the inflated figures uncritically: for example, BdU accepted 325,000 GRT as the "colossal success" figure for the "Night of the Long Knives" (17–19 October 1940) when the actual tonnage was 152,000 GRT. The same degree of discrepancy between claimed and actual tonnage was found in the U.S. Navy's submarine force, where skippers' total claims of 4,000 ships and 10 million tons were revised downward after the war to 1,314 ships and 5.3 million tons; Blair, Jr., *Silent Victory,* pp. 877–78.

31. *Ciltvaira* survivors' reports are in OA/NHC, "SS Ciltvaira 19 Jan 42," in "Fifth Naval District Intelligence Office," p. 36; "S/S Ciltvaira" in "War Record of the Fifth Naval District, 1942," pp. 42–43; *New York Times,* 22, 23 January 1942.

32. BFZ, *Schussmeldung* U-*123,* 19 January 1942, No. 4795, p. 4.

33. Hardegen, "*Auf Gefechtsstationen!*", p. 184.

34. Survivors' reports are in OA/NHC, "War Record of the Fifth Naval District, 1942," pp. 39–41: "The S/S Malay is Shelled and Torpedoed"; *New York Times,* 20, 21 January 1942. An account of *Malay's* successful run to port under her own power is also given in Moore, *Needless Sinking,* "SS Malay," n.p.

35. Ibid., 20 January 1942.

36. Morison, *Battle of the Atlantic,* pp. 127–28.

37. *New York Times,* 21 January 1942.

38. Abbazia, *Mr. Roosevelt's Navy,* p. 370.

39. Morison, *Battle of the Atlantic,* p. 119.

40. ESF, March 1942, pp. 238–40.

41. *New York Times,* 21 January 1942.

42. Ibid.

43. NHC Library, Rare Books, MS No. 138 dated 1946, Naval Administrative History, "Commander in Chief, U.S. Atlantic Fleet," vol. 1, p. 274.

44. *New York Times,* 22 January 1942.

45. Ibid.

46. NHC Library, Rare Books, MS No. 138 dated 1946, Naval Administrative History, "Commander in Chief, U.S. Atlantic Fleet," vol. 1, p. 261.

47. Ibid.

48. Ibid., p. 274; *New York Times,* 24 January 1942.

49. Ibid.

50. Ibid., 30 January 1942.

51. OA/NHC, Action Report, Commander Destroyer Squadron Seven, Serial 004, 31 January 1942.

52. Ibid.

53. BFZ, *Schussmeldung* U-*130,* 21 January 1942, No. 5124, p. 5.

54. BFZ, *Schussmeldung* U-*66,* 22 January, No. 4778, p. 16; Rohwer, *Axis Submarine Successes,* p. 75.

55. Ibid., p. 75.

56. BFZ *Schussmeldung* U-*66,* 24 January 1942, No. 4778, p. 20.

57. BFZ *Schussmeldungen* U-*66,* 24 January 1942, No. 4791, pp. 8, 12, 16.

58. OA/NHC, "War Record of the Fifth Naval District, 1942," pp. 44–49, "M/V Empire Gem" and "S/S Venore Torpedoed."

59. BFZ *Schussmeldung* U-*130,* 25 January 1942, No. 5124, p. 9; *New York Times,* 26 January 1942.

60. BFZ *Schussmeldung* U-*125,* 26 January 1942, No. 5126, p. 7.

61. Cremer, *U-Boat Commander*, p. 221.
62. BFZ *Schussmeldung U-130*, 27 January 1942, No. 5124, p. 13.
63. OA/NHC, "Fifth Naval District, District Intelligence Office," pp. 41–43; *New York Times*, 28, 29 January 1942.
64. BFZ *Schussmeldung U-109*, 23 January 1942, No. 5129, p. 16.
65. The exchange of fuel took place on the night of 6–7 February (CET). Nineteen cbm were transferred in seventy minutes' time while both boats faced the wind at 50 degrees with E motors on dead slow. KTB-*130* and KTB-*109*, 6–7 February 1942. Decrypts of wireless messages from BdU to the two boats are in NARA, RG 242, PG 30105/4 and PG 30120/2, 27 January 1942 ff.
66. BFZ, *Schussmeldungen U-109*, 1 February 1942, No. 5130, p. 3; 5 February 1942, No. 5130, p. 8.
67. Rohwer, *Axis Submarine Successes*, p. 76.
68. Nicholas Monsarrat, *The Cruel Sea* (New York: Alfred A. Knopf, 1952), pp. 329–33.
69. *New York Times*, 24 January 1942. When one "blond giant" survivor of the Norwegian *Norness* was asked would he ship out to sea again, he said, "Sure, I go!" Ibid., 17 January 1942.
70. Ibid.
71. Ibid., 23 January 1942.

10. Course Home!

1. KTB-*123*, 19 January 1942. A fragment of a shell fired by U-*123* at *Malay* is on exhibit at the Maritime Museum in Islesboro, Maine, birthplace of Master Dodge.
2. U-*123* crew interviews, Bad König/Odenwald, November 1985.
3. Dialogue in the *Kosmos II* incident has been reconstructed by the writer on the basis of KTB-*123*, 19 January 1942; Hardegen, *"Auf Gefechtsstationen!"* pp. 185–86; U-*123* crew interviews; and *New York Times*, 7 February 1942.
4. KTB-*123*, 19 January 1942. To this entry Hardegen added a sentence recounting a news report that he had just heard on U.S. radio: "For example, all private telegram traffic of Jews at sea stopped altogether." It is not believed that a significant number of Jews served in the U.S. or foreign merchant fleets. At the date of this writing Hardegen cannot recall why a cessation of Jewish messages occurred or why he thought it was important. He made no mention of the fact in his *"Auf Gefechtsstationen!"*
5. "AN DEN PAUKENSCHLÄGER HARDEGEN. BRAVO! SEHR GUT GEPAUKT." KTB-*123*, 20 January 1942.
6. Literally, "Man, Don't Shoot Yourself," a board game like Parker Brothers' Trouble.
7. U-*123* crew interviews, Bad König/Odenwald, November 1985.
8. KTB-*123*, 22 January 1942.
9. NARA, RG 457, Box SRGN 5514-6196, 23 January 1942.
10. Hardegen was also mentioned by name, as he quoted the broadcast later in *"Auf Gefechtsstationen!"* p. 188: "As already stated in a special bulletin, German U-boats inflicted heavy losses on enemy supply shipping with their first appearance in North American and Canadian waters. Directly off the enemy coast they sank 18 merchant ships totalling 125,000 GRT. An additional ship and navy vessel were torpedoed. One U-boat in particular, that of Com

mander Hardegen, distinguished itself by sinking eight ships, including three tankers, over 53,000 GRT off the New York coastline." Hardegen added: "This way our boat, which many had seen in the movie *Uboote westwärts*, became very well known. And, really, we could not go much farther westward."

11. NARA, RG 457, Box SRGN 5514-6196, 24 January 1942.

12. Hardegen, *"Auf Gefechtsstationen!"*, p. 192.

13. KTB-*123*, 25 January 1942. This incident, with the dialogue, is reconstructed from the KTB, *"Auf Gefechtsstationen!"* and from the interviews with Hardegen.

14. Interview with Wilfred Larsen by Ariid Mikkelsen, *Familiebladet Hjemmet* [Oslo, Norway], 28 December 1981, pp. 66–67, 73–75; 5 January 1982, p. 28.

15. Ibid., 28 December 1981, p. 73.

16. KTB-*123*, 27 January 1942. Just three days before, and not far distant in BC 4700, a similar humanitarian act occurred. Kptlt. Peter Erich Cremer (U-*333*) sank the Norwegian motorship *Ringstad*, then assisted the crew with directions to land. Of Cremer one of the survivors said thirty-seven years later: "The man was very humane. . . . He was a seaman, one of the type that we [Norwegians] produce. He behaved according to the code of seamen who take no oath on it but know: help one another when in trouble at sea!" Cremer, *U-Boat Commander*, pp. 42–43. Helmut Schmoeckel has described humanitarian actions by 121 U-boats during the war in *Menschlichkeit im Seekrieg?* (Herford, West Germany: Verlag E.S. Mittler & Sohn GmbH, 1987).

17. KTB-1/Skl, 19, 26, 28 January 1942. Point *Sperber* was also known as *Erpel* and *Willi*.

18. NARA, RG 457, Box SRGN 5514-6196, 27 January 1942.

19. Ibid., 28 January 1942.

20. KTB-*123*, 31 January 1942.

21. NARA, RG 457, Box SRGN 5514-6196, 31 January 1942.

22. Ibid., 31 January 1942. An account of the *Spreewald* sinking, with his explanation how the error occurred, is given by Cremer in his *U-Boat Commander*, pp. 43–47.

23. KTB-1/Skl, 31 January 1942.

24. Cremer, *U-Boat Commander*, p. 45.

25. Ibid., p. 47.

26. Ibid., pp. 46–47.

27. Up to 9 February the Ziethen boats sank twenty ships, 87,398 GRT, either in Newfoundland and Canadian waters or in transiting to and from those stations.

28. NHC Library, Rare Books, MS No. 138 dated 1946, Naval Administrative History, "Commander in Chief, U.S. Atlantic Fleet," vol. 1, pp. 273–74; Hadley, *U-Boats Against Canada*, pp. 71–72; *New York Times*, 31 January 1942.

29. KTB-BdU entry, quoted in Doenitz, *Memoirs*, p. 203.

30. Beesly, *Special Intelligence*, pp. 110–11.

31. PRO, ADM 223/15, 100820, "U-Boat Situation," 26 January and 2 February 1942.

32. Quoted in Farago, *Tenth Fleet*, pp. 58–59.

33. Kimball, ed., *Churchill and Roosevelt*, vol. 1, p. 348.

34. Hardegen, *"Auf Gefechtsstationen!"*, p. 197.

11. Last Patrol

1. ESF, October 1943, chapter 2.

2. See E. Keble Chatterton, *Q-Ships and Their Story* (Annapolis, Md.: Naval Institute Press, 1972).

3. ESF, October 1943, chapter 3.

4. Andrews to King, New York City, 29 January 1942; OA/NHC, Microfilm Roll No. 478, "Q-Ships. Documents on WW II Actions [hereafter cited "Q-Ships"]."

5. Ibid., Captain Glenn W. Legwen USN to Admiral Horne USN, San Juan, Puerto Rico, 15 June 1946.

6. Ibid., Commandant, Navy Yard Portsmouth NH to OpNav (Rear Admiral W. S. Farber, USN), Portsmouth, 6 March 1942; ESF, October 1943, chapter 3.

7. Ibid., October 1943, chapter 3.

8. OA/NHC, "Q-Ships," Captain Legwen USN, to Admiral Horne USN, San Juan, Puerto Rico, 15 June 1946.

9. OA/NHC, "Q-Ships," Captain Thomas J. Ryan, Jr., USN, to Vice Admiral W. S. Farber, USN, Annapolis, Maryland, 12 February 1946.

10. ESF, October 1943, chapter 3.

11. F. H. Hinsley, *British Intelligence,* vol. 2, p. 179. The blow was doubly hard in retrospect since February was the same month in which the German B-Dienst completed the reconstruction of the British North Atlantic convoy code (Naval Cypher No. 3).

12. Rohwer, *Axis Submarine Successes,* pp. 77–82. The numbers do not include additional sinkings during the same period by boats operating in Canadian and Newfoundland waters or by boats transiting in mid-Atlantic.

13. PRO, DEFE-3, Kals to BdU, 13 January 1942; Hadley, *U-Boats Against Canada,* p. 68.

14. Ibid., pp. 70–71.

15. ESF, chapter 7, February 1942.

16. KTB-1/Skl, 22, 24 January 1942. Doenitz, *Memoirs,* pp. 206 ff.

17. Roskill, *War at Sea,* vol. 2, pp. 101, 104.

18. Crew interviews, Bad König/Odenwald, November 1985.

19. Wolfgang Lüth, "Command of Men in a U-Boat," Harald Busch, *U-Boats at War* (New York: Ballantine Books, 1955), pp. 160–72.

20. Crew interviews, Bad König/Odenwald, November 1985.

21. KTB-*123,* 22 March 1942; BFZ, Schussmeldung, U-*123,* 22 March 1942, No. 5557, page 4.

22. Although the U.S. Navy and the U.S. Maritime Commission were soon aware of the loss of *Muskogee,* no effort was made to notify the next of kin. Forty-five years later Mr. George H. Betts, of Milo, Maine, sought the facts surrounding the death of his father, William Wright Betts, who was master of the vessel, and communicated his findings to the brother and sister of the radio operator and to five other family survivors whom he could discover. On 9 October 1987, Mr. Betts met with Reinhard Hardegen and his wife Barbara on a cruise ship visiting Quebec, Canada, and later, from photographs in Hardegen's possession, was able to identify two and possibly a third survivor on one of the rafts that got away. Betts pronounced Hardegen to be "a decent former foe of this nation"; letter to the present writer, Milo, Maine, 7 March 1988.

23. KTB-*123,* 22 March 1942.

24. The attack on *Empire Steel* is reconstructed from ibid., 23–24 March 1942; BFZ, Schussmeldungen U-*123*, 24 March 1942, No. 5557, pp. 9, 12; Hardegen, *"Auf Gefechtsstationen!"* pp. 199–201; the Hardegen and crew interviews.

25. A kindness that would be remembered for a lifetime by the crewman, who moved to the United States after the war. In 1985 while en route to a U-*123* crew reunion he, his wife, and his daughter-in-law were killed in an automobile accident in Flensburg, West Germany. Hardegen: "Two years ago we really laughed together about this incident. It's really quite sad." Crew interviews, Bad König/Odenwald, West Germany, November 1985.

26. OA/NHC, "Q-Ships," Communications Third Naval District, 27 March 1942.

27. The *Carolyn* sinking is reconstructed from KTB-*123*, 26–27 March 1942; *"Auf Gefechtsstationen!"*, pp. 201–4; BFZ Schussmeldungen U-*123*, 27 March 1942, No. 5556, pp. 3, 7; the Hardegen and crew interviews. As in the cases of *Muskogee* and *Empire Steel* there were no survivors from whom to learn the other side of this fateful encounter.

28. KTB-*123*, 30 March 1942; BFZ Schussmeldung U-*123*, 30 March 1942, No. 5556, p. 11.

29. OA/NHC, "Q-Ships," Communications Third Naval District, 27 March 1942.

30. ESF, chapter 2, October 1943, p. 8.

31. OA/NHC, "Q-Ships," Lt. Comdr. Glenn W. Legwen to Admiral Andrews, New York, N.Y., 3 May 1942, "Narrative of First Cruise of USS ASTERION (SS EVELYN)."

32. Ibid., Captain Glenn W. Legwen USN, to Admiral Frederick J. Horne, USN, San Juan, Puerto Rico, 15 June 1946.

33. The broadcast was recorded by the Associated Press and appeared in the *New York Times* on 10 April 1942.

34. OA/NHC, "Q-Ships," Captain Legwen to Admiral Horne, San Juan, 15 June 1946; Admiral Horne, Memorandum for the Secretary of the Navy, 18 March 1946.

35. Ibid.

36. One parent in particular, Mrs. Paul H. (Eunice) Leonard, of Columbia, South Carolina, took exception to the Navy's handling of the status of her son, Ensign Edwin Madison Leonard, one of *Atik*'s officers. She was particularly angered that it was only through the *Post* article in 1946, nearly four years after the disappearance of the crew, that she learned that her son had been sent to sea "on an old ship unable to defend itself." Her pungent questions about the entire project, together with supporting letters of inquiry from both her state senators, as well as the various Navy responses drafted to her heartfelt protestations are found in OA/NHC, "Q-Ships." Among the documents is a memorandum from Admiral Horne to Secretary of the Navy James V. Forrestal, dated 18 March 1946, in which Horne hypothesized: "It is quite possible that the submarine then surfaced and liquidated all survivors to assuage the curious German sense of justice."

37. ESF, chapter 2, October 1943, p. 13, where further structural details are given.

38. Ibid., October 1943, p. 34.

39. Roskill, *War at Sea*, vol. 2, p. 98.

40. This could have been U-*105*, *160*, or *754*, all of which were patrolling in the area.

41. NARA, RG 38, Chief of Naval Operations [hereafter cited CNO], Armed Guard Files, "Liebre."

42. ESF, Enemy Action Diary, 1 April 1942, 0141 hours; OA/NHC, War Record of the Fifth Naval District, 1942, pp. 157–59, "Shelling of the S/S Liebre Suggests Surface Raider, April 2, 1942."

43. The attack on *Liebre* is reconstructed from ibid.; KTB U-*123*, 2 April 1942; BFZ, Schussmeldung U-*123*, 2 April 1942, No. 5556, page 18; Hardegen, *"Auf Gefechtsstationen!"*, pp. 204–5; NARA, RG 38, CNO, Armed Guard Files, "Liebre"; and Moore, *Needless Sinking*, "SS Liebre."

44. OA/NHC, War Record of the Fifth Naval District, 1942, pp. 157–59; NARA, RG 58, CNO, Armed Guard Files, "Liebre." At the date of this attack *Liebre* was not armed; subsequently she would be.

45. KTB-*123*, 8 April 1942. The attacks on *Oklahoma* and *Esso Baton Rouge* from the U.S. perspective are described in NARA, RG 80, CNO, Armed Guard Files, "Oklahoma" and "Esso Baton Rouge"; and Moore, *Needless Sinking*, "SS Oklahoma," "Esso Baton Rouge." Neither ship was armed at the time.

46. KTB-*123*, 8 April 1942.

47. U-*202* herself was reported sunk by HMS *Starling* on 1 June 1943 with eighteen killed and thirty captured. U-*532* survived the war and was sunk after German capitulation in the British disposal program, "Operation Deadlight."

48. For the sinking of *Esparta* see KTB-*123*, 9 April 1942; BFZ, *Schussmeldung* U-*123*, 9 April 1942, No. 5658, p. 8; NARA, RG 38, CNO, Armed Guard Files, "Esparta." *Esparta* was not armed.

49. NARA, RG 242, Collection of Foreign Records Seized, 1941, *Handbuch der Ostküste der Vereinigten Staaten, 2. Teil* (1941), p. 206. The contents had been abstracted from U.S. and British publications.

12. The Navy Stirs

1. Quoted in Buell, *Master of Sea Power*, p. 287.
2. Churchill, *Hinge of Fate*, p. 111.
3. Quoted in Costello and Hughes, *Battle of the Atlantic*, p. 196.
4. Ibid., p. 196.
5. Quoted in Roskill, *War at Sea*, vol. 2, p. 99.
6. Quoted in Lewin, *American Magic*, p. 234.
7. Roskill, *War at Sea*, vol. 2, p. 99.
8. Interview with Patrick Beesly, Lymington, England, 9 July 1986.
9. Churchill, *Hinge of Fate*, p. 119.
10. Kimball, ed., *Churchill & Roosevelt*, vol. 1, p. 424.
11. Beesly, *Special Intelligence*, pp. 113–14. And interview with Beesly.
12. Ibid., p. 114.
13. Ibid., p. 115.
14. Telephone interview with Captain Kenneth A. Knowles (USN, Ret.), 7 July 1986.
15. Rear Admiral Alan R. McCann, quoted in Buell, *Master of Sea Power*, p. 298.
16. ESF, March 1942, chapter 1, p. 1; April 1942, p. 302.
17. Ibid., April 1942, chapter 7, pp. 3–4.
18. Ibid., March 1942, pp. 232, 258–60.
19. Ibid., March 1942, chapter 1, p. 230; August 1943, p. 33. When the oil industry suggested that *it* be permitted to fly land-based aircraft along the

tanker routes it was turned down "because of technical and practical considerations."

20. Ibid., November 1943, p. 36.
21. Ibid., March 1942, p. 231.
22. Ibid., November 1943, pp. 31–32.
23. Ibid., November 1943, p. 31.
24. Ibid., p. 32.
25. Ibid., p. 37.
26. Ibid., p. 37.
27. Ibid., p. 38.
28. *Miami Herald*, 8 July 1942.
29. ESF, March 1942, pp. 238–40.
30. Ibid., February 1942, p. 168.
31. Ibid., March 1942, pp. 234–36.
32. Ibid., April 1942, p. 306.
33. Ibid., April 1942, p. 307.
34. Ibid., March 1942, p. 255.
35. King, quoted in Buell, *Master of Sea Power*, p. 287.
36. ESF, February 1942, p. 130.
37. OA/NHC, United States Naval Administrative Histories of World War II; No. 114: "Commandant Seventh Naval District, 'Administrative History of the Seventh Naval District, 1 February 1942—14 August 1945'"; Gulf Sea Frontier War Diary [hereafter GSF], July–October 1942 (microfilm); Morison, *Battle of the Atlantic*, pp. 135–44.
38. Ibid., pp. 135–44; Rohwer, *Axis Submarine Successes*, pp. 92–99. Depending how one defines the boundaries of the Gulf of Mexico the first ship sunk in the Gulf could have been the American tanker *Federal*, 2,881 GRT, lost to U-boat *507* five days earlier on 30 April south of the westernmost tip of Cuba. The writer is indebted to Allen Cronenberg, Department of History, Auburn University, for the use of his paper, "U-Boats in the Gulf: The Undersea War in 1942"; and to Carl Vought, of Huntsville, Alabama, who has created a map displaying Gulf sinkings.
39. ESF, June 1942, "Enemy Submarine Campaign," p. 3.
40. Ibid., April 1942, pp. 304–5.
41. This is the certain conviction of Kapitän Hans Meckel, who as director of all U-boat communications in the period was in position to know if there was any such rendezvous. Meckel's recollections were communicated to the present writer by Hardegen, interviews, May 1985, December 1986.
42. Doenitz, *Memoirs*, p. 219; Beesly, *Special Intelligence*, p. 120. Of the seven hundred tons of fuel a tanker would have to reserve about one hundred for her own operations.
43. Quoted in Cremer, *U-Boat Commander*, p. 82.
44. ESF, April 1943, p. 9.
45. Ibid., January 1942, chapter 3, p. 68; April 1943, chapter 2, p. 6.
46. Ibid., April 1943, chapter 2, p. 7.
47. Ibid., March 1942, p. 255; April 1943, chapter 2, p. 6.
48. Ibid., April 1943, chapter 2, p. 6.
49. Morison, *Battle of the Atlantic*, p. 135.
50. OA/NHC, GSF, "Composition of Forces," 1 July 1942. For earlier air strength levels in the GSF see ibid., 30 April 1942.
51. NARA, RG 38, Box 245 (Records of the CNO), Headquarters COMINCH 1942, Memorandum, King to Stark, 7 March 1942.

52. ESF, March 1942, p. 254.

53. NARA, RG 38, Box 35 (Records of the CNO), Headquarters COM-INCH 1942, Memorandum, King to the President via the Secretary of the Navy, 22 December 1942; Box 111, Rear Admiral Russell R. Waesche, Commandant, United States Coast Guard, to COMINCH, 25 June 1942. 566 Coastal Picket patrol vessels were operational during 1942.

54. ESF, May 1942, chapter 3, p. 7.

55. Ibid., July 1942, Coastal Picket Operation Plan No. 11-42, 14 July 1942, p. 145.

56. Ibid., July 1942, chapter 10, pp. 6–7, King to Commanders ESF and GSF, 17 June 1942.

57. Ibid., July 1942, chapter 10, pp. 1–10.

58. LC, King Papers, Container 34, Wilford G. Bartenfeld, Cleveland, Ohio, to King, 26 June 1942. For the swordfish fleet and Cruising Club of America initiatives see OA/NHC, ESF, March 1942, pp. 266–78; July 1942, pp. 82 ff.; and Morison, *Battle of the Atlantic*, pp. 268–76.

59. LC, King Papers, Container 34, Memorandum, Assistant Chief of Staff Rear Admiral Willis A. Lee, Jr. to King, 29 June 1942.

60. Morison, *Battle of the Atlantic*, pp. 269 ff.

61. Philip Wylie and Laurence Schwab, "The Battle of Florida," *Saturday Evening Post* (March 11, 1944), pp. 14 ff.

62. Morison, *Battle of the Atlantic*, pp. 275–76.

63. LC, King Papers, Container 34, Miller to King, 17 February 1942; Lee to Miller, 27 February 1942.

64. NARA, RG 38, Box 245 (Records of the CNO), Headquarters COM-INCH 1942, Memorandum, Andrews to King, 12 March 1942.

65. NARA, RG 38, Box 245 (Records of the CNO), Headquarters COM-INCH 1942, Memorandum, Edwards to King, 15 March 1942.

66. ESF, August 1943, p. 33.

67. OA/NHC, GSF, July–October 1942 (microfilm), "Composition of Forces," 1 July 1942. Interview with former CAP pilot George Newell, who later in 1942 flew patrols out of Sarasota, Florida.

68. ESF, August 1943, p. 40.

69. The present writer, having hosted that particular late afternoon radio program while a high school student in the city, remembers the theme music and opening lines.

70. Hardegen, *"Auf Gefechtsstationen!"*, p. 209.

71. BFZ, Schussmeldung U-*123*, 11 April 1942, No. 5653, p. 20; also the KTB-*123* under the same date. Both record that only one torpedo was launched, despite reports of certain tanker survivors. Details of this as of all other attacks are given in narrative form in the *Schussmeldung* and KTB, on which the writer relied for this reconstruction of the attack on *Gulfamerica*.

72. Hardegen, *"Auf Gefechtsstationen!"*, p. 211.

73. Ibid., p. 124.

74. Interview with Edward Mussallem, 14 May 1989. An Eastern Air Lines plane sighted the flames and "flares 400–500 feet high"; ESF, Enemy Action Diary, 10 April 1942.

75. OA/NHC, "History of U.S. Naval Auxiliary Air Station Mayport, Florida, 1 December 1944," pp. 22–23.

76. Interview with George W. Jackson, Saint Augustine, 17 May 1989.

77. *Florida Times-Union* (Jacksonville), 15 April 1942. It bears repeating that the shooting of survivors in lifeboats was not a common German

practice and that it never happened under Hardegen's command. Suggestions that inhumanity of this kind occurred off the U.S. mainland appeared first in Morison, *Battle of the Atlantic*, p. 130 and n., and most recently in John Terraine, *U-Boat Wars 1916–1945* (New York: G. P. Putnam's Sons, 1989), p. 498; but in the absence of documented evidence it is hard to credit these statements.

78. *St. Augustine Record*, 14 April 1942.
79. NARA, RG 38, CNO Armed Guard Files, "Gulf America."
80. *New York Times*, 15 April 1942.
81. *Florida Times-Union*, 15 April 1942.
82. *St. Augustine Record*, 12 April 1942.
83. ESF, April 1942, chapter 7, p. 5.
84. OA/NHC, GSF, 10 April 1942.
85. Ibid., 11 April 1942.
86. KTB-*123*, 11 April 1942. *Evelyn*'s report of the sighting is recorded in both the GSF for 11 April and in skipper Lt. Comdr. Legwen's "Narrative of the First Cruise of USS ASTERION (SS EVELYN)," 3 May 1942, in OA/NHC, "Q-Ships."
87. KTB-*123*, 11 April 1942. Fritz Rafalski confirmed to the writer that the screw noises were definitely those of a *Zerstörer* (destroyer); interview, Bonn, 21 December 1986. Hardegen's statement that the crewmen flew about the boat—*Leute fliegen durch die Gegend*—appears in conflict with the recollections of crewman Lorenz; see chapter 2.
88. Hardegen, *"Auf Gefechtsstationen!"*, p. 212.
89. Interviews with Hardegen, December 1986. The attack of *Dahlgren* on U-*123* is reconstructed from the interviews; KTB-*123*, 11 April 1942; *"Auf Gefechtsstationen!"*, pp. 212–13; NARA, RG 80, General Records of the Department of the Navy, Log of USS "Dahlgren," 11 April 1942; and OA/NHC, GSF, 11 April 1942. There are discrepancies between the *Dahlgren* log and the KTB-*123* with respect to times and positions.
90. KTB-*123*, 11 April 1942.
91. NARA, RG 80, Log of USS "Dahlgren," 11 April 1942.
92. Interview with Rafalski, n. 87.
93. KTB-*123*, 12 April 1942.
94. The attack on *Leslie* is recorded in KTB-*123*, 13 April 1942; BFZ, Schussmeldung U-*123*, 13 April 1942, No. 5657, p. 6; OA/NHC, "Summary of Statements by Survivors, SS 'Leslie,' " 29 April 1942; OA/NHC, GSF, 13–14 April 1942.
95. Interview with Rafalski; see n. 87.
96. The attack on *Korsholm* is recorded in KTB-*123*, 13 April 1942; OA/NHC, "Summary of Statements by Survivors, MV KORSHOLM," 5 May 1942; OA/NHC, GSF, 13–14 April 1942. In May the Florida waters would be visited successfully by two commanders mentioned previously in this narrative, Bleichrodt (U-*109*) and Cremer (U-*333*), as well as by Reinhard "Teddy" Suhren (U-*564*), whose four Florida sinkings would help win him Diamonds to his Oak Leaves.
97. KTB-*123*, 13 April 1942.
98. Ibid.

13. Final Reckoning

1. Farago, *The Tenth Fleet*, pp. 69–70. For his part, Winston Churchill was also not above creating and inflating U-boat sinkings; see William Manchester, *The Last Lion: Winston Spencer Churchill*, volume 2, *Alone, 1932–1940* (Boston-Toronto: Little, Brown and Company, 1989), pp. 565, 574.

2. Dönitz is quoted in Morison, *Battle of the Atlantic*, p. 157. See *Congressional Record, Proceedings and Debates of the 77th Congress Second Session*, vol. 88, part 4, May 25, 1942, to June 30, 1942 (Washington, D.C.: U.S. Government Printing Office, 1942), p. 5332, 30 April 1942.

3. See, e.g., Eugene Rachlis, *They Came to Kill: The Story of Eight Nazi Saboteurs in America* (New York: Random House, 1961); Leon O. Prior, "Nazi Invasion of Florida," *The Florida Historical Quarterly* (October 1970), pp. 129–39.

4. Morison, *Battle of the Atlantic*, p. 127.

5. OA/NHC, "War Record of the Fifth Naval District, 1942," pp. 12–14, 460.

6. OA/NHC, "War Diary of the Operational Intelligence Branch of the District Intelligence Office, Fifth Naval District," pp. 14–17.

7. *Roper*'s attack on U-*85* is described in ESF, April 1942, pp. 320–23. The trawler *Bedfordshire* would be sunk by U-*558* on 11 May; Royal Navy crews had remained on board the trawlers despite Admiral King's intention to replace them with USN personnel.

8. Ibid., May 1942, chapter 3, pp. 8–14. A fuller account of the sinking, with U-*352* crew list and record of interrogations, is given in OA/NHC, Microfilm, NRS 1973-106, "U-*352* Sunk 9 May 1942."

9. An account of the desperate plight of U-*701*'s survivors is given in ESF, July 1942, chapter 9.

10. An additional boat, U-*166*, would be sunk in U.S. waters during the remainder of 1942. On 1 August a Coast Guard aircraft from Houma, Louisiana, made the kill in the Gulf of Mexico. As late as 4 September one last German boat, U-*171*, was operating in the Gulf. It had entered the Gulf sometime before 26 July when it sank its first vessel off the Mississippi. On its return through the Bay of Biscay it struck a mine and sank on 9 October.

11. Abbazia describes the low readiness state of ASW crews that was noted in prewar maneuvers; *Mr. Roosevelt's Navy*, pp. 18–21. For ASW advances see ESF, May 1942, chapter 2.

12. NHC, Rare Books, United States Naval Administrative History No. 138, Manuscript, "Commander in Chief, U.S. Atlantic Fleet," vol. 1 (bound in 2 vols.), 1946, pp. 279–80.

13. Ibid., pp. 290–91.

14. ESF, February 1942, p. 142.

15. Ibid., pp. 141, 144–45.

16. Roskill, *War at Sea*, vol. 2, p. 97; Love, "King," in Love, ed., *Chiefs of Naval Operation*, p. 154.

17. Terraine, *U-Boat Wars*, p. 413. Terraine demonstrates that in this respect the U.S. Navy ignored the wisdom of one of its own, Rear Admiral William Sowden Sims, USN, who had persuaded Britain to adopt the convoy for antisubmarine warfare in World War I; pp. 92, 413. Cf. Rear Admiral William Sowden Sims, U.S. Navy, *The Victory at Sea* (Garden City, New York: Doubleday, Page and Company, 1921), chapter 3, "The Adoption of the Convoy," pp. 88–117. Morison, *Battle of the Atlantic*, p. 200, laid responsibility for

the original lack of small craft solely at the feet of the admirals: "Blame cannot justly be imputed to Congress, for Congress had never been asked to provide a fleet of subchasers and small escort vessels; nor to the people at large, because they looked to the Navy for leadership. Nor can it be shifted to President Roosevelt, who on sundry occasions prompted the Bureau of Ships and the General Board of the Navy to adopt a small craft program; . . ." The 1940 volume of James about German U-boats in World War I, *German Subs in Yankee Waters*, pointedly warned that Germany again could send a fleet of U-boats to U.S. shores at the outbreak of a war, and added: "Those who cry for peace when there is no peace and bemoan the enormous expenditures for capital ships to be used offensively, could have little grievance toward a naval program that provided for the construction of fleets of destroyers, subchasers, patrol boats and mine-sweepers, which could be used solely for defensive purposes," p. 187.

18. Roskill, *War at Sea*, vol. 2, p. 97.

19. John Keegan, *The Price of Admiralty: The Evolution of Naval Warfare* (New York: Viking Penguin, Inc., 1989), pp. 218–19. Love, "King," in Love, ed., *Chiefs of Naval Operation* noted that independently steaming merchantmen made faster time than weakly escorted convoys could have made in the months of January and following; hence, he theorized, "premature introduction of coastal convoys in 1942 would have reduced gross carrying capacity far beyond the tonnage losses inflicted in the spring by the U-boats" (p. 154 and n. 46). Yet he went on to state that the coastal convoy system, once instituted using small patrol craft, "was an immediate success" (pp. 154–55). Love attributed the theory's origin to King, but gave no citation for the source. The midshipman on whose statistics Love relied for his "proof" of King's theory made no use of these statistics himself when, three years later, he published his own study of the merchantmen losses: Lieut. (jg) Thomas J. Belke USN, "Roll of Drums," *United States Naval Institute Proceedings* (April 1983), pp. 59–64.

20. ESF, March 1942, pp. 307, 311, 313.

21. Ibid., March 1942, pp. 249–53.

22. Ibid., May 1942, chapter 4; June 1942, chapters 1, 3; Morison, *Battle of the Atlantic*, pp. 252–65.

23. ESF, June 1942, chapter 2.

24. KTB-BdU, 19 July 1942. Anticipating these developments, the ESF war diary for June expressed its "hope that the most disastrous period of submarine warfare on this coast is now over"; chapter 1, p. 6, June 1942. Ironically, Dönitz's withdrawal occurred in a period when he was receiving thirty new boats on operational status per month, a new high, and all the more striking an increase in view of the fact that he had lost only twenty-six boats in the previous six months; Terraine, *U-Boat Wars*, p. 459.

25. King and Whitehill, *Fleet Admiral King*, p. 457.

26. Samuel Eliot Morison, *History of the United States Naval Operations in World War Two*, vol. 3, Revised Edition, *The Rising Sun in the Pacific* (Boston: Little, Brown and Company, 1954), p. 132; Edward L. Beach, Captain, USN (Ret.), *The United States Navy: 200 Years* (New York: Henry Holt and Company, 1986), p. 447; Layton, "*And I Was There*," pp. 498, 507. Admiral of the Fleet the Lord Hill-Norton and John Dekker, *Sea Power* (London: Faber and Faber Limited, 1982), pp. 51–52. Admiral Nimitz told Gordon W. Prange: "It was God's mercy that our fleet was in Pearl Harbor on December 7, 1941"; Prange et al., *Miracle at Midway* (New York: McGraw-Hill Book Company, 1982), p. 9.

27. Quoted in King and Whitehill, *Fleet Admiral King*, pp. 455–56. The

original of Marshall's memorandum can be found in the George C. Marshall Research Library, Lexington, Virginia, Marshall Papers, Box 73, Folder 12, "King, Ernest J. 1942 May–1942 August," 19 June 1942.

28. Ibid., p. 456. King's former deputy chief of staff Admiral Richard S. Edwards wrote to King on 19 November 1951: "I like the antisubmarine chapter of your book, particularly the inclusion of your correspondence with Marshall"; LC, King Papers, Container 31.

29. King, *U.S. Navy at War*, p. 80.

30. Robert H. Ferrell, ed., *The Eisenhower Diaries* (New York: W.W. Norton & Company, 1981), p. 50. Upon rereading this entry after the war Eisenhower commented: "In justice I would say that all through the war, whenever I called on him for assistance, he supported me fully and instantly"; ibid., p. 403.

31. Samuel Eliot Morison, *History of the United States Naval Operations in World War Two*, vol. 10, *The Atlantic Battle Won, May 1943–May 1945* (Boston: Little, Brown and Company, 1956), p. 32, n. 3; King and Whitehill, *Fleet Admiral King*, pp. 445–48.

32. KTB-BdU, 21 August 1942. Cf. Middlebrook, *Convoy*, pp. 310–15; Roskill, *War at Sea*, vol. 2, pp. 362–64; Costello and Hughes, *Battle of the Atlantic*, pp. 240–41; Dan van der Vat, *The Atlantic Campaign: World War II's Great Struggle at Sea* (New York: Harper & Row, Publishers, 1988), p. 326.

33. Morison, *Atlantic Battle Won*, p. 362 and n. 21.

34. Simpson III, *Harold R. Stark*, pp. 150–51.

35. Richard M. Leighton, "OVERLORD versus the Mediterranean at the Cairo-Tehran Conferences (1943)," Kent Roberts Greenfield, ed., *Command Decisions* (New York: Harcourt, Brace and Company, 1959), p. 185 and n. 2.

36. Hugh P. Willmott, *Sea Warfare: Weapons, Tactics, and Strategy* (Strettington, Chichester, England: A. Bird, 1981), cited in Keegan, *Price of Admiralty*, p. 210.

37. Middlebrook, *Convoy*, pp. 302–4 and passim.

38. Roskill, *War At Sea*, vol. 2, pp. 367, 371.

39. Doenitz, *Memoirs*, p. 341.

40. Costello and Hughes, *Battle of the Atlantic*, p. 302.

41. Morison, *Atlantic Battle Won*, p. 361.

42. NARA, RG 457, Box No. 15, K. A. Knowles, "Memorandum for the Director of Naval History [3 pp.]," 23 October 1945.

43. Morison, *Battle of the Atlantic*, p. xiii.

44. Hinsley, *British Intelligence*, vol. 2, p. 549.

45. KTB-*123*, 14 April 1942.

46. Ibid., 17 April 1942.

47. OA/NHC, War Record of the Fifth Naval District, 1942, "S/S Alcoa Guide Shelled and Sunk, April 16, 1942"; ESF, Enemy Action Diary, 16, 19 April 1942; NARA, RG 38, CNO, Armed Guard Files, "Alcoa Guide" [no armed guard was aboard]; Moore, *A Careless Word*, "SS Alcoa Guide," n.p. When he read this survivor's account in the present manuscript Hardegen commented: "It was terrible for me to read the fate of Souza and his comrades." Hardegen to the writer, Bremen-Oberneuland, West Germany, 20 September 1989.

48. U-*107* (Kptlt. Harald Gelhaus) would sink six ships on this patrol in the Caribbean, Gulf, and mid-Atlantic; Rohwer, *Axis Submarine Successes*, pp. 99–106.

49. KTB-*123*, p. 38, undated.

50. KTB-*123*, *Besondere Erfahrungen*, pp. 36–37.

51. Hardegen interviews with the writer. The minutes of Hitler's conference with Grossadmiral Raeder at Rastenburg on 13–14 May 1942, record: "The Fuehrer expresses his belief that it is impossible to build up a naval air force during the war." *Fuehrer Conferences on Matters Dealing with the German Navy*, 1941–1942, vol. 2 (Washington, D.C.: Office of Naval Intelligence, Navy Department, 1947), entries of 13, 14, and 16 May 1942.

52. Reinhard and Barbara Hardegen's children, all still living at the date of this writing, are: Klaus-Reinhard, born 5 April 1939; Jörg, born 28 January 1941; Ingeborg, born 31 January 1944; and Detlev, born 23 October 1945. Barbara, maiden name Petersen, was born in Kiel on 18 October 1915.

Afterword

1. Samuel Eliot Morison, *The Two-Ocean War: A Short History of the United States Navy in the Second World War* (Boston: Little, Brown and Company, 1963), pp. 71–75.

2. Roberta Wohlstetter, *Pearl Harbor: Warning and Decision* (Stanford, Calif.: Stanford University Press, 1962), pp. 386–96; Layton, *And I Was There*, passim.

3. There is not sufficient evidence for deciding to what extent in January King's mind was fixed on Jutland-type fleet actions that he expected in the Pacific, or to what measure he may have forgotten that one of the principal functions of a navy is to protect the nation's trade and communications. Fifteen years afterward Henry L. Stimson, who had been secretary of war during the entire conflict, complained about King's priorities: "With rare exceptions anti-submarine warfare received only the partial attention of the first-rate officers, while actual operations were left to commanders not always chosen from the top drawer"; Henry L. Stimson and McGeorge Bundy, *On Active Service in Peace and War* (New York: Harper & Brothers, 1947), p. 515. This contention was rebutted "*in toto*" as a "slur" by Navy loyalist Morison in *Atlantic Battle Won*, p. 30. King was promoted to the five-star rank of fleet admiral in December 1944.

4. Simpson, *Stark*, p. 268.

5. Rebecca West, *A Train of Powder* (New York: Viking, 1955), p. 49.

6. Winston Churchill, *Hinge of Fate*, p. 125.

7. Mikkelsen, *Familiebladet Hjemmet*, 5 January 1982, pp. 28 ff.

8. Emory Holloway, ed., Inclusive Edition, Walt Whitman, *Leaves of Grass* (Garden City, N.Y.: Doubleday & Company, Inc., 1962), pp. 221–22.

APPENDIX C Operation of the Schlüssel M (Enigma) Machine

Operation of the three-rotor Schlüssel M is described in F. H. Hinsley, *British Intelligence*, vol. 2, pp. 163, 170, 487; Lewin, *Ultra Goes to War*, pp. 31–33, 206–7; Calvocoressi, *Top Secret Ultra*, pp. 26–33, 54–55; Rohwer, *Convoy Battles*, pp. 232–35; Ralph Bennett, *Ultra in the West: The Normandy Campaign 1944–45* (New York: Charles Scribner's Sons, 1979), pp. 2–5; Beesly, *Special Intelligence*, pp. 64–68; and (the most technical account) Gordon Welchman, *The Hut Six Story: Breaking the Enigma Codes* (New York: McGraw-Hill Book Company, 1982), pp. 38–52. The Schlüssel M, commonly called in English language literature the "Enigma M" machine, was a cryptographic device of German invention and manufacture, dating from a design by Dr. Arthur Scherbius in 1923. Its development is recounted in Lewin, *Ultra Goes to War*, pp. 25 ff.

GLOSSARY

AA: antiaircraft.

AAF: (U.S.) Army Air Forces.

Abaft: toward the stern of a boat or ship.

Adressbuch: a U-boat code book for disguising grid (Marinequadrat) positions on an ocean chart in radio (wireless) transmissions.

aft: rearward, or toward the stern of a vessel.

air gap: the mid-Atlantic region that, until spring 1943, was not covered by British and American ASW aircraft.

Alarm!: order for an emergency dive by a U-boat, corresponding to U.S. Navy submarine usage, "Dive! Dive!"

angle-on-the-bow: the difference between the U-boat's line of sight and the heading of its target.

Armed Guard: a U.S. Navy gun crew stationed aboard a merchant freighter or tanker.

ASDIC: an acronym standing for Anti-Submarine Detection Investigation Committee (British), commonly used to describe the apparatus housed in a dome on the underside of an antisubmarine vessel's hull, which sent out sound waves in pulses that, striking an underwater object such as a U-boat, returned a signal that gave the range and bearing (and after 1944 the depth) of the object. *See* sonar.

ASV: airborne microwave (10- and 3-cm) radar.

ASW: antisubmarine warfare.

"Auf Gefechtsstationen!": "Battle stations!"

ballast tanks: tanks outside the pressure hull of a U-boat which, when flooded with water, enabled the boat to dive.

B-Dienst (Funkbeobachtungsdienst): the German radio-monitoring and cryptographic service.

466

BdU (Befehlshaber der Unterseeboote): Commander in Chief, U-boats. Though specifically denoting Admiral Karl Dönitz, the abbreviation was also commonly used to identify the Admiral's staff or headquarters.

bee: (*Biene* in German) U-boat nickname for aircraft.

Befehlshaber der Unterseeboote: Commander in Chief, U-Boats. See BdU.

Biscay, Bay of: a bay of the Atlantic Ocean between northwestern France and northern Spain.

Bletchley Park: a mansion in Buckinghamshire, northwest of London, officially called Government Code and Cipher School and secretly called Station X, where cryptanalysts attacked intercepts of German wireless (radio) traffic.

bombe: word used to describe the electromechanical scanning machine constructed from a series of Enigmas yoked together at Bletchley Park.

***Bootskanone* (also *Bordkanone*):** the deck gun, or artillery piece, carried forward on a U-boat.

bow: the forward end of a vessel.

bows: the forward exterior hull of a vessel, sloping back from the stem.

BP: Bletchley Park (q.v.).

Bridge: the raised structure from which a power vessel on the surface is navigated.

bulkhead: a wall-like structure inside seagoing vessels used to subdivide space, form watertight compartments, or strengthen the interior framing.

bunkers: on a U-boat, the exterior tanks that contained diesel fuel.

capital ship: a term used throughout World War II to define the most significant warships in a fleet.

CINCLANT: Commander in Chief, Atlantic Fleet.

cipher: basically, a secret system of communication that substitutes letters for letters (*see* code).

cloud cover: the presence of clouds was recorded in a U-boat's KTB on an ascending scale from zero to ten.

code: basically, a secret system of communication that substitutes ideas for ideas (*see* cipher).

COMINCH: Commander in Chief, United States Fleet.

conn: as a noun, steering responsibility for a boat or ship, or (as a verb) the act of steering or maneuvering. Also spelled *con*.

conning tower (*Kommandoturm*): the low observation tower of a U-boat, containing the helmsman's steering controls and topped by an open bridge. In Type IX U-boats the tower also contained the attack periscope eyepiece and the torpedo deflection calculator.

control room: see *Zentrale*.

convoy: an organized formation of merchant ships in disciplined columns escorted by warships.

crash dive: U.S. Navy term for an emergency dive by a submarine (U-boat).

cryptanalysis: the process of "breaking" (solving) a code or cipher by uncovering its key.

cryptography: the science or study of code and cipher systems employed for secret communication.

CSF: Caribbean Sea Frontier (U.S. Navy).

DD: U.S. Navy abbreviation for the destroyer-class ship.

DE: destroyer escort–class ship.

deckhouse: an enclosed structure raised above the weather deck of a vessel.

decrypt: a deciphered or decoded message.

diesel: the compression-ignition type engine used on U-boats; also the combustible petroleum distillate used as fuel.

DR: dead reckoning, the calculation of one's position at sea based on course, speed, and elapsed time since the last observed position, taking into account currents, winds, and compass declinations.

Dräger Tauchretter: a U-boat crewman's personal underwater escape apparatus (Dräger was the name of the manufacturer).

eel: in German *aal*, a U-boat nickname for torpedo.

Einbaum: literally "dugout canoe," a nickname for the small, coastal-training U-boat Type IID.

Eins Zwei Drei: *123.*

E-Maschinen: electric motors (E motors).

E motors: battery-powered electric motors on a U-boat.

encryption: an enciphered or encoded message (*see* cipher and code).

Enigma: another name for the *Schlüssel M* cipher machine. The term was also used to denote the machine's encrypted product.

ESF: Eastern Sea Frontier (U.S. Navy).

ETO: G7e (electric) torpedo.

F-21: the U.S. Navy Atlantic Section, Intelligence Center, first called OP-20-G, at Main Navy; an exact clone of the OIC Submarine Tracking Room of the British Admiralty, it began operations in spring 1942.

Fächerschuss: a simultaneous spread, or fan, launch of two or more torpedoes.

Fähnrich zur See: Midshipman.

Fangschuss: a finishing shot, or coup de grace.

fathom: six feet or 1.829 meters.

Feindfahrt: operational patrol.

5ND: Fifth Naval District (U.S. Navy).

500-tonner: Type VII U-boat.

flag officer: a naval officer holding rank higher than captain, for example, rear admiral, who is entitled to display a flag bearing the insignia of his or her rank.

flank: the extreme right or left side.

flotilla: a small fleet of small vessels.

Flugboot: German term for a flying-boat aircraft, such as the British Sunderland or the U.S. PBY-Catalina.

fore: forward, or toward the bow of a vessel.

Fregattenkapitän: Captain (junior).

Frontboot: a U-boat at sea that has crossed into an operational area.

F.T.: see Funk-Telegraphie.

Funk-Telegraphie (F.T.): German term for Wireless Telegraphy (W/T) generally; for a wireless (radio) transmitter/receiver specifically. The abbreviated form F.T. was used to denote a wireless message.

Funker: German Navy radioman (wireless operator).

G7a: torpedo with a 380-km warhead driven by a compressed air-steam propulsion system.

G7e: electric (battery-driven) torpedo, the more commonly used German torpedo in 1942. The seven-meter-long weapon, sometimes designated T-2, had a speed of thirty knots, a range of five thousand meters, and (its principal advantage) it left no wake. The warhead weighed five hundred kilograms.

Geheime Kommandosache: "top secret."

general quarters: on U.S. Navy vessels, a call to action stations and battle readiness.

Great Circle: the shortest route, or track, following the arc of the earth's surface and appearing as a curved line on a Mercator chart of the oceans.

green: starboard (*Steuerbord*), that is, right (U-boat usage).

gripes: the canvas bands and fastenings that secure a lifeboat in its cradle.

Gröner: the merchant fleet handbook, with silhouettes of all known freighters and tankers of all nations, compiled by German nautical authority Erich Gröner.

Grossadmiral: grand admiral, corresponding to fleet admiral (U.S. Navy) or admiral of the fleet (Royal Navy).

gross register tonnage: the measurement of all the enclosed spaces in a ship expressed in hundreds of cubic feet. (See chapter 2, n. 5.)

GRT: *see* gross register tonnage.

Gruppe: literally, "group"; a patrol line or operation of U-boats usually given a particular name, for example, Gruppe Schlagetot (Hacker) or Paukenschlag (Drumbeat).

GSF: Gulf Sea Frontier (U.S. Navy).

guerre de course: French term meaning a war on seaborne trade or commerce.

Handbuch der Ostküste der Vereinigten Staaten: German sailing directions, abstracted from U.S. and British publications, for the East Coast of the United States.

hatch: circular opening on the deck or in interior bulkheads of a U-boat through which crewmen and cargo pass.

HE (hydrophone effect): underwater sound, for example, propeller cavitation of a surface ship or the path of a torpedo, detected by hydrophone and shown on instruments as having a certain bearing and range. (*See* hydrophone.)

head: toilet (WC).

HF/DF ("Huff-Duff"): high-frequency/direction finding.

Hilfskreuzer: German term for an armed merchant cruiser of the Royal Navy.

Huff-Duff: nickname for HF/DF (q.v.).

hull: the primary, hollow, flotable structure of a boat or ship.

hull down: the appearance of a ship at great distance when only its masts and smokestack can be seen over the horizon.

HYDRA: the cipher used by operational U-boats in establishing the daily setting of the Schlüssel-M cipher machine.

hydrophone: underwater sound detection device employed by both U-boats and surface warships. In German, *Horchgerät.*

hydroplanes: extended surfaces fore and aft on a U-boat's outboard hull that directed the pitch of the boat underwater.

in ballast: a ship steaming "in ballast" has empty holds, having discharged its cargo, hence rides high in the water.

Kaleu: diminutive form of the rank Kapitänleutnant (Lieutenant Commander).

Kapitänleutnant: Lieutenant Commander.

Kapitän zur See: Captain.

keel: the central structural member of a boat's or ship's hull that runs fore and aft along the bottom of the hull for the full distance from stem to sternpost.

keep: *see* "seakeeping."

Keroman: protective U-boat bunkers, or pens, at Pointe de Keroman near the harbor entrance at Lorient, France.

Kleines Boot: a small U-boat used primarily for training, such as the Type IID.

knot: A unit of speed equivalent to one nautical mile per hour. *See* nautical mile.

Konteradmiral: Rear Admiral.

Korvettenkapitän: Commander.

Kriegsmarine: the World War II German Navy, so named from 1935 to 1945.

Kriegstagebuch **(KTB):** German war diary kept by ships and boats at sea, also by shore-based headquarters staffs.

KTB: see *Kriegstagebuch.*

Kurzsignale: a U-boat's short-signal position report by radio (wireless).

Leutnant zur See: Lieutenant junior grade.

LI: Leitender Ingenieur, "Chief engineering officer."

Lotapparat: a U-boat's equipment for determining depth in fathoms or in meters.

Luftwaffe: German Air Force.

Main Navy: Navy Department main headquarters building at Seventeenth St. and Constitution Avenue in Washington, D.C.

MAN (Maschinenfabrik Augsburg-Nürnberg AG): manufacturer of the diesel engines on both Type VII and IX U-boats.

maneuvering room: electric motor room on a U-boat, aft of the diesel engines, which housed the battery-powered dynamotors (E-motors), used to propel the boat when submerged.

Marinequadrat: naval square, an arbitrarily drawn rectangular region of the ocean drafted to Mercator's projection permitting the organization of the ocean surface into a grid chart where the many individual naval squares were identified by letter digraphs and numbered zones.

Mehrfach: a multiple, though not simultaneous, launch of torpedoes.

meter: 39.37 inches.

"mixers": torpedo mates on a U-boat.

MOMP: mid-ocean meeting point south of Iceland, where U.S. and British naval escorts exchanged responsibility for guarding Atlantic convoys. Also called "chopline" (change of operational control).

monkey island: the flying bridge on the top of a ship's enclosed pilot house, or wheelhouse.

Morse code: a message system of dots and dashes, clicks and spaces, or flashes of light that represent letters of the alphabet.

NAS: (U.S.) Naval Air Station.

nautical mile: 1.1516 statute miles.

NOB: (U.S.) Naval Operating Base.

Oberfähnrich zur See: Ensign.

Oberleutnant zur See: Lieutenant senior grade.

OKM (Oberkommando der Kriegsmarine): German Naval High Command.

OKW (Oberkommando der Wehrmacht): German Army High Command, also Supreme Command of the Armed Forces.

ONI: (U.S.) Office of Naval Intelligence.

painter: a line, usually at the bow, for attaching a boat to a ship.

Papenberg column: a shallow depth-pressure gauge for close-to-the-surface periscope work.

PC: patrol craft, 173-foot submarine chaser, steel hull (U.S. Navy).

periscope: an extendable tubelike optical device containing an arrangement or prisms, mirrors, and lenses that permitted a U-boat to view the surface of a sea from a submerged position.

PG: gunboat (U.S. Navy).

Plimsoll mark: the load line marked on the hulls of British cargo vessels to indicate the safe limit to which the vessel could be immersed.

port: the left-hand side of a vessel as one faces forward.

pressure hull: the U-boat cylinder containing personnel and essential operating systems that was designed to withstand many atmospheres of water pressure when submerged.

Puster: German Navy nickname ("blower") for a radioman (wireless operator) (see *Funker*).

Q-ship: a decoy merchant ship with flotation cargo and hidden deck armament designed to lure a surfaced U-boat to close-in destruction.

quarter: the arc of 45 degrees to either side horizontally from the stern of a vessel.

R-boat: *Räumboot,* motor minesweeper.

Rade de Lorient, La: roadstead (protected anchorage) at Lorient, France.

RAF: (British) Royal Air Force.

rake: a patrol line across the path of a convoy formed by several or many U-boats. (See *Rudeltaktik.*)

Räumboot: motor minesweeper.

red: port (*Backbord*), that is, left (U-boat usage).

Reichsmarine: the German Navy in the period 1919–35.

Ritterkreuz des Eisernen Kreuzes: Knight's Cross of the Iron Cross.

road(s): a protected anchorage less enclosed than a harbor.

Rohr: torpedo tube.

RPM: revolutions per minute.

Rudeltaktik: the nighttime "wolf pack" technique of massing U-boats in a patrol line across a convoy's course and of engaging the convoy's formations in a radio-coordinated attack.

Samson posts: posts at the stern or bow of a vessel for supporting cargo booms.

SC: 110-foot submarine chaser, wooden hull (U.S. Navy).

Schlüssel M (Marine-Funkschlüssel-Machine M): Kriegsmarine version of the electromechanical cipher machine used by the German armed forces for telex and wireless (radio) traffic. *See Enigma.*

Schnorchel: a valved air pipe that protruded above the surface and allowed a U-boat to proceed underwater on diesel power.

Schussmeldung: a U-boat's required "shooting report" on each torpedo action.

sea force (sea state): Seas were recorded in a U-boat's KTB on an ascending scale from zero to ten.

seakeeping: ability to stay at sea safely.

sea state: *see* sea force.

700-tonner: Type IX U-boat.

Sonar: an acronym standing for Sound Navigation, Ranging, the U.S. Navy echo-ranging sound apparatus equivalent to the British ASDIC (q.v.).

Spargel: literally, "asparagus"; U-boat nickname for the periscope.

Special Intelligence: decrypted German wireless (radio) traffic from Bletchley Park. Also called "Z" and, when transmitted to operational commanders, "Ultra."

splinter camouflage: a paint scheme characterized by long, thin, sharp-edged bands of various colors that obfuscate the form of a warship at sea.

Standzielsehrohr: the attack-periscope sight in a U-boat conning tower.

starboard: the right-hand side of a vessel as one faces forward.

stem: the forward bladelike end of a vessel to which the bows, or side plates, are joined.

stern: the after (rear) part of a vessel.

T-Schu: *see Torpedo-Schuss-Empfänger.*

TETIS: a U-boat cipher used in wireless (radio) transmissions by new U-boats training in the Baltic.

Tiefenmesser: a U-boat's depth-pressure gauge, or depth manometer.

tonnage war: the attempt by U-boats to sink more ships than the Allies could build.

Torpedo-Schuss-Empfänger: torpedo launch receiver, which, in the fore and aft torpedo rooms of a U-boat, received target data from the Vorhaltrechner and fed it into the guidance systems of the torpedoes. Abbreviated T-Schu.

Torpedoerprobungskommando (TEK): Torpedo Trials Command at Kiel and Eckernförde.

Torpedokommando: German Navy Torpedo Command.

torpex: a high-explosive mix of Cyclonite, TNT, and aluminum flakes.

trim: the balancing of a submarine's (U-boat's) weight and equilibrium underwater.

TRITON: a U-boat cipher employing four rotors instead of three, introduced on operational boats in February 1942 and not solved by cryptanalysts at Bletchley Park (where it was called "Shark") until December of the same year.

Uboot-Zieloptik **(UZO):** surface target-aiming binoculars with luminous graticule attached to a bridge post that automatically fed target line-of-sight bearing and range to the *Vorhaltrechner.*

Ubootwaffe: the German submarine (U-boat) fleet.

Unterseeboot: "submarine" in German, abbreviated as U-boat in English.

USCG: United States Coast Guard.

USN: United States Navy.

USNR: United States Navy Reserve.

UZO: see *Uboot-Zieloptik.*

Vorhaltrechner: A Siemens-made electromechanical deflection calculator in the U-boat conning tower that fed attack headings into the gyrocompass steering mechanism of the torpedoes in their tubes.

W/T: Wireless Telegraphy (radio).

Wabo: German nickname for *Wasserbombe* (q.v.).

Wasserbombe: German term for a depth charge dropped on U-boats by British and American surface ships and aircraft.

way: the motion or speed of a ship or boat through the water.

Wehrmacht: German Army.

Weyer: a U-boat's identification manual for warships of all nations.

wind force: wind velocities were recorded in a U-boat's KTB on an ascending scale from zero to ten.

Wintergarten: the open, railed platform on the after part of a U-boat bridge.

Zentrale: U-boat control room, directly below the conning tower and bridge, containing all diving controls.

SELECT BIBLIOGRAPHY

The writer has relied primarily on original archival documents, which are identified in the notes. Those sources he supplemented with material drawn from interviews with surviving principals and from published works: documentary collections, official histories, technical reports, autobiographies, and secondary accounts of various kinds. All of the published works utilized in the writing are cited in the notes. Those found to have been particularly useful are named in the select list below:

Abbazia, Patrick. *Mr. Roosevelt's Navy: The Private War of the U.S. Atlantic Fleet, 1939–1942.* Naval Institute Press, Annapolis, Md., 1975.

Bailey, Thomas A., and Paul B. Ryan. *Hitler and Roosevelt: The Undeclared Naval War.* Free Press, New York, 1979.

Beach, Edward L., Captain, USN (Ret.). *The United States Navy: 200 Years.* Henry Holt and Company, New York, 1986.

Beesly, Patrick. *Very Special Intelligence: The Story of the Admiralty's Operational Intelligence Centre 1939–1945.* Hamish Hamilton, London, 1977.

Bennett, Ralph. *Ultra in the West: The Normandy Campaign, 1944–1945.* Charles Scribner's Sons, New York, 1979.

Blair, Jr., Clay. *Silent Victory: The U.S. Submarine War Against Japan.* J.B. Lippincott Company, Philadelphia and New York, 1975.

Brennecke, Jochen. *The Hunters and the Hunted.* W.W. Norton and Company, New York, 1957.

Buchheim, Lothar-Günther. *U-Boat War,* trans. Gudie Lawaetz. Alfred A. Knopf, New York, 1978.

Buell, Thomas B. *Master of Sea Power: A Biography of Fleet Admiral Ernest J. King.* Little, Brown and Company, Boston, 1980.

Buell, Thomas B., et al. *The Second World War: Europe and the Mediterranean.* United States Military Academy, Avery Publishing Group, Inc., Wayne, N. J., 1984.

Busch, Harald. *U-Boats at War.* Ballantine Books, New York, 1955.

Calvocoressi, Peter. *Top Secret Ultra.* Ballantine Books, New York, 1980.
Chatterton, E. Keble. *Q-Ships and Their Story.* Naval Institute Press, Annapolis, Md., 1972.
Churchill, Winston. *The Second World War*, Vol. 1, *The Gathering Storm.* Houghton Mifflin Company, Boston, 1948.
————. Vol. 3, *Their Finest Hour.* Houghton Mifflin Company, Boston, 1949.
————. Vol. 4, *The Hinge of Fate.* Houghton Mifflin Company, Boston, 1950.
Costello, John, and Terry Hughes. *The Battle of the Atlantic.* Collins, London, 1977.
Craven, Wesley Frank, and James Lea Cate. *The Army Air Forces in World War II*, Vol. 1, *Plans and Early Operations, January 1939 to August 1942.* University of Chicago Press, Chicago, 1948.
Cremer, Peter. *U-Boat Commander: A Periscope View of the Battle of the Atlantic.* Naval Institute Press, Annapolis, Md., 1985.
Doenitz, Karl. *Memoirs: Ten Years and Twenty Days*, trans. R. H. Stevens in collaboration with David Woodward. World Publishing Company, Cleveland, Ohio, 1959.
Dorwart, Jeffrey M. *Conflict of Duty: The U.S. Navy's Intelligence Dilemma, 1919–1945.* Naval Institute Press, Annapolis, Md., 1983.
Farago, Ladislas. *The Tenth Fleet.* Ivan Obolensky, Inc., New York, 1962.
Frank, Wolfgang. *The Sea Wolves: The Story of U-Boats at War.* Rinehart & Company, Inc., New York, 1955.
Gasaway, E. B. *Grey Wolf, Grey Sea.* Ballantine Books, New York, 1985.
Greenfield, Kent Roberts, ed. *Command Decisions.* Harcourt, Brace and Company, New York, 1959.
Hadley, Michael L. *U-Boats Against Canada: German Submarines in Canadian Waters.* McGill-Queen's University Press, Kingston and Montreal, 1985.
Hardegen, Reinhard. *"Auf Gefechtsstationen!" U-Boote im Einsatz gegen England und Amerika. Mit einem Geleitwort von Grossadmiral Dönitz.* Boreas-Verlag, Leipzig, 1943.
Hearings Before the Joint Committee on the Investigation of the Pearl Harbor Attack, Congress of the United States, Seventy-Ninth Congress. Government Printing Office, Washington, D.C., 1946.
Heinrich, Waldo. *Threshold of War: Franklin D. Roosevelt & American Entry into World War II.* Oxford University Press, New York, 1988.
Herwig, Holger H. *Politics of Frustration: The United States in German Naval Planning, 1889–1941.* Little, Brown and Company, Boston, 1976.
Herzog, Bodo. *60 Jahre Deutsche Uboote 1906–1966.* J.F. Lehmanns Verlag, Munich, 1968.
Hezlet, Vice Admiral Sir Arthur. *The Electron and Sea Power.* Peter Davies, London, 1975.
Hinsley, F. H., et al. *British Intelligence in the Second World War: Its Influence on Strategy and Operations*, 3 vols. Cambridge University Press, New York, 1979–1988.
Jäckel, Eberhard. *Hitler in History.* Brandeis University Press and University Press of New England, Hanover, N.H., 1984.
Jacobsen, H. A., and J. Rohwer, eds. *Decisive Battles of World War II: The German View*, trans. Edward Fitzgerald. G.P. Putnam's Sons, New York, 1965.
James, Henry J. *German Subs in Yankee Waters: First World War.* Gotham House, New York, 1940.

Karig, USNR, Commander Walter, et al. *Battle Report: The Atlantic War,* Farrar and Rinehart, Inc., New York, 1946.

Keegan, John. *The Price of Admiralty: The Evolution of Naval Warfare.* Viking Penguin, Inc., New York, 1989.

Kimball, Warren F., ed. *Churchill and Roosevelt: The Complete Correspondence.* Princeton University Press, Princeton, 1984.

King, Ernest J., and Walter Muir Whitehill. *Fleet Admiral King: A Naval Record.* W.W. Norton & Company, Inc., New York, 1952.

King, Fleet Admiral Ernest J. *U.S. Navy at War, 1941–1945: Official Reports to the Secretary of the Navy.* United States Navy Department, Washington, D.C., 1946.

König, Kapitän Paul. *Die Fahrt der Deutschland: Das erste Untersee-Frachtschiff.* Hearst's International Library Co., New York, 1916.

Langer, William L., and S. Everett Gleason. *The Undeclared War, 1940–1941,* published for the Council on Foreign Relations. Harper & Row, New York, 1953.

Larrabee, Eric. *Commander in Chief: Franklin Delano Roosevelt, His Lieutenants, and Their War.* Harper & Row, New York, 1987.

Layton, USN (Ret.), Rear Admiral Edwin T., with Captain Roger Pineau, USNR (Ret.), and John Costello. *"And I Was There": Pearl Harbor and Midway—Breaking the Secrets.* William Morrow and Company, Inc., New York, 1985.

Lewin, Ronald. *The American Magic: Codes and Ciphers and the Defeat of Japan.* Farrar, Straus, Giroux, New York, 1982.

————. *Ultra Goes to War: The First Account of World War II's Greatest Secret Based on Official Documents.* McGraw-Hill Book Company, New York, 1978.

Lloyd's Register of Shipping, 1942–43. Society's Printing House, London, 1942.

Love, Jr., Robert William, ed. *The Chiefs of Naval Operation.* Naval Institute Press, Annapolis, Md., 1980.

Mahan, Alfred Thayer. *The Influence of Seapower upon History 1660–1783.* Sagamore Press, New York, 1957.

Manchester, William. *The Last Lion: Winston Spencer Churchill, volume 2, Alone, 1932–1940.* Little, Brown and Company, Boston-Toronto, 1989.

Metzler, Jost. *Sehrohr südwärts! Ritterkreuzträger Kapitänleutnant Jost Metzler erzählt, niedergeschrieben von Otto Mielke.* W. Limpert, Berlin, 1943.

Middlebrook, Martin. *Convoy.* William Morrow, New York, 1976.

Moffat, Alexander W., Captain USNR (Ret.). *A Navy Maverick Comes of Age, 1939–1945.* Wesleyan University Press, Middletown, Conn., 1977.

Monsarrat, Nicholas. *The Cruel Sea.* Alfred A. Knopf, New York, 1952.

Moore, Captain Arthur R. *A Careless Word . . . A Needless Sinking.* American Merchant Marine Museum, Kings Point, New York, 1983.

Morison, Samuel Eliot. *History of the United States Naval Operations in World War II,* Vol. 1, *The Battle of the Atlantic September 1939–May 1943.* Little, Brown and Company, Boston, 1964.

————. Vol. 3, *The Rising Sun in the Pacific.* rev. ed. Little, Brown and Company, Boston, 1954.

————. Vol. 10, *The Atlantic Battle Won, May 1943–May 1945.* Little, Brown and Company, Boston, 1956.

————. *The Two-Ocean War: A Short History of the United States Navy in the Second World War.* Little, Brown and Company, Boston, 1963.

Mowat, Farley. *The Grey Seas Under*. Little, Brown and Company, Boston, 1958.

Mulligan, Timothy, ed. *Records Relating to U-Boat Warfare, 1939–1945: Guides to the Microfilmed Records of the German Navy, 1850–1945: No. 2*. National Archives and Records Administration, Washington, D.C., 1985.

Padfield, Peter. *Dönitz: The Last Führer*. Panther Books, London, 1985.

Parrish, Thomas. *The Ultra Americans: The U.S. Role in Breaking the Nazi Codes*. Stein and Day, Publishers, New York, 1986.

Porten, Edward P. Von der. *Pictorial History of the German Navy in World War II*. rev. ed. Thomas Y. Crowell Company, New York, 1976.

Prange, Gordon W., in collaboration with Donald M. Goldstein and Katherine V. Dillon. *At Dawn We Slept*. McGraw-Hill Book Company, New York, 1981.

————, with Donald M. Goldstein and Katherine V. Dillon. *Miracle at Midway*. McGraw-Hill Book Company, New York, 1982.

Raeder, Erich. *My Life*. United States Naval Institute, Annapolis, Md., 1960.

Rattray, Jeannette Edwards. *Perils of the Port of New York: Maritime Disasters from Sandy Hook to Execution Rocks*. Dodd, Mead & Company, New York, 1973.

Rich, Norman. *Hitler's War Aims: Ideology, The Nazi State, and the Course of Expansion*. W.W. Norton & Company, Inc., New York, 1973.

Rohwer, Jürgen. *Axis Submarine Successes*. Introductory material trans. John A. Broadwin. Naval Institute Press, Annapolis, Md., 1983.

————. *The Critical Convoy Battles of March 1943: The Battle for HX.229/SC122*. Ian Allan Ltd., London, 1977.

Rohwer, Jürgen, and G. Hummelchen. *Chronology of the War at Sea, 1939–1945*, Vol. 1, *1939–1942*, trans. Derek Masters. Arco Publishing Company, Inc., New York, 1972.

Rohwer, Jürgen, and Eberhard Jäckel, eds. *Kriegswende Dezember 1941*. Bernard & Graefe, Koblenz, 1984.

Roskill, DSC, RN, Captain Stephen W. *The War at Sea, 1939–1945*, 2 vols. Her Majesty's Stationery Office, London, 1954, 1956.

Rössler, Eberhard. *The U-Boat: The Evolution and Technical History of German Submarines*. Arms and Armour Press, London, 1981.

Sherwood, Robert E. *Roosevelt and Hopkins*. Harper & Brothers, New York, 1958.

Showell, Jak P. Mallmann. *The German Navy in World War Two*. Naval Institute Press, 1979.

————. *U-Boats Under the Swastika*. Naval Institute Press, Annapolis, Md., 1987.

Simpson III, B. Mitchell. *Admiral Harold R. Stark: Architect of Victory, 1939–1945*. University of South Carolina Press, Columbia, 1989.

Stern, Robert C. *U-Boats in Action*. Squadron/Signal Publications, Inc., Carrollton, Texas, 1977.

Stick, David. *Graveyard of the Atlantic, Shipwrecks of the North Carolina Coast*. University of North Carolina Press, Chapel Hill, 1952.

Stimson, Henry L., and McGeorge Bundy. *On Active Service in Peace and War*. Harper & Brothers, New York, 1947.

The Story of the U-505. Museum of Science and Industry, Chicago, 1981.

Terraine, John. *The U-Boat Wars 1916–1945*. G.P. Putnam's Sons, New York, 1989.

Thursfield, Rear Admiral H. H., ed. *Brassey's Naval Annual*. The Macmillan Company, New York, 1947.

Trial of the Major War Criminals Before the International Military Tribunal, Nuremberg, 14 November 1945–1 October 1946, Vol. 40. Allied Control Authority for Germany, Nuremberg, 1949.

Vat, Dan van der. *The Atlantic Campaign: World War II's Great Struggle at Sea.* Harper & Row, New York, 1988.

Wagner, Gerhard, ed. *Lagevorträge des Oberbefehlshabers der Kriegsmarine vor Hitler 1939–1945.* Bernard und Graefe, Frankfurt am Main, 1972.

Weinberg, Gerhard L. *World in the Balance: Behind the Scenes of World War II.* University Press of New England, Hanover, N.H., and London, 1981.

Welchman, Gordon. *The Hut Six Story: Breaking the Enigma Codes.* McGraw-Hill Book Company, New York, 1982.

Werner, Herbert A. *Iron Coffins.* Bantam Books, New York, 1978.

West, Rebecca. *A Train of Powder.* Viking, New York, 1955.

Wohlstetter, Roberta. *Pearl Harbor: Warning and Decision.* Stanford University Press, 1962.

Wreck Information List Compiled by the U.S. Hydrographic Office from All Available Sources, Corrected to March 10, 1945. Government Printing Office, Washington, D.C., 1945.

INDEX